RUSSIA

in 2020

MARIA LIPMAN
NIKOLAY PETROV
EDITORS

RUSSIA
in 2020

Scenarios
for the Future

CARNEGIE ENDOWMENT
FOR INTERNATIONAL PEACE

WASHINGTON DC ▪ MOSCOW ▪ BEIJING ▪ BEIRUT ▪ BRUSSELS

Carnegie Endowment for International Peace
1779 Massachusetts Avenue, N.W., Washington, D.C. 20036
202-483-7600, Fax 202-483-1840
www.ceip.org

The Carnegie Endowment does not take institutional positions on public policy issues; the views represented here are the authors' own and do not necessarily reflect the views of the Endowment, its staff, or its trustees.

To order, contact:
Hopkins Fulfillment Service
P.O. Box 50370, Baltimore, MD 21211-4370
1-800-537-5487 or 1-410-516-6956
Fax 1-410-516-6998

Library of Congress Cataloging-in-Publication Data for this book are available

ISBN 978-0-87003-263-9 (pbk.) – ISBN 978-0-87003-264-6 (cloth)

Cover design by Mission Media
Composition by Oakland Street Publishing
Printed by United Book Press

16 15 14 13 12 11   1 2 3 4 5   1st Printing 2011

TABLE
of CONTENTS

FOREWORD

For more than ten years, the signal characteristic of Russian politics has been stability. It is a stability that has exacted a serious price with regard to hopes for reform yet also brought reassurance to many Russians unsettled by the events of the prior decade. Russia's leaders appear set on trying to maintain that stability throughout the present decade as well. Whether they will manage to do so is a defining question for the country. It is also the question that animates this book.

In 2010 Maria Lipman and Nikolay Petrov assembled a remarkable group of experts on Russian politics, economics, and security and tasked them with analyzing what Russia will look like in the year 2020. They urged them to explore the forces for change and the imperatives of continuity, the potentials and the pitfalls, not for the goal of predicting but instead for understanding the range of possibilities and the most likely determinants of the country's path. The result is a kaleidoscopic study not just of Russia's future but also its present situation. True to its subject, it is a sprawling, multilayered account, steeped in the complexities that make the study of contemporary Russia such a compelling and also challenging task.

Lipman and Petrov proceed from a core belief—that in the face of varied internal pressures that are likely to increase, the political system Vladimir Putin built over the last ten years cannot be maintained in its present form for another decade—that in effect the Putin era as we understand it is ending even as Putin enters a new period as president. From this outlook many important arguments and conclusions follow, as the richly diverse chapters by the different experts show.

The commitment that the Carnegie Endowment made to Russia and U.S.-Russian relations when it opened the Carnegie Moscow Center in the early 1990s endures. This book is a happy exemplar of that commitment and reflects its core principles. It brings together scholars and policy researchers from Russia, the United States, and Europe, across disciplines, national boundaries, and ideological perspectives, united in the common endeavor of deep-reaching exploration and elucidation. It takes seriously the task of understanding Russia on its own terms, but also equally seriously the challenge of communicating that understanding to others outside Russia in the hope of contributing to a better future for Russia and for Russia's relations with the world.

Thomas Carothers
Vice President for Studies
Carnegie Endowment for International Peace

ACKNOWLEDGMENTS

This book is a joint effort of many people, and we are deeply grateful to all those who made it possible, even if we cannot list everyone on this page. First of all, we want to thank our team for their contributions and for the terrific participation that ensured a creative, thought-provoking, as well as warm and friendly atmosphere at our joint events.

Carnegie Endowment Vice President Thomas Carothers took part in some of our discussions and helped us throughout the project; we are indebted to him for his profound insights, his advice, and his moral support. Ambassador James F. Collins, director of the Carnegie Russia-Eurasia Program in Washington, D.C., was a wonderful chair at our events at the Endowment and offered useful comments at various stages of our project. Carnegie Moscow Center Director Dmitri Trenin not only contributed to our project, but also greatly encouraged us throughout our work.

We would like to thank Senior Publications Manager Ilonka Oszvald and her team of editors and proofreaders for the excellent organization of the production process and for their patience with our 20-plus authors. Marina Barnett and Ann Stecker of the Carnegie Russia-Eurasia Program in Washington, D.C., were infinitely helpful organizers of our D.C. events.

Thane Gustafson, our intellectual role model in the Russia forecast endeavor, generously shared his experience with looking into Russia's future. We are grateful to all those scholars and experts who at various times took part in our discussions, especially Sergey Aleksashenko, Harley Balzer, Aleksey Berelovich, Timothy Colton, Boris Dubin, Stephen Holmes, and

Ivan Krastev, whose sharp comments and honest critiques added depth to our analysis.

Several prominent institutions provided their venues and generous assistance for our discussions: Rob Garris and Pilar Palacia at the Rockefeller Foundation's gorgeous Villa Bellagio; Alex Nice at Chatham House, and Gertraud Auer Borea d'Olmo at the Bruno Kreisky Forum. We deeply appreciate their hospitality and perfect organization, which made our stay at all these places productive and enjoyable.

Our special thanks go to the Open Society Foundation for sponsoring this project. Lenny Benardo took a personal interest in our project at the early stages and provided valuable advice. Our project also benefited from a grant of the C.S. Mott Foundation, and we are grateful for that.

Tatiana Barabanova, Maria Lipman's assistant, and Yelena Sheetova, Nikolay Petrov's assistant, worked indefatigably to help this project happen and committed much effort to the preparation of this book for publication.

We would like to express our gratitude to Carnegie Endowment President Jessica T. Mathews for her interest in our project and for her support from the very beginning and through the publication of this volume.

RUSSIA *in* 2020— DEVELOPMENT SCENARIOS

Maria Lipman and Nikolay Petrov

Russia–2020, a project of the Carnegie Moscow Center, was officially launched in early 2010. On the tenth anniversary of Vladimir Putin's model of state governance and on the eve of the next election cycle, it seemed like a logical time to analyze and reevaluate Russia's prospects for development. How sustainable is the political and economic system put in place by Putin? Can the status quo be maintained for the long term, or does Russia face major changes? These were the fundamental questions that underlay this work on development scenarios for Russia in the coming decade. Ten years was chosen as the optimal period for forecasting. A decade is not too short term—in which case there would be a risk that current problems and temporary conditions might cloud a long-term view—and yet also not too long term, in which case it would be impossible to responsibly propose realistic scenarios.

Nearly three dozen experts took part in the Carnegie Moscow Center's scenario development research project. Each participant offered his or her "thematic" view of Russia's prospects in various spheres. The group of participating authors was both interdisciplinary and international, representing Russia with fifteen experts, the United States with ten, and Europe with five. In most cases, each topic was considered by a pair of experts, one Russian and one Western, to provide breadth of vision and methodological diversity. Periodically during their work, the authors gathered for public discussions to ensure that many external experts would also have an opportunity to contribute to the final outcome.

The main thematic divisions of the project were as follows:

- *Russia and the world:* Georgi Derluguian, Thomas Graham, Fyodor Lukyanov, Arkady Moshes, Dmitri Trenin, Thomas de Waal, and Immanuel Wallerstein.
- *Political economy and economics:* Clifford Gaddy, Vladimir Milov, Kirill Rogov, and Daniel Treisman.
- *The political system and parties:* Vladimir Gelman, Henry Hale, Boris Makarenko, and Richard Sakwa.
- *The state and political elite:* Pavel Baev, Alexander Golts, and Nikolay Petrov.
- *Federalism and the regions:* Alexandr Kynev, Alexey Malashenko, Robert Orttung, and Natalia Zubarevich.
- *Social development and civil society:* Sam Greene, Lev Gudkov, Maria Lipman, Alexey Sidorenko, Jens Siegert, and Igor Zevelev.

The project participants first gathered in October 2010 in Bellagio, Italy, where they discussed their preliminary work on the chapters and had a brainstorming session on integrated development scenarios. The experts broke into three teams (so that all the main thematic divisions were more or less represented) and made forecasts in the form of trajectories of development with milestones, crossroads, and the like. This collaborative teamwork was the most vibrant and memorable aspect of this meeting. Work on the combined scenario analyses and descriptions was continued in the next stage of the project. The results of this work are presented in the final, concluding chapter of this volume.

The project was kept as open as possible. Anyone who was interested could participate along with the experts. And even before the participants gathered for discussions, a special website (http://russia-2020.org/ru) was inaugurated, with texts specially produced by the project experts. More detailed versions of the thematic scenarios were published in two issues of the journal *Pro et Contra*. And a significant part of the material from the collective discussions was published as a series of articles in the newspaper *Vedomosti*.

In recent years, several other projects have attempted to predict and project Russia's future, including projects at the Center for Strategic and International Studies,[1] New York University,[2] and the Finnish Parliament.[3] Russia–2010 differs from these projects in two main ways: It was conducted later and thus could use the materials these earlier projects generated; and it is larger in scale and scope. Furthermore, most development scenarios focus primarily on economics and politics. This project, in contrast, also devoted significant attention to society. Indeed, the social factor was given as much attention as the state.

This project of the Carnegie Moscow Center is also distinguished by its renowned participants. The monographs by the members of the project's large collective of authors are, without exaggeration, a veritable library of topics connected with Russia—and not only Russia. The project's "orchestra" of authors—or rather, its group of soloists—included staff members from practically all the major world centers and schools that produce studies of contemporary Russia, both theoretical and practical. This gave the project broad access to analyses conducted by researchers all over the world and ensured that the ideas proposed by its team of experts would be disseminated even before its joint work was published. The synergy that was so vibrant at the conference in Bellagio was to a great degree preserved in the subsequent stages of the work.

Scenario analysis differs from prognostication primarily in that the goal is not to predict the future or to determine the likelihood of various future events. Instead, the task is to provide the entire picture—to show the probable future and the relationship of all the elements in the entire picture. Each author considered a spectrum of possible trajectories of development; the factors that might affect these trajectories; and possible points of bifurcation, where the trajectory might dramatically change. The authors tested the trajectories' resilience under the influence of external factors and determined their corridors—the boundaries of the trajectories' fluctuation—as well as opportunities for exerting direct influence on them. The results were not utopias, nor were they anti-utopias. They were not images of the "desired future" but rather études on the same theme, written in a variety of manners and from a variety of positions.

The Russia-2020 team was particularly interested in the fascinating scenario analysis of Russia's future by Daniel Yergin and Thane Gustafson.[4] It is a unique example of constructing noninertial scenarios, and it combines precise scholastic forecasting with the consideration of minuscule details, transforming the scenario into something close to a work of art.

In early 2011, the question of Russia's future changed from a strictly analytical subject to a broader social topic. A great number of scenarios, strategies, and predictions were published and avidly discussed in the Russian expert community. Of course, this trend was not accidental; it was spurred by the upcoming election cycle and growing uncertainty. Anxiety about the future impelled experts to try, if only on paper, to change the adverse course of events. The most noteworthy publications in early 2011 were a fundamental, 300-page text produced by the Institute of Contemporary Development (Russian acronym: INSOR), *Attaining the Future: Strategy 2012*; a report from the Center of Strategic Research, *The Political Crisis in Russia and Possible Mechanisms for Its Development*; and materials from a large group of experts in the state-formed commission revising *The Strategy of Economic Development 2020*.[5] In addition to concerns about the domestic situation—the exhaustion of reconstructive economic growth and the deterioration of the Soviet-era social and physical infrastructure—there are serious concerns about the international situation: financial and economic crises, social upheaval, and regime change in North Africa.

These are difficult times for many governments. For the Russian government, which values control above efficiency, the challenge may be roughly seen as a Gorbachev–Mubarak dilemma. Gorbachev opted for reforms, yielded some control, and lost it all. Mubarak would not yield and stayed in power for much longer, but in the end he, too, lost it all. The parallels may not be fully accurate, but they give an idea of the risks and the fears of the Russian leadership. Putin as we know him will not choose the Gorbachev option. But the model of governance that he relied on in the 2000s is unlikely to hold for another decade. The coming years will reveal whether the Russian leadership has the political vision and statesmanship to succeed where Gorbachev and Mubarak failed.

Notes

1. Andrew C. Kuchins, ed., *Alternative Futures for Russia 2017*, Report of the Russia and Eurasia Program (Washington, D.C.: Center for Strategic and International Studies, 2007), http://csis.org/files/media/csis/pubs/071214-russia_2017-web.pdf. The contributors to this volume include Charles Ryan, Anders Åslund, Thomas Graham, Henry Hale, Sarah Mendelson, and Cory Welt.

2. Center for Global Affairs, "Russia 2020: CGA Scenarios 4, Spring 2010," www.scps. nyu.edu/export/sites/scps/pdf/global-affairs/russia-2020-scenarios.pdf.

3. Osmo Kuusi, Hanna Smith, and Paula Tiihonen, eds., *Russia–2017: Three Scenarios* (Helsinki: Committee for the Future, Parliament of Finland, 2007), http://web.eduskunta.fi/dman/Document.phx?documentId=lt14107123156950&cmd=download.

4. Daniel Yergin and Thane Gustafson, *Russia 2010: And What It Means for the World* (New York: Random House, 1993).

5. Institute of Contemporary Development (Institut Sovremennogo Razvitiya), *Obretenie buduschego: Strategiya-2012* (Attaining the Future: Strategy 2012) (Moscow: INSOR, 2011), www.insor-russia.ru/files/Finding_of_the_Future%20.FULL_.pdf; Sergey Belanovskiy, Mikhail Dmitriev, *Politicheskiy krizis v Rossii i vozmozhnie mekhanizmy ego razvitiya* (The Political Crisis in Russia and Possible Mechanisms for Its Development) (Moscow: Center of Strategic Research, 2011), www.csr.ru/index.php?option=com_content&view=article&id=307%3A2011-03-28-16-38-10&catid=52%3A2010-05-03-17-49-10&Itemid=219&lang=en; and materials from a large group of experts in the state-formed commission revising *The Strategy of Economic Development 2020*; see the commission's websites http://strategy2020.rian.ru and http://2020strategy.ru.

RUSSIA *in*
the WORLD

PART I

CHAPTER ONE

RUSSIA *and* THE WORLD

Thomas Graham

Russia emerged as a major European power in the eighteenth century. It was a huge success for nearly three hundred years, until the collapse of the Soviet Union in 1991—if success is measured in terms of augmentation of territory, expansion of political sway, or accumulation of military victories. Indeed, no other country can match that three hundred years of geopolitical advance; few have mattered as much in international affairs. The Russian victories over Napoleon and Hitler and the Russian Revolution—all events with world-historical consequences that enhanced Russia's power—are only the high points of a remarkable story.

At the beginning of the eighteenth century, Russia was already the largest state in the world, with a territory of more than 10 million square kilometers.[1] Its borders extended from Smolensk in Europe to the Pacific Ocean, and from the Arctic Ocean to the Sea of Azov, the northern reaches of Central Asia, and China. From this enormous base, Russia continued to expand in subsequent centuries.

In the eighteenth century, Russia gained control of the Baltic Sea coastline from the Gulf of Finland to Riga and hastened Sweden's fall from the ranks of the major powers with its victory in the Great Northern War (1700–1721). Along with Prussia and Austria, it slowly undermined, dismembered, and eventually eliminated Poland as an independent state. It pressed southward, finally driving the Ottoman Empire from the northern littoral of the Black Sea with the annexation of the Crimea in 1783, while it began to encroach on Ottoman lands in the Balkans.

This march continued in the nineteenth century with Russia's victory over Napoleon in the decisive campaign of 1812–1814. Russian troops drove as far west as Paris, and Russia remained the dominant power in the eastern half of the continent—the "gendarme" of Europe—until its defeat in the Crimean War in the middle of the century. Russia continued its expansion into the Balkans, annexing Bessarabia, and consolidated its control over the South Caucasus. As Great Britain, France, and lesser European powers divided up Africa and pushed into South Asia, Russia moved swiftly into Central Asia. Along with the other great powers, it participated in the dismemberment of China toward the end of the century.

Finally, in the last century, the collapse of the Russian Empire at the end of World War I proved to be but a momentary retreat. The new rulers, the Bolsheviks, quickly regained most of the empire's lost territory during the bitter civil war that followed their seizure of power. With victory in World War II, the Soviet Union effectively regained all the territory once controlled by the Tsarist state, with the exception of Finland and Alaska (sold to the United States in the mid–nineteenth century). For forty years after that victory, the Soviet Union dominated the eastern half of the continent and attracted client states in the Americas, Africa, and Southeast Asia. Its superpower rivalry with the United States provided the essential geopolitical framework for world affairs.

Russia as a European Power

Russia's emergence as a great power coincided with the formation of the European balance-of-power system. As the eighteenth century evolved, European politics came to be dominated by five powers: France, Prussia, and Austria at the center, and Great Britain and Russia on the western and eastern flanks, respectively. This system provided the framework for European politics—and indeed for global politics, because European powers dominated the global system—until the end of World War I. In its place, after World War I, emerged the bipolar superpower rivalry between the United States and the Soviet Union, which struggled for primacy in Europe and beyond.

Despite Russia's large role in European affairs, the past three hundred years have witnessed a constant debate on Russia's relations with Europe: Was it part of European civilization, or an Asiatic intruder into European affairs? Statesmen and intellectuals have answered that question in various ways over time, depending on developments in both Europe proper and Russia. But the key point is that, no matter how different Russia might have been from other European states in the character of its internal regime (and on this matter, too, there is a lively historical debate), its foreign policy was driven by the same goals as the great powers of Europe—control of territory, resources, and trade routes; defensible borders and geopolitical advantage; and dynastic prestige—and its behavior abroad differed little from that of those powers in the pragmatic, nonideological pursuit of its national interests. For this reason, the other great powers had little difficulty accepting Russia as an integral member of the European system, no matter how they might at times have feared Russian power. In short, Russia was a European great power, not simply a great power operating in Europe.[2]

Russia's essential European character did not change during the Cold War—even if, in the guise of the Soviet Union, it emerged as an existential threat to the West. Soviet ideology was grounded in a socialist worldview with deep roots in European thought and tradition. Soviet external behavior fell well within European diplomatic traditions, once the goal of near-term global revolution was abandoned in practice if not in rhetoric (by the end of the 1920s, at the latest).

Russia's Insecurity

Despite Russia's history of success, its central role in the European balance-of-power system, and its superpower status during the second half of the twentieth century, it has historically been an insecure power, prone to see powerful enemies along its borders and skeptical of the loyalty of its own population.[3] As Tsar Aleksandr III once quipped over a century ago, "Russia has no friends but its army and navy."

The sources of this insecurity were twofold. The first was Russia's geopolitical setting. Russia's borders have been unsettled and contested, even if it has generally had the upper hand. In the eighteenth century, it was engaged in almost constant struggle with first Sweden and then Poland and the Germanic powers in the northwest and with Turkey in the southwest, and with Persia to the south and China to the east. In the nineteenth century, Polish unrest destabilized the western border and insurgencies buffeted the Caucasus. The late nineteenth century witnessed the rise of a powerful united Germany on Russia's western flank and a modernizing imperial Japan on the eastern one, both of which were to become deadly foes in the twentieth century. During the Cold War, there were repeated challenges to Soviet domination of Eastern Europe (East Germany in 1953, Hungary and Poland in 1956, Czechoslovakia in 1968, and Poland again in the 1980s) and the border with China was unsettled, with a brief armed conflict breaking out in 1969.

At the same time, Russia's success against external foes pushed its borders outward and brought ever greater numbers of non-Russians into the empire, concentrated along Russia's periphery. By the end of the nineteenth century, according to the 1897 census, ethnic Russians accounted for less than half the population. Initially, this situation posed little trouble for the state, but the challenge grew rapidly in the nineteenth century with the rise of nationalism across Europe. The late-nineteenth-century Russification campaign only exacerbated the tensions between the state and its non-Russian subjects, particularly in European Russia, and raised the cost of providing security along the borders. The Soviet decision to build the state system along ethnoterritorial lines initially eased the pressure. But it also created national elites in the various republics of the Soviet Union, which were to play central roles in the Soviet Union's dissolution in 1991 along ethnoterritorial lines.

The second source of insecurity was the character of state power. The defining trait of the Tsarist state was the combination of state sovereignty and economic ownership, the sole source of political legitimacy and the sole owner of economic resources, in the person of the tsar. The population, whether noble or peasant, served him to a greater or lesser degree. By the time Russia emerged as a great power, the tsar had effectively done away with private property for nobles—who were allowed to use property contingent on providing service to the tsar—and enserfed the peasants, binding them to specific lands.

These bonds were loosened over time—in 1762, for example, Catherine the Great relieved nobles of the obligation of compulsory service to the state while leaving them with their property, and in 1861 Alexander II emancipated the serfs. But none of this changed the fundamental character of the state. Most nobles continued to enter state service to supplement their income and maintain social rank, in part because the Russian practice of equal division of inheritance precluded the long-term survival of private fortunes.[4] The serfs were emancipated in a way that left them impoverished and beholden to their noble landlords. As a result, no strong social classes emerged independent of the state to put significant political or legal constraints on the tsar, who ruled as an autocrat until the end of the empire. The Bolsheviks may have overthrown the tsar, but once in power they recreated the traditional tsarist relationship between state and society, only with a more onerous and pernicious form of state servitude undergirded by a totalitarian ideology.

The character of the state militated against the formation of a strong sense of national identity and allegiance to the state during the Tsarist period. If there was any loyalty at all, it was to the tsar. For the nobles, he anchored the system in which they competed for favor and privilege.[5] For the peasants, he was the protector against the arbitrary power of local landowners and officials, that is, the local representatives of state power. Peasants saw no contradiction between rebellion against these representatives and loyalty to the tsar.[6]

During the Tsarist period, there were too few officials to effectively administer the country's vast territory and scattered population of dubious loyalty. A large army was needed to garrison the state against domestic unrest. Despite the large sums devoted to the army (in bad years, more than 70 percent of the budget in the eighteenth century and more than 50 percent in the nineteenth[7]), its resources were stretched thin. When wars erupted, Russia had to move soldiers from the interior to the borders, thus attenuating the defenses against domestic disorder. Not surprisingly, the most serious outbreaks of disorder tended to emerge during times of war. The great Pugachev peasant rebellion of the eighteenth century, for example, broke out while Russia was engaged in a major war with Turkey.[8] As a result, the tsars found themselves in a constant struggle to balance the resources needed for external defense against those required for domestic tranquillity.

Russia's Soviet rulers went to an extreme in trying to solve this problem, promoting Soviet patriotism while building a massive state bureaucracy to administer the country, one of the world's largest militaries to protect against external foes, and a pervasive internal security organization to guard against domestic unrest. That approach appeared to bear fruit in the early decades after World War II, as the Soviet Union seemingly closed the gap in power and fortune with the United States. Ultimately, however, that effort drained the state's resources; created an environment inimical to the discovery, development, and mastery of new technologies critical to economic growth, particularly in the information and communications sectors; fostered corruption; and alienated the population. The system collapsed under its own weight in 1991.

The Sources of Russian Power

Although history demonstrates otherwise, Russia as it emerged as a great power did not appear destined for success. A state with a vast territory, hard-to-defend borders, an impoverished population of dubious loyalty, an overstretched bureaucracy and army, and powerful foreign enemies, behind which it lagged technologically, hardly seems a recipe for success. But Russia did succeed. Why? What were the sources of its power?

Paradoxically, the sources of insecurity also provided the ingredients of great power. Russia's vast geographic expanse gave it strategic depth, which in turn made it nearly impossible to conquer, at least from the West, as Charles XII discovered in the eighteenth century, Napoleon in the nineteenth, and Hitler in the twentieth. When Russia was strong, its hard-to-defend borders allowed it to move aggressively into neighboring regions. Moreover, particularly in the eighteenth century, Russia found itself faced by powers that were in decline—Sweden, Poland, the Ottoman Empire—and it expanded until it came up against the rising Germanic powers—Prussia and Austria—in the middle of Europe. In the nineteenth century, it moved rapidly into the geographically accessible and weakly organized territory of Central Asia, expanding its sway up to the borderlands of the unconquerable Afghanistan and the British Empire on the Indian Subcontinent.

The state structure provided effective mechanisms for mobilizing resources for state purposes, allowing Russia to more than hold its own against other European powers, even though it was impoverished and technologically backward by European standards for most of the past three hundred years. During the Tsarist period, the state used its nobles to recruit a huge peasant army that was a match for any of its rivals. Peasants were generally conscripted for twenty years (in effect, for life). Torn from their native villages, they developed a deep sense of identity with and loyalty to their units. They turned out to be brave, disciplined, and able soldiers, something on which non-Russian observers repeatedly commented. At the same time, the state was able to provide the instruments of war and, when necessary, launch a concerted campaign to modernize the country so that it did not fall catastrophically behind its major rivals. Peter the Great's effort to Europeanize Russia transformed Russia into a great power; Stalin's forced industrialization was critical to Russia's victory in World War II.

Finally, for a brief period in the mid–twentieth century, Marxism-Leninism provided Russia with considerable soft power. Foreign communist parties loyal to Moscow extended its reach across the globe. Its ideological opposition to colonial powers gave it high standing among the national liberation movements that proliferated during the 1950s and 1960s.

The Current Challenge

Nearly twenty years after the breakup of the Soviet Union, after a decade of socioeconomic collapse and a subsequent decade of recovery, Russia finds itself in a situation reminiscent of 1700. Although it remains the largest country in the world, its borders are nearly identical to the 1700 borders. The political system that was consolidated under Putin bears the characteristics of the traditional Russian system: a centralized, authoritarian state, with considerable military and security forces, ruling over a passively loyal and profoundly apathetic population. The country's leadership, despite the rhetoric of Russia's return and "rising from its knees," still feels insecure, seeing multiple external challenges and lacking trust in its own people. During a trip to the Russian Far East in 2008, for example, President Dmitri Medvedev warned that Russia could "in the end lose everything" quite unexpectedly in the region, pointing to the collapse of the Soviet Union as a cautionary tale.[9] A year later, launching his campaign to modernize Russia, Medvedev issued another warning: "We must start the modernization and technological renewal of all productive spheres. I am convinced that this is a question of the survival of our country in the contemporary world."[10]

In these circumstances, the question begs itself: Is today's Russia a rising power, as Peter's was three hundred years ago, one that will write new chapters in Russia's long history of success? Or is Russia, like many successful empires and great powers before it, on an irreversible path to middle- or lesser-power status after having enjoyed a brief respite in the past decade? There is no clear answer, only suppositions and arguments. No matter what the answer, one thing is certain: Russia faces the most formidable challenge to its great power ambitions that it has confronted in the last three centuries.

First, the geopolitical context has changed dramatically to Russia's disadvantage. For the first time since it emerged as a great power, it is surrounded (beyond the former Soviet space) by countries and regions that are more dynamic than it is—economically, demographically, and politically:

- To the east lies China, which is quickly emerging as a global power on the foundation of robust economic growth. China's GDP overtook Russia's in the early 1990s and has now grown to be more than four times as large. Moreover, the quality of China's growth has been far superior to Russia's: While Russia was putting back into productive use Soviet-era infrastructure that had fallen idle in the 1990s, China was building new modern infrastructure. Finally, the ongoing global economic crisis is only widening the gap between China and Russia.[11]
- To the south lies the Middle East, a region of great religious and sectarian ferment and robust demographic growth with a primeval energy (*passionarnost*) lacking in Russia. The historic struggle in the Muslim world between modernity and tradition has spawned militant radical groups—most notably al-Qaeda—with ambitions that extend well beyond the Middle East. Conflicts in Afghanistan and Iraq and internal disquiet in Pakistan and Iran, among other

factors, have created pools of centrifugal energy that threaten Central Asia and the Caucasus, and through them, Russia itself.

- To the west lies Europe, which remains engaged in the grand historical project of building a united Europe (minus Russia), no matter the recent setbacks and current drift. The European Union already dwarfs Russia in population and economic capacity, and the threat to Russia is that the EU will eventually develop a unified foreign and security policy that will dramatically increase its geopolitical weight. (Moreover, the reversal of this grand project would augur ill for Russia, depriving it of a potential partner in dealing with the graver challenges from the south and east.)

- Finally, global warming has opened up a northern front, the Arctic, which could become a major zone of competition between Russia and, among other nations, the United States. No matter what difficulties the United States might be facing at this point, the resources it can command dwarf by orders of magnitude those that Russia can mobilize.

In these circumstances, the historical pattern of power has been reversed. Instead of flowing out from the Russian core into the surrounding regions, power is flowing into Russia's neighborhood and into Russia itself from abroad. Chinese investment, for example, is moving into Central Asia to such an extent that China has probably already overtaken Russia as that region's major commercial partner.[12] Radical Islam has penetrated into Central Asia and the Caucasus and with time threatens to infect the Muslim-dominated parts of the Urals-Volga region, particularly Tatarstan and Bashkortostan, two resource-rich regions that lie astride the lines of communication between European Russia and Siberia and the Far East. And the European Union—despite its current economic difficulties—still proves to be a pole of attraction for the former Soviet states situated in Europe.

Second, the nature of power itself has changed. Until the latter part of the twentieth century, hard power was the coin of the realm in international affairs. The constant threat of war—and territorial changes—put a premium on a country's being self-sufficient in the resources needed to conduct warfare successfully. The advent of nuclear weapons ironically eroded the value of military power—even if it remains the ultima ratio in world affairs—and, at least in relative terms, raised the importance of other kinds of power—economic, commercial, financial, cultural, and ideational. Globalization renders self-sufficiency unattainable, even in advanced military systems. The ability to manipulate interdependence is now at least as important as physical control of resources as an element of power. The postindustrial era puts a premium on creativity and flexibility in building and sustaining a competitive economy; within broad limits, the quality of the workforce is of greater consequence than its size. Earlier the coercive power of the state could to a great degree compel a population to provide the instruments of state power. Now the state must to a great degree inspire society to be creative if it is to maintain its standing in the world.

The question is whether the Russian system is capable of replicating its historical success under current conditions. Can a system that proved quite capable of mobilizing human and natural resources to produce overwhelming military force now produce the wide range of powers Russia needs to succeed in the twenty-first century? Will tinkering with the system suffice, or does it need a radical overhaul or, at the extreme, replacement? At a minimum, given the changing nature of power, it would appear that the system will have to open up to generate the active support from a significant segment of the population that it will need so that Russia as a state can prosper in an increasingly competitive and unsettled global system.

Scenarios to 2020

Building scenarios for Russia's role in the world is exceedingly complicated because there are myriad independent variables. In particular, the rise and fall, the change in relative standing, of the other great powers will have a huge impact on what Russia can do in the world, and Russia has little, if any, influence over those developments. This is all the more challenging now that the world has entered a period of great upheaval and uncertainty until a new global equilibrium emerges.

Nevertheless, seven assumptions about global developments to the end of 2020 appear reasonable to frame the possibilities and challenges facing Russia:

- There will be no great power war, but there will be considerable conflict among lesser powers and nonstate actors, particularly in the broader Middle East stretching from Morocco to Afghanistan and Pakistan.
- The great powers will pragmatically pursue their national interests; no significant ideological divide will emerge between them to sharpen competition among them.
- Global dynamism will continue to shift from Europe and the Atlantic region to Asia and the Pacific region, with China and India continuing to rise as great powers.
- The United States will remain the only truly global power with the capability to intervene anywhere in the world, although its margin of superiority will narrow, and budget deficits and mounting debt will compel it to prioritize its goals more strictly than it has for the past several decades.
- Europe will continue to muddle its way toward greater unity.
- Globalization will continue to define the international environment. The global economy will remain relatively open. There will be no massive retreat toward protectionism and the fragmentation of global markets.
- There will be no technological breakthrough that will fundamentally alter the nature of power or the relative standing of states by 2020.

Any, or all, of these assumptions may turn out to be mistaken. China's rapid economic growth could stall, for example, from the loss of external markets or internal contradictions. The United States could lose its margin of superiority or find that it could not exploit it effectively, because of a debilitating debt burden, burgeoning deficits, political gridlock, or ill-conceived or ineptly executed policies. The grand project of building a united Europe could come to an end because of a prolonged economic downturn or the reckless economic policies of certain member states. And a prolonged global economic crisis could reignite protectionist passions around the globe, putting an end to globalization, at least in the economic realm. What precisely such developments would mean for Russia is uncertain, but none are likely to alter the fundamental challenge facing

Russia—to build the domestic sinews of power usable on the global stage—although all could sharpen that challenge.

Given these assumptions and the challenges facing Russia, what place in world affairs can it reasonably hope to occupy by 2020, and what does it need to do to reach its goals?

During the past decade, Russia has regained much of the stature as a major power that it lost during the first post-Soviet decade. Its goal for the next decade should be to consolidate that status by seeking to be:

- The dominant power in the former Soviet space. Russia should aspire to be the keystone in any security architecture for the region or its subdivisions (Europe, the Caucasus, and Central Asia) and the engine of economic growth with a large and growing commercial presence. Russian should remain the region's lingua franca.
- A major partner of all other leading powers, including the United States, China, and India.
- A key pillar in European security architecture, along with NATO and the European Union, a leading supplier of energy to Europe, and a major destination for Europe's trade and investment.
- A leading player in the management and development of Arctic resources.
- A first-tier member of all the key global rules-making organizations, including the United Nations, International Monetary Fund, World Trade Organization, Group of Twenty, and any other that might be established.
- A central player in global energy issues, as a world leader in the oil and gas sector, in civil nuclear energy, and in the development of new technologies.

To progress toward those goals, Russia will need:

- Robust economic growth based on a revival of Russia's manufacturing sector and the emergence of a strong, cutting-edge technology sector.
- Reform of the military to create a force that is capable of maintaining strategic stability vis-à-vis other nuclear powers, protecting

Russia's borders, and projecting power into neighboring regions to deal with instability and low-level violence.

- Sufficient national cohesion to be able to mobilize the necessary resources to cope with any national emergency, including economic and political modernization.
- A pragmatic foreign policy based on the pursuit of national interests that minimizes the number of potential enemies and helps create a benign international order in which Russia can focus its energies on domestic reconstruction, renewal, and growth.

The Consequences of Inertia

There is an elite consensus that Russia must modernize to survive as a major power during the next decade and beyond. That does not mean that modernization will come, however. Failure of imagination at the highest policymaking levels; bureaucratic infighting, resistance, or inertia; or societal conservatism could undo any modernization effort. The consequences of inertia would be at least relative, if not absolute, decline vis-à-vis the other major powers; the reinforcement of centrifugal forces across the former Soviet space; and a diminishing voice for Russia in world affairs.

This does not necessarily—in fact it probably does not—end in catastrophe within the next decade. The Russian leadership is still young and aggressive and confident of its right to rule Russia; the population has shown little appetite for active protest, and it fears a return of the unrest and instability that marked the end of the Soviet Union and the first decade of the new Russia. This is not a revolutionary situation. At the same time, even without modernization, Russia will retain sufficient military capacity, including in particular its nuclear forces, so that no outside power would be tempted to seize Russian territory or resources. Nor would any be interested in Russia's demise—that would create a zone of instability with vast amounts of nuclear material in the heart of Eurasia. There may be extremist forces that would seek to exploit further weakness, particularly in the North Caucasus, which could become ungovernable and parts of which could become de facto independent (as Chechnya was for a brief time in the 1990s), but that would hardly mark the collapse of the system as a whole. In short, in the absence of modernization, the most likely scenario for the next decade is muddling downward, with the breaking point further in the future if the trend is not reversed.

The Optimal Scenario: What Must be Done?

The optimal scenario would entail a careful balancing of the needed economic modernization, political mobilization, military reform, and pragmatic foreign policy. Economic modernization is the sine qua non of an enhanced Russian role in the world. It will give Russia the capability it needs to strengthen its presence in the former Soviet space in a way that will not appear to threaten the other major powers, and to cooperate productively with them on a broad range of global issues. It will also earn Russia considerable respect. It will demonstrate a seriousness of purpose, a willingness to give national interest precedence over private gain, of which many in the West believe the Russian leadership is incapable.

Economic modernization is a multifaceted effort entailing renewal of the country's infrastructure, much of which was left over from the Soviet period and starved of investment thereafter; revitalization of the industrial base on the basis of global best practices and world-class technologies; investment in fostering cutting-edge technologies; the creation of deep, effective domestic financial markets; and reform of the health and education systems necessary to grow a competitive workforce, especially because Russia's working-age population will almost certainly continue to decline during the next decade.[13] Success will require a concerted national effort, with skilled leadership at the top and active support from the most energetic segments of the population. It will also require considerable investment, at least several trillion dollars during the next decade,[14] which Russia cannot generate from domestic sources alone.

Although Russia clearly needs to diversify its economy, energy will remain a critical component for years to come, and the income from the energy sector will continue to supply a large share of budget revenues and could help fund the larger modernization effort. In this regard, Russia needs to undertake a greater effort to explore and develop resources east of the Urals and offshore, particularly in the Arctic. Developing new resources will be crucial to Russia's ability to honor its contracts with European customers during the next decade, and to meet surging demand in China and elsewhere in Asia. The management skills and technology Russia needs to succeed in this effort are not currently available from domestic sources.

Good relations with the West will be imperative. Russia can obtain some of the investment it needs from China and a few other non-Western states during the next decade, but the technology and know-how it requires, both to modernize its economy and to develop its energy sector, can only be found in the West, particularly in the United States. Good relations have two aspects. First, Russia will need to continue to reduce tensions with the West, building on the reset in relations with the United States and removing further irritants in relations with European states (along the lines of the resolution of the decades-long dispute with Norway over boundaries in the Barents Sea and the rapprochement with Poland in 2010). But Russia will need to move beyond the simple reduction in tensions to the development of mutually beneficial cooperation with the West on a broad range of security challenges and economic opportunities. In this regard, agreement on the key elements of a European security architecture should be a priority (although these do not necessarily have to be based on President Medvedev's proposal), as will be eliminating the political issues that have led to cut-offs in Russian energy flows to Europe in recent years. Finally, Russia will need to work closely with the United States, Canada, Norway, and Denmark to ensure cooperation in the development of the Arctic's resources and limit the risk of dangerous geopolitical competition.

Second, Russia will need to build an attractive investment climate. What needs to be done is well known—less bureaucracy; less corruption; independent, competent, and fair courts; better protection of property rights, particularly of intellectual property. Russia's entry into the World Trade Organization will send a powerful signal to foreign investors about its commitment to integration into the global economy and interest in foreign trade and direct investment. Likewise, its membership in the Organization for Economic Cooperation and Development would help persuade Western businessmen that it is an attractive place to do business.

Good relations with the West will not suffice for Russia's purposes, however. Russia must also work to promote as benign an international environment as possible, especially along its own periphery, so that it can concentrate its effort on modernization at home. That will require a continued effort to build constructive relations with China, a more active role in helping to stabilize the situation in and around Afghanistan, and vigorous diplomatic efforts to prevent the outbreak of war in the Middle East, particularly with regard to Iran, and contain the instability unleashed by the Arab Spring.

On the domestic front, the Russian leadership will need to mobilize both the elite and a substantial part of the rest of the population for the modernization project. Because creativity, flexibility, and risk taking will be critical to success, the political system will have to be opened up. Open debate will be needed to find the right way forward on a range of issues, to engage the more creative, risk-taking elements of the population, and to overcome the general public's apathy about national affairs. In addition, the benefits of modernization will need to be spread broadly to build the support necessary for long-term success. That will mean in part instituting policies to produce greater social equality. Finally, steps will need to be taken to reinforce the sense of political community, that is, the sense that all Russians are bound by a common fate. That will almost certainly entail the promotion of some form of nationalism. Great care must be taken in this task. To avoid alienating the nearly 20 percent of the population that is not ethnic Russian, a civic nationalism should be preferred to an ethnic one. To avoid jeopardizing needed foreign investment, energy should be focused on rebuilding Russia and improving living standards rather than on mobilizing against an external enemy. A repeat of the anti-Western rhetoric of the 2007–2008 electoral cycle in the future would quickly cut off the much-needed cooperation with Europe and the United States.

All these steps must be taken without destabilizing the political system. In particular, the leadership needs to build confidence among the elites and the population as a whole so that it can manage modernization without fueling the kind of unrest that undid Gorbachev's perestroika and destroyed the Soviet Union. The challenge is undoubtedly less formidable now than it was twenty to twenty-five years ago: Russia is not seething with latent ethnic unrest as the Soviet Union was; the current leadership is young, energetic, and self-confident, not old, slothful, and unsure of itself as the Soviet elite was; and popular discontent is now far below the levels of the late Soviet period. Nevertheless, the Russian leadership must take care that the political system's opening does not outrun its capacity to absorb new participants. This needed political opening up will also pose a challenge to the most progressive elements of Russian society, which will need to find a way to work with the state, even if policies are not as bold, nor the opening of the political system as rapid, as they would desire. Radical opposition to the regime by progressive forces throughout Russian history has tended to create conditions more conducive to authoritarian practices than democratic advance—witness the late Tsarist period and the refusal of the Kadets to work with the regime, or the late Soviet period and the progressives' opposition to Gorbachev.

Finally, Russia needs to conduct a thorough military reform that will create the type of forces needed to deal with the contingencies that Russia will most likely face—low-intensity conflict along its borders—rather than large-scale conventional war among major powers. The reliability of the strategic deterrent needs to be maintained, albeit at lower levels, to ensure Russia's security in a rapidly changing geopolitical environment with a likely increase in the number of states with nuclear forces. Building a military capable of dealing with the most likely threats will help improve relations with the West, and the United States in particular. Such reform will provide convincing evidence that Russia has moved away from Cold War threat analysis and that it is developing the capabilities to partner with the United States in confronting a wide range of contingencies, particularly in Eurasia and the broader Middle East.

The Critical Junctures

The optimal scenario for 2020 would be steady, mutually reinforcing progress along the lines outlined above on four tracks—economic, political, foreign policy, and military. To approach this scenario, Russia will need skilled leaders who comprehend the interrelations among the four tracks, can maintain the delicate balance among them, and are flexible and resourceful enough to parry the challenges and crises that will inevitably occur during the next decade. For this reason, the critical juncture will be those times when the question of power is on the agenda, that is, during the 2011–2012 and 2016–2018 electoral cycles.

The upcoming electoral cycle is more important: It comes at the beginning phases of the modernization effort, which is associated most prominently with Medvedev, even though Putin also has long recognized the need for such an effort. The election campaign and the outcome should build support for modernization, in part by reinforcing reassurances that the effort will continue unabated and along the same general lines well into the future. That would be especially important if Putin returned to the presidency.

In this regard, it is worth reviewing the benefits that Russia has derived so far from the Medvedev-Putin tandem. It took a strong effort to weather the challenges that emerged with the war with Georgia in 2008 and the subsequent sharp deterioration in relations with the West. It managed the impact of the global economic crisis as well as most other countries, and did so in a way that sparked remarkably little social unrest.

From the standpoint of the challenges lying ahead, two points are worth making:

- First, even if Putin clearly remains the dominant political figure, Medvedev as president has created space for a more open political debate and Medvedev's rhetoric on corruption and legal nihilism, as well as his commitment to modernization, have encouraged a much broader discussion than might have otherwise been the case. At the same time, Putin has restrained the more conservative elements of the elite by providing reassurance that Medvedev's policies will not slip out of control and spark the widespread instability that doomed Gorbachev's perestroika.
- Second, Medvedev's more "modern" face has facilitated rapprochement with the West. In the United States, given Putin's harshly negative image, the Obama administration would have encountered much fiercer domestic opposition to its reset policy if Putin had stayed on as president. At the same time, Putin in the background has led the United States to make more concessions to Russia than it would have otherwise in the belief, or hope, that that would bolster Medvedev's position.

In other words, a continuation after 2012 of the tandem in its current configuration, with Medvedev as president and Putin as prime minister, and Putin as the clearly dominant figure, would offer good prospects for continued progress on Russia's modernization. Putin's return to the presidency would not end the modernization effort, but it would almost certainly slow it down, because Putin as president could not play both of the roles he and Medvedev have played in the past two and a half years. He cannot be both an impulse to modernization and a reassurance to conservative forces. Nor can he be a friendly face to the West, given the recent past.

Russia's Fate in a Changing World

The world is in the midst of a fundamental reordering. Not only has the Cold War system finally come to an end—a generation after the end of the Cold War itself—with the recognition that even the last remaining superpower could not dominate global affairs; so has Europe's centrality to global affairs, after a run of some five hundred years. The central drama of the next decade and beyond will be the struggle for the creation of a new global equilibrium, one that will likely endure well into this century. For Russia, the central drama will be whether it can generate the imagination it will need to find a respectable place for itself in this new world order, the creativity to devise the policies that can bring it to that place, and the political will to execute those policies. That will ultimately determine whether Russia is at a new beginning or at the end of a remarkable run of success.

Notes

1. See Richard Pipes, *Russia Under the Old Regime* (New York: Charles Scribner's Sons, 1974), 83.

2. See Martin Malia, *Russia Under Western Eyes: From the Bronze Horseman to the Lenin Mausoleum* (Cambridge, Mass.: Belknap Press of Harvard University Press, 1999), 21–27; Dominic Lieven, *Empire: The Russian Empire and Its Rivals* (New Haven, Conn.: Yale University Press, 2000), chap. 8; and William C. Fuller Jr., *Strategy and Power in Russia 1600–1914* (New York: Free Press, 1992).

3. This section draws heavily on my earlier work, "The Sources of Russia's Insecurity," *Survival: Global Politics and Strategy* 52, no. 1 (February–March 2010): 55–74.

4. See Walter M. Pinter and Don Karl Rowney, "Officialdom and Bureaucratization: Conclusion," in *Russian Officialdom: The Bureaucratization of Russian Society from the Seventeenth to the Twentieth Century*, edited by Walter McKenzie Pinter and Don Karl Rowney (Chapel Hill: University of North Carolina Press, 1980), 377–8.

5. As Edward Keenan wrote, "The *idea* of a strong tsar was essential both to the princely clans and to the non-princely bureaucrats as the warrant of their own power and of the legitimacy of their position—and as protection against one another. . . . It mattered little, in most generations, who was at the center of this system, but it was crucially important that *someone* be, and that the common allegiance to him be at least nominally unconditional" (italics in the original). Edward L. Keenan, "Muscovite Political Folkways," *Russian Review* 45, no. 2 (April 1986): 141–2.

6. What Richard Pipes wrote of the peasant of 1900 was true earlier; he "owed loyalty only to his village and canton; at most he was conscious of some vague allegiance to his province. His sense of national identity was confined to respect for the Tsar and suspicion of foreigners." Richard Pipes, *The Russian Revolution* (New York: Alfred A. Knopf, 1990), 91–92. See also Pipes, *Russia Under the Old Regime*, 161–62; and Ilya Prizel, *National Identity and Foreign Policy: Nationalism and Leadership in Poland, Russia, and Ukraine* (Cambridge: Cambridge University Press, 1998), 166–79.

7. Fuller, *Strategy and Power*, 105; Geoffrey Hosking, *Russia: People and Empire, 1552–1917* (Cambridge, Mass.: Harvard University Press, 1997), 190–91; Martin Malia, *The Soviet Tragedy: A History of Socialism in Russia, 1917–1991* (New York: Free Press 1994), 370–73.

8. Fuller, *Strategy and Power*, 94–98, 132–39.

9. Dmitri Medvedev, "Zaklyuchitel'noye slovo na soveshchanii po voprosam sotsial' no-ekonomicheskogo rasvitiya Kamchatskogo kraya" [Concluding Remarks at the conference on issues of the socioeconomic development of Kamchatskiy Kray], Petropavlovsk-Kamchatskiy, September 28, 2008, http://news.kremlin.ru/transcripts/1518.

10. Dmitri Medvedev, "Poslaniye Federal'nomu Sobraniyu Rossiyskoy Federatsii" [Address to the Federal Assembly of the Russian Federation], Moscow, November 12, 2009, http://kremlin.ru/transcripts/5979.

11. Gross national income figures at purchasing power parity are derived from World Development Indicators available at www.worldbank.org; see also "China vs. Russia: Wealth Creation vs. Poverty Reduction," *Hoover Daily Report*, April 25, 2005, www.hoover.org/pubaffairs/dailyreport/archive/3582641.html#n1.

12. See Sebastien Peyrouse, *The Economic Aspects of Chinese-Central Asia Rapprochement*, Central Asia–Caucasus Institute, Silk Road Studies Program, Silk Road Paper, September 2007.

13. According to United Nations projections, Russia's population could decline from 140.4 million in 2010 to as low as 132.3 million in 2020. See United Nations, *World Population Prospects: The 2009 Revision*, Population Database available at http:/esa.un.org/unpp/index.asp.

14. See Alexey Zayko, "Strategiya 'maloy Rossii'" ["Little Russia's" strategy], *Ekspert* 39, no. 723 (October 4–11, 2010), www.expert.ru/printissues/expert/2010/39.

CHAPTER TWO

RUSSIA *in* WORLD-SYSTEMS PERSPECTIVE

Georgi Derluguian and Immanuel Wallerstein

Since its formulation as a critique of modernization theory in the early 1970s, world-systems analysis has met with considerable resistance in Russia and among Russia experts. The reasons were mainly ideological. Official Soviet ideology, which in the 1970s and 1980s proclaimed the existence of a "world socialist system," certainly could not accept that the USSR was merely a semiperipheral state still facing the perennial problems of technological development, even if this state was ideologically eccentric and exceptionally militarized.[1] Needless to say, in the 1970s Soviet censors found scandalizing the prediction that Moscow might soon abandon its obsolete official ideology and burdensome arms race for the sake of admission into the club of core capitalist states.

In the 1990s the majority of Russian intellectuals converted to the neoliberal "Washington Consensus." This new creed, presumably the opposite of erstwhile Marxism-Leninism, looked like a powerful political weapon against the nomenklatura as well as the ideological destination of post-Soviet "transition." Our theoretical claim that Russia was still a semiperipheral country, of course, could not be acceptable to the people who believed that they were moving their country toward the heights of communism or, after 1991, toward the heights of capitalism. The most bitter irony is that virtually all East European rebels of 1989–1991 were blinded by their ideology to the fact that the state-minimizing neoliberal agenda was taking their countries not to the promised land of North America but rather to the harsher realities of South America. More recently some elements of the Russian ruling elite have shown interest in the predictions of world-systems analysis regarding the crisis of Western capitalism. This interest, however, seems to be fed mostly by nationalist sentiments, which might be ignoring the further implications of the global crisis. But we are not engaging in futile ideological polemics. Instead, we simply want to state where we locate Russia in world-systems perspective.

Three Waves of Despotic Modernization

Let us begin with what we all should know. At the end of the nineteenth century, Russia appeared unsure of its status vis-à-vis the West and was beset by myriad problems—including enormous disparities between rich and poor; the political discontent of the liberal intelligentsia, dominated classes, and nationalities; the blind inertia and corruption of the ruling bureaucracy; police brutality; the embarrassing insufficiency of technological progress, despite the efforts of excellent scholars and engineers; and a persistent dependence on the export of primary commodities. In short, Russia seemed to be falling behind the West. And now, at the turn of the twenty-first century, the long list of problems besetting postcommunist Russia looks largely the same—if not worse. Does nothing ever change? Yes and no. These are the typical dilemmas of semiperipheral countries.

Yet Russia has always managed to stay balanced on the outer edges of the capitalist core. In 1900, the Russian Empire was a world power. This must be judged a remarkable exception compared to similarly semiperipheral states. The real losers at that point in history seemed to be China, India, Persia, Turkey, and, for that matter, Poland and Spain—which arguably had been among the greatest powers back in 1600.[2] One way or another, all these once-formidable states failed in the geopolitical competition of previous centuries.[3] By contrast, Russia has experienced several successive bouts of vigorous efforts to foster a new army, state apparatus, tax flows, and productive economic bases. In the past, such efforts brought to the fore such hyperactivist despots as Ivan the Terrible, Peter the Great, and Stalin.

The recurrence of despotic activist rulers is the typical semiperipheral strategy of compensating for the lack of concentrated capitalist resources with heightened coercion.[4] In all three instances, in the sixteenth, eighteenth, and twentieth centuries, Russia's leaps to a higher stage of state centralization and military force relied on hugely oppressive measures to squeeze peasant producers for labor and economic surplus. Each major effort to upgrade Russia's world-systemic position had to start by undoing the old elites and replacing them with new cadres whose group organization, skills, and identities were articulated in alignment with the goals of state reformation. Each Russian "modernization" thus meant some kind of revolution from above.

In 1917, the Bolsheviks were just one among several radical currents of intelligentsia, that is, the frustrated educated cadres whose professional careers were either stymied by the aristocratic order or structurally nonexistent. The Old Regime since the 1860s had attempted various reforms but they all ran into political blocs. Today, the technocrats in the Russian government might find painfully familiar the dilemmas of Count Sergei Witte, Russia's greatest promoter of industrialization before the Bolsheviks. The last tsar, as we all also know, grew aloof in the face of conflicting elite pressures and popular discontent.

The Bolsheviks proved anything but indecisive. They put forth an inspiring, universalistic ideology, which made them (and even many opponents) believe that they were the vanguard of world revolution. Surrendering state power, even temporarily for the sake of democratic rotation, was absolutely out of the question because it would equal failing in their historical mission. The purges, the Gulag, and the Iron Curtain flowed from this quite logically, if not inevitably.[5] In fact, the Bolsheviks pushed forward the reforms of Count Witte by different means. They simply had no other option if they wanted their state to be a serious player in a world system torn by world wars and depression. Arguably the most consequential irony of the last century is that the capitalist world system itself survived the Nazi bid for world-imperial domination largely thanks to the improbable turn of events in Russia after 1917.[6]

The Leninist strategy of state building took very little from classical Marxism. Instead, the adherents of Leninism relied on the fusion of three advances in the contemporary organization of social power: an ideologically inspired and disciplined party fostering mass political participation through career promotion from the lower ranks of society; the mass-producing and planned industrial economy, which required mass urbanization, education, and welfare provisions (or what may be called global "Fordism"); and a mechanized army staffed by mass conscription.[7] Stephen Hanson aptly defined this as a kind of power that "Max Weber himself could not have imagined: a charismatic bureaucracy."[8]

The success of this developmentalist strategy was certified by the victory over the Nazis in 1945 followed by Russia's recognition as the special superpower rival to America. The lightning-fast transformation of an erstwhile agrarian empire into a military-industrial superpower elicited numerous emulations around the world in various socialist or nationalist colors. Even if the rapid dismantling of colonial empires after 1945 and the resurgence of countries like China and India were not direct results of Soviet foreign policy, such epochal shifts in the global balance were mightily assisted by the very existence of the Soviet example. Moreover, the workers in the capitalist core itself would have probably not obtained such a generous bargain after 1945 if it had not been for the ruling elite's anxieties associated with the Cold War.

The Limits of Soviet Growth

The Soviet success, however, sowed the seeds of its own undoing. Geopolitically, after 1945 the USSR found itself responsible along with America for the durable pacification of Europe and, to some extent, also much of Asia. This achievement (about which Count Witte could only dream) put the enormous mechanized armies of the Soviet Bloc in a positional stalemate. Moreover, by inspiring and directly helping various developing states that thrived in the competitive bipolarity of the Cold War, the USSR hugely if inadvertently contributed to the containment of violent disruptions on the periphery, mainly of the varieties now represented by terrorist groups, warlords, transnational mafias, and eccentric regimes seeking to obtain their own nuclear deterrent. Yet the prestigious arms race and the upkeep of so many foreign clients presented Moscow with huge costs on a truly superpower scale.

The other source of escalating costs was domestic and social in nature—in fact, a direct result of successful industrialization. These costs had three distinct components, which corresponded to the main social classes of mature Soviet society: nomenklatura, intelligentsia, and workers. After 1991 Russia shed most of its erstwhile superpower burden, albeit in very chaotic and painful ways. However, its sociopolitical and demographic dilemmas, in many respects, became significantly worse.

The members of the bureaucratic nomenklatura, like any ruling elite, carried an ingrained psychological tendency to secure their privileged status for themselves and their children and simply to enjoy the fruits of power with less fear.[9] The denunciation of Stalinism in 1956 made overt the nomenklatura's rebellion against the terrorist methods that kept them on a short leash. Nikita Khrushchev's personality overdramatized the rupture, but the members of the nomenklatura were certainly moving in the same direction, at least since the execution of the dreaded Lavrenty Beria.

With the removal of the hyperactive Khrushchev, the members of the nomenklatura obtained their paradise. The result, however, proved collectively irrational. A command economy, forgive the tautology, requires a supreme commander. In his absence, bureaucratic pathologies of all familiar kinds rapidly proliferate through the ranks. The state apparatus becomes corrupt, fragmented by patronage networks, and blindly inertial and wasteful. It is sometimes claimed that the USSR failed to keep up with the advances in microelectronics and computers because of the intrinsically democratic, flexible, and "network" qualities of this new technology. Yet neither the U.S. Department of Defense, where the Internet was invented, nor the famed Japanese corporations can be considered democratic institutions. The Soviet economy, having once achieved impressive rates of growth and technological innovation, began stalling precisely when Moscow was transformed from the commanding heights of a despotically centralized war economy into a marketplace of bureaucratic lobbying for resources. This dissipation of centralized power was conducive to the ever softer "budget constraint," which, unlike the earlier heroic-terrorist period, now brought rapidly diminishing returns.[10]

The majority of Soviet workers, whether in factories or on state farms, also obtained their kind of lesser paradise. Significant concessions in real wages were derived in the main from the structures of Soviet industrialism and changing demographics. Whatever the specific causes, for the first time in history Russian rulers could no longer dispose of the inexhaustible reservoir of labor and military recruits provided by the peasantry. Autonomous labor organizing remained strictly outlawed, but this could not prevent collective bargaining in tacit forms, including a decrease of labor input in the forms of slackening, absenteeism, or, for that matter, alcoholism. By the 1960s, the nomenklatura could no longer rely on the old Stalinist tools, at least nowhere near earlier levels. What remained was the tactic of buying labor compliance with increased consumption and toleration of inefficiencies. This is the political economy behind the sarcastic expression "they pretend to pay, and we pretend to work."

Looming in the background was the ultimate reason for the nomenklatura's concessions to workers: the specter of a political alliance between socialist proletarians and the intelligentsia that could materialize in cross-class rebellions like Poland's Solidarity movement in 1980. The present-day absence of such potentiality is what renders the behavior of the post-Soviet "post-nomenklatura" so brazenly egotistical.

The post-1945 period was also marked by the coalescence of a new Soviet intelligentsia. This was an occupationally and ethnically quite diverse class of educated specialists who shared a common desire: to reform the political and cultural structures of the Soviet state in accordance with their now vastly increased proportional and functional importance in society. Potentially, this was a force for renewed economic dynamism on the basis of what at the time came to be called the Technoscientific Revolution. These youthful romantic urges (it would be an overstatement to call them a project) almost immediately ran into the resistance of the nomenklatura. The problem was obviously political. The young intelligentsia, though ideologically still predominantly socialist and Soviet patriotic, nevertheless expected to get a say in the selection of state personnel and the discussion of policies. In effect, this challenged the nomenklatura's control at all levels, from education and industrial enterprises to foreign policy, if not only in what was regarded as the highly restrictive isolation of the Soviet citizenry from prestigious foreign goods, contemporary cultural practices, personal contacts, and travel.[11]

This kind of pressure peaked with the ebullient antiauthoritarian activism of 1968. The brewing revolt was promptly suppressed, but the further costs of suppression proved staggering indeed. The sclerosis personified by Leonid Brezhnev was hardly a medical condition. The Soviet rulers, in effect, shut down the emergent public arena along with all the inventiveness, social energy, and perhaps even renewed legitimacy it could generate. What remained were stultifying dogmatic inertia, institutionalized hypocrisy, pervasive withdrawal into private life, apathy, and cynicism. Such costs are hardly quantifiable. Their hugely damaging and lasting effects, however, would come to light both in the catastrophic failure of perestroika and what ensued in its aftermath. The few remaining circles of the intelligentsia still nurturing dissident political ambitions turned to the ideologies that seemed the most antithetical to Soviet officialdom: nationalism and the neoliberal market individualism. It is a very bitter irony that dissident ideologies both provided salvation strategies to the nomenklatura while destroying the geopolitical and organizational advantages that could have moved the USSR closer to the capitalist core.

Recoiling to the Periphery

In retrospect, perestroika appaears a confusing or even painfully embarrassing episode pushed outside the pale of serious discussion. This seems to us simply dangerous because the lessons have not been learned. But what are the lessons?

First, it is necessary to recall the international context. In the early 1970s, America was suddenly weakened by the combination of defeat in the Vietnam War, domestic unrest, and economic crisis. In the meantime, the West European allies and Japan fully recovered from wartime devastation and grew into strong economic competitors of America. Predictably, they began pushing for a more independent role in world politics, including the relaxation of Cold War tensions at their borders and the right to establish direct commercial relations with communist countries. Moscow, having long exhausted the potential of developmentalist dictatorship, now seemed very interested in gaining access to foreign loans, consumer goods, and above all productive technologies. In exchange, the Western Europeans were promised access to the USSR's vast markets, natural resources, and educated yet still comparatively underpaid labor force.

Also predictably, the détente was strongly opposed by the elite factions of both superpowers who stood to lose from it: namely, the nomenklatura of the Soviet military-industrial, or rather military-industrial-ideological, complex; and their analogous "Cold Warrior" adversaries across the Atlantic. They stalled the process and even provoked a brief reversal in the early 1980s. Generational change in Moscow's leadership, epitomized by Mikhail Gorbachev, helped to unblock the process of rapprochement. Washington had to reciprocate largely out of realism in the face of declining influence among its allies. For a moment, the road seemed open for an honorable inclusion of the USSR in the core capitalist networks of power, wealth, and prestige. This would have been a spectacular crowning achievement for a formerly semiperipheral country. In the twentieth century only Japan and, to some extent, Italy and Spain have managed to run the full developmental sequence.

Gorbachev was intuitively seeking a political alliance between several different social forces, both outside and inside Soviet borders. Externally, these were primarily the Western European capitalist elites whom Gorbachev promised to deliver from the long-standing communist menace, liberate from American tutelage, and make partners in the joint control of huge new markets (remember that China was not yet a serious player). On the home front, Gorbachev sought to bolster the nomenklatura's reformist and more cosmopolitan faction, located primarily in advanced industries, against its more provincial and conservative factions. His main political strategy was quite traditional for Soviet rulers intent on changing course: a purge of cadres combined with an ideological campaign. But the key promoters and the mass audience of his ideological campaign were certainly novel—they were the intelligentsia and specialists whose aspirations had been kept under tight lid since 1968. In this sense, 1989 became a continuation of 1968 throughout the whole Soviet Bloc.[12]

Gorbachev dropped the ball—although, let us note, quite late in the game, when success seemed near. His achievements of the previous five years were nothing short of amazing, which should instruct and inspire future Russian reformers. The West, for all its ideological and material advantages, was forced to accept the unimaginable fact that Moscow was single-handedly reordering post-1945 geopolitics. This pointed to a powerful new bloc in continental Europe centering on an alliance between

Russia and now-unified Germany. Of course, Gorbachev had to learn and accept many realities that were new to him, too. Yet he was a quick learner. Eventually, he let go of the Baltic republics, a minor loss in the grand scheme of things, and even reconciled himself to the inevitable fragmentation of the Communist Party of the Soviet Union, his original platform of political power and a major constraint.

Gorbachev is usually regarded as a reckless liberal reformer, but he was in fact a visionary conservative. His goal was to preserve the Soviet Union as a major power, with the necessary cost-cutting concessions, and to transform the nomenklatura into capitalist technocrats collectively and thus more securely ensconced in the large state and semistate corporations partially open to foreign capital through joint ventures. This strategy would have strengthened the position of the former communist elite vis-à-vis their Western partners and especially their own population. If it had come to pass, the end result would not have looked too different from what had emerged in Western Europe and Japan in the postwar decades. Hence the intuitive affinity often felt between Moscow, Paris, Bonn, and Tokyo.

The structural constraints on perestroika were primarily negative, that is, the relative dearth of self-organizing, effective support from the social groups of its potential beneficiaries, the reform nomenklatura, and educated specialists. In turn, constraints flowed immediately from the early suppression of social energies in the late 1960s rather than the more remote legacies of Russian despotic tradition or Stalinism, which had long been undone by the success of Soviet developmentalism. Here, comparisons with other communist states will allow us to compress the argument.

First of all, let us discount an anachronistic analogy. Unlike China, the USSR was no longer an agrarian country whose rural populations could provide a large pool of cheap labor and small-scale entrepreneurs with minimal state intervention. It was plain ideological naïveté, or worse, to expect that the employees of huge and technologically complex Soviet industries could readily obtain the social skills and capital or market opportunities for transforming themselves into productive businessmen once this was decreed by reformers or, as often happened in reality, the state enterprises simply stopped paying wages. A central irony of the Soviet situation was that any successful transition to markets had to be carefully planned and supervised by the state bureaucracy.

Unlike Hungary, where since the late 1960s socialist managers had been permitted to engage in various joint ventures with Western capitalist firms, Soviet industrial managers had too little experience in such matters to immediately appreciate the opportunities of perestroika and begin projecting their career aspirations into the reform movement. And unlike Poland and Czechoslovakia with their recent memories of mass mobilization, the political skills and organizing networks of the Soviet intelligentsia remained limited. Surely there was a lot of symbolic activism in the public arena fostered by glasnost and coming mostly from celebrity intellectuals and journalists, but it was not yet enough to reach into the larger population for sustained support.

Such alliances of the intelligentsia with larger popular strata and a few defecting nomenklatura elements began emerging as a credible political force toward 1989. By this time Gorbachev, the last general secretary, in a common mistake of authoritarian reformers, seemed increasingly disoriented. For good reason always fearing a reactionary coup, he proved too slow to appreciate the rapidly rising political potential of the emergent social movements. Instead, he put too much hope in his international prestige and foreign loans, vainly expecting that this would allow him to weather the rising storm on the domestic front.

In the aftermath of the August 1991 coup and Gorbachev's failure to show force, the previously inert or obedient majority of the nomenklatura finally dared to act on their own. Their desperately defensive action translated into a panoply of haphazard improvisations seeking survival in the shortest run. Breaking the long-standing Soviet taboos, the members of the nomenklatura deployed three strategies, each of which they preemptively hijacked from the demands of oppositional social movements: parliamentary elections, the privatization of state enterprises, and national sovereignty. Because in many situations the nomenklatura still controlled the state organizational resources and economic assets at the level of their immediate administrative jurisdiction, they could use elections for self-promotion into Parliament speakers or presidents; privatization for self-enrichment, the cultivation of clients, and creating safe landing strips; and last but not least, national sovereignty for barricading local rulers against another purge coming from Moscow and harnessing the short-lived mobilizations of national intelligentsias.

In 1990 and 1992, the nomenklatura essentially disassembled the USSR into parts—republics and provinces or industrial sectors and enterprises. The loss of state and economic integrity led to the rampant proliferation of bureaucratic pathologies, which have never been absent from the Soviet past. But the scale itself now made a qualitative difference. Shady patronage became the main or even the sole organizing principle of politics in which the granting of corruption rents grew into the main form of reward and control. In addition, two other institutions of control and extraction emerged in the areas where direct political control was infeasible or undesirable: organized crime and business oligarchs, intersecting realities especially in the early stages of disintegration, and using sheer force and corrupt connections to create business opportunities.

The outcome of the nomenklatura counterrebellion proved collectively irrational. Significantly weaker successor states could never expect an invitation to join the capitalist core because they could not maintain the levels of industrial coordination and investment, science, educational and welfare provision, or, for that matter, military force and diplomatic influence previously achieved by the USSR. It is fantasy to imagine such states eventually normalizing and establishing property rights and the rule of law. This runs against the hard reality of their morphology and functioning. The state itself serves as the main or even sole viable source of profits as well as the arena of business competition, which is invariably dirty and often also violent. The loudest calls for the rule of law and punishing "fat cats" typically come from the elite factions that currently find themselves on the losing side. But once they get into power in some sort of coup or popular uprising, which periodically happens because the states are relatively weak, former oppositionists discover that the corrupt system is too hard to change and that it actually works for them by offering the means of control and enrichment. The negative dynamic tends to become self-reinforcing by rendering almost any productive enterprise too precarious and unprofitable. The locus of accumulation then durably shifts into pillage via the abuse of state offices and subordinate intermediary alliances with large foreign interests that can organize their own protection. This is what one may call the trap of peripheralization. This picture has been long familiar from the experiences of many states in the what was once called the Third World, and now joined by fragments of the defunct "Second World." Instead of moving the USSR closer to the capitalist core, the messy demise of the Soviet state produced a recoiling to the periphery.

Back from the Nadir?

On the basis of the arguments given in this chapter, our prognosis must be moderately pessimistic. Let us first explain the reasons for pessimism and then qualify them by suggesting what could be an unapparent alternative for the future.

In the past, Russia had enjoyed a relatively high status in the modern world-system due to a fortuitous geographic position, formidable armies, and a large enserfed peasantry. During this long stretch of history, from the 1500s until the 1960s, Russia spectacularly succeeded in three major surges of state power associated with early gunpowder monarchy, bureaucratic absolutism, and the revolutionary military-industrial transformation. The main measure of this success was that Russia remained a major player long after its fellow noncapitalist empires—China, Spain, Poland-Lithuania, Iran, and Turkey—succumbed to subordinate incorporation into the capitalist world economy. The Russian and mainly Soviet success finds any reasonable comparison only in the example of Japan, and still it is a lesser example considering that Japan made its final spurt into the capitalist core after 1945 as an American special dependency. The Bolshevik achievement per se had no direct bearing on abstract human freedom or the pursuit of happiness. Nevertheless, the Soviet Union played an enormously consequential role in defeating the Nazis, speeding up decolonization, and bolstering the twentieth-century developmentalism around the world. All this certainly could serve as a matter of national pride.

For the USSR to have continuity with the despotic past became impossible with the completion of Soviet industrialization. The traditional sources of Russian power were exhausted in the period shortly after 1945, which was marked by the rapid disappearance of peasantries (as, in fact, part of a worldwide phenomenon) and the durable pacification of core geopolitics. What remained, however, was still an extremely large and tightly centralized state with exceptional armed forces, first-class science and education, formidable industrial bases, and an enviable endowment of natural resources. The next logical step in the trajectory of Soviet developmentalism would suggest using these assets to negotiate admission into the world system's core. In effect, various Soviet leaders since the death of Stalin have sought just this. Today it still remains the hope, albeit a more distant one than twenty years ago.

The biggest political problem of mature Soviet society stemmed from its own success. Instead of the peasantry, whose sporadic rebelliousness was countered by geographical dispersion and a lack of modern political ideology, contemporary Soviet rulers had to deal with the strategically concentrated, literate, mobile, still mostly young and active masses of workers and members of the new intelligentsia. The dilemma of Soviet rulers was exactly this: How could they acquire core-like features for the economy and technology while preventing the intelligentsia and workers from forging a rebellious alliance and restructuring political institutions in accordance with their aspirations for greater autonomy and dynamism in every social sphere? In other words, how could they continue developmentalism in a bureaucratic-authoritarian mold minus state terrorism, because this would threaten the members of the nomenklatura themselves. No positive solution was ever found. In the meantime, the contradiction peaked in 1968, and again, far more broadly and openly, in 1989.

The uncoordinated series of nomenklatura counterrebellions in 1991 and 1992 delivered a disastrously Pyrrhic victory in this class struggle. The sudden collapse left the intelligentsia and workers demoralized, insecure, and impoverished. The former members of the nomenklatura, with some unluckier or simply less nimble exceptions, largely preserved their control over sources of wealth and political power. But the collapse scattered and undid the Soviet assets on whose strength one might have hoped that post-Soviet Russia could achieve a better position in the capitalist world economy. Instead of a place like Europe or North America, the Russians found themselves essentially in South America.

A totally pessimistic scenario suggests that, from here on, the movement would be a downward spiral. The process of "undevelopment" would be driven by the continuing erosion of state structures, and by the fragmentation of the ruling class into rival oligarchies and provincial bailiwicks that become unable and therefore unwilling to support the institutions and social groups that once embodied the core-like features of Soviet developmentalism. There is, however, a certain "stickiness" to both past success and failure that should moderate our pessimism regarding Russia. Specifically, this might mean two quite different political possibilities taking shape in the coming decade.

The first possibility is the recovery of state power from within and above. Russia arguably has a long history of such recoveries by authoritarian means, embodied by the fractions of the ruling class most directly associated with the erstwhile superpower service and status positions that are meaningless to privatize. In the mid-1990s, we predicted that the next Russian president would likely be a man wearing epaulets, a military general, or, as it happens, a KGB colonel.[13] That interview concluded with a series of short questions and answers:

- *Will Russia become an American satellite?* No. Russia is destined to stick with Europe.
- *Will Russia remain semiperipheral?* As always, since at least the reign of Catherine the Great.
- *In ten years, will Russia become more assertive geopolitically?* Yes.
- *Catch up with the West?* No.
- *Will democracy survive?* Perhaps.
- *And the free market economy?* Doubtfully.
- *Corruption?* No doubt.

Sixteen years later, we still stand by these predictions. Vladimir Putin achieved primarily two things: He brought to heel the oligarchs and provincial governors. And he made the West count with Russia again. Can he, or some appointed successor, move further? That would depend on the ability to discipline the state apparatus. The usual talk of corruption and economic crime in Russia misses the key point. Putin forcefully limited the nonstate possibilities for private accumulation, including those relying on the use of coercion (that is, organized crime in its many shades). But in doing so, he had to "pay" his subordinates by essentially granting them a license to collect rents from office. Sanctioned venality is nothing new in the repertoire of state rule. Recall the absolutist monarchies of Europe. But this is a blind and wasteful kind of governance fraught with the danger of provoking strong opposition from society, including the elite factions who find themselves on the losing side.

The Russian political regime today could be called a "sovereign bureaucracy." It indeed became sovereign from foreign dictates or any domestic elite interests. The state has regained at least a theoretical possibility to act independently. But can it really act? Bureaucracy tends to become "sovereign" not only from foreigners and the common population but also from its own superiors. State servants, especially those in the middle ranks, have a structural interest in, and possibilities to insulate themselves from any interference and supervision, especially when private gain is allowed to become their key motivation. Such situations commonly create periods of stagnation because superiors prefer to go along and personally profit from the shameful state of affairs. But once an activist ruler attempts to exercise power by making his subordinates do what they would otherwise not do, it invariably provokes resistance in the form of foot-dragging or even a palace coup.

The typical way of overcoming such resistance is a purge from above. This tactic was intrinsic to Soviet governance. But neither Stalin nor Gorbachev in the early years of perestroika could assault the cadres by violence alone. A purge is always accompanied by an intensely ideological campaign not merely for propagandistic justification but mainly for the purposes of targeting the opponents and promoting the loyalists. Still, a purge (or any radical reshuffling) poses a direct risk to the ruler, as Khrushchev and later Gorbachev found out. It remains a largely empirical question whether Russia's present leaders can find anywhere an alternative supply of "cleaner," more professional cadres and, moreover, devise the political framework to identify, promote, and keep in line the new appointments.

An alternative push to rationalize and discipline the state could come from below. Some Arab countries serve as the most recent example of how unexpectedly this can happen. For all the changes, and even more so the talk of big changes since 1991, the social structure of Russian society remains basically similar to what emerged in the 1960s. On one side is a sort of nomenklatura whose members are now recruited, promoted, and held together by personal patronage and cronyism rather than by the Communist Party. This "post-nomenklatura" possesses infinitely less cohesion and ésprit de corps in comparison with its Soviet predecessors. The ritual invocations of state patriotism meshing with the imitative rituals of de-

mocracy look unconvincing if not downright cynical because the contrast
with actual practices and dispositions is too great to disguise. All this certainly makes rulers more vulnerable to popular contestation. Nevertheless,
a country of such size and forcefulness as Russia—which still has nuclear
weapons, a large coercive apparatus, and the rents from natural resources
available for political patronage and a degree of social redistribution—
might be able to avoid a successful revolution for some years to come.
The result would then resemble a diminished version of Brezhnevism that
never produced its Gorbachev.

On the other side are the politically disunited workers who no longer
enjoy job security, the members of the intelligentsia who lost much of their
institutional base along with their lofty group ideology, and now also the
numerous and motley strata of subproletarians, mostly young people with
no prospect of stable employment, who can be ferocious street fighters
but hardly anything else on their own. The hopes often vested in the new
middle class of businesspeople seem to us largely false. The members of
this class, by virtue of their occupations, are too prone to strike personal
deals with representatives of the existing power structures. Some could
join or even sponsor protests, but they are as likely to defect from the
cause once it becomes too dangerous or their individual ambitions have
been met. Add to this a large—by any measure—gap between Moscow
and the provinces. This typical sociogeographic cleavage is found in many
semiperipheral countries where the capital city becomes the exclusionary
concentration of higher incomes and careers. All in all, Russian society
does not appear to be a very promising site for contentious mobilizing,
despite the large but disparate pools of discontent.

The liberal Westernizers, although a ubiquitous and vocal presence
in the intelligentsia circles of the capitals of all countries frustrated by
their semiperipheral status in the world system, could hardly ever tap into
popular discontent on their own. For this purpose, the imitative liberals
seem too esoteric and removed. Moreover, their elitist and individualist
ideology is not particularly suited to the demanding work of building parties and movements. Nor is social democracy a suitable import. This is a
political strategy and regime type found only in stable times and in the
wealthy countries where the capitalist elites can afford a degree of internal redistribution to support their legitimacy, social peace, and consumer

demand. Social democracy, in short, is a core luxury. Nationalism seems the likeliest sentiment to hold together enough people in an uprising. After all, nationalism played a major unifying role in the 1989 rebellions across Eastern Europe. But in an imperial country with large ethnic and immigrant minorities, nationalism is an extremely tricky proposition.

What then remains? May we say the unutterable: Leninism. We certainly do not mean a return to the defunct official ideology. We mean instead what one might call a new progressive patriotism. Today in Russia, Vladimir Lenin is largely forgotten, despite the lingering monuments. For the time being, this actually works to Lenin's benefit. But things could change rapidly. We believe that Lenin is bound for a political resurrection because there seem few acceptable alternatives in the Russian historical pantheon. Any successful nation needs national founders and great heroes. Peter the Great was cast for the role but found to be too remote. Stalin, for obvious reasons, will ever remain too divisive, despite the attempts to bring him back. Besides, he is just not a founder.

Lenin brings five political advantages. First, he was an improbably successful state builder who wrestled the remnants of the Russian Empire from defeat, foreign interventions, and local separatisms.

Second, he removed the political obstacles and pushed forward the reforms of Count Witte. Lenin was a modernizer dreaming of electricity (the part of the slogan referring to communism will be creatively forgotten).

Third, Lenin resolved by deed the Westernizers–nativists debate by being simultaneously both. He showed how a non-Western country could regain its dignity and at the same time adopt Western technology. So now, in the face of a growing China in the twenty-first century, Russians might take pleasure in reminding the ever-respectful Chinese who had inspired their own modern founders.

Fourth, national heroes must be decisive and farsighted leaders. Lenin took whatever train could transport him to Petrograd, without hesitation made difficult compromises, and in the end won. He brought organization to the enormous chaos where the power was "lying in the streets." He knew when to shift gears, by at various times accepting the peasants' demands for land, the cultural aspirations of nationalities, or the market's restoration under the New Economic Policy.

Fifth and finally, Lenin proclaimed and practiced democracy, if just within his own party. And did he not warn about Stalin?

Lenin might turn in his sarcophagus from such patriotic praises; but that will not matter. Nobody except a few ideologues and pedantic historians will worry what Lenin really thought about himself and his politics. What will matter is that he was a world figure, a resolute and astutely inventive state builder, and a national unifier and modernizer who never (notice) succumbed to Russian chauvinism. We predict that the political force that first proves capable of grasping the potential of Leninism and projecting it into the future could come out on the winning side.

Will this mean socialism? We do not believe that anyone today can really know what a future equivalent of socialism might be in practice. History is full of ironies—that is, failures to predict further outcomes. Lenin believed he was in the vanguard of world social revolution, but in fact he mightily continued the reforms of Count Witte, launching Russia into another upswing of power and prestige in the capitalist world-system. Today Russia seems to be emerging from another historical nadir, with its political fortunes still looking very uncertain. Our counterintuitive emphasis on the near success of Gorbachev's perestroika and the untapped future potential of Leninism is meant to provoke a reasoned and serious debate. Russia must walk a narrow path between the extremes of reactionary imperial nationalism and globalist neoliberalism.

Notes

1. Immanuel Wallerstein, "The Rise and Future Demise of the World Capitalist System: Concepts for Comparative Analysis," *Comparative Studies in Society and History* 16, no. 4. (September 1974): 387–415.

2. William McNeill, *The Pursuit of Power: Technology, Armed Force, and Society Since A.D. 1000* (Chicago: University of Chicago Press, 1982).

3. Immanuel Wallerstein, *The Modern World-System, Vol. 1: Capitalist Agriculture and the Origins of the European World-Economy in the Sixteenth Century* (New York: Academic Press, 1974; updated edition, Berkeley: University of California Press, 2011).

4. Charles Tilly, *Coercion, Capital and European States, A.D. 990–1992* (Oxford: Blackwell, 1992).

5. Immanuel Wallerstein, "Social Science and the Communist Interlude, or Interpretations of Contemporary History," in *The End of the World as We Know It: Social Science for the Twenty-First Century* (Minneapolis: University of Minnesota Press, 1999), 7–18.

6. Eric Hobsbawm, *The Age of Extremes: A History of the World, 1914–1991* (New York: Vintage Books, 1996).

7. Michael Mann, *The Sources of Social Power, Volume 2: The Rise of Classes and Nation-States, 1760–1914* (Cambridge: Cambridge University Press, 1993).

8. Stephen Hanson, *Time and Revolution: Marxism and the Design of Soviet Institutions* (Chapel Hill: University of North Carolina Press, 1997), 17.

9. Immanuel Wallerstein, "The Bourgeois(ie) as Concept and Reality," *New Left Review*, January–February 1988, 91–106. Also in *The Essential Wallerstein* (New York: New Press, 2000).

10. Ivan T. Berend, *From the Soviet Bloc to the European Union: The Economic and Social Transformation of Central and Eastern Europe Since 1973* (New York: Cambridge University Press, 2009).

11. See analytical-historical chapters 3 through 5 in Bourdieu's *Secret Admirer in the Caucasus: A World-System Biography*, by Georgi Derluguian (Chicago: University of Chicago Press, 2005).

12. Giovanni Arrighi, Terence K. Hopkins, and Immanuel Wallerstein, "1989, The Continuation of 1968," *Review* 15, no. 2 (Spring 1992).

13. Georgi Derluguian, "Russia: Trying Hard. A Conversation with Immanuel Wallerstein," *Medved*, no. 4 (1995): 22–24.

CHAPTER THREE

RUSSIA'S FOREIGN POLICY OUTLOOK

Dmitri Trenin

If, in the future, the European project is able to overcome its current difficulties, it would strengthen Moscow's "European vector" policy and would encourage Euro-Russian integration. The failure of the project, on the contrary, would deprive Russia of a natural "anchor" in the world arena.

Since 1992, Russian foreign policy has gone through several stages. Initially, until about 2003, it focused mainly on the country's integration into the Western community. During the Yeltsin years, there was talk of Russia's immediate integration into transatlantic and European institutions. At the beginning of Vladimir Putin's administration, emphasis was placed on alliances with the United States and NATO under the flag of the war against international terrorism, and on rapprochement with the European Union within the framework of Russia's "European choice."

For various reasons—both internal to Russia and international—the policy of integration was unsuccessful. A sharp deflection took place in 2003 and 2004. The vector of Russian foreign policy was unfolded by the United States' invasion of Iraq, the "Yukos affair" and the retaliatory campaign of Western media and international organizations to "fight against Putinism," the Beslan tragedy and the United States and Britain granting asylum to Chechen separatist leaders, and, finally, the Orange Revolution in Ukraine. Putin's famous speeches related to the terrorist attack in Beslan (September 4, 2004)[1] and at the Munich Security Conference

(February 10, 2007)[2] became the ideological basis for the U-turn from the original policy. And the material foundation of this new course was the continuous steady rise in oil prices starting in 2003.

The Time of Self-Affirmation

The evolution of Russian foreign policy that began in 2003–2004 was marked by Moscow's abandonment of its attempt to follow the process of integration with the Western community. Instead of this, Russia has focused on strengthening its own position as a great power. This course— this "solo voyage"—has brought limited results.[3] Thanks to favorable economic conditions, Russia has achieved financial independence from the West; reestablished its political presence after a long hiatus in regions like Asia, Africa, and Latin America; and founded the semblance of a non–Western world alliance with China, India, and Brazil—in the framework of the Shanghai Cooperation Organization and virtual structures like the BRICs and RIC.

In the 2000s, the Russian economy engaged with global markets. Having gotten rid of the crutches of loans from the International Monetary Fund, and having settled the accounts of its sovereign debt, Moscow was already able to stand on its own feet politically. Nevertheless, it became clear that Russia was stuck on the periphery of the global economy, and its political weight and influence in the world continued to decline. In the dynamics of development and recovery in the international arena, Russia began to give way not only to China and India but also to countries like Brazil, Indonesia, Mexico, Turkey, and South Africa.

The stage characterized by slogans like "sovereign democracy" and "energy superpower" was completed in 2008. The war between Russia and Georgia almost led to a clash between Russia and the United States. The global financial and economic crisis of 2008–2009 hit Russia harder than any other major economy in the world. In the backdrop of falling global GDP, China's steady growth drove the "scissors" even wider between Russia and its great eastern neighbor. At the same time, Russia's position in scientific and technical capacities sank in major world ratings. Perhaps the biggest factor for this—along with the outflow of investments—was the sharp decline and subsequent stabilization of oil prices. The combination of these adverse events and processes forced the Russian government to modify its foreign policy.

In 2009, President Dmitri Medvedev declared a policy of modernizing Russia. This decision confirmed that Medvedev and Putin recognized that hopes of the ongoing oil boom would return Russia to a leading position in the world would not materialize.

Features and Limitations of the "Modernization" of Foreign Policy

In my opinion, the decision to embark on the course of modernization was driven by the Russian ruling class's anxiety over the country's great power position in the world. The progressively increasing economic and techno-logical backwardness not only threatened the country's hard-earned re-newed personality but also its international independence. Similarly, a fall in Russia's international weight undermined opportunities for the Russian elite, including financial ones.

The very concept of a "power" refers to an independent state. In the view of the Russian leadership, it is necessary to guarantee Russia's in-dependence with respect to the global leading power of the United States and the rising world power of China. At the end of 2008, Putin could have applied Churchill's saying, that he "would not preside over" the loss of Russia's status as a great power.[4] The conclusion that "something must be done" followed.

It is important to highlight the fact that the Russian government looks at modernization most of all as a significant increase in the technological level of the economy, and development as its innovative component—with a role for the government as the entity that leads, organizes, and controls like a ruling corporation. On the one hand, this sets rather narrow limits for modernization policies. In this way, all modernization can be reduced to a formula: money plus engineers. The political system thus becomes clamped up; the current model completely meets the needs of the elites. Accordingly, the drawbacks of this system—in particular, corruption—are regarded as a "virus," not a salient phenomenon of the system. On the other hand, the current attempt to modernize—unlike that of, say, Stalin—clearly has a nonmilitary, nonconfrontational, and open-minded character, even though it runs parallel to the military reforms and initiated the reequipment of the Russian armed forces—after two decades of virtual negligence.

The starting point of the "connection" between the modernization agenda and foreign policy is the government's realization that left to its own devices, Russia will not be able to cope with the challenges of the time. Vladislav Surkov, who coined the term "sovereign democracy," has acknowledged this publicly, and in precisely these terms.[5] From this realization, a logical conclusion was derived: Foreign policy, which earlier had served as a means of Russia's self-affirmation, will now become the instrument to search for external resources for the country's modernization. The geographical direction of this search is clear—it is toward the developed countries, which are a part of the Organization for Economic Cooperation and Development, primarily the member countries of the European Union and the United States. Russia hopes to negotiate with these countries what Dmitri Medvedev called "modernization alliances."[6]

The process of the "reset" between Russia and the United States is associated with the policy of modernization. However, it must be kept in mind that this "reset" was started by Washington, where after a change of administrations in 2009, its foreign policy priorities also changed. Without any preconditions or negotiations, President Barack Obama unilaterally eliminated all the main irritants that had destabilized United States–Russia relations during the second term of George W. Bush's presidency: advancement of Ukraine's and Georgia's memberships in NATO, political and military support extended to Mikheil Saakashvili, and plans to deploy a missile defense system in Central Europe.

Moscow responded to the U.S. president's initiatives positively, but with general caution. By the fall of 2010, Russia had reciprocated America's "reset" by significantly modifying its position on Iran. This became evident with Russia's support for UN Security Council Resolution 1929, which toughened sanctions on Iran—restricting the Kremlin in supplying Iran with S-300 antiaircraft systems for which Iran had already paid. (The cost of the affair was approximately $1 billion.) Russia also granted permission to use its territory and airspace for the transit of U.S. and NATO forces to access Afghanistan. In March 2011, Moscow abstained from UN Security

Council Resolution 1973 on Libya, and thereby created a legitimate basis for NATO's military operation against Muammar Gaddafi's regime, which ended in his being ousted. Under these conditions, there is some level of mutual trust between the Kremlin and the White House. The ratification and implementation of the new Strategic Arms Reduction Treaty (New START), and enforcement of agreements on cooperation vis-à-vis nuclear energy ("123 Nuclear Cooperation Agreement"), formed the practical results of the "reset." Furthermore, the United States removed the remaining obstacles stalling Russia's accession to the World Trade Organization.

In the European direction, President Medvedev has advanced his proposal for a European Security Treaty, the idea for which emerged before the war with Georgia. This initiative represents Moscow's desire to achieve a balance of interests in the Euro-Atlantic area. The promotion of the European Security Treaty is evidence that Russia seeks to consolidate the status quo rather than revise it. However, the chances of this project's being realized in the form proposed by Medvedev are practically zero. A more promising means of building confidence between Russia and the United States-NATO is cooperation in the area of missile defenses. Medvedev's participation in NATO's Lisbon Summit became a symbol of this emerging strategic turn. Vladimir Putin, for his part, suggested to the German business community a partnership based on the integration of German (European) technologies and Russian resources.

It is clear that the most important condition for the modernization of partnerships is a strategic turnabout in relations between Russia and the United States–NATO. Without such a shift, a modernization of partnerships cannot be realized. The other condition is the reconciliation between Russia and its eastern neighbors, which would overcome the imperial and communist past. In the mid-2000s, bad relations with Poland, which joined the European Union in 2004, became a serious hindrance to Russia's relations with the EU. Having become convinced of the futility of trying to put pressure on Poland through Moscow's principal partners—Berlin and Paris, especially after the political departure of Chancellor Gerhard Schröder and President Jacques Chirac—Vladimir Putin has personally led the line of normalization of relations with Poland.

The crash of the Polish president's aircraft in Smolensk immediately after a joint ceremony with the two leaders in Katyn was a brutal test of the new relationship. The words and actions of the Russian authorities in relation to the death of President Lech Kaczynski and dozens of others who died on board, and the reactions of the Polish politicians and public, showed that as of now, both sides have passed the test despite additional complications arising from the investigation of the complex reasons for the crash of the presidential aircraft.

Yet another example is the Arctic.[7] In 2007–2008, the media actively discussed the topic of a division of Arctic resources. Russian and Western politicians exchanged harsh, even belligerent, statements. But in 2009, this rhetoric came to a halt, and in 2010, Russia signed an agreement with Norway on the delimitation of economic zones in the Arctic—the forty-year dispute ended in a compromise based on the principle of 50/50. This agreement signaled Moscow's willingness to resolve disagreements on a contractual basis. In early 2011, the state-owned company Rosneft signed an agreement with BP on asset swaps and joint development of oil fields in the Kara Sea. When the project fell through because of the position of the Russian business partner of BP from the AAR group, the American company ExxonMobil became Rosneft's new partner in the Arctic.

With regard to new states, Moscow has taken a generally moderate course. The rhetoric about "privileged interests" and "protection of Russian citizens abroad" has become rarer and duller. After the departure of the main irritant in Kiev—President Viktor Yushchenko—Russia began to settle its gas disputes with Ukraine. Promoting its own interests—for example, in relation to the Black Sea Fleet—Moscow went to Kiev with financial concessions and abandoned its previous plans (which it had had until 2004) to integrate Ukraine into a single economic, military, and political space with Russia.

A voluntary integration was carried out—predominantly from Kazakhstan's side—in the framework of a Customs Union that came into effect in 2010. The situation was more difficult with Belarus. Moscow has applied economic, political, and psychological pressure on Belarusan president Alexander Lukashenko with the purpose of getting him to "open" the Belarusan economy to Russian capital. Here, it seems, Moscow managed the impossible. One the one hand, Medvedev harshly criticized Lukashenko, and the Kremlin-controlled Russian media gave a platform to the opposition candidates, many of whom positioned themselves as pro-Russian. Outwardly, it seemed that Lukashenko stopped being someone Moscow considered capable of dialogue, and Moscow deleted him from the list of Russia's partners. Yet on the other hand, these unusual pressures on "the last dictator in Europe" were only a means to extract the maximum concessions from him. Before the elections, Lukashenko was invited to Moscow to discuss contentious issues. Finally, on election night, the Belarusan security forces showed unprecedented cruelty—even for Minsk—in the persecution of the opposition. This, at once, destroyed the Western vector of Belarusan politics, which Lukashenko had industriously built up over the past years as a counterbalance to dependence on the Russian Federation. As a result, toward the beginning of 2011, Belarus seemed more strongly attached to Russia than ever before. At the same time, Moscow avoided all accusations of supporting the Minsk autocrat—because earlier Moscow had criticized him as severely as had the West.

In 2010, Russia morally and politically supported the overthrow of Kyrgyzstan's authoritarian president, who proved to be an unreliable partner for Moscow. However, Russian officials refused to intervene in the political and ethnic conflicts in the country despite the willingness of the new authorities, and the apparent willingness of the West, to support such an intervention. This demonstrates Moscow's unwillingness to do any heavy lifting, political or military, unless truly vital interests are involved—while at the same time wanting to be seen as a mediator wielding its soft power for the sake of conflict resolution, as evidenced by its diplomatic efforts to support dialogue between the conflicting sides in the Nagorno-Karabakh and Trans-Dniester conflicts.

With respect to Georgia, Russia's position has remained adamant: Abkhazia and South Ossetia are independent states and no meaningful dialogue can take place with Tbilisi as long as Mikheil Saakashvili remains in power in Georgia. Meanwhile, since the end of the 2008 war, the situation on the borders of Georgia has remained calm. Previous disagreements over the Georgian issue between Russia and the United States, on the one hand, and the European Union, on the other hand, have managed to be "weeded out."

When the Russian state-owned companies Rosneft and Transneft became large debtors to Chinese state-owned banks, a program of close economic cooperation was developed between the eastern regions of Russia and the neighboring provinces of China, a pipeline was built from Russia to China, and positions on future gas supply came closer. But no strategic shift from Russia's side toward China took place.

The main strategic task before Russia is to maintain control over the regions of Siberia and the Far East. Smooth and friendly relations with China are extremely important, but one-sided dependence on an increasingly powerful neighbor is considered unacceptable. The pipeline construction project, launching sites, and preparation for the Asia-Pacific Economic Cooperation Summit in Vladivostok serve precisely this purpose. In 2010, an important conclusion was reached in Moscow: The Chinese leadership has moved away from the covenant to carry out Deng Xiaoping's nonconfrontational foreign policy and is ready to press claims with other countries.[8] This calculation makes Russia seek balanced relations with Beijing through linkages with other countries—India, South Korea, and Vietnam. Moscow cautiously formulated its approach to the Korean problem, banking on Seoul, and took a neutral stance on the territorial dispute between China and its neighbors—countries belonging to the Association of Southeast Asian Nations (ASEAN) and Japan.

Russia's relations with Japan remain difficult, especially because of Tokyo's unwillingness to compromise on the territorial problem, and Moscow's opposition to meeting the Japanese claim. As a result, the Southern Kuril Islands have become a subject of domestic consumption in both countries. Medvedev's ostentatious trip to the Kuril Islands was a move in his fight for the right to participate in the 2012 elections. He clearly does not want to be perceived as a "new Gorbachev" because he has been overly compliant with the West. Against the backdrop of a clear "thaw" in the relations between Russia and the United States and the European Union, rigidity between Russia and Japan will be seen as dissonance. As a result, in the short and perhaps medium terms, Moscow's main partner in the modernization of northeastern Asia will be Seoul.

Development Scenarios Until 2020

Theoretically speaking, there are three scenarios for Russia's foreign policy during the second decade of the twenty-first century: the inertial (base), the bearish, and the bullish.

All these scenarios cannot ignore developments in the world's situations. I have already pointed out what adjustments the financial and economic crisis of 2008 brought to Russia's foreign policy, which influences played out in Russia with Barack Obama's rise to power in the United States and Viktor Yanukovych's in Ukraine. One might add that the war in the Caucasus in 2008 was triggered by the Georgian president. In constructing future scenarios, I believe that in the next decade, Russia will join the World Trade Organization, China will pursue a more assertive foreign policy, and oil prices will see moderate growth. At the same time, many other factors remain unknown. Until the end of 2010, few imagined that there would be a fundamental change in the Arab world in the short term. Russian foreign policy over the last two decades has been primarily reactive, and the circumstances in the outside world will be a major influence on Moscow's foreign policy behavior.

Along with this, I believe that the most important source of any country's—including Russia's—foreign policy is its domestic needs and priorities—and how those are determined by its government's leadership.

The Inertial Scenario

The inertial scenario assumes the continuation of the "modernization" of Russia's foreign policy. Even though this course is associated with the personality of Dmitri Medvedev, in principle, it can still be implemented in the likely event that Russian prime minister Vladimir Putin once again becomes the president in 2012. However, it is clear—and one must include the prime minister himself on this list—that the modernization-integration and promotion of Putin's performance will be directly confronted by great skepticism in the West, but the very return of Putin to the Kremlin will not make the West radically change its position toward Russia.

The "modernized" foreign policy, therefore, has sufficient resources for the medium term—up to the mid-2010s.

Of course, this path has dangers and risks—above all, domestic Russian ones. The reaction in the political circles of the EU and the United States on the new sterner sentence for Mikhail Khodorkovsky indicates a growing pessimism in the West about the prospects for a "soft transformation" of Russia's political system. Despite assurances to the contrary, the movement toward the rule of law has stalled, the authorities use the judicial system in their own interest, and the opposition's speeches in the streets are harshly repressed by the police. All expectations linked to Medvedev's figure are weakening. If, in its turn, these factors intensify repressive tendencies in Russian domestic policies, then the resources dedicated to the "reset," "partnership for modernization," and other efforts will be significantly reduced.

The central significance in this regard will be the deciding factor on the possibility (or impossibility) of cooperation in the field of missile defense between the United States and NATO on one side, and Russia, on the other. A move toward a variant of a joint (coordinated, conjugate) missile defense system could ultimately lead to the transformation of the strategic relationship between Russia and the West. However, the failure of such attempts—while continuing to work toward building a global missile defense system with a subsystem in Europe (excluding Russia)—could lead to a further aggravation of relations and to Russia's strategic exclusion from the West. Putin and Medvedev have warned that in response to the prospect of "the US acquiring capabilities of a first nuclear strike and effective defense against significantly suppressed Russian response," Russia will be obliged to expand its strategic nuclear weapons. This is not a bluff; to maintain strategic independence is a Russian foreign policy constant. Moscow's ultimate position—"either a joint missile defense system or an expansion of offensive arms"—in these circumstances is very risky, above all for Russia itself. An arms race would lead to the disappearance of external sources of modernization and the rapid depletion of domestic resources for development. Tighter security in Europe and the United States would increase uncertainty about Russia's international role, and complicate its relations with countries like Iran and China.

There are also other risks. Although the development of Iran's nuclear program has slowed down, the possibility of a military strike against Iran, either by the United States or by Israel with U.S. support, remains. Such an attack could easily cause a rift between Moscow and Washington, and consequently bring Russia and China together. In such circumstances, one could expect a correction of the Russian position on the Korean nuclear issue—in the direction of a rapprochement with Beijing's position. There are also immediate risks to the borders of Russia. Despite the change of regime in Kiev in 2010, Russian-Ukrainian relations are not unproblematic, and the question of Ukraine's NATO membership is not completely closed indefintely. The U.S. administration, under pressure from the critics of "Putin's Russia," may allow the delivery of heavy artillery to Georgia, which would immediately aggravate the situation in the Caucasus. President (and perhaps, future prime minister) Saakashvili could arouse Moscow's anger by playing a dangerous game in the direction of the North Caucasus. In any case, the issue of restoring Georgia's territorial integrity as it was at the time of the Georgian Soviet Socialist Republic has not been removed from the agenda in Tbilisi. For its part, Moscow under certain conditions could interfere with the development of the situation in neighboring countries—from Belarus to Uzbekistan—possibly reviving the notion of Russia's foreign policy as being aggressive and neo-imperialist.

Developments in Asia are already leading to increased tensions between China and its neighbors on the one hand, and between China and the United States on the other. Although Russia would almost certainly maintain its neutrality, its tactical maneuvering in the absence of a coherent strategy—"neither favoring one nor the other"—would also have a price. A specific risk is that in a serious crisis on the Korean Peninsula, where Russia will encounter both Chinese and U.S. interests, Moscow would need to maneuver, and possibly improvise on the fly.

The fundamental risk is the uncertainty of Russia's official position toward the West, and the uncertainty of the U.S. and EU positions toward Russia. Russian elites have not made a clear strategic choice in favor of confrontation with the United States, though competition for resources with America is clearly not enough. The dominant view of Russia in the United States is that of a country in a long-term decline, and whose value for the United States is constantly dwindling. The EU is absorbed in its own financial, economic, and political problems, and it has no unified strategy or domestic leadership. In these circumstances, "negative politics" has a greater pull than a constructive stance for each of these three players.

Explicit or implied mistrust and lack of interaction of institutions must be kept in mind and always remembered. This fact reinforces the importance of psychological factors. Installing Russian officials to cooperate with the West is not based on an awareness of the common vital interests and core values of the Russian Federation, the United States, and the European Union. In stark contrast is the anti-Western "breed." It is fair to add that the image of Cold War stereotypes has not completely eroded from the consciousness of the political classes of Europe and America. In these circumstances, an event can cause one to be "knocked out" of the rut, leading to drastic alienation and even hostility. Therefore, there is a chance that the inertial scenario "falls into a negative." This calls for a closer look at the bearish scenario.

The Bearish Scenario

The bearish scenario would primarily be determined by events in Russia. The country's leadership could be pushed toward a further stiffening of the political regime by the growing inefficiency of public administration, corruption in the government, and its ties with criminals; the resulting discontent and social unrest; and finally, the impossibility of a significant improvement in the system without posing a serious obstacle to the interest of the ruling groups. And this stiffening of the regime would likely be accompanied by the radicalization of the opponents of the regime, excesses on the part of its protectors, and the expansion of the practice of political repression, from the targeted killing of opponents to the mass suppression of active dissidents.

Reaching a certain point, such a course of events could radically change the attitudes of the public and governments of the United States and countries of the EU toward Russia. This could include Germany—the leading economic and, in the long term, political power of Europe. Russia's trajectory would look dangerous to these countries. Under these circumstances, the programs of technological ("modernization") and economic ("integration") cooperation with Russia would be limited and would gradually wind down. In the area of security, the focus would shift from including Russia in some kind of general system to maintain stability in the Euro-Atlantic area and protecting the Eastern European countries from Russia.

In the framework of this scenario, Belarus and Moldova could become "theaters of political action." Finally, part of the bearish scenario can exacerbate the situation in the Caucasus, both in the South and the North. "Fighters against Russian imperialism," beginning with Saakashvili, see the Caucasus as the "Achilles' heel of the Russian regime." In this regard, the 2014 Winter Olympic Games could become a convenient excuse for a variety of actions that could provoke a hard response from Moscow.

Under such circumstances, the forty-fifth U.S. president, who will replace Obama in 2016 (or, less likely, in 2012) would be forced to conduct a full-scale revision of relations with Russia. The revision of policy could lead the White House to conclude that an authoritarian and aggressive Russia is a midscale threat to U.S. interests. This conclusion, in turn, would have a range of effects: from a revival of NATO's role as an instrument to contain Moscow to the proclamation of a policy of "supporting freedom" in authoritarian regimes.

Aggravated relations between Russia and the United States, and a sharp "freezing" in relations between Russia and the EU, would force Moscow to seek help and support from other centers of power. Under these circumstances, it would be logical to assume Russia's movement toward closer relations with China, and the transformation of the current strategic partnership into a quasi-union between the two—under the leadership of Beijing.

Furthermore, Russia, in dire need of financial resources, would be forced to recognize China's leading role in the bilateral relations, and make other concessions—from granting Chinese state-owned companies access to Russian resources and military technology to the recognition of Central Asia and Kazakhstan as the sphere of state interests in China. To reduce its dependence on China, Moscow would be interested in any event that could lead to an increase in the price of oil. This interest could lead to a change in Russia's approach toward Iran, and the situation in the Middle East in general.

Another possibility of the bearish scenario would be the opposite of the aforementioned "reactive" path, which could mean a "soft" disintegration of the country. In this case, the government, economy, and social sphere would lose their unity and integrity, with some regions plunging into "neo-feudalism" while others would become appendages of neighboring, more successful economies. Overall, there would be growing chaos in the country, leading to extremely dangerous consequences.

These opportunities and risks point to the instability of the "modernization" of foreign policy. Its sound point—pragmatism—is simultaneously its greatest weakness (that is, value "rootlessness" and hence instability).

Another apparent advantage—the concentration of decisionmaking in the hands of top officials with the practical exclusion of other actors—turns into extreme vulnerability, not only in case of a change of these individuals but above all in that the isolation of "problem-solvers" from society, and even from the ruling group as a whole, increasing the likelihood of errors and mistakes.

The Bullish Scenario

In describing the bullish scenario, I do not operate under the assumption of the Russian elites' and society's "miraculous healing" from all the ills that are inherent in them. I speak of that Russia that exists today at the beginning of 2011, and who will remain at the helm of power for the foreseeable future—perhaps even until 2020. The main condition for the realization of the bullish scenario is the readiness of specific managers— by virtue of any reason whatsoever—to act on the basis of national interest rather than group, clan, or corporate interests. Thus, in my opinion, the realistic bullish scenario is moderate, with the clear expression of a nationalist component.

In fact, it is the willingness to realize the very same ideas expressed by President Dmitri Medvedev, and former President Vladimir Putin at the start of his term: building legal state institutions, making a significant improvement in the investment climate, and creating a shift in the political system toward greater competition within the law and the established rules of the game that are respected by all, including the ruling elites. Such a shift can be called "constitutionalist." It would not threaten the position of the "first persons" of the country but would return Russia to the path of economic, social, and political transformation, from which the country was derailed and which led into a dead end.

However, it is clear that even if the top management took upon itself the tasks of sanitizing (decriminalizing) the current regime "from above," thus increasing the efficiency of public administration and widening the perspectives of society as a whole, then such transformations would meet with extremely serious obstacles in the form of the interests of the specific clans and groups on which the senior management depends.

Ahead of a crisis, the proximity to the one-hundredth anniversary of the events of 1917 not only creates a psychological framework but also offers a model for a revolutionary way out—either a "February" or "October" revolution. However, both these models came with great risks and huge costs. And a hundred years later, revolutionary upheavals would still be fraught with disastrous consequences for Russia. As of now, as in 1911, there still exists an evolutionary path, but it does not assume linear development. For it to succeed, it is essential that it take place within the backdrop—and under the influence—of a modern rising social movement, and along with those patriotic sentiments, the thinking part of the ruling class recognize itself as the core of the political class that is capable of thinking in terms of national interests. If this group is able to prevail in political leadership, it could become a partner in the national public dialogue (the model of "roundtables"), and alongside these lay the foundations of civic republicans—as the "common affair" of Russians.

It must be taken into account that such a turn in domestic politics would be possible only with substantial advancement in the direction of four main objectives—geographically arranged—of Russian foreign policy: pacification in the West, stabilization in the South, consolidation in the East, and integration in the center.

Pacification in the West. The immediate major task in the direction of the West is reliably stabilizing relations with the United States and the EU, given the current positive inertia of their irreversible character. The possibility of integration—into NATO or the EU—is either premature or unpromising, and, therefore, inappropriate. Instead, there is a need to modify the modernization agenda so as to demilitarize the course of political relations and economic rapprochement with the West. In this case, the Russian economy would be integrated with the world economy in the capacity of a cooperative partner—a member of the global production chain.

The fundamental steps in taking this course are:

- The real demilitarization of relations with the United States and NATO and the formation of a Euro-Atlantic security community, in which war as a means of resolving conflicts must be categorically excluded.

59

- The transformation of the strategic relationship between Russia and the United States, possibly toward the creation of a missile defense system based on Russia's cooperation with the United States and NATO.
- The implementation of a historic reconciliation with the countries of Central and Eastern Europe: Poland, the Baltic states, and others.
- The creation of a common economic space with the European Union, the creation of a pan-European energy partnership; industrial integration (in the fields of energy, aviation, space, military technology, and other fields), the formation of a common humanitarian space (the abolition of visas), and cross-border regional cooperation.
- The formation of close cooperative relations with, and mutual respect for, the new European states: Ukraine, Belarus, and Moldova.

In the longer run (after 2020), it would be necessary to establish relations with the European Union in a new capacity—not in the format of a "union with Europe" but with free trade economic zones, European cooperation in foreign policy initiatives, and a Euro-Atlantic security community.

Stabilization in the South. The situation in the Near East, Middle East, Central Asia, Eastern Europe, and the South Caucasus will continue to be extremely fragile and explosive. The beginning of revolutionary unrest in the Arab world further complicates the picture of this macro region. For the stabilization of southern Russia, it is imperative to form a strategic partnership with Kazakhstan, and establish close relations with the new states of Central Asia and the South Caucasus.

Outside the post-Soviet space, Russia's main strategic partner is India. Moscow–Delhi relations can become a major factor of stability in Central and South Asia. On the basis of the Collective Security Treaty Organization and relations with India, Russia can increase the effectiveness of the Shanghai Cooperation Organization as a factor for stability and development in the inner regions of Asia. Interaction with China will also be crucial for this.

Other factors for the stabilization of the South include relations with Turkey, especially with the Caucasus on the agenda; constructive cooperation between Russia and other countries on Iran's nuclear issue and building relations with Tehran in the long run; Russia's participation, alongside that of other nations, stabilizing the situation in Afghanistan under the condition of the withdrawal of U.S. and NATO troops; dialogue with moderate forces in Pakistan; and a constructive role in the Middle East "quartet."

Consolidation in the East. In the case of a shift of the central theater of international political and economic relations to the Asia-Pacific region, Russia would need to recognize itself as a Euro-Pacific country. The main task to be accomplished by 2020 is to start the development of Eastern Russia (Pacific Russia and Eastern Siberia) per the model of "double integration": domestic and Asia-Pacific. Russia's partners are not limited to China alone, though it is essential to strive for a balanced partnership with China. It will also be crucial to turn Japan into a "Germany of the East" and thus gain economic and technological support for Russia's modernization, an equally important policy for Moscow. The rise of China could also help this modernization. Other partners for resource and technology modernization are South Korea and Singapore. Finally, a projection of the Pacific region's foreign policy also considers the United States, Canada, Australia, and New Zealand as regional partners. The more of these partners Russia has, the higher its tricolor will fly on the Pacific coast.

Integration in the Center. The development of Russia's relations with former states of the USSR is an important indicator of the modernization of Russian foreign policy. From Moscow's side, the basic principle of this relationship should have been the comprehensive development of economic, scientific, technical, cultural, and humanitarian cooperation without political attempts to integrate these countries into a single bloc with Russia, and turning that bloc into a regional "power center." The development of supranational institutions makes sense precisely to the extent that it is driven by economic necessity. The Customs Union, a single economic space, a free trade area, and other forms of integration should be created to facilitate the development of Russia and its partners, and not as a foundation for a political superstructure with the Kremlin as its center.

If this is recognized as the main aim of Russian policy in the region, then the Eurasian Economic Community can become the foundation for operating a free trade area; the Collective Security Treaty Organization can be transformed into a modern multilateral and multidisciplinary structure of security in Central Asia and Kazakhstan; and the Commonwealth of Independent States can strive to allow travel among its members without visas, as well as cultural cooperation. An important condition for the success of Russian foreign policy in this geographically central area is its ability to resolve—in collaboration with its stakeholders—the "frozen" conflicts from twenty years ago with Trans-Dniester, and to normalize relations with Georgia.

If Russia wants to become a regional leader, which in principle is both possible and desirable, it must turn to "soft power," and it must learn to produce—at least on a regional scale—"international public goods." A purely self-interest-based policy, and an inability or unwillingness to live for others, is incompatible with claims to leadership. It is important to learn not only how to take but also how to give.

Summing Up

In addition to foreign policy's traditional geopolitical angles, it also has global dimensions. As foreign policy constantly expands, it comes to cover common problems for all humanity, such as climate change and threats to the world's ecology; energy and energy efficiency issues; problems related to values, norms, and principles; intercultural and intercivilizational relations; and new dimensions of security—from the war against international terrorism and cybersecurity to the proliferation of weapons of mass destruction to the need to ensure people's rights and freedoms. This new agenda for foreign policy in many ways has changed the components of international relations.

Under these circumstances, Russia must learn to act as a "global citizen," organized as a collection of not only states but also business corporations, nongovernmental organizations, and international organizations. Individuals connected to each other through social networks also make up a big part of the "global community." Russia's participation in international organizations and forums—from the United Nations to the Group of

Twenty—should not only be a "demonstration of the flag" but should also set for itself the goal of producing tangible and sought-after "international public goods" at the global level.

Conclusions

Several main factors that will influence the formation of Russia's foreign policy are, in domestic politics, the choice between modernizing the country's development and the stagnation of inertia, relying on the proverbial "pipe"; and in the external environment, U.S. policy, which will either continue to provoke the "besieged fortress" syndrome among Russian leaders or engage Moscow in cooperation on terms acceptable to Russia. Another external factor will be China's policy—its degree of assertiveness, or, conversely, flexibility with regard to Russia. However, the leading factor in the formation of Russia's foreign policy will be Europe. If, in the future, the European project is able to overcome its current difficulties, which have come to be symbolized by the euro crisis, a further development of the European Union will strengthen Moscow's "European vector" policy and facilitate Euro-Russian integration. On the contrary, the failure of this project would deprive Russia of its natural "anchors" in the world.

The bullish scenario is unrealistic, the bearish one is terrible, and the inertial course is dull and joyless. In reality, there is a possibility that none of the three will be realized—and there is a possibility that one of them will. After all, these are scenarios—not predictions. Nevertheless, it makes sense to act in time to prevent or reduce the trends leading to the negative scenarios and to increase the factors that may facilitate the positive ones. From this perspective, it is very important to conduct a serious discussion among all the parties—conservative, socialist, and liberal—that are responsible for Russia's national political trends on the primary principles, scope, and objectives of its foreign policy.

Foreign policy, of course, strongly depends on the situation inside the country—the economy, society, and politics. However, it is not a simple continuation or reflection of the interior. It has its own logic and dynamics. At the same time, it is true that Russia's international positions—most of all, its relations with the West—drive the conditions for the functioning of its domestic processes. Thus, when there is an atmosphere of a "besieged fortress" and when the mode is to fight on two fronts—against foreign enemies, and against the internal enemy—the opposition authorities begin to look like the "fifth column" of external forces, thereby reducing their influence and power, which makes it possible to monopolize patriotism. On the contrary, given the presence of good international relations and Russia's general openness to the West, the Russian regime finds itself in a comfortable and relatively safe spot, although it is more important that society has access to the resources for development. Under these circumstances, the real prerequisites will have been met for the transformation of not only the social environment but also, in the end, of the political system.

Notes

1. "Message from the Russian President Vladimir Putin," Moscow, September 4, 2004, http://archive.kremlin.ru/appears/2004/09/04/1752_type63374type82634.

2. "Speech and Discussion on Security Policy at the Munich Conference," Munich, February 10, 2007, http://archive.kremlin.ru/appears/2007/02/10/1737_type63374type63376 type 63377type63381type82634_118097.shtml.

3. For more information see Dmitri Trenin, *Odinochnoye plavanie* (Solo Voyage) (Moscow: Carnegie Moscow Center/R. Elinina, 2009).

4. This refers to Winston Churchill's phrase delivered in November 1942 in connection with the successful actions of British troops in Egypt: "I have not become the King's first minister in order to preside over the liquidation of the British Empire."

5. See, for example, "Renew Yourselves, Gentlemen!" *Results*, October 26, 2009. Vladislav Surkov met with the community "Futurussia" on April 7, 2010; see http://state.kremlin. ru/face/7495.

6. See, for example, the speech by President Medvedev at a meeting with Russian ambassadors and permanent representatives in international organizations in Moscow, July 12, 2010, http://news.kremlin.ru/transcripts/8325. The turn toward the West can be traced in the statements of Russian foreign minister Sergei Lavrov in London in February 2011 during a press conference after talks with the foreign minister of the United Kingdom, William Hague; see www.mid.ru/brp_4.nsf/0 / 5E7F059B024CDC39C32578 380070D2AF. Previously, the publication of certain internal documents of the Russian Foreign Ministry in *Russian Newsweek* was evidence of new trends in foreign policy. See "K. Haase and M. Zygar Change the Foreign Policy of Russia," *Russian Newsweek*, no. 20, 2010.

7. Regarding the Arctic, see Dmitri Trenin and Pavel K. Bae, *Arctic: The View from Moscow* (Moscow: Press Club Service, 2010).

8. A demonstration attack on September 7, 2010, by Chinese fishing boats on a Japanese coast guard vessel near the Senkaku islands raised tensions around the Pacific coast of Asia. Clear evidence of China's claims to the islands in the South China Sea worried Vietnam.

CHAPTER FOUR

RUSSIA'S PLACE *in the* WORLD OF UNINTENDED CONSEQUENCES, *or* MURPHY'S LAW AND ORDER

Fyodor Lukyanov

When a simple system tries to regulate a complex system, you often get unintended consequences.

— *Andrew Gelman, director of the Applied Statistics Center at Columbia University*

Anything that can go wrong will go wrong.

— *Murphy's Law*

During the past quarter of a century, Russia has repeatedly found itself at a historical crossroads: strategic, when the future of its statehood was at stake, and tactical (but no less crucial), when the long-term scenario depended on a decision yet to be made. At some point—after the collapse of the Soviet Union, and at the dawn of the new Russia—it seemed that the main choice had already been made; but the more time passed, the clearer it became that this is not exactly so. Russia, together with the whole world, has entered a period of fundamental change with an unpredictable ending, when it is simply impossible to "freeze the frame" (as television people would put it) for making a final decision that will determine the further march of events.

The second decade of the twenty-first century is the next, already very advanced, stage of global transformation. Its distinguishing feature is the fact that even the most powerful and influential players no longer lay claim to the ability to control the course of events. They confine themselves to attempts to respond to external impulses and minimize the costs associated with the challenges of globalization.

The international environment is getting more complex in many ways. First, there is the growing gap between the world economic system, which is becoming increasingly integrated and global, on the one hand, and the system of political relations, on the other.[1] The latter is still based on national priorities and also shows signs of the weakening influence of all international and supranational (to a greater degree) bodies in contrast to national sovereignties. This combination of economic interdependence with political and ideological incompatibility is becoming quite commonplace. The intricate relations between Russia and the European Union, and especially those between the United States and China, are the most obvious examples.

Second, international relations have been becoming more "democratic," and individual countries have been becoming more "emancipated." Bloc discipline, typical of the Cold War era, is finally giving way to independent policies by not only large players but also medium-sized ones. Countries that just fifteen years ago remained loyal members of stable alliances (for example, France and Turkey), and of systems of relations (Egypt and Pakistan), or did not show any far-reaching ambitions (Brazil and Iran) are now ever more often determined to play their own game. At the same time, the desire to participate in international relations does not necessarily mean the ability to play a constructive and effective role in them. The level of ambition often exceeds real competence, which contributes to the overall turbulence. In any case, the growing activity of hitherto low-profile actors is reducing the already diminished resources of the leading powers to control current developments and reduce the potential of global governance, calling into question the very possibility of handling global processes.

Third, the erosion of integrationist and governance institutions— NATO, the European Union, the International Monetary Fund, the World Trade Organization, the Organization for Security and Cooperation in Europe, and the like—that were inherited from earlier periods, and have proven unable to adapt to the rapid changes that appeared at the beginning of the twenty-first century, raises a question that only five years ago elicited a plain answer: Is integration the key to political and especially economic problems? The lesson of the misconceived principle of an entity that is "too big to fail" that governed the global financial markets and led to the all-too-well-known consequences in 2008 is, in fact, applicable to relations between states. As a result, cyclical economic crises are spreading with the speed of a pandemic and are being catalyzed by the problems of individual countries, which are experiencing a dangerous resonance. Attempts taken to save at all costs some elements of the system for the sake of the whole system impede structural reform and merely defer an even deeper crisis.

The most striking example of this is the situation in the euro zone in the context of the debt crisis in Greece and other similarly economically and fiscally troubled EU member countries. Obviously, if Greece were not a member of the European Monetary Union and enjoyed sovereignty over its own money, it would long ago have found ways to overcome the current catastrophic situation. However, its participation in a major integration project has made the state of affairs more than hopeless. The situation is steadily getting worse as a result of actions by the leading countries and financial institutions of the euro zone, which in fact completed the transformation of Greece into a failed state—in order to take no drastic measures to reform the entire union.

The already-mentioned contradiction between the different levels of economic and political integration also illustrates the case of European integration. The European Monetary Union, which represents the highest degree of economic and financial integration, also requires appropriate standardization in the political domain. However, the EU's intentions for political integration, as expressed in the draft European Constitution, have run up against a wall—the European nations are unprepared to agree to any further limitations of their sovereignty.

According to an assumption that had long been considered an axiom, in the era of globalization small and medium-sized actors have no prospects on their own, so the sole way out for them is to join large unions. However, there is a downside to globalization, which, as the Greek experience shows, can have fatal consequences for weak economies. The implementation of the principle of solidarity between the larger and smaller members of integration organizations is doomed to stay within the realm of the interests of the "heavyweights," which will always act to minimize their own costs. Therefore, "keeping hands free" from external constraints (that is, retaining an opportunity to use a broader set of tools, which has traditionally been considered a privilege of the great powers) may prove a basic condition of survival for less significant actors.

Fourth, the principles on which the international environment is structured will continue to change. Because the universalist approach to political and economic governance cannot cope with the ocean of challenges, there has emerged a trend toward regionalization as a way of structuring the global processes. But the approach to forming alliances will change dramatically. Stable alliances, cemented by common values (that is, ideology), were a product of the twentieth century, when ideologies played an exaggerated role in world politics. The twenty-first century, judging by many indications, will see a return to normality in this sense: Geopolitical and geoeconomic interests will prevail over the sharing of values. The latter, of course, will not disappear, but it will be rather an additional factor that facilitates or, conversely, complicates cooperation. Donald Rumsfeld's maxim, "The mission determines the coalition," will long survive its author, who quit active politics a while ago. Flexible alliances created for specific missions, which the very same Rumsfeld described as "coalitions of the willing," look more promising in an environment where problems can be quite unexpected—both in their content and place of action.

The fundamental problem of the current world situation is rooted in the fact that despite the complication of the entire complex of instantaneously communicating international media, the forms and methods of its interpretation remain exactly as they were in the twentieth century. Newfangled fantasies by political fiction writers revolving around the theme of a "networked world" (interestingly enough, the same degree of love for them is demonstrated by the most progressive American liberals and the most reactionary Russian fans of geopolitics, ranging from Anne-Marie Slaughter to Sergei Kurginian) offer nothing that might help better explain the ongoing processes. The use of traditional theories of international relations also runs against new phenomena, in particular, the repeatedly mentioned contradiction between the nature of world politics and economics. Attempts to make decisions based on an inadequate analysis of complex systems lead to a situation where the law of unintended consequences becomes the basic rule of modern politics. Thus politics turns into an inverted pyramid, where state officials have to exert tremendous effort to resolve the many new problems arising from the improper methods they had employed in their attempt to solve what originally seemed to be a very specific problem. The multilateral operation in Libya in 2010 and 2011 is probably the most convincing example of this dynamic.[2]

In practical policymaking, there remains the ideological inertia of the 1990s, when the tide of euphoria following the Cold War made further developments look predetermined. The leading players simply do not have time to evaluate the surge of change and to at least develop a tactically correct response, let alone a long-term strategy.

To a certain extent, post-Soviet Russia is better prepared for such a model of behavior, because its foreign policy has always, under all three presidents, been almost exclusively reactive—largely due to the lack of any kind of conscious and coherent foreign and domestic political identity. Amid the current complete uncertainty about the prospects for world development, such flexible tactics seem to be the only rational option—the more so, because the problems with Russian identity have gone into the next phase but still remain unresolved. Furthermore, the public consensus on foreign policy, which was one of the obvious achievements of Vladimir Putin's rule, is likely to erode in the coming years. But this will be due not so much to changes in the international arena as to the complex processes within Russian society, which has entered a period of postimperial transformation of the collective consciousness. This is fraught with both positive and sharply negative factors.

Among the likely major political trends in the coming years, three stand out: the shift of the focus of world politics to Asia, the disappearance of Europe as a strategic player of global significance, and the United States' adaptation of its understanding of global leadership to the multipolar reality and the need to cut costs. Each of these trends will have a decisive influence on the shaping of Russia's foreign policy.

The Search for a Place in Asia

It has become commonplace to observe that the drift of the global strategic platform in the twenty-first century to Asia and the Asia-Pacific region will play the same role that the Euro-Atlantic area played in the twentieth century. Europe paid for its central position in the global system with centuries of violent and bloody conflicts. The last century alone saw two world wars and a systemic confrontation verging on mutual annihilation. Potentially, there are preconditions for similar scenarios in Asia—its countries have accumulated a considerable potential of historical claims on each other.

However, there are two new factors today that were absent a hundred years ago. One is the global economy, which keeps all countries closely linked in a single economic and political conglomerate; if it collapsed, everybody would stand to lose. The other is nuclear arms. By virtue of their tremendous power to annihilate, they make opponents more disciplined. In a sense, however, the situation of Asia vis-à-vis nuclear weapons is still inchoate—both the region's existing nuclear deterrence realtionship—India and Pakistan, and those likely in the future—Iran and Israel—have no experience in strategic brinkmanship that the Soviet Union and the United States gained in the middle of the last century.

Whatever the case, Russia is not entering the Asian century as a serious actor in this part of the world. Its sole major asset vis-à-vis Asia is its territory. It is true that this is a considerable asset indeed—13.1 million square kilometers of land, more than three-quarters of its national territory, and rich in a variety of resources. However, in the context of Russia's demographic decline and one-sided raw-materials-pegged economy, which is poorly adapted to intensive and innovative development, this territory creates not only opportunities but also risks. The underdeveloped Asian part of Russia, against the background of impressive growth in many countries of the region, especially in neighboring China, is fraught with soaring economic imbalances, which sooner or later will become political ones. And although the fear of Chinese expansion that is widespread in Russia is highly exaggerated, one should have no doubt that the economic and demographic vacuum will be filled somehow.[3]

Moscow's policies during the post-Soviet decade have been exceptionally centered on the West, and thus aimed at proving to the West that

Russia had been written off too early and that it will regain its position as a significant global player. Now Russia faces the task of regaining at least some role in Asian affairs (a leading one should not even be dreamed of). At present, Moscow's participation in the Asia-Pacific region's politics is not noticeable, except for some imitations and token events (such as the 2012 Asia-Pacific Economic Cooperation summit, the demarche over the Kuril Islands, and the plans for the deployment of Mistral helicopter carriers there). Russia's membership in most regional organizations does not mean that it plays any significant role in any of them. The region's countries do not perceive Russia as an Asian power.

The situation in Central Eurasia and South Asia is slightly better, but there (except, perhaps, in the case of India), Russia's influence stems from the fact that the solution to certain problems of the United States depends on it. In other words, Russia is not a policy actor but a circumstance. The vagueness of such a state of affairs is particularly noticeable in the case of Iran, where Moscow's policy is, in essence, a derivative of the current relations between Russia and the United States, which is absolutely wrong in view of the geographical proximity of the two countries and the apparent growth in Iran's influence in Middle Eastern and Eurasian affairs.

Meanwhile, it is quite clear that most of the threats and opportunities for Russia will emerge in the large Asian region. The opportunities will arise from chances to use Asian economic dynamism for the development of Russia's Siberian and Far Eastern regions. In the most general terms, the threats of the coming decade can be summarized as pertaining to three key issues, each of which deserves a brief subsection.

Iran's Striving for Nuclear Capability

The first key issue is the rapid deterioration of stability, associated with Iran's striving for nuclear capability and attempts by the United States and Israel to finally resolve this problem by force. The crisis over Iran will become a strong external shock, which will affect neighboring regions, especially the South Caucasus. This is precisely what could potentially unbalance the status quo over Nagorno-Karabakh (Iran is an important partner of both Azerbaijan and Armenia), putting Russia in the very bad position of having to choose between Baku and Yerevan. Moscow is unable to make this choice in principle; both countries are too important for future development. Another option of such an external shock would be the spill-over of social and political instability in North Africa and the Middle East to countries that play a fundamental role in the South Caucasus—again, Iran and Turkey (which is unlikely), or the collapse of the Bashar al-Assad regime in Syria. In the latter case, the instability in the region could increase, or ethnic Armenians could start to flee a Syria ravaged by civil war.

The Genesis of the Afghan Conflict

The second key issue is the genesis of the Afghan conflict, which, apparently after the inevitable withdrawal of the United States and NATO contingents, will turn Afghanistan into a scene of total civil war of "all against all," very much like the one that raged from 1992 to 1995 after the fall of the pro-Soviet Najibullah regime. This time, the internecine conflict could be much larger and more dangerous, because each of the opposing groups will most probably have sharply competing foreign interests—those of Pakistan, India, Iran, China, the United States, Russia, and the Central Asian countries.[4]

The scenario for a new consolidation of Afghanistan under Taliban rule looks less destructive than the one sketched above. In this case, one can expect attempts by the Taliban to channel the anger of the active part of non-Pashtun populations outside the country, stimulating their expansion to the north—into Uzbekistan, Tajikistan, and Kyrgyzstan. This will surely create a big problem, but it, at least, has a solution—the strengthening of the Collective Security Treaty Organization in order to transform it into a full-fledged military and political alliance.

The scenario of a civil war could provoke the most negative sequence of events. Intra-Afghan feuding would be a powerful catalyst for competition among the regional powers, especially India and Pakistan.[5] In view of the nuclear status of both countries and the likelihood that the other two regional powers—Russia and China—would be unable or reluctant to distance themselves from such developments, an unfavorable outcome in Afghanistan could be the harbinger of truly global turmoil.

Growing Rivalry Between the United States and China

The third key issue is the growing rivalry between the United States and China. In the context of the relative weakening of the United States and China's continued growth, Washington and the countries leaning on it may have the suspicion (irrational, perhaps) of a rapid growth of the threat from Beijing. In this case, one cannot exclude active measures of deterrence, retaliatory steps, and so on.

Theoretically, the position as an important onlooker is advantageous for Russia. But in practice, resisting attempts, inevitable in this case, by both parties to win Moscow to their side would be very risky, for the two opposing powers are much stronger than Russia—the more so because a United States–China confrontation would unfold on a broad regional front, involving other countries (Southeast Asia, those on the Korean Peninsula, Japan, India, and Pakistan), threatening a grave destabilization.

Russia would only have limited opportunities to influence events to reduce the likelihood of negative scenarios. Bearing in mind the range of risks and proceeding from the possibility that each of them could materialize, the rational mode of behavior may follow three steps.

The first step would see the intensifying of a diplomatic process with Iran by all means and seeking alternatives to war, because any scenario involving the use of force would have far more negative consequences for Russia than hypothetical benefits (for instance, those in energy markets). One should keep in mind the lessons of the military interventions of the late twentieth and the early twenty-first century, from Yugoslavia to Libya— the unintended consequences sometimes distort the original plans beyond recognition.

The second step would be assistance to the United States and NATO in stabilizing the situation in Afghanistan, but without direct involvement, because the interests are, in fact, not quite the same. The task of the Western coalition would be to create the most favorable political and military conditions for withdrawal. The problem for Russia and neighboring countries would be focused on balancing the interests and pressure from different groups for long-term stability around Afghanistan. The latter requires more active steps to build up regional institutions—primarily the Collective Security Treaty Organization and the Shanghai Cooperation Organization.

And the third step is an active policy to strengthen ties with the key players in the Asia-Pacific region—the United States, China, Japan, South Korea, and the members of the Association of Southeast Asian Nations, both individually and collectively as a regional organization. This is difficult and laborious work, which in many respects would need to be started from scratch. Settling the North Korean nuclear issue would be an ideal way for Russia to assert itself in the Asia-Pacific region. Moscow is in an advantageous position, because in this matter it is perceived by all stakeholders as a fairly neutral force. If Russia's assistance helped break the deadlock, this would be a major contribution to regional stability, which would be appreciated by all participants, yielding economic benefits (for example, transportation and energy projects). In general, although the main country in Asia is, of course, China, Moscow must avoid a situation in which Beijing would be the reference point for its Asian policy. Asia, even East Asia, is greater and more diverse than China.

It is worth mentioning that the shift of general strategic attention to Asia could also open up new prospects for U.S.-Russian relations. In the Euro-Atlantic zone, the two powers are overburdened with the legacy of their Cold War rivalry, and this inertia is bound to last, although Europe itself has ceased to play the role in the world that it once did. In Asia there is no such tradition. A future positive agenda between Russia and the United States could begin to be formulated there, especially given that the issue of how to deal with the new China is relevant to both countries.[6]

Europe as a Source of Uncertainty

For centuries, Europe served Russian society and its elite as a source of impetuses for internal transformations, if not a model to be replicated— Russian reformers have never wanted to borrow the European model in its entirety—or an image of some better reality. Although Russia, unlike its neighbors, has never seriously considered the question of joining the European institutions, the very idea of Europe as an obviously more progressive and successful community influences the Russian political process.

Today, however, the situation has changed dramatically. The seemingly inevitable institutional, sociopolitical, and ideological transformation of the European Union means that the collective behavior of Europe as a regional actor will undergo major changes, and this creates a completely different framework of conditions for the post-Soviet states and Russia.

The failed transformation of the EU into a global political player, which was one of the goals of the Lisbon Treaty, does not mean that the European Union, having dropped its global ambitions, will be focused only on its "neighborhood." The experience of the past eighteen months since the treaty took effect shows that the EU's real interest in its frontier regions and willingness to spend any major political and financial resources on them have sharply diminished. This becomes evident even vis-à-vis the Middle East and North Africa, where acute crises are blazing in an area of Europe's immediate interests.

The apparent rightward shift in public sentiment in Europe, which has been manifested in the elections in virtually all European countries, is by no means conducive to the revival of interest in the European periphery, let alone support for its expansion. In the Old World, protectionist tendencies in the broadest sense have been gaining the upper hand. Voters, whose opinion politicians have no chance or right to ignore, are extremely concerned about the wave of change that globalization brings. They instinctively take a defensive stance. They seek to protect the socioeconomic, cultural, and political status quo, which in the current international situation is impossible.

As Europe loses the role of a leading international force and even the central scene of world politics, it can still generate turmoil on a global scale, and this sudden awareness may ruin the customary peaceful image and self-perception of modern Europe. And this, by and large, is not the fault of Greece but a consequence of an unprecedented and—as it has turned out—risky historical experiment that the major European states, which have been unable or unwilling to enforce their own set of rules, have dared stage.[7]

The critical moment in the development of the EU coincided, on the one hand, with European voters' fatigue and boredom over the problems of unification and, on the other, with very weak political leadership in virtually all countries of the Old World. And it is against this background that the authorities need to make urgent and very unpopular decisions, while the voters, whose opinions cannot be ignored, are increasingly unwilling to pay for the "freeloaders"—whether they are "sloppy" Greeks or "crowds of new migrants."

The critical state in which the European Union is likely to remain up to 2020 means:

- An emphasis on domestic issues and less interest toward external initiatives, except for those directly related to the union's economic prosperity and political stability;[8]
- A complication of relations with the United States, which is insisting on a more uniform sharing of the burden within the transatlantic security alliance. Brussels is not ready for this—psychologically, politically, or financially—so Washington will intensify its search for other partners to address the problems that are of fundamental importance to it in different parts of the world;[9]
- A change of the dominant political paradigm in the leading European countries toward a more nationalist and protectionist line in an attempt to prevent voters who are uncertain about their own future from drifting toward radical political forces.

The decline in Europe's interest in its eastern neighbors dramatically reduces the opportunities available to the countries that built their policies on maneuvering between Russia and the EU in order to derive the maximum dividends.

Europe, which is living through difficult times, will most likely opt for a frankly mercantile line. The post-Soviet space will be of interest to European countries only in terms of the benefits and advantages that they can garner—whether a market for goods, a target for profitable investment (to the extent that this is possible in the murky post-Soviet investment climate), or a source of raw materials. In this sense, the common values mantra will finally turn into an empty nutshell.

The main problem for the development of post-Soviet states in this regard is that the "European choice" would disappear even as a common reference point. In contrast to Central Europe, the former post-Soviet countries have never been very good at goal setting. Nor have they had a clear prospect of accession to Western institutions. But they could at least operate with the term "European model."

Of course, this very model would still be in place as a set of specific and quite effective principles of government and economic structure. However, the economic problems of the euro zone and the inability to reform the social system—which does not match the realities of today and, particularly so, of tomorrow—raise doubts about the prospects of a European approach. The basis upon which the European "welfare state" has rested since World War II has seriously malfunctioned in the world's new economic conditions and against the background of current demographic trends in Europe.

For Russia, the crisis of European integration is both a challenge and a window of opportunity. Relations with the EU would finally cease to be strategic, their purely political element would shrink, and they would become almost exclusively socioeconomic. With the renationalization of politics in Europe, which is likely to grow as the influences of the EU's central institutions weaken, would allow Moscow to finally get back to the familiar one-to-one game with individual European countries. These countries, which are interested in strengthening their own economic position, will tend to seek beneficial agreements, such as energy deals or the recent sale of French Mistral helicopter carriers to Russia. Given the peculiarities of the Russian business environment, especially that its big businesses are closely associated with the state, European interests are likely to merely strengthen Russia's corrupt monopolies-based system.

Europe's possible transformation from a sociopolitical benchmark, with its powerful ability to project "soft power" into a political introvert immersed in domestic issues and seeking to dissociate itself from growing external challenges, would create a completely different dynamic in the post-Soviet space.

During their twenty years of independence, the states that emerged from the ruins of the Soviet Union have lived through several stages of development. The birth pangs were mostly over by the turn of the century. Next, there was a period of seeking final self-determination and accession to larger projects. But this did not happen, because instead of growing stronger and more developed, the international structures and institutions plunged into an era of weakening and erosion, just as did the entire world order, and failing to adapt to new realities.

Russia is the only country that regards neighboring countries as exceptionally important. This, however, does not mean that it has a clear action plan and an integration program. But it surely means that no other fundamental integration projects for post-Soviet countries are anywhere in sight; and even if some appeared, Russia would probably have enough clout to block them.

Relations With the United States:
Overpowering the Inertia of the Past

Relations with the United States continue to take center stage in Russia's foreign policy, although their nature has changed dramatically many times during the past quarter century. The reset, undertaken in 2009–2010, eased the sharp tensions that had developed toward the end of the 2000s and normalized the situation, but it clearly had a limited agenda, which has been implemented successfully. The future depends on various factors, both objective and subjective. It is quite natural that the reset has come to an end because the two powers have stumbled on the missile defense issue, which is the essence of the existing type of relationship.

The theme of missile defense, which has been on the agenda for several decades, and will still be there, despite the dramatic and rapid changes in the international scene. And it is not just intellectual inertia and remarkably stable stereotypes that are to blame. As long as the United States and Russia have huge arsenals of nuclear weapons, many times greater than those of all other countries, the logic of deterrence, which is based on the principle of "mutual assured destruction" will be preserved. The reason being that such huge arsenals can have no use other than to maintain parity—evincing the legacy of the arms race, because a tenth of this amount would be more than enough for any self-defense. But because they are in place, the understanding of "strategic stability" has not changed since that period. Moscow's categorical demand for establishing an interconnection between defensive and offensive strategic weapons is quite explainable. Indeed, by this logic, the inevitability of retribution is a guarantee against a first strike, whereas the ability to screen oneself from it (in theory, this is precisely the task of the missile defense system) will be a temptation for the aggressor.

Today, even the most inveterate hawks never discuss in full seriousness the possibility of a nuclear war between Russia and the United States. But mutual assured destruction is a clear and understandable principle, and nothing as clear and understandable has replaced it to this day. All speculations to the effect that Moscow and Washington do not regard each other as enemies, and that NATO poses no threat to Russia and the other way round, are nothing but fine words, whereas the existing sense of the two powers' destructive potential is an obvious reality. And this sensation is so stable that, for example, repeated demonstrations of NATO's incapability are unable to persuade those in Russia who faithfully believe in the aggressive nature of the bloc, that the Alliance is closing its pincers around Russia. Incidentally, legal guarantees stating that the planned missile defense system will not be directed against Russia—something on which Russian diplomacy has been insisting on—will not solve anything. There is no single document that cannot be simply canceled or ignored, if necessary.

In other words, sidestepping this problem is impossible, however anachronistic it might seem in the second decade of the twenty-first century. And this is all the more true because with the reduction of the overall Russian potential—both economic and demographic—the psychological value of nuclear weapons as a guarantee of Russia's sovereignty and integrity will grow.

The debate on a joint European ballistic missile defense strategy that unfolded in late 2010 and early 2011 ended inconclusively, and this outcome could have been easily predicted. However, there will be a chance in the coming years that the missile defense issue will not become an insurmountable obstacle to the development of relations, but on the contrary contribute to finding a new framework for them.

Both parties acknowledge the existence of threats from third countries. Provocative behavior by Iran and North Korea, the existence of missile capabilities in India and Pakistan, the growth of China's military might, and the inevitable appearance of other sources of threats in the future make the issue of protection more than relevant for both Russia and the United States. But this does not and will not eliminate the mutual suspicion of the two main former enemies. Is it possible to combine two opposite forms of interaction—each other's strategic deterrence, and strategic cooperation against third countries? This will seem absurd only if one relies on the paradigm of the second half of the twentieth century, when alliances and confrontations were immutable, being based on ideologies. In the twenty-first century, as was stated above, most likely everything will change. In a very chaotic environment, international coalitions will be formed to address specific problems, and the similarity of values shared will hardly serve as the determining factor. Expediency is more likely to be seen under these circumstances. And in this scheme of things, deterrence in one area and joint efforts to counter threats in another can be imagined.[10]

In the 2010s, U.S. foreign policy will be defined by the following general conditions:

- The need to cut costs for the sake of reducing the huge public debt and budget deficit. Although public opinion is beginning to gravitate to less U.S. involvement in international affairs, full isolationism in the global environment will be impossible and dangerous to U.S. interests. However, a lack of funds will require the more careful selection of priorities and analysis of actions to be taken.
- The value of Europe will continue to decline with the decrease in its ability to fulfill its alliance commitments, with the drift of U.S. security interests further eastward. This will require new supporting partners.
- The analysis of what system of balances Washington should seek in Asia is likely to become a major strategic challenge in the coming years. The answer to this question will be critical in determining the U.S. position toward and relations with the world's other major regions and countries that have an important role in the balance of force.

The period extending up to 2020 will be crucial for getting rid of the old type of relations between Russia and the United States, which were determined by the inertia of past confrontation. In Asia, as was noted above, Moscow and Washington do not have the tradition of rivalry that persists in Europe. Changes in the international arena will require a rejection of old stereotypes and a search for new forms of cooperation on issues of importance to both sides, despite the ideological differences and divergent interests. Thus far, there are no prerequisites for the relationship to cease being purely one-sided, geostrategic, and instead be supplemented by intensive economic cooperation.

There is a risk, however, that there may be unpredictable political developments inside the United States. Because of its acute political polarization, American society is in a state of confusion, and the traditional pendulum of politics may thus begin to sway with a greater amplitude and velocity. Traditionally, the American political system has successfully absorbed the shocks of extreme manifestations and identified the permissible mainstream. However, in response to the uncertainty arising from globalization, the mainstream may drift toward more radical positions, as is the case in Europe. Consequently, attempts at sharp steps in foreign policy may follow, which will have a strong destabilizing effect on the rest of the world. However, due to financial and economic constraints, an adventurist attempt cannot be a long-term one, if it is ever made.

Conclusion

The 2012 presidential election will be a turning point for Russia, regardless of the name of the person who will lead the country after it. The stakes are too high—of the next presidential term, and in general of the period up to 2020. It will not be a time for self-determination or of choosing a path into the future. On the contrary, the coming years will see the final disintegration of the old structures and a possible succession of regional crises, resulting from chaotic developments.

Russian foreign policy during the twenty years after the Soviet collapse was always reactive; it responded to external signals with varying degrees of success. There is no reason to believe that some kind of strategy will emerge in the forthcoming term. This is so not because of the inability of the domestic elite but because strategic planning is impossible in general. The leading players simply need to adapt themselves to rapid and unpredictable events. In this sense, Russia, with its extensive experience of responding, may even be relatively better prepared than other countries.

What trends will dictate a mode of behavior for Russia on the international scene? First, the erosion of all the institutions that were created in the era of the former balance has entered the final stage. However, no new structures or rules have appeared, because the global system's transition state remains far from completion, with the final destination still unknown. Accordingly, the question arises of how appropriate and effective will be the integration into existing institutions. At the same time, attempts by the leading players to strengthen these institutions, to adjust them to the flow of change, may have the opposite effect—in strict accordance with the law of unintended consequences.

Second, it is becoming clear that flexibility and adaptability are valued above permanent commitments. Growing worldwide interdependence promotes the understanding that global problems cannot be solved at the national level. But because political consciousness is still unable to overcome national boundaries, the real answer to more and more challenges is not the pooling of efforts but more and more stubborn attempts to retain room for individual maneuvering. In a rapidly changing environment, stable alliances may not expand opportunities but narrow them.[11]

Third, there is a notable desire for national emancipation. The number of significant players is growing. Medium-sized countries are beginning to act independently and with great vigor, although not always professionally enough or with the expected results. This complicates the overall formula, because a much larger number of variables are added to it.

Fourth and finally, there is a change of the systemic vector. Until now, relations with the West have served as the starting point for Russian politics; but as the focus of world events moves toward Asia, this approach begins to lose sense. Against a background of politically crumbling Europe and the increasing attention that the United States is paying to South Asia and the Pacific, Russia's lack of an intelligible understanding of its place in Asia would be tantamount to giving up any active role in international affairs.

Given this extremely diverse and complex palette, there are two models of behavior. One is to be guided by the medical principle "Do no harm," that is, to be careful enough to avoid radical steps and irreversible decisions, and wait for the situation to become clear. Or, conversely, one may take risks and use confusion to strengthen positions, with the aim of taking a more privileged place in a future world order.

The latter model, however, requires passion (which cannot be seen anywhere in Russian society), professionalism (its overall level is declining), and a solid internal political and economic base (with which there are also obvious difficulties). So, most likely, the principle of reasonable sufficiency and moderation will be the keynote of Russian foreign policy during the next presidential cycle—unless some unexpected and sudden outside impulses require equally sharp responses, or if, due to some unforeseen domestic circumstances, some radical and adventurous-minded force rises to power. The exhaustion of the post-Soviet agenda will affect Russia's relations with its neighbors, which in previous years caused the most significant challenges to Russian policy. Classical imperial instincts are giving way to other emotions—in particular nationalistic isolationism, which in Russia's case is fraught with internal turmoil.

As many experts have rightly noticed, in the context of high external turbulence and global interdependence, which cannot be ignored, the task of maintaining internal stability and balance will be essential for a country's survival and development. Any domestic disasters, even in societies that only partially free and not fully open, resonate immediately and are intensified sharply due to modern communication. In Russia, the task of maintaining internal stability requires an upgrade of the political system, which apparently no longer has the safety margin of flexibility and sustainability that is required in the event of such resonance. Finding a reasonable balance of openness and control, for which all the world's nations without exception have been looking these days, is a major challenge for Russia. The critical parameters for the entire political structure of Russia are thus set by the morale of Russian society, which is faced with the problem of demographic decline and the rise of ethnic, cultural, and religious heterogeneity, along with the strength of the state's social texture. And this same Russia will need to look for a place in a world governed by the law of unintended consequences.

Notes

1. For more on this, see Timofei Bordachev, "Foreign Policy Comeback," *Russia in Global Affairs*, July–September 2010, http://eng.globalaffairs.ru/number/Foreign-Policy-Comeback-14994.

2. Conn Hallinan, "Libya and the Law of Unintended Consequences," *Huffington Post*, April 8, 2011, www.huffingtonpost.com/conn-hallinan/libya-and-the-law-of-unin_b_846005.html.

3. These conclusions were confirmed by a survey titled "The Far East: Untapped Potential" and conducted by the Russian investment company Troika Dialog. "The man in the street in Moscow or Nizhni Novgorod is afraid of a Chinese invasion much more than the man in the street in Vladivostok or Khabarovsk is," the survey says. "There are few signs of Chinese presence in the region. There are fewer Chinese in the streets of Khabarovsk than in London, and Chinese companies do not have firm positions in the region. There are few examples of investment by Chinese companies; this issue is complicated by legal obstacles." See www.sia.ru/?section=484&action=show_news&id=111792 (in Russian).

4. Omar Nessar, "Afghanistan: Trapped in Uncertainty," *Russia in Global Affairs*, April–July 2011, http://eng.globalaffairs.ru/number/Afghanistan-Trapped-in-Uncertainty-15246.

5. For more on this, see the excellent book by Anatol Lieven, *Pakistan: A Hard Country* (New York: PublicAffairs, 2011).

6. As the authors of the National Military Strategy of the United States state, "We seek to cooperate with Russia on counter-terrorism, counterproliferation, space, and ballistic missile defense, and welcome it playing a more active role in preserving security and stability in Asia." It is interesting that the only mention of Russia in this document refers to the Asian context. See U.S. Joint Chiefs of Staff, *National Military Strategy of the United States of America 2011: Redefining America's Military Leadership*, www.jcs.mil//content/files/2011-02/020811084800_2011_NMS_-_08_FEB_2011.pdf.

7. For an analysis of European decline, see, for example, Charles A. Kupchan, "The Potential Twilight of the European Union," Council on Foreign Relations Working Paper, September 2010, www.cfr.org/eu/potential-twilight-european-union/p22934.

8. As the Reflection Group called by the European Council to review EU perspectives noted in its report, 2010 could have marked the beginning of a new phase for the European Union, and the next fifty years could be about Europe's role as an assertive global actor; or, alternatively, the European Union and its member states could slide into marginalization, becoming an increasingly irrelevant western peninsula of the Asian continent. In 2010 and 2011, the situation continued to worsen. See *Reflection Group on the Future of the EU 2030, Project Europe 2030: Challenges and Opportunities—A Report to the European Council* (Brussels: European Union, 2010), www.european-council.europa.eu/home-page/highlights/project-europe-2030.aspx?lang=en.

9. See Robert Gates, speech in Brussels, June 10, 2011, www.washingtonpost.com/world/the-security-and-defense-agenda-as-delivered-by-secretary-of-defense-robert-gates-brussels-belgium-june-10-2011/2011/06/10/AGqlZhOH_story.html.

10. For more on the ballistic missile defense issue between the United States and Russia, see Dmitri Trenin, "A European Missile Defense System to Replace the Great Game," *Russia in Global Affairs*, April–July 2011, http://eng.globalaffairs.ru/number/A-European-Missile-Defense-System-to-Replace-the-Great-Game-15241.

11. Dmitri Yefremenko, "After the Tandem: Russian Foreign Policy Guidelines," *Russia in Global Affairs*, April–July 2011, http://eng.globalaffairs.ru/number/After-the-Tandem-Russian-Foreign-Policy-Guidelines-15236.

CHAPTER FIVE

RUSSIA *and the* NEW "TRANSITIONAL EUROPE"

Arkady Moshes

Many experts have described the political development of Ukraine, Belarus, and Moldova—the nations in the western part of the post-Soviet area—during the past two decades as the emergence of a "strategically unviable no man's land between a united West and an increasingly hostile Russia."[1] They argue this point of view by saying that, on the one hand, Ukraine, Belarus, and Moldova have no visible prospects of joining the European Union and NATO, but on the other hand, Russia has not gained full control over developments in the region. Moscow can block what in its point of view are completely unacceptable foreign policy decisions by the region's governments, but it cannot completely dominate them, draw them back into a reintegration process, or secure international recognition of its exclusive sphere of influence in the region.

This accurately describes the situation, but the problem with this approach is that it follows nineteenth- and twentieth-century thinking, which saw the fate of disputed territories determined by the balance of power between the great powers. In today's world, however, even small countries can be significant actors on the international stage and have the right and possibility of choice. These possibilities are even greater when individual countries' actions are placed in a regional context. Such was the case in the 1990s, for example, in Central Europe and the Baltic states, and today we are starting to see a similar process taking shape to the west of the Russian-Ukrainian and Russian-Belarusan borders.

What is emerging is an informal grouping based on a European self-identity, as opposed to Russia's self-identity in its "Eurasian" and "Euro-Pacific" variants, and also on the perception of Russia as a challenge to these countries' sovereignty. More recently, an awareness has also begun to emerge of common economic interests as energy-dependent and energy-transit countries, as opposed to Russia's interests as an energy producer and exporter. It would make sense to call this region "interim Europe," or the "new Eastern Europe." These terms are debatable, of course, but they reflect the main aspects of, first, an emerging commonness in which a European or "quasi-European" identity is gradually replacing the post-Soviet element in their identities, and second, their interim geopolitical situation, separate from both Russia and the West.

At the same time, a new possibility is taking shape now that lets us stop looking at Ukraine, Belarus, and Moldova, whether separately or together, solely as an area of geopolitical competition between Russia and the West, and see them instead as a triangle in which the regional actors are independent, though not yet strongly defined, entities. Russia's current policy pursues clear goals (maintaining its sphere of influence), but it has relatively limited means with which to achieve its aims. The West, on the contrary, has big economic levers at its disposal, but it has not put together a strategic vision of its goals. In this situation, the region's future depends more on the choice that its countries themselves make, and on their ruling elites' ability to allocate effectively the resources they are offered.

The methodological framework described above forms the basis for the attempt that this chapter makes to forecast developments in Russia's relations with the "interim European" countries through to 2020.

A scenario of inertia or "soft" disintegration seems the most likely prospect. This course was set by the fundamental and in many ways irreversible changes that took place during the period 1991–2010, and which are analyzed below. This scenario would see Russia's influence in the region gradually decline over the medium and long terms. Of course, this could be a wavelike process (with possible periods of rapprochement), but on the strategic scale, interaction would become less intensive. It would not be possible to break free of the path-dependency paradigm.

From Russia's point of view, "soft" disintegration is not the worst option. It makes it possible to maintain a natural level of mutually advantageous economic cooperation and avoid having inevitable private differences grow into open and general conflict with the region's countries and the European Union. Russia would find itself in a more difficult predicament if centrifugal development accelerates, rather than following its current inertia, but this would require the combination of several different conditions, which is unlikely. The optimum scenario would be one of far-reaching changes within Russia itself and the return to the "European choice" policy that was announced but not carried out at the start of the 2000s. This would automatically defuse tension along the lines of potential division. But this is a nigh-impossible scenario in the short-term perspective, and delaying internal reform even for a few years could make it ultimately impossible to break free of the centrifugal paradigm.

The Dynamic of Internal Change: Piling Up the Differences

In today's world, two decades is a realistic length of time for forming an independent state in Europe. During these last twenty years, the post-Soviet area has seen a whole new generation of people born in independent countries and without memory of the Soviet Union entering adulthood, while the older generations have become used to living separately from Russia and the other former Soviet republics. The local ruling elites have needed to justify their being in power by emphasizing the advantages of living in an independent state, and this has led to concerted attempts to spread ideological platforms and historical interpretations through the education system and the media that differ from Russia's interpretations, though they are not necessarily in direct opposition to them.

Identity

With the partial exception of Moldova, the value of independence has become firmly cemented in people's minds throughout the region. Annual public opinion surveys conducted by the Razumkov Center in Ukraine, for example, show that, if a referendum on the issue were to be held, the number of people in all age groups and all parts of the country who would vote for independence outweighs the number of opponents, although supporters of independence form an absolute majority in central and western Ukraine but a relative majority in the eastern and southern regions. The overall figures are much lower than those from the 1991 referendum (in which 90 percent voted for independence, and 8 percent against, whereas in 2009, the overall figures were 52 and 22 percent, respectively), but even so, opponents of independence are in a clear minority. In a survey in Belarus in December 2009 that asked if declaring independence had been a good thing for the country, 66 percent of respondents said yes, and only 20 percent took a negative view.[2]

Thus, the idea of political reintegration with another country is something that only a minority of people support. Even in Belarus, the number of people willing to vote in a referendum for "union" with Russia (the term is deliberately abstract, allowing more concrete use ranging from the current Russia-Belarus Union State to integration along the lines of the European Union), dropped during the last decade from 47 percent (the peak came in 2003, at 53 percent) to 32 percent in March 2010. In Ukraine in 2007, only 6 percent of people expressed support for the idea of this or that region of the country seceding and joining an unnamed country (10 percent in the east, 12 percent in the south, 3 percent in the west, and 1 percent in the center).[3]

The situation in Moldova differs from that in Ukraine and Belarus in that support there is mostly for the idea of Moldova's being a part of bigger groupings. A survey conducted in November 2009 by the Public Policy Institute (the survey did not cover the Trans-Dniester region, but the results are still clear enough) showed that more than 43 percent of respondents would be willing to vote in a referendum for the country's return to a restored Soviet Union, whereas 30 percent said they would vote against such a proposal. But at the same time, 63 percent of this same group of respondents said they want Moldova to join the European Union. These results reflect big contradictions in public opinion in general, and they also indicate quite clearly that people are not very comfortable with the idea of Moldova existing as a small country on its own, outside any bigger grouping.[4] Another survey gave convincing evidence, however, that Moldovan young people under the age of thirty years overwhelmingly share the view that the country's post-Soviet history confirms that Moldova's choice to separate from the Soviet Union and pursue its own independent development was the right one.[5]

It is noteworthy that the sizable ethnic Russian and Russian-speaking population in the country does not change this picture in any critical way. As Russian scholar Dmitri Trenin has rightly pointed out, for the Russian-speaking communities in the post-Soviet area, the Russian Federation is a country of the past and not a country of the present or the future. "Russians in Ukraine or Kazakhstan might consider themselves Russian in the cultural sense," he writes, "but they have accepted that they live in countries in which they form a minority. In other words, nowhere do we see any particular yearning for 'reunification' with Russia."[6]

What makes the "interim Europe" region specific compared with the other former Soviet regions is that the emergence of a new identity here is going hand in hand with a rejection of the idea of Russia as the only possible center around which integration in the region can be based. The idea that these countries might accept, say, China or Turkey as an integration center is hard to imagine. Indeed, from quite early on, these countries started giving this role to the European Union and the West in general, and this lends the whole process an added political overtone. Throughout the 2000s, the level of support in Ukraine and Belarus for a geopolitical course looking toward Europe was similar to the support level for a Russian-oriented course. In Moldova, as was mentioned above, support for integration with Europe was dominant, partly because of its greater geographical distance from Russia, and partly because of a sense of belonging not just to the post-Soviet area but also, historically speaking, to the Balkan region, which was opening up to new prospects for entering Europe.

The Political System

In the 2000s, all the countries in the region saw the emergence of political regimes capable of continuing or changing government without Moscow's help and without reference to Russia's position. This was a significant change. Russia lost its "kingmaker" role in the political campaigning sense and also in the sense of being the one to ensure the local regimes' international legitimacy. The domestic policy situation started to count for more than relations with the Kremlin.

Ukraine provides the clearest example. Viktor Yushchenko became president of Ukraine in 2005 despite Russia's open resistance. Subsequent developments showed that Moscow could not prevent its former favorite, Viktor Yanukovych, from entering a government coalition with Yushchenko in 2006, or prevent a return to power of the "Orange Coalition" formed by Yushchenko and Yulia Tymoshenko, who became prime minister for the second time in 2007. In the end, during the 2009–2010 presidential campaign, Russia decided not to make any clear political bets. This line of conduct was very much justified given that the two main candidates—Tymoshenko and Yanukovych—were both seen as being capable of pragmatic cooperation, and it also freed the winner of the election from having to "thank" Russia for its support. There is no longer any systemic dependence on Moscow for victory in Ukrainian elections.

Moldova's political ups and downs and changes of government have received less attention, though events there have been in some ways even more surprising. In 2001, Vladimir Voronin, the leader of Moldova's communists, was elected president on a platform of closer relations with Russia. But when his administration rejected the Russian-backed Trans-Dniester settlement plan in 2003, his relations with Moscow soured fast. He took a critical stance toward Moscow in the 2005 elections and won, but the communists did not manage to pull off a reverse transformation in the 2009 election. Although they had reached an understanding with the Russian authorities and received promises of economic assistance that was badly needed in the economic crisis, in the parliamentary election the communists failed to secure a majority big enough to allow them to elect a president. A repeat election saw them lose their majority altogether to a coalition that declared a combination of national-democratic values and a European choice.

The Belarusan leader Alexander Lukashenko, who has been president without interruption since 1994, has also consolidated his independence over time. In the 1990s, domestic political considerations made it to his advantage to present himself as an integrator in favor of uniting the post-Soviet area and building a bilateral union with Russia. These aims required Moscow's public support. But in the 2000s, responding to shifts in Belarusan public opinion, Lukashenko started appealing to the rhetoric of sovereignty and independence. In this situation, it was more important to underscore the differences rather than the similarities between Belarus and Russia, and this became the main leitmotif of Lukashenko's political campaigns in 2004 (the constitutional referendum), 2006, and 2010 (presidential elections).

In Ukraine's and Moldova's case, the emergence of political systems different from Russia's current system is a fundamentally significant development in the overall centrifugal drift. Ukraine and Moldova are elected democracies with constant, ongoing political competition that reflects a pluralism of opinions, and where disputes and clashes are resolved through free elections certified as such by international observers. The opposition came to power in Moldova in 2001 and 2009, and in Ukraine in all four elections during the past five years (the presidential elections of 2005 and 2010, and the parliamentary elections in 2006 and 2007). To some extent, one can say that this is a somewhat mechanical system in which the protest platform is always certain to win. But at the same time, the system is flexible enough overall to guarantee the opposition's rights and protect these countries from changes of government through revolution. This sort of system is objectively difficult to influence from outside because striking a deal with one force does not guarantee continued fulfillment of the obligations the ruling group has taken on in the country's name. In both Moldova and Ukraine, the president has only limited power, and both countries' political systems are closer in type to those of Central Europe rather than the classic post-Soviet models.

Belarus's system is closer in type to Russia's, and a casual glance would suggest that their common "values" should help to bring them closer together. Paradoxically, however, it is precisely the closely consolidated nature of the Belarusan regime that makes it hard for Russia to have an influence. If Russia fails to reach agreement with President Lukashenko, there is simply no one else around to apply effective pressure on him at home in support of Russia's position.

Russia as a Challenge to Sovereignty

In the immediate wake of the Soviet collapse, the countries in the region of the former Soviet Union chose completely different models of relations with Russia. Ukraine started its geopolitical drift away from Russia almost straight from the start. Kiev was active in developing alternative formats for international relations: a special partnership with NATO, cooperation with its neighbors in Central Europe, especially Poland; and stronger ties with the Commonwealth of Independent States (CIS) member countries that had problematic bilateral relations with Russia. Belarus took the opposite road of political reintegration with Russia, going as far as establishing the Russian-Belarusan Union State. Moldova searched for a middle road, aware that it would neither be able to develop its economy nor restore its territorial integrity without Russia's support.

But all three countries currently have complicated bilateral relations with Russia, and this in itself is worthy of attention. Furthermore, they all see Russia to a considerable extent as a threat to their sovereignty. All three countries therefore seek to establish a counterweight to Russia in the form of outside players, and not follow in Russia's wake.

Belarusan politics has seen the most radical turnaround. President Lukashenko frequently describes Russian policy in what amounts to hostile terms in his speeches.[7] Clearly, Belarusan political circles perceive a number of the steps that Russia has taken as being aimed at weakening Belarus's sovereignty, if not dismantling the country's independence altogether. In 2002, the proposal was made publicly that Belarus join the Russian Federation as six regions; and in 2004, Belarus became the first CIS country against which Russia used the "energy weapon" of turning off gas supplies as a negotiating tool. In 2008–2009, Moscow pressured Belarus to recognize Abkhazia and South Ossetia as independent countries, which the Belarusan authorities perceived as an attempt by Russia to set limits on Belarus's sovereign foreign policy. After Belarusan attempts to guarantee energy security by giving Gazprom control of pipelines did not bring the hoped-for results—energy prices continued to rise, and Belarus lost its preferential energy resource processing conditions—it became clear that the country needed to diversify its economic and general political ties with the outside world.

Moldova spent more time veering first one way and then another, rather than making consistent and concerted efforts to weaken Russia's influence on its domestic situation. But it nonetheless found itself facing Russian economic sanctions in the mid-2000s, when Russia imposed an embargo on imports of Moldovan wine. These actions made it clear to public opinion in Moldova that Russia was part of the problem rather than the solution (even if not all political forces, for understandable reasons, were willing to admit so publicly).[8] Russia is no longer seen as an objective mediator in the Trans-Dniester conflict. The parties in the conflict perceive Russia as a player that supports the Trans-Dniester regime, and this complicates relations between Moscow and Chisinau, while at the same time giving the Tiraspol regime a free hand. This situation makes Russia a hostage rather than the master of the situation.

As for Ukraine, there is a cyclical pattern of sorts. The rapprochement of 2001–2004 did not last long because Ukraine did not want to concede in any form control of its gas transportation system, which served as Kiev's main lever for applying pressure on Moscow. Furthermore, Ukrainian big business preferred the prospect of membership in the World Trade Organization to the idea of joining a common economic space with Russia. In 2005, Viktor Yushchenko came to power and set a course of taking Ukraine into NATO, which ushered in a period of open confrontation with Russia, which was reflected not just in the "gas wars" of 2006 and 2009 but also in Russia's recall of its ambassador to Kiev. In 2010, Yushchenko lost the presidential election to Viktor Yanukovych, who represented eastern Ukraine and had been prime minister from 2002 to 2004, and this sent the pendulum swinging back the other way. Russia and Ukraine signed a deal exchanging gas price discounts for the Russian navy's right to extend its lease of the Sevastopol base from 2017 to 2042. But a new period of stagnation set in soon after. Divergent economic interests will only increase fears with regard to Russia's intentions. In all likelihood, Moscow will try to take advantage of the current economic difficulties to establish control over important economic assets, and at the same time will use gas pipelines that bypass Kiev to weaken its monopoly on the transit of Russian gas to Europe. Kiev, of course, will attempt to resist this by whatever means it can.[9]

Limiting Factors in Russian Policy

The preceding period showed that, although Russia is much stronger than any of the region's countries taken separately, its possibilities for expanding its influence are nonetheless quite limited. The results of the policies followed in the 2000s are clearer in this respect because, unlike in the 1990s, Moscow did indeed try to play a tougher hand in the region during this time, but it still failed to gain the degree of control over the situation that it hoped to achieve. This is because several fundamental factors limit the effects that Russia's policy can have.

First, although Russia's foreign policy is now quite centralized, there is not, and in principle cannot be, any full consensus in today's Russia on its foreign policy's specific aims and content. Its foreign policy has become "market focused," and this makes it harder to harmonize the different domestic players' various interests. Even among the state actors, there is a clear basic conflict between the desire for geopolitical and military-political advantages and the reluctance to commit to paying potential allies' big expenses. Private business is even less interested here. Some private companies, when they try to expand into the region's markets, pin their hopes on making use of Moscow's political support, whereas others find it more to their advantage to avoid excessive politicization and reach agreements with the local authorities. Finally, widespread corruption and various opaque intermediary organizations also play a negative part in this process. The result is that there is no one common course, and Russian policy often pursues mutually incompatible goals.

Belarus is a very instructive case. Moscow shows interest, on the one hand, in keeping Belarus as a military ally and partner in resisting expanding Western geopolitical influence and launching new integration projects. But on the other hand, it is gradually depriving Belarus of income from energy resources processing and transit, periodically engaging in trade wars over various products with Belarus, and not showing any desire to take on clear spending commitments for its military presence. Taken separately, these two lines are easy to explain and are logical enough, but put together they undermine each other and give Lukashenko room for diplomatic maneuvering and using lobbying channels within the Russian corridors of power.

Second, no matter what policy goals are pursued, there is the problem of limited resources. Even leaving out of the equation the long-term tendency that will see the region's countries, including Russia itself, diversify their trade ties, it is obvious that economic pressure cannot be applied indefinitely. Sanctions are a double-edged sword. If they are used too often and for too long, they only deepen the rifts between countries and increase the desire to find new allies and new markets. Friendly feelings for Russia in the countries subjected to this pressure drop sharply. The "stick" policy's direct results often fall far short of what was hoped for, as was made eminently clear by the 2009 gas crisis, in which Russia came no closer at all to establishing control of Ukraine's gas transportation system. What is more, this policy damages Russia's own economic interests and reputation.

But if used solely as a means of buying the loyalty of post-Soviet regimes, economic incentives such as cheap energy supplies, preferential access to markets, and an open labor market cannot reliably tie down a client state. This policy provokes a parasite mentality, with client states starting to take subsidies for granted, and it does not guarantee that they will not "sell" their loyalty to some other patron in the future. As Belarus's reaction shows, any attempt to reduce the subsidies triggers immediate conflict. At the same time, the recipient countries are increasingly aware of the difference in Russia's economic power compared with that of the Western players.[10] The economic power of the European Union and the Western financial institutions is becoming an ever more important factor in weakening Russia's "soft power."

These identity shifts in Russia's neighbors make it hard for Russia to try to win over the hearts of people there through the use of "soft power" components such as the Russian-language media, the Orthodox Church, and opportunities for studying in Russia.

Russia maintains and to some extent is even strengthening its range of levers for wielding an indirect influence on the region through its Western partners. NATO's Bucharest summit in 2008 showed that in critical situations—the case in question was the idea of NATO offering membership action plans to Ukraine and Georgia—Moscow can exert quite effective influence on the position on key European capitals in order to quash decisions with which it does not agree. But at the same time, this only highlights the lack of instruments for direct control in Moscow's hands. The fact that Kiev, despite all the pressure, did not recall its application for a membership action plan in 2008 is extremely significant in this context, and left Moscow with no choice but to appeal to the Western countries and leave the decision in their hands.

Third, Russia's policy toward Ukraine, Belarus, and Moldova is no longer a purely bilateral matter. Russia must take into account its own relations with the European Union, and this acts to restrict it from applying tougher pressure. In cases when Russia's actions do not affect Western vital interests, as during the Georgian conflict in 2008, the EU limits itself to rhetorical condemnation. But when energy security is at stake, the EU takes a more active position. The EU responded to the Russian-Ukrainian gas war of 2009, for example, not only by suddenly stepping up its search for new ways to diversify energy supplies but also by fixing its intentions in documents, signing a bilateral agreement with Ukraine on March 23, 2009, in which it expressed its willingness to develop bilateral cooperation with Ukraine and help it to modernize its pipeline network, despite Russia's objections.

The European Union: A New Center of Gravity

The European Union has changed its approach to the region substantially during the past several years. Before it expanded eastward from 2004 to 2007, the EU's interests went little beyond maintaining stability and developing economic cooperation. There were various cooperation formats in place, but overall, the EU did not see the need to take on responsibility for the region's development. What is more, among the countries that had applied to join the EU, even Ukraine, Belarus, and Moldova's direct neighbors did not seek to develop genuine integration relations with these countries, fearing that it would slow down their movement toward EU membership.

But once the EU's borders reached the western limits of the "interim Europe," it lost the possibility of simply watching from the sidelines. The fundamental reason for the EU's increasing activeness on its new eastern periphery is a new awareness in Brussels that without successful transformation, these countries will never manage to catch up in living standards and would thus be at risk of turning into a source of "soft security" threats. As the experience in Central Europe showed, the reform and construction of a functioning market economy and political democratization greatly reduce this risk and create new opportunities, including for economic penetration. Reform will become more likely if the EU can offer its partners a series of incentives.

There is also an awareness that without guarantees for the region's energy security and transparent rules of the game in the energy sector, energy security in a number of EU member countries would also be at risk, and this too plays a big part in policy motivation.

The backtracking on plans for possible further NATO expansion in 2008 has also had an effect. Up until that point, European capitals placed development of relations with the region primarily in the context of relations with NATO. But after the Bucharest summit, a passive position on the EU's part would have been a disadvantageous move in image terms, amounting to a "double rejection" and overall negative reaction to the region's hopes for institutional rapprochement.

Gradually, the EU has declared its willingness to engage in integration and not just cooperation with willing potential partners in the region. The EU has not gone as far as offering the prospect of full-fledged membership, but it has expressed a real ambition to include interested nations in its economic and legal space. That this will be a lengthy process has been clear from the start. But traditionally, the EU has emphasized the consistency of direction rather than the actual pace, and steady progress rather than the final result, and the new policy thus fits well with the EU's typical foreign policy approach.

The EU's regional initiatives have gone in a short time from the abstract notion of a "neighborhood" to the Eastern Partnership Program, launched in May 2009, and in which Ukraine, Belarus, and Moldova are taking part, along with Armenia, Georgia, and Azerbaijan. This initiative's significance should not be underestimated. First, for the first time in Europe's east, a format for cooperation between the EU and the post-Soviet countries that does not include Russia has taken shape. This formally cements a reduction in Russia's possibilities for directly influencing decisions that also often concern it. Furthermore, the fact that Moscow's traditional partners did not seek to block the program's launch and preferred to avoid open conflict with the countries backing the project also reflects a reduction in Russia's indirect influence. In reality, the EU would welcome Russia's inclusion in specific projects, but the program's basic texts make no reference to the need to coordinate the initiative with any strategic partnership ties with Moscow. Work on the program accelerated after the Russian-Georgian conflict, clearly demonstrating that it reflects an approach that does not want to let EU policy be hostage to relations with Russia.

Second, the Eastern Partnership Program focuses on building relations based on political association and economic integration. The EU and the external participant countries have declared their intention to create an deep and comprehensive free trade zone (something that Russia has never offered its regional partners, even within the framework of the customs unions), liberalize visa relations, and pursue legislative harmonization that will lead to convergence with EU laws and standards—in other words, adoption of these laws and standards by the participating countries. If this partnership goes ahead in even just a few economic sectors, the legislative gap with Russia will start to widen. The interim objective and the basis for continued future integration is an association agreement.

Third, the EU is encouraging its partners to engage in multilateral co-operation, and it stresses that it is implementing a regional policy, and not a mechanical combination of several bilateral formats.[11]

As for the region's countries themselves, a real shift in relations between the EU and Belarus took place after 2008. The authorities in Minsk came to the conclusion that the EU's policy was not about trying to change the regime but about encouraging its gradual evolution through a coordinated policy approach. Lukashenko responded by freeing political prisoners, thus removing the main formal obstacle to getting dialogue started, and outlined prospects for economic liberalization, which drew the interest of European economic actors. Clearly, continued progress in relations will not be a linear process and will probably have its share of setbacks and crises, such as those that have unfolded since the presidential election in 2010, but Minsk is highly unlikely now to ever return to a policy focused on Moscow alone. It is far more likely to try to weave a middle course between Moscow and Brussels.

Relations between Chisinau and Brussels have recently undergone a positive change.[12] The EU was swift to react to the arrival of pro-European politicians in power in Moldova, increasing its economic aid and overall involvement in the country's affairs. Negotiations on an association agreement began in 2010, and Romania's membership in the EU will also help to keep Brussels' attention on Chisinau.

It is with Ukraine that the EU's cooperation has gone farthest. However, these relations are the greatest source of disappointment in Brussels because they have long since gone beyond the stage of declarative partnership, and taking the rapprochement further would require Ukraine to adopt transparent European rules within the country, and this is something that part of the Ukrainian elite resists. Even so, the arrival in power of Viktor Yanukovych and the eastern Ukrainian business groups that back him will more likely see the country come to a standstill for a while rather than go into reverse. Yanukovych will attempt to maintain balanced relations with both Russia and the West, trying to get economic benefits from both. It was not by chance that his first trip abroad as president was to Brussels. It is likely that disappointment with prior results and difficulties in breaking through the resistance within Ukraine itself will oblige Brussels to wait and see what results Yanukovych's economic policy brings, and see what outcome the 2012 parliamentary election produces, and only then going ahead with reformatting bilateral relations. Also possible, however, is that the EU will speed up efforts to conclude an association agreement with Ukraine in order to give it greater possibilities for balancing.

The Severance Test

On the basis of the analysis given above, developments in the region look most likely to follow an inertia scenario that would see Russia's cooperation with the region's countries continue its gradual decline. But one cannot exclude the possibility that centrifugal tendencies will gather pace in the second half of the decade and perhaps provoke a rapid disintegration scenario. The following combination of events could bring this about.

The first combination of events would be the arrival in power in the region's countries of a new generation of politicians seeking consensus in the name of European integration. In the right circumstances, this could happen as early as 2015–2016. Yanukovych's term in office would be over by then. In 2010, he became the first Ukrainian president who did not get even 50 percent of the vote in the second round. If his bet on improved relations with Moscow does not improve the country's economic situation, he could end up losing his electoral support, and as early as 2012 a new parliamentary majority could put a new government in place that is not loyal to Yanu-kovych. The foreign policy preference pendulum would then swing back toward a European choice. If a new pro-European coalition learns from past mistakes and manages to ensure internal consolidation, by 2015 it could be strong enough to elect a president with a similar ideological platform.

By 2016, Alexander Lukashenko might be pushed out of power. This could follow two possible scenarios. The less likely one is that Belarus liberalizes and the opposition wins power in an election, and the more likely is that the country's officials reach an agreement among themselves, with the EU's approval, to guarantee Lukashenko's immunity if he volun-tarily steps down. This would bring to power a group of technocrats and bureaucrats with an interest in getting the West to recognize them as the ruling elite of an independent eastern European country. The situation in Moldova is not entirely clear yet, but if the current pro-European coalition keeps power, the country's pro-European course will only grow stronger.

Second would be for the EU to start implementing a consistent "condi-tions-based" policy that sets in motion a process of step-by-step integra-tion of the region's countries in the EU's political and legal space (through a deep and comprehensive free trade zone based on EU standards and visa-free travel). Association agreements with Ukraine and Moldova could be signed within two or three years, and this would raise the question of taking cooperation further than what the Eastern Partnership Program of-fers. Relations with Belarus would develop a lot more slowly, but the coun-try is not likely to remain completely outside the process, at least as far as visa liberalization is concerned.

Third would be for Russia to remain stuck in its economic crisis while facing negative social and demographic trends. The instruments at Rus-sia's disposal and its ability to support neighboring countries economi-cally—and ultimately have some control over the situation—weaken even further, and growing nationalism, terrorist threats, and police corruption and high crime rates worsen its image. Even worse is the possibility that—either in an attempt to boost the regime's prestige at home, or as a result of uncontrolled provocation—armed conflict breaks out between Russia and one of its neighbors, or there is a border clash such as the Tuzla incident in 2003, when Russia's actions were perceived as an attempt to use force to change the sea border with Ukraine.

Fourth would be that differences between Russia and the EU increase to the point that Russia definitively ends up on the periphery, an outside force not integrated in any fundamental way either into the EU or into Europe in the broader sense, confined to the role of raw materials supplier with some of the features characteristic of developing countries. Such a development would not in itself lead to conflict between Russia and the EU, but it would force the EU to realize that it needs to take on more responsibility for maintaining stability and fostering economic development along its eastern borders.

Into Europe Together With Russia

One good scenario with regard to preventing the further erosion of cooperation between Russia and the region's countries would be for Russia itself to renew its rapprochement with Europe through far-reaching internal democratization and economic reforms, and by adopting European norms and standards. This scenario would create opportunities for greatly reducing the impact of several of the aspects contributing to the current centrifugal trend. Successful reforms in Russia (liberalization, ending protectionism, making progress toward the rule of law, reducing corruption, and fighting nationalism) would make Russia more attractive in its neighbors' eyes. Ending the postimperial claim to a zone of primary influence would help to change current perceptions of Russia as the main challenge to its neighbors' political independence. If Russia were to take a leadership role in the realm of regional reform, it would become the EU's main policy priority, because successful reform in Russia would result in other countries' following in its wake. More closely aligned norms and laws would make cooperation natural and help to develop new ties between Russia, the region's other countries, and the EU. It would no longer be possible, and indeed would make no sense, to ignore Russia and leave it outside the emerging cooperative framework.

Given the real situation today, however, this scenario is only a hypothetical possibility, if not a utopian vision. It is hard to imagine Russia's domestic politics undergoing any far-reaching transformation any time before the 2012 presidential election. At the very least, years would be needed before the results of such a transformation would really become clear. In its current foreign policy, Russia does not view the European Union as the priority. Relations between Russia and the EU have been stagnating as far as agreements are concerned, going no further than declarations on partnership.

At this point in time, one cannot expect to see a situation favorable to all parties emerging in the "interim Europe." There is even less reason to anticipate, however, that having lost undisputed control over territories once under its authority, Russia would make then once again look its way and forever exclude the possibility of them joining a different integration project, if such is their choice, simply because it would exclude this possibility for itself.

Notes

1. Alexander J. Motyl, "End of Ukraine and Future of Eurasia," *Kyiv Post*, May 7, 2010, http://kyivpost.com/news/opinion/op_ed/detail/66065. The quotation given applies to Ukraine in the source, but it can be fairly applied to the entire western part of the CIS.

2. Here and below, I cite the results of surveys conducted by the Independent Institute for Socio-Economic and Political Studies; see www.iiseps.org.

3. "Formation of a Common Identity of the Citizens of Ukraine: Prospects and Challenges—Analytical Report of the Razumkov Center," *National Security and Defense*, no. 9 (2007): 20.

4. For the details, see Barometer of Public Opinion (Institute of Public Policy), November 2009, www.ipp.md/public/files/Barometru/2009/BOP_noiembrie_2009_English.pdf.

5. "Perceptions of Soviet and Post-Soviet Era History Among Young People in the New Independent States: Non-Profit Partnership, International Research Agency," *Eurasian Monitor*, April–May 2009, 21–22, www.eurasiamonitor.org/rus/research/event-155.html; http://www.eurasiamonitor.org/rus/research/event-162.html.

6. Dmitri Trenin, "Rossia v SNG: Polye interesov, a ne sfera vliyaniya," *Pro et Contra*, nos. 5–6 (September–December 2009): 94.

7. In his address to the Belarusan people and Parliament in April 2010, for example, Lukashenko said that Russia's policy amounts to "deliberately planned action that threatens our country's very survival." *Kommersant*, April 21, 2010.

8. The current acting President of Moldova, Mihai Ghimpu, said in an interview: "If Russia says that it recognizes our territorial integrity it should settle this issue. There [in Trans-Dniester] the situation depends 99 percent, if not 100 percent, on Russia." *Kommersant*, May 5, 2010.

9. In mid-May 2010, discussing the prospects for the South Stream gas pipeline, Yanukovych said, "If this is a means of putting pressure on Ukraine, we understand this. But if this is about competition, we are ready for it." *Vremya Novostei*, May 14, 2010.

10. In the spring of 2010, when the Ukrainian authorities reached a deal that Russia would provide $3 billion in economic aid in the form of subsidized gas prices, they simultaneously obtained from the International Monetary Fund $12 billion in loans to stabilize the budget. Even in theory, Russia could clearly not have provided such a sum to Ukraine.

11. For more details see "Joint Declaration of the Prague Eastern Partnership Summit, Prague, May 7, 2009," Council of the European Union, Brussels, 8435/09 (Presse 78).

12. For the details, see Stanislav Secrieru, "Integration Reloaded: Streamlining Moldova's European Course," FIIA Briefing Paper 56, March 23, 2010.

CHAPTER SIX

THE SOUTH CAUCASUS *in* 2020

Thomas de Waal

Since 1991, the South Caucasus has embarked on an entirely new historical path. The name "South Caucasus" itself indicates that the era that began in 1801—during which the region was called by its Russocentric name, the "Transcaucasus," and was implicitly linked to Russia—is now over. The region has regained the "in-between" status it had in 1918–1921, whereby it is no longer part of any neighboring power but the object of the competing interests of several. However, this time there is an important difference: The independence of the three states of Armenia, Azerbaijan, and Georgia is internationally recognized; and they are being given the chance, slowly, to build viable states. This is the long-term trajectory within which all other developments fall. State building will be slow and painful, and the three states will still lag economically and politically behind Turkey and the western Balkan countries, let alone the EU member states. There is a small chance of renewed fighting. But there is at least no prospect of a return to the complete collapse of 1918–1921. The three countries' sovereignty is no longer in question, and state institutions have the capacity to deliver basic services to citizens.

However, a number of uncertain factors make for a picture of "predictable unpredictability." The borders of Azerbaijan and Georgia are still disputed. The Nagorno-Karabakh conflict is a dormant volcano, which, if it erupts, would have a disastrous impact on literally every other aspect of life in the region. A new Russia-Georgia crisis, a crisis in Iran, or a major terrorist incident could all quickly destabilize a region where state authority is fragile and democratic institutions are weak or nonexistent.

Of all these shocks, the most obvious and probably the most dangerous is renewed fighting over Nagorno-Karabakh. This could happen because of a deterioration on the cease-fire line (the Line of Contact) or a direct Azerbaijani offensive. A resumption of the conflict would be very dangerous and highly unpredictable. The only thing that could be safely assumed is that it would be very destructive, causing ripples far beyond the immediate region, and that neither side would fully win. Outside powers, Russia and the United States in the first instance, would act to suppress the conflict but not before much damage had been done. The "five-day war" over South Ossetia illustrates how catastrophic even a limited conflict can be.

Russia and the Region

A long-term trend that will be more marked by 2020 is the region's growing detachment from Russia. Russia's dominance of the region, both in the Tsarist and Soviet eras, was always much weaker than it was perceived to be. Saint Petersburg and Moscow relied on co-opted elites to govern and, with some exceptions, accommodated national aspirations and built local institutions within a colonial project. Since the turbulent early 1990s, when the Russian military (as opposed to the Russian state) was a major actor in the region, Russia's influence has been in steady decline, although Russian assumptions that the region is "ours" are still prevalent among the members of the older generation.

"De-Russianization" manifests itself in a number of ways. Ethnic Russians now number less than 2 percent of the population—a strong contrast to Kazakhstan or the Baltic states. The Russian language is in decline, despite being a lingua franca for the older generation and in part because the Russian government does little to support linguistic and cultural initiatives. Russian television channels are still watched in Armenia, but hardly in Azerbaijan and Georgia. The younger generation, even in Armenia, derives its cultural diet from globalized and national media and decreasingly from Russia.

In their foreign policy choices, the three countries are less reliant on Russia than they were, and this trend is also set to continue. Georgia has made a strong break with Russia, and the Russian economic embargo has forced it to diversify exports away from Russia. In the next few years, links of some kind will resume—and Russian business in fact still has a strong presence in Georgia. But the events of the last few years have ensured that in outlook at least, Georgia and Russia have moved far apart. Baku balances its relationship with Moscow with its relations with Brussels, Washington, and Ankara. Russia is Armenia's closest ally, and the two countries signed an agreement extending Russia's lease of the military base in Gyumri until 2042. Notwithstanding that, Yerevan is also careful to cultivate other relationships, being a big recipient of U.S. aid, an active participant in NATO's Partnership for Peace program, and a partner of Iran.

All this is slowly forcing Russia to enter into new "rules of engagement" in the South Caucasus with other powers, understanding that the locals want to balance their interests and other outsiders are here to stay. It is part of Russia's painful transition to being what Dmitri Trenin describes as a "postimperial power," which seeks be the most powerful actor in its neighborhood but no longer wants to reestablish an empire, with all the colonial burdens that that would bring.

Russia's influence on the region will increasingly be as an economic actor. Russians own or manage most of Armenia's major assets, including its railways, telecommunications companies, and nuclear power plant. Russia still owns assets in Georgia. It is now buying gas from Azerbaijan and is offering to buy more. This approach corresponds to the strategy outlined in the leaked Russian foreign policy doctrine, whereby the Foreign Ministry increasingly sees its main goal to be in forging "modernization alliances" to facilitate the economic transformation of Russia. Even Armenia fits within this vision, given that the doctrine sees the expertise that Russia gains from Yerevan's relations with the EU and NATO as an asset and identifies Armenia as a useful conduit for importing technology into Russia.

Migrants

The subject of migration to Russia deserves special attention because this is likely to be the main way ordinary Russians and South Caucasians interact over the next decade. There may be up to 5 million Armenians, Azerbaijanis, and Georgians living in Russia, both as new Russian citizens and as migrants. This in effect creates a "mini-Caucasia" on Russian territory, which has both good and bad consequences for both sides.

On the positive side, the migrants make for a healthy interdependence between the South Caucasus and Russia. Opinion polls suggest there is a more positive attitude among the general population in Azerbaijan and Georgia toward Russia than among the political elite. Economically speaking, the migrants provide a vital source of revenue to the three South Caucasian countries through remittances; estimates vary, but they may be more than $1 billion a year for each country, or equivalent to almost half the Armenian state budget. In Russia, these migrants perform the role of *gastarbeiter* anywhere, doing the jobs that locals would rather not do and providing much-needed labor power for agriculture and the construction industry.

One negative aspect of this phenomenon is that migration drains the South Caucasus of its most useful workers. The main category of migrants is young men between the ages of twenty and thirty-five years, who leave a big gap in the workforce back home and consequently make small towns and villages across the South Caucasus (but not the capital cities) dismal semi-abandoned zones. Other professionals seek to assimilate in Russia, rather than returning home. A bigger problem is that "people of Caucasian nationality" are a major target of racial and xenophobic discrimination and violence. This applies equally to everybody from the region—a skinhead will not discriminate between an Armenian student and an Azerbaijani market worker. It only takes a small spark to ignite ethnic violence, as happened during the Georgian-Russian crisis of 2006, when hundreds of Georgians were forcibly deported from Russia. So what economics brings together, politics can still drive apart. A domestic nationalist backlash in Russia, caused by an economic downturn, in which Caucasian migrants were victimized or forced to flee, could spark a serious crisis in bilateral relations with all three South Caucasus countries.

Abkhazia and South Ossetia

Abkhazia and South Ossetia are the big exceptions to the trend of diminishing Russian influence in the South Caucasus, having been de facto annexed by Russia since 2008. Arguably, the Russian takeover began long before that, and it could be argued that in 2008 Moscow was not so much redrawing the map as aggressively reasserting the status quo that had been in place since 1992–1993, when the two territories de facto seceded from Georgia.

Both territories are now parts of the Russian economic, military, and media space, although Abkhazia's political institutions are still basically autonomous. However, the prospect of the two ever formally joining Russia is very remote. Currently, there is far less engagement between the West and Georgia with South Ossetia than with Abkhazia, but during the next decade that is likely to reverse. South Ossetia is small and poor and of far lesser strategic importance to Russia than Abkhazia, whereas Ossetians and Georgians have much stronger traditions of intermarriage and trade than do Abkhaz and Georgians. That suggests that if and when a small thaw occurs in Georgian-Russian relations (something that both sides need to happen but that is unlikely to occur before Mikheil Saakashvili leaves office in 2013), they will begin to make a deal on South Ossetia and open up South Ossetia to trade from Georgia. Abkhazia is stronger, bigger, and more strategically important to Russia. Its population of Georgian internally displaced persons is bigger and less welcome to return. This means that a breakthrough on conflict resolution is very unlikely and the best either side can hope for is that Abkhazia achieves the status of the Turkish Republic of Northern Cyprus, a peaceful territory with certain links to the south and to the international community and certain opportunities to develop economically.

Two factors will bear on the future of Abkhazia and South Ossetia. The first is the unstable situation in the North Caucasus. Russia has increasingly lost levers of control in the North Caucasus, and there is no sign of the low-level insurgency abating there. The Russian government's recognition of the independence of Abkhazia and South Ossetia has only complicated matters there, sowing resentment in Chechnya, Ingushetia, and the three Circassian regions of Adygeia, Kabardino-Balkaria, and Karachaevo-Cherkessia about Russian "double standards" in suppressing nationalism on its own territory while encouraging it on the territory of Georgia. At some point, Russia may need to turn to both Georgia and Western countries for help in stabilizing the North Caucasus—which will in turn require it to be more flexible over Abkhazia and South Ossetia.

The second factor is the Sochi Winter Olympics in 2014. The Russian government wants to be able to rely on Abkhazia, which is just a few kilometers to the south, to help make them work. On the one hand, Russia wants to be able to depend on infrastructure in Abkhazia to supplement what is available in and around Sochi, whether it is the Sukhumi airport (which is better able to receive airplanes than the Adler airport near Sochi) or hotels that can accommodate thousands of guests. This means that in the short term, Russia will continue to try and consolidate its economic hold on Abkhazia. On the other hand, the Russian government will want to invite foreign as well as Russian visitors to stay in Abkhazia—which would involve some kind of consent from the Georgian government on the use of what most of the world still regards as sovereign Georgian territory. For both these reasons, there will be an incentive for Russia to be more flexible after 2013.

State Fragility

Governments in the South Caucasus are strong but brittle. Power is mainly exercised through a classic post-Soviet "state vertical," beginning with the president. There are few safety valves (with the partial exception of Georgia), with the result that elections still have the potential to turn into crises, as happened in Azerbaijan and Georgia in 2003 and Armenia in 2008.

Azerbaijan

Azerbaijan presents the starkest case of this duality of strength and weakness, and is the strongest candidate for a major crisis before 2020. Increasing energy wealth and sharpening social divisions go hand in hand. The Azerbaijani elite looks much stronger and richer than it was a decade ago. The old opposition has been marginalized, and political space has narrowed to the point that even a dozen people cannot demonstrate in favor of the Musavat Party in central Baku without being detained by police. The removal of presidential term limits from the Constitution means that Ilham Aliev (who will turn 58 in December 2019) can be elected leader of Azerbaijan almost indefinitely. Even if he were to leave the scene, a successor (perhaps his wife) can be found from his family or network.

The future stability or instability of Azerbaijan depends in large part on how far its oil and gas revenues will stretch. According to one projection, the country could earn as much as $400 billion over the next twenty years from the Azeri-Chiraq-Guneshli oil fields in the Caspian Sea, whose oil is exported through the Baku-Tbilisi-Ceyhan pipeline. When it comes to oil revenues, there are two main variables: Will the price of oil hold up? And how long will reserves last? The first question is unanswerable; suffice it to say that if the oil price dips to below $50 a barrel, revenues will also fall considerably. When the world oil price fell sharply in 1998, a string of foreign companies left Azerbaijan.

As for oil reserves, two recent predictions say that "at 2009 production levels, the country's oil reserves will be depleted in eighteen years" and that they will be exhausted in twenty to twenty-five years barring new discoveries. The decline of "peak oil" is expected to begin in about 2014. BP has indicated that it may be able to increase the life of the Azeri-Chiraq-Guneshli field by deeper drilling and thus extend peak oil until about 2019.

Azerbaijan's hope is that by that time, rising gas revenues will have filled the gap left by falling oil revenues. The country has plentiful reserves of gas, and production is expected to increase to about 20 billion cubic meters a year in 2015 and beyond that when the second phase from the Shah Deniz field begins in about 2017. This should potentially give Azerbaijan a stable source of income—although not as spectacular as that from oil. However, Azerbaijan's hopes for gas prosperity are dependent on factors completely beyond its control—the changing gas market and, in particular, whether new shale-gas technology will open up a new worldwide energy source and cause a dramatic dip in world gas prices.

All this underlines the reality that Azerbaijan's future is much too reliant on an unpredictable commodity. A worrying omen is that Azerbaijan's once-rapid growth of gross domestic product has slowed considerably in the last few years. After growth averaging more than 21 percent a year in the period 2005–2009, growth in 2010 was a modest 5 percent and International Monetary Fund predictions put it at below 3 percent in 2011. The creation of a State Oil Fund, SOFAZ, was supposed to mitigate the effects of this. The government drew heavily on SOFAZ in 2009, spending almost AZN 5 billion to close the budget deficit, but it cannot intervene this heavily every year without rapidly depleting the fund.

Worryingly, beyond energy products, the rest of the economy is extremely weak. In 2009, oil and gas contributed 95 percent of Azerbaijan's total export revenue. Agriculture and the non-oil industry are both very poorly developed. Even at the moment, this creates problems as oil and gas are not good creators of employment, providing only about 1.5 percent of jobs in the economy. Oil and gas have also skewed the situation by concentrating almost the entire economy of Azerbaijan in the capital, Baku. According to various estimates, between 55 and 80 percent of the population now lives in and around the city.

Islam and Iran

Surveys of Azerbaijani youth indicate high levels of cynicism and a worrying "values gap." Young people believe that money and connections are more important attributes than natural talent. They take little interest in politics and show distrust for both Russia and the West.[1] Whereas Russia has the taint of being the former colonial power, the West has the associations of being the friend of the ruling elite and the oil companies. These attitudes as well as the country's growing social divisions and the prospect of falling oil revenues in about 2020 are bound to boost political Islam as a force in Azerbaijan.

Up until now, political Islam has been weak in Azerbaijan, in comparison with Uzbekistan, for example. But a social base for it is now forming. In 2006, a poll by the Far Center in Baku found that 19 percent of respondents favored establishing an Islamic state in Azerbaijan and 30 percent more favored introducing more Islamic elements into public life. Since then, such attitudes will undoubtedly have been strengthened. The government has acted clumsily, closing several mosques, while continuing to ally itself closely with the official clerical establishment it inherited from the Soviet era. New, younger articulate and educated mullahs are emerging. Most are moderate, but some are not.

Political Islam comes from both the north and the south. In the north, it is Sunni and linked to the most Islamic part of the Russian Federation, Dagestan. New instability in Dagestan could have a direct impact on Azerbaijan via their shared Lezghin population. In the south, political Islam is Shia and intersects with Azerbaijan's other major challenge in the next decade, Iran. Iran and Azerbaijan—which used to be part of the same empire until the early nineteenth century—are vulnerable to one another, and a crisis in one is likely to have an impact on the other. There are upward of 20 million Azeris in Iran (the numbers are strongly disputed because most are heavily assimilated), and occasional unrest in northern Iran suggests that many of them want more rights to speak and teach their language than are being given them by the Iranian government. The Republic of Azerbaijan has the capacity to manipulate this.

For its part, Iran has the capacity to disturb Azerbaijan by preaching its strong Shia Islam to what is both a Shia and a secular state. The television channel Sahar-2 broadcasts in Azeri to southern Azerbaijan and sends the propaganda message that the current ruling elite in Baku are "friends of Israel" and "enemies of Islam." Opposition leaders such as Isa Gambar, who are now barred from the mainstream media, give interviews to Sahar-2. The Iranians also influence the Talysh minority, who are estimated to be 200,000 to 250,000 strong. They speak a language related to Farsi and live in southern Azerbaijan.

In theory, Azerbaijan and Iran have a shared interest in mutual stability. When tensions were high between Iran and the United States in 2006, the Azerbaijani government reaffirmed that it would stay out of any potential U.S. military action against Iran. However, events have a tendency to get out of control, and there are plenty of possible flashpoints. In the last decade, there have been a number of serious incidents—including an Iranian warship confronting an Azerbaijani survey vessel in the Caspian Sea in 2001; up to 60,000 Iranian Azerbaijanis crossing the border into Nakhichevan in 2005–2006, when Iranian-U.S. tensions were high; and demonstrations and mutual accusations after cartoons that Azerbaijanis found insulting were published in an official Iranian newspaper in 2006.

All this underlines the fact that Azerbaijan currently has what the International Crisis Group aptly calls "vulnerable stability." The present system is built to accommodate the political and economic agenda of the current elite. By 2020, the system is likely to be more fragile and vulnerable to internal and external shocks. The risk this poses is not just to Azerbaijan itself, because if there is a domestic crisis inside the country, a leader may be tempted to play the "Karabakh card" and unite Azerbaijanis around the prospect of a new war with Armenia.

Armenia

Armenia is the most ethnically homogeneous of the three states but is also politically fragile. Serzh Sarkisian came to power as president amid arrests of the opposition, following the violent street clashes in Yerevan on March 1, 2008, and he has established himself as the undisputed leader of the country. But his perceived legitimacy is still low, although the opposition has not managed to keep up the momentum of protest against him. Disastrous economic news (a double-digit fall in gross domestic product) and the halting of the Armenia-Turkey rapprochement mean that he is still vulnerable. The chances of an opposition candidate being able to mobilize street power and take office in 2013 or 2018 are not insignificant. There is also a possibility of a split within the governing elite—a factor that reinforces Sarkisian's very cautious attitude to both the Turkey and Nagorno-Karabakh issues, because he does not want to be challenged by anyone playing a "patriotic card" against him.

Armenia's survival as a state is assured—something that could not have been said with certainty during the cold, dark winters of 1991–1993. Yerevan is a properly functioning city, although the surrounding regions are still sunk in poverty. The main issue facing the country is whether it can break out of regional isolation through the normalization of relations with Turkey and resolution of the Nagorno-Karabakh conflict. In particular, Armenia needs the route to Europe that lies through Turkey to have any hope of future prosperity.

However, Armenian leaders of all parties are clear that they will not make what they regard as unjust concessions over key issues of Armenian identity to Azerbaijan and Turkey for the sake of economic benefits. Specifically, they would rather pay the price of isolation than unilaterally give up Azerbaijani territories conquered during the Karabakh conflict that they say are an essential "security zone" to protect the Karabakh Armenians. This does not inspire any hope for the resolution of the Nagorno-Karabakh conflict—particularly given that the Azerbaijani side is, if anything, even more intransigent.

There is more cause to be optimistic over Armenia-Turkey normalization. Here the cards are very much in Turkey's hands. Opening the Armenia-Turkey border and establishing diplomatic relations with Armenia would hurt Ankara's relations with Baku, but would bring Turkey other benefits. It would rid Turkey of the continuing agony of genocide resolutions in foreign parliaments and take the country one step closer to the European Union. However, Turkey's decisions will stem from domestic political factors. Currently only the Justice and Development Party (AKP) would take this step, and even it feels constrained by Azerbaijani lobbying. Effectively, this means that Armenia must wait for events beyond its control—a better political climate in Turkey—to be assured of open borders to the West and its own economic transformation.

Georgia

Georgia is a much more open society than its neighbors, but it is still a long way from being a full democracy. Its system of government has been aptly called a "pluralistic feudalism," in which politicians are allowed to compete for power but are barely accountable to the public when they achieve it. Centralization never fully works in Georgia, and there are competing interests and players, both from the opposition, in the regions and within the ruling elite who can challenge Saakashvili's grip on power and ability to name a successor. The president is working hard to ensure that his people inherit the levers of power when he leaves office in January 2013, but he needs to do so in a way that does not invite Western condemnation. Constitutional amendments have enhanced the future powers of the prime minister so that Saakashvili can emulate Putin and switch roles, if he wants to.

Barring a new flare-up over Abkhazia or South Ossetia (which is not in the strategic interests of either Georgia or Russia, and which Western powers and the European Union Monitoring Mission will do their best to avert), Georgia is unlikely to face a major conflict in the next decade. The major issue facing the country is whether it can make progress economically and politically or whether the current governing elite will merely entrench itself in power, leaving Georgia as a hybrid country, still relatively pluralist but neither fully democratic nor fully European. Currently, Georgia is basically a one-party democracy of extremely youthful politicians, who will not be easily dislodged and still have a solid base of popular support. Their presentation skills and useful friends (especially in Washington), and the fact that they are relatively more democratic than Georgia's neighbors, spare them from strong criticism.

The country is proud of its economic record, of having posted double-digit growth figures and massively increased the state budget. But the easiest part is now behind them. Much of the growth in state revenue was due to parts of the gray or black economy being legalized in 2004–2005. The major privatizations—which former economics minister Kakha Bendukidze described as "selling everything except our conscience"—have now all gone through. U.S. and EU aid, which Georgia was lucky to receive before the world financial crisis hit in the autumn of 2008, is unlikely to be given again in such large quantities. The economy has improved substantially in the last few years but still faces major problems—90 percent of businesses are concentrated in Tbilisi, and unemployment remains high. This suggests that Georgia needs a sustained long-term strategy for economic transformation. Currently, the government seems insufficiently professional to come up with one. The appointment of an inexperienced twenty-eight-year-old from Canada to be economics minister does not inspire optimism.

The key challenge for Georgia is whether it can and wants to pursue economic integration with the European Union, as the Baltic states did in the early 1990s. Currently, there is an ideological divide within the Georgian governing elite. Some want to pursue European integration, beginning with a free trade agreement with the EU. Others (led by the libertarian Kakha Bendukidze) see European integration as a straitjacket and dream that Georgia will become, in President Saakashvili's words, "Switzerland with elements of Singapore." In practical terms, this has resulted in disputes in Brussels and Tbilisi about the launch of negotiations on a Deep and Comprehensive Free Trade Area that would grant Georgia privileged access to the EU single market.

Optimistic Scenarios

There is a strong pull toward inertia in this region. Ruling elites are well established and see little incentive to invite change that would unseat them.

Optimistic scenarios for the South Caucasus rest on the twin interrelated goals of a resolution of the region's economic and security problems. The most benign scenario is an economic transformation from below, with the region following the path of Turkey during the past decade in achieving strong economic growth. The drivers for this would be the owners of small and medium-sized businesses given the political space and incentives to pursue their natural entrepreneurialism. Turkey itself could play a positive role in helping make this happen, but only if it succeeds in normalizing its relations with Armenia and becoming a neutral regional power.

The main actor that could help make this kind of transformation happen would be the European Union, if it robustly pursued free trade and association agreements that opened up European markets, gave the countries a stronger legal framework, and empowered local businesspeople. Successful EU engagement in the South Caucasus requires goodwill from both sides. From Brussels, it means the will to offer better visa facilitation and trade privileges and to be willing to engage with a region that defies easy solutions. From the South Caucasian side, it means a willingness to strike a bargain that involves economic and political liberalization (with the accompanying weakening of power of elites) in return for the economic and security benefits that the EU can offer.

When it comes to security, the benign role here could be played jointly by Russia and the United States, as well as the EU, if relations continue to improve, in agreeing on a shared security arrangement that could jointly support Armenia, Azerbaijan, and Karabakh. In other words, the latter-day great powers could agree on a robust peacekeeping force or security regime that would be sufficient to persuade the Armenians to give up the Azerbaijani-occupied territories in favor of a status solution for Nagorno-Karabakh that falls short of independence. In this way, the "reset," combined with Russia's acceptance of the end of its dominant role in the region, could pave the way for a more stable regional security framework.

Note

1. See, for instance, "Public Opinion Survey on Moral and Social Stance of Azerbaijani Youth," *Turkhan's Blog: Independent News from Azerbaijan*, June 4–July 4, 2009, http://turkhan.wordpress.com/2010/06/12/public-opinion-survey-on-moral-and-social-stance-of-azerbaijani-youth.

POLITICAL ECONOMY *and* ECONOMICS

PART II

the "third cycle":
IS RUSSIA HEADED
BACK TO THE FUTURE?

Kirill Rogov

Russia has entered the third cycle of its post-Soviet history. Although this cycle's contours are not yet clear, we are already in it, and its results will be summed up around 2020—and precisely these results will then form the country's image.

Indeed, if one looks at the twenty years of post-Soviet history from a bird's-eye view, one is struck primarily by the presence of two periods whose main characteristics are as different as night and day. The first period, the 1990s, and can rightfully be called *transformational*. It consisted first and foremost of large-scale institutional changes and a no less substantial restructuring of the economy. The first outlines of post-Soviet Russia's major political and economic institutions were formed during these years. At the same time, restructuring the economy occurred in the form of a deep transformational recession (Russia's gross domestic product contracted by as much as 35–45 percent), which was accompanied by a dramatic fall in living standards (real disposable income in 1999 was 46 percent of its 1991 level). Yet another characteristic of the transformational cycle was the chronic budget deficit (in the absence of sources with which to cover it). This indicator, in fact, reflected the high degree of political instability and the weakness of the state, along with its inability not only to adequately collect taxes but also to oppose pressure demanding an increase in expenditures. The population's extremely low level of

FIGURE 7.1 *Dynamics of real disposable income, GDP, and the state of affairs in the country*

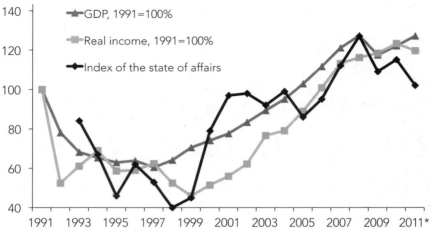

* The index of the state of affairs in the country is calculated as the difference between the affirmative and dissenting responses to the Levada Center question: "Are matters moving in the right direction, or will external events take us to a standstill?"—plus 100 points; this means that a value below 100 points indicates that the difference between affirmative and dissenting responses is negative.

** For the year 2010 – data for a total of 10 months.

support for the acting leadership and its policies during the second part of this period completes the picture: Public opinion ran the spectrum from extreme reformist enthusiasm in 1991 to extreme negativity in 1994–1998 (see figure 7.1).

Then, as if by magic, everything seemed to begin changing in 1999. The second period of post-Soviet history can rightfully be called *stabilizing*—stabilization was its main slogan and goal. This period was characterized by consistent and impressive growth in the country's GDP (at an average rate of about 7 percent annually), and by the fast-paced growth of incomes. Moreover, the growth rate of incomes exceeded the GDP growth rate, whereas in the 1990s, its rate of decline outpaced the GDP's fall. Additionally, the period was characterized by a consistent budget surplus, evincing the reversal of fundamental political tendencies—the government was no longer under siege. Further evidence of this reversal were changes in the population's evaluations of the state of affairs in the country and the direction of its development (see figure 7.1). Finally, according to experts, yet another feature characterizing this second, stabilizing cycle, was the deceleration and attenuation of institutional reforms (compare, for example, the behavior of Russian figures in the Bertelsmann Foundation Transformation Index; according to the Status Index, Russia moved from 41st place in 2003 to 65th place in 2010, while it moved from 31st to 107th place on the Management Index).[1] The political direction was also changing: If at the beginning of the period the idea of consolidation of power was associated with reforms (for example, the "Gref program"), then in the second half it acquired a distinctly authoritarian spirit, and political development and democratization indices showed a rapid regression.

The financial crisis of 2008–2009 marked the conclusion of the second cycle. Having noted the striking differences between the two eras, the features of which mirrored each other almost exactly, one cannot ignore the fact that the trends that so clearly marked the second cycle had been broken, or at least been enfeebled. For the first time since 1998, GDP did not increase in 2009 but contracted; moreover, the extent of the reduction (by 7.9 percent) was comparable only to the pace of economic decline in 1992–1994. In 2010 and 2011 Russia demonstrated economic growth, but its pace (about 4 percent of GDP) is substantially more modest than that of the post-crisis recovery of 1998–1999 and the pre-crisis growth of 2006–2008.[2] Despite high oil prices, capital outflow, rather than inflow (as was the case before the crisis), is being observed. The budget has once again been saddled with a deficit and income growth has not recovered. If from 2000 to 2007 the annual income growth of the population was in the range of 9 to 15 percent, then in 2008–2009 it was 2–4 percent per year, and in the first half of 2011, a decline of real income by 4 percent has been recorded (this is in sharp contrast to the picture of the 1998 crisis: at that time, incomes fell sharply, but then turned toward a sustained recovery). As a whole, the economy has not yet managed to enter a pre-crisis trajectory; experts (including those in the Russian government) do not expect a return to the previous situation of growth in the economy and incomes, and the government hopes to balance the budget no earlier than 2015. It is logical to assume that these changes in fundamental trends will—as was observed in the first and second cycles—have implications for the social and political spheres.

Cycles and Cyclicity: A Theoretical Framework

In the 1990s, the processes under way in the postsocialist countries were primarily considered within the framework of the transitology paradigm, according to which these processes had a defined, well-known end point, and the empirical investigation of their development was conceptualized as a story of intermediate stages and various deviations along the trajectory toward this goal. Disillusionment with this paradigm in the early 2000s was rapid,[3] and its unpopularity during the following decade is comparable only to its popularity in the preceding one. As Russia pushed away from this paradigm, a new position on Russia and the other countries that belong to the Commonwealth of Independent States became increasingly widespread. According to this view, the period of reformist "disturbance" associated with the collapse of the socialist economy and the Soviet empire is regarded as an anomaly and a result of an imbalance and a general loss of equilibrium, rather than as a prelude to a qualitatively new stage. The postsocialist regimes of the CIS countries were now seen as "competitive authoritarianisms": the fall of the Soviet Union provoked open competition for domination among the elites, which ended with those elites who had captured the dominant positions undertaking consolidation based on the restoration of traditional hierarchies.[4] Thus, the concept of the existence of a certain authoritarian/totalitarian/paternalistic archetype of Russian statehood—immutable, organic, and the only fully realized system of power relations that can survive periods of crisis or decline, but which remains essentially unchanged—once again acquired popularity.

However, the clear antisymmetry of the first and second approaches, which consider one of the two states of society as abnormal and the other as normal or normative, as well as the series of color revolutions on the territory of the former USSR, gave impetus to a third view of development—to the argument about the oscillatory nature of the historical and political evolution of the post-Soviet countries—and refreshed interest in the idea of cyclicity.[5] "Cyclicity," in this context, means the instability of hybrid regimes associated with a divided elite and weak institutions; fluctuations between periods of dominance of authoritarian and paternalistic practices, on the one hand, and democratic bursts, on the other, are explained by the elite's inability to achieve consolidation on the basis of established conventional rules of coexistence and cooperation.[6]

There is, however, a broader, more general interpretation of cyclicity that is not related to the problem of hybrid regimes, and which could be called sociohistorical. Here I primarily have in mind the famous description of the cycles of American history undertaken by Arthur Schlesinger Jr., which was based on an empirical analysis of Arthur A. Schlesinger Sr.[7] According to this view, cyclicity is regarded not as an aberration (an inability to find a state of equilibrium, as is handled in the previous case) but as the natural model of society's historical existence—moving, as if by tacks, so that periods of public exaltation and of focusing on the social and the rationalization of social interests (liberalism, in the American sense of the term) are followed by periods of concentration on private interests, of social apathy, and of preferences for the proven "old" forms and the prevailing status quo over any reforms and innovations (conservatism).

Although soft, "electoral" authoritarianism seeks to reduce society's direct influence on the government, it is in fact very concerned with the issue of public opinion, which it views as an important resource in maintaining power (in the terms of Robert Dahl, such a regime should be handled as an "inclusive hegemony.")[8] In turn, public opinion in semiauthoritarian regimes (in contrast to the situation in totalitarian regimes) enjoys significant autonomy from the government (in this, such regimes also differ from totally authoritarian and totalitarian regimes) and is inclined to view its relationship with authority as a contract, in a sense. In other words, under conditions of electoral authoritarianism, when the population is included in the procedures for legitimizing authority (though with very limited rights), the oscillation of public opinion between alternative politicians and priority systems present in the public consciousness has a place, despite the fact that these alternative politicians might be weakly institutionalized.[9]

Finally, the dynamic of the business cycle can be considered a widely recognized factor in the cyclicity of political development: changing economic trends lead to significant changes in levels of employment and income and to corresponding changes in public sentiment. This relationship was clearly in evidence during the transition from the first to the second period of Russia's post-Soviet history (table 7.1).[10] Economic performance

TABLE 7.1 *Answers to the question "In which direction is the political life of Russia currently heading?" (Levada Center)*

	1997	2000	2005	2006	2007	2009	2010
The development of democracy	14	26	32	33	36	36	37
The restoration of the Soviet system	12	14	7	6	9	9	9
It is becoming a dictatorship	4	6	12	14	13	14	19
Growing chaos and anarchy	54	37	30	22	14	21	12
Difficult to respond	17	17	18	24	28	20	24

influences not only the assessment of the current situation and politicians in power, but also the assessment of the political and economic doctrines and concepts associated with these politicians.

However, if the subject of our attention is a specific historical period in the life of society and the analysis of possible points of bifurcation during this period, then we find that the three interpretations of cyclicity discussed above, in fact, are directed at three important sites of social interaction that in reality are connected by strands of mutual influence, interdependence, and interpenetration. Macroeconomic fluctuations violate the established forms and modes of cooperation and coexistence among the elite, and stimulate the reconsideration of widely held views rooted in the previous period; in turn, shifts in social attitudes stimulate political activism among elite groups and form a demand for programs that involve changing the rules of the game and changing the priorities of the economy in order to reverse economic behavior. In essence, these are three vertices of a single triangle.

I attempt in the following pages to provide insight into the problem of cycles in the post-Soviet history of Russia from the perspective of the three indicated interacting levels: (1) changing macroeconomic trends, 2) the evolution of the prevailing attitudes of public opinion, and 3) changing rules of interaction among the elite.

In general we can say that over the course of the first two cycles, the country's image changed quite radically, albeit in entirely different senses.

At the end of the first cycle, a market economy had developed in the country, but the significant material difficulties of this process brought about society's deep disillusionment with the basic concepts that had driven the transformations. In the second cycle, by contrast, citizens' welfare steadily increased, positive changes took place at the micro level (see Daniel Treisman's chapter in this volume), at the same time that the evolution of social and political practices was inspired by the "spirit of reaction" to the "boisterous 1990s."

The Third Cycle: The Macroeconomic Dimension

In scrutinizing the differences between the first two cycles of the post-Soviet history of Russia and the character of the transition from one to another, it is necessary to make one essential observation. The crisis of 1998 undoubtedly triggered this transition: It struck a powerful blow to the potential of oligarchic groups and cleared the way for a policy of financial stabilization, while the devaluation of the ruble allowed the government to sharply reduce its debts and the economy to quickly transition to a phase of dynamic growth in order to meet the domestic demand connected with the reduction of imports.

At the same time, the transition to a phase of growth was not exclusively the result of these changes. It is significant that all the countries of the former Soviet Union—independent of the economic policies they pursued, their economic structure, or their political situation—moved toward economic growth from 1997 to 2000. The reason clearly lies in the fact that by the end of the 1990s, the process of the primary restructuring of the main sectors of the economy and of property relations had largely been completed, and a new system of internal and external markets had been constructed that paved the way for the recovery of economic growth; it is indicative that economic growth was first recorded in Russia following results from the second half of 1997.[11] The crisis of 1998 played the role of a sort of trigger mechanism: The beginning of a new, recovery phase of the transformational cycle in the economy coincided with the beginning of a new political cycle.

How does the Russian crisis of 2008–2009 look against this background? From the very beginning, it was the subject of sharp controversy among those who believed that it was caused primarily by the external impact of the global financial crisis and those who believed that this impact was only the pin that popped the "internal bubble." However, the cumulative effect of the crisis leaves supporters of the first point of view without a chance; in 2009, Russia demonstrated the maximal reduction in GDP among the 25 largest world economies (−7.9 percent, while the GDP of Russia's closest "competitor," Mexico, fell by 6.5 percent), whereas the amplitude of the fall from its precrisis growth rate (8.1 percent in 2007) to the "bottom" of the crisis amounted to a 16-percentage-point loss (its closest "competitors," Mexico and Turkey, endured falls of 9.8 and 9.4 percentage points). The trade, construction, and financial services sectors in Russia were particularly affected in comparison with other economies; Russia also led the way in the decline of consumer demand. All this points both to a general overheating of the economy before the crisis, along with the direct overheating of consumer demand.[12]

Indeed, economic growth in Russia at the turn of the 1990s and 2000s had a restorative character and relied on the expansion of exports as well as on domestic demand (import substitution). In the mid-2000s, it was supported by significant capital inflows into the country, which enabled the rapid growth of incomes and consumer demand as well as the fast expansion of credit to both enterprises and consumers. However, the rapid growth of incomes and domestic demand led to a swift expansion of imports, as a result of which the further growth in incomes had less and less of a stimulating effect on industry. The growth model based on the rapid expansion of domestic demand hit the ceiling, and the financial crisis yanked out from under it support in the form of massive capital inflows. In other words, we are dealing with a crisis of the very model of growth that had ensured the successes of the 2000s. However, the crisis of 2008–2009 did not lead to structural changes in the economy, and the rapid recovery of oil prices led to a situation in which postcrisis growth is largely similar to the previous scenario. If this hypothesis is true, then we are in a maturation phase of preconditions to a new structural crisis, combined with the impossibility of continued sustained economic growth without a new stage of restructuring.

Low rates of economic growth (2.5 to 4 percent per year) and low rates of growth or the stagnation of real income look today to be the most likely inertial scenario for the coming years, attainable only given a sufficiently favorable situation in the commodity markets. Additionally, the government will lack the means to simultaneously stimulate the economy and fulfill its social obligations, a fact that will be expressed in the budget deficit. The exhaustion of the possibilities of the previous model of economic growth signals not only the necessity of finding a new model but also the inevitable correction of prevailing social attitudes, assessments, and expectations, as well as of the possibilities and strategies of the elite groups. This correction and its social and political consequences, in my opinion, will primarily decide the basic substance of the third cycle of Russia's post-Soviet history, and will determine its trajectory.

Liberal and Conservative Phases: The Russian Version

If we again turn our gaze to Russian history during the past twenty to twenty-five years, but now examine it from the angle of trends in social expectations and preferences as well as those effects to which these trends gave rise in the political sphere, then we again see several stages and two major tendencies. The first stage, from the late 1980s to the early 1990s, is characterized by the dominance in public opinion and public discussion of two fundamental political concepts that in many ways determined the direction of political development. The first concept is that of "reform." The past and current state of affairs are assessed extremely negatively and are characterized as a "standstill" and as "stagnation," while the alternative and the desired future are associated with deep "reforms." The second major trend of social ideas is the preference for decentralization. I define "decentralization" here extremely broadly—in the sense of the autonomy of enterprises, the expansion of citizens' economic and political rights, and the independence of different branches and institutions of power, of nongovernmental organizations, and of the press. In general, decentralization should be understood as the idea of transferring rights and powers from higher levels of hierarchical structures to lower-level structures, and thus as the idea of splitting and distributing power among different levels and institutions. Preferences in favor of decentralization found their logical reflection in the political upheaval of 1991 and the policy of the first post-Soviet government of Russia: free elections, a free press, the liberalization of prices and of economic life, the provision of significant autonomy to the regions, and the reduction of the central government's powers and zone of authority.

However, during the next five years (1993–1998) there was growing disappointment with the results of movement in this direction, and accordingly, with the key concepts that defined the direction ("reform," "markets," and so on). This disappointment reached its peak in 1998–1999, and the preferences and political doctrines dominant in the public consciousness in the 2000s ultimately proved to be diametrically opposed to those noted in the first stage. To put it even more precisely, the new preferences and political doctrines were formed in repulsion to the preceding ones. Two central concepts of the new period were "stability" and recentralization, which were given, in the political language of the time, a common label: "the vertical of power." The "stability" of the value system becomes an absolute priority compared with the idea of changes and "reforms," whereas the latter are recognized only to the extent that they do not contradict the interests of "stability" (this is why, for example, the population's complaints about the low quality of institutions is not accompanied by demands for their reform). In parallel, the return of authority from the lower floors of the social hierarchy to the higher ones is invariably met by an approving or neutral attitude on the part of society. If in the previous cycle the underlying trend was the pursuit of "splitting" power (one can recall the significant role that the Duma, the Constitutional Court, the gubernatorial framework, and independent media played in political life, along with the executive authorities), now the guarantor of "stability" seemed to be a certain image of syncretic power exerting a decisive influence on most areas of social life. Accordingly, the value and significance of the separation of powers and of the autonomy of territories, of unrestricted media, and of political competition were sharply reduced in the eyes of society.

FIGURE 7.2 *Dynamics of market support, reform, and the state of affairs in the country*

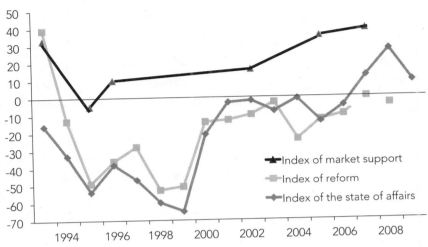

The index of market support is calculated from the breakdown of responses to the Levada Center question on the behavior of transition to the market: from the sum of twice the value of the responses that expressed in favor of quick transition, and the value of the responses that expressed in favor of gradual transition, is subtracted twice the value of responses that voted against a transition, and the value of responses that said the question was difficult to answer.

The index of reform is calculated from the breakdown of responses to the Levada Center question on the necessity to continue or stop the reforms: from twice the value of responses that support the continuation of reforms is deducted twice the value of responses that support their termination, and the value of responses that found the question difficult to answer.

The Preconditions of the Second Transition: The Erosion of Values

Deep disappointment with the results of the policy associated with the concepts that had received preference in public opinion during the preceding era became the most important factor for the popularity of the new political ideology that has dominated the past decade. But it is equally clear that as the policy of "stabilization" achieves its goals, demand for "stabilization" begins to decline. The forfeited positions on the notions of "reform" and "markets" gradually return (see figure 7.2). Analyzing the trends in the attributes that people used to describe the political process during the 2000s, one sees a sharp reduction in the beginning of the period among those who defined the situation as "chaos and anarchy," and an equally fast rise in the number of people who defined it as the "development of democracy." Since the mid-2000s, the share of answers for "chaos and anarchy" has continued to decline rapidly, but the share of answers for the "development of democracy" is no longer rising—on the contrary, the share of those who answered "it is difficult to decide" is quickly rising (see table 7.1). If the very process of reducing uncertainty and turbulence looked during the first stage to be unquestionably valuable, then during the second stage, the issue of the quality of the "stabilization" achieved and its prospects becomes increasingly relevant. Thus, for a hungry person the cost of food is limited by practically nothing—he is prepared to spend all his resources on it, but as he grows full, the question of the cost of food becomes central for him: the question of his future, of moving forward—this is the possibility of reducing the price paid for food in the first cycle.

Although the political practices of the 2000s consistently follow the recipes for "recentralization" and generally receive approval from the population, in examining the behavior of social preferences, one can find evidence of shifts in the opposite direction. For example, supporters and opponents of a multiparty system formed fairly equal groups, and in the early 2000s opponents were in the minority (50:40); in the late 2000s, supporters of a multiparty system increased consistently, reaching a ratio of 70:20 (table 7.2). This is all the more remarkable since in the official political rhetoric of the second half of the 2000s, the idea of the "dominant party" was advocated ever more persistently. A similar trend can be observed in the responses to the question "do we need a strong opposition party that can influence the government?": the share of positive responses over the course of the 2000s increases consistently (table 7.3).

Also indicative is the trend in assessments of the notion of "order." The importance of this concept looks in the second half of the 2000s to no longer be as absolute as it was at the turn of the 1990–2000s. In answering the question "what is more important: order or human rights?" in 1997 the distribution of responses in favor of order was 60:27; in the late 2000s, supporters of order make up just over 50 percent of the respondents, while supporters of human rights constitute about 40 percent of respondents (see table 7.4). Finally, presented with the extremely tough choice between democracy associated with "disorder," and order associated with the suppression of freedoms, respondents at the turn of the 1990–2000s made

TABLE 7.2 *Distribution of responses to the question "How many political parties are necessary in Russia?" (Levada Center)*

	1994	1999	2004	2008	2010
One strong ruling party	31	43	34	32	18
Two or three large parties	30	35	44	45	58
Many small parties	9	5	6	8	10
Political parties are not necessary	10	5	6	6	3
Difficult to respond	20	12	9	6	11
Balance: for/against a multiparty system	39 / 41	40 / 48	50 / 40	53 / 38	68 /21

TABLE 7.3 *Distribution of responses to the question "Is it necessary to have social movements and parties that could be in opposition to the president and could assert a serious influence on the life of the country?" (Levada Center)*

	2001	2002	2005	2007	2009
Necessary	59	56	61	66	71
Not necessary	23	24	25	20	16
Difficult to respond	18	20	14	14	13

TABLE 7.4 *Distribution of responses to the question "What is more important now: order in the state or human rights?"*

	1997	2007	2009
Order in the state	60	54	51
Human rights	27	36	39
Difficult to respond	13	10	10

the choice in favor of order at a ratio of 75–80 percent against 9–11 percent staunch supporters of democracy; in the late 2000s, the former group constituted 60–70 percent, while the share of unconditional supporters of democracy was about 20 percent (see table 7.5).

TABLE 7.5 *Distribution of responses to the question "What is more important: order, even if it means violating democratic principles, or democracy, even if it means giving free rein to destructive elements?"*

	1993	2000	2004	2006	2007	2009	2010
Order	75	81	75	68	68	59	56
Democracy	11	9	13	11	18	18	23
Difficult to respond	14	10	12	21	15	22	21

Even these figures show, however, that what is at issue is not some sort of decisive shift in the views of society; furthermore, one can point out a number of other polls definitively demonstrating that the choice in favor of paternalistic models dominates. (It is worth remembering that the ideological and political pluralism of the largest Russian media is significantly and artificially restricted; society is effectively cut off from the arguments of those who support decentralization and political pluralism.) At the same time, the data presented here, in my opinion, demonstrate that the idea of the benefit introduced by centralism and "syncretic" power is problematized in public opinion—the preference for the corresponding models loses its energy and certainty, and the logic of centralization seems largely exhausted. One could say that just as the pluralistic practices of the 1990s continued to exist at the end of that decade even though they did not respond to public demand, so the political practices of the late 2000s have been oriented, in reality, toward the public demand of the beginning of this decade.

That being said, the popularity of the political concept of "centralization" during the 2000s was supported not only by the repulsion from previous experience but also by the stable and rapid growth of the economy and incomes. The latter, as a result, looked like a consequence of the former. The crisis of 2008–2009 broke the causal relationship between these processes that had been formed in the mass consciousness in the 2000s, and demonstrated that the "centralization" (verticalization) of power is not in and of itself the engine of economic and income growth. The sharp slowdown in economic and income growth could have a no less dramatic effect on the public perception of "stability." "Stability" appears unquestionably beneficial while society is leaving a period of high uncertainty, or during a period of positive economic growth; in the latter case, "stability" implies "the stability of positive changes." When both it and other factors cease to act, then "stability," when placed against a background of low or negative income growth, will increasingly and inevitably take on a different color in the perception of society and will increasingly be thought of as "stagnation."

In this instance, I want not so much to correct the picture of Russians' social attitudes in the late 2000s as to point to the significant contextual dependence of preferences made during a concrete historical period of some political paradigm. Russians as a whole were in no way staunch democrats at the turn of the 1980s and 1990s, but it is also unlikely that they are innate supporters of the idea of the "strong hand" and centralism today. The changing parameters of the social and economic context (the presence or absence of instability, and the presence or absence of economic growth) will lead to a shift in the dominant political preferences and a reweighing of the value of certain sociopolitical doctrines.

The Elite: An "Imposed Consensus" and Public Competition

The influence of economic behavior on political trends occurs mainly along two interacting channels: on the one hand, the social well-being of the population changes, and, accordingly, its political assessments and preferences change in step (strong empirical data demonstrating this relationship are presented, in particular, in the work of Daniel Treisman). On the other hand, economic behavior affects the mood and strategies of elite groups, which have the resources to protect their economic interests. As is well known, it is the divisions among the elite, projected onto mass expectations and assessments, that form political demarcations and lead to the emergence of political competition (such is the general rule of Schumpeter's model of political competition). To assess the trajectory of possible changes in the plane of interactions among the elite, we again must resort to retrospection.

And here we once again find two periods marked by opposing tendencies. In Russia in the second half of the 1990s, a system was taking shape under which elite groups with resources could form their political "delegation" and the corresponding political infrastructure (media, political parties, and civil society organizations), in order to consolidate public support and use it in competition with other elite groups in the battle for resources and authority. This occurs both in the federal political arena and at the regional level—including in the big cities, where the economic differentiation of the elite is at its proper level.[13] In the 2000s, the reverse system was formed; it was precisely elite groups' abandonment of claims to political representation and their refusal to appeal to the people in the struggle for their interests that became the condition for maintaining their resources and authority ("the rejection of politics"). The ones who attempted to use political leverage—that is, to mobilize public support—had the resources enabling them to do this taken away (this explains why the empires of some oligarchs were destroyed by the Kremlin, while others had the possibility not only to preserve, but also to strengthen their positions).

This new situation constitutes one of the foundations of the "Putin system"; in its application to Russian circumstances, I have proposed calling it an "imposed consensus."[14] Such a consensus relies on the ability of the dominant player, representing "power," to block the politicization of inter-elite conflicts and their transmission into the public sphere with the help of sticks and carrots.[15] However, this "consensus" was formed and maintained in a situation of continuous economic and income growth, which significantly reduced the severity of the inter-elite conflicts; opting for confrontation did not look rational, because maintaining the status quo or even enduring a slight loss amid a growing economy is a significantly more attractive result than the prospect of losing one's "market position." It is no accident that the beginning of the transition from the public confrontation of the 1990s to a new system of relations coincides with the transition to a phase of economic growth. In turn, as one might expect, the new economic situation and the stagnation of incomes and of the economy as a whole will likely lead to the disintegration of this system. As long as the market grows, the division of additional income is at the center of the game and the majority of participants are winners. But in a stagnant market, actors have nothing to share but the resources they already have, and any winnings represent another's loss. Finally, in a shrinking market, the game is reduced to a battle for the redistribution of losses, and there are always more losers than winners. Additionally, during a phase of growth, the population is inclined to look favorably upon the acting authorities and the established status quo, which reduces the potential efficacy of elite groups' appeals to authority, and vice versa—during a phase of stagnation or of a decline in income, the population's attitude toward the established rules and hierarchies becomes increasingly critical, and, accordingly, the effectiveness of the aggrieved elite groups' actions in the public sphere increases.

Thus, in a phase of economic stagnation or weak growth, the combined effects of these factors will contribute to the destruction of the "imposed consensus" and to the aspiration of the elite to return to the practice of public competition by politicizing inter-elite conflicts (one of the "first signs" of this kind can be seen in the conflict surrounding the resignation of the mayor of Moscow, Yuri Luzhkov, who had openly defied the Kremlin and subsequent pressure to resign). In turn, public competition among the elite will stimulate the polarization of public opinion and the formation of groups supporting the new political factions and the concepts they advance against a background of gradual disillusionment with the values of the previous era ("stability" and "centralization").

"Deferred Problems" and the Effect of "Weak" Growth

To a certain extent, it is appropriate to understand the Russian crisis of 2008–2009 and the impending phase of Russian history in the context of the analogous crisis of the South Asian countries in the late 1990s. Rapid growth in developing countries frequently allows society and the ruling groups to ignore the unfinished transformational changes and pushes the problem of bad institutions onto the back burner. Economic growth goes hand in hand with the growth of corruption, which for a certain period even looks like a stimulating factor—it helps overcome institutional barriers, contributes to the accelerated concentration of capital, and allows for the redistribution of social costs and the use of "purchased" advantages in order to break into new markets.[16] The negative effects of corruption look like an "acceptable evil" against the background of the obvious successes of the economy and the fast growth in incomes of the most active social strata and groups. However, a slowdown or cessation in this growth would fundamentally change the situation; institutional problems would again be at the center of public attention, while corruption and the principles of "friendly capitalism" (in the Russian version, it is more correct to speak of "clan-bureaucratic" capitalism) would turn into a major social irritant.

Accumulated reserves allowed the Russian government to alleviate the immediate financial and social consequences of the crisis of 2008–2009, but the crisis in Russia can only be considered to have reached its final end upon a return to high rates of economic growth. Low rates of growth, while entirely adequate for developed economies, are not acceptable when it comes to maintaining social stability in developing countries with a weak institutional structure. With a distribution of income that is characteristic for the Russian economy (about 50 percent of total revenue goes to the most affluent twentieth percentile), slow growth rates will not be able to secure tangible gains for the majority of the population, and will look like stagnation. And the attempts of the "market barons" to reallocate the costs associated with deteriorating market conditions lead to a sharp rise in discontent.

If the slowdown in economic and income growth awakens "sleeping problems," then what are the weak points that could arise at the center of public attention and consolidate the discontent? First of all, as has already been mentioned, corruption and the principles of "clan-bureaucratic capitalism" should be the focus of public attention. Russia's return to a period of open political confrontation and mass politicization will, with a high probability, be carried out under slogans associated with the notion of "fairness." Demand for democracy in Russia at the turn of the 1980s and 1990s was associated with the desire to be rid of total control, to acquire more rights and freedoms, including the freedom of enterprise, and to gain independence from the state and from the authority of the government. The new demand for democracy may be fundamentally different in substance; it is entirely likely that it will involve the pursuit of more equitable income distribution, greater equality of opportunity, and greater control of society over the government. In this sense, it is also entirely likely that in its substance and spirit, it will be significantly more left-leaning than its predecessor twenty years ago. However, it is precisely the entrance into the political arena of "mass interests" that is capable of preventing a repeat of the situation of the 1990s, where the benefits of democracy and public competition were largely privatized by the leading elites.

The second most important and most likely line of development of the new political conflicts is the opposition of the "center" and the "regions." Regionalism as a factor in Russian politics, having arisen in the second half of the 1990s, has a powerful potential; the attempt made in the 2000s to arrest and restrain this factor, effectively depriving the regions of political representation, could be purely temporary in nature and could cause a recoil in the future.

It is significant that the issue of the effective autonomy of the regions has been one of the few political issues (likely the only one) over which, even in the late 2000s, the opinion of the majority of the population has fundamentally broken with the opinion of the central government and of Vladimir Putin personally. Thus, during the second half of the 2000s, 60 to 65 percent of respondents expressed support for returning to the election of regional governors, while the official position (and the position of Vladimir Putin), which consists of the unswerving defense of the new order, was supported by only 25 to 30 percent of the population. This distribution of responses is typical, however, given the formulation of general political questions ("What kind of system do you think is better?"); when people are asked whether they want their governor or mayor to be elected by popular vote or appointed by a higher authority, the number of supporters of direct elections (at least in the big cities) grows to 75 to 80 percent, while the number of supporters of appointment falls to 8 to 15 percent.[17] Clearly, in such a situation the question about the election of governors will return to the political agenda at the first signs of significant weakness in the central government's position; moreover, this issue looks like the ideal focal point for the consolidation of dissent and passive dissatisfaction, as well as a point of intersection for the interests of the regional elites and the disillusionment of the population.

Internal regional conflicts—that is, conflicts between appointed governors and local elites—have the greatest potential for the politicization of society, linking together the regional (local) and federal political arenas. For example, this was quite in evidence during the events in Kaliningrad in early 2010. The conflict of part of the regional elite with the governor, Georgy Boos, who had been appointed by Moscow (Boos had previously worked in Moscow City Hall) led to a massive rally at which demands for the resignation of Prime Minister Putin were voiced. Quite apparent in this situation were the political risks that appointed governors carry for the central government amid the deteriorating economic situation. Here, even a purely internal regional conflict takes on the character of regional opposition to the center, and causes an escalation of distrust of the federal government's policies in general.

One can list a number of other issues that could generate conflicts with broad implications. Here I mention just one: the likelihood of a crisis of corporate management in major companies, regardless of whether the major shareholder is the state or a private entity. The influence of the nominal owners on the activity of such companies has weakened in recent years, and the influence of management has grown, while the mechanisms of external control have been poorly aligned. Favorable circumstances have allowed these companies to exist in a state of constant expansion in recent years, relying both on political support from the government and on the high availability of external financing. As a result, the companies have effectively lived under soft budget constraints, justifying them with hopes for future profits. Changes in external conditions coupled with reduced demand could lead to a sharp deterioration in their financial situation. That being said, it is worth bearing in mind that today these companies are acting as the "wallets" of the central government, paying for the political infrastructure of "soft authoritarianism." Such a situation, where there are conflicts of interest among various levels of a company's management, can quickly spread into "politics," thereby causing the infrastructure's erosion.

In this case, however, the specific points of bifurcation are not as important as the systemic causes giving rise to these points. Upon completing the phase of restorative growth and the period of overheating associated with the significant influx of foreign capital—amid conditions of "difficult growth" and, correspondingly, of lower growth rates—the methods of "manual control" and excessive centralization will reveal their growing inefficiency.

Conclusion: The Baseline Scenario—A Return to the Future

To conceptualize the theoretical framework of Russia's institutions concerning the coming decade, it is worth paying attention to the fact that, as is usually true for prognoses, an inertial scenario implies a linear extension of existing trends. My attempt to examine the forthcoming period in the context of the two preceding cycles—"transformation" and "stabilization"—allows us to approach the issue from a somewhat different perspective. The transition from the first cycle to the second looks like quite a sharp and deep turnaround in terms of both economic and social trends—like a radical rejection of the previous period. In turn, the logic of economic processes—much like the logic of social expectations and preferences—and the general "agenda" of the second cycle as of today all appear to be largely exhausted. In this regard, as the inertial scenario for 2010, I anticipate some sort of general reverse motion—a partial return, on a new level, to the preferences and problematics of the 1990s. The period of rapid growth in the 2000s was a period, returning to the terminology of Schlesinger, primarily of "private interest" coupled with conservative skepticism regarding the possibility and necessity of social and institutional changes. The lack of easy recipes for economic growth will with great likelihood force society once again to revert to a search for solutions in the institutional and social spheres.

The second feature of my analysis is the assumption that the deterioration of economic behavior will have an impact not only on the population but also (and primarily) on the elite, who today are connected with the rules of the "imposed consensus." This means that the diffusion of the current political system could take place against the background of an economic picture that, at first glance, does not seem to be a crisis. The system of political and economic interactions prevailing in Russia today is very young, having been formed "just in time" under extremely favorable external circumstances. Its ability to adapt to other economic conditions is unknown, and the impulses that enabled its formation appear to have been largely squandered. Thus, I list my main conclusions and assumptions:

1. The reaction to the transformations of the early 1990s, having built up in public opinion during the period from 1993 to 1998, gave impetus to the movement in the opposite direction (recentralization instead of centralization, stability instead of reforms).

2. The consolidation of new political practices consistent with the values of "order," "stability," and "recentralization" provided significant support to the economic growth of the 2000s.

3. At the same time, in public opinion in the 2000s, the energy of the preferences for the values expressed in these practices gradually faded and the relevance of this option declined, while signs of demand for more balanced political mechanisms began to appear.

4. The crisis and the subsequent long slowdown or cessation of growth stimulated demand for alternative models of political and social organization; thus the idea of "centralization" will quickly—and the idea of "stability" will more slowly—lose value in the eyes of society.

5. The deterioration of economic conditions will lead to the erosion and collapse of the regime of the "imposed consensus" in elite relations, while inter-elite conflicts will again break out into the public sphere, stimulating the collapse of ideological consensus surrounding the doctrine of the previous cycle.

In my opinion, this inertial baseline scenario is unlikely to be altered by the local efforts of domestic players—for example, by tightening censorship and political control, by exerting pressure on the opposition, or by further centralizing the mechanisms of control. Such measures (and the probability that they will be employed in the near future seems to be quite high), against a background of weak economic conditions, either will not have any effect or will lead to an escalation of the basic contradictions between old political and administrative practices and new public demand. As is the case during the "dusk" of a political trend, even chance events will "play" against it in the form of natural and human-made disasters (such as the wildfires during the summer of 2010). New shocks in the commodity markets are capable of quickly turning the scenario into a crisis.

To alter the baseline scenario, there will need to be events that can once again deploy society in favor of supporting a mobilizing agenda. In the 1990s, the war in the Caucasus played the role of an external stimulus that could secure support for such an agenda. However, such events simultaneously inflicted a heavy blow on Putin's reputation and decisively deprived him of his role as the "guarantor of stability." In turn, the loss of this role and the fall of his "ratings" would undermine the effective legitimacy of his tenure in office, and would lead to a rapid reduction in the loyalty of the state apparatus and the elite.

Notes

1. The Bertelsmann Foundation Transformation Index can be found at http://www.bertelsmann-transformation-index.de/en/bti.

2. According to results from the first half of 2010, real income growth (by the first half of 2009) amounted to more than 4 percent; however, the acceleration of inflation since August 2010 will lead to a reduction in that figure for the year. It should also be borne in mind that the income statistics were influenced by the valorization of pensions at the beginning of the year—i.e., a one-time event that will not be repeated in the next period.

3. See the notable debate in the *Journal of Democracy* in 2002.

4. One of the ingenious developments of this viewpoint was the concept of "competitive authoritarianism": the period of democratization in the USSR is considered to be a consequence of the destruction of the existing hierarchy, which provoked an open competition for dominance among the elite; this competition ends when the elite who captured the dominant positions begin to consolidate them on the basis of restoring the traditional hierarchies, given that qualitative changes in the system do not occur; Steven Levitsky and Lucan Way, "The Rise of Competitive Authoritarianism," *Journal of Democracy*, vol. 13, no. 2, April 2002, 51–65.

5. See, for example Henry Hale, "Regime Cycles: Democracy, Autocracy, and Revolution in Post-Soviet Eurasia," *World Politics*, vol. 58, no. 1, October 2005, 133–65.

6. For a description of such cycles based on the example of the Latin American countries, see Guillermo O'Donnell, "Delegative Democracy," *Journal of Democracy*, vol. 5, no. 1, 1994.

7. Arthur Schlesinger Jr., *Tsikly Amerikanskoy Istorii* (Cycles of American History), trans. from the English (Moscow: Izdatel'skaya gruppa "Progress," Progress-Akademiya, 1992).

8. Robert A. Dahl, *Polyarchy: Participation and Opposition* (New Haven, Conn.: Yale University Press, 1972).

9. Attempts were made to apply this scheme to Soviet-Russian history as well (see George W. Breslauer, "Reflections on Patterns of Leadership in Soviet and Post-Soviet [Russian] History," *Post-Soviet Affairs*, vol. 26, no. 3 (2010): 263–74), but the mechanisms for influencing public demand for political practices in the Soviet Union and in post-Soviet Russia differ significantly.

10. Alberto Alesina, Nouriel Roubini, and Gerald Cohen, *Political Cycles and the Macroeconomy* (Cambridge: MIT Press, 1997). For an analysis of the effects of the

political business cycle in Russian policy of the 1990s, see Daniel Treisman and Vladimir Gimpelson, "Political Business Cycles and Russian Elections, or the Manipulations of 'Chudar'," *British Journal of Political Science*, vol. 31, April 2001.

11. Yegor Gaidar, *Dolgoe Vremya. Rossiya v Mire: Ocherki Ekonomicheskoy Istorii* (Lasting Time: Russia and the World—A Study of Economic History) (Moscow: Delo, 2005), 399–409.

12. For more details on this argument, see S. Smirnov, "Faktory Tsiklicheskoy Uyazvimosti Rossiyskoy Ekonomiki" (Factors of Cyclical Vulnerability of the Russian Economy), *Voprosy Ekonomiki*, no. 6, 2010.

13. For a discussion of the role of "splits" in the formation of political regimes in the Russian regions, see Vladimir Gelman, "Politicheskie Rezhimy Perehodnogo Perioda: Rossiyskie Regiony v Sravnitel'noy Perspektive" (Political Regimes in Transition: Russia's Regions in Comparative Perspective), in *Rossiyskiy Konstitutsionalizm: Politicheskiy Rezhim v Regional'nom Kontekste* (Russian Constitutionalism: The Political Regime in the Regional Context) (Moscow: Center for Constitutional Studies, 2000).

14. For the details, see Kirill Rogov, "Democracy 2010: The Past and Future of Pluralism in Russia," *Pro et Contra* 13, nos. 5–6 (September–December 2009).

15. The notion of an "imposed consensus" in the Russian case was examined by Gelman, where the issue at hand, however, was the electoral cycle of 1999–2000; my use of the term "electoral cycle" differs somewhat from the interpretation proposed in his pioneering work. See Vladimir Gelman, "Vtoroy Elektoral'niy Tsikl I Transformatsiya Politicheskogo Rezhima v Rossii" (The Second Electoral Cycle and the Transformation of the Political Regime in Russia), in *The Second Electoral Cycle in Russia, 1999–2000*, edited by Vladimir Gelman, Grigorii V. Golosov, and Elena Y. Meleshkina (Moscow: Ves Mir, 2002).

16. For more on the different roles of informal institutions in developing countries, see Gretchen Helmke and Steven Levitsky, "Informal Institutions and Comparative Politics: A Research Agenda," *Perspectives on Politics*, vol. 2, issue 4 (2004): 725–40; on the role of corruption in economic development in East Asian countries, see D. C. Kang, *Crony Capitalism: Corruption and Development in South Korea and the Philippines* (Cambridge: Cambridge University Press, 2002).

17. See the surveys by the Levada Center in Moscow and Perm in 2010 (www.levada.ru).

CHAPTER EIGHT

RUSSIA'S POLITICAL ECONOMY: THE NEXT DECADE

Daniel Treisman

Prognostication has a bad name. When it comes to predicting how societies will evolve, the record of forecasters is poor, and specialized knowledge does not appear to help very much. In a recent twenty-year study, psychologist Philip Tetlock tracked "the accuracy of hundreds of experts for dozens of countries on topics as disparate as transitions to democracy and capitalism, economic growth, interstate violence, and nuclear proliferation." He found that the specialists' forecasts rarely outperformed the guesses of "dilettantes, dart-throwing chimps, and assorted extrapolation algorithms."[1]

There are obvious reasons why deducing the future of complex systems is close to impossible. A country's political and social trajectories result from the interaction of large numbers of individual players, who respond to multiple, changing sources of information and often behave strategically. At any moment, one can identify patterns in the recent past. But there is no guarantee that these will continue to hold—often their very recognition creates incentives for change. Nor is it easy to aggregate the local patterns to produce macroscopic forecasts. This does not mean that no predictions will be correct; if enough are made, some will turn out to be right. But that will not help much if one only discovers which ones are correct after the fact.

So why bother? Even if one cannot say which of many paths history will go down, it is still useful to think about the layout of the paths, their forks and intersections. If nothing else, this prepares one to interpret rapidly what is happening as events unfold. At the same time, the attempt to think systematically about the future imposes a certain discipline and perspective that are helpful for understanding the present. One is forced to think about how different aspects of current reality fit together.

I begin, therefore, with a brief account of Russia's current political economy. What one sees depends, of course, upon how one looks. What a photographer records is a function of the breadth of angle of his lens and the duration of his exposure. In a famous essay, the French historian Fernand Braudel contrasted three kinds of history.[2] The traditional histoire événementielle paid attention to individuals and events. It saw the past as a "mass of minute facts," a series of days and moments, which it gathered up into narratives that were "precipitious, dramatic, and short of breath." In Braudel's day, this style had been challenged by a history of "cyclical oscillations," which carved out ten-, twenty-, or even fifty-year tranches of the past. Finally, there was the history of the longue durée, which focused on whole centuries at a time.

To identify patterns in Russia's political economy, I look first at what I call "the big picture," examining the change between today and twenty years ago, and comparing the country's trajectory to that of other former communist states. I then focus in on the "close-up view," exploring short-run dynamics.[3] On the basis of these reviews, I argue that how politics develops is likely to depend on economic performance, and I suggest several scenarios, each of which seems possible. I close by reviewing some "known unknowns," which could alter the direction of developments, and offer brief conclusions.

Russia's Political Economy Since 1992

The "Big Picture"

How have Russia's politics and economics changed during the last twenty years? In politics, one sees a tide of democratization rising during the early

1990s, reaching high tide around 1994 and then gradually retreating. But "democratization" is probably the wrong word. This was, essentially, a tide of disintegration, dissolution, and dismantling of Soviet era institutions and practices. However, the Soviet institutions that were dismantled were replaced everywhere by formally democratic ones. Practices also became much more democratic. Not only the central structures of government changed. The disintegration also affected the links between levels of the state. First authority decentralized, then it recentralized; administrative hierarchies were first flattened, and then rebuilt into a "vertical of power," a process that began several years before Vladimir Putin thought to popularize this phrase.

These trends in Russia's polity need to be seen in their geographical context. The same tide of disintegration and reintegration swept all the postcommunist countries, from Slovenia in the west to Tajikistan in the east. The effects varied in a way that correlated with the country's location on an east–west axis.[4] In Central and Eastern Europe, administrative structures were rebuilt and hierarchies were reconstituted in a predominantly democratic context. This was also the pattern in the Balkans, although reintegration was delayed by a decade or so of war. By contrast, in Central Asia, the Soviet era institutions were only superficially dismantled, and then were repaired and repainted with a thin veneer of popular rule. Reconsolidation took place in an authoritarian setting, resulting in autocracy. The Caucasus (Armenia, Azerbaijan, and Georgia) and the European members of the Commonwealth of Independent States (Russia, Ukraine, Belarus, and Moldova) saw a much greater variation in outcomes, both across countries and over time. The re-creation of order was essentially authoritarian in Belarus and Azerbaijan. In Moldova, it was mostly democratic. In the other states—including Russia—it produced hybrids that combined elements of both genuine and formal democracy with some authoritarian features. Whether—and, if so, how fast—the hybrid regimes will gravitate to one pole or the other, becoming full-fledged democracies or consolidated autocracies, remains to be seen. Figure 8.1 plots the average *Polity* scores—a measure of the extent of democracy—for the different groups of postcommunist countries over time.

With regard to the economy, the last two decades have transformed Russia in three ways—marketization, modernization, and globalization.

FIGURE 8.1   *Democracy in the Postcommunist World (Polity Scores)*

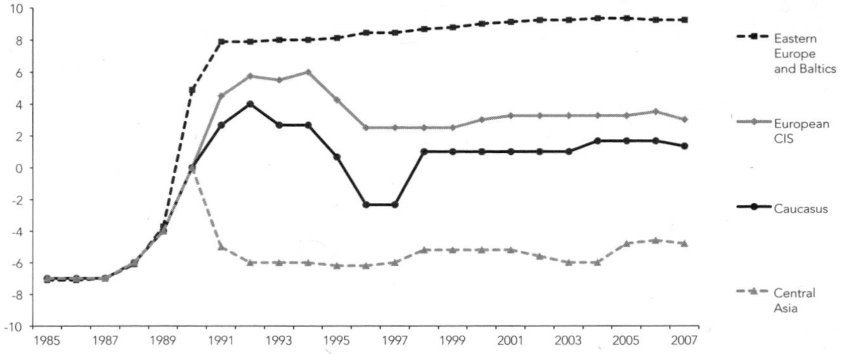

Note: Polity scores range from 10 for pure democracy to −10 for pure autocracy. Eastern Europe and the Baltics includes Bulgaria, Czech Republic, Hungary, Poland, Romania, Slovakia, Estonia, Latvia, and Lithuania. European Commonwealth of Independent States includes Belarus, Moldova, Russia, and Ukraine. Caucasus includes Armenia, Azerbaijan, and Georgia. Central Asia includes Kazakhstan, Kyrgyzstan, Tajikistan, Turkmenistan, and Uzbekistan.

Source: Polity IV, September 2009 revision, www.systemicpeace.org/polity/polity4.htm.

First, a centrally planned economy has been replaced by one dominated by markets and private ownership. A total of 69 percent of Russian workers today have jobs in the nonstate sector, compared with 17 percent in 1990.[5] Since that year, the housing stock has gone from about 30 percent to 82 percent privately owned.[6] By 2009, Russia had the world's thirteenth-largest stock market.[7] Along with marketization, output increased. Even going by the official statistics for gross domestic product (which exaggerate the value of output before the Soviet collapse), GDP per capita adjusted for purchasing power parity grew from about $8,000 in 1990 to $19,000 in 2009. Real final consumption by households more than doubled between 1990 and 2008.[8]

Since 1990, Russia has also undergone a dramatic modernization. For most Russians in 1990, personal computers were the stuff of science fiction. By 2008, every second family owned one.[9] Almost 40 percent of households are now connected to the Internet, and more than two-thirds of households in Moscow and Saint Petersburg. In 1989, fewer than one Russian family in three had access to a telephone of any kind.[10] By 2008, there were 1.4 cell phones per person in Russia, up from 0.004 in 1992.[11] The number of institutions of higher education has more than doubled since 1990, with the most rapid growth occurring among nonstate colleges and universities.[12] Gross enrollment in tertiary education increased from 52 percent of school leavers in 1991 to 75 percent in 2007—a higher rate than in France, Italy, or the United Kingdom.[13] In 1990, 401,000 Russians completed higher education; in 2008, 1.4 million did.[14] Since 1992, the proportion of the employed population with a college degree has risen from 16 to 28 percent.[15]

At the same time, Russia has reengaged with the world, especially Europe. One can see this in statistics on trade, travel, and other kinds of contacts. Russia's exports grew from $54 billion in 1992 (12 percent of GDP) to $472 billion in 2008 (28 percent of GDP), while imports increased from $43 billion (9 percent of GDP) to $292 billion (17 percent of GDP).[16] The number of Russians traveling abroad to countries beyond the former Soviet Union almost tripled, from 8 million in 1993 to 22 million in 2009.[17] The most popular destinations were Finland (3.0 million), Turkey (2.4 million), Egypt (1.8 million), China (1.7 million), and Estonia (1.6 million). In 1990, Russians made 41 million international phone calls; in 2002, they made 1.1 billion. In 2007, they talked on international phone lines for 29 million hours—about 12 minutes per person.[18]

An increasing number of Russians study abroad. According to UNESCO, the number rose from 20,000 in 1999 to 41,000 in 2008, of which 20,000 were studying in Western Europe and 10,000 in Central and Eastern Europe.[19] Russians have been investing in real estate abroad—$10 billion worth each year, by one estimate—and not just in the French chateaus of the oligarchs: realtors report major demand for inexpensive apartments around London, Berlin, and Stuttgart.[20] These days, a majority of Russians—53 percent—say they would like their country to join the European Union if given the chance.[21]

Thus, the "big picture" shows a powerful trend toward marketization, modernization, and integration into the world, especially Europe. Yet, at the same time, it reveals a political system stuck somewhere between the democratic and authoritarian poles. Those who believe, as argued by Seymour Martin Lipset, that modernization tends to engender more political freedom expect that at some point, if the economic trends continue, politics will evolve toward greater openness. Just as democracy moved south into the Balkans in the 1990s, it will move east into the European members of the Commonwealth of Independent States. Others think the authoritarian elements in the current regime will stifle the positive economic trends. Although both trajectories are possible, the first seems to me more likely.

The "Close-Up View"

What if one looks from a closer vantage point, focusing not on long-run trends and processes but on shorter-term dynamics? Consider first economics. Although the long-run trend is toward modernization and development, the shorter run has seen extreme volatility. Russian income fell sharply in the early 1990s, before rising rapidly after 1998, only to stall in the throes of the global financial crisis of 2008–2010 (see figure 8.2). The initial fall was caused by a combination of external shocks and homegrown weaknesses. The main external shock was the plunge in the oil price in the 1980s and its subsequent dip to less than $9 a barrel in 1998. This combined with the chronic economic problems inherited from the Soviet era (poorly designed and obsolete capital stock, illogical geographic configuration of industry) and the legacy of Gorbachev's disastrous improvisations (which tripled the money supply between 1985 and 1991, accrued large foreign debt, and destroyed central coordination without sufficiently

FIGURE 8.2 *Gross Domestic Product per Capita in Russia, 1990–2009*

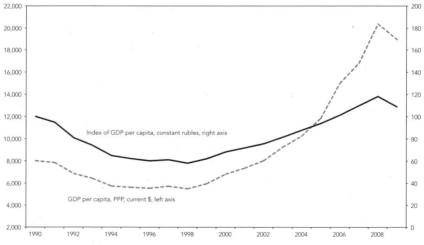

Sources: World Bank, *World Development Indicators*, October 2010; Rosstat data, October 2010.

liberalizing markets). The rebound after 1999 resulted from, first, the positive effect of devaluation in 1998; second, the rise in oil and gas prices; and, third, the positive impetus of the market reforms of the 1990s. And since 2005, as argued by Vladimir Milov in chapter 10 of this volume, growth has also been supported by large inflows of foreign capital.

This cycle in economic performance had notable effects on politics. Changes in the state of the economy, as perceived by the Russian public, influenced the level of popular support for the incumbent political leaders. As in other countries, when citizens saw the economy prospering, the incumbent leaders were popular. When the economy performed poorly, the leaders' ratings plummeted. Other factors also mattered. Both Chechnya wars on balance cost the Kremlin support, although at moments of terrorist attacks or intense fighting, the public sometimes rallied behind the flag. The 2008 war in Georgia prompted a jump of 10 to 15 percentage points in the ratings of both Putin and Medvedev. But economic perceptions have done a consistently good job of predicting the trends in presidential approval.[22]

At the same time, the capacity of leaders to implement policies has increased or decreased in tandem with their approval ratings. Falling ratings have encouraged opposition, prompting elites and special interests—in Parliament, regional governments, the federal bureaucracy, the media, business, and elsewhere—to press mutually contradictory demands and block implementation of any coherent policy. By contrast, at times of high presidential popularity, obstacles to the president's agenda have largely disappeared.

Consequently, when the leader was popular, the country's policy course and the style of government depended strongly on that leader's views and objectives. During his early years of high popularity (1987–1989), Mikhail Gorbachev chose to loosen social controls, experiment with economic decentralization, and move slowly toward democratic political institutions. In his moment of acclaim (1990–1992), Boris Yeltsin opted to introduce fully competitive elections, to support self-determination for other Soviet republics and significant autonomy for Russian regions, and to lay the foundations of an economy based on private property and free enterprise. And during his ten years of sky-high ratings, Putin has chosen to empower law enforcement agencies, erode civic rights and protections, and manipulate elections, while enacting conservative macroeconomic policies and assisting Kremlin associates in their business endeavors.

Changes in formal institutions have had far less effect on the outcomes of politics than changes in the economic context and in public opinion. The enactment of the 1993 Constitution did not, as critics feared, empower the president to impose whatever policies he liked on a reluctant Parliament. On the contrary, reforms were even more thoroughly blocked than before by opposition-minded deputies, governors, and business interests. Conversely, the major recentralization of power in 1998–2002 occurred without any significant change in the nature of political institutions. What changed was how politics worked, both within and outside the confines of the formal institutions.

For example, the formal mechanism for filling top offices has remained the democratic election. Over time, however, the practice has degenerated. Various tricks, pressures, and devices have been used more and more blatantly to favor incumbents in elections at all levels. Because the national incumbents have been genuinely popular, such manipulations have not yet produced outcomes in national elections that were very different from those implied by credible opinion polls. If the country's leaders tried to use the same techniques at a time when they were very unpopular, it is not clear that these techniques would still work. This is a major source of uncertainty for the future.

Most of the time, Russia's presidents have sought to increase their popularity by (1) fostering growth—or, at least, preventing decline—in the population's real incomes, even at cost to longer-term goals, and (2) choosing policies that the public favored on a variety of issues. Yeltsin's decision to proceed with rapid economic reform in 1991 matched public opinion at the time, as did his decision to slow reforms down the next year. His use of force against the Parliament in October 1993 was backed by a majority. Putin's rhetorical support for "order," his (moderate) expansion of the state's role in the economy, his reinstatement of the Soviet era music to the national anthem, and his assaults upon the oligarchs were all popular.[23] In fact, Putin went against the public's declared preferences primarily when this was necessary for accomplishing the first objective; his more liberal economic policies were the least popular of his initiatives.

To summarize, the dynamics of politics in the last twenty years, when viewed from close up, have been shaped by the interaction of two things: first, economic performance; and, second, the goals and, to some extent, the tactical skill, of the Kremlin incumbent. Public opinion on specific issues has also seemed to matter at various times. Changes in these factors have been more important than changes in the formal institutions.

Looking Ahead

On the basis of the last two decades, it seems likely that formal institutions will not strongly determine the character of Russia's politics in the immediate future. There is enough flexibility within the current Constitution and other laws for much more—or somewhat less—democratic practices to emerge. We also see that wars or other traumatic events can affect the dynamics of politics.

But if the next ten years resemble the past twenty, a great deal will depend on the pace and pattern of economic growth. The impact of growth is complicated by the fact that it has different—even contradictory—effects at the two levels I have discussed. In the big picture, more rapid economic advances will tend to speed up the country's modernization and integration into Europe, rendering the task of controlling society ever more complicated. As the population becomes still more highly educated, wired to the Internet, and bourgeois and cosmopolitan in outlook, managing information flows and elections will become harder. However, looking from close up, the picture is quite different. Higher growth is likely to sustain the popularity of the current political incumbents, consolidating and entrenching their less-than-democratic regime.[24]

The net result is likely to be a contradictory situation in which economic advances both strengthen the current political regime and help society to outgrow it. Better economic performance will not in itself hasten a regime transition. On the contrary, it will help the current incumbents hold onto power, perhaps even enabling them to increase repression without much resistance. But it will prepare society for a rapid transition to more democratic government when—as is bound to happen eventually—a serious economic reversal occurs. At that point, the "mole of history" will be seen to have done its work.

By contrast, a fall in economic growth would slow the evolution of Russian society toward greater modernity and autonomy (the big picture), yet would likely provoke more vocal opposition, splits within the ruling elite, and perhaps a turnover in the leadership (the close-up view). Such a turnover would increase the competitiveness of the political process, at least initially. What happened next would depend—other things being equal—on whether the economy continued to decline or began to recover. The former would tend to produce continuing instability; the latter would help the new leaders to consolidate their authority. The more modern and globally integrated Russian society was at this point, the more likely that such a consolidation would occur in a relatively democratic framework.

What is likely to happen in the economy in the next ten years? As Vladimir Milov and others suggest, by the time of the global financial crisis, growth had come to depend on a rising oil price and increasing foreign investment. The Kremlin would like to catalyze a new kind of high-technology-driven growth by means of state support for nanotechnology and other scientifically advanced sectors. However, given the difficulty of competing with the world leaders in these fields and the fact that high technology sectors currently make up only about 3 percent of Russian GDP, it seems unlikely that such projects will boost Russia's growth appreciably in the short run.[25] I suggest three possible scenarios, which might, in fact, be combined.

The first scenario assumes slow or even zero growth. If raw materials prices do not rise—or even fall—and a new era of tight money replaces the cheap money environment of recent decades, and especially if the bureaucracy's inefficient regulation and corruption are not cut back with effective reforms, then the kinds of increases in demand and/or productivity that would stimulate growth on a national scale would be unlikely. This is probably the scenario that most economy watchers judge most likely.

But there are other scenarios, the probability of which is also not negligible. One is that of a more rapid economic collapse. At present, Europe's demand for Russian gas is thought likely to remain quite strong for the next ten years; increased supplies of liquefied natural gas will no more than offset the fall in output from North Sea sources. Plans to mine shale gas within Europe will run into ecological opposition. If these expectations prove wrong and demand for Russian energy falls more sharply, this would have serious consequences for Russia's exports, budget revenues, and economic growth.

A more positive scenario relates to China. As China's economy develops, many expect its demand for Russian raw materials to surge. How rapidly this will happen is hard to predict. It is at least possible that Chinese demand will rise fast enough to more than offset falling European demand, driving up the prices of Russia's exports. Chinese investment in the development of Russian oil and gas fields, mines, and smelters could also provide for some investment-led growth. Thus, piggybacking on Chinese economic progress might sustain Russia's growth at least for a while.

A second positive scenario has been less widely recognized. I would not say that it is likely, but it is possible. When the financial markets crashed in 2008, many economists declared the era of cheap money to be over. Banks would no longer provide large loans at very low interest rates to emerging market companies. However, as of 2010 many expect the Federal Reserve to keep U.S. interest rates close to zero for a considerable time. Money will, in other words, be not just cheap but almost free. This could prompt the emergence of a new "carry trade," with investors borrowing in the United States and investing in companies in countries like Russia that have implicit government guarantees and reasonable prospects for profits. With investment opportunities in the United States and Europe looking relatively unattractive, it is conceivable that, especially in countries like Russia that still have large currency reserves and low government debt, foreign investment would resume fast enough to sustain reasonable growth.

Whether such a scenario materializes will depend in considerable part on investors' psychology, as well as on how the aftermath of the global crisis continues to play out in Europe and the United States. According to preliminary estimates, foreign direct investment in Russia reached $40 billion in 2010, its highest level ever.[26] Figures were not yet available for total foreign investment, but those for the first nine months of 2010 had been less encouraging. Putin promised in December 2010 to introduce amendments to reduce obstacles to foreign investment in "strategic" sectors. Earlier, the government had already announced plans to privatize stakes in state-owned companies worth some $10 billion annually for five years.

Known Unknowns

Besides the rate of economic growth, a variety of other factors may influence Russia's politics during the next decade. First, not just the rate of growth but also its timing and distribution matter. Whether growth is low or high on average, and how the rises and falls correspond with the electoral cycle (presidential elections in 2012 and 2018; Duma elections in 2011 and 2016), will be important. So too will how average growth is shared across different social and geographical constituencies. A situation in which income growth was high for some regions and economic groups but stagnant for others could lead to outbreaks of unrest and increased social tension.

Externally caused social or political shocks could also change the dynamics. If (as currently seems unlikely) NATO were to advance toward admitting Ukraine or Georgia, this would very likely prompt a rallying behind the Kremlin and pressure to oppose this move. A military confrontation of some kind could have a similar result. Another outbreak of war with Georgia remains possible. More natural disasters like the fires of the summer of 2010 might eat away at the regime's popularity. Terrorist attacks could have a variety of effects, depending on the extent to which the authorities appeared unprepared and incompetent in defending the population.

If external shocks or economic deterioration erode the popularity of the leadership, provoking challenges from lower down, much will then depend on the strategies that the Kremlin chooses in response. One can imagine mistakes that could turn a chronic weakening of the regime into a sudden collapse—for instance, the use of significant force at the wrong moment, in a way that catalyzed rather than intimidated opposition. An article by Yevgeny Gontmakher, published in 2008, outlining a "Novocherkassk 2009" scenario was widely discussed in Russia.[27] Of course, the real Novocherkassk events did not result in a serious challenge to the regime; in some ways, a better analogy might be to Tbilisi in 1989.[28] Another deadly mistake, from the Kremlin's point of view, might be a political liberalization at a time of growing economics-based discontent, leading to competitive mobilization of opposition by political entrepreneurs, and rapidly undermining the regime à la Gorbachev.[29] It is also possible that economically rational but unpopular efforts to increase efficiency could spark unexpected protest, as occurred with the monetization of social benefits in January 2005. A major pension reform would be particularly dangerous. Leaders who have been in office for a long time often do make mistakes.

Even in a high-growth scenario, political instability could result from quarreling among top members of the regime. One can imagine the emergence of intense factional rivalries within the Kremlin entourage. To date, Putin has always succeeded in managing any such conflicts, with only relatively muffled cries audible to those outside the tent. But that could change.

Conclusion

Various factors—some currently known, others as yet unrecognized—could change the logic that has governed Russia's political economy during the last twenty years. If, however, the basic relationships remain unchanged, much will depend on how the economy performs. In the long run (decades, rather than years), the logic offers some reasons for optimism. Assuming the current trend toward integration with Europe continues, it will give elite Russians—and, gradually, a larger share of the population—a stake in openness and good relations. As more and more Russians travel to vacation, study, work, and trade in Europe, their increasing ties to the Western world will render them less responsive to isolationist, authoritarian impulses.

This does not mean that in the short run economic growth will lead to a softening of Russia's political practices. On the contrary, higher growth at present is likely to sustain mass support for the current incumbents, to weaken any voices in the Kremlin calling for economic or political reform, and to encourage the incumbents to indulge their instinct to tighten control over society. Although it might stabilize an increasingly authoritarian regime, rapid economic growth would simultaneously create the conditions for a more successful jump to democracy if that economic growth were to falter. As Russia becomes richer, more modern, and more globally integrated, the probability will increase that a sharp economic reversal would prompt political change in the direction of greater freedom.

Notes

1. Philip E. Tetlock, *Expert Political Judgment: How Good Is It—How Can We Know?* (Princeton, N.J.: Princeton University Press, 2006), 20.

2. Fernand Braudel, "Les modalités du temps historique," in *Écrits sur l'histoire* (Paris: Flammarion, 1969), 44–51.

3. In this chapter, I draw on several previous works: Daniel Treisman, *The Return: Russia's Journey from Gorbachev to Medvedev* (New York: Free Press, 2011), esp. chap. 7; Daniel Treisman, "Russian Politics in a Time of Economic Turmoil," in *Russia After the Global Economic Crisis*, edited by Anders Åslund, Sergei Guriev, and Andrew C. Kuchins (Washington, D.C.: Peterson Institute, 2010); and Andrei Shleifer and Daniel Treisman, "The US and Russia: They Don't Need Us," manuscript, University of California, Los Angeles, 2010.

4. Daniel Treisman, "Twenty Years of Political Transition," UN-WIDER Working Paper, 2010, www.sscnet.ucla.edu/polisci/faculty/treisman/Papers/Final%20Helsinki%20paper %20nov%2009.pdf.

5. Goskomstat Rossii, *Rossiiskiy statisticheskiy yezhegodnik* (Moscow: Goskomstat Rossii, 2009).

6. Goskomstat Rossii, *Sotsial'noe polozhenie i uroven' zhizni naseleniia Rossii* (Moscow: Goskomstat Rossii, 2009).

7. World Bank, *World Development Indicators, 2010*. The total market capitalization of listed Russian companies came to $861 billion.

8. Calculated from ibid.

9. Goskomstat Rossii, *Rossiiskiy statisticheskiy yezhegodnik*. There were 47 personal computers per 100 families.

10. Goskomstat Rossii, *Sotsialnoe polozhenie i uroven zhizni naseleniya Rossii* (Moscow: Goskomstat Rossii, 1996).

11. Goskomstat Rossii, *Rossiya v tsifrakh* (Moscow: Goskomstat Rossii, 2009); Goskomstat Rossi, *Sviaz v Rossii* (Moscow: Goskomstat Rossii, 2003).

12. Goskomstat Rossii, *Rossiiskiy statisticheskiy yezhegodnik*.

13. World Bank, *World Development Indicators, 2010*.

14. Goskomstat Rossii, *Rossiiskiy statisticheskiy yezhegodnik*.

15. Ibid; Goskomstat Rossii, *Rossiiskiy statisticheskiy yezhegodnik* (Moscow: Goskomstat Rossii, 1996).

16. Goskomstat Rossii, *Rossiiskiy statisticheskiy yezhegodnik*, 1996 and 2009; World Bank, *World Development Indicators*, 2010.

17. Goskomstat Rossii, *Rossiya v tsifrakh* (Moscow: Goskomstat Rossii, 1996 and 2010).

18. Goskomstat Rossii, Sviaz v Rossii; Goskomstat Rossi, Sviaz v Rossii (Moscow: Goskomstat Rossii, 2008).

19. Statistics from UNESCO at http://stats.uis.unesco.org.

20. Gordon Rock, "Aktivnost rossiyan na rynke zarubezhnoy nedvizhimosti: Itogi 2009 goda," February 10, 2010, http://gordonrock.ru/news/?tema=97&news_id=488; Svetlana Kononova, "The Russians Are Buying," *Russia Profile*, February 2, 2010.

21. Levada Center, *Obshchestvennoe mnenie 2009* (Moscow: Levada Center, 2009), 176.

22. Daniel Treisman, "Presidential Popularity in a Hybrid Regime: Russia Under Yeltsin and Putin," *American Journal of Political Science*, forthcoming, 2011.

23. For the details, see Treisman, *Return*, chap. 7, and Daniel Treisman, "Russian Politics in a Time of Economic Turmoil," in *Russia After the Global Economic Crisis*, ed. Åslund, Guriev, and Kuchins.

24. That the same economic factors can have opposite effects when considered at different levels and in different time spans is not a new idea. It recalls the dialectical materialism of Marx. Although Marx was wrong on many things, and referring to him is hardly fashionable, he was right to point out that economics and politics interact in nonlinear and sometimes contradictory ways.

25. Keith Crane and Artur Usanov, "Role of High-Technology Industries," in *Russia After the Global Economic Crisis*, ed. Åslund, Guriev, and Kuchins, 95–123, at 119.

26. See "Russia to Ease Foreign Investments in 2011—Putin," Reuters, Moscow, December 28, 2010, www.reuters.com/article/idUSLDE6BR10W20101228.

27. For the article in English, see www.riocenter.ru/en/_news/analytics/3236.

28. Although not in others—there is currently nothing like the threat of anti-Russian nationalisms confronting a weakened center that existed in the late 1980s.

29. Yet, here again, the analogy does not seem quite appropriate. Russian society in 2010 is so different from Soviet society in 1985 that one cannot assume the political effects of a social "liberalization" would be very similar.

the russian economy through 2020: THE CHALLENGE of MANAGING RENT ADDICTION

Clifford G. Gaddy and Barry W. Ickes

Russia was one of the best-performing economies in the world in the first decade of the 2000s. But this success was an anomaly, based on the extraordinary rise in the world prices of the primary sources of Russia's wealth, its oil and gas. Russia will not see another decade with those kinds of price rises. This will make for a radically different situation in the future, with implications for politics as well as economics.

In the coming decade, problems that were largely ignored during the decade of windfall resource wealth will become unavoidable. The most important problems stem from the fact that today's Russian Federation has yet to overcome the nonmarket industrial structure it inherited from the Soviet Union. For all the remarkable changes that have occurred in the twenty years since the collapse of the communist economy, the structure of the Russian economy's industrial core, along with its legacy of misdevelopment and mislocation of production and population, remains intact.

Because this inherently noncompetitive structure lays claim to physical and human assets that otherwise could be allocated to fundamentally new uses, the only way for Russia to achieve sustainable growth is to dismantle it. It is not just deadweight on the economy, or a lump sum tax. The more resources that are used to prop it up, the stronger are its future claims on those resources. The more it gets, the more it needs. It creates an addiction.

Russia in the first decade of the 2000s did worse than merely fail to dismantle this structure. For the sake of job preservation and social stability, it used its windfall wealth to reinforce it. The country will thus need to devote an ever-increasing amount of oil and gas wealth to maintain the status quo in terms of output and jobs in the industrial core sectors. Meanwhile, the overall amount of resource wealth—commonly referred to as resource rents—is not going to grow as fast as would be needed for that. At some point during the next eight to ten years, it is likely that rent-addicted Russia will experience withdrawal symptoms. This will be painful. It will stress the current system for managing the distribution of its oil and gas wealth and perhaps will cause changes.

As long as stability is the leadership's priority, there will be no fundamental reform of this noncompetitive industrial structure. The reform efforts that are commonly called "modernization" will instead focus on improving the static efficiency of the existing structure. The dilemma is that upgrading the current structure in this way will make the more fundamental challenge of restructuring even more difficult.

Russia has been governed by a model of political economy that worked during the decade of the rent boom. It even served well to weather the deep crisis of 2008–2009 on the basis of the reserves it had built up. But the coming decade will be different. Expectations and aspirations will be tempered. A decade of abundance will be replaced by one of trade-offs, tightness, and tensions.

The Russian Economy's "Addiction" to Resource Rents

The basic problem of this inherited industrial structure is that it was never meant to be viable on the terms of any market economy. The industrial economy of the Soviet Union was built to meet the goals of a dictatorship obsessed with the idea of increasing its military strength and reducing its economic vulnerability to a hostile outside world. This produced a costly, hypermilitarized economy that was further penalized because it was disconnected from the international division of labor. Internally, the allocation of resources was irrational. Plants, cities, and infrastructure were built in locations that defied market logic. But because there were no market prices, the true costs of this grand project could not be directly recognized. Recognized or not, however, these costs were real and had to be borne by someone. Ultimately, they fell on individuals and households, which were denied the right of free choice of where to work and live. The extreme form of this denial of free choice was the system of mass prison labor, the Gulag.

The Soviet industrial structure was erected through coercion. It was a structure that would not have been built with free labor. It could then only be maintained by either continued coercion or by infusion of value from the outside. During Stalin's lifetime, coercion dominated. The Gulag was the main source of labor to build the infrastructure for industry—the railroads, canals, mines, and the plants themselves. After Stalin's death, the role of coercion was reduced. Initially, this was due to Lavrenty Beria's insight that the Gulag was economically counterproductive. Industrial serfdom was more efficient than industrial slavery. Therefore, Beria released hundreds of thousands of Gulag prisoners from camps but still required them to live and work as severely underpaid "wage workers" in the same cold and remote regions. Their productivity was higher, and the costs of camps and guards had been eliminated. Brutality lessened, but labor remained unfree.

The more fundamental reason why coercion could be reduced was the growth of resource rents in the Soviet Union in the 1960s and 1970s. Oil and gas rents served to cover the hidden costs of the hypermilitarized, mislocated industrial structure. Thanks to this additional value, the structure was expanded and deepened—in terms of the size, number, and geographical distribution of plants and supporting towns and cities. But each expansion phase also increased the dependence on further rent infusions to enable the structure to survive. This was a dependence that deepened and developed into something resembling addiction to a drug.

The term "addiction" is probably overused and misused in referring to resources like oil. So it is important to clarify that we have a specific reason for using it here. The term is admittedly not a precise one, and its use is in fact discouraged by the medical community, which prefers to speak of varying degrees of "dependence." Nevertheless, as an analogy for the Russian economy's predicament, the concept of addiction to a substance is useful. There are three main features of this addiction. First, the addict's craving for the substance is so strong that he or she is willing to sacrifice or

BOX 9.1   *Rent Addiction and Tolerance*

Why did production enterprises in the Soviet system become addicted to rents; specifically, why did they develop tolerance? That is, why did the enterprises require increasing,
rather than just constant, rent flows? It might seem that maintaining the existing level of
rents would be sufficient to sustain an economy with rent-dependent enterprises. To understand why this was not the case, one needs to examine the incentives and risks facing
the enterprises.

A rent-dependent enterprise needs an infusion of rents to survive. It would seem that
the best strategy for the enterprise would then be to minimize its need for rents—say, by
modernizing its plant and equipment and becoming more efficient. Although this might be
true for an enterprise in isolation, it is exactly the wrong strategy when one considers the
equilibrium of the game that these enterprises must play. Enterprises compete for rents.
And particularly when rents are scarce, the enterprises that will continue to have access
to rents are those that are most dependent on them. They will be the ones that are most
integrated with the supply and distribution chains that rent managers must preserve, the
ones that have augmented their importance to the rent managers by further investing in
the supply and distribution chain.

To illustrate, let us imagine three enterprises—A, B, and C—that received rents during a boom and employed different strategies for using these rents:

- Enterprise A used previous rents to modernize production and reduce its
  dependence.
- Enterprise B used previous rents as a transfer to workers.
- Enterprise C used previous rents to increase capacity and now employs more workers or requires supplies and inputs from more enterprises in the supply chain.

Suppose now that rents decline. Which enterprise will have the best claim to rents in
the downturn? Clearly, enterprise C's claim is the strongest. But forward-looking enterprise directors understand this game. Indeed, they have survived precisely because they
are good at playing this game. Hence, they will choose strategy C over strategies A and B.

This means that, in equilibrium, the economy as a whole needs ever more rents to
satisfy addicts. The problem is that the addicts' behavior results in more dependence. A
constant flow of rents will not satisfy the increased needs.

run risks (to the point of self-destruction) to obtain the substance. Second
is the phenomenon of withdrawal, the intense suffering that results from
discontinuing use of the substance. Third, and most pernicious, is tolerance: The addict craves more and more of the substance (see box 9.1).[1]

Addiction changed the very nature of the Soviet economic system. Increasingly, what was in principle an economy controlled and administered
from the top (the so-called command-administrative economy) evolved
into one driven by forces from the bottom up. The real economic priorities

were not set by policymakers at the center but rather were driven by the imperative to support the otherwise unsustainable sectors. Rather than policy shaping the structure, the structure drove practical policy. This remains true today, and it is the most important legacy Russia has from the Soviet Union. As we show below, the imperative to share the rents persists and is even more powerful than the forces of the market system that replaced Soviet central planning.

An "Inverted Funnel"

As the oil and gas rents grew, and as they were used to sustain a growing structure dependent on them, the industrial economy began to assume a peculiar shape. At the top was a concentrated source of wealth—oil, gas, and other mineral resources—whose wealth was distributed to sectors that were much broader, in terms of people, plants, and territories. This broad base depended on the rent flowing down from the resource sectors in order to survive. It was like an inverted funnel.

The funnel's neck is dominated by oil and gas. In terms of the numbers of people involved, the oil and gas sector is a narrow segment of the economy. The sector employs barely half a million workers, or only 1.1 percent of the total labor force.[2] Its corporate structure is similarly concentrated. Even today there are only about 175 companies operating in the oil and gas extraction sector in Russia. (The United States has more than 20,000.) But the value they produce is huge. Oil and gas currently account for nearly two-thirds of Russia's total export revenues and almost half of federal budget revenues.[3] But we must remember that the past decade has been an extraordinary period with respect to the value of oil and gas. It is important to be aware of how much it has changed over time. Figure 9.1 depicts the evolution of Russia's oil and gas rent in real (inflation-adjusted) prices since 1970.[4] The figure puts the decade of the 2000s in perspective. The period 2000–2008 saw the biggest growth in rents in Russia's history. But the process resembled what had happened earlier. From the mid-1970s to the early 1980s, the rents exploded and were claimed by the addicts. The inverted funnel economy was consolidated. Similarly, the rent explosion of the 2000s infused new life into the old Soviet structures.

FIGURE 9.1 *The Value of Russian Oil and Gas, 1970–2010*

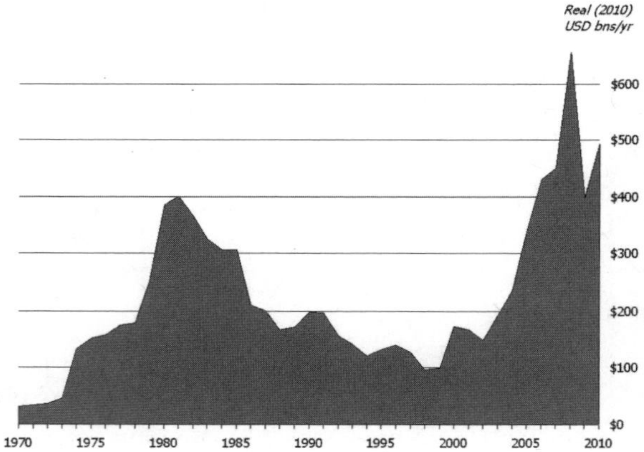

Real (2010)
USD bns/yr

Source: Clifford G. Gaddy and Barry W. Ickes, "Russia After the Global Financial Crisis," *Eurasian Geography and Economics* 51, no. 3 (2010): 281–311.

Rent Distribution Chains

If oil and gas is the narrow part of the inverted funnel, the broad base is dominated by the heavy manufacturing sector, what was traditionally known as machine building. This includes the defense industry. The mechanisms whereby the oil and gas rent is distributed to the base vary. Some rent flows through formal channels, notably the part that is collected in the form of taxes and redistributed by subsidies or other budget allocations. A larger portion of total rent is distributed informally. Some of this distribution can be considered informal taxes, such as bribes paid to government officials and payments made for the support of public-sector needs that are nominally voluntary but in fact are mandatory for businesses—for example, payments made by enterprises to support the social sector of towns and regions, cultural programs, philanthropic giving, and so on.

The most distinctive, the most opaque, and the most important form of informal rent distribution in this inverted funnel economy is the constraint placed on resource companies to directly participate in the production and supply chains linking the enterprises inherited from the Soviet economy. It

FIGURE 9.2   *Schematic Version of Rent Distribution through Production*

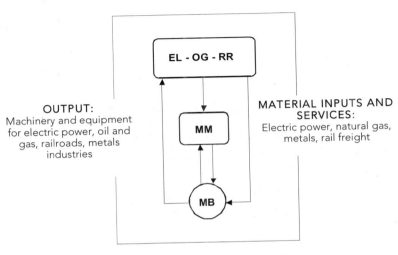

Note: This is a schematic version of the flows involved, encompassing five core industrial sectors: (1) oil and gas = OG; (2) machine building (including the defense industry) = MB; (3) transportation (mainly railroads) = RR; (4) electric power = EL; and (5) metals and materials = MM.

is this constraint that ensures that rent is distributed in the form of excess costs of production. Suppliers of material inputs (fuel and energy, metals, and components) and services (railroads and pipelines) are bound to serve the machine-building enterprises. The produced machinery and equipment are then shipped, predominantly to these very same input sectors. Figure 9.2 shows a schematic version of the flows involved, encompassing five core industrial sectors: (1) oil and gas; (2) machine building (including the defense industry); (3) transportation (mainly railroads); (4) electric power; and (5) metals and materials. And figure 9.3 arranges these sectors according to their positions in the "funnel."

As regards rent distribution, the importance of the scheme depicted in figure 9.2 is that rather than having the oil and gas rents exclusively collected as formal taxes and redistributed by the center, the oil and gas producers provide much of them directly, in either a physical form (as inputs) or a monetized form (as payment for orders) to the equipment manufacturers, or via intermediate production sectors that serve the oil and gas industry, such as transport infrastructure construction, the electric power

FIGURE 9.3   *The Inverted Funnel*

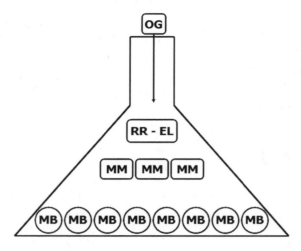

Note: *This schematic inverted funnel shows the five core industrial sectors: (1) oil and gas = OG; (2) machine building (including the defense industry) = MB; (3) transportation (mainly railroads) = RR; (4) electric power = EL; and (5) metals and materials = MM.*

sector, or the processing (refining) industries. The supply and production chains can thus be regarded as rent distribution chains. They are mechanisms to disperse rent in the form of excess costs from the narrow part of the inverted funnel to the broad base. The distribution of rent through production is the most important way in which rent is shared in today's Russian economy, and it is all informal: It is not prescribed by law; it does not proceed through the budget; and no formal taxes are involved.

Strategic Planning Replaces Central Planning

It is useful to compare and contrast the current Russian system of rent distribution through production with previous systems. The Soviet system, the interim system of the 1990s, and the post-2000 Putin system all had almost the same rent distribution chains. In the Soviet economy, rent was centrally allocated. Then as now, the rents were produced by the oil and gas sector. But the Soviet central authorities (the Communist Party, Gosplan) could allocate the rents wherever they wanted because they (the "state") owned all the enterprises. The nominal priorities for rent distribution in the Soviet system were arms production and food production. The actual driver was the same as today: the imperative to give orders to heavy industry (machine building).

The difference is who initiates the chain. In the Soviet era, Gosplan commanded the machine-building enterprises to deliver arms and agricultural equipment for the military and farms. In the Putin era, orders for equipment from machine builders come directly from corporations.[5] In the Soviet period, the mechanism for organizing and managing this rent distribution was five-year plans, which were administered by central planners and Communist Party officials. Today, there is still a pretense of direction from the top, as the various industrial ministries at the center draw up long-range (10–20 year) "strategic" programs for sectors, regions, and large corporations.[6] In reality, however, the key decisions are made by the corporations. The strategic programs are mainly compilations of the corporations' own plans, enhanced by wishful thinking on the part of bureaucrats.

The Role of Private Ownership

The particular role of private owners in this system begs comment. Ownership of most of the companies in Russia's core industrial sectors shifted from the state to the private sector in the 1990s. Most of these changes persisted in the 2000s. (The only significant exception is the oil company Yukos, which was effectively renationalized after the 2003 arrest of its owner, Mikhail Khodorkovsky.)[7] The lucrative metals and mining sector is almost entirely in private hands.[8] The Putin leadership strongly believes in the superiority of private over state ownership to achieve economic efficiency. The highest priority for the regime with respect to private owners is to ensure that they continue to support the rent distribution chains.[9] The political economy system of today's Russia is in effect a rent management system, in which the corporation owners (the "oligarchs"), certain top government officials, and the governors of the most important regions are on nearly equal footing—they all are "rent management division heads" in the gigantic enterprise of "Russia, Inc." This is a system aimed at combining the virtues of stability (by ensuring that rent is distributed to the socially and politically most important regions, cities, and plants—the broad base of the funnel) and efficiency (by giving the private owners of rent-generating industries incentives to maximize profits and thereby create more rents).

The commitment to share rents through support of the production chains is a central feature of the peculiar Russian version of the market economy. In a normal market economy, private ownership is based on secure property rights and a system that gives owners both the power and incentives to be fully efficient by choosing optimal location, product range, volume of production, and mode of production, including the choice of suppliers and partners. In the Russian economy, the nominal owners of the companies operating in the key sectors are highly constrained in all these critical choices because they are subject to the imperative to preserve the rent distribution chains. Suppliers of material inputs are locked into the chain. They are constrained to deliver their electricity, gas, steel, aluminum, and so on, and to provide their rail freight and other services to the core machine-building enterprises. This means that one of the main features of the system is to eliminate competition among suppliers and autonomous decisionmaking on the part of companies in the supply chain.

To appreciate how well developed the notion of rent distribution chains is, consider the statements made by Prime Minister Putin in April 2011, as he presented plans for the future development of a key subsector of the machine-building industry, the sector that builds heavy machinery and equipment for Russia's electric power generating plants (see box 9.2). His comments make it clear that he understands the two key steps to lock in the rent distribution chains discussed above: (1) Buyers of the equipment are locked in with guaranteed orders to machine building from oil and gas and electric power; and (2) input suppliers are locked in by guaranteed supply contracts to machine building from oil and gas, electric power, the railroads, and metallurgy.

The Next Decade

The notion of addiction discussed above gives a framework for thinking about Russia's near- and middle-term future. The political economy we have described was a model that served its purpose well during the

BOX 9.2 *Putin on Locking in the Rent Distribution Chains*

Comments by Prime Minister Vladimir Putin at a meeting on "Measures to Develop the Energy Machine-Building Sector in the Russian Federation," Saint Petersburg, April 8, 2011.

On guaranteed orders:

"[The] largest guaranteed customers for these products are budget-funded entities. Look no further than the investment programs for Russia's electric power production, oil, and natural gas companies. Let me cite some figures. Russian power generating companies alone intend to purchase energy machine-building products worth 1 trillion rubles in the next three years, and grid companies another 500 billion rubles worth of equipment. Natural gas companies intend to spend 600 billion rubles, and oil production companies another 1 trillion rubles. It's not difficult to add this all up to get an impressive amount of 3.1 trillion rubles."

On guaranteed inputs:

"In addition to this system of long-term contracts between energy companies and equipment manufacturers, we need to develop a system of long-term contracts for the entire production chain connected to the energy machine-building sector— suppliers both of fuel, and of iron and steel, and of nonferrous metals."

"[We need to] thoroughly build out the entire chain of relationships with subcontractors and suppliers of raw materials[,] . . . railway transportation, . . . electricity, primary raw materials, and gas."

previous decade. It could meet the demands of the addicts by sharing the rents broadly while at the same time allowing relatively strong fiscal and macroeconomic discipline, and building reserves. That is, it could both ensure domestic stability and protect Russia against shocks from outside. But that was during a decade of abundant rents. How well can it work in times of scarcity, when trade-offs are more sharply defined across the board—especially the fundamental trade-off between protecting financial sovereignty vis-à-vis the outside world and preserving stability at home?

To start thinking about Russia's future in this framework, one must ask about how much rent will be available in the coming decade. Recall that the very essence of *addiction*, in contrast to mere *dependence*, is that the rent flows need to grow to maintain the status quo. Addiction deepened during the boom decade. The addicts now demand more. If the rent flows do not continue to grow, and grow fast enough, it will lead to withdrawal symptoms. There will be pain, and this pain will mean discontent and instability.

Future Rent Flows

As we have explained, we compute rent as the quantity of oil and gas produced in Russia times the world prices of these commodities less the cost of extraction. The government's aim is to keep output on about the same level as today for at least the next ten to fifteen years. This will not be easy. The Russian oil industry was able to expand production in the late 1990s and early 2000s thanks to Soviet-era investments in exploration and infrastructure. Companies could launch greenfield projects in those established regions and expand output in existing fields with low depletion rates. There are still some margins for growth, but they are diminishing.

In any event, the growth or decline of Russia's rents in the coming decade will depend much less on how much oil and gas it produces than on the prices. Russia's dilemma is that it can neither influence the oil price nor (any more than anyone else) accurately predict where the price is headed over any period of time, long or short. For 120 years (1880–2000), the average price of oil in today's dollars was below $25 a barrel. The consensus for the past few years has been that it will not return to that level, that oil has entered a new price regime. Bodies like the U.S. Energy Information Agency and the International Energy Agency estimate that, on average, oil will be worth nearly $100 a barrel for the next couple of decades.[10] Only a few months ago, these seemed like conservative and reliable estimates. But as prospects for the overall global economy dim, more observers are questioning them. And when these forecasts are plotted in a chart showing the historical development of oil prices since 1880, it becomes clear that a prediction of $100 oil is rather bold (see figure 9.4).

The future of gas prices remains virtually as uncertain as that of oil prices. Historically, gas prices have closely tracked world oil prices, but with a lag. In coming years, gas prices may decouple from oil, owing to expanded production of liquefied natural gas and shale gas. More gas from a wider range of suppliers will make the market more competitive and push prices down. At the same time, climate change considerations are likely to

FIGURE 9.4   *The World Oil Price, 1870–2010 (Actual) and*
2011–2035 (Forecasts)

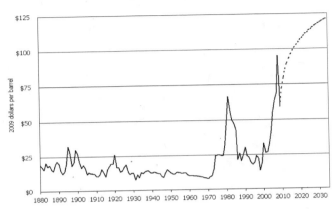

Note: The 2011–2035 data are forecasts from the U.S. Energy Information Agency.

Source: Clifford G. Gaddy and Barry W. Ickes, "Russia After the Global Financial Crisis," *Eurasian Geography and Economics* 51, no. 3 (2010): 281–311.

raise the demand for natural gas as consumers switch to gas as a cleaner alternative for power generation (instead of coal) and for transportation (instead of oil).

In short, price uncertainty for both oil and gas means that there is simply no way to reliably predict how Russia's resource rents will evolve during the next decade. All one can do is posit scenarios based on various hypothetical price trends. So we offer one: Suppose that the world oil price does behave as in the U.S. Energy Information Agency's reference price scenario. What would Russia's rent flow look like? Figure 9.5 gives the picture.[11] At first glance, it looks very positive. On average, for the next twenty to twenty-five years, Russia would receive more oil and gas rent each year than in the boom year of 2008. But remember that in an economy afflicted by addiction, what is important is not the *level* of rents but the *rate of growth* of these rents. Here, the picture is much less positive. Rents in the 2000–2008 period grew at a rate that was several times faster than what we see for the post-2010 period in figure 9.5.[12] This means that even in what many would deem an optimistic price scenario, there will not be enough rent to satisfy the reinvigorated addicts.

FIGURE 9.5   *Soviet/Russian Oil and Gas Rents, 1970–2010 (Actual)
and 2011–2030 (Forecasts)*

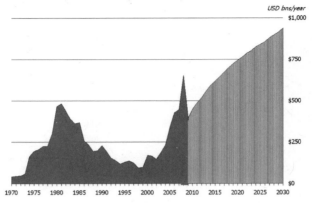

Source: Clifford G. Gaddy and Barry W. Ickes, "Russia After the Global Financial Crisis," *Eurasian Geography and Economics* 51, no. 3 (2010): 281–311.

Managing Addiction

There are those who say that a drastically lower oil price is the best thing that could happen to Russia. That, they argue, would automatically reduce rent seeking and force both the government and businesses to follow better policies. However, this argument ignores the reality and the power of addiction. A shrinkage of rents in itself will not cause a healthy change; whether the rent flow is large or small, addicts typically have the priority claim. In a time of relative rent scarcity, the rest of the economy is crowded out even more as resources are claimed by addicts. Addiction does more damage when rents shrink than when they grow.

Hoping that addicts will accept a reduction of rents without resisting is like expecting a hard-core drug addict to passively accept being denied his fix. That does not happen, because the pain of withdrawal is too severe. In the case of the Russian economy, this pain takes the form of closed-down enterprises and lost jobs.[13] No regime whose priority is social and political stability will allow this. To avoid this outcome, the leadership has been compelled to deal with the problem of addiction in different, and sometimes contradictory, ways. One general approach has been to tackle addiction head on, to try to "cure" it, in effect. Another approach has been to more or less ignore addiction and concentrate on the nonaddicted part of the economy.

Curing Addiction

Unlike a "cold turkey" approach that would simply cut off the flow of rents to the addicts and let them perish if they cannot survive on their own, the idea of curing addiction is to give the companies a makeover that will make them more efficient and therefore reduce their need for the rents. Because it is assumed that the main reason for their inefficiency is their worn-out and outmoded capital stocks, investment in new technology is the answer. This is the heart of Putin's "modernization" effort, a massive investment program aimed at thoroughly upgrading the production apparatus of the Russian economy.

The flaw here should be obvious. Trying to reduce the cost of addiction through greater efficiency sounds logical, were it not for the fact that the most egregious forms of inefficiency constitute the very essence of the addictive structure: the excess costs that result from the mislocation of the enterprises and the compulsory supply and production chains. Because they cannot be touched, this leaves only efficiency enhancements at the margin. Channeling more investment into the Soviet-era factories today to prevent them from demanding more tomorrow is like trying to reduce a substance abuser's craving for a drug by giving him more—asking only that he promise to refrain from abuse in the future.[14]

Developing Nonaddicted Sectors

Rather than trying to deal with the addicts, the second approach purports to do the opposite. It concentrates on creating new, competitive industries that will not be dependent on rent sharing. The goal is to have these new sectors grow fast enough to outpace the addiction and ultimately reorient Russia's economy away from oil and gas. This is the "innovation" approach associated with Dmitri Medvedev. Its model is the combined research park, university, and business incubator in the Skolkovo region of Moscow. Businesses that participate in the Skolkovo project will have access to state-of-the-art facilities and infrastructure, and they will enjoy special protection from the legal and regulatory abuses that plague the rest of Russian business.

Critics of the Skolkovo approach typically question whether it differs from other industrial policy efforts in which the government, rather than the market, chooses certain types of economic activity as more worthy than others and then intervenes to give them support. Such efforts do not have a good track record in general, and the preconditions for success in Russia are particularly weak. But viewing Skolkovo in the context of addiction makes it clear that the main question about Skolkovo is not whether it can succeed on its own terms—that is, whether the businesses there can develop innovative products. The question is whether these businesses can ever be fully protected from the influence of the addicts. Skolkovo is not a bootstrapping exercise. It requires subsidies and other support, all of which ultimately come from oil and gas rents. This puts Skolkovo businesses in competition with the addicted sectors for those rents. Indeed, the competition extends beyond oil and gas rents to all the resources of the Russian economy. Resource rents enable expanded production of the addicted sectors and therefore increase their demand for all factors of production. There cannot be a level playing field when the addicts' production and supply chains continue to claim resources.

As a result, it is in the end more likely that the innovative firms will choose to conform to the addicted system than fight against it. To the extent that those investing in and managing innovative firms recognize that the addicts and their claims to the rents dominate the system, they are forced to play that game, like it or not. The innovators present their case for support from the government not by arguing that they represent an alternative to the existing rent-dependent enterprises, but on the contrary, that they are important for the addicts' survival. They look for ways to integrate themselves into the production chains. The owners/directors of the innovative start-ups thus mimic the behavior of the successful directors of the addicted enterprises.[15]

Attracting Foreign Investment

The modernization campaign emphasizes the importance of attracting foreign direct investment (FDI). On the surface, it would appear that Russia has been successful in attracting FDI.[16] However, nearly all of that went to the resource and retail sectors. The main target of the modernization efforts, the machine-building sector, attracted less than 5 percent of total FDI. Moreover, the overwhelming share of that relatively small sum was made by foreign companies (notably automobile firms) that needed to establish a manufacturing presence in Russia as an "admission ticket" to the Russian market.[17]

The government's stated objective in bringing in more FDI to Russia is to provide needed "capital, technology, and management practices" to the core sectors of Russian industry.[18] But these goals can be properly understood only in the context of the constraints described above. Foreign investors—like domestic private investors—will not be allowed to compete or interfere with the rent distribution chains. Efforts to sell off state-owned assets in the core sectors, whether to Russians or foreigners, are perfectly consistent with the prevailing system. New equity holders, whether as majority or minority owners, will be subject to the same rules of the game as current owners. They must not challenge the rent distribution chains.

The privatization in 2008 of Russia's electric power monopoly, UES, is a classic case. The power generation assets were disaggregated and sold off to private owners, including non-Russian companies. The transmission grids remained in state hands. The reform was hailed as a major market-oriented reform by many observers. In fact, the move merely served to consolidate the system we describe here. What can private owners do with their share, even if it is a majority share, of Russian power plants? They cannot choose prices. They cannot choose their customers. They cannot choose their product—obviously. They cannot even choose their investment program. Above all, they cannot choose their suppliers. They must stick to the existing chain. They can only contribute money, technology, and management expertise.

Conclusion

Russia's past performance under the model of economic management that we have described has been good. In the decade leading up to the global financial crisis in 2008, Russia's economic growth outpaced those of almost all other countries. Figure 9.6 compares Russia with the other members of the so-called BRIC group—Brazil, India, and China—by growth of GDP in dollars. From a baseline in 1999, Russia by 2008 had grown more than twice as fast as China, and more than three times as fast as Brazil and India.

FIGURE 9.6   *BRICs' Relative GDP Growth, 1990–2010*
(growth in dollars; 1999 = 100)

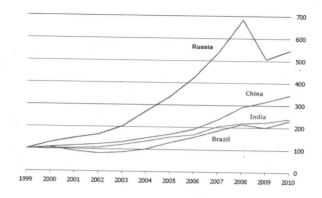

Source: Clifford G. Gaddy and Barry W. Ickes, "Russia After the Global Financial Crisis," *Eurasian Geography and Economics* 51, no. 3 (2010): 281–311.

But this dramatic performance was an anomaly. It led to skewed views of the Russian economy from the outside. The very idea of the BRICs is one such view. Russia is not a young, dynamic, "emerging" economy. It is an old economy still burdened by a legacy of sixty years of misallocation and faulty development. The misallocation was not weakened and reversed but rather reinforced by a decade of rent abundance. The first decade of the 2000s was a time of stability and welfare gains. Now, however, as Russia enters a decade of trade-offs and tensions, it is caught in a trap. To achieve sustainable development, it needs to fundamentally change the structure of its economy. But such change would be highly destabilizing, socially and politically. And the Russian leadership cannot risk destabilization.

Does the preceding discussion mean that all the modernization efforts in Russia are doomed to fail, that Russia will not reform at all? The answer depends on one's definition of reform. Measures to increase efficiency can be introduced in the sectors that create the rents (oil and gas), the ones that serve to transmit the rents (transportation, electric power, and construction), and the ones on whose behalf the entire rent-sharing system works (heavy manufacturing). But these changes will be subject to one basic constraint: The rent-distribution chains must be preserved. The type of change that will not be permitted is the kind that would disrupt the chain or negate its purpose by allowing companies to be shut down when they are inefficiently operated or located, restructuring supply chains to minimize costs, and so on.

As long as the rents suffice, Russia's heavy manufacturing enterprises will continue to benefit greatly from Putin's modernization campaign. They will expand production to fill the guaranteed new orders from oil and gas companies, the electric power companies, the railroads, and so on. The expanded market will also attract some foreign investors, who seek to share in the flow of rents. These international corporations will help retool Russian enterprises with modern equipment and introduce progressive new business practices. As a result of all this, GDP may be boosted in the short to middle term. But because the priority will continue to be to support the production enterprises inherited from the Soviet system, with their non-market legacies of location and organization, the long-term result will not be modernization in the true sense but rather an even more deep-seated lack of competitive ability.

As for the innovation approach, if the government pours enough resources into Skolkovo-type projects, new firms, and even entire sectors, may emerge over the next few years. They, too, will attract some foreign investors. On the whole, however, the development of innovative firms will be difficult, slow, and costly. And the net value they generate will be too small relative to oil and gas to change the economy's overall profile.

Notes

1. For discussions of the concept of addiction, see Clifford G. Gaddy and Barry W. Ickes, "Russia's Declining Oil Production: Managing Price Risk and Rent Addiction," *Eurasian Geography and Economics* 50, no. 1 (2009): 1–13; and Clifford G. Gaddy and Barry W. Ickes, "Russia After the Global Financial Crisis," *Eurasian Geography and Economics* 51, no. 3 (2010): 281–311.

2. The employment and value-added measures are from the state statistics service. They include the categories of "oil and gas extraction," "oil and gas services," and "oil products manufacturing."

3. The average share of crude oil, natural gas, and oil products in Russia's overall export revenues for the years 2005–2010 was 63 percent; data from the Central Bank of Russia. The share of federal budget revenue classified as "oil and gas revenues" was 48.0 percent in 2010, according to the Ministry of Finance. This share has risen steadily since 2000, when it was only 20 percent. "Oil and gas revenues" come from five taxes: the mineral extraction taxes on oil and gas, and export duties on crude oil, natural gas, and petroleum products. They do not include taxes on the profits of oil and gas companies.

4. We discuss the concept of resource rent in greater detail in our earlier publications; see Clifford G. Gaddy and Barry W. Ickes, "Resource Rents and the Russian Economy," *Eurasian Geography and Economics* 46, no. 8 (2005): 559–583; and Gaddy and Ickes, "Russia After the Global Financial Crisis." As we describe there, we calculate resource rent as the quantity produced times its market price (regardless of whether or not it was actually sold at that price), less what we refer to as the natural cost of extraction. The latter is the cost of production that would be incurred in a competitive market with free entry.

5. One might ask: But in the decade after the Soviet era but before Putin, who ordered? The answer, quite frequently, is "nobody." See Clifford G. Gaddy, *The Price of the Past: Russia's Struggle with the Legacy of a Militarized Economy* (Washington, D.C.: Brookings Institution Press, 1996), 92–96; and for the story of how the rent distribution chains survived the 1990s, see Clifford G. Gaddy and Barry W. Ickes, *Russia's Virtual Economy* (Washington, D.C.: Brookings Institution Press, 2002).

6. The five core industrial sectors fall under the purview of three different ministries. Oil and gas and electric power are under the Ministry of Energy (MinEnergo); the railroads are under the Ministry of Transport (MinTrans), and machine-building and metals and materials are under the Ministry of Industry and Trade (MinPromTorg).

7. We stress that the Yukos case was exceptional. The popular notion that Putin has pursued a campaign of renationalization of companies and wholesale expropriation of the oligarchs is wrong.

8. The dominance of resource sectors as the source of wealth for private owners can be seen by studying the list of the richest Russians according to *Forbes* magazine. Of the 46 Russians with personal wealth of more than $2 billion on the 2011 list, all but

3 made their fortunes in the oil, gas, and mining, metals, and materials sectors. See "200 bogateyshikh biznesmenov Rossii 2011," www.forbes.ru/rating/100-bogateishih-biznesmenov-rossii/2011; and "The World's Billionaires," www.forbes.com/wealth/billionaires/list.

9. The assertion made in this sentence reflects the central problem of political economy in today's Russia, namely, how can privately owned resource companies be compelled to share so much of the rents via the informal schemes described here? We term this enforcement mechanism "Putin's protection racket." See Clifford G. Gaddy and Barry W. Ickes, "Putin's Protection Racket," in *From Soviet Plans to Russian Reality*, edited by Iikka Korhonen and Laura Solanko (Helsinki: WSOYpro Oy, 2011).

10. For our examination of the history of price forecasts by private individuals and companies as well as by government and multilateral agencies, see Clifford G. Gaddy and Barry W. Ickes, "Russia's Declining Oil Production: Managing Price Risk and Rent Addiction," *Eurasian Geography and Economics*, 50, no. 1 (2009): 1–13.

11. This assumes that Russia can maintain its current output level for oil (about 500 million tons a year—10 million barrels per day) and increase gas production modestly.

12. To be exact, this is 5.8 times faster. Between the third quarter of 1999 and the second quarter of 2008, Russia's oil and gas rents grew at an annual pace of 26.6 percent. In figure 9.5, rent grows at only 4.6 percent a year in the period 2010–2030.

13. This is especially true because of the concentration of manufacturing in one-company towns and similar regions without mixed economies. Hence the loss of jobs is particularly threatening.

14. It is instructive to think why this differs from using methadone to treat a heroin addict. Methadone programs are also based on giving a drug to addicts in order to wean them. The difference is the degree of leverage over the addicts. Methadone program administrators typically have great power over the addicts undergoing treatment. In Russia, it is the addicted enterprises that have the leverage.

15. Putin, especially, seems to see the innovations as a part of his campaign to modernize the defense enterprises, machine-building enterprises, and so on. See, for example, the discussions between Putin and entrepreneurs at the launch of his Strategic Initiatives Agency in April 2011, where a number of the businessmen begged him to help them secure contracts from defense plants.

16. According to World Bank data, in total FDI flows per year, Russia is second after China among the BRIC nations (Brazil, Russia, India, and China). On a per capita basis, Russia has been number one each year since 2005.

17. Thanks to its oil wealth, Russia had emerged during the past decade as a major market for imported goods, especially high-end consumer goods. But when the oil price fell, a collapse of imports followed. Investment plans were scrapped. In the future, Russia's population of 140 million will provide a substantial market, but the decision to move beyond selling to producing inside Russia will not be so obviously attractive as it appeared to be before the crisis.

18. Cf. Putin's statement at the meeting of the Government Commission on Monitoring Foreign Investment on March 25, 2011: "Above all, Russia needs high-quality investment
for development and modernization so that our industry can obtain, along with capital,
advanced technologies and efficient systems for organization and management of production." See http://premier.gov.ru/eng/events/news/14630.

the RUSSIAN ECONOMY *in* LIMBO

Vladimir Milov

Since it was hit hard by the global financial crisis, things have been difficult for the Russian economy, which needs to somehow return to sustainable growth, beyond just postcrisis recovery. Such a return to growth is essential for the survival of the social and political model that was established in Russia during the early 2000s. Almost a decade of unstoppable and impressive economic growth from 1999 to 2008, which had resulted in sharp rises in real personal income and improvements in the quality of life, were an extremely important factor in the gradual elimination of political competition in Russia, and the establishment of an authoritarian environment and the political monopoly of the ruling clan. There is a strong consensus among observers that the high popular approval ratings of Vladimir Putin, which made possible the gradual dismantling of Russia's various democratic institutions and the emergence of the current authoritarian political regime, were largely a result of the strong economic performance that has made society tolerant of the regime's limiting of civil liberties.

Although the economic growth of the early 2000s resulted in increased income inequality—the income gap between the 10 percent richest and 10 percent poorest Russians grew from 13.9 times in 2000 to as much as 16.9 times in 2008 (according to Rosstat)—nevertheless, it is impossible to deny that all groups of Russian society benefited from the decade of growth in one way or another.

The economic decline and stagnation of 2009–2010 had already led to political and social changes never experienced before—mass protests in the Russian regions with demands for Putin, among others, to resign; and a serious decline of the ruling party, United Russia, in the results of regional and municipal elections. Although these changes still have a limited scope, they nevertheless represent an important new trend.

If Russia is caught further in a limbo of low growth, stagnation, and economic decline, disappointment with the government's policies will inevitably spread to more groups in society, sparking dissatisfaction with the current political system. Arguably, only Russia's return to strong and sustainable economic growth similar to that of 1999–2008, from which all social groups would benefit in one way or another, would ensure the continuation of the current political model. Otherwise, it may be strongly challenged by disappointed groups experiencing growing discontent.

However, it appears that the factors driving the Russian economy's impressive growth from 1999 to 2008 have gone, and are not likely to come back any time in the near future. Therefore, to be able to return to economic growth, Russia needs to considerably revise its economic policies to stimulate investment and efficiency, which, in turn, are confronted by the rent-seeking political and governance model that developed under Putin's rule.

A Closer Look at the Russian Economic Development Model of 1999–2008

Russian economic growth of the last decade can be clearly divided into two historical phases. During the first phase, which roughly corresponds to Putin's first presidential term, growth was based on the postcrisis recovery, being driven by the effects of the ruble's sharp depreciation and the availability of substantial unutilized manufacturing capacities. A significant contribution to growth was the increase in international commodity prices (Urals crude oil prices increased to an average $24 per barrel in 2000–2002 from $17 per barrel during the 1990s), as well as increases in the physical volumes of commodity exports.

However, by 2002–2003, the potential positive influence of these factors on economic growth had largely expired for the time being, and there was a consensus among many experts that further gross domestic product (GDP) growth rates would slow down over the years from 5–7 percent to 3–4 percent and then to no more than 1–2 percent. To ensure higher growth rates, it was widely believed that more fundamental policy measures would be required—that is, stimulating fixed investment through the creation of a more favorable investment climate, stimulating the growth of labor productivity and the economy's efficiency through structural reforms of the "nonmarket sector" (as defined by Yevgeny Yasin)[1]—privatization of state-owned enterprises, restructuring of infrastructure monopolies, and so on.

The government's comprehensive economic reform program, launched in 2000 and pursued further with regular updates (known as the "Gref program"), seemed to be aimed at just that. However, its implementation during the years 2000–2007 had turned out to be fragmentary and inconsistent, and brought little effect, as fixed investment remained almost flat at about 20 percent of GDP, compared with well above 40 percent of GDP in China (up from 35 percent in 2000) and above 30 percent of GDP in India (up from 25 percent in 2000), where economic growth was really investment based. The situation with labor productivity remained no better; during the entire recent decade, it grew, too, but almost two times slower than real personal income.

During 2003–2005, annual GDP growth was temporarily boosted again to 6–7 percent due to a sharp increase in the price of Urals crude oil—to an average of $27 per barrel in 2003, $34 in 2004, and the previously unimaginable $50 in 2005. This had undermined substantially larger capabilities for continuing rent-based economic growth without reliance on potentially painful structural reforms. By the end of 2004, the newly created Government Stabilization Fund had reached 500 billion rubles.

It is important that, at that time, more of a stimulus had emerged for the government to slow down the structural reform agenda: on one hand, its own appetite for control over strategic assets and a partial renationalization of the economy (marked by takeovers of Yukos and other formerly privately owned companies, which had largely caused the decline in the share of GDP produced by the private sector from 70 to 65 percent, according to the European Bank for Reconstruction and Development—a pattern quite uncommon for other transition economies), and, on the other hand, the grim perspective of social instability and protests. The latter perspective had became visible during the early 2005 social unrest related to the government's efforts targeted to monetize social benefits.

In any case, in the years 2005–2008, the massive inflow of foreign capital emerged as a new factor supporting economic growth in Russia, apart from the growing revenues from oil exports, that once more supported rent-oriented policies and allowed the government to postpone the necessary structural reforms. Before 2005, Russia had been a net exporter of capital—more capital had fled the country than was invested in it. However, in 2005, the situation changed—though the net inflow of capital was then still relatively insignificant—when the inflow was $1.1 billion, and that marked the change of the multiple-year trend. Further figures were even more impressive: In 2006, net capital inflow was $41.6 billion; in 2007, it was $82.3 billion; and during the first half of 2008, it was $17 billion.

This period of excessive global liquidity and underestimated risks was marked by large flows of Western capital to all major emerging market economies; however, the atypical situation for Russia was that, unlike, say, other BRIC countries (that is, Brazil, Russia, India, and China—the world's fast-growing, very large, emerging market countries), capital came mostly in the form of loans to Russian corporations and banks (60–70 percent), not foreign direct investment.[2]

This latter factor was an indirect indication of the lack of confidence of foreign investors in direct investment in Russia, as well as high direct investment entry barriers imposed by the new government policies of renationalization and of seeking control over strategic sectors of the economy. It was also an indirect indication that investors preferred debt investments to equity investments, because they believed that the government would use its impressive accumulated financial reserves to directly or indirectly bail out potentially problematic debtors if problems emerged (which was proven true during the active phase of the latest global financial crisis in 2008–2009). The government's financial reserves in this case were largely considered a pledge under this rapid credit expansion.

As a result, the total foreign debt of Russia's corporate and banking sector skyrocketed from about $108 billion by January 1, 2005, to $505

FIGURE 10.1 *Russian Corporate Debt, 2005–2010 (billions of dollars)*

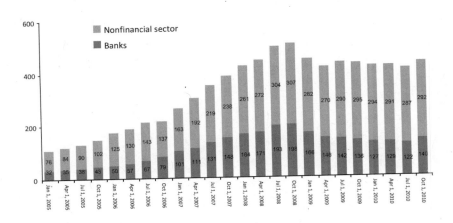

Source: Russian Central Bank.

billion by October 1, 2009 (figure 10.1). During the years 2005–2008, the average share of loans in overall foreign debt had constituted 67 percent for banks and 76 percent for nonfinancial enterprises, whereas during the active phase of the 2008–2009 financial crisis, these levels jumped to 73 percent and 81 percent, respectively.

This expansion of cheap foreign credit into the Russian market was the country's main source of economic growth in the years 2005–2008— the second historical phase of the last decade's growth, as defined in this chapter—surpassing oil export revenue as the major contributor, and countering earlier pessimistic forecasts of a potential slowdown. It has also largely accounted for the impressive growth in real wages (10–16 percent a year), which has far exceeded the growth of labor productivity and has contributed to the country's political stability. Conversely, this factor significantly undermined the country's limited economic competitiveness. As suggested above, growth was largely driven by massive inflows of "easy money" into the country rather than by the economy's increasing efficiency and productivity. When the global financial crisis began, these factors mattered a great deal (figure 10.2).

FIGURE 10.2   *Real Personal Income and Labor Productivity Growth in Russia during the "Prosperity Years," 2003–2008*

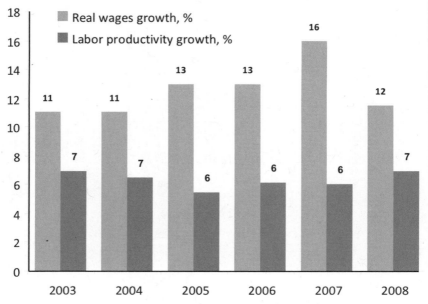

Source: Rosstat.

The Recent Global Crisis

The economic crisis of 2008–2010 revealed that Russia's development model based on expanding foreign corporate debt was clearly unsustainable. Starting in the second half of 2008, along with the active phase of the global financial crisis, capital had started to rapidly exit the country, along with other emerging markets, leaving Russia with huge corporate foreign debt, most of which was short-term.

Capital flight began in the second half of 2008, when $150 billion had fled the country, and continued through 2009, when the net outflow had reached $52 billion, and through the first nine months of 2010 (when the net outflow was about $13 billion). In total, more foreign capital has left the country during the recent crisis than came into Russia earlier, in the years 2005–2008.

Only starting in the second quarter of 2010 did net capital inflow become positive, constituting $4.5 billion—however, this was lower than the government's initial forecast (about $10 billion). And in the third quarter of 2010, capital flight reappeared; net capital flight was $4.2 billion in the third quarter of 2010. Overall, in 2010, the government expected net capital inflow to be zero (the surplus in the second through fourth quarters will not exceed the capital flight recorded in the first quarter).

This massive outflow of liquidity forced the government to use its accumulated reserves to substitute for it. The Russian Central Bank had lost about $200 billion of its hard currency reserves trying to slow down the ruble's sharp depreciation and thus ease the repayment of some of the foreign-currency-denominated loans for Russian banks. By July 1, 2008, the foreign debt of Russian banks exceeded foreign-currency-denominated cash by about $100 billion, which was seen by many experts as the real cause of the Central Bank's "gradual" ruble depreciation approach, contrary to the fast depreciation that would have seemed natural due to the sharp change of the Russian foreign trade balance.[3] The government had committed to keep and even increase its spending to help the economy through the crisis. The total estimates of the government's anticrisis aid vary from 3 percent of GDP in 2009 (the official estimate) to 7 percent of GDP, which takes into account the measures followed at the end of 2008.[4]

For this reason, the Russian federal budgets for 2009 and 2010 were adopted with a deficit. In 2009, the actual federal budget deficit made up 5.9 percent of GDP, and it was planned to be 6.8 percent of GDP for 2010 (the actual figure is now predicted to be slightly lower—about 5 percent of GDP, which is nevertheless a high deficit in itself). The federal budget deficit for 2011 is still projected to be 3.6 percent of GDP, even with planned tax increases of more than 2 percent of GDP, and the Ministry of Finance estimates that the budget deficit will continue through 2012 (3.1 percent of GDP) and 2013 (2.9 percent of GDP), under the assumption that international oil prices will remain at the level of $75 per barrel. It is quite clear that even massive government aid did not help prevent the major plunge of the Russian economy.

Despite this enormous amount of aid, the country's GDP in 2009 contracted by 7.9 percent—the largest contraction in fifteen years, since 1994, even surpassing the 1998 default (when GDP had contracted by just

FIGURE 10.3 *Russian GDP Contraction During the Three Largest Economic Crises of the Last Two Decades*

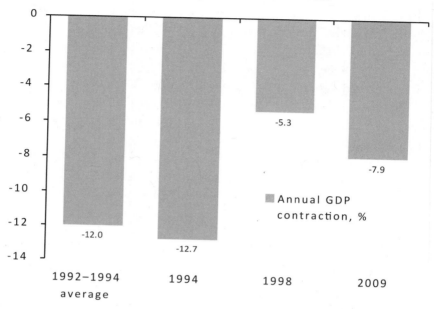

Source: Rosstat.

5.3 percent) (figure 10.3). During the first quarter of 2010, Russian GDP had climbed by a moderate 2.9 percent, compared with the disastrous first quarter of 2009, when GDP had plunged by a gloomy 9.8 percent compared with the first quarter of 2008. Most indicators—industrial output, investment, entrepreneurial activity—indicate that, despite some formal recovery compared with the disastrous numbers for the worst months of the crisis in early 2009, the economy mostly finds itself in stagnation, "hanging" at the levels of 2007.

It is quite clear that massive government spending, leading to a rapid erosion of the government's financial reserves, does not particularly help the economy. And quite soon, even this opportunity will have expired. The Ministry of Finance's Reserve Fund (the successor to the Stabilization Fund) had shrunk dramatically during the crisis (see below), and will be very likely fully spent in the upcoming months, if it is to be used further to finance the huge budget deficit. There is also the Ministry of Finance's

National Wealth Fund (another part of the split former Stabilization Fund) of about $90 billion, but a substantial part of it is committed to pension system spending, and in any case, it cannot prolong the life of the reserve-based deficit-financing policy for more than a year or so.

All this led finance Minister Alexei Kudrin to openly call in April 2010 for reconsideration of budget-financed recovery policies, and the government will have to cut budget spending by 20 percent by 2015. However, as it appears from the draft 2011–2013 federal budget developed by the Ministry of Finance later in 2010, the best Kudrin was able to do against lobbyists is to keep budget spending at the current level—which means cutting it in real terms due to inflation, but without risking nominal cuts so as not to "disturb" the opposing lobbyist groups.

It is quite remarkable that even the relatively high Urals crude oil prices—about $75 per barrel during most of 2010, well above the 2000–2008 average of $46 per barrel—did not help to save the government's Reserve Fund from major shrinking; during the months January–April 2010, it shrank by one-third, from $60 billion to $40 billion, flattening out later on. Since peaking in fall 2008, the Reserve Fund had lost more than 70 percent of its value (figure 10.4). This means that, given the government's current size and the extent of its direct involvement in recovery efforts, even if oil prices were to stay at $70–80 per barrel, that would not be enough to avoid large budget deficits and further erode the state's financial reserves, not to mention any opportunity for building a new reserve.

The "Oil Dependence" Hypothesis

It has been widely claimed by both the Russian authorities and independent observers that the depth of Russia's economic crisis from 2008 to 2010 can be explained by its strong dependence on oil and gas production and exports. In fact, this explanation is an extrapolation of an earlier attribution of the growth of 1999–2008 to the rise in international oil prices. However, as shown above, neither the growth of the previous decade nor the recent crisis can be fully explained by the oil price factor alone, and thus this factor does not have as much relevance as is commonly attributed to it.

FIGURE 10.4 *Russia's Reserve Fund and National Wealth Fund During the Crisis (billions of dollars)*

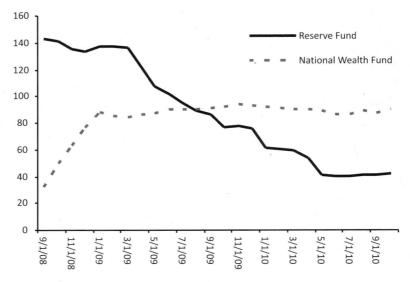

Source: Rosstat.

As illustrated above, the growth of 1999–2008 was driven by a combination of factors, among which oil prices played significant, but not dominating role—particularly in 2005–2008, when a key contribution to growth was played by incoming foreign capital. It is true that the capital expansion into the Russian market would not have been possible if the government had not accumulated significant financial reserves, originating from oil and gas export windfall profits. And it is also true that the windfall profits and emerging reserves had weakened the stimulus for the government to carry out important structural reforms. Therefore, though the oil factor has strongly influenced the development of the Russian economy in the past decade, it would still be fundamentally wrong to primitively explain this development solely with this factor.

It is even more misplaced to seek to explain Russia's recent economic crisis by pointing to its overdependence on oil and gas exports. Several reasons can be cited against this theory:

- Russia was among the countries hit the hardest by the global financial crisis; in 2009 its GDP fell more than that of any of the Group of Twenty countries, but some economies far more dependent on oil exports than Russia—Saudi Arabia, and, even more comparably, Azerbaijan and Kazakhstan—were GDP positive in 2009;
- The sectors of the Russian economy where value added fell more than anywhere else were manufacturing and construction (in both sectors, value added fell by about 21 percent during the first half of 2009, according to Rosstat), which are largely irrelevant to oil and gas production and exports.
- In the extractive industries, value added fell by just about 3.7 percent during the first half of 2009—the most difficult period of the crisis—when GDP had contracted by 10.4 percent.
- The current oil export taxation system is built that way so most of the revenues above $40 per barrel go to the state's budget, which makes the oil extractive industry and the rest of the economy objectively less sensitive to global oil price shocks that normally should be fully absorbed by the state's financial system in the short term (something contrary to what happened in Russia in 2008–2010, when the state's financial system had suffered strong blows but remained solid with a substantial financial reserve surplus, whereas the economy had contracted dramatically).

Figure 10.5 illustrates that the oil and gas production industry was not among the leaders of contraction of the Russian economy—instead of the manufacturing and construction sectors. These points suggest that the explanation for the recent Russian economic difficulties is far more complex than the "oil dependence" factor, and the discussion about the recent crisis should not be simplified to that plain explanation. Moreover, there are clear signs that the nature of the recent Russian economic crisis bears little direct relevance to the oil price collapse of the second half of 2008.

This phenomenon is important to understand while trying to predict Russia's economic future for the upcoming decade. The overall conclusion that "everything will be OK if the oil prices climb back to $100 per barrel" is wrong. Even currently, oil prices at the level of $75 to $80 per

FIGURE 10.5 *Contraction of Value Added by Sector of the Russian Economy During the First Half of 2009*

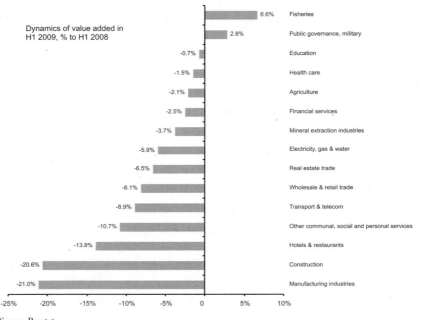

Dynamics of value added in H1 2009, % to H1 2008

Source: Rosstat.

barrel are still *higher than in any of the previous years except 2008*, but the economy faces severe difficulties finding a path to recovery, and the budget for 2011–2013 is planned with sizable deficits. The reader should be reminded that in 2000–2007, when oil was much cheaper, a federal budget was adopted with surpluses—and the dramatic reverse of this situation reflects the price that Russia is forced to pay for the growing size of the government during previous years.

What were the reasons for such deep a crisis, then, and for the fact that massive and unprecedented state aid did not help prevent the biggest plunge of the Russian economy since 1998? The principal factors seem to be the limited competitiveness of the Russian economy, which turned out not to be able to sustain itself (not to mention even to develop) without massive injections of cheap foreign money, and the counterproductive policies of the government, which influenced the situation in two ways:

- These policies seriously damaged the fundamentals of the country's investment climate (private property rights, independence of the judiciary, law enforcement, and so on), which had predetermined both the dominant role of short-term speculative capital and loans (as opposed to direct investments) in the structure of capital that flew into Russia in 2005–2008, along with the speed of exit of capital from Russia at the beginning of the crisis, even comparing it with other emerging markets.
- And these policies led to the enormous growth of the size of government, imposing a severe burden on the economy and creating a strong impediment to future growth, which is now problematic even with oil staying at $75 per barrel.

These two factors combined—the economy's limited competitiveness and the negative role of the government—have contributed to the recent crisis much more than the oil price collapse, which arguably could only have caused limited damage to an otherwise more competitive and risk-free economy.

What does this situation mean for the future? It means that even high oil prices may only questionably serve as a factor in Russia's sustainable economic growth in the future, given that there are too many impediments for it—an ineffective but expansionist government, a poor investment climate, a noncompetitive economy. As the period 2008–2010 has shown, even the high price of oil—$75 per barrel, or substantially higher than in 2000–2007, not even mentioning the 1990s—could not help prevent the deepest crisis in fifteen years, and is not particularly helping to ensure a strong recovery (as will be shown below).

It is important to note that, if international oil prices rise again above $100 per barrel and continue to increase further, the government's financial strength and capability to assist with economic development will turn out to be somewhat greater than under the current circumstances, which gives way to a more optimistic scenario of Russia's economic development within the current model. These different scenarios are considered in more detail below.

The Postcrisis Recovery

Although many economists and observers rushed to pronounce the economic crisis in Russia to be "over" and a "matter of the past," the reality is much more complicated. It is true that the recovery of the Russian economy in the first half of 2010 was quite rapid; GDP grew by 2.9 percent in the first quarter of 2010 and by 5.2 percent in the second quarter, and industrial output grew by 5.8 percent in the first quarter of 2010 and by 10.2 percent in the second half of 2010.

However, it should be remembered that these growth figures only represent a comparison with the disastrous figures from the economy's freefall during the first half of 2009, when GDP contracted by 10.4 percent, and industrial output by 14.5 percent. According to Rosstat, neither GDP nor industrial output reached precrisis levels, and recently the recovery has been significantly flattening out. For instance, seasonally adjusted quarterly GDP growth in fixed 2003 prices slowed down substantially in 2010 compared with the second half of 2009, the most active stage of recovery; and throughout all of 2009, seasonally adjusted quarterly GDP growth was steady, increasing by 1.42 percent and 1.87 percent in the third and fourth quarters respectively, while during the first and second quarters of 2010, the growth of seasonally adjusted GDP in fixed prices was not only substantially lower (0.9 percent) but also slowing down.

The ruble-denominated, seasonally adjusted quarterly GDP in fixed 2003 prices is also currently lagging behind the 2008 precrisis peak levels by 5–6 percent, with the clear flattening of the curve into more of an "L"-type rather than a "U" or "V" one (figure 10.6). Industrial output, which demonstrated sizable growth on a month-to-month basis from June 2009 through March 2010 (with a seasonal January pause), had largely flattened out in April–September 2010, as can be seen from figure 10.7. Therefore, despite some basic partial recovery, the economy still visibly lacks the engine to drive its further potential growth.

There was also a significant slowdown in month-to-month growth in fixed investment; from December 2009 through June 2010, it had demonstrated healthy double-digit growth (again, with a seasonal January pause), which, however, has sufficiently slowed down lately. It is quite clear that

FIGURE 10.6   *10.6 Russian Quarterly GDP Seasonally Adjusted in Fixed 2003 Prices, 2009–2010*

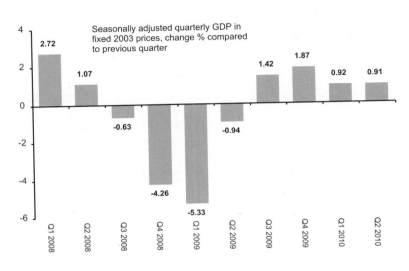

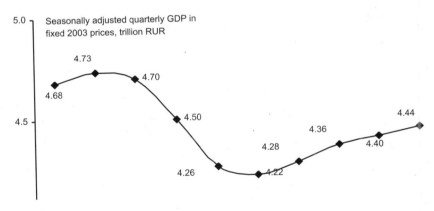

Source: Rosstat.

fixed investment has difficulties breaking through beyond just plain post-crisis recovery (figure 10.8). The recovery also seems to be very clearly driven not by the domestic factors but by the growth in exports, which had picked up significantly during 2009 but had absolutely flattened out at the level of about \$32 billion (but not truly reaching precrisis levels): This

FIGURE 10.7 *Industrial Output Month to Month, 2009–2010*

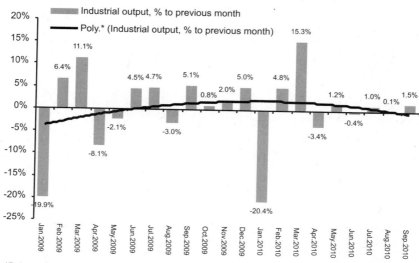

*Polynomial regression.

Source: Rosstat.

FIGURE 10.8 *Fixed Investment Month to Month, 2009–2010*

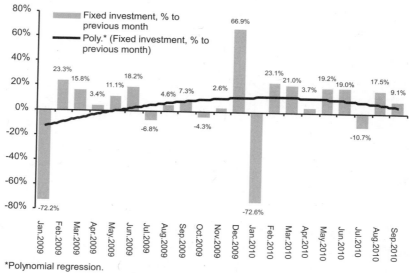

*Polynomial regression.

Source: Rosstat.

FIGURE 10.9 *Russian Exports by Month (billions of dollars)*

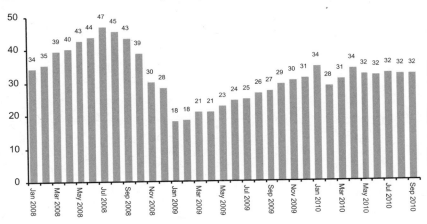

Source: Rosstat.

flattening strikingly corresponds to the slowdown in the month-to-month growth of industrial output and fixed investment (figure 10.9).

However, as shown above, without being supported by fundamental positive changes in the domestic situation, even an increase in the volume of exports alone cannot ensure that the Russian economy will return to the path of sustainable growth. Flattening out the level of exports almost ultimately excludes the possibility of resumed growth. Domestic demand dynamics also clearly became weaker in the second half of 2010, reflecting the slowdown of the economic recovery (figure 10.10).

So far, therefore, the recovery from the 2008–2010 economic crisis in Russia has not proven sustainable. And this is a stark contrast to the 1998 crisis, when the economy began to rapidly grow less than twelve months after the outbreak of the crisis—a growth that proved to be sustainable and virtually never stopped for more than nine years thereafter. This is something different from what we are observing right now. After the start of a moderate recovery during the second half of 2009 and the first half of 2010, the Russian economy is clearly flattening out, with every reason to expect that stagnation or a low-growth environment will be the dominant scenario, unless the economy finds a new engine to power further growth, which apparently is not in sight at the moment.

FIGURE 10.10 *Volume of Retail Trade Month to Month, 2009–2010*

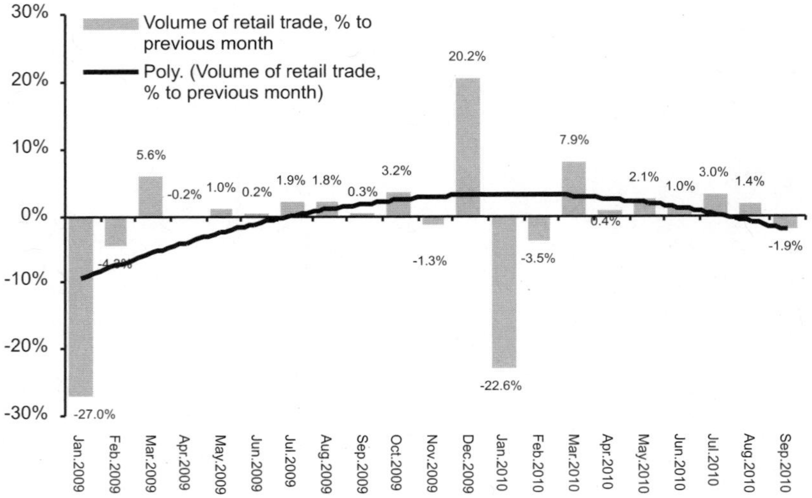

Source: Rosstat.

What Is Next?

Again, what is left to stimulate a return to sizable economic growth in the upcoming decade? It is quite clear that, due to ongoing global financial troubles, foreign capital will not return to Russia—at least not any more in the form of the massive cheap loans of the years 2005–2008. In fact, capital is still exiting the country, despite constant rosy forecasts by government officials about the "expectations of turnaround" of the trend. Corporate debt remains high; according to the Russian Central Bank, it is still more than $430 billion, having started to climb in the second half of 2009. Foreign loans make up more than two-thirds of this debt. This factor will significantly complicate the ability of the Russian corporate and banking sector to further borrow a significant amount on international markets, particularly given the continuing global credit crunch and the remaining overall limited availability of credit. Repayment of foreign loans will also negatively influence the structure of capital flows.

As indicated above, oil prices also can hardly be considered as a potential source of growth—at the levels of $70–80 per barrel, they are not sufficient for that, given the current enormous size of the government. General government spending remains at the level of 40–41 percent of GDP, compared with 33–36 percent at precrisis levels. It should be also mentioned that the Russian oil and gas industry is confronted by a totally new level of expenses related to the development of new greenfield oil and gas provinces and fields, something not experienced in the early 2000s. This means that this sector can no longer be considered the same source of easy rents as during the past decade, when the bulk of production was delivered from depreciated old fields with few investment and operational costs. The debate on fully lifting export duties on oil exported through the new Eastern Siberia–Pacific oil pipeline, as well as the lifting of export duties on gas to be exported via the Nord Stream and South Stream gas pipelines, is a clear illustration of that.

There is always a possibility that oil prices may rise above $100 per barrel and further upward again, providing the Russian government with a renewed opportunity for continuing its dirigiste economic course. However, that perspective is quite far from being certain, given the current situation in the international oil market, where there is a clear excess of spare oil production capacity that is forecast to last well beyond 2015 even in the optimistic case of a global economic recovery (about which a more detailed discussion follows). A new sharp rise in global oil prices can be considered a scenario for analyzing Russia's economic future, but the probability of that scenario does not appear to be high.

In previous years, it was debated that growing government spending (particularly investment-related) may also become a new source of growth and modernization of the economy, but the actual consequences of a sharp increase in federal spending in 2006–2010 do not support this theory. Government spending turns out to be quite inefficient and does not deliver any practical results in terms of stimulating economic growth in any way comparable with the private sector's power.

Increases in government spending during recent years also contributed to spiking inflation in 2007–2008, a process that may resume due to continuing high government spending. Another problematic issue related to the excessive size of government and budget deficits are suggested severe increases in taxes—a unified social tax, excise gasoline taxes, and regional property taxes, which may amount to more than 3 percent of GDP in 2011–2013. That would complicate recovery even further.

The only source of a potential resuming of significant economic growth in Russia may still be significant increases in the economy's efficiency, productivity, and stimulation of fixed investment—the agenda abandoned several years ago together with the whole set of much-needed structural reforms. However, this would require a considerable revision of the mainstream government's policies compared with the period—changing from renationalization and the creation of state-owned "national champions" to privatization; changing from a restrictive attitude toward foreign direct investment in strategic sectors of the economy to a favorable attitude; and changing from further expanding the government's size and regulatory powers, as is currently being pursued, to radically reducing them, ensuring true independence of the judiciary and private property protection, and so on.

The Impact of the Global Economy

Russia is not isolated from the global economy; instead, it is fundamentally linked to it, which determines much regarding the nation's economic future, to say the least. However, it is not possible to analyze the perspectives of the global economy within the framework of this chapter—it requires a more focused and detailed analysis. Nor it is possible here to analyze the perspectives of the global oil market, which will determine the level of international prices of oil—an important factor that may help the government sustain the current economic model.

What is possible, however, is to make two assumptions, which will be used below to further project several scenarios for the development of the Russian economy. The first assumption is imperative and largely not questioned in this chapter—some readers may disagree with it, but the author believes that the reality will more or less correspond to this assumption:

- The situation in the global economy will not, under any scenario, allow new opportunities for massive international cheap credit expansion into the Russian market similar to that experienced in

2005–2008. The difficulties of sustaining global economic recovery, the ongoing global credit crunch, and the perspectives of double dip recession are factors that largely rule out that possibility, at least in the next several years.

The second assumption is a variable:

- International oil prices will either stay at the level below $100 per barrel for at least several years to come (the author believes that this option is the most realistic to expect), or they will rise to $100 per barrel and above, and possibly continue to rise further (a less realistic, but still possible scenario).

The author's opinion about the greater likelihood of the "below $100 per barrel" oil price scenario is based on several factors:

- There is no fundamental deficit of physical oil in the global market in the medium-term perspective, even in a ten-year perspective under the optimistic scenarios of global economic recovery. The sharp contraction in global oil demand during the financial crisis has led to the emergence of unprecedented spare oil production capacity among the Organization of the Petroleum Exporting Countries (OPEC) of about 5.5 million barrels per day (about 6 percent of daily global oil demand), even without taking Iraq, Venezuela, and Nigeria into account (they would add another 1 million barrels per day of spare capacity). New capacity additions for OPEC countries expected in 2010–2014 should add about 2 billion barrels per day to global production, and non-OPEC oil output (by countries like Brazil, Kazakhstan, and Azerbaijan) is also expected to rise. Even under optimistic scenarios of global economic recovery, which suggest returning to annual world oil demand growth at a level of about 2 percent, all these factors would help to keep the OPEC spare oil production capacity at a level of 3.5 to 4 million barrels per day, at least for the next four or five years. Further ahead, the global oil market may get tighter, but we still are not talking about an actual physical scarcity of oil until 2020.

- It is possible that financial investors may try to overheat the commodities markets again, just as they did in early 2008, driving up the prices of oil and other commodities. But given the experience of the oil price collapse in the second half of 2008, and the widely recognized evidence for speculation in the international commodity markets as the main factor driving prices upward in 2008, the author expects much more caution from market players if some financial speculators once again try to heat up oil prices without sufficient fundamentals behind such an upward drive.

- Some radical scenarios forcing oil price spikes—like a United States– or Israel-led war with Iran, or an intentional holding back of oil production by Saudi Arabia—are possible. But given the experience of past crises of similar types, for various reasons these events will only be able to influence the oil market in the short term, whereas the fundamental sufficiency of oil through the period up to 2020 will not be challenged, and short-term oil price spikes will not last for a long period.

The Outlook for the Future

It is not clear whether the Russian authorities will finally have the will to consider fundamentally changing the country's economic (and political?) course. However, if they do not do so, there appear to be no more "silver bullets" on which to rely for economic growth similar to those that have boosted Russia's economy during the past decade—growth in oil export revenues and massive inflows of cheap foreign loans. However, if new silver bullets cannot be found, and the current dirigiste course is not radically changed, the country's economy faces a very uncertain course—most likely, very low growth or stagnation for years.

These policy crossroads—between the "business-as-usual" dirigiste course and a radical change of the economic policy agenda—will shape Russia's economy until 2020. Therefore, in the end, the three scenarios that can be suggested here for consideration are a "business-as-usual scenario," a "lucky" scenario (with a new, sharp rise in global oil prices to a level well above $100 per barrel, which may help to sustain the current political and economic system), and a "radical change" scenario (some kind of radical transformation of the political and economic system, most widely discussed as the return to more radical market-oriented structural reforms). Now these scenarios are considered in some detail.

The Business-as-Usual Scenario

The business-as-usual scenario suggests the continuation of major current trends in economic policy, with international oil prices staying at current levels or moving slightly higher (but still largely below $100 per barrel) for at least several years:

- A continuing dirigiste approach to economic policy, at least in the strategic sectors, an absence of serious privatization, and a reopening of state-controlled sectors of the economy to private investment;
- Government spending largely at the current levels, with the state's financial reserves being used up to finance budget deficits; and
- A bad institutional environment—a lack of structural reform, an absence of an independent judiciary, poor law enforcement, an arbitrary and inefficient regulatory environment, increasing taxes, and so on.

Under this scenario, economic growth will remain at zero or at low levels (an annual average of less than 3 percent).

The business-as-usual scenario may also be implemented under different political circumstances—for example, with the rise to power of more left-wing, paternalist political forces, which would further opt to increase the government's presence in the economy. The author considers this a variation of the base case scenario, despite serious potential political reshuffling—the critical factor here is that the general policy trends, though being radicalized, would still follow similar patterns to the current situation—with budget deficits, increasing taxes, big government, and refraining from privatization and maintaining state control over strategic industries.

The Lucky Scenario

The "lucky" scenario has basically the same characteristics as the business-as-usual scenario, except that the new, sharp rise in global oil prices to a level well above $100 per barrel may take place, giving the government more room for maneuver under the same economic course, and providing the economy with an evident source of growth through an increasing volume of exports. Under this scenario, economic growth is likely to be substantially higher than under the business-as-usual scenario, which will predetermine the greater sustainability of the current economic model.

The Radical Scenario

The radical scenario envisages a serious reconsideration of economic policies promoting market-oriented structural reforms, encouraging private investment, improving the institutional and regulatory environment, decreasing the role of government in the economy, and further opening and liberalizing markets. This scenario is considered "radical" because it would represent an impressive turnaround from the policies of the past five or six years, even if the scale of distancing from the current economic course will be limited. (However, it needs to be significant—and the recent government suggestions to privatize several minor equity stakes in big state-controlled companies in the amount of about $10 billion per year do not qualify, because they can barely influence the structure of the economy and will be no more than fund-raising exercises needed to sustain old-style "big government" policies.)

The radical scenario will likely encourage private investment, allow a reduction in the size of the government, and avoid increasing taxation. Its overall impact on the economy is expected to be rather positive, leading to economic growth much higher than in the "business-as-usual" scenario.

Probabilities of Each Scenario

Under present circumstances, the business-as-usual scenario seems most likely, given the government's remaining resource potential, which is sufficient to support the old course. However, the rapid expiration of this potential increases the probability of the radical scenario, even if significant changes are not made to the political system. And even if such changes are made, the radical scenario is still not guaranteed and is just one option. The actual outcomes will depend on which political forces take control over the Russian government after such potential changes to the political system—if these are left-wingers or reshaped centrists under a new umbrella, the business-as-usual scenario would still dominate; but if a more reform-committed coalition comes to power, the radical scenario would be more possible.

In any case, the probability of the lucky and radical scenarios appears to be limited to 10 to 20 percent, with the business-as-usual scenario so far still dominating the forecasts. These appear to be the main patterns and dilemmas of Russian economic development and economic policy for the upcoming years.

Notes

1. Yevgeny Yasin, *Nerynochny sector: Strukturnye reformy i ekonomichesky rost* (Nonmarket sector: Structural reforms and economic growth), (Moscow: Liberal Mission Foundation, 2003.

2. Kirill Rogov, "Investitsii: Kreditnaya bolezn" (Investments: A credit disease), *Vedomosti*, January 23, 2008, www.vedomosti.ru/newspaper/article/140193.

3. Aleksey Mikhaylov, "Koshelek ili rubl" (Wallet or ruble), gazeta.ru, December 15, 2008, www.gazeta.ru/comments/2008/12/15_a_2910919.shtml.

4. Sergey Aleksashenko, "Prozhorlivy suslik" (A gluttonous gopher), Vedomosti blogs, February 14, 2010, www.vedomosti.ru/blogs/saleksashenko.livejournal.com/621.

POLITICAL SYSTEM

PART III

CHAPTER ELEVEN

INSTITUTION BUILDING and "INSTITUTIONAL TRAPS" in RUSSIAN POLITICS

Vladimir Gelman

As the Nobel Prize winner Douglass North has stated, "Institutions are not . . . usually created to be socially efficient; rather, . . . [they] are created to serve the interests of those with the bargaining power to devise new rules."[1] In other words, the deliberate creation and maintenance of inefficient institutions that lead society toward institutional decay should be perceived as a norm of institution building rather than an exception. The countries of post-Soviet Eurasia, meanwhile, can serve as a sort of "laboratory" for testing partial and temporary solutions that lead to cyclical unstable patterns of institution building,[2] and also of the deliberate creation of stable, inefficient institutions designed to maximize the ruling elites' advantages and help them keep a monopoly on rents and political benefits. Comparative studies of the post-Soviet countries show that this latter solution became inevitable when major conflicts between key political actors were resolved as "zero-sum games" according to the "winner takes all" principle.[3] But the outcomes and consequences of institution building in the post-Soviet countries actually offer a variety of different trajectories of institutional change, and of the degrees of inefficiency of these institutions themselves.[4] In this respect, Russia's case is different even in comparison with its post-Soviet neighbors. First, the country's pathway toward the "institutional trap" was quite complex and winding; and second, the possibilities for a gradual way out of this dead end are looking increasingly ephemeral.

Toward the "Institutional Trap," Episode 1: Elite Conflicts and "Cartel-Like Deals"

The politics of institution building in the post-Soviet countries was in many ways a side effect of the conflicts between key political actors—various segments of the elites, whose resources and political orientations (partly inherited from the Soviet period) affected the choice of institutions and their political consequences.[5] The "Soviet legacy" has shaped the constellation of actors in Russia's institution building in two important dimensions. First, Russia, unlike many of the other post-Soviet countries, offers the case of extreme fragmentation among subnational actors because of the large number of relatively strong regional elites.[6] None of them had the power to systematically affect the national political agenda on their own, and their attempts to create stable interregional coalitions failed because of the irresolvable problems of organizing collective action.[7] Second, the limited number of key national economic actors also created the conditions for conflicts between sectoral-based interest groups. These two interest groups—regional and sectorally based—serve as subordinated actors, and although they were the major rent-seekers and had considerable influence on shaping institutional choices in the 1990s, they were unable to contend for the real power that was up for grabs after the Soviet Union's collapse.[8]

Fierce conflict between the Russian elites flared up in 1992–1993, against the background of the severe economic recession and high inflation that followed the Soviet Union's collapse. The elites were divided into two camps, one grouped around President Boris Yeltsin, and the other around the Supreme Soviet.[9] Aside from major economic policy differences, the core of contention between the two camps was the uncompromising aspiration of each to the dominant position. The distribution of resources was clearly unequal. Yeltsin was much stronger than his opponents, he had broader public support, and the costs to pay for coercion toward his rivals looked relatively small. In September 1993, he declared the Parliament's dissolution, but the Parliament refused to bow down and instead attempted to impeach him. The result was that tanks shelled the Parliament building, which was finally forced to surrender. This victory in a "zero-sum game" was a turning point in terms of institutional choice; in December 1993, faced with little resistance, Yeltsin was able to get a draft Constitution adopted in a referendum that guaranteed him broad powers and an almost complete lack of checks and balances.[10] The provision limiting the president to two consecutive four-year terms was about the only formal institutional constraint still in place.

One would have thought that according to the "winner takes all" principle, the institutional solution resulting from this outcome of elite conflict would have enabled Yeltsin to use the lack of institutional constraints to take advantage of his dominant position to coerce his opponents (similarly to Alexander Lukashenko's regime in Belarus after 1996). But in practice, despite the seeming institutional opportunities for unchecked arbitrary rule, the increasing fragmentation of elites and the weakness of the Russian state forced Yeltsin to abandon coercion after 1993. His fragile ruling coalition splintered into several competing cliques, which raised the relative costs of coercing opponents, especially with the increasing decay and fragmentation of the coercive and in particular distributive capacity of the Russian state. Roughly speaking, Yeltsin had neither the strength nor the resources (including support from the elites and society in general) to wipe out his potential opponents in all areas, while his potential opponents, along with other actors, had neither the incentives nor the resources to organize stable cooperation among themselves on a "negative consensus" basis. Institutions were thus rather poor filters for strategies of political actors during this period, and preserved the status quo nearly by default. This constellation maintained the partial and ineffective equilibrium that had spontaneously emerged.

In this situation, Yeltsin, as the dominant actor in Russian politics, changed his strategy from coercing the opposition to a cheaper cooperation with subordinated actors, including some of his former opponents, which had a major impact on the politics of institution building. Starting in 1994, Yeltsin's camp initiated a series of tacit "cartel-like deals" with the elites. A number of regional leaders who were willing to agree to sell their loyalty to Yeltsin signed bilateral agreements with the federal authorities, which in turn gave them various tax breaks and control over key assets.[11] Opposition parties and politicians were brought into the new regime's framework without threatening to undermine it,[12] and even when they had the majority in the State Duma (in 1996–1999), they preferred political maneuvers and compromises with the executive authorities to open confrontation with the ruling group.[13] These compromises were reflected in the politics of institution building. Many of the laws and decrees adopted at this time (including laws regulating center–regional relations, and electoral laws) were full of compromises, omissions, gaps, and loopholes.

The 1996 presidential election played a key role in supporting the "cartel-like deals" and maintaining the status quo. The possibility that the election might be canceled or its results overturned if Yeltsin lost was a critical aspect of his campaign,[14] and his team even attempted to dissolve the Duma. But the cost of undermining the existing institutions and ensuring the ruling group's survival by coercing the opposition (and not holding the election) was too high. Such moves could aggravate conflicts among the elites even deeper than that of 1993. In the end, the president's team was forced to accept the preservation of the existing institutions, and it thus accepted costly cooperation with subordinated actors as the lesser evil. The election was considered clearly unfair, not to mention facts indicating fraud in Yeltsin's favor,[15] but the various political actors, including the opposition, did not challenge the result.[16]

Paradoxically, even though many observers noted the weakening of the Russian state, its political institutions temporarily preserved some democratic elements. But the major troubles of Russian politics and governance became the price to pay for maintaining this status quo. For example, experts criticized Russia's party system for its high fragmentation due to the oversupply in all segments of the electoral market, and a high level of electoral volatility. Nonparty politicians aligned with regional or sectorally based interest groups played a key role in national and even more so in subnational electoral politics.[17] Center–regional relations demonstrated trends of spontaneous devolution of major leverages of power, including institutional regulation powers;[18] administrative resources, including the regions' capacity to influence appointments to federal agencies, even the security and law enforcement agencies such as the prosecutor's office and the police, with, in a number of cases, de facto control over them passing to regional political-financial (and sometimes even criminal) groups;[19] and economic resources, including control over property rights and over budget flows, the subnational component of which rose as a share of the total national budget to almost 60 percent in 1998 through a reduction in the share of public funds directly under the federal authorities' control.[20] The regional elites were soon transformed into "veto actors" in federal elections, and thereby forced the federal authorities to make new concessions to them with regard to decentralization. Finally, the "divided government" situation in terms of executive–legislative relations led to the postponement or suspension of many important and much-needed laws, thus making it impossible to carry out vital reforms. The ineffective institutional equilibrium in Russia ultimately contributed to the 1998 financial crisis.[21]

The partial equilibrium of inefficient institutions was accompanied by fierce conflicts between the elites, which flared up on the eve of the 1999–2000 parliamentary and presidential elections, when a loose coalition of regional leaders and "oligarchs" was ready to seize the position of dominant actor and was looking for victory in competitive elections. But this scenario was not implemented in the end. The reason for this was not just the spontaneous shift in the balance of power that took place when Vladimir Putin and his entourage managed to win the backing of regional and business leaders, who played a key role during the election campaign.[22] The problem was also that the inefficiency of Russia's political institutions (which became notorious in the wake of the 1998 financial crisis) was severely criticized by the Russian political class, which sought not only to maximize its own benefits but also to overcome the partial institutional equilibrium that had spontaneously emerged in the 1990s. This situation gave rise to the "demand for recentralization"[23] that dominated among the Russian elites after 1998; the ideas of strengthening the Parliament and limiting the presidential powers, and consolidating the party system, were presented during the 1999 parliamentary election campaign in the programmatic statements of major political parties, regardless of their political orientations.[24] But the demand for institutional change was satisfied in such a way that the medicine proved worse than the disease itself.

Toward the "Institutional Trap," Episode 2: "Imposed Consensus"

Yeltsin's handover of presidential power to Putin in early 2000 should have opened up new opportunities for successful institution building in Russia—or so one would have thought. But once in place as the dominant actor, Putin had no incentive to weaken his own role. On the contrary, his efforts to resolve the institutional problems were concentrated not on making institutions more efficient but on weakening the subordinated actors and reducing their autonomy. This was the goal of the institutional changes in the 2000s that aimed to recentralize the state and governance and reframe Russia's electoral and party systems. Formal distribution of power between the president and the other actors in Russian politics did not change initially, but the nature of their relations changed considerably. "Cartel-like deals" with the elites collapsed during Yeltsin's time because of institutional inefficiency that incited the subordinated actors to search for autonomy vis-à-vis the dominant actor. Under Putin, the new cartel-like deals took on the principle of "an offer you can't refuse," to quote the (in)famous statement in the film *The Godfather*. The loyalty that most of the subordinated actors showed Putin in return was determined by their lack of resources for "voice."[25]

Putin's initial preference for cooperation rather than coercion was determined by the circumstances of his rise to the position of dominant actor in the political arena. At the start of the decade, Putin had only relative and not absolute control of the resources, and the costs to pay for coercing other actors would have been too high, especially after the preceding decade of intense conflict between the elites, inefficient institutions, and a high degree of uncertainty. It was to Putin's advantage to cooperate with the subordinate actors, to strengthen his hold on resources, and to weaken his subordinated partners through the use of "divide and rule" tactics. The resulting political deal was for the most part shaped by bargaining between the subordinated actors with the dominant actor and between themselves within the framework of the "imposed consensus," and not through an open electoral competition.[26] But the terms of this fragile agreement were violated once the dominant actor succeeded in concentrating a major share of the resources in his hands, thus dramatically reducing the costs of coercion strategy.

From the start of the decade, the State Duma supported almost all the presidential bills, regardless of their content,[27] and United Russia, now transformed into the "party of power," held the majority of seats in the Parliament.[28] United Russia's implicit coalition policy in the 2003 parliamentary elections, the changes in parliamentary bylaws and regulations, and the formation of a "manufactured supermajority" gave United Russia more than two-thirds of the Duma seats.[29] United Russia had no autonomy from the presidential administration, which ran it according to the "external management" principle,[30] and it thus had no incentive to strengthen the Duma. Indeed, the "party of power" willingly turned the Duma into an institution with little influence and significance.

Putin also divided the country into federal districts, appointing his envoys to coordinate the federal ministries and agencies in the regions and control the use of federal property and federal budget funds. The regional leaders, who had formerly wielded full power in their "fiefdoms,"[31] now found their resources seriously limited, and they were replaced in the Federation Council—the upper house of Parliament—by appointed officials, which left the upper house with no real political importance. Putin, for his part, got the right to dissolve regional parliaments and remove from office regional governors if they failed to comply with federal laws.[32] At the same time, Putin launched an offensive against the independent media, with most media outlets forced to resort to self-censorship and/or coming under the direct or indirect control of the state and its allied business groups. Putin declared a policy of "equal distance" in the state's relations with business, in exchange for business's renunciation of taking part in making key political decisions. Those who opposed this decision were punished, as the Yukos affair vividly illustrated.[33] To sum up, after 2000, Putin managed to reduce the open competition between political elites and to make institutional changes that weakened the position of all actors except the dominant one. The presidential administration became the sole agent for institution building in the country, and the major goal of these changes was to formally consolidate the ruling group's monopoly on power and help it maximize its rents.

During the initial stage, the recentralization and reform of the electoral and party system had the side effects of some weakening of subnational authoritarianism and led to a certain increase in political competition in regional and local elections. But the new round of institutional changes led to institutional decay. Starting in 2003, the Kremlin initiated a new wave of reforms aimed at further narrowing the field for political competition between the different actors. This included raising the threshold for gaining seats in the State Duma from 5 to 7 percent, and the adoption of the new law on political parties that tightened organizational and membership requirements for registering political parties and obliged parties established to reregister earlier under the new conditions. This substantially raised the entry barrier for political parties. It became extremely difficult to create a new party, and the number of parties fell from 46 to 7 during the period 2003–2008. Finally, the reform of the parliamentary election system (replacing the mixed electoral system with a closed party list proportional representation) not only raised party discipline within United Russia and made its parliamentary deputies more loyal to the Kremlin,[34] but also enabled the party to dominate the 2007 parliamentary election. The Duma's adoption of new laws that tightened state control over nongovernmental organizations and changed the rules for holding public events (such as rallies and demonstrations) gave the authorities a free hand to prevent antisystem mobilization through public civic initiatives and to use force to put down acts of protest (which never reached a large scale in post-Soviet Russia in any case).

Starting in 2002, the presidential administration began pursuing an initiative that forced elections for regional parliaments to take place using the mixed electoral system. This change was designed to increase the national parties' influence in the regions, and above all that of the Kremlin's major weapon—United Russia.[35] But this measure was only partially effective in tightening federal control over regional and local leaders. In the regional and local elections in 2003–2004, United Russia was successful only in those regions where its party branches were under the control of the governors or mayors. The regional and local leaders, for their part, had little incentive to put all their eggs in one basket and preferred to divide their support among the various parties and blocs that the national parties had established under their control.[36] Encouraging competition between parties could in itself have expanded the range of political alternatives at the regional and local levels, and eventually begun to erode subnational authoritarianism,[37] but these developments did not fit in with the plans of the Kremlin, which was primarily concerned with holding onto power in the federal elections in 2007–2008. This outcome could be ensured by, among other things, drawing the subnational "political machines" into the national "echelon." The federal authorities' decision in 2004 to cancel the elections of regional governors was a logical continuation of the recentralization policy in this respect.[38] Essentially, the appointment of regional governors signified a new informal contract between the federal authorities and the regional and local leaders, which settled the two-sided commitment problem that had previously prevented United Russia from becoming the dominant party in the regions.[39] It is therefore no surprise that in the 2007 parliamentary elections, 65 of 85 governors were on the United Russia list,[40] although fewer than half were on the list in the 2003 parliamentary election. Thus, the ability to control the local electoral process by whatever means, rather than the efficiency of regional and local governance, was what ensured the survival of regional leaders appointed by Moscow during the federal elections in 2007–2008 and the subsequent period. The compromise between the federal authorities and the regional and local leaders reached through keeping a "monopoly hold on power in exchange for 'the right' results of voting"[41] became the major important element in Russian authoritarianism and was institutionally consolidated.

In the end, the institutional changes in the 2000s strengthened the "imposed consensus" between the Russian elites, eliminating possible alternatives to the status quo and/or raising their costs to prohibitive levels for all actors. Putin, the dominant actor, was able to consolidate monopolist control and had relatively little trouble passing office on to a loyal successor—Dmitri Medvedev. The institutional changes carried out since he took office have been more a case of fine-tuning designed to partially rectify a few "excesses" in the transformations pursued by his predecessor. His moves such as requiring the Cabinet of ministers to make formal reports to the Duma, lowering the registration requirement for political parties from 50,000 to 45,000 members, setting aside a couple of seats in the Duma for parties that obtained from 5 to 7 percent of votes in elections, and giving the parties that win regional elections (literally, United

Russia) the right to submit to the president their nominations for the post of regional governor (along with bringing in some new names to replace old governors) were obviously cosmetic. And his several moves to inject some new life into second-order political institutions created earlier (the Public Chamber, various consultative councils, and so on) were clearly imitative. His most significant institutional change was the amendment to the Constitution extending the presidential term in office from four to six years, and the Duma's term from four to five years. This move clearly pursued the objective of maintaining the status quo in the country's political regime. Medvedev's presidency has demonstrated the consolidation of the Russian political elite in the lack of meaningful alternative actors able to challenge it. Even the severe economic troubles brought on by the 2008–2009 global financial crisis posed no substantial threats to the status quo and/or incentives to carry out new institutional reforms. In other words, the major result of the last decade's institutional changes has been a deliberate decay of political institutions and maximizing of the ruling group's rents.

The Institutional Trap: The Dead End of "Stability"

One of the major outcomes of the institution building in Russia during the last two decades has been the establishment and subsequent consolidation of three important formal institutions (the institutional core)[42] of the Russian political regime:

1. a monopoly of the de facto federal chief executive over key aspects of political decisionmaking;
2. a taboo on open electoral competition among the elites; and
3. the hierarchical subordination of the subnational authorities to higher levels of government (the "power vertical").

If one examines these institutions in terms of how well they fit the "interests of those with the bargaining power to devise new rules," the results are imperfect because they involve temporary or unavoidable "defects": At the federal level of authority, a dual power system has begun to emerge (president versus prime minister); in some cases, minor parties have emerged as genuine opponents to United Russia in subnational elections; and the "power vertical" is not all encompassing because it is does not include local self-government in a full-fledged manner.[43] These institutions also face the inherent and inevitable problem of inefficiency, which is reflected in extremely high levels of corruption (which also creates incentives for loyalty among all segments of the elite[44]), hidden but nonetheless very fierce battles between interest groups (so-called Kremlin towers) for access to rents and resources, and the ruling groups' inability to carry out major reforms that could break the current institutional equilibrium (which explains why efforts at modernization policy from above have been so inefficient so far).

The institutional equilibrium that had emerged in Russia by the end of the century's first decade proved self-enforcing, not just because of the lack of meaningful actors able to challenge the status quo but also because of the institutional inertia of the 1990s, and especially the 2000s. Furthermore, given the fact that inefficient institutions shortened rather than extended time horizons for all meaningful actors, no one was interested in launching major institutional changes, which could have brought positive effects in medium- or long-term perspective. Yet some scholars suggest that the major part of the Russian elite is deeply dissatisfied with the state of affairs in the country and considers some possibilities of their collective actions to change the status quo.[45]

However, at the moment, such a development looks unrealistic not just because the various actors are deeply fragmented but also because of the existence of major institutional barriers. In fact, the existing institutional equilibrium has created a situation where preserving the status quo in state power and governance at any cost (the regime's "stability") has become a goal itself for the ruling groups rather than simply a means for maintaining their hold on power. Even if one supposes that any group within the country's elites voluntarily pursues changes aimed at making government more efficient, these good intentions would almost certainly run up against the risk of involuntarily worsening its own position by undermining the status quo, and this risk would outweigh the possible benefits of reforms for the ruling groups themselves and for the country in general. The result is that Russia finds itself in a situation where even if the elites and society in general agreed about the urgent need for key institutional changes, not only are there no real incentives for the political actors to undertake such changes, but they would in any case realize the impossibility of implementing these changes "here and now" without considerable losses for those who risk actually launching meaningful transformations.

This kind of institutional equilibrium, which is reminiscent in many ways of Soviet political practice in the 1970s and early 1980s, can be described as an "institutional trap": a highly stable but inefficient equilibrium, which none of the significant actors is interested in breaking.[46] Thus, the longer today's institutional "stability" continues, the more Russia falls into a vicious circle that increasingly reduces its chances of finding a successful way out of the "institutional trap."

The Agenda for Tomorrow

Is there a way for Russia to extricate itself from this "institutional trap"? And if there is a way, then how? Can it abandon the current political institutions based on inefficient authoritarianism and develop more efficient and stable democratic institutions? The answer to this question is far from clear, at least in the short-term perspective. The problem is not just that the conditions for this kind of institutional changes do not exist in Russia today (none of the actors are able or willing to conduct them), but also that extrication from the institutional trap usually happens as a result of major exogenous shocks, and it is a useless task to attempt to predict how such events would influence the actors' actual behavior. In any case, even if one leaves aside the speculations about this kind of exogenous shocks (until 2020, at least), the likelihood of major reforms looks rather slim. Realistically speaking, political institutions in Russia look more likely to follow a different developmental trajectory.

Two basic scenarios look most likely in the short term. The first entails preserving the current status quo—an institutional "rotting," to use Soviet-era jargon. The second would attempt to overcome institutional inefficiency and/or eliminate possibilities of challenging the ruling group by resorting to more authoritarian means—wielding "the iron fist." It is hard to really assess the chances of either scenario at the moment, and things will probably become clearer only after the national presidential and parliamentary electoral cycle of 2011–2012.

Under the "institutional rotting" scenario, Russia's political institutions would remain unchanged throughout the coming decade, with only minor and insignificant adjustments made here and there. This inertia-based scenario looks likely if the constellation of key actors and their rent-seeking opportunities remain roughly the same as now. In this case, one could expect to see the rise of principal–agent problems within the "power vertical," increasing corruption at all levels, and regular clashes (but by and large managed and settled) between the different interest groups for access to rents. Institutions' efficiency will continue to decline, but one could expect to see at the same time cosmetic changes designed to boost the importance of second-order institutions so as to maintain and to some extent consolidate the political regime's institutional "core." Today, these institutions (such as the Public Chamber or Kremlin satellite parties) are largely a facade and imitative, but it is possible that over time they could attain a certain degree of autonomy and play the role of full-fledged political arenas and/or subordinated actors that not only do not undermine the ruling group's monopoly but, on the contrary, also help to consolidate it.

More far-reaching moves in this direction could include adjustments to the separation of powers by, for example, delivering to United Russia relative rather than absolute majorities of seats in the regional parliaments, a majority rather than supermajority of seats in the State Duma, expanding the national and regional parliaments' powers (for example, by requiring the majority's approval of candidates for the posts of ministers), and so on. Cosmetic changes could even perhaps go so far as to introduce more or less open electoral competition in local elections (with participation limited to "loyal" parties and candidates and the retention of centralized control over local governments through the "power vertical"). These kinds of changes would make it possible overall for the ruling group to co-opt autonomous actors rather than trying to coerce them. But all these moves are more likely to raise the costs of maintaining the institutional equilibrium (including by increasing the side payments to subordinated actors claiming their share of the political rents), rather than actually making institutions more efficient. This policy can continue as long as these costs do not become prohibitively high.

The other possible scenario is that the ruling group could attempt to make institutions more efficient and/or deal with real or potential challenges to their dominant position (these aims can be pursued simultaneously) by wielding an "iron fist"—in other words, fully or partially replacing some of the existing institutions, with their quasi-democratic facade with purely authoritarian mechanisms of government while keeping the institutional core in place. It is hard to predict what specific moves the Kremlin might make in this direction, but options include restricting political parties' activities (including those of "loyal" parties), a thorough overhaul of legislation to expand the law enforcement and security agencies' powers and further restrict civil rights and liberties, and letting second-order institutions fall into further decline and have their activities cease. More radical options could include further narrowing the Parliament's powers by having it "voluntarily" delegate to the executive authorities the power to adopt laws, with subsequent approval by the Duma and Federation Council; similarly, regional authorities would delegate some of their powers to the federal authorities.

Finally, a logical consequence of this institution-building approach could be the adoption of a new Constitution free of such remnants of the "wild 1990s" as the declarations on civil rights and liberties and provisions on the primacy of Russia's international obligations over domestic legislation, and other liberal provisions. These changes will not make Russia's political institutions more efficient; on the contrary, corruption, the "battles between the Kremlin towers" for access to rents, and the increasing principal–agent problems will not go away but will only take on new forms, but they could dramatically raise the costs of maintaining the institutional equilibrium because of the increase of side payments to the coercive apparatus. At the same time, these kinds of institutional changes in themselves will not necessarily challenge the equilibrium, even if the expansion of repressive practices starts to threaten a large section of previously loyal actors or various "dissenting" groups within the ruling elite— at least, not as long as "exit" in the form of leaving the country remains a more viable alternative for them; in the lack of a realistic alternative, even inefficient authoritarian regimes can maintain institutional equilibrium over a long period of time, preserving the status quo nearly "by default."

The "institutional rotting" and "iron fist" options described above are apparently "ideal-type" scenarios. In reality, institutional change in Russia could be based on a combination of both approaches or an inconsistent alternation of their various elements. But is there an alternative road that would see Russia's political institutions take on a genuinely new quality and move from authoritarianism to democracy? The answer to this question looks negative, judging by the way Russia's political institutions operated throughout the 1990s, and especially in the 2000s. They are clearly incompatible with democracy, good governance, and the rule of law; and democratization, when it occurs in Russia, would require not just some changes to the current political institutions, but their major dismantling and replacement with new institutions suited to the tasks of political reforms and new governance mechanisms. At the same time, there is no guarantee that complete overhaul of the institution-building process would be a success, and in fact, the quality of the institutions themselves, during the first stage at least, could even worsen. These costs could rise steeply the longer efforts continue to maintain the current institutional equilibrium in Russia.

Almost two decades of politics of institution building in postcommunist Russia have led the country into an "institutional trap" dominated by inefficient political institutions of authoritarianism. These self-enforcing institutions became embedded in Russian politics because of efforts of the current political regime, and they play an important role in keeping it functioning. But these institutions are also seriously impeding Russia's development, preventing open political competition between the elites, and creating barriers to making governance more efficient and governments at all levels accountable, open, and transparent to the public. Improving Russia's political institutions in their current form is impossible. The only choice is to destroy them. It will become clearer over the coming years whether they can be dismantled and replaced using peaceful means.

Notes

1. Douglass North, *Institutions, Institutional Changes, and Economic Performance* (Cambridge: Cambridge University Press, 1990), 16.

2. Henry Hale, "Regime Cycles: Democracy, Autocracy, and Revolution in Post-Soviet Eurasia," *World Politics* 58, no. 1 (2005): 133–65.

3. Timothy Frye, "A Politics of Institutional Choice: Post-Communist Presidencies," *Comparative Political Studies* 30, no. 5 (1997): 523–52; M. Steven Fish, *Democracy Derailed in Russia: The Failure of Open Politics* (Cambridge: Cambridge University Press, 2005); Hale, "Regime Cycles"; Vladimir Gelman, "Out of the Frying Pan, Into the Fire? Post-Soviet Regime Changes in Comparative Perspective," *International Political Science Review* 29, no. 2 (2008): 157–80.

4. Andrey Zaostrovtsev, "Modernizatsiya i instituty: Kolichestvennye izmereniya" [Modernization and institutions: Quantitative dimensions], in *Puti modernizatsii: Traektorii, razvilki, tupiki* [Pathways of modernization: Trajectories, turning points, and dead ends], edited by Vladimir Gelman and Otar Marganiya (St. Petersburg: European University at St. Petersburg Press, 2010), 151–83.

5. Gelman, "Out of the Frying Pan."

6. Peter Rutland, *The Politics of Economic Stagnation in the Soviet Union: The Role of Local Party Organs in Economic Management* (Cambridge: Cambridge University Press, 1993), 91–108.

7. Henry Hale, *Why Not Parties in Russia? Democracy, Federalism, and the State* (Cambridge: Cambridge University Press, 2006).

8. Andrei Shleifer and Daniel Treisman, *Without a Map: Political Tactics and Economic Reform in Russia* (Cambridge, Mass.: MIT Press, 2000).

9. Lilia Shevtsova, *Yeltsin's Russia: Myths and Reality* (Washington, D.C.: Carnegie Endowment for International Peace, 1999), 31–78; Michael McFaul, *Russia's Unfinished Revolution: Political Change from Gorbachev to Putin* (Ithaca, N.Y.: Cornell University Press, 2001), 121–204.

10. Frye, " Politics of Institutional Choice."

11. The Chechen Republic in the 1990s in this respect was just an exception that proves the rule. See Daniel Treisman, *After the Deluge: Regional Crises and Political Consolidation in Russia* (Ann Arbor: University of Michigan Press, 1999); Kathryn Stoner-Weiss, *Resisting the State: Reform and Retrenchment in Post-Soviet Russia* (Cambridge: Cambridge University Press, 2006).

12. Vladimir Gelman, "Political Opposition in Russia: A Dying Species?" *Post-Soviet Affairs* 21, no. 3 (2005): 226–46.

13. Thomas Remington, Steven Smith, and Moshe Haspel, "Decrees, Laws, and Inter-Branch Relations in the Russian Federation," *Post-Soviet Affairs* 14, no. 4 (1998): 287–322.

14. McFaul, *Russia's Unfinished Revolution*, 300–304.

15. Shevtsova, *Yeltsin's Russia*.

16. Gelman, "Political Opposition in Russia."

17. Grigorii V. Golosov, *Political Parties in the Regions of Russia: Democracy Unclaimed* (Boulder, Colo., Lynne Rienner, 2004); Hale, *Why Not Parties in Russia?*

18. Stoner-Weiss, *Resisting the State*.

19. Vadim Volkov, *Violent Entrepreneurs: The Role of Force in the Making of Russian Capitalism* (Ithaca, N.Y.: Cornell University Press, 2002). ·

20. Vladimir Gelman, "Leviathan's Return: The Policy of Recentralization in Contemporary Russia," in *Federalism and Local Politics in Russia*, edited by Cameron Ross and Adrian Campbell (London: Routledge, 2009), 1–24.

21. Shleifer and Treisman, *Without a Map*.

22. · Timothy Colton and Michael McFaul, *Popular Choice and Managed Democracy: The Russian Elections of 1999 and 2000* (Washington, D.C.: Brookings Institution Press, 2003); Hale, *Why Not Parties in Russia?*

23. Gelman, "Leviathan's Return," 7.

24. Yevgeniya Popova, "Programmnye strategii i modeli elektoral'nogo sorevnovaniya na dumskikh i prezidentskikh vyborakh 1995–2004 godov [Programmatic strategies and models of electoral competition in the parliamentary and presidential elections, 1995–2004], in *Tretii elektoral'nyi tsikl v Rossii, 2003–2004* [Third electoral cycle in Russia, 2003–2004], edited by Vladimir Gelman (St. Petersburg: European University at St. Petersburg Press, 2007), 156–95.

25. Albert O. Hirschman, *Exit, Voice, and Loyalty: Response to Decline in Firms, Organizations, and States* (Cambridge, Mass.: Harvard University Press, 1970).

26. Michael McFaul and Nikolay Petrov, "What the Elections Tell Us," *Journal of Democracy* 15, no. 3 (2004): 20–31.

27. Thomas Remington, "Presidential Support in the Russian State Duma," *Legislative Studies Quarterly* 31, no. 1 (2006): 5–32.

28. Hale, *Why Not Parties in Russia?*

29. Grigorii V. Golosov, "Sfabrikovannoye bolshintsvo: Konversiya golosov v mesta na dumskikh vyborakh" [A manufactured majority: Conversion of votes into seats in State Duma elections], in *Tretii elektoral'nyi tsikl v Rossii*, ed. Gelman, 39–58.

30. Vladimir Gelman, "Party Politics in Russia: From Competition to Hierarchy," *Europe-Asia Studies* 60, no. 6 (2008): 913–30.

31. Stoner-Weiss, *Resisting the State*.

32. Peter Reddaway and Robert W. Orttung, eds., *The Dynamics of Russian Politics: Putin's Reform of Federal-Regional Relations*, vols. 1–2 (Lanham, Md.: Rowman & Littlefield, 2004–5); Gelman, "Leviathan's Return."

33. William Thompson, "Putting Yukos in Perspective," *Post-Soviet Affairs*, 21, no. 2 (2005): 159–81; Vadim Volkov, "Standard Oil and Yukos in the Context of Early Capi-

talism in the United States and Russia," *Demokratizatsiya: The Journal of Post-Soviet Democratization*, 16, no. 3 (2008): 240–64.

34. Remington, "Presidential Support"; Regina Smyth, Anna Lowry, and Brandon Wilkening, "Engineering Victory: Institutional Reform, Informal Institutions and the Formation of a Hegemonic Party Regime in the Russian Federation," *Post-Soviet Affairs*, 23, no. 2 (2007): 118–37.

35. Ora John Reuter and Thomas Remington, "Dominant Party Regimes and the Commitment Problem: The Case of United Russia," *Comparative Political Studies* 42, no. 4 (2009): 501–26.

36. Grigorii V. Golosov, "Elektoral'nyi avtoritarizm v Rossii" [Electoral authoritarianism in Russia], *Pro et Contra* 12, no. 1 (2008): 22–35; the citation here is on 28.

37. Ibid., 29.

38. Gelman, "Leviathan's Return."

39. Reuter and Remington, "Dominant Party Regimes."

40. Gelman, "Party Politics in Russia."

41. Golosov, "Elektoral'nyi avtoritarizm v Rossii," 33.

42. Article 6 of the 1977 Soviet Constitution gave the Communist Party the official status of "the core of the political system"—which was entirely true. Similarly, one can speak of an "institutional core" at the heart of the political regime of contemporary Russia.

43. The recently frequent practice of replacing elected mayors by city managers appointed on a contract basis is supposed to rectify this "flaw."

44. Sergei Ryzhenkov, "Lokal'nye rezhimy i 'vertikal' vlasti'" [Local regimes and the "power vertical"], *Neprikosnovennyi zapas*, no. 2 (2010): 63–72.

45. Mikhail Afanas'ev, *Rossiiskiye elity razvitiya: Zapros na novy kurs* [Russia's developmental elites: Demand for a new policy] (Moscow: Liberal'naya missiya Foundation, 2009).

46. Victor Polterovich, "Institutional Trap," in *The New Palgrave Dictionary of Economics Online* (New York: Palgrave Macmillan, 2008), http://dictionaryofeconomics.com/article?id=pde2008_I000262doi:10.1057/9780230226203.0809.

CHAPTER TWELVE

TRANSITION *as a* POLITICAL INSTITUTION: TOWARD 2020

Richard Sakwa

Russian political institutions often appear mimetic, mere copies of Western institutions that lack an inner vitality of their own. This is a problem common to all societies that have engaged in radical transitions in the recent era, yet most soon engage in adaptive practices that ensure that the "transplants" take root in different societal contexts, thus tempering their specifically mimetic character. The context of the transplantation of what we can call the "standard package" of constitutionalism, liberal democracy, and free markets varies widely. Three fundamental types can be identified: an *imposed* process, such as those that took place in postwar Germany and Japan; a *necessary* adaptation, evident in the so-called third wave of transitions since April 1974 as previously secure authoritarian orders broke down in Southern Europe, Latin America, and Eastern Europe; and the *self-imposed* transitions in post-Soviet Eurasia. The second type is dubbed "necessary" for the simple reason that the previous orders demonstrably proved themselves unviable as they dissolved in one way or another, accompanied by the growing domestic consensus in favor of adopting the standard package. In the third type, the transition process was part of the dissolution of the communist order, but the reception of the standard package was not necessarily the default option. The complex relationship between transition and state building in the post-Soviet states (including to a degree the Baltic republics) led to an enduring stalemate as state and nation building tempered the adaptive process. The transition in all three cases is about the transfer of existing institutions from one social context to another, but the central argument of this chapter is that in the end in all three cases, although in different ways, the process itself became an institution in its own right.

The Self-Imposed Model and Scenarios for Change

When the mode of adaptation is imposed or necessary, the transitional institutions gradually lose their distinctive—mimetic—character as they are absorbed to create an enduring new order. However, during the self-imposed transition they remain dominant and act as an impediment to the adaptive process that they were intended to achieve. Thus, the third category of self-imposed transitions has proved to be the most problematic in terms of the consolidation of the standard package. The use of the word "imposed" already signals some typological coincidence with the post-war category, yet ultimately the attempt to graft the standard package in the post-Soviet space represented autochthonous transformations and, to a greater degree than the other two, self-contained ones. Despite the crowing of Western triumphalists, the dissolution of the communist regime in the USSR was overwhelmingly an endogenous process, whereas the disintegration of the country itself, although far less of a voluntary event, was also driven overwhelmingly by domestic factors. Thus, in this region the autochthonous element has far greater saliency than in most other transition processes; but even here it is far from exclusive. All three of the categories delineated above are present, because none of these ideal types is applied in a pure form, giving rise to hybrids in which the imposed, the necessary, and the autonomous sit together uncomfortably.

Aspects of each type are given different emphasis in the various countries of the region. Ukraine, for example, for long liked to think of itself as part of a classic necessary transition, whereas Uzbekistan at the other extreme insisted on the autonomous and relatively insulated self-imposed nature of its trajectory. The extreme hybridity of the process in post-Soviet Eurasia is to a large degree a determinant of the hybrid nature of the regimes. In other words, the pronounced triple character of the transition as an institution in the region endows the actual institutions of the standard package with an accentuated hybrid quality as they are transferred to the area.

The Endless Russian Transition: Three Levels of Change

This situation helps explain why in Russia the adaptive process has been particularly traumatic and long drawn out, and the "grafting" is still not firmly grounded. It is the nature of this partial failure of adaptation that will determine Russia's fate in the medium term. Even though there have been persistent assertions that "the transition is over" and that what has emerged in Russia is some sort of end point of that process, the structural ambivalence of the transition as an institution is far from having been transcended. The standard package—constitutionalism, liberal democracy, and free markets—certainly now represents the dominant formal framework for social life in the country. However, at every level the porous manner in which the three elements operate demonstrates the contradictions of the grafting and adaptive process. As we shall see below, this gives rise to the emergence of a dual state in which the formal constitutional order and its systemic ramifications are balanced by an informal administrative regime. Out of this emerges a distinct world of practices, undermining the formal institutions of the standard package.

It is out of these contradictions that a fundamental argument of this chapter emerges. Here I identify three levels of political action: the constitutional, the systemic, and the practical. Reflecting the hybrid nature of the transition as an institution, I argue that Russia is undergoing neither a constitutional nor a systemic crisis but a crisis of practices. The institutions that have been crafted in the last two decades (derived from the standard package) may not be perfect, yet they are capable of acting perfectly adequately if they were able to operate in an autonomous manner without the "manual management" of the administrative regime operating at the level of practices. The social power of this regime (leaving aside a detailed historical account of how the regime was from the first able to liberate itself from the democratic movement that brought it to power and from the formal institutional constraints of the political order that it is pledged to maintain) is derived from the self-created nature of the political realm and the enduring quality of "transitional" institutions.

Democracy and the market had to create the conditions for their own existence, and thus did not represent the gradual maturation of the polity, economy, and society. The accelerated nature of the Russian transition meant that there could be little evolutionary growth into a market democracy. The relative weakness of the imposed and necessary elements in the transition allowed the autonomous element to become exaggerated, taking the form of an elemental discourse on "sovereignty." Although couched in the language of Russia as an independent great power and as master of its own destiny, this discourse only reflects the self-imposition element in the transition, allowing the regime a freedom to maneuver lacking in most other third-wave, let alone postwar, transitions.

Given this structural interpretation, it follows that any amount of detailed institutional engineering would probably lead back to the same place—a relatively autonomous power system standing outside the institutions created by the transition process itself. Below, I will describe the appropriateness of the institutions that have been grafted on to the Russian political order, because it certainly does make a difference whether Russia is a presidential or a parliamentary republic or something in between, but certain political practices will remain, although adapted to the new institutional context. Equally, there has been profound development since the late Soviet years, notably the creation of an extensive framework for private property and civic engagement. Both are consolidated in the Constitution and are operational at the systemic level. However, at the level of practices, their work is vitiated by the arbitrariness of the administrative regime and its sociobureaucratic ramparts that extend deep into the daily life of business and society.

Three Scenarios

It is in this context that we can examine the dynamics of medium-term change.[1] Three scenarios for Russia's development to 2020 are currently prominent. The first focuses on the "inertia" model: The existing situation continues for the next decade or so, accompanied by sluggish economic growth, a managed political scene, and continued muddling through in foreign policy in which there is neither a breakthrough in relations with Russia's key Western partners (the European Union, the United States, and

NATO) nor a radical deterioration in relations. The domestic institutional framework continues along the course of "path dependency" established in the period of "phony democracy" of 1991–1993, whose roots lie deep in the Soviet order and were then given form by the peculiar nature of the post-Soviet transitional process (as was discussed above).

The second model is rather more pessimistic, and suggests a breakdown of the present system prompted by the worsening of the world economic crisis and accompanied by an increasingly unmanageable domestic political situation, characterized above all by widespread popular mobilization. The third scenario, the breakthrough option, envisages that the present discussion about economic modernization and political liberalization is finally translated into decisive action, which would transform Russia's domestic politics and economy and its place in the world. This would represent a period of intensified adaptation that would gradually erode the transitional (mimetic) character of institutions.

Each of these three scenarios—muddling through, breakdown, and breakthrough—is associated with a distinctive political program. The logic of the "transition as an institution" model may suggest that only a thorough breakdown of the old transition model would allow a new one to emerge in which the "necessary" features of classic third-wave transformations would predominate. The "regime of transition" would finally be subordinated to the constitutionalism and other features of the standard package of political order created by the process of change. However, the contrary argument is equally cogent. It suggests that a radical rupture would only reinforce the contingent and subaltern character of political institutions, once again subordinating them to a directed process of change from above.[2] There is a strong historical basis to such an argument. Advocates of this view would point to the numerous revolutions in Russia in the early part of the century (notably 1905 and 1917), and the renewed bout of revolutionary institutional development from 1988 to 1993, and then once again in the 1990s under Boris Yeltsin. Russia is a postrevolutionary society undergoing a revolutionary political transformation, and this colors social relations, patterns of political demobilization, and perceptions of necessary change.

Although the political character of the changes was very different, in structural terms they were remarkably similar in that a leadership group

managed a self-imposed transition that ensured its own systemic autonomy. In other words, every radical constitutional and systemic rupture
has only reinforced the "emergency" character of the extraconstitutional
and suprasystemic practices of the institutionalized transition. The political essence of the third scenario is precisely to overcome this feature,
which throughout Russia's modern history has generated a set of practices
that undermine the lofty principles enshrined in the formal constitutional
and systemic order. From this perspective, it is the practices that need to
change, and not the constitutional or systemic framework. Only the tran-
scendence of the transition as an institution will allow the formal constitutional and systemic levels to operate autonomously. That at least would
be the argument of those in favor of the gradualist breakthrough model.
Indeed, the corollary is that only an evolutionary process would allow a
long-term breakthrough that could begin to dismantle the practices of institutionalized transition.

From this it is clear that scenario building is a deeply political exercise,
reflecting attempts at an empirical evaluation of probabilities as well as
expressing a set of normative preferences. It is almost impossible to separate the two, and the methodology to do so is not clear. This has been the
perennial problem of the comparative democratization literature, and is in
part responsible for the discrediting of some of the cruder transitological
models. The assertion of this chapter is that if we view transition as an
institution, then fruitful lines of analysis open up. It also helps provide
an analytical key to assessing various medium-term forecasts of political
change.

The Party System and the Dual State

The potential for all three scenarios is seen most vividly when it comes to
the operation of the party system, and hence I begin with a brief analysis of the current situation with some prognostications for future development, as well as a brief outline of the notion of the dual state. I then
examine the broader reasons for the "crisis of practices," and how this in
turn feeds back to undermine the constitutional order and systemic viability. The breakdown model, of course, is less of an agent-directed process

and would emerge out of the structural flaws of the present system. These flaws, I stress, emerge primarily out of practices rather than structural or systemic flaws. If the practices of the administrative regime become so dysfunctional (for example, if electoral manipulation provokes a color revolution), then this will reach back and become a systemic crisis and ultimately, possibly, provoke constitutional collapse. The logic of the administrative regime expands to encompass all available space. Unlike in some semiauthoritarian system where this process takes on hypertrophic forms, however, in Russia there are countervailing pressures. The language of political "modernization" in the Dmitri Medvedev era was an attempt to give voice to the ideology of constitutionalism through political liberalization. At the heart of this is an awareness that the development of a genuinely competitive party system has the potential to resolve the systemic features of the crisis of Russian democracy.[3]

There are two main approaches to explaining Russia's distinctive party development. The first focuses on social and cultural factors "from below": the weakness of an independent civil society, blurred class identities, a cultural resistance to party affiliation, and weak civic subjectivity. The second prioritizes institutional design "from above," notably the "superpresidential" system towering above the government, Parliament, and the judicial system while reproducing a "monocentric" system to which all sociopolitical life is subordinated.[4] These are exogenous factors. But there is also the endogenous approach, focusing on the behavior of parties themselves—of which one of the best examples is the work by Riggs and Schraeder, who argue that the sudden fall of the Soviet system in 1989–1991 disrupted the evolutionary emergence of a stable party system by cutting its links to society, and thus the party system was reconstituted from above by elites, a pattern that was reinforced by subsequent elections. Thus the party system was largely the outcome of elite interactions and will remain stunted until parties are able to reestablish genuine reciprocal links with society.[5] In a later study of the 2003–2004 electoral cycle, Riggs and Schraeder concluded that the elite-driven party system had only intensified and accelerated the "Mexicanization" of Russian politics—that is, the establishment of a one-party dominant political system.[6]

Clearly, any convincing study of the Russian party system must combine endogenous and exogenous factors. In the 2000s, however, as the

regime took an increasingly active managerial approach to party development, exogenous factors became decisive. Despite the regime's assertion
that the transition is over and the country has become "normal," its practices were precisely redolent of the "normalization" period in post-1968
Czechoslovakia. In contemporary Russia, parties have been unable to become system forming but remain a subordinate feature of a dominant power system. It is precisely this dominant system that emerged out of Russia's
self-adapting transition process. The tension between the dominant system
and the dominant party is unstable. This is unlike the system in Egypt up
to the revolution of February 2011, where the ruling National Democratic
Party (created by President Anwar El Sadat in 1978) was clearly subordinated to the presidency, and in general the features of the dual state were
less pronounced, in large part because Egypt was formally in a state of
emergency since 1967, except for a brief eighteen-month period in the
early 1980s. Following his re-election in 2005, President Hosni Mubarak
appeared to be grooming his son Gamal for the succession, while the regime's willful manipulation of the December 2010 parliamentary elections
by banning the participation of the main opposition grouping, the Muslim
Brotherhood, helped precipitate the popular uprising in 2011. In Russia,
as in Egypt, therefore, the onset of each election represents a potential
moment of rupture.

For this reason, the complexity of social and political relations should
not be reduced to a simplified model of regime dominance. Although the
practices of the administrative regime remain dominant, the adoption of
the standard package (however mimetic the character of its institutions)
means that a constitutional state has also emerged and represents a permanent reproach to the arbitrariness of regime politics. In the dual state,
the normative/legal system based on constitutional order is challenged by
shadowy arrangements (here dubbed the "administrative regime") that are
populated by various conflicting factions (see below).[7] The tension between the constitutional state and the administrative regime is the defining characteristic of contemporary Russian politics.[8] No society is without
such features, but in Russia (unlike in the Egyptian example) dualism has
assumed systemic forms. As the succession struggles in 1999–2000 and
again in 2007–2008 demonstrated, neither of the two orders predominates.
The interaction between the constitutional state and the administrative

regime is the critical process that shapes politics. As long as each retains a distinctive identity, then Russian political evolution remains open-ended, retaining the potential for further democratization but not precluding the possibility of an overtly authoritarian turn.

The dual state model helps operationalize the three scenarios outlined above. The strengthening of the constitutional state—accompanied by the reining in of the practices that undermine the consolidation of genuine constitutionalism, political pluralism, and competitiveness, and the regulated market order—is associated with the breakthrough model. Of course, the association of the administrative regime with the breakdown scenario, though entirely appropriate, could be misleading if one assumes that there will be a speedy dissolution of the political order with which it is associated. There is no reason why the authoritarian and corrupt practices associated with the administrative regime could not perpetuate themselves for a significant period of historical time—the inertia model. But at a certain point, such heavily managed systems collapse under the weight of their own contradictions. At present, the administrative regime and the constitutional order are relatively evenly balanced, and neither one can consolidate its authority to the systemic exclusion of the other. It is precisely this stalemate that strengthens the inertia scenario. The stalemate reflects not equilibrium but a blockage, a type of developmental impasse that encourages corruption, bureaucratic arbitrariness, and political degradation but also provokes a response in defense of the pluralism and political openness characteristic of a mature constitutional state. Thus the tension between the two pillars is the matrix through which the Russian political landscape can be understood.

Factionalism and Political Stalemate

The underdevelopment of the party system is a common refrain of commentators on Russian politics, and in the medium term the emergence of a dominant party system in the form of United Russia may act as a mechanism to externalize and manage conflicts within the regime. The party system operates at the systemic level, and its stunted development acts as a proxy to measure the extent of the systemic crisis. I argued above that the practices of the administrative regime impede the autonomous operation of party competition. Instead, the struggle about control over policy and the ideological orientations of the system takes a factional form. If parties are the characteristic systemic feature of a modern constitutional state, factions are the medium in which conflicts within the administrative regime are conducted. When factional conflict is brought within the systemic ambit of party politics as part of the standard package, this would indicate that the transition really is coming to an end in Russia, and with it the undeclared "emergency" practices of the institutionalized transition.

The term "faction" rather than "clan" is used advisedly. In the mid-1990s, Thomas Graham suggested that clan-type structures had emerged as the shaping force of Russian politics, in which various economic structures struggled for access to the president and thus to state resources in order "to engineer a political stability that would ensure their hold on power and the country's financial resources."[9] The notion of clan politics was probably an exaggeration even then, although undoubtedly there were various interests seeking to impose their views on policy. These included the traditional industrialists, represented by Prime Minister Viktor Chernomyrdin; the Moscow group headed by the city's mayor, Yuri Luzhkov; the "party of war," including Yeltsin's confidant and bodyguard, Alexander Korzhakov, which had encouraged Yeltsin to launch a full-scale war in Chechnya; and the various "Westernizers" who shaped Russia's liberal economic program. The dominance of the "family"—a grouping of oligarchs, relatives, and administration officials in Yeltsin's last years—was always unstable and represented little more than a fluid grouping based on immediate interests, although sharing in broad terms a commitment to a set of policy preferences (above all, keeping the communists and their allies out of power). Factions are far less substantive and enduring than clans.

Viktor Sheinis points out that the influence of what he calls "shadow structures" remains strong: "The defining feature of the organization of power under both Russian presidents is the characteristic interaction of official and shadow structures. People from the president's 'inner circle,' because of their personal ties, gain influence that far exceeds the authority granted by law to their post. Under Putin such people have become the organizers of both houses of Parliament. Thus it is not surprising that in such a system the highest legislative body takes on a subaltern role."[10] For Shevtsova, the extraction of all live forces in Russian politics, except for the bureaucracy, accompanied by the weakness of the opposition, created conditions for the development of all types of radicalism—liberal, left, or nationalist—and threatened the presidency itself: "All-powerful power-lessness—this axiom was demonstrated by Yeltsin and by many others in history."[11] Even the most benign view of Vladimir Putin's system, as some sort of "enlightened absolutism," raises problems of regime coherence and continuity.

Various forms of sociopolitical structures favor different political out-comes. Ukraine's more strongly institutionalized clans imbued that country with an entrenched fragmentation that favored a more pluralistic political environment. One result of this was the greater uncertainty of political out-comes. The clan phenomenon is far less defined in Russia than in Ukraine and some other countries. Unlike in Ukraine—where clan-type structures represent a combination of social, regional, economic, and even ideological differences[12]—in Russia the political regime is more dominant and inter-ests are less defined. This difference is an important factor determining divergent democratization trajectories in the two countries. In some Central Asian countries, clan structures (based on kinship ties and regional identi-ties) and political administrations have for all intents and purposes merged, and this in turn gives rise to yet another type of political regime.[13] Collins argues that they are not a perverse inversion of standard accounts of institu-tional development but a rational way for social groups to interact in a spe-cific collectivist institutional and cultural setting characterized by late state formation, weak national identities, and underdeveloped capitalist market relations. She is at pains to stress that clans should not be reduced to state organizations or ethnic ties.[14]

Although in Ukraine there is a clear regional and sectoral basis for rela-tively stable groupings with a defined stance on public policy issues, the degree to which a stable "clan" system has emerged can be questioned. Similarly, the attempt to apply a clan model to Kazakhstan politics has been questioned on the basis of the lack of empirically testable evidence.[15] The applicability of this model to Russia is even more problematical, be-cause there things are far more situational, permeable, and malleable. Executive authorities in the center and the regions build up their own factions through personalized patterns of appointment, as seen most vividly in Putin's "tail" from Saint Petersburg, and it would be farfetched to call them a "clan." Elsewhere in the country, the recruitment mechanism of the great majority of regional officials does not conform to any Weberian stereotype and is far from competitive, being dominated by "informal relations and personalized practices."[16] The reason for this partly lies in the absence of what one scholar calls "instruments of mass vertical mobility," primarily effective political parties, and thus "politics"—that is, "activity to achieve influence and power"—"is hostage to the amorphous structure of Russian society [*sotsium*]."[17]

Under Putin and Medvedev, the presidency maintained its preeminence by standing above factions. As Andrei Ryabov puts it, "In postcommunist Russia the presidency, in which all fundamental authoritative functions are concentrated, is traditionally balanced, and often even opposed, to the interests of various elite groups. Conflicting groups have to appeal to the supreme arbiter for support. The president also wishes to maintain such a state of affairs, which works to strengthen his power and extends the field for political maneuver."[18] This reflects a Bonapartist model of politics, but the fundamental question is the nature of the groups above which the presidency stands. According to Glebova, "The ruling layer of the new Russia is divided into groups engaged in a permanent 'war' for access to resources and superprofitable output. All these groups participated (and participate) in the creation of supermonopolies—raw materials, telecommunications and so on, which are easily controlled. The state is one of the players in this field and always wins any fights."[19]

The emergence of a relatively autonomous power system appealing to a centrist ideology has the potential to degenerate into unprincipled expediency. The administrative regime purports to stand above the historic divisions of the modern era, and indeed claims to reconcile the forces that had torn Russia apart in the twentieth century. The democratic process was managed by a force standing outside democracy, co-opting elements of political society willing to compromise and marginalizing the rest. This is a type of passive revolution, which for Antonio Gramsci entailed "an abortive or incomplete transformation of society," and can take a number of forms—including one where an external force provokes change but lacks a sufficiently strong domestic constituency and runs into the resistance of entrenched interests. When the forces are equally balanced, a stalemate emerges, giving rise to a situation of "revolution/restoration."[20] Russia today is characterized by a Bonapartist situation where class forces are equally balanced—above all the bureaucracy, the "securocracy," the business class, and the protobourgeoisie, as well as their factional manifestations—allowing the regime to act with autonomy. The Russian government continues the revolution in property and power begun in the late Mikhail Gorbachev years, but at the same time has restored elements of the previous regime. The system, though promoted as the ideology of reconciliation, had an inconclusive nature that took the form of an entrenched transition and the ensuing dual state, with all its inherent contradictions and accompanying stalemate.

The Ontology of the Crisis of Practices

In any political system, there is a tension between the intrinsic features of a political institution and how it operates in interaction with exogenous political practices, culturally patterned modes of behavior, and the policy framework. For example, in a period of emergency or crisis, different practices will prevail than in a "desecuritized" and peaceful environment. Because Russia since its inception as an independent nation-state has faced an almost permanent crisis (or so it has been perceived or constructed by its governing elites), it is difficult to assess the relationship between cause and effect: Has a flawed institutional design contributed to stunted democratic development, or have exogenous factors—notably the crisis conditions faced by the leadership, the political aggrandizement of self-seeking elites, or simply the personality flaws of the individuals who came to head the Russian state—been predominant? Here I advance a rather more structural logic of causation, in which the transition itself institutionalized a bifurcated social order. Let us see how this works in practice.

Historical Origins and Practices of Constitutional Conservatism

The fundamental process here is unevenness. A remarkable feature of Russian institutional development since 1993 has been the stability of the black letter Constitution, that is, the formal structures outlined in the December 1993 Constitution. This is in sharp contrast to the earlier period and demonstrates that the transition is over—at least at the constitutional level. Gorbachev inaugurated a period of rapid constitutional change in 1988, and this accelerated in 1991 and 1993 when, under Yeltsin, the Russian Parliament found itself locked in conflict with a presidency that it had itself created. Parliament sat as a permanent constitutional convention, and institutions themselves became the central actors in the struggle as Parliament lined up against the presidency. Lacking a clear ideological configuration other than "for or against democracy," political conflict was contoured by the struggle between institutions rather than being contained by the institutions themselves. Earlier, the institutions of the Soviet state had come into conflict with the Russian ones, and by late 1991 Russia had effectively taken over the core institutions of the Soviet Union. The subsequent, and understandable, attempt to constrain institutional conflict had the perverse effect of deinstitutionalizing politics in general, giving rise to a rich variety of paraconstitutional innovations and the politics of practices that are identified above.

The experience of the period of "phony democracy" between 1991 and 1993, when social movements and aggregated political constituencies were marginalized by the struggle between institutions, shifted Russia's elites toward a position of constitutional conservatism. This froze the victory of a particular faction and the politics of a distinctive moment in time, but it has the advantage of ensuring that the plane of political contestation is not returned to that of interinstitutional rivalry. The 1993 Constitution is hard but not impossible to amend, but even with a constitutional majority, the Putin administration did not make any amendments, adopting a strict line of constitutional stability. The changes made by the Medvedev administration have been relatively limited, extending the presidential term to six years and that of Parliament to five years.

This is in sharp contract, for example, with Brazil, which like Russia also has a long and detailed Constitution enumerating various social and economic provisions. In the twenty years following its adoption in 1988, the Brazilian Constitution was amended 62 times, typically modifying an aspect of public policy rather than a fundamental principle.[21] This was Brazil's eighth Constitution since gaining independence in 1822, so the country is characterized by instability both within and between constitutions. Putin was quite explicit in his attempt to create a platform for constitutional stability in Russia, and he rejected all plans for constitutional change. He thus favored Buchanan and Tullock's restrictive view of the need to protect constitutions from fleeting majorities,[22] as opposed to Waldron's more flexible position.[23]

However, instead of politics taking the form of normal infraconstitutional routine, it has recourse to paraconstitutional strategies. In other words, politics is played out in a parallel terrain as well in the constitutional sphere, an aspect of the dualism in Russian politics discussed above. At the close of the period of phony democracy, both government and to an even greater extent opposition policies were constitutionalized by the adoption of the relevant amendments. But after 1993, this aspect of Russian politics—also characteristic of the final two years of the Soviet system from 1989—came to an abrupt end. Instead, changes in politics took paraconstitutional forms, such as in the creation of the seven (now eight) federal districts or the Public Chamber. These institutions exist without formal constitutional sanction, yet they do not repudiate the existing constitutional order. With the transition itself having become an institution, actual political institutions can be left largely unchanged. This is a measure of the degree to which the administrative regime can manage a parallel sphere of paraconstitutional practices.

Structural Problems of Russia's Institutional Order

For Robert Elgie, the key feature of semipresidentialism is the way that a government is formed or a prime minister is appointed, irrespective of the power of the president.[24] By contrast, Matthew Shugart and John Carey focus precisely on the relative strength of the president, prime minister, and Parliament. Russia's semipresidential constitution approximates the "presidential-parliamentary" type of mixed system that Shugart and Carey consider the most unstable.[25] They distinguish between semipresidential systems that oscillate between presidential and parliamentary predominance. They call the French Fifth Republic "premier-presidential," whereas systems that give the president greater powers to form and dismiss governments independently of Parliament are dubbed "presidential-parliamentary."[26] The former are considered more likely to create a stable democratic system because there is greater accountability to Parliament, whereas in a presidential-parliamentary system the government is torn between accountability to both the president and Parliament.

Although the French system's ability to flip between a presidential and parliamentary mode creates a "safety valve" that ensures that political tensions between president and Parliament do not degenerate into constitutional conflict,[27] Russia's "presidential-parliamentary" system engendered endemic conflicts under Yeltsin, and under Putin it seemed that the only way to resolve the problem of divided government was to ensure a compliant legislature. Now, under Medvedev, the problem has been resolved by appointing a strong prime minister at the head of a huge parliamentary majority, and for that prime minister to become the head of the dominant party. Russia executed a "half-flip"—not quite a turn to a premier-presidential republic, but the balance shifted from a wholly presidential toward a more presidential-parliamentary system.[28] Although the presidency was stripped of none of its formal powers, informal evolution toward greater party-parliamentary authority provided an institutional base for the tandem.

The Constitution does, however, contain structural problems. Colton and Skatch note that "Russian semi-presidentialism was of the most conflict-ridden subtype—divided minority government."[29] Krasnov argues that the Constitution itself acts as the source of pathological behavior, above all in promoting the excessive presidentialization of politics.[30] As he notes in a later coauthored work, there is even a question if the presidency is a branch of power or whether it stands entirely outside the separation of powers. A strict reading of the Constitution suggests that the presidency does not even head the executive but stands above and beyond the governmental system.[31] The weak—or, indeed, absent—separation of powers was accompanied by the strong concentration of power in the administrative system. This means that Parliament has not acted as the focus of consensual politics but instead has veered from sullen resistance in the 1990s to passive obeisance in the 2000s. A great mass of reformist legislation was passed even in the 1990s, but in institutional terms the Duma is at the margins both of decisionmaking and of national political identity.[32]

The practice of prerogative powers by the regime was in part provoked by flaws in institutional design, reinforced by perceived political imperatives in what was seen to be a hostile geopolitical environment and an underdeveloped political society. The "stateness" question in new democracies is fundamental, and in Russia took three forms: the questioning of the basic legitimacy of the new state by those opposed to the forced breakup of the Soviet Union; the weakness of the managerial capacity of the new state, above all in relations with the regions and big business; and the overt challenge posed by various secessionist movements, which in Chechnya took the form of an armed insurrection. The classic stateness problem, moreover, is accompanied by the "great power" problem: Russia's claim to be a major actor on the world stage and in its region. The Constitution certainly endows the presidency with extensive powers, but these are embedded in a system that forces the executive to operate through complex instruments. Putin's mastery of factional politics (a key facet of the politics of practices) was a political response to a constitutional dilemma; but it was also determined by the political challenges facing the country.

The duality of the system was reflected in what Montesquieu recognized as the "distribution des pouvoirs [powers]" rather than the "séparation des pouvoirs." Putin did not set out to undermine the constitutional separation of powers, but in the political sphere he systematically undermined divided government, defined by Elgie, inter alia, as the "absence of simultaneous same-party majorities in the executive and legislative branches of government."[33] Putin's technocratic managerialism blurred functional differentiation between the various branches of government, but did not repudiate the distinct logics on which executive, legislative, and judicial authority was based. Key constitutional principles are not sustained by political practices; but the Constitution still constrains behavior and acts as a normative boundary setter for the system as a whole (although, when it comes to executive powers, the borders admittedly are set rather wide, but in formal terms remain within accepted democratic limits). Putin's successor was faced not only by economic modernization tasks but also by the objective requirement to modernize the political system by increasing the effectiveness of existing institutions, and one of the key ways to do this was by reducing the informal powers of the factions and allowing more autonomy to public politics. In other words, the fundamental challenge is to ensure that political practices at the systemic level are brought into greater conformity with constitutional norms, above all by limiting the prerogative powers of the regime and thus reducing the duality of the system.

Conclusion

Contemporary Russia is a classic case of uneven political development. The transition is over at the constitutional level, with a viable normative framework for the development of the rule of law and genuine constitutionalism more broadly. But at the systemic level, the picture is rather more mixed, with the emergence of the classic institutions of representative democracy (various executive bodies, together with parties, Parliament, regular elections, and civil associations), but the autonomous operation of all these is undermined by the emergence of an administrative regime. The informal practices of this regime are characterized by the development of paraconstitutionalism and factionalism, together with rampant corruption and the abuse of law. The entrenchment of transition as an institutional form is the terrain that allows the administrative regime to consolidate its power. Rather than openly declaring a state of emergency, as Egypt had done, the Russian regime informally applied emergency practices through the administrative apparatus.

A fundamental feature of the model of the dual state delineated here is the potential for existing institutions and processes to become autonomous in their own right. Just as the Soviet system nurtured institutions—notably union republics based on a titular nationality, which emerged as independent actors when the regime, seized by a democratizing impulse, weakened in the late 1980s—so today there remains a powerful latent potential in the formal institutions of postcommunist Russian democracy.[34] Parties, Parliament, the judiciary, and the whole juridico-constitutional system established in the early 1990s have the potential to evolve within the existing system. The federal system under Putin lost its autonomous character, but federal institutions have been preserved and could come to life in different circumstances. The tension between constitutional federalism and unitary political practices, as in the Soviet system, provokes a permanent contradiction. In both this sphere and in others, there is a conflict between the latent and the actual.

The breakdown and breakthrough models of development have become institutions in their own right. And the unstable zone of inertia politics between them, caught in a stalemate, has emerged as the central terrain for politics to be conducted. This distinctive form of "centrism" can guarantee neither modernization nor political coherence, but that does not mean that this stalemated situation cannot endure indefinitely. There will be no immediate breakthrough to the full adoption of the standard package, yet the necessary institutional features of the transition ensure that by the same token a complete reversion to the arbitrariness and authoritarianism of the administrative regime is unlikely. After all, the self-imposition of the standard package entails an extensive process of grafting and adaptation, even if accompanied by an immutable quotient of practices that subverts the consolidation of the classic package. Russia remains trapped in the transitional logic outlined in this chapter, yet this logic can be transcended not by launching yet another transitional process but by allowing the institutionalized transition to gradually be exhausted. At that point, the mimetic institutions of the standard package will gradually gain an autonomous life of their own, and the constitutional state will overcome the arbitrariness of the administrative regime.

Notes

1. For a comparable analysis, see Andrew C. Kuchins, *Alternative Futures for Russia to 2017* (Washington, D.C.: Center for Strategic and International Studies, 2007).

2. Peter Reddaway and Dmitri Glinski, *The Tragedy of Russia's Reforms: Market Bolshevism Against Democracy* (Washington, D.C.: US Institute of Peace Press, 2001).

3. See Richard Sakwa, *The Crisis of Russian Democracy: The Dual State, Factionalism, and the Medvedev Succession* (Cambridge, Cambridge University Press, 2011).

4. For a discussion of these two approaches, see Boris Makarenko, "'Nanopartiinaya' sistema," *Pro et Contra* 11, nos. 4–5 (July–October 2007): 43–57.

5. Jonathan W. Riggs and Peter J. Schraeder, "Russia's Political Party System as an Impediment to Democratization," *Demokratizatsiya* 12, no. 2 (Spring 2004): 265–93.

6. Jonathan W. Riggs and Peter J. Schraeder, "Russia's Political Party System as a (Continued) Impediment to Democratization: The 2003 Duma and 2004 Presidential Elections in Perspective," *Demokratizatsiya* 13, no. 1 (Winter 2005): 141–51.

7. Sakwa, *Crisis of Russian Democracy*.

8. Richard Sakwa, "The Dual State in Russia," *Post-Soviet Affairs* 26, no. 3 (July–September 2010): 185–206.

9. Thomas Graham, "Novyi russkii rezhim," *Nezavisimaya gazeta*, November 23, 1995, 5.

10. V. L. Sheinis, "Dvizhenie po spirali: Prevrashcheniya rossiiskogo parlamenta," *Obshchestvennye nauki i sovremennost'*, no. 5 (2004): 43–52; the quotation here is on 47.

11. L. Shevtsova, "Vpered, v proshloe! Ili manifest stagnatsii," *Izvestia*, February 25, 2004.

12. See Kimitaka Matsuzato, "Semipresidentialism in Ukraine: Institutionalist Centrism in Rampant Clan Politics," *Demokratizatsiya* 13, no. 1 (Winter 2005): 45–58; and Kimitaka Matsuzato, "A Populist Island in an Ocean of Clan Politics: The Lukashenko Regime as an Exception Among CIS Countries," *Europe-Asia Studies* 56, no. 2 (March 2004): 235–61. Our argument is that Lukashenko's regime is not quite so exceptional; and this of course raises questions about the degree of comparability between Belarus's personality-based "populism" and Russia's regime-based version.

13. See, for example, Edward Schatz, *Modern Clan Politics: The Power of "Blood" in Kazakhstan and Beyond*, Jackson School Publications in International Studies (Seattle: University of Washington Press, 2004); and Edward Schatz, "Reconceptualizing Clans: Kinship Networks and Statehood in Kazakhstan," *Nationalities Papers* 33, no. 2 (2005): 231–54.

14. See Katherine Collins, *Clan Politics and Regime Transition in Central Asia* (New York: Cambridge University Press, 2006); Katherine Collins, "Clans, Pacts, and Politics in Central Asia," *Journal of Democracy* 3, no. 3 (2002): 137–52; and Katherine Collins, "The Logic of Clan Politics: Evidence from the Central Asian Trajectories," *World Politics* 56 (January 2004): 224–61.

15. Jonathan Murphy, "Illusory Transition? Elite Reconstitution in Kazakhstan, 1989–2002," *Europe-Asia Studies* 58, no. 4 (June 2006): 523–54.

16. A. E. Chirikova, "Ispolnitel'naya vlast' v regionakh: Pravila igry formal'nye in neformal'nye," *Obshchestvennye nauki i sovremennost'*, no. 3 (2004): 71–80; the quotation here is on 73.

17. A. G. Vishnevskii, "Modernizatsiya i kontrmodernizatsiya: Ch'ya voz'met?," *Obshchestvennye nauki i sovremennost'*, no. 1 (2004): 17–25; the quotation here is on 23.

18. Andrei Ryabov, "Poslanie prezidenta kuda podal'she," *Novaya gazeta*, May 4–10, 2006.

19. I. I. Glebova, "Politicheskaya kultura sovremennoi Rossii: Obliki novoi russkoi vlasti i sotsial'nye raskoly," *Polis*, no. 1 (2006): 33–44; the quotation here is on 40.

20. Antonio Gramsci, "Notes on Italian History," in *Selections From the Prison Notebooks of Antonio Gramsci*, edited and translated by Quintin Hoare and Geoffrey Nowell Smith (London: Lawrence & Wishart, 1971), 104–20. See also Robert W. Cox, "Civil Society at the Turn of the Millennium: Prospects for an Alternative World Order," *Review of International Studies*, 25 (1999): 16.

21. Cláudio G. Couto and Rogério B. Arantes, "Constitution, Government and Democracy in Brazil," *World Political Science Review* 4, no. 2, article 3 (2008): 9.

22. J. M. Buchanan and G. Tullock, *The Calculus of Consent: Logical Foundations of Constitutional Democracy* (Indianapolis: Liberty Fund, 1999; orig. pub. 1962).

23. Jeremy Waldron, *Law and Disagreement* (Oxford: Clarendon Press, 1999).

24. Robert Elgie, ed., *Semi-Presidentialism in Europe* (Oxford: Oxford University Press, 1999). For later reflections, however, see Robert Elgie, "A Fresh Look at Semipresidentialism: Variations on a Theme," *Journal of Democracy* 16, no. 3 (July 2005): 98–112.

25. Matthew Soberg Shugart and John M. Carey, *Presidents and Assemblies: Constitutional Design and Electoral Dynamics* (Cambridge: Cambridge University Press, 1992).

26. Ibid., 23–27.

27. Ezra N. Suleiman, "Presidential and Political Stability in France," in *The Failure of Presidential Democracy: Comparative Perspectives*, edited by Juan J. Linz and Arturo Valenzuela (Baltimore: Johns Hopkins University Press, 1994), 137–62.

28. Cf. Ivan Rodin and Aleksandra Samarina, "Gryzlovu nashli zamenu," *Nezavisimaya gazeta*, March 28, 2008.

29. Timothy J. Colton and Cindy Skatch, "The Russian Predicament," *Journal of Democracy* 16, no. 3 (July 2005): 117.

30. Mikhail Krasnov, "Konstitutsiya v nashei zhizni," *Pro et Contra* 11, nos. 4–5 (July–October 2007): 30–42, esp. 32.

31. M. A. Krasnov and I. G. Shablinskii, *Rossiiskaya sistema vlasti: Treugol'nik s odnom uglom* (Moscow: Institut Prava i Publichnoi Politiki, 2008), 30.

32. Paul Chaisty and Petra Schleiter, "Productive but Not Valued: The Russia State Duma, 1994–2001," *Europe-Asia Studies* 54, no. 5 (2002): 701–24. See also Paul Chaisty,

Legislative Politics and Economic Power in Russia (Basingstoke, UK: Palgrave Macmillan, 2006).

33. Robert Elgie, "What Is Divided Government?" in *Divided Government in Comparative Perspective*, edited by Robert Elgie (Oxford: Oxford University Press, 2001), 2.

34. Cf. Valerie Bunce, *Subversive Institutions: The Design and the Destruction of Socialism and the State* (Cambridge: Cambridge University Press, 1999).

can the machine come to life? PROSPECTS FOR RUSSIA'S PARTY SYSTEM *in* 2020

Henry Hale

The post-Soviet political history of Russia can largely be understood as the construction of a giant political machine with a monopoly on the national electoral market. This machine itself is not a continuation of the Communist Party's monopoly on power in the USSR, but was constructed out of the detritus the Soviet Union left as it dissolved. President Boris Yeltsin played the key role in creating and arranging the essential elements of the machine, though it was his apprentice and successor Vladimir Putin who tightened both design and implementation to produce the system that existed at the end of the 2000s.[1] This system left little room for party competition, though it has been important that it was never eliminated entirely; thus, opposition parties have been allowed to compete in every major election since the Soviet breakup. The system was simply weighted strongly in favor of a single party, whose formal electoral dominance both preserved and resulted from coordinated political behavior among the most powerful figures in Russian society in support of the machine. This party, United Russia, is often dismissed as nothing but an empty shell that these powerful figures (elites) populate, but in fact its genuine popular appeal is essential for its success in marginalizing alternative parties, keeping the country's elites united around the incumbent leadership, and stabilizing the regime. Although United Russia's appeal is not yet such that one would call it "robust," it grew and deepened relatively consistently throughout the 2000s, strengthening the system.

It is entirely possible that this basic state of affairs could continue, with United Russia increasingly anchoring a political machine monopoly in Russia, though one can envision at least three scenarios that would inject "life" into Russia's political party system, potentially transforming it from one that serves primarily to bolster the political machine to one that structures political competition and a strong connection between state and society. One is if the leadership itself chooses to liberalize the political system, voluntarily breaking its own machine's electoral monopoly and encouraging elites to compete for top offices by appealing to voters, not to the machine's leaders. A second is if the genuine appeal that Putin and United Russia have cultivated drops significantly, unhinging the system. A third is if the top leadership makes some kind of major managerial mistakes that create doubt as to the likely future endurance of the regime and thereby disrupt elite unity.

The first scenario is the most positive because with the application of political skill, the transition could be managed and kept peaceful. The second and third scenarios involve a great deal more uncertainty, and a greater likelihood that the ultimate winners would be populist or nationalist parties who could take Russia in radical new directions. These latter two scenarios would also be much less beneficial to the current rulers, who, having lost control instead of "going out on top," would become much more vulnerable to future prosecution or worse at the hands of those who win the ensuing political battles. As things look now, with leadership popularity still high but signs that this may not last, the leadership would have a strong chance of successfully pulling off the first scenario. A delay risks a future drop in popularity or a major managerial mistake, which could result in the second or third scenario in 2017–2018 or 2022–2024 (depending on whether Putin returns to the presidency). Of course, one cannot rule out unforeseen developments, as Russia has consistently taught prognosticators throughout its history.

This chapter discusses what it means to have a healthy party system, examines the nature and development of Russia's party system, and outlines scenarios whereby Russia's current system could evolve into a healthy one.

What Is a Healthy Party System?

Political parties are not generally desirable ends in and of themselves. People from Russia to the United States complain about their party systems and frequently see parties as sources of division and corruption, as did even the American "Founding Fathers."[2] Parties, then, might be best characterized as *means* for achieving *other* desirable ends. In democracies, parties serve to structure political competition, simplify choice, add predictability to policymaking, and provide vested interests against the usurpation of power by any one person. Scholars have also noted the importance of dominant parties for hybrid and authoritarian regimes, observing that party-based nondemocratic systems tend to be more stable.[3] Levitsky and Way observe that such dominant parties might actually facilitate long-run democratization in these same regimes.[4] Although social scientists have studied a wide variety of party system features, this analysis focuses on those party system traits that have the most relevance to parties' ability to serve these larger functions:

- *Sturdiness*: The degree to which parties are able to weather shocks in the institutional environment and to survive beyond their original leaders;
- *Representativeness*: The degree to which parties represent genuinely different interests and viewpoints on major issues facing society;
- *Penetration*: The extent to which parties structure competition for and policymaking in the most important institutions of the state;
- *Contestation*: The degree to which a governing party faces the real prospect of removal from office in the event that its performance is judged wanting by substantial shares of the electorate.

Drivers of the Russian Party System's Development

Political parties can be usefully understood as one product of a market for the goods and services needed for election to state posts: Candidates seeking office are the consumers; political entrepreneurs who create parties out of the stock of existing political capital are the suppliers; and the state plays the role that the state usually does in markets, which is to set the rules of the game (formal and informal), to create enforcement mechanisms, and occasionally to enter the market directly or indirectly itself.[5] Parties are created by political entrepreneurs who trade on some form of starting political capital, which in Russia has usually meant some kind of initial connection to the state as a source of money, reputation, or organization.

One of the most important features of the Russian political landscape in the 1990s was that political entrepreneurs found that they could create new forms of political organization that were not parties by any typical definition but that still were able to strongly influence the political process. That is, they served some of the same functions that parties did, helping candidates win election to office, without serving many of the functions considered to be important for improving the quality of voter–state connections, especially the aforementioned qualities of sturdiness and representativeness. In effect, then, they were "party substitutes" that helped candidates win office while freeing themselves from the burdens of accountability and ideological consistency that a healthy party system tends to promote.

Although these "party substitutes" took on a wide variety of forms, three types deserve special mention. One was the regional political machine, typically the assemblage of administrative resources that Russia's governors accumulated by manipulating privatization and regulatory authority so as to gain control over much of the economy and by using the authority of executive office to co-opt, repress, or divide and conquer local opposition, if not establish control over election commissions so as to engage in outright fraud.[6] During most of the 1990s, in assessing a candidate's chances for regional-level office, it usually mattered far more that he or she secured the support of the governor than that he or she gained the backing of any particular political party.[7] A second major form of party substitute was politicized financial-industrial groups (PFIGs)—giant financial-industrial networks that reached stratospheric levels of wealth through the 1990s privatization process and that influenced politics not only by distributing money and buying off politicians but also by mass media holdings that could convey political messages (as with Boris Berezovsky's stake in ORT and Vladimir Gusinsky's NTV), by controlling the fates of major enterprises that employed large numbers of voters in many regions, and by placing their representatives in political positions. The third and ultimately most important form of party substitute, however, was the Kremlin itself. Functioning at the national level much as governors did at the regional level, Russia's presidents found that they could successfully contest elections without depending primarily upon a presidential party and instead relying mainly on all the levers that national executive office could mobilize. Although the Kremlin controlled many of its own vital assets, such as the state-owned RTR television channel and national government revenues, one of its most important advantages was the ability to mobilize regional political machines and PFIGs to its advantage when it needed them in national elections.

The electoral market and the associated party system that emerged in Russia by the late 1990s was thus extraordinarily complex, properly conceived of as featuring not only the parties represented in the Duma or other legislatures but also a wide range of party substitutes that often competed directly against party-backed candidates for many important offices. One result was a party system that was reasonably representative, in the sense that parties developed reputations for advocating views that captured major public sentiments on the most important issues of the day (roughly half of Russian voters even expressed some form of attachment to a political party), but were very weak in terms of both penetration (where "independents" dominated government and large parts of legislatures) and sturdiness (where parties rarely survived their initial leaders or simply did not change leaders even after disappointing performances).[8]

This situation changed radically in the 2000s, and the catalyzing event was the 1999 Duma elections, which at the time were generally seen as a kind of "primary election" for the 2000 presidential race that would determine Yeltsin's successor.[9] It was catalytic because as of August 1999, the favorite to win was a coalition of PFIGs and powerful regional political machines organized in opposition to the Kremlin by Moscow mayor Yuri Luzhkov and the popular recent prime minister Yevgeny Primakov under the banner Fatherland–All Russia (OVR). This coalition was defeated only by an absolutely wild set of events, notably the shocking mass murder by explosion of some 300 sleeping citizens in apartment buildings in Moscow and elsewhere and the ensuing military action that Putin led in Chechnya that sent his popularity soaring. By late November, assisted by a highly effective Kremlin television campaign directed against Luzhkov and Primakov, Putin had become the clear favorite in the presidential race. It was at this point that Putin effectively entered the "primary" by endorsing the hastily created Unity Bloc, which then formed the core of a countercoalition of party substitutes (PFIGs and regional political machines) backing Putin instead of OVR. When Unity surged to a close second place behind the Communist Party in the final vote count, the Kremlin came to realize two things: First, though a dominant party can be constraining, it can also help prevent elites from coordinating in opposition to incumbent authorities; and second, Unity's success hinged on Putin's own popularity, and OVR's failure had much to do with the Kremlin's success in undermining its public support.

In this light, Russia's party system history during the 2000s can be seen as Putin's effort to rein in party substitutes and create a new structure that would facilitate the Kremlin's ability to coordinate their future electoral efforts and thereby ensure they did not work against Kremlin interests. This new structure became the United Russia Party, which was formally founded in 2002 through the merger of the Unity Bloc and the defeated and demoralized OVR. The PFIGs were brought into line by prosecuting a few leaders (Berezovsky, Gusinsky, and Khodorkovsky) and cowing the others into submission while promising them the opportunity to capture megaprofits as long as they engaged in politics only at the Kremlin's bidding.[10] The governors were tamed through a series of reforms that stripped them of their direct electoral mandates, made them more financially dependent on allocations from the central government, subjected them to monitoring and active coordination through a series of seven new federal districts, and reduced their capacity to coordinate activities against the central government. By mid-2011, almost all the former heavyweight governors had been removed from office, replaced by lower-profile figures who were far less capable of playing an autonomous national or local political role, often not having substantial roots in the regions that they now represented.[11]

Underpinning this success was the strong connection Putin sustained with the electorate, which rewarded him with approval and electoral support for perceptible economic growth and more general performance in office. His regime has also regularly shaken things up to keep the party from growing stale in the eyes of voters, including not only the tandem arrangement with Medvedev, but also its rotation of formal leaders from Shoigu to Gryzlov to Putin. Putin's May 2011 creation of the All-Russian Popular Front under United Russia's aegis can also be understood partly in this light.

A combination of the Kremlin's administrative resources and widespread public approval of the performance of Putin and his associates in office contributed mightily to the marginalization of all genuine alternatives to United Russia during the 2000s. For one thing, the Kremlin's supporters in the Parliament (including United Russia) instituted a whole series of laws that made it difficult for parties to maintain registration and get on the ballot; provided multiple points at which individual candidates or parties could be selectively denied places on the ballot; and raised the threshold of votes needed for party lists to win seats in proportional representation contests. Additionally, the Kremlin created, nurtured, or encouraged a series of "virtual parties" that purported to represent a wide range of political viewpoints while in reality being closely connected to and not very critical of Putin. These served not only to sap votes from "genuine" parties (as Patriots of Russia and the Pensioners' Party arguably did from the Communist Party of the Russian Federation [KPRF]) but also to preemptively fill various ideological niches in which genuine parties might one day seek to form (as the Party of Life did with postmaterialist values) and simply to capture votes for the regime from people who liked Putin but did not care much for United Russia.[12] Divisions within genuine opposition parties were also sometimes exploited, producing splits that eventually led either to the complete capture of the party (as with the Democratic Party of Russia) or to its merger with existing virtual parties to form a larger virtual party, as happened with the Union of Right Forces (SPS) (which merged with the DPR and another virtual party to become the virtual Pravoe Delo) and Rodina (which merged with the Party of Life and the Pensioners' Party to become Spravedlivaia Rossiia). Opposition parties, by one pessimistic account, appeared to be a "dying species."[13]

The party system that emerged by the end of the 2000s, then, featured seven parties: One dominant party, United Russia; one true opposition party capable of consistently winning seats in both national and regional legislatures, the KPRF; two virtual parties consistently winning seats at both the national and regional levels, the Liberal Democractic Party of Russia (LDPR) and Party of Socialists-Revolutionaries (SR); two minor virtual parties, Pravoe Delo and Patriots of Russia; and one genuine opposition party facing severe challenges of winning office yet clinging to existence and 1 to 2 percent support in reliable opinion polls, Yabloko. No new party has been successfully registered since 2009.[14]

One might thus distill the following as the primary drivers of both stasis and change in Russia's political party system during the past two decades:

- *Russia's single-pyramid political system.* The combination of pervasive patron–client relations concentrated around a single "vertical" of executive power facilitated the accumulation of vast amounts of formal and informal power by the president into a single "pyramid" of political machine power that then strongly influenced the party system. Dmitri Medvedev's accession to the presidency and Putin's transfer to the prime ministership did not substantially alter the single-pyramid nature of the system because he and Medvedev remained in tight coordination, with most agreeing that Putin calls the shots.

- *Regime performance, especially in the economy.* One of this system's anchors is Putin's (and, increasingly, United Russia's and now Medvedev's) ability to convince the public that something is being provided by the government that is desirable.

- *Political strategy and skill.* The popularity of Putin, United Russia, and Medvedev is a result both of the political strategy of the top Kremlin leaders (who are determined to weed out undesirable candidates and parties and keep them from gaining support, for example) and their skill in making connections with the population, managing intricate elite games, and understanding the complex interaction between formal and informal institutions, using the former to influence the latter in ways that sustain their own power.[15]

Evaluating Russia's Party System as of 2011

So how did Russia's party system stack up as of 2011 on the four metrics established above for evaluating the "health" of a party system?

Penetration

Political parties came increasingly to structure political competition and policymaking in Russia, but this "progress" came mainly by legislative fiat and left many major gaps:

- *State Duma*: A reform effective as of 2007 eliminated single-member-district (SMD) elections to the State Duma and instituted party-list elections in which only party nominees could compete. Previously in SMD Duma elections, parties had shown little ability to systematically defeat nonparty rivals backed by powerful "party substitutes" like governors' political machines or major corporate groups.
- *Regional legislatures*: Through 2003 legislation, party-list elections were instituted for at least half the seats of at least one legislative chamber in elections for each region's legislature. SMD deputies also increasingly affiliated themselves with parties as governors' political machines (increasingly subordinated to the Kremlin) themselves affiliated with parties (by 2010, this was always United Russia).
- *Regional executives*: Although the Kremlin was increasingly successful in pressing governors to formally join United Russia during the 2000s, the 2005 elimination of direct gubernatorial elections made governors' fates formally dependent on majorities in their regions' legislatures, which in turn were increasingly dominated by United Russia. Unsurprisingly, nearly all governors had become members of United Russia by 2010.
- *Government*: Only some of the government's chief representatives are formally party representatives, and few observers regard United Russia itself as playing the dominant role in government formation. Instead, this role has regularly been assigned to Prime Minister

Putin and his apparat or, during his presidency, his presidential administration. Although Putin is the chairman of United Russia, he has also demonstratively refused actually to become a "member" of the party, thereby refusing to govern on what one might genuinely call a partisan basis.

- *The presidency*: The dominant pattern for most of post-Soviet Russian history has been for the president to refuse party affiliation, aspiring instead to be "president of the whole people." During their presidencies, both Yeltsin and Putin were willing to support "parties of power," but neither would lend his unequivocal support in the form of accepting party membership (formal law could have easily been changed to facilitate this) or even in the form of running for Russia's top office as a party nominee. Putin took a major step in the 2007 Duma election, becoming the first sitting Russian president to head the candidate list of a political party in any election (United Russia), though he still refused in the process to become a party member. Medvedev took another step in 2008, becoming the first president to have won the office as an official party nominee (United Russia's), though, like Putin, he too refused actually to become a party member. Thus, whereas Russia's chief leaders have brought United Russia closer to the heart of power than ever before, they have still kept it at arm's length, refusing to lend it their full personal authority.
- *Who is doing the penetrating*: By the end of the 2000s, United Russia had so far eclipsed other parties that it was hard to talk about any other party displaying significant penetration. The KPRF became the main rival, typically occupying a weak minority (under one-third) of the seats in legislatures and having virtually no representation in executive bodies except at the most local of levels.

Sturdiness

The United Russia Party has generally become sturdier during the 2000s, while all other parties have weakened, with only the KPRF demonstrating anything like substantial staying power, though with imperfect institution-

alization due to its continued dependence on its founding leader, Gennady
Zyuganov:

- *United Russia*: In the 2000s, United Russia became the first Russian party of power to be featured for more than one federal election cycle. It developed increasingly robust connections with the electorate, even to the point of cultivating a core set of loyalists—approximately 30 percent of the population by 2008 by one measure, reported in table 13.1. Survey evidence finds that United Russia is associated with certain ideational stands (including a broadly rightist orientation against a return to socialism and for partnership with the West; see tables 13.2 and 13.3) and support for authorities that are seen as performing well both generally and in the economy—things that have been found to build durable party loyalties over time in countries around the world. These same orientations are associated both with Putin and with his closest allies, including Medvedev and Sergei Ivanov.[16] The party does not boil down to Putin alone; views on major issues and economic trends have also been important.[17] The party's fortunes (like those of its leaders) have also weathered some major shocks that might have hurt a weaker party of power, including the global financial crisis that hit in 2008 and a new bout of terrorist attacks in nonperipheral areas of Russia in the latter 2000s.[18] Despite ups and downs in regional legislative elections, the very striking trend has been United Russia's stability.

- *Other parties*: Only the KPRF and LDPR have demonstrated any real staying power in Russian politics during the last two decades, though of these only the KPRF can be said to have formed anything like an enduring electorate of actual loyalists. Surveys reinterviewing the same sets of people over time have shown that the LDPR's electorate in Duma elections tends to change almost completely from election to election at the same time that the party is consistently able to cobble together a roughly stable proportion of supporters (that is, it might get 5 to 15 percent of the vote each election, but the people making up this 5 to 15 percent appear to be different each time).[19] With only legislative minorities and

TABLE 13.1   *Percentage[1] of the Population Found to be "Transitional Partisans"[2] for Different Parties in Different Years,[3] Russian Election Studies (RES) Surveys[4]*

PARTY	1995	1999	2003–4	2004	2008
United Russia & Parties of Power Joining It	5	10	22	26	30
Our Home Is Russia	5	1	-	-	-
Fatherland-All Russia	-	5	-	-	-
Unity	-	4	-	-	-
Communist Party	15	17	13	8	8
LDPR	5	3	5	4	4
Russia's Democratic Choice/ SPS	2	2	2	1	0
Yabloko	5	6	3	2	1
SR (Motherland)	-	-	5	4	2
Agrarian Party	2	-	-	-	0
Women of Russia	4	-	-	-	-
Total for all major parties	38	38	50	45	45

1.   The figures presented from RES surveys are computed using the weighting technique designed by Leslie Kish to take into account the disproportionately frequent occurrence of certain categories of respondents who appear in the sample design used. For details, see Timothy J. Colton, *Transitional Citizens* (Cambridge, Mass.: Harvard University Press, 2000). Column totals may be a bit imprecise due to rounding.

2.   Transitional partisanship is a concept developed by Colton, *Transitional Citizens*. The survey first asks voters: "Please tell me, is there any one among the present parties, movements, and associations about which you would say, 'This is my party, my movement, my association'?" Respondents replying yes are asked to name a specific party without being presented with a list to choose from. Those replying no are asked: "Please tell me, does there exist a party, movement, or association which more than the others reflects your interests, views, and concerns?" Those replying affirmatively are then asked to name a specific party (also without the help of a list). People answering affirmatively to either of those questions and naming an actual party are categorized as that party's transitional partisans.

3.   Note: Listed are the years when most of the survey questionnaires were administered. The 1995 and 1999 surveys were both administered in the autumn prior to those years' parliamentary elections; the 2003–2004 survey was administered during the winter that straddled the new year (that is, between the parliamentary and presidential elections); the 2004 and 2008 iterations were undertaken shortly after the March presidential voting.

4.   Unless otherwise indicated, the survey results given in this chapter come from RES surveys. At different times, the RES has received funding from the National Council for Eurasian and East European Research (NCEEER) under authority of a Title VIII grant from the U.S. Department of State, the Carnegie Corporation of New York, and the National Science Foundation, to each of which the author expresses gratitude. Nevertheless, the views expressed here are those of the author alone and are not the responsibility of the U.S. government, the NCEEER, the Carnegie Corporation of New York, the National Science Foundation, or any other entity. See Colton, *Transitional Citizens*, and Hale (2006) for more on the surveys. All RES surveys were carried out by Demoscope, led by Polina Kozyreva and Mikhail Kosolapov of the Russian Academy of Sciences' Institute of Sociology. Citations for the first two surveys, available through ICPSR, are Timothy Colton and William Zimmerman, *Russian Election Study, 1995–1996* [computer file], ICPSR version (Moscow: Russian Academy of Sciences, Institute of Sociology, Demoscope Group [producer], 1996). Ann Arbor, Mich.: Inter-university Consortium for Political and Social Research [distributor], 2002.

TABLE 13.2 *What is United Russia's Position on Whether Russia Should Pursue Continued Market Reform or a Return to Socialism? Percentage of the Russian Population Giving Each Response, RES Surveys.*

POSITION	2003	2008
Return to socialist economy	4	1
Leave as is	10	7
Continue, deepen market reforms	61	77
Various nonanswers	25	16

TABLE 13.3 *What is United Russia's Position on Whether Russia Should Treat the West as an Enemy, Rival, Ally, or Friend? Percentage of the Russian Population Giving Each Response, RES Surveys.*

POSITION	2003	2008
As an enemy	0.3	0.4
As a rival	6	11
As an ally	63	65
As a friend	9	8
Various nonanswers	21	16

no significant access to executive power, however, even these relatively successful parties of nonpower are unable to develop reputations based on policy performance and so have increasingly lost the ability to develop sturdy electorates or stable administrative bases of support, as table 13.1 demonstrates.

Representativeness

If popular support in elections (or in polls reproducing expected electoral choices) is a measure of representativeness, then one can conclude that United Russia has come successfully to represent the majority of the

TABLE 13.4   *Should Russia Pursue Continued Market Reform or a Return to Socialism? Percentage of the Russian Population Giving Each Response, RES Surveys.*

RESPONSE	2003	2008
Return to socialist economy	25	17
Leave as is	12	11
Continue, deepen market reforms	53	58
Various nonanswers	10	14

TABLE 13.5   *Should Russia Treat the West as an Enemy, Rival, Ally, or Friend? Percentage of the Russian Population Giving Each Response, RES Surveys.*

RESPONSE	2003	2008
As an enemy	2	3
As a rival	18	22
As an ally	62	61
As a friend	14	10
Various nonanswers	5	6

population, and the KPRF a significant minority, with the LDPR and SR representing most of those who are left. A relatively stable situation has developed in which United Russia attempts to represent the whole population in party politics (including allowing the creation of "clubs" within the party representing leftist, rightist, and "patriotic" ideas), while the Kremlin simultaneously promotes a series of "virtual parties"[20] to "represent" those who are either left out (for example, local elites not selected for local United Russia leadership posts) or who generally support Putin and Medvedev but who are uncomfortable with the ideas or other personalities with which United Russia is associated (the classic example is SR). The KPRF has become virtually the only party available in the party system to represent those dissatisfied with the leadership more generally, and its association with Russia's totalitarian past and its communist ideology prevent many from utilizing it as a vehicle for representation. United Russia has done an adequate job positioning itself at the points on major issue divides that have the most support among the population, as a comparison of tables 13.4 and 13.5 with tables 13.2 and 13.3 illustrates on two important issues. In short, those satisfied with the regime and its outputs are well represented in the Russian party system, whereas others are not.

Contestation

For a party system to have the most positive effects for state–society relations, it must also produce free and fair competition between parties, competition that enhances representation by providing opportunities for people to fully explore what their interests are and who might best represent them. Party systems everywhere constrain this process; no system can be perfectly competitive or representative. But in Russia, at least, it is fair to say that the trend in the 2000s has been the constraining of political choice through the weeding out (through formal or informal means) of many alternatives and through tilting the playing field away from certain options, as described above. In particular, the Kremlin has done an effective job narrowing the set of players to a particular collection of rivals that reinforce the way that United Russia chooses to position itself on major issues rather than challenge its positioning. The KPRF is in this case the perfect "rival," representing (or easily portrayed as representing) a past to which most Russians clearly do not want actually to return, abstract feelings of nostalgia notwithstanding. Independent SPS, conversely, was a problematic rival, representing a genuine claim to modernizing market-oriented reform that at least somewhat undercut United Russia's ability to capture the whole antisocialist segment of the population. Of course, SPS was highly unpopular during the 2000s, but it was still deemed by the Kremlin to be more deserving of outright co-optation and turning into a virtual party than the KPRF, resulting in the creation of Pravoe Delo. The overall trend, therefore, is that the Kremlin has essentially been able to define the principal lines of cleavage along which people define their choices of representation, and this has broken heavily in favor of United Russia. Even more fundamentally, of course, is the fact that only two genuine opposition parties remain officially registered as of 2011 (Yabloko and the

KPRF), at the same time that there exist very high hurdles for the registration of new parties, not to mention their actual participation in elections, as described in the previous section. This means that even if the number of people wanting to vote for a pro-regime party drops precipitously, they will have only two real choices for some time to come: Yabloko and the KPRF. Although these are certainly legitimate options for many, they hardly represent the range of views and interests that might demand representation in such a situation.

The Inertial Scenario

If Russia's leadership sustains its single-pyramid political system, experiences further steady economic growth, and continues to flexibly find ways to react to major crises to connect with the population and to keep itself from growing stale in the eyes of the public, then it is most likely that Russia's party system will continue to develop along the current trajectory—barring a major exogenous shock, which cannot be ruled out. This inertia would involve a continued gradual increase in the sturdiness, penetration, and representative capacity of United Russia (including the deepening of its connections with a substantial share of the population) and the simultaneous stagnation of all other parties on these same dimensions, with the accompanying lack of contestation. In this sense, Russia could come to resemble other authoritarian or hybrid regimes that (have) endured for decades through the state-supported dominance of a single party, such as Singapore or Mexico.

Can Rose-Colored Glasses Produce 2020 Vision?

Focusing on the three primary drivers of stasis and change discussed above, one might conceive of three basic paths to a healthy party system that would feature sturdy and representative parties that compete vigorously and win control of the most important policymaking positions in Russia. All three involve a dismantling of the single-pyramid system, which by its nature does not facilitate contested, highly representative party politics.

The most positive of the three would involve a voluntary dismantling of the single-pyramid system by the top leadership itself. In this scenario, the Kremlin would initiate the construction of a sound legal-institutional basis for robust party competition, including dramatically lowering the barriers to entry into the electoral market by new parties. This might occur if Russia's top leadership realizes that the linchpins of the current system—including high popularity and skilled and energetic hands-on management—are extraordinarily hard to sustain over long periods of time and that the costs of a breakdown could be catastrophic for individual regime leaders personally in terms of their ability to avoid reprisals (as some current and former Arab leaders have recently disovered). With this in mind, it may be better in the long run for incumbent leaders to construct a system that leaves them with a safe exit option, which could be by opening up political competition while they and United Russia still wield popularity and a strong organization, which could then serve to protect them even if it goes into opposition.

A second scenario would be more like the recent Egyptian experience, where some kind of exogenous shock, deep social fatigue with a long-ruling clique, or sustained economic decline causes the leadership to lose its ability to dominate politics by electoral appeal and to have to rely almost entirely on administrative resources. This can work for a while, but even the strongest administrative resources—when not undergirded by genuine popular support—can break down in the face of a succession crisis or other events that start to make the leadership look likely to be short-lived. One possible point for such a crisis could be the 2017–2018 election cycle because it could become a natural rallying point for those dissatisfied with the regime, an especially likely development if this becomes a succession election (that is, if the incumbent president does not or cannot run for reelection and thus becomes a lame duck). A very unpopular regime would then be forced either to shift to a full-fledged dictatorship along the lines of Uzbekistan, to liberalize hastily in a last-ditch effort to salvage a safe postelection position, or face overthrow. If 2017–2018 does not turn out to be a succession election, then the more likely timing for such developments would be the 2022–2024 election cycle. Depending on which one, 2020 could see either the early period of new multiparty politics in Russia or the first cracks in the system leading to such a development. Under this general scenario, legalized opposition parties like the KPRF and Yabloko could see a sudden surge in support (as happened with the long-marginalized PAN in Mexico with its historic 2000 election to the presidency) along with the coming to life of virtual parties, as their elite leaders would have an incentive to "abandon the sinking ship" and claim independence. The latter prospect could be rather dangerous because their most effective appeals would likely be populist or nationalistic stances that might distract people from looking at their records as stooges of the unpopular former regime. And because this process would not be controlled or prepared for with proper legislation, the kind of competition that would emerge could be rather wild, and unless it were to also somehow involve the construction of a true balance of power in place of the overweening presidency, there would be a strong chance of reconsolidation into a new single-pyramid system under new leadership. But there would be a chance that what emerged from the chaos would be a set of battle-tested parties that could develop genuine appeals to the public and successfully negotiate an enduring competitive party system.

A third scenario resembles the second except that the regime loses control over events not because its popularity drops but because it makes some kind of major blunders that fail to maintain unity among the various elites on which the regime depends for its political monopoly. This could happen, for example, by grossly favoring one set of elites over others. Although the current leadership has demonstrated remarkable skill during the 2000s, the fact remains that the current system hinges on a tremendous degree of micromanagement of intra-elite relationships by Kremlin leaders.[21] This means that there are myriad opportunities for small mistakes, and small mistakes in such a system can rapidly magnify into large ones.[22] The existence of the Putin–Medvedev "tandem" arrangements make this scenario more likely, because it complicates elite coordination by creating uncertainty as to who exactly is and will be in charge and what relationships must be cultivated for success in the system. A result could be the coming to life of virtual parties and high levels of contestation, though representation would accordingly be weak due to the flimsy nature of these parties' claims to public support. As with the second scenario, there would also be a strong chance that whoever won the national battle would restore a single-pyramid system, but there would at least be a chance that this new contestation could put Russia on a path to a healthier party system as the "born again" parties seek public support to help their election efforts.

Conclusion

None of the optimistic scenarios sketched here is likely. But then again, no single scenario of any kind is likely: Given the complexity of possibilities, each of hundreds of individual scenarios has a fraction of a chance of occurring. Nevertheless, thinking as this chapter (and volume) has done helps us to consider possible pathways to reaching a healthy party system for Russia. In this case, Russia's best hope by 2020 is for its leaders to recognize a long-term personal (and national) interest in adopting reforms now, while they still wield immense political authority anchored in genuine popularity. Of course, this is also the time when leaders are often least amenable to adopting such reforms, because they feel themselves invincible and do not understand the fragility of their system. The lesson is typically learned too late, as with the leaders of Tunisia, Egypt, and Libya, not to mention Eduard Shevardnadze, Leonid Kuchma, Askar Akaev, and Kurmanbek Bakiev. In the long run, well beyond 2020, as Daniel Treisman observes in chapter 8, economic development and ties with the West are likely to erode some of the foundations of Russia's single-pyramid system, notably the extensive patron–client relations that are its essence, thereby promoting a healthier party system.[23] But for those who do not wish to wait, there is still hope.

Notes

1. Henry Hale, "Prezidentskii rezhim, revoliutsiia, i demokratiia: Sravnitel'nyi analiz Gruzii, Kyrgyzii, Rossii, i Ukrainy," *Pro et Contra*, no.1 (January–February 2008): 6–21.

2. Richard Hofstadter, *The Idea of a Party System* (Berkeley: University of California Press, 1969).

3. E.g., Barbara Geddes, "What Do We Know About Democratization After Twenty Years?" *Annual Review of Political Science* 2 (June 1999); Jason Brownlee, *Authoritarianism in the Age of Democratization* (New York: Cambridge University Press, 2007).

4. Steven Levitsky and Lucan A. Way, *Competitive Authoritarianism: Hybrid Regimes After the Cold War* (New York: Cambridge University Press, 2010).

5. For elaboration, see Henry E. Hale, *Why Not Parties in Russia? Democracy, Federalism, and the State* (New York: Cambridge University Press, 2006); and Russian-language book manuscript on parties, draft 2011.

6. M. N. Afanasiev, *Klientelizm i Rossiiskaia Gosudarstvennost'* (Moscow: Moscow Public Science Foundation, 1997); M. Steven Fish, *Democracy Derailed in Russia* (New York: Cambridge University Press, 2005).

7. Henry Hale, "Reformy i Razvitie Politicheskikh Partii," in *Federal'naia Reforma 2000–2004, T.2. Strategii, Instituty, Problemy*, edited by Nikolai Petrov (Moscow: Moskovskii Obshchestvennyi Nauchnyi Fond, 2005), 268–307.

8. Grigorii V. Golosov, *Political Parties in the Regions of Russia: Democracy Unclaimed* (Boulder, Colo.: Lynne Rienner, 2003); Hale, *Why Not Parties*.

9. Olga Shvetsova, "Resolving the Problem of Pre-Election Coordination: The 1999 Parliamentary Election as Elite Presidential 'Primary,'" in *Elections, Parties and the Future of Russia*, edited by Vicki Hesli and William Reisinger (New York: Cambridge University Press, 2003).

10. Hale, *Why Not Parties in Russia?*

11. Vladimir Gelman and Sergei Ryzhenkov, "Local Regimes, Sub-National Governance, and the 'Power Vertical' in Contemporary Russia," *Europe-Asia Studies*, vol. 63, no.3 (May 2011): 449–65; J. Paul Goode, *The Decline of Regionalism in Putin's Russia: Boundary Issues* (New York: Routledge, 2011).

12. Graeme B. Robertson, *The Politics of Protest in Hybrid Regimes: Managing Dissent in Post-Communist Russia* (New York: Cambridge University Press, 2011).

13. Vladimir Gelman, "Politicheskaia oppozitsiia v Rossii: vymiraiushchyi vid?" *Polis*, no. 4, 2004.

14. Alexandra Odynova, "Pirate Party Refused Registration Over Name," *Moscow Times*, March 22, 2011, 3.

15. Nikolai Petrov, Maria Lipman, and Henry E. Hale, "Overmanaged Democracy in Russia," Carnegie Paper 106, Carnegie Endowment for International Peace, February 2010.

16. RES Survey results for 2008; see table 13.1 for the source information.

17. Henry E. Hale and Timothy J. Colton, "What Makes Dominant Parties Dominant in Hybrid Regimes? The Unlikely Importance of Ideas in the Case of United Russia," revised edition of paper presented at the Annual Meeting of the American Association for the Advancement of Slavic Studies, Boston, November 12–15, 2009.

18. For example, Levada Center Press Release, "24.02.2010. Doverie politikam i partiiam," www.levada.ru/press/2010022401.html.

19. Timothy J. Colton and Henry E. Hale, "The Macro-Micro Puzzle of Partisan Development in Post-Soviet Russia," paper presented at the Annual Meeting of the Midwest Political Science Association, Chicago, April 2–5, 2009.

20. Andrew Wilson, *Virtual Politics: Faking Democracy in the Post-Soviet World* (New Haven, Conn.: Yale University Press, 2005).

21. Petrov, Lipman, and Hale, "Overmanaged Democracy."

22. See James C. Scott, *Seeing Like a State: How Certain Schemes to Improve the Human Condition Have Failed* (New Haven, Conn.: Yale University Press, 1998).

23. See also Herbert Kitschelt and Steven I. Wilkinson, "Citizen-Politician Linkages: An Introduction," in *Patrons, Clients, and Policies: Patterns of Democratic Accountability and Political Competition*, edited by Herbert Kitschelt and Steven I. Wilkinson (Cambridge: Cambridge University Press, 2007), 1–49.

CHAPTER FOURTEEN

SCENARIOS
for the EVOLUTION *of the* RUSSIAN POLITICAL PARTY SYSTEM

Boris Makarenko

The 2011 parliamentary elections have become an unavoidable point of the Russian political party system's bifurcation into two possible scenarios: "moderate liberalization," or "stagnation." A scenario-based study of the party system as a whole—and of the party system of today's Russia in particular—presents a special challenge, given that it is difficult to define both the dependent and the independent variables in the analysis of the parties. Like the lobsters in the mad quadrille from *Alice in Wonderland*, they long to be swapped (in Carroll's book, lobsters are changed, not swapped). There are three main reasons for this.

First, political party systems, to a greater extent than other political institutions, are at once both a *product* of the political system and its *creator*, which is especially true for the nascent political systems of the third-wave democracies.[1] In Russia, parties (in the literal sense—that is, not in the archaic sense of factions at court) played a limited, albeit very important, role in the establishment and development of the political regime. Today, the dominance of the executive branch in Russian politics is all the more undeniable. This turns the development of the party system into a variable that is dependent on the general evolution of the state system, and that is being instigated and directed from the Kremlin. If the Russian political system evolves toward democratization, then parties will gain the possibility of shifting from being the objects of policy to being the subjects; without this, democratization will simply not take place. Whether or not the country will develop policies that can take advantage of this opportunity, and whether this attempt will be successful, is another question.

Second, if we continue to examine the political party system as a variable that is dependent on other institutions (such as the executive branch, the electoral system and its enforcement, the balance between the executive and legislative branches, and the balance between Moscow and the regions), then a problem arises: Which of these things in particular should change, and to what extent? What combination of changes in each of these institutions could foster different scenarios of development in the party system?

The third main reason is the institutional nature of political parties: On the one hand, they are players in "big politics," consolidate the elite, forge the political agenda, promote leaders, and compete with other elite groups. On the other hand, parties are institutions of civil society, aggregating elements of the public interest. This brings us to the same question: Could parties, even in a favorable scenario, master the role of political actors, having retained and redefined the one function they somehow manage to carry out today—the expression of, if not the will, then at least the emotions and prejudices of their constituents?

This chapter explores these issues for the evolving Russian political party system under five themes.

What Kind of Life Have We Built for Ourselves?

The first theme is "What kind of life have we built for ourselves, and is there any escape from our current situation?" The genre of scenario forecasting requires that one begin by analyzing the current state of the research subject and perhaps even referring to the issue's historical background—though the sad story of the decline of Russian political parties has been described many times before.

Political parties emerged in Russia during a time of acute crisis of state legitimacy and socioeconomic reforms that divided both elites and the rest of society. For nearly a decade, the authorities carried out reforms, and moreover, they did so while the opposition constituted the majority of the legislature—a unique occurrence throughout all the postcommunist space. This led to a constitutional design with a weak Parliament and a limited role for political parties. Nevertheless, during this period the multiplicity of parties played a positive role. Through the parties and their parliamentary representation, a wide variety of groups from throughout the population were initiated into the realities of the new politics: those who were nostalgic for the Soviet regime (through the Communist Party, the KPRF), those who felt more at home with right-wing populist opposition with a nationalist tinge (through the Liberal Democratic Party of Russia [LDPR]), pro-Western liberals (through Yabloko and the forebears of the current Right Cause, Pravoe Delo), as well as the center-left supporters of paternalism (through a number of small left-wing parties).

With all the inconsistency of the institutional role of the State Duma in the 1990s, it became an instrument through with the country created a new pluralistic political community and filled (albeit not optimally) the legislative field. The "party of power," still small at the time, played its role in these processes, as did opposition parties of various persuasions and independent single-mandate deputies, who constituted a quarter to a third of all deputies during the first three convocations.

However, this configuration of the political space, in helping to overcome the crisis of the legitimacy of the state, gave rise to the complexity of the next stage. First, the "cost of reforms" that had been carried out without relying on a consensus of the public and elites was quite high. The relationship between the state and property that was formed in the first decade of the country's postcommunist development had an insufficient, waning legitimacy: The transfer of authority to any other political force created the risk of a large-scale revision, which in turn carried the threat of a complete destabilization both of the country's politics and of its economy. A correction in the relationship between state and property could only be accomplished by the strengthening of the party-independent federal center.

Moreover, the issue was one of a correction within strictly defined bounds—in particular, it was an issue of being isolated from the power of the "politicized oligarchs," of bringing about the "equal distancing" of big business, and of the weakening of the political autonomy of regional leaders. The distanced individuals themselves did not have the possibility of going over to the opposition parties, because the latter did not have a real chance to come to power—for the most part, they were antagonistically disposed toward political and business figures who had risen to power in the past decade. The reform of the Federation Council in 2000–2001, the "Yukos affair" (whose leaders had provided financial support to various parties) in 2003, and the abolition of the popular election of governors in 2004 brought to an absolute minimum the strategy of "placing one's eggs in different baskets"—that is, the diversification of party connections throughout big business and among regional leaders.

Thus, within the political and business elite, a single-channel system for the expression of political interests was created—through the "party of power," United Russia. This situation effectively persists to this day. For the purposes of a scenario-based prediction, it is useful to briefly note those features of the party system that are most important for understanding the possible alternative tracks of development.

The Party System

The party system arrived at its current state after December 2007: Spearheading the United Russia party list, Vladimir Putin for all intents and purposes—though nothing was ever said about this explicitly—strove for a result comparable to his own landslide victory in the 2004 presidential elections. In fact, he aimed to reproduce his presidential majority in the parliamentary elections, which are carried out under the proportional system. With regard to December 2007, such a decision is understandable, at least: The outgoing president wanted to get a "fresh legitimacy." However, the target of the regional authorities and of United Russia to get an outcome of "60 percent in favor" in the next regional elections of 2008–2009—without Putin, and moreover, during a period of economic crisis rather than of growth—finally finished off the already declining party pluralism. Competition among the parties gave way to competition among regional and district leaders to attain the highest result in favor of United Russia in their districts. Administrative resources reached their maximum, while the political resources of the opposition fell below a critical level; together, all opposition parties have fewer than one-third of all seats in the federal legislature, and in most regional legislatures. The effective number of parties,[2] according to the author's own calculations, for the majority of elections in the Russian Federation, fluctuates between just above two for electoral parties (that is, participants in the election) and just below two for parliamentary parties (those represented in the legislature). In other words, it has effectively ceased to be a multiparty system.

Main Messages

In such a party system, parties cannot fully carry out their functions, which are familiar to any normal party system. In some approximations they serve only to represent the interests of the voters who vote for the "main message" of the major parties. In simplified form, these "messages" might look like this: *support for the state, nostalgia for the Soviet past, populist protest against the state*, and *a sense of social injustice*. Other functions—in particular the struggle for power—are not performed by parties. The weakness of parties and their inability to serve the political elite—to aggregate interests, to manage the development and realization of political lines, to promote party and government leaders, to serve as a mechanism for the peaceful resolution of elite conflicts—severely limits the influx of promising politicians and other resources into opposition parties. This state of parties in the country's political system took shape during the last decade, and today is only getting worse.

Strong and Weak Parties

Weakness of opposition parties does not imply strength of the "party of power." Having attained an absolute majority in all parliaments, United Russia remains a "feature" of the executive branch (see the explication of the third theme below), which does not negate the fact there is real support for the "party of power" from a significant portion of the population.

Several factors prevent one from considering this system to simply be a dry run with no chance of success: Parties are actually performing the function of representing interests; society has become used to the legitimization of government by means of the election process; and finally, there is the modernization message espoused by the Russian leadership, which at least rhetorically suggests the democratization of the country, albeit slowly and through a process of evolution.[3]

The Development of the Party System

The second theme, to quote Anna Akhmatova, is "If only you knew to what trash gives rise. . . ." When considering the development of the party system, one must bear in mind that none of the existing parties is capable of independent, high-quality development. Here it is useful to briefly consider each of the main parties.

United Russia: Membership and Career Advancement

Despite the fact that United Russia enjoys substantial electoral support, that membership in the party is a factor of career *advancement*, and that its members include a large number of high-status and professional politicians, the "party of parliamentary majority" has never ceased to be a feature of the executive branch. Key decisions in United Russia, whether they concern personnel or policy decisions, are made outside the party itself. If the party is able to develop and defend any independent political line at all, then it is the line to "protect" its dominant position and resist fundamental reforms in the political system. Only when instructions were passed down from the top did the party adopt laws to ensure that the opposition would at least have some sort of existence and take steps toward maintaining a minimal level of vitality in "internal party life" (for example, participation in debates and primaries, and the work of parties' political clubs).

The KPRF and LDPR

The KPRF and LDPR are parties without a future, as their existence depends upon a single factor. For the KPRF, this consists of maintaining support among the "nostalgic" and not reproducible elderly electorate, for the sake of whom the KPRF has consistently refused to undertake internal reforms. It is these voters to which the "orthodox" wing of the party holds on, squeezing out all the "reformers" from the upper echelons of the party hierarchy. With the reduction in the numbers of this voting base that should take place over the course of one or two electoral cycles, the party will face the problem of undertaking a radical restructuring of its electoral niche. This process will be significantly hampered by the conservatism and ideological intransigence of a significant part of the party's core. Furthermore, there is very limited space in which to maneuver: In the center-left field, there are other players (in particular, A Just Russia, Spravedlivaya Rossiya), while a withdrawal into "leftism" or "patriotism" does not guarantee the communists enough electoral support; their "turn" away from communism to nationalism cannot be sharp, because they will need to preserve the remnants of the current electoral core that "don't get" the transformation of Zyuganovists into Rogozinists.

The future of the LDPR depends on the political longevity of Vladimir Zhirinovsky: The right-wing populist party with a nationalist "tinge" certainly has a right to exist, but this electorate and electoral core, selected "on the basis of sponsorship," has nothing to hold it together besides the unique phenomenon of Zhirinovsky himself. Even today, according to the polls of the Russian Public Opinion Research Center (VCIOM), without Zhirinovsky the party would lose about half its voters,[4] while the "case of Malyshkov," the candidate from the LDPR in the 2004 presidential elections who received a paltry 2 percent of the votes, suggests that this proportion will prove to be even greater.

A Just Russia

A Just Russia was established as a "spare party of power," and in the electoral field it is closer to United Russia than to the KPRF. However, any influx of real politicians into the party was limited by the rigid position of the bureaucracy (both regional and federal) that resisted "mainstream" competition.

In fact, it is precisely such competition between nonantagonistic political programs and politicians that can form the basis for real pluralism. No matter how the party was conceived "at the top," its real political asset is the people who are completely compatible with the current political regime but have not been included in the "party of power" either because of an inability to "march in step" or because of a serious conflict with the authorities on the federal—or more often, the regional—level. The party's stated platform for social justice is potentially elastic: It can accommodate European-style social democrats, social liberals, and populists who are not pleased with the fact that a single force has monopolized power in the country and that it is closed to criticism. But today, A Just Russia is not ready to exist in the context of pluralism due to its insufficient weight, both in terms of elites and the electorate.

Right Cause and Yabloko

The liberal parties Right Cause (Pravoe Delo) and Yabloko have not demonstrated an ability to escape from a state of deep crisis. In addition to the traditionally cited reasons—the crisis of leadership, the lack of new, striking personalities, and the authorities' hostile relationship to the parties—it is necessary to note the most important: Although the number of liberal-minded citizens in Russia is not small (various polls give numbers ranging from 10 to 20 percent), only for an insignificant portion of these do the values of liberalism and freedom play a "system-forming role," serving as the driving motivation behind their electoral choice. Today, people of this persuasion are more independently oriented, believe in neither politics nor elections, and are generally not inclined to "play these games." The liberal parties themselves are unable to build a coalition or to escape beyond the confines of their narrow right-wing liberal and social-liberal niche.

Patriots of Russia

The Patriots of Russia (Patrioty Rossii) party deserves a minimum of attention in this context: The party can attain only "isolated points" of success on the regional level, where it leases its flag in franchise to any local elite group.

Factors of Change—or of Hope?

The third theme is "Factors of change, or factors of hope?" The inertial development of the current situation is unlikely to continue, for several reasons.

Current Shifts in the Party System

The current party system cannot remain in a state of equilibrium. Without "external influences," the administrative machine (the regional authorities and United Russia) are set on a course of constant expansion. Even the limited "manual control" of party politics by the federal center—that is, with regard to measures creating minimal guarantees of propagation for the "legal opposition" and the installation, initiated from above, of all four parliamentary parties into regional parliaments in March 2010—was perceived by the nomenklatura of United Russia as unjustified defeatism and provoked a strong emotional response, as evidenced by the discussions of the party-based clubs of United Russia, for example.[5]

Recently, a trend toward soft control of administrative resources has become noticeable in the Kremlin's politics, though for now such resources are still leveraged in regional elections. If in the 2011 federal elections, in the name of ensuring the "continuity of government," the scenario of the 2007 Duma campaign is repeated and a similar result is achieved (that is, a constitutional majority for United Russia, and no competition), then the stagnation of the party system will become practically inevitable. We will have to wait five years until the next "bifurcation" in the federal elections, and with high probability, it will be affected by the approach of a new operation to ensure the "continuity of government" in the 2018 presidential elections.

Thus, the 2011 parliamentary elections have become an unavoidable point of bifurcation into two possible scenarios: "moderate liberalization," or "stagnation" (see below).

A Distributive Coalition

A "secret to success"—but of course, not the only one—in building a monocentric regime in Russia lies in the nature of the elite coalition that was created against the backdrop of the long-standing growth of state revenues from the rising price of hydrocarbons. In essence, the regime is a *distributive coalition* that has been steadily expanding for several years, and that was attractive both for paternalistically oriented voters (and this is the absolute majority of Russians) and for elite players seeking to "lean on the state" even under terms in which they are integrated into a tightly controlled "power vertical."

However, the financial crisis is impeding the further construction of such a power vertical: The government has been forced to choose between investment programs and fulfilling its social obligations, to reduce its reserve funds, and to make unpopular decisions (such as raising utility tariffs and the transportation tax). One can assume that, in the future, the "distributive coalition" will be forced to accept a less vertical character and to demand the formation of "social pacts" with the economically and politically active part of society. This could lead to a relative increase in the autonomy of political actors within United Russia (first and foremost among the single-mandate deputies), as well as create an incentive for a less confrontational attitude on the part of the "party of power" toward its opponents—first and foremost, toward A Just Russia, which attracts what are, by and large, "mainstream" political figures.

Are Parties Necessary?

But are parties necessary for society? The data from sociological surveys, in particular from the Levada Center, reveal a number of significant nuances of the demand for pluralism in Russian society (see tables 14.1 and 14.2). For Russians, the phrases "opposition to government" and "opposition parties that seriously affect the life of the country" are not synonyms, as one would expect, but are different concepts. In their view, since the beginning of this decade the "opposition to government" in the country has weakened substantially (from 53 percent who acknowledged its existence at the turn of this century to approximately 40 percent in the last six years), but at the same time, the share of those who claim that "significant opposition parties" are present in the country even increased slightly, from approximately 30 percent in the first half of this decade to about 40 percent in recent years.

At the same time, the demand both for "an opposition to government" and for the presence of influential parties and movements has changed: First of all, it has grown since the beginning of the decade; and second, in recent years the portion of those claiming a "need" for an opposition exceeded at all times the share of those stating an actual presence of real

TABLE 14.1 *Demand for Opposition to the Government,*
2000–2009 (percent)

SURVEY QUESTION	2000	2004	2005	2006	2008	2009
Is there currently political opposition to the government in Russia?						
Definitely yes / probably yes	53	42	41	37	46	39
Definitely no / probably no	25	38	35	39	35	38
Does Russia currently need political opposition to the government?						
Definitely yes / probably yes	47	61	63	56	62	57
Definitely no / probably no	29	17	14	20	21	19

Source: "Rossiyane o politicheskoi oppositsii" (Russians on the political opposition), press release from Levada Center, July 28, 2009, www.levada.ru/press/2009072802.print.html.

TABLE 14.2 *Demand for Opposition Parties, 2002–2009 (percent)*

SURVEY QUESTION	2002	2004	2005	2007	2009
Does Russia have significant opposition parties and movements?					
Yes	31	30	30	41	38
No	42	47	47	33	47
Does Russia need or not need public movements and parties that would be in the opposition and that could have a serious impact on the life of the country?					
Needs	56	66	61	66	71
Does not need	24	21	25	20	16

Source: "Politicheskaya oppozitsiya v obshchestvennom mnenii" (Political opposition in public opinion), press release from Levada Center, October 23, 2009, www.levada.ru/press/2009102306.print.html.

opposition parties in Russia. The demand for such parties has risen significantly, and in 2009 consisted of 71 percent of respondents.

The apparent contradiction has a logical explanation. On the one hand, the majority of Russians in the 2000s had gained confidence in the highest authority and clearly did not want to change it (this is with regard not to the personalities of the presidents but rather to the majority's preference for a representative of the current government over any of the opposition figures in taking the role of president). As a result, many of our fellow citizens accept the official picture of the alignment of political forces in which the opposition parties are considered to be "influential" (in 2007, the number of those who held such views even exceeded the number of supporters of the opposing point of view). On the other hand, however, a feeling of a "lack of pluralism" is growing alongside the consolidation of the current government; an increasing portion of Russians are speaking out about the necessity both of having "an opposition in general," as well as of having influential parties.

A significant and growing part of Russian society—undoubtedly including government supporters—is recognizing the necessity of a political opposition. However, they understand the opposition not as an antagonist to the current government that seeks to take its place at the helm but rather as a sort of counterweight, a limiter, and a critic (and possibly even a whistleblower)—in other words, as an opponent, but a fundamentally "constructive" one. This explains the apparent contradiction between the dominance of the progovernment sentiments and the statements regarding the necessity of a "strong opposition." The latter is credited with strength not in the struggle for power but rather in the opposition to it on the Duma floor. Qualiative sociological studies (focus groups and in-depth interviews) give approximately the same picture.[6]

Thus, the nature of Russian society's demand for political pluralism is inconsistent. On the one hand, the high level of confidence in government encourages the majority of Russians to recognize and accept the current state of affairs (this is evidenced by the growth in the ratings of United Russia, the leading party force in the country, as described below), while on the other hand, the parties in existence today do not fully meet the demand for the presence of a real and influential opposition—that is, the available "supply" in the political market does not entirely correspond to the demand for pluralism.

In the surveys of the Levada Center, which have been conducted regularly since 1999, the ratio of supporters and opponents of a multiparty system in recent years is approximately 50 to 40 percent (10 percent do not have an opinion) (table 14.3).[7] However, a definite shift took place in 2009: The proportion of supporters of a multiparty system grew to 68 percent, while the share of opponents fell to 21 percent.[8]

TABLE 14.3 *How Many Political Parties Are Necessary in Russia Today? (percent)*

SURVEY QUESTION	2001, IX	2004, IV	2004, IX	2005, X	2006, VII	2007, IV	2008, VI	2009, X
One strong ruling party	34	34	34	38	32	30	32	17
Two or three big parties	41	41	44	39	42	46	45	59
Many relatively small parties	4	8	6	4	5	7	8	9
In general, we do not need political parties	9	7	6	7	7	6	6	4
It is difficult to answer	13	11	9	12	14	13	10	11

Note: The roman numerals following the dates refer to the months the surveys were conducted.

Source: *Obshchestvennoe mnenie—2009: Ezhegodnik* (Public opinion—2009: Yearbook), (Moscow: Levada Center, 2009), 99.

Limitations of the "Vertical" Model

The "vertical" model of the party system, with limited pluralism and opportunities for discussion—not to mention the possibility of influencing the policymaking process "from the bottom"—increasingly contradicts the sentiments and interests of the politically active part of society. This concerns the "new middle class" and, more precisely, that part of it that is dissatisfied with the lack of "social mobility," bureaucratic and police pressure on business, the lack of opportunities to influence the "political machine," and the archaic style of communication between the state and society. In essence, this amounts to a "nonpartisan protest." These people are not ready to vote for the "party of power," but at the same time, they do not see any of the existing opposition parties as representing their interests. As is shown in a recent study of the "middle middle" and "upper middle" classes, part of this group maintains a pragmatic external loyalty to the political leadership, and part is oriented toward the opposition, but the common theme for the overwhelming majority of this stratum is an open cynicism in their perception of the political sphere and a lack of belief that the bureaucracy is able to listen to and understand their aspirations.[9] How ever, as is shown in the same study, the themes of conformism, of protest, of the desire for more democracy, and of fear of the loss of stability are so intertwined even within this stratum that no form of quantitative sociology is able to give an intelligible picture of just how widespread such sentiments are. Even such a shock as the 2008–2009 global financial crisis only highlighted these sentiments a bit more clearly, but did not lead to the emergence of new social movements.

By the admission of United Russia party members,[10] their party is experiencing serious difficulties in communicating with these groups of citizens.

Such a situation is anomalous even for regimes with limited political pluralism: It is usual for them to restrict the "leftists"[11]—the Communists, socialists, trade unions, and the working class—in order to allow the establishment to develop and implement its strategy. In Russia, the situation with pluralism is "turned on its head": The favorable economic conditions that prevailed in the middle of this decade allowed the authorities to rely precisely on the paternalistic "lower classes" and allow the isolation (or self-isolation) of the active minority. When abundance is replaced by the "postcrisis situation" and the government declares a strategy for modernization, such an inverted support structure becomes dangerous; the state loses control over the "new opposition" and does not include the active minority in the political coalition for modernization.

The future of the Russian party system depends on how this contradiction is resolved: Will the policy of rejecting the active minority continue, and if not, will the "party of power" be able to attract them—or will they find their own political representation through another party structure or structures?

Scenario Bifurcations in the Evolution of the Party System

The fourth theme is the scenario bifurcations in the evolution of the party system. Looking at the situation today, it is extremely difficult to predict along the lines of which scenario the party system will develop: The "linear" or "inertial" scenarios of development seem primitive; they amount to a general form of "stagnation," turning into either a scenario of "authoritarianism" or "collapse" (or successively from "authoritarianism" into "collapse"), and finally, the "miracle" scenario—a pivotal shock to the development of the party system.

The "miracle" scenario should be excluded immediately. Even in the event that the will to undertake substantial liberalization appears "from the top," neither the existing parties nor civil society (see the second theme above) can effectively engage in political life. But one needs to express a reservation: Liberalization in Russia is necessary and even possible, but full-fledged political parties can be only an "intermediate product" of this system.

"Stagnation" is the most likely scenario: The given party system is convenient for the executive branch, because it secures it with absolute dominance not only over the legislative branch but also over the entire system of political representation. The degree of loyalty of the registered political parties is extremely high, because the opposition fears that its already extremely limited existence will be limited even further, while the "party of power" depends too heavily on the resources (administrative, financial, and public) that are concentrated at the federal center or with the Kremlin-appointed governors. At the same time, in such circumstances, any opposition or alternative political movements are pushed out either "onto the street" or onto the Internet, which will be the only available means for them to communicate (especially through the blogs) and mobilize (for example, a gathering of participants in drivers' protests organized through social media). Street-based and Internet activity today annoys the authorities and provokes strong reactions within their ranks; there are crackdowns on the "Dissenters' Marches," unsubstantiated accusations against the opposition, and attempts to use legislation to increasingly restrict the freedom of public protest (for example, the establishment of permit requirements even for single picketers, and attempts to tighten the regulation of the Internet). Although this reaction is very awkward at times, given the current small scale of alternative political activities, the government considers such costs acceptable. At the same time, the current party system to a minimally sufficient degree reflects the structure of mass preferences and enables the creation of a "facade of a multiparty system" that the government, the ruling party, and the experts and journalists that are loyal to it declare is "fully formed and established" (see the remarks of the president in his Address to the Federal Assembly, the interview of

Boris Gryzlov with *Gazeta.ru*, and the reports of Dmitry Badovsky, Mikhail Vinogradov, and Dmitry Orlov.)[12]

Such a "multiplicity of parties" can be maintained only in a regime under "manual control" that does not allow the logic of administrative resources to "put the squeeze on" a loyal opposition and leave in parliaments only one opposition party "required by law," and preferably with a minimal strength. This is a state of stagnation. The cost for the government of maintaining the current status quo depends on the strength of resistance not so much from "within" the existing party system as much as from alternative forms of political action. If it grows to a larger scale, then the authorities can make a move either toward partial liberalization or toward a further restriction of pluralism, cutting off all alternative channels of collective action and restraining the "legal" opposition within the current narrow framework. The more powerful the alternative protest grows, the greater the risk of increasing authoritarianism.

Strictly speaking, rational scenario planning should end at this point. There are two ways out from authoritarianism: either through a new attempt at liberalization, or through "collapse" or "revolution." But given such a course of events—for which, among other things, it is difficult to define a time frame—all or the majority of objective or subjective factors of the preceding period cease to apply. Institutions and parties cease to be "simulations," but this does not mean they will comply with the letter or spirit of democratic constitutional design.

It is rationally possible to make only the following assumptions:

- "Revolution" in such a scenario cannot be "colored" or "orange." That assumes a far greater degree of political pluralism than is present in today's Russia (and most likely, than will be present in tomorrow's, either): "Color" revolutions take place where the electoral potential of the opposition is comparable to the strength of the "party of power." In those places where the opposition attempted not to defeat the authorities in elections but rather to "compete" with them (for example, where they challenged the victory of the president in the first round, as happened in Georgia and Armenia in 2008), the attempt at "orange action" fails—the "street" does not have enough motivation to persevere.

- A military coup of the sort seen in Latin America, where the military takes power in order to eventually give it to the strongest party in future elections, is also impossible. First of all, the Russian military does not possess the political thinking and ambition (and thank goodness—otherwise the risk of military coups would be too high at every moment of modern Russian history); and second, there is no one to whom to pass authority after the fact. The elite does not have the skill to undertake independent collective action not "ordered" from above.[13]

- Consequently, the revolutionary scenario in Russia's future is possible only in either "hard" form, where it converts latent and soft authoritarianism into a hard form, or as a "collapse," or, in Alexander Herzen's words, a "senseless and merciless Russian rebellion." After this, with an unpredictable time lag, a new (but certainly not predictable) liberalization will take place.

The Possibilities and Limits of Partial Liberalization

The fifth theme is the possibilities and limits of partial liberalization. The scenario of partial liberalization is also difficult to predict; however, it is the only one that gives some sort of hope for the positive evolution of the party system. For this scenario to be realized, the logic briefly explained in the following subsections should be implemented.

The Role of the Executive Branch

The executive branch should recognize the necessity of changing the nature of the coalition and should step in to support it. Specifically, it should come to the conclusion that ignoring the "active minority" and the "new opposition" is dangerous, and that in the long term it could be useful to incorporate these trends into the political mainstream and create a "coalition for modernization." It is very difficult for the leaders in the Kremlin to make such a decision; it contradicts all the logic of past years and requires revitalizing their political bargaining skills, and, more important, requires greater openness and equality of opportunity in electoral campaigns, which would most likely result in a decrease in support for United Russia to a level nominally defined at 50 percent.

The Changing Logic of Parliamentary Elections

The situation described above effectively means that the logic of parliamentary elections should once again break with the logic of presidential elections, as was the case in Russia until 2007. The presidential elections in the foreseeable future (not only in 2012, but also most likely in 2018) will continue to have low levels of competition; defending his position from the opposition party nominees, the "Kremlin candidate" will have a 100 percent chance of winning. At the same time, in 2012, for the first time in Russian history, the candidacy of the future election winner will depend not on the will of one person (a full analogue of the Mexican "political rite" of *el dedazo*, where the president points a finger at his successor[14]) but on the agreement of the president and the prime minister—that is, it will depend on at least two people. This requires their agreement concerning a number of other characteristics of the country's direction and of the configuration of the political regime—that is, what is de facto a sort of "proto-institutionalization" of these characteristics.

In particular, this concerns the definition of the role of the "party of power" in the future political system. The "tandemocrats" will search for a way out of this contradiction: On the one hand, they are guided by the inertial desire to "secure stability" (this wish, according to Juan Linz, is one of the innate deficiencies of presidential power[15]) with the help of the comfortable majority of the party of power at all levels; on the other hand, given the aim of advancing the modernization of the country, the need to give the party system greater flexibility and variety grows increasingly evident.

The decision to liberalize is further complicated by a reverse-chronological progression (a "chronological inversion"): The party system will become one of the parameters of the next president's regime, but its fate will be decided by parliamentary elections that will take place earlier than the presidential ones—and moreover, with high probability, Vladimir Putin will once again lead United Russia in the elections. What configuration the "tandem" will take in the next electoral cycle and who is more capable of taking on the risk of liberalization—the "conservative Putin" or the "liberal Medvedev"—is an important point of scenario bifurcation that today does not admit of an obvious solution.

The Evolutionary Steps Toward Moderate Liberalization

The choice in favor of "moderate liberalization"—if it is made—will be expressed in a set of evolutionary steps, which could include

- weakening administrative resources for elections and effectively abolishing "target figures" for the outcome of the "party of power";
- excluding from electoral law regulations that openly "play into the hands" of the party of power: reducing the cutoff barrier to 5 percent, discouraging the practice of "engines," abolishing the method of "Imperiali quotas" used to allocate seats in regional elections,[16] and simplifying the processes and procedures for registering parties and candidates in elections;
- changing the law enforcement practice in elections so as to enable the opposition to control the electoral process. It is useful to note that in all three directions in the last two years, definitive steps have been taken, but they could not substantially change the situation, because they either expected to be applied under "manual control" (compare the situation of some limitation of administrative resources in the March 2010 regional elections) or they were too soft in nature (for instance, providing one or two seats to parties that received from 5 to 7 percent of votes);
- repealing or weakening the informal but rigorously observed bans on the introduction of "mainstream" figures from the opposition parties, having financial support of parties that is independent of the Kremlin, and allowing the opposition access to federal television channels, and so on; and
- restoring the proper parliamentary procedure of review and passage of bills, that is, effectively turning Parliament into a "place for discussion"—in particular, giving real meaning to the newly established constitutional norms on the regular reports of the government to the Parliament, both at the federal and regional levels.

The Effects of These Measures

For the party system, the effects of these measures would not be radical. First of all, if the first stage of such a scenario is realized (which might last one to two six-year "presidential" cycles), political pluralism would be limited by the "parliamentary platform," with the dominance of the presidential party and more active and procedurally fair activity on the part of the opposition. This, among other things, would create incentives for the parties (both for the "party of power" and for the opposition parties) to compete for the electorates of the "new opposition" and the "active minority."

Second, United Russia would remain the dominant party for at least the short to medium term (for the next six to twelve years). This is not necessarily a deficiency or shortcoming of the party system; the dominant or predominant (in the classification of Sartori[17]) party is a frequent phenomenon in transitional and modernizing societies. The problem is that in order to perform this role, United Russia must become a real party, with greater autonomy in decisionmaking, "internal party democracy," and a real (and not simply stated) responsibility for their actions. Such an evolution of the "party of power" is the first necessary condition for the development of a party system in Russia.

Third, the remaining parties must demonstrate an ability to use the "partial liberalization" to attract promising elite figures into their ranks and learn to formulate and defend their political program in competition with the "party of power." That being said, the competition should be real—that is, it should not only have a real impact on forming the policies and ensuring the accountability of the executive branch but should also remain within the consensus regarding the basic foundations of the country's political and economic life.[18] In other words, a "limited uncertainty" should be produced in politics, which Philip Schmitter and T. L. Karl called the main principle of a functioning democratic society.[19]

Fourth, this evolution of the party system would bring about a change in the role of the legislative branch in the system of checks and balances, as well as in the federal structure of the state. However, forecasting these movements lies outside the scope of this chapter.

Of the existing "nonpower parties," A Just Russia has the biggest window of opportunity in this scenario; its "starting kit" of elite resources is better than that of other parties. There is a hypothetical niche for the liberal parties in this environment, but everything depends on whether they can overcome their internal defects in order to take advantage of it. The KPRF and LDPR in any scenario run into the problems described above concerning their dependence on one resource—on an aging electorate in the first case, and on a leader who is not growing younger in the second case.

In the event that such a scenario is successfully realized, the next two parliamentary election cycles will be a time of growth and formation for the party system, which in ten years will require a new restructuring, because by that time at least three questions will have arisen:

- In the new party system, will the dominance of one party be preserved, or will the system become fundamentally more competitive?
- What parties will inherit the niches currently filled by the KPRF and the LDPR—will these parties themselves, having undergone a fundamental "rebranding," survive, or will there be new players?
- How will the niche of liberal voters be filled in the party system?

Notes

1. A. Gryzmala-Busse, *Rebuilding Leviathan: Party Competition and State Exploitation in Post-Communist Democracies* (Cambridge: Cambridge University Press, 2008).

2. The effective number of parties is a political science indicator that assesses the aggregate political heft of parties participating in elections (the effective number of electoral parties) and in parliamentary activities (the effective number of parliamentary parties). See M. Laakso and R. Taagepera, "Effective Number of Parties: A Measure with Application to West Europe," *Comparative Political Studies*, no. 12 (1979). It shows the degree of real, and not formal, party pluralism in the country:

$$N = \frac{1}{\sum p_i^2}$$

where p_i is the share of votes (seats) received by the ith party in elections or during the distribution of seats in parliament.

3. See, for example, D. Medvedev, "Rossiya, vpered!" (Onward, Russia!), http://news. kremlin.ru/news/5413: "As in most democratic states, the leaders in the political struggle will be the parliamentary parties periodically replacing each other in the government. Parties and their coalitions will form federal and regional executive authorities (and not vice versa), and nominate candidates to the post of the head of state, as well as nominating regional leaders and local authorities. They will have long-standing experience with civilized political competition."

4. "LDPR bez Zhirinovskogo: Est li u nee budushchee?" (The LDPR without Zhirinovsky: Is there a future?), Press Release 1394, VCIOM, December 21, 2009, http://old.vciom. ru/arkhiv/tematicheskii-arkhiv/item/single/12945.html.

5. Center for Social-Conservative Politics, "TsSKP: Stenogramma zasedaniya politicheskikh klubov partii 'Edinaya Rossiya' na temu 'Actualnaya povestka diskussii politklubov' v Tsentre sotsialno-konservativnoi politiki" (The CSKP: A transcript of the meeting of the political clubs of the United Russia Party on the subject of "the current agenda of political club discussions" at the Center for Social-Conservative Politics), March 28, 2010, www.cscp.ru/clauses/6/397/c/4238.

6. B. Makarenko, *Partiinaya sistema Rossii v 2008–2009* (Russia's Party System 2008–2009) (Moscow: INION, 2009), 17.

7. "Politicheskaya oppozitsiya v Rossii" (Political opposition in Russia), press release, Levada Center, July 31, 2008, www.levada.ru/press/2008073102.print.html.

8. Levada Center, *Obshchestvennoe mnenie—2009: Ezhegodnik* (Public opinion—2009: Yearbook) (Moscow: Levada Center, 2009), 99.

9. L. Grigoriev, B. Makarenko, et al., *Middle Class after the Crisis. Express-Analysis of Political and Economic Positions* (Moscow: MAKS-Press, 2010).

10. Center for Social-Conservative Politics, "TsSKP: Stenogramma zasedaniya politicheskikh klubov partii 'Edinaya Rossiya.'"

11. G. O'Donnell, "On the State, Democratization, and Some Conceptual Problems: A Latin American View with Glances at Some Postcommunist Countries," *World Development* 21, no. 8 (August 1993): 1355–69.

12. See, for example, D. Orlov, D. Badovsky, and M. Vinogradov, *Ekvator ili Rubikon? Analiticheskii doklad* (The Equator or the Rubicon? An analytical report) (Moscow: Agency for Political and Economic Communication, 2010); and D. Orlov and D. Konyaev, "Rossiiskaya partiinaya sistema: Deistvuyushchie igroki, aktualnye vyzovy i vybory—2011" (The Russian Party System: Active Players, Current Challenges, and the 2011 Elections), in *Slaboe zveno i novaya strategiya Kremlya* (The Weakest Link and the Kremlin's New Strategy), www.regnum.ru/news/1318646.html.

13. In a similar situation half a century ago, there were Nasser's "Free Officers" in Egypt, who were honestly attempting to give power to any party that could carry out full-fledged agrarian reform. However, by a process of elimination, the Egyptian soldiers concluded that there was no one to undertake modernizing reforms but themselves—the landlords and compradors were not interested in them.

14. V. Gelman, "Perspektivy dominiruyushchei partii v Rossii" (Prospects for the dominant party in Russia), *Pro et Contra* 10, no. 4 (July–August 2006): 62–71.

15. J. Linz, "The Perils of Presidentialism," *Journal of Democracy* 17, no. 1 (Winter 1990): 51–69.

16. "Imperial division" is the increasingly widely applied method of allocating deputies' seats in regional elections, which favors large parties. On the effects of its application, see N. Shalaev, "Opyt ispolzovaniya systemy delitelei Imperiali v regionakh Rossii" (Experience using the system of Imperial Division in Russia's regions, *Rossiiskoe elektoralnoe obozrenie*, no. 1 (2009): 4–12.

17. G. Sartori, *Parties and Party Systems*, vol. 1 (Cambridge: Cambridge University Press, 1976).

18. I. Yu. Yurgens, ed., *Demokratiya: Razvitie rossiiskoi modeli* (Democracy: The development of the Russian model) (Moscow: Ekon-Inform, 2008), 33.

19. Philip C. Schmitter and T. L. Karl, "What Democracy Is . . . and Is Not," *Journal of Democracy* 2, no. 3 (Summer 1991): 39–52.

STATE

PART IV

the EXCESSIVE ROLE *of a* WEAK RUSSIAN STATE

Nikolay Petrov

The Russian state is big but weak. Its weakness is related to its internal ineffectiveness and omnipresent facade, given the inadequacy of its legal institutions, the functions of which have become "privatized" and are used to further individual, group, or corporate interests. Finally, the state is weak because of overcentralization, whereby the center of gravity during all important decisionmaking processes rests at the top and the entire system becomes sluggish.

The Russian state system is afflicted by administrative paralysis—it can only stand in place by resting on raw returns. To move it in any direction, it is necessary to restore its lost ability to "walk." First of all, it is the ability to arrive at decisions accounting for the priorities of major interest groups—including corporate and regional, coordinating the actions of the different blocks of state machinery, and establishing two-way communication channels with citizens to ensure stability and flexibility through the transfer of authority to the lowest possible hierarchical level.

The viability of the current Russian state is determined by how much one can live without moving—in other words, when the recovery of lost functions becomes an urgent necessity. I believe that in the near future, one can expect significant adjustments or even a reversal of trends.

Evolution of the State

The general trend of the state's evolution in recent years has been the "primitivization" of the government's machinery, from which the "extra" parts have been ejected. As a result, the machinery has been losing maneuverability and flexibility, because it is locked in under a single mode of motion—downhill on a straight road—with a single driver. One of the consequences of "primitivization" is awkwardness, so long as separate facilities are built, instead of generic units. The institutional logic for management, especially when determined by framing legislation, is unlikely to offer anything else.

In recent years, while the state system has been simplified, the circumstances in which it functions have become more complicated, especially with the onset of the global financial and economic crisis. This has led to a widening gap between the system's capabilities and what it requires from the external environment. Until now, faced with increasingly complex problems, the system responds through manual adjustments, but this cannot and will not last.

With the arrival of Vladimir Putin as president, the government became more centralized and unitary. However, whereas during his first term (2000–2003) this had a positive impact, in the last few years its effect has been the opposite. If at first the pendulum of relations between the center and regions rested in the middle—then, in the previous period, it swung too far in the direction of the regions—in recent times it has again swung strongly to the center. The dominance of the regions over the center extended beyond the rational framework and reached the limit of the conceivable, leaving behind even the Soviet Union's centralization. Now there is only one way to go—backward.

The State's Excessive Role

The excessive role of the state has been entrenched in Russia throughout its history and continues, with the exception that in the current situation, many government functions have been practically privatized by bureaucrats. After the collapse of the Soviet Union, the Russian government was drastically weakened, which resulted in the partial strengthening of autonomous social processes. But in recent years, there has been a steady increase in state ownership in various spheres of society and the country as a whole. The state, acting through bureaucrats, has subjugated political parties, has tightened control over civil society groups, and has taken advantage of the recent crisis to increase its control over big business.

Since the state has assumed the customary role of the all-powerful sovereign and universal moderator, its dominance has been considered a given and has not encountered any resistance. During the 2000s, the centralized state, through bureaucrats, has steadily expanded the scope of its authority—including both breadth, in various spheres of social life, and depth, to regional and municipal levels. In the absence of control not only from the bottom, in the form of democratic accountability, but also from above, as under the Soviet model, the bureaucracy has become "disengaged." Now, only the bureaucracy can say with complete legitimacy, "The state—that's me!"

The "Primitivization" of the Regulation of the State

Not only has the quantity of the state machinery changed but also its quality. Alongside the alignment of many corporate and departmental vehicles, especially security enforcement, there was a weakening of party-administrative horizontal constraints. In the USSR, two major elements of reinforcement supported the entire structure: the Communist Party and administration in the main position, and KGB officials, who did not let the party completely monopolize power and "privatize" it, that is, use the power exclusively for group and personal interests—the interests of the system notwithstanding. In the case of a nontransparent government and an uncontrollable society, this system of two fiercely competing "verticals" was the Soviet system's version of "checks and balances," which prevented the entire structure from shaking. At the same time, the highest echelons of the central party and administrative apparatus exercised tight control over the powerful. In the 1990s, the whole state apparatus greatly weakened, and was strengthened only with Putin's arrival, based on the secret police and more broadly, the power of its constituents. The party-administrative apparatus had lost its former autonomy and was practically absorbed by the political police, or Cheka. The Cheka (from "Extraordinary Commission to fight against Counterrevolution"), was established in 1917 and is a predecessor of the Soviet KGB or current FSB – State Security Service, and thus the Chekists are those who work in the Cheka-KGB-FSB.

The weakening of internal tension in a system, along with the liquidation of one of its two supporting rods, leads to the weakening of the structure as a whole. Without overt, outside competition, the sharp reduction of internal competition inevitably leads to a rapid and sustained degradation of the system.

Another consequence of the new configuration of power is a sudden decline in external control over the observance of rules, which has been made especially dangerous by the legal relativism of the "Chekist" verticals. Internal corporate rules and regulations (military and paramilitary, with a rigid line of command, undivided authority, "the organization charter of internal services," acting in a specific capacity in the state machinery) become the norm for the entire machinery. This structural insufficiency of the system, which now appears on all hierarchical levels, will become even more integral with the continuing deterioration of the regions.

The Dominance of Security Enforcement

The Russian security enforcement units, first of all, represent an independent set of interests; second, they act as the tool for the achievement of the goals of other elite groups; and third, they fulfill state duties, that is, the coming together of fundamental groups for the sake of common interests. Earlier, in the context of decentralization, security enforcement resources were more fragmented, and their use was more balanced. Now, these resources are the skeleton of a system with excessive verticals and underdeveloped horizontals. And the large and growing investment in the security enforcement verticals will not lead to the strengthening of the system as a whole.[1]

Internally, the security enforcement units are not homogeneous—they are not so much a single corporation but instead form an association of several corporations that are functionally close to each other. The Federal

Security Service (FSB) forms the core and the inner shell—and thus other security structures fall under its formal or informal control. The outer shell is formed by civilian structures, whose leadership is strengthened by the representatives of the FSB; the latter often serve as "commissioners" for civilian specialists. Such a system, in popular context, reminds one of an organ that swells to the size of an organism, producing associations from the Russian author Nikolai Gogol with his famous story "The Nose" to the contemporary art-group Voina with their performance "Penis captured by the FSB." The role of the "Chekists" in this structure can be explained in terms of systemwide "network corporations," and the essence of this phenomenon somewhat transmits the modus operandi that "there is no such thing as a retired Chekist."

With the expansion of the Chekist components, related changes have occurred not only in the system but also in its functioning. Given the circumstances where the security forces dominate, a further weakening of institutions is under way, as is the crumbling of relatively autonomous actors—public discussions and transparency in decisionmaking are being displaced by special operations; the state's security resources are not controlled by society but are instead dedicated to corporate, group, and individual tasks;[2] and the selection and promotion of staff members are conducted on the basis of personal loyalty and bondage, as is joining the private clientele of the "chief" (one of the ways to ensure loyalty is "compromise" when the discovery of violations does not lead to dismissal or prosecution of the employee but reinforces his complete dependence on the chief's faithfulness).

The Network State

If formal institutions are weak, imitation versions of them also exist, which guarantee the existence and functioning of the enormous state organism, albeit inefficiently. This function is served by the network, sometimes in more formal ways by taking the shape of substitutes, and sometimes in less formal ways that include criminals. "Putin's political bureau," which runs the country, is a network structure consisting of nodes of a nationwide nexus of key sites and corporate connections. These nodes include the government and its departments, the presidential administration and its staff, key law enforcement agencies, major state-owned corporations, and business empires. Precisely this network structure—not the official government, and not even the Parliament—makes the country's most important decisions. Putin's famous "power vertical," in fact, represents a beam of departmental verticals—this is the hierarchical network.

The concept of "network state" was coined by Manuel Castells in the context of the European Union. He is also the originator of the concept of "network society." For Castells, the network state is characterized by the sharing of power (even the possibility to exercise legitimate violence) within a certain network. However, in the case of Russia, the network aspect of the state is to be understood differently—as the interception of parts of the state's functions pertaining to formal institutions by certain network structures. In other words, the state acts as a part of the network, and the network as a part of the state.[3]

Therefore, going back to the state police, during Soviet times, the KGB was a powerful network structure, which had its representatives in the army and all major institutions and businesses. During Boris Yeltsin's rule, when state security structures had been radically weakened (on Yeltsin's initiation, the giant department was divided into various parts; furthermore, to a large extent, it was concerned with measures to reduce funding for government agencies), many KGB officers began looking for new opportunities. Since the beginning of the transition to an open market economy, some secret service officers have used a "gold party" to open their own businesses, and others—as active reserve officers—have been asked to manage major banks and businesses. Additionally, the emerging oligarchs have hired "secret service professionals" as managers of their own security departments. The biographies of many current FSB officers feature work experience in commercial organizations.

Beginning in the early periods of Russian capitalism, symbiotic relationships between businesses and security officials were only strengthened, and "protection rackets" and state racketeering were only one side of the problem. Vadim Volkov, who developed the concept of "violent entrepreneurship," says that the "gangster" phase of the 1990s was replaced by the stage of "nationalization," in which we now live.[4] The bandits were involved in a historical turnaround between 1999 and 2003, and "when the process of building large, vertically integrated, state holdings was going on, these holdings were already being run by people with much higher qualifications, coming from different walks of life, with an army of lawyers, and with serious security services that included current and former FSB officials."[5] The problem, however, is that the state's power resources are used not in the interest of the state as a whole but in the interest of the network structure, which in this way extracts revenue from the state.

The "Chekists" form a network megastructure, working all across the country. In this case, the "network" is often understood in the abstract sense—real functioning network structures are more compact and more concrete, and they are characterized by clear functional relationships, whereas in the case of a nationwide "Chekist" network, one should talk of the mental and genetic proximity and ability to recover, if necessary, and use the connections that do not apply in everyday life (unlike FSB officers). Putin's entire career has been a trampoline of different network structures: the Leningrad KGB, the Judo team, the "Dresdeners," the mayor's office in Saint Petersburg, the Ozero cooperative, Saint Petersburg liberals, and existing "Chekists" in the Russian establishment. The very question "Who is Mr. Putin?" asked with regard to the official leader pertains not so much to a person as to nodes of a network—or, more precisely, many different networks.

From the point of view of promoting national interests, the network state is ineffective in principle. It may be a reliable tool for maintaining the status quo when it is necessary to ensure the performance of routine functions, but it is much less suited to respond to changing conditions. Hence there appears a breakdown in decisionmaking and the notorious regime of "manual control," which has been observed in the past few years. Moving forward will require the strengthening of institutions, and therefore, a weakening of network structures. The problem is that at a time when the power genie has been summoned from the bottle, state power resources "disengage" and move to a network structure, and are already unsuitable to perform state duties.

The Dualism of the Tandem's Effect

The emergence of the ruling tandem of Vladimir Putin and Dmitri Medvedev in 2008 led to divergent tendencies in the administrative system. In relation to the economy, the effect was rather positive: Putin, after becoming prime minister, as one would expect, eliminated the dual-leadership executive branch (which previously had been divided into presidential and prime-ministerial) and, furthermore, began to improve the approval procedures in the administration of various interest groups. In the absence of full-fledged institutions, especially an effective Parliament, the mechanism of the simultaneous adjustment of interests of the key players is not working. This task is fulfilled by "Putin's arbitration," whereby the concerned elite groups are able to bring their point of view to the arbiter. This method of coordination takes much longer, which is why "Putin's arbitration" has skidded into crisis when decisions need to be made quickly.[6]

If in foreign policy, the tandem promoted greater freedom for maneuvering and improved the country's image, at least for a while, then in domestic politics, the tandem's effect was negative. Having left the formal post of the presidency, Putin has built a fairly complex system, where he has continued to keep all levers of power under his control, without being the formal center of power. At the same time, he has blocked all attempts at serious political reform, rightly fearing that they will destroy the structure he created and will not be useful to him.[7] Additionally, the tandem has led to further deinstitutionalization, because Putin's move to the position of prime minister has weakened the role of the only powerful institution—presidential power. Besides, "double-headedness" has made the decisionmaking system even more cumbersome, going from clumsy to partly paralyzed. Among the other adverse effects of the tandem are a shortened planning horizon and increased political uncertainty, which further increases as we get closer to the 2012 elections. On the positive side, one can note some expansion of public debate and the government's introduction of standard liberal rhetoric.

In the Russian governmental system, where strategy development and decisions about political issues have traditionally been settled by the Kremlin and the president, and economic issues have been decided by the government, the dramatic shift in the center of gravity leads to a weakening of the strategic component, even in the case when operational management could be made more effective. However, it is impossible not to notice the system's ability to regenerate and its structural adaptability; in particular, important management structures previously tied to the president—for example, the presidential council—were quickly adapted to function under the prime minister (the prime minister led the working presidium in this council, and the president was left with the representative function in the large council that meets once or twice a year). In any case, where such a "switch" was not possible—for example, in the government council—the premier created similar analogous structures.

It appears that the tandem as a structure has exhausted itself. In the future, the maintenance of separate functions for the de facto and de jure leaders will be ineffective in all respects, and hence it is a less realistic scenario.

The State's Nine Most Important Problems

The most important problems associated with the state include the following nine issues. First, the existing system of the state machinery is inadequately complex—as the very tool of administration, and as resolving its tasks and those of the country; the machinery is like a car, from which all essentials have been stripped, including the engine, and it has been left to go downhill on a straight road. The only option to maintain the system is to restore its complexity, or at least some of its dismantled parts and mechanisms.

Second, in fact, there is not one single state machinery but a collection of separate units that are accustomed to working on their own. Any attempt to change this mode of operation is fraught with failure both within those units and in the connections between them. Hence the effect of sticky persistence is not just a rut but a rut in a swamp with slippage.

Third, parts of the state machinery have in essence been privatized by corporations—both those concerned with power generation and industrial production, and in the top layers of these corporations, people close to the "national leader" have been appointed. These can be business corporations—both state-owned and formally private ones, though they are strictly controlled by the state (for example, Noril'skii Nikel), as well as government agencies. This primarily relates to security officials, with their characteristic dissonance and conflict—both internal and between offices in the Ministry of Internal Affairs, the Ministry of Defense, and the Investigation Committee.

Fourth, the Russian Federation is not a federation of regions but of corporations. In the framework of a weak state institution, the government is organized and works as a network—with informal contacts and agreements, and with internal norms ("understandings") and loyalties. The consequences of this are "nonpublicness" and nontransparency, because the very structure of the state eliminates normal interactions with society. At the same time, along with the change of regionalization to 89 regional kingdoms came the "corporatization" of the kingdom-corporations.[8] Thus one can speak of a two-dimensional model that preserves regional and corporate aspects, but these aspects are partly reversed—that is, corporations have become the major force.

Fifth, the corporate structure, whose building blocks are closely looped corporations that have little contact with each other, causes the lack of, or even the complete absence of, specialization, which leads to the duplication of functions in different parts of the system and becomes a reason for the low effectiveness of the system as a whole. The actions of corporations are often mismatched, and the competition between them outside the domain of public politics often damages the system.

Sixth, the lack of effective separation of powers and the weakness of institutions compounded the dismantling of well-functioning "foolproof" mechanisms, which are designed to protect society and the administrative system from bad decisions. Since 2000, the representatives of such mechanisms have been sequentially removed:

- mass media, relatively free from the government apparatus;
- a relatively independent and pluralistic Parliament;
- independent governors, serving for terms of four to five years;
- direct elections at all levels;
- nongovernmental organizations operating independently of vertical powers at various levels;

- representatives of federal agencies in positions that demanded dual—national and regional—loyalties.

In fact, the reduction of governance mechanisms to a system with hard verticals, the refusal to conduct public discussions and other conciliatory procedures in decisionmaking until the time these decisions will be enforced is a strict control of the final outcome—this is the result of disabling the "foolproof" mechanism.

Seventh, the current government itself has been constructed following the corporation model, in such a way that the key word always turns out in favor of the shareholder. However, having no relations with the management, it is difficult to maintain the position of a major shareholder—you can be thrown out. Therefore, shareholders sometimes, though not necessarily, act as managers. Putin is not just the arbiter but also the main shareholder—or, more correctly, is the arbiter and therefore the main shareholder. Ordinary citizens of this circuit are cut off from the corporation engaged in the recovery and redistribution of natural resource revenue—they are a burden, with the exception of the small parts that cater to the car.

Eighth, an important reason why state reforms are necessary is the accumulation of systemic problems related to technical and social infrastructure. Chronic underfunding over the years has led to a situation in which the strained infrastructure has become unsuitable. This is more noticeable in the case of technical infrastructure—in recent years, major accidents and disasters have become almost common. With regard to the social infrastructure, where negative effects have accumulated, the wear and tear is less obvious, but nevertheless it threatens a collapse. Recovery is possible, but it will take at least as much time as it took to destroy it (in this case, it is not apparent if the system has enough time). The same can be said about the entire state infrastructure.

Ninth, a serious problem arising from these features of the system is a short planning horizon. Keeping in mind the instability of the system, it is not rational to invest in long-term projects and implement strategic economic or political plans. As a result, the system is not capable of either strategic vision or strategic behavior. On the one hand, the short horizon is due to weak institutions and the system's "personal" nature; on the other hand, it further breeds weak institutions. The problem is worsened by the fact that certain key decisionmakers are ready with exit options—such as departure to the West, where they have property, children, and families. They do not share a sense of belonging to any system, not even with the country, and thus they act as temporary workers.

These nine problems delineate the system's ineffectiveness, even at the central level. At the regional level, the various federal agencies streamline their actions even less, and sometimes directly compete with each other.

Political Mechanics

An analysis of the "mechanics" of the current Russian state identifies the following characteristic flaws:

- Because of the "mechanistics" of the entire power structure, with numerous verticals, it procreates only at the top. This situation resembles that of the Martian tripods in the movie *War of the Worlds*, which were unstable due to a lack of horizontal mass and a high center of gravity.

- The lack of cushions and the stiffness of connections lead to the fact that isolated bumps and shocks can be transmitted to the top of the system, and even potholes in roads can shake the entire structure.

- The lack of checks and balances that were dismantled for the ease of control leaves the system potentially unstable: Any thoughtless or accidental decision can have tremendous consequences.

- The state's monocentricity gives it a long and extended hierarchical chain of making and implementing decisions with a large number of transfer units, in each of which can occur the loss or distortion of a signal. This lack of autonomous administrative controls slows the system and makes it inflexible and vulnerable to changing conditions;

- The state's high anisotropy means that corporate structures with independent information-gathering systems form numerous, unrelated units working toward subsistence. The design does not have the integrity of an organism's system, but it has the flexibility and variability in population.

- The state's poor location means that there are sites of conjugation between hierarchical levels—federal and regional (governors), and regional and municipal (mayors). There appears significant friction and a loss of information, and management impulses fade away.
- The primitivization of the administrative system does not indicate its simplicity or orderliness. On the contrary, ephemeral, ad hoc, individual devices without further harmonization and codification are cluttering the system, making it obscure, interfering, and lean. Many sites and blocks live their lives without being operationally connected to the rest of the mechanisms, or by duplicating analogous units and competing with them, thereby exacerbating the chaos and disorganization.

One could say that such a system is extremely inefficient and enormously time consuming—if not for a "but": It is inefficient from the point of view of a "normal" state, whose apparatus is designed to perform important functions and thus is controlled from the outside. However, in the Russian bureaucratic regime, which is based on natural resource revenues, the considerations of external systemwide competitiveness are not too important, and, conversely, internal competitive motives—between the different subsystems and networks—have been heightened. The fact that the whole system is costly and ineffective for its separate units, the interests of which run systemwide, is the revenue and spirit of their activities. Exactly the same things that can be seen as costs and signs of ineffectiveness for the whole system are the meaning of existence forming revenues of its separate units whose interests dominate over systemic ones.

The situation is precarious because of the weakness of the state's controlling mechanisms, and the fact that the rampant yet fragmented government apparatus is not capable of identifying a systemwide interest, let alone implementing it. We can expect that in the coming years, it will undergo major changes—either in stages leading to a series of major crises, or simultaneously and dramatically—as a result of a crisis in the entire system.

Effective major changes in the government apparatus must be systematic and universal—chief among them a radical reduction in the functions performed by the state machinery. Parasitic functions—feeding the bureaucracy instead of solving national problems—that interfere with the existence of business and society must be eliminated, and the remaining functions should be redistributed among hierarchical levels according to the principle of subsidiarity, with a simultaneous eradication of disparities between the horizontal and vertical elements.

The Interaction Between Central and Regional Levels of Government

In Russia, a vast country with large regional differences, a crucial role is played by the interaction between two key levels of administration: the top and the middle. This is where the government has been most significant and consistent—but counterproductive—in its efforts to restructure the entire system of relationships among different levels.

Today, the actions of the various departments (verticals) with respect to each particular region are not well coordinated, and in some cases the coordination is completely missing. Once upon a time, all actions were routed through the governor, who acted as a mediator between the regional elites and the center. Thereafter, the role of the coordinator of federal agencies was to some extent served by the chief federal inspector. Now, the senior official in the region is once again the governor, but many reports made into the center verticals bypass him. This implies problems of representation of regional political elites at the center. As soon as this role was taken away from the governor, the role of the speaker of the regional legislative assembly strengthened, and he began acting as the senior representative of the regional elite. With the transition to a new structure in 2010, when it was decided to appoint secretaries of the United Russia Party's political council as the speakers, there was a mass replacement of these speakers, and since then the ability of the system to function has been drying up. Meanwhile, just because regional elites have articulated regionwide or general interests, one should not think that these concerns have disappeared. It only points to the likelihood that administrative errors such as those that led to the mass protests in Vladivostok in 2009 will occur more often, and even more time will be spent correcting them.[9] Repeated errors of this sort carry the threat of political destabilization. Here, regions had acted as a stronghold and had managed to balance all interests—private, corporate, and public; vertical and horizontal.

In recent years, the system of horizontal rotations has been restored—a system that came into force under Stalin. Gradually, it spread to nearly all key positions in the federal region, starting with prosecutors, police chiefs, and the chief federal inspector, and now also includes governors and judges. The point of the rotation is to destroy any horizontal ties and break the regional loyalty of key officials to ensure that they are guided by the interests of the center and its disposition. In fact, instead of strengthening control, this has led to its decline; although Moscow now controls more seats allocated to the "Varangians," they themselves control the situation—in regions that are unfamiliar to them—which is much worse than before. Problems have worsened, when due to a lack of coordination between the verticals, several officials in the same region have been simultaneously replaced.[10] Such a horizontal rotation is an example of the dismantling of the "foolproof" mechanisms.[11]

The emphasis on improving the governance of the "Moscow–Federal District–Region" link is a double-edged sword. Governance would be better if the "change of political appointees" were accompanied by a "permanent device," but any newly appointed head, rightly, takes his team with himself, crippling the region from which he came, and the region to which he has been appointed. This undermines the possibility of making strategic decisions at the regional level.

As a result, in order to achieve lighter maneuvering, the center breaks the bonds between the steering wheel and the tires. In general, this is a losing game for the center, but the first move—sending "their" person to the region—gives an apparent win, but concerns about the second and third stages, as has already been said, are not taken into account.

This gives birth to a paradox: On the one hand, the system has shown its inability to act strategically, and, on the other hand, the imposition of horizontal rotation has been consistently and purposefully conducted for many years. The bottom line is that we are not dealing with a long-term strategy but with many shortsighted practices that give the appearance of a strategy, so long as there is no change in the present conditions. Such tactics can be called "Putin's dead ends." It can be described as the ascent of an Alpine climber: With each step, he wants to go higher and higher; and if the slope is smooth, he indeed gets to the top. However, it is easy to imagine a situation where the climber ascends a secondary peak, retreating from the main one, so that in the near future, it may be possible to do the entire return journey.

Similarly, the system almost certainly needs a substantial restructuring in the relations between the center and the regions—federalism is not only necessary but also inevitable. Alternatively, it either becomes a dysfunctional state like right now (though the current situation is unstable) or shows the lack of a unified de facto and de jure government. There are insufficient resources to build a normal, functioning, centralized, authoritarian state in a country on the scale of today's Russia; given current circumstances, it is not possible in principle.

From the USSR to Russia: Legacy and Change

In the time since the collapse of the Soviet Union, many changes have occurred in the public administration system. Table 15.1 lists what has been dismantled, and conversely, what has been created in the post-Soviet period. Since changes in many spheres that took place in a certain direction during the first decade after the collapse have now moved in the opposite direction, I separately examine what happened in the 1990s and in the 2000s.

The post-Soviet development has been inconsistent and uneven. In some cases, the advancement or deterioration in key directions of public administration can be estimated by summing up the signs of trends in these sections, each of which featured five to six different directions. The summation indicates that the only section where the trend of the past ten years has been more positive than in the previous decade is the section on propagation. In all other cases, there has been a sharp reversal in these trends.

Putin's Dead Ends

In addition to the extreme deterioration of Russia's infrastructure caused by long-standing factors, there are also Vladimir Putin's dead ends, time

TABLE 15.1 *Trends in Public Administration in the Post-Soviet Space (+ - and - + respectively denote the sequence of changing trends, and zero indicates constancy)*

THE INTERNAL ORGANIZATION OF POWER (+6 –4)	
Separation of powers as a whole: + –	In the early 1990s, the division was strengthened after the execution of the Supreme Council, and acceptance of the new Constitution was weakened to de jure status, though in parts preserved its de facto powers, and then virtually disappeared altogether.
Institutionalization: + –	All institutions of state administration that appeared in the 1990s were drastically weakened in the 2000s, with the exception of presidential power, and its turn came with the tandem's accession.
Parliamentarianism: + –	It appeared, continued, and disappeared at the federal level. The situation was somewhat better at the regional and local levels.
The Constitutional Court and Competitive Elements in the Higher Courts' System: + +	The emergence of the constitutional court and the strengthening of commercial courts, Russia's inclusion in the European Court of Human Rights, as well as consideration of many business disputes in Stockholm, London, and other courts. All these factors have strengthened the judiciary; however, it cannot be independent because of the strengthening of monocentric power in the 2000s.
Magisterial Courts and Juries: + -	Starting in 1993, the system was introduced for a long period of time, in the 2000s, the scope was reduced.
Party Structure, the Role of KGB and FSB: + –	If in the 1990s, the country went through a process of liquidation of monopoly power, as represented by the Communist Party of the Soviet Union, and oversaw a weakening and fragmentation of previously all-powerful state security organs, then in the 2000s, both of them were reestablished.
TERRITORIAL ORGANIZATION (+3 –2)	
Program for Administrative-Territorial Division: + 0	Continuous separation of the territory at all levels of the administrative-territorial composition, formalization of an intermediate floor—between the top and middle levels—which exists in the administrative hierarchy but is not guaranteed any resources.
Unbundling: enlargement of the regions: + –	In place of the process of fragmentation of regions that was characteristic of the 1990s, came the process of their unification; the total number of regions of the first level, increased from 73 "Soviet" regions to 89, and then decreased to 83.
Federalism and regionalism: + –	Regionalism, with elements of federalism, had headily flourished during the 1990s against the backdrop of a weakening center, but thereafter, the process was abruptly discontinued. This trend is especially pronounced with respect to the status (electivity and relative independence) of the regional heads.

Asymmetry of the regions—legal entities of the federation: + −	High-profile economic and political asymmetries of the regions sharply increased in the 1990s, and then began to weaken, although until the present there have been contradictions in the Constitution related to "Matreshka-like" regions, when, for example, corporations themselves are legal entities and at the same time are a part of other legal entities.
Total character of the administrative boundaries of the legal entities: + −	In the 1990s, the simultaneous strengthening of the regional level of government and the reduction of the spatial movement of citizens because of dramatically increased "friction space" led to political and socioeconomic "encapsulation" within the administrative boundaries of the regions; in the 2000s, this situation changed.

PROPAGATION (0 +3)

Dismantling the nomenclature system as a whole: + −	The nomenclature system by virtue of revolutionary changes in the state and society weakened sharply, at first, and then began to quickly recover, with no means of propagation and selection/elimination, that is, without components that limit the power of the nomenclature.
Layered system of education, selection and training of cadres: − +	A replacement for the Komsomol (Young Communist League) did not appear in the 1990s, or the 2000s, although individual elements can be found in the Nashi, Young Guards of United Russia, and other projects developed in the mid-2000s.
System of professional training of party-administrative functionaries: − +	The network of party high schools was almost ruined, but was then reinstated at the top level in the form of public service academies.
Exchange of cadres between Moscow and the regions: − +	In the 2000s, this became a two-way process; it is a continuous exchange and does not run on impulse. The encapsulation of regional elites has been liquidated.
Mechanism of rotation of federal agencies' heads in the regions: + +	Regional replacement and promotions are carried out rigorously, as is inviolable retirement once a person reaches a certain age.

CONSIDERATIONS OF INTERNAL AND EXTERNAL COMMUNICATION SYSTEMS (+6 -6)

Representation of regional and corporate interests: + −	Intelligible system formulation and representation of group interests, which began to emerge in the 1990s, is now virtually nonexistent; this serves as a vivid illustration of the transformation of the Federation Council.
Proportionality of the system of connections: + −	As compared with the 1990s, when both vertical and horizontal (interregional) connections were weakened, the 2000s saw the enlargement of vertical connections, alongside the shrinkage of horizontal ones.
Presence of decisionmaking taking into account interests of major groups: + −	After having been created in the 1990s, the mechanisms of public policy were destroyed, and those from the Soviet system were not restored; currently, there are no mechanisms to coordinate the interests of major groups.

Primacy of statewide interest in case of conflict with its parts: + −	The articulation and realization of systemwide interest, by political and business elites, especially in cases of conflicts with individual, group, or corporate interests gained strength during the 1990s; and practically disappeared in the 2000s.
Nature of communication between levels of the system: + −	The anisotropy of connections in vertical links are much more lightweight when moving from top to bottom, and are hindered when going from the bottom to the top; after a radical "shaking up" of the system in the 1990s, in particular, because of the political turbulence, mechanisms of straight and two-way connections between the society and different levels of the government functioned not too badly; in the 2000s, some of these connections, such as referendums, were completely dismantled, and the others converted into certain rituals.
Distribution of power functions among various levels of the government on the principle of subsidiarity, where each function is performed at the lowest hierarchical level: + −	The center's drastic absolute and relative gain, which took place in the 2000s, turned the pyramid upside-down. Now the principle of power distribution can, instead, be described as reverse subsidiarity, that is, from top to bottom.

RELATIONS BETWEEN AUTHORITIES AND CITIZENS (+6 -5)

Effectiveness of one-way and two-way channels between the government and society: + −	In the 1990s, de-bureaucratization of the system, alongside a dramatic renewal of the elite and competitive elections, provided multiple channels of communications between the government and the society. Then there was a clogging of all mechanisms, barring the restoration of the Soviet method "complain to the top" (a clear example is the protests that have become the only way to convey the aspirations of citizens to the government).
Competitive relations between the levels and agencies of the government: + −	Competition dramatically increased in the 1990s with the demolition of the old system, which provided space for citizens' evolution; as of the present day, this space has almost completely evaporated (if the 1990s were characterized by some sort of competitive delegative democracy, then in the conditions of tight centralization, no space is left for competition, as well as "fathers of the regions").
Noninterference in the private lives of citizens: + +	The abolition of single-party monopoly, there has been a dramatic increase in the space for personal life, free from state interference, and now includes the possibility for citizens and elites to emigrate (even within the country). In the 2000s, due to the increased material well-being of citizens, the ability to choose another country to live transformed from "escape" forever to the concept of a "global citizen."
Elections and referendums as means of direct communication: + −	If the 1990s was a time of rapid rise of electoral democracy, the 2000s saw a decrease in the number and role of feedback mechanisms, going from a supporting structure to merely an aesthetic one.

Political parties as the mechanism of interaction between the government and the society: + -	If the formation of a multiparty system started in the 1990s, then toward the end of the next decade, there was a complete reduction in the space of public politics, displayed by the sharp decline in the formation of political parties.
Media as a channel of communication between government and society: + −	The freedom from formal government censorship, as in Soviet times, that began during perestroika and continued during the 1990s with the development of a market economy led to the professionalization of the mass media and supported its pluralism, even at a nationwide level. In 2000, effective control over media with the highest proportions of audience was reinstated; national television channels that had been effective in shaping public opinion had been turned into a political resource of the government. Pluralism and freedom of speech still exist over the Internet and media with a relatively small audience; however, the function of these channels is limited to "steam release" for the critically minded minority of the population. With the consolidation of the elites, and reduction in the spheres of public policy, these media have practically no influence on the political process and decisionmaking.

bombs ticking against the country due to the incorrect strategic decisions made in the last decade. It is useful to briefly consider each one.

The Caucasus

The main problem in the Caucasus is the absence of a serious strategy related to Chechnya, and the Caucasus as a whole, along with the model of "indigenization" of conflict and "disindigenization" of federal troops that is implemented on its territory. Before the 2004 elections, when Putin had to urgently demonstrate that the problem had been successfully resolved, ventures into "Chechenization" were made. But even then, it did not help resolve the conflict, and instead pushed it to the periphery of public consciousness based on the cynical formula "let the Chechens kill the others." After handing over power to "good bandits" in exchange for their symbolic loyalty, and tentatively assisting them to suppress all other bandits, Moscow at some point became a hostage of this decision, and has since been forced to agree to all major concessions. Meanwhile, during the relatively unbalanced stabilization in Chechnya, the conflict spread to other republics and engulfed the entire Northern Russian Caucasus. The 2014 Sochi Olympic Games will require certain costs in the short term to ensure control over the situation—yet another example of how the government prefers tactics over strategy, exacerbating an already difficult situation. The status quo in the form of a low-intensity civil war can hardly be maintained for another ten years. To come out of this dead end, the country will end up paying very dearly.

Deinstitutionalization

By deinstitutionalization, I am speaking of the extreme deterioration of all independent institutions and the reduction of their authority and autonomy, which leads to a complete undermining of citizens' confidence in them. The system of institutional checks and balances was replaced by the ultimate arbiter; and this process was accompanied by the deliberate fragmentation of corporations and agencies (particularly security and law enforcement units), with the alignment of "conflict management" systems between them as well as within them. Due to the lack of autonomous players with a certain amount of empowerment, the system is not in a condition to automatically respond to emerging problems, and each time requires "manual control" and first-person intervention. For a long time, the basis for building the government was the high popularity of the leader, and the country could do without institutions, but sooner or later his popularity would begin to fall and become a reason for destabilization.

Paternalism

At the moment, a paternalistic model for relations with the public exists on both sides. The problem with this model is that it makes the state hostage to its populist promises, forcing it to live beyond its means—in fact, at the expense of the future—and additionally, the model prevents the development of initiatives from and independence of the citizens. Moreover, another problem is in the drastic inconsistency of not only the modernization processes but also the elementary conservation of sustained economic development.

Depoliticization

The eradication of public policy and politics made the government's life easier for some time. But after decades of using this tactic, it is turning negative—with the increasing ineffectiveness of the government itself because of a reduction in political competition and the lack of accountability at all government levels, the inability to develop a realistic agenda for the country and get popular support on its basis, a shortage of talented personnel, and the like. Political technologies as substitutes for policies could somehow work in the "fat" years, but now the situation is changing rapidly and the absence of adequate responses from the authorities serves as evidence of its shortsightedness and arrogance. Repoliticization in the next year or two is inevitable, and in many ways depends on the government—whether it will follow an evolutionary path or an explosive one, as in the last days of the Soviet Union.

Oil and Gas

Russia's chosen governing model of an "energy superpower" attracts enormous investments in its pipelines, which are considered a tool of geopolitical expansion. This method of realizing personal and corporate interests and ambitions at the cost of the country consolidates the resource-oriented and coherently redistributive character of the Russian economy, prolonging the impact of the "resource curse" for an indefinitely long future. As a result, outside the oil and gas sectors, and the services sector, which is fueled by oil and gas money, a rapid degradation of the industrial complex is under way. Furthermore, the most sophisticated and enterprising people, who could have become the backbone of diversified model, are being "washed" from the country.

Defederalization

Over the course of the last decade, there has been consistent excessive centralization and unitarization with the deprivation of both minimally autonomous and independent regions, a process that has reduced the huge diversity of the country, which used to be a source of competition, to a heavy burden. Attempts to manage a vast country from a single center with varied solutions, without taking into account the varied regional political interests, leads to a "leveling to average" in politics, and in economics, it creates the chronic subsidization of an overwhelming majority of the regions. The top manager of the regional elites, who is an influential and respected figure with experience in public-political activities, gets replaced by bureaucrats, whose management effectiveness is extremely limited—especially in a crisis situation or for the realization of modernization. And the bureaucrats worsen the problem, which can no longer be solved by a simple redistribution of powers.

It is not difficult to see that all these "private" dead ends are interconnected and form one big dead-end demodernization. In the optimistic scenario, with the intensification of efforts, the authorities can find a way out of this grave situation, to which they drove themselves along with the country. However, the longer the country is moving toward an impasse, the longer it will take to come out. This begs the question: Have we not overshot the point of no return? Moreover, the problem is often compounded by the vicious circle that only a large-scale crisis can break.

Against the backdrop of the many varied challenges faced by the state, there is a triad of the major state challenges that are not just the most important but are so important that they can affect the very existence of the system, and even the country, and where a critical situation can arise at any time:

- The North Caucasus
- A breakdown of technological and social infrastructure
- Administrative collapse

First, in the North Caucasus, conflict has built up over the many decades, and the situation has reached such a level that it could explode at any moment. There is no quick resolution to the Caucasus problem, and such a solution will not come. It is essential to implement a long, difficult, and very painful strategy to solve the actual problems of the Caucasus, and those that are inherent in the entire country, but in the Caucasus these problems are of a supernormal magnitude. These include weak institutions, personalism and cronyism, corruption, and so on. Moscow's current tactic, on the one hand, relies on archaic local political elites, whereby Moscow buys their loyalty with generous financial injections, and on the other hand, controls over federal law enforcement officials are tightened, and regulatory agencies are headed by immigrants from other regions. Not only does this tactic not contribute to any improvement in the situation, but by itself can lead to a blast.

Second, the system invests tremendous forces and means in geopolitical and geoeconomic infrastructure, which in itself is a source of income for many corporations and can increase future revenues. At the same time, it acts as the temporary owner of an enterprise that seeks to extract maximum benefit from it right now and not consider the future. In the case of technological infrastructure, this is more pronounced: The scrapping of roads exceeds the construction of new ones in such a way that large-scale technological catastrophes and accidents are a monthly affair. In the case of social infrastructure, and primarily in the areas of health and education, it is not clear why neither the government nor society pays enough attention, thereby exacerbating negative effects in the future.

And third, in recent years there have in fact been two one-way processes: the risk management failures due to the crisis and fast-changing environment; and the decreasing adaptability of the system along with its worsening ability to take a punch. The system is designed so that, on the one hand, it can provoke a crisis, at the drop of a hat, without any external shocks; and so that, on the other hand, by virtue of its inability to manage the crisis, a local problem can easily escalate into a systemwide crisis.[12] This model of creating and spreading the crisis, therefore, could be seen as the "grassroots" and the "horseman," and lead to the most extreme implications for the system.

Some experts, citing Russian history, believe that, first, it is possible to live with these problems for quite a long time; and, second, that it is impossible to fix the system. It seems that the comparison with the period of the "Brezhnev stagnation" is not quite correct. First of all, for various reasons, the processes of development and expansion are much faster now, and Putin's regime has passed the full cycle of development—from birth to senile degeneration—in just ten years. Furthermore, right now there is no stiffness, uniformity, rigidity, or lack of an alternative, all of which were characteristic of the Soviet state. And even when the situation has changed for the worse, vivid memory and experience remind one that they can contribute to a rapid improvement within the frame of change.

Notes

1. The canonical example is huge; there has been a near fifteenfold increase in security spending in the last ten years (from $2.8 billion in 2000 to $36.5 billion in 2010), and in this backdrop, there has also been a sharp increase in terrorist activities over recent years. "Putin: Volume IV—The Caucasus Deadlock," www.rusolidarnost.ru/video/2011-02-07-putin-itogi-chast-iv-kavkazskii-tupik.

2. Recall the story when in August 2008, Air Force commander General Shamanov sent special air forces to disrupt the activities of the Investigative Committee investigator working on the case of his son-in-law—an "authoritative businessman"—wanted on suspicion of an attempted murder.

3. Such an understanding of the network state can be found in the recently published book: V. Kononenko and A. Moshes, eds., *Russia as a Network State: What Works in Russia When State Institutions Do Not?* (London: Palgrave Macmillan, 2011).

4. V. Volkov, "Silovoe predprinimatel'stvo," *Letnyi Sad*, 2002, 282.

5. V. Volkov, "Silovoe predprinimatel'stvo budet vsegda," *Delo*, April 15, 2011, http://sia.ru/index.php?section=412&action=show_news&id=123790&issue=165.

6. In recent years, virtually not a single major decision at the state level affecting the interests of various agencies and corporations was accepted once and for all. It has become commonplace that a decision is first formally made, only to be reconsidered, postponed, or canceled altogether. A striking example of this is the replacement of unified social tax insurance premiums. In fall 2008, the government took the decision to sharply increase the tax burden on businesses so as to reduce the pension fund deficit. This decision was finalized with the support of the Ministry of Health, Ministry of Finance, and Ministry of the Economy, but the business community remained opposed to it. Initially, the date of enforcement was pushed back from January 2010 to January 2011. Then, when the new program came into force, its drawbacks became clear, and, conversely, with elections approaching, the president gave an urgent order to revise the proposal and reduce the downward pressure on businesses.

7. This was especially evident at the meeting of the State Council for the political system on January 22, 2010, when representatives of almost all parties came out in favor of reforms in one form or another. Putin urged avoiding the "Ukrainization" of political life in Russia, and said, "Any effective political system should be characterized by a healthy degree of conservatism. The political system should not shake the liquid jelly every time you touch it"; http://edinros-37.ru/ceo/speaker435.php.

8. The latter were noticeable in the 100 Most Influential Politicians rating put together by *Nezavisimaya Gazeta*; earlier, the number of regional leaders in this list was about two dozen, and now it has dropped to just a few persons. Instead, there has been a dramatic increase in the number of corporate executives, especially security officials.

9. Some of the decisions were made by different industries (wood, metal, right-hand-drive cars) that overlapped with one another, and as a result deprived the coastland of a large part of its means of livelihood. If someone had taken into account the consequences,

mass protests could have been prevented, if the implementation of these solutions had been accompanied by some kind of compensation for the Far East.

10. One of the first regions where a number of federal officials were replaced by the "Varangians" was the Tver region on the eve of the arrival of the new governor, Dmitri Zelenin, in 2003. It is clear that effective control of the situation not only did not increase, but also rapidly weakened. In 2010, after a series of social protests and failed elections, there was practically a simultaneous replacement of newcomers by control police bosses and FSB heads in the Irkutsk region.

11. Interestingly, the power is still not particularly worried about the change in rotation of the federal officials working in the regions that was made in accordance with the July 2011 Duma government bill. The principle of rotation for a period of three to five years covers a broad range of heads and deputy heads of territorial bodies of departments exercising control and supervisory functions.

12. An illustrative example of events in such a scenario is given by Yevgeny Gontmakher. See "Stsenarii: Novocherkassk-2009," *Vedomosti*, November 6, 2008, www.vedomosti.ru/newspaper/article/167542.

CHAPTER SIXTEEN

CENTER-PERIPHERY RELATIONS

Robert Orttung

The conduct of center–periphery relations in Russia is a battle over resources between the federal government and the regional elite. The amount of resources available for contestation grows and shrinks and the balance between the center and the periphery constantly changes, but the struggle continues endlessly.

This chapter examines recent trends in Russia's center–periphery relations and seeks to explain how these trends will evolve over the next ten years. It first looks at key drivers in the relationship between the federal government and the regions. It then examines how these trends have evolved from the collapse of the Soviet Union through 2010. A subsequent section examines the questions that these trends raise for the further development of center–periphery relations over the next decade. Finally, the chapter lays out two potential scenarios for these relations to 2020.

Key Drivers

There are several important drivers in Russia's center–periphery relations. First is the degree of unity among central leaders. A second driver,

I am grateful for the numerous comments on an earlier draft provided by Nikolay Petrov. Additionally, this chapter benefited greatly from the discussion among the project participants at the conference in Bellagio. Of course, I remain responsible for any errors or omissions.

closely related to the first, is the activeness of the regional elite. A third driver is the state of the overall economy in Russia.

Although analysts tend to focus on either federal decisionmakers or regional initiatives, the key driver in center–periphery relations is really the interaction between the two. The federal executive usually takes into account the likely regional reaction to its policies before introducing them. Similarly, regional actors are well aware of what is going on in Moscow, and their perceptions of the federal situation shape their actions at the local level.

If there is a split among the elite in Moscow, the regional elites can play central leaders against each other and exert greater influence on policy-making processes. However, if the central elite is relatively unified, there is less room for the regional elites to maneuver. But the simple unity of the federal elites does not necessarily determine the nature of central policy toward the regions because this can vary from accommodationist toward regional interests or aggressively seeking to implement a federal policy that does not take regional interests as its primary motivation. Even when the central elite is unified, it cannot necessarily put together a policy to keep the regions under control. In these cases, the problem is not that one or more regions fights with the center but that the center fails to define and implement a coherent and effective policy.

A key policy tool for the federal leaders is changing the rules of the game to suit the immediate needs of the center. Currently, there is no con-sistently applied long-term set of democratic rules at the regional level.[1] By manipulating elections, political parties, and the level of freedom in the media, the central elite shapes the level of democracy in the country as a whole. In the post-Soviet period, Russia's leaders have frequently re-sorted to this technique. From 1991 to 2010, the way Russia chose its gov-ernors swung from appointments to elections and back. The institutional arrangements have also changed, such as the electoral formula used to elect the members of the State Duma and to select members of the Federa-tion Council. In the last decade, the center has created a political party, United Russia, that improves its ability to control the regions. Similarly, it has reduced the level of freedom in the media. When the center frequently changes the rules, it has the impact of unsettling the regional elite and forcing it to adjust to the new situation.

The actions of the regional elite and populations are equally important. In center–periphery relations, the governors are crucial for their role in defining and protecting regional interests vis-à-vis the rest of the country as well as extracting resources from the federal government and bringing them back to their regions. In a situation when resources are scarce and the center and each individual region must contend for its interests, center–periphery relations are competitive. When Moscow appoints the governors, it becomes more difficult for the regional elites to express their interests because the governor primarily represents federal interests. These regional groups can either try to capture the appointed governor so that he expresses regional, rather than federal, interests, or they can resist the governor as an outsider who does not represent them.

If they choose to actively pursue their interests, the regional elite have three main choices depending on the level of unity in the center. First, if the center is weak, the regional elite can try to take advantage of it. Second, if the center is strong, the regional elite can push back against aggressive federal policies or carry them out in a subversive manner that primarily serves regional rather than federal interests. If the regional elite see no point in fighting the center, it can accept and implement federal policies without much resistance. The third possibility is for the regional elite to remain inert in the face of federal preferences. In this mode, regional leaders may choose to simply ignore federal orders or implement them slowly.

Regional civil society plays a role either by actively supporting or protesting the policies of federal and regional leaders or by remaining passive. Because of the lack of institutions through which ordinary people either can hold regional or federal officials accountable or influence policymaking processes, civil society groups typically need to resort to street demonstrations to express their opinions and seek to influence policy. In most cases, therefore, an active civil society is one focused on protest.

The state of the overall economy serves as a driver for center–periphery relations because the level of resources available determines the degree and nature of the competition between the center and the individual regions. When the economy is doing well, resources are relatively plentiful and there is less competition. In poor economic conditions, when individual standards of living are not continuously rising and the center lacks sufficient resources to distribute to keep regional elites satisfied, there is likely to be a revival of regional politics as the regional elites seek more resources to compensate for the problems of their local constituents. In this sense, Russia's federal institutions, which have been "sleeping" since 2000 because of the relatively good economic times, could "wake up" and start to live a life of their own as regional elites across Russia seek to increase their share of the resource base.[2] Such a change is most likely if the price of oil drops, and thus fewer investors send their money to Russia and the country's overall income plummets.[3]

The Evolution of Relations

Center–periphery relations have evolved through several distinct stages during the post-Soviet period. During the Soviet era, Moscow exerted extensive control over regional affairs. It appointed the powerful oblast committee (obkom) party secretaries who controlled each region. It also controlled the flow of money from the regions to the center and then back to the regions in the form of state programs and support.

The Yeltsin Era

The collapse of the Soviet Union in 1991 left a power vacuum at the federal level, which provided an opening for regional elites to assert their interests. As Boris Yeltsin fought Mikhail Gorbachev for control over Russia, he appealed to the regional elite to help consolidate his power. In an effort to swing the regional elite to his side, he famously told them to "take as much sovereignty as you can swallow," and many regional leaders began to do just that, running their regions according to their personal whim and often in violation of Russian law. During this period, Yeltsin appointed most governors, a situation that did not prevent many of them from trying to assert their independence. Hoping that his regional envoys would serve as counterweights to the local Communist establishments that continued to dominate regional politics in most places, Yeltsin generally appointed reform-minded individuals as governors. His appointees came from the local elite and represented local interests.[4]

Yeltsin relied heavily on the regional elite during his time in office and depended on them to guarantee victory in the 1995–1996 electoral cycle. To gain this support, he made two concessions to the governors. Starting in 1996, the governors and regional legislature chairmen automatically gained seats in the Federation Council, the upper house of the national Parliament. Additionally, starting in 1996, once the presidential elections were over and Yeltsin had been safely returned for a second term, he allowed all governors to be elected directly by their constituents.[5]

The gubernatorial elections, combined with the governors' strong connections to local businessmen, made them powerful players at the local level and gave them considerable leverage at the federal level as well. The governors' effort to take power reached its apogee in the 1999 State Duma elections, when a group of powerful regional leaders, including Moscow's Yuri Luzhkov and Tatarstan's Mintimer Shaimiev, set up the Fatherland–All Russia political bloc and seriously challenged Yeltsin's handpicked designee, Prime Minister Vladimir Putin, for control of the Parliament's lower house. However, drawing on his apparently successful prosecution of the second Chechen war, Putin won the election. His rise to the presidency, following Yeltsin's resignation at the end of 1999, launched a new phase in center–periphery relations.

Yeltsin had to cede considerable power to the regional elites in part because the Russian economy was in poor shape during the 1990s. Sustained economic growth only began after the financial crisis of 1998 and when oil prices started to rise at the beginning of the next decade. Accordingly, Yeltsin had few resources to distribute to the regional elites, and most residents remained discontented because their living standards had fallen considerably from what they remembered of the Soviet era.

The Putin Era

When Putin became president, he quickly moved to consolidate and centralize power in the Kremlin. He effectively changed the rules of the game to hand much greater authority to the federal government and reduced the ability of the regional elite to influence federal policy. With a strong reliance on his colleagues in the Federal Security Service, he established seven new districts to monitor the actions of the governors and ensure that they obeyed Russian law and implemented federal policy. He also removed the governors and regional legislative chairs from the Federation Council and replaced them with appointees who were easier for the Kremlin to manipulate. In 2004, he changed the rules of the game again, by canceling future gubernatorial elections. Henceforth, the president had the power to appoint the governors. Additionally, the president reformed the electoral system used to pick members of the lower chamber of the Parliament. Starting with the 2007 State Duma elections, Russia switched from a system in which it elected half the members of Parliament directly from single-member districts to a system in which all members are elected on a proportional basis through party lists. As with the upper house appointees, the members of Parliament selected from party lists are more likely to represent federal interests than those elected by regional voters in territorially defined districts. Putin also reorganized Russia's fiscal federalism so that the center gained much greater control over the country's finances. In short, during Putin's eight years as president, regional interests lost much of their ability to exert a direct influence on federal policies.

Even though Putin took considerable power from the regional elite in subordinating the governors directly to the president rather than making them accountable to their voters, he pursued a very careful personnel policy. Although he could theoretically fire any governor at will, in practice he left most of the governors in place. For this reason, Russia's governors did not protest their direct subordination to the president. Also helpful in maintaining their quiescence was the fact that the federal government provided them with sufficient funds to meet their primary political needs.[6]

Despite having installed this new system, Moscow continued to pursue an ad hoc policy toward the regions, treating each one according to its specific needs. Typically, powerful local leaders were able to conduct themselves as they wished at the regional level with little federal intervention into their policies. As long as the situation remained stable and they delivered the necessary votes in parliamentary and presidential elections, the Kremlin asked few questions about the governors' ties to the local business elites and corrupt dealings.[7]

Even though Putin took a cautious approach toward replacing incumbent governors with people of his own choosing, his decision to appoint rather than elect governors changed the tenor of center–periphery relations in Russia. Because they are now appointed by Moscow, governors no longer primarily represent regional interests. Rather, they serve as implementers of federal policies in the regions. Because Putin's goals were maintaining stability and guaranteeing his ability to remain in office or choose a political heir, policymakers did not pay attention to the goal of regional development beyond what was necessary to prevent protests and achieve other short-term political goals. Thus, though the appointment of governors has simplified Russia's political system and made it easier to control the regional executives, it has not improved actual management of the regions. In particular, the new system does not seem to contribute to economic growth outside the capitals of Moscow and Saint Petersburg.[8]

The practical consequence of appointing the governors from 2005 onward was to make the federal authorities directly responsible for what happens at the regional level. Accordingly, when regional residents express anger at what is taking place at the regional level, they are as likely to target the federal leadership, typically Putin, as the appointed governor. In this way, problems that might have remained purely local take on the character of a center–periphery battle.[9]

During Putin's presidency, he benefited from a strong economy. The price of oil was rising and the living standards of the average person were constantly increasing. This economic growth made it possible for him to extract considerable power from the regions without causing much of a reaction. In many cases, though the regions lost control over their own finances, there actually was more money available at the regional level so the regional elite did not feel that they were worse off.

During the Putin era, the president could count on his governors to ensure strong victories for United Russia in the 2007 State Duma elections and the election of Dmitri Medvedev, Putin's chosen successor, as president in 2008. The regional populations were also relatively passive during this period, with the only major exception being the 2005 protests against the monetization of benefits, which considerably shrank state subsidies to key groups within the population.

The Putin/Medvedev Era

Although the federal executive did not lose any of its powers over the regions during the period 2008–2010, the context for Russia's center–periphery relations changed considerably. Following the economic crisis that began in 2008, the size of the Russian economy shrank by 7.9 percent in 2009 and only achieved slow growth in 2010. The crisis caused economic pain in many regions and stopped the consistently improving living standards that people had come to take for granted during the Putin presidency. The result was that the political passivity of the population that characterized the Putin era came to an end. The clearest signal of this change was the large protest in Kaliningrad in January 2010, which brought 10,000 people on to the street, with demonstrators demanding the resignation of Putin and Governor Georgi Boos.

In response to these changing conditions, after 2008 the Putin/Medvedev leadership team adopted a new policy toward the governors. In contrast to Putin's conservative preference for leaving in place experienced leaders who had proven their ability to maintain stability and deliver votes, since taking office Medvedev (with Putin's backing) has removed the so-called heavyweight governors who defined the regional leadership during the Yeltsin and Putin presidencies. These leaders have included Orel's Yegor Stroev, Sverdlovsk's Eduard Rossel, Tatarstan's Mintimer Shaimiev, Bashkortostan's Murtaza Rakhimov, and, most prominently, Moscow's Yuri Luzhkov.

Instead of working with locals deeply embedded in regional networks, in many cases Medvedev began to appoint leaders from outside the region (developing a trend that began under Putin).[10] These leaders have no personal or business ties to the regional elite where they are appointed. The center expects them to stand above the local political scene and carry out federal directives rather than pursue the interests of the regional groups that could otherwise capture the governor and use his office to serve their purposes. Locals perceive these governors as temporary residents of the regions where they are assigned.

Over time, the federal government has become more confident in its ability to correctly choose the type of leaders needed for each region. In selecting the governors, the federal authorities seem to make decisions on a case-by-case basis, taking into account a variety of local factors rather than pursuing a consistent list of criteria across regions. In most cases, however, the Kremlin has relied on appointing younger leaders than had been in place before. The average age of the governors has dropped from sixty-three to forty-eight years.[11] This break from past practices clearly signals that the new governors primarily represent Moscow rather than the regions where they are working.

Under the old system, the governor was seen as a patron who could distribute resources to his allies and supporters. The governors' offices controlled the key financial flows in the region, as well as property rights and access to the media. The governor could give his friends lucrative state contracts and access to other resources. For any regional business, having good relations with the governor was essential to achieving success. But under the new system of appointing outsiders, the governor is no longer a patron for the region. He is not dependent on the local elites and is not necessarily interested in promoting their particular interests. Rather, his primary goal is to serve Moscow well so that he will eventually be given a new appointment, either in a more prestigious region or in the federal government based in Moscow. Using this system, the federal government can move people in and out much more flexibly, taking into account federal interests rather than regional ones.

A major drawback to the new system is that central officials are having trouble identifying new regional leaders. In the absence of free and fair elections, the Russian authorities must rely on other forms of leadership recruitment. In particular, they have turned to the creation of a presidential cadre reserve, similar to the Soviet-era nomenklatura system, as a way of identifying and promoting new leaders. Such a system is not likely to promote politicians who can articulate and integrate various interests. More likely, it will advance bureaucratic managers who have support from existing leaders. Often the officials that Medvedev appointed were not able to communicate effectively with the residents of the regions they led. Early reviews of Sergei Sobyanin's performance as mayor of Moscow, for example, complained about his lack of desire and inability to explain the logic of his actions to Moscow residents, petty tyranny, and other problems reflecting his preference to work behind closed doors rather than through public processes.[12] An analysis of the use of the cadre reserve during Putin's first term as president concluded that it served to consolidate authoritarian rule rather than promote democratic systems.[13]

In another innovation, Medvedev has moved to replace governors quickly when they fail to meet his political needs. Medvedev fired Luzhkov in September 2010 after Luzhkov publicly challenged his authority. The president did not reappoint Boos to a second term after the January 2010 demonstrations in Kaliningrad demonstrated that the governor did not have a popular base there. Similarly, Medvedev had to replace Nikolai Kolesov as governor of Amur under pressure from the population.

The appointment of Nikolai Belykh in Kirov Oblast marks another novel way that the Kremlin has used gubernatorial appointments to neutralize the opposition in Russia. Even though Belykh once led the liberal Union of Right Forces party, he was willing to accept an appointment from Medvedev to manage one of Russia's poorest regions in an effort to demonstrate that he could convert his ideology into effective practice and that it would produce results by improving the quality of life even in the most difficult conditions. If Belykh is successful, his efforts will support the current system, in part by infusing it with some of his reformist ideas; if he fails, the Kremlin can simply remove him as an ineffective leader.

One area where Medvedev has not relied on outsiders is in the ethnically defined regions such as Tatarstan.[14] In these republics, it is important to have someone from the titular ethnic group as the leader. In this sense, Russia seems to have continued its policy of ethnofederalism, in which it treats the republics differently than the other regions. For example, when Shaimiev left office, Medvedev appointed one of his deputies as his successor, Rustam Minnikhanov. In Bashkortostan, however, Medvedev replaced Rakhimov with another member of the local elite, Rustem Khamitov, but one who was in opposition to the former president.[15] In Karachaevo-Cherkessia, Medvedev brought in a new leader who had long lived in Moscow; however, he was not sensitive to the nuances of local ethnic politics, and the result was ethnic-based discontent.

Ironically, the new reliance on outsider governors creates a depersonalized system at the regional level, while Russia's political system remains highly personalized at the federal level. Power in the center remains a function of one's ties to Putin. At the same time, Moscow is working assiduously to break the similar kinds of personal relationships that once existed between the governors and the local elites within each region. Effectively, such a system could reduce the level of corruption in the regions while leaving it unchecked at the federal level. Medvedev claimed that the appointment of outsiders would make it easier to fight corruption and that the outsiders could make the hard decisions necessary to revive local business, create jobs, and deal with any discontent created by the poor performance of the economy.[16] Such a system would likely result in great tensions as the regional elite saw that they were forced to play by one set of rules while those in Moscow operated under a different set.

Even as Putin and Medvedev have repeatedly made clear that they will not replace the system of appointing governors with elections,[17] the public demonstratively does not support them on this issue. In fact, it is one of the few issues where there is a clear difference in public opinion polls between official policy and popular desires. Currently, a majority of the population favors restoring gubernatorial elections. According to Levada Center public opinion polls, 57 percent back the return of such elections, 20 percent prefer the current practice of appointments, and 23 percent had no opinion.[18]

The United Russia party serves as a mechanism for Moscow to exercise control over the regions. The party manages access to state resources; distributes key public offices; supplies goods and services to leaders, elites, and voters; helps ambitious politicians rise to more important offices; and resolves disputes among elites.[19] As of the beginning of 2010, 78 of 83 governors were members of the party, and it controlled 81 of 83 regional assemblies. The party serves as a system for distributing rents, patronage, and the spoils of incumbency through vote trading. In regional legislatures, key decisions are made in United Russia's fractional meetings. Thanks to one of Medvedev's political reforms, the majority party in each regional legislature has the right to present the president with a list of possible governors, from which the president can choose the next governor. Because United Russia controls all the legislatures, it now holds this power, although in practice the federal leaders of the party, rather than regional representatives, pick the gubernatorial candidates.[20]

Key Questions for Determining Future Trends

The center–periphery policies of the Putin/Medvedev administration raise many questions about how they will shape future trends—among which it is useful to focus here on four key questions. First, how effective will the policy of appointing governors be, particularly as Medvedev moves away from the past practice of leaving elected governors in place and appoints younger outsiders? The benefits of this system mainly accrue to the federal leadership. Appointing governors has increased the Kremlin's ability to manage the regions and has reduced the governors' dependence on the local business elite, according to a survey of 50 experts.[21] The president and prime minister no longer have to deal with elected officials who have a base of legitimacy in the regions. Instead they work with officials whose position is dependent on their approval.

However, there are many downsides to appointing governors. This system continues Putin's enterprise of building an authoritarian state. Although some democratic countries such as France do not elect their governors, in Russia the gubernatorial elections provided a basis for building democracy across Russia's vast territory. Elected governors are more flexible in reacting to the situations in their regions, closer to public opinion, and more independent in making decisions.[22] Because Medvedev has relied heavily on outsiders, under the new system of appointing governors, Russia may soon be governed by people who have no relationship to the regions where they are working. An examination of past experience with such appointed leaders shows that they have produced greater political instability in their regions and reduced public and elite support.[23] The outsiders create conflict because they represent a change in the rules of the game. They provoke alienation among regional elites and publics, polarization of the bureaucracy, and resentment toward Moscow, all of which foster feelings of subregional nationalism. The arrival of a new governor makes regional elites nervous because they depend on the governor as their main ally in securing resources from the federal bureaucracy. Governors chosen for their loyalty to the center may not prove very effective at the task of developing the regional economies they oversee. Finally, the power of federal agencies operating in the regions will now be unchecked because appointed governors will not want to oppose their federal colleagues. Elected governors often served as an informal check on the power of such agencies, including the police. Such unchecked power could ultimately lead to even higher levels of corruption than are apparent now. Appointed governors also reduce the amount of media freedom at the local level.[24]

The second key question affects the conduct of future elections at the regional level: How much do the political machines in each region depend on the governor to operate? Is each machine the personal creation of one man, or something that will continue to function in more or less the same way after the governor who established it is no longer there? This question is particularly important because the new governors typically are not politicians with the same kinds of public skills as their predecessors, but usually bureaucrats working to serve Moscow. The new governors may not have the personal authority to apply the administrative resources as well as the old ones did.

Third, what are the roles of the ethnic factor and nationalism? Will there be ethnic uprisings? During the 1990s, regional leaders in Tatarstan and other republics used the threat of ethnic conflict to extract greater resources from the Kremlin. In most of these cases, the regional elite could control the level of ethnic protest, generally using it as a bargaining chip in their effort to win more money from Moscow. Today such protests are less visible, though many ethnic groups feel aggrieved that they do not receive sufficient support from the center. It remains an open question whether ethnic identity will be a mobilizing factor between 2010 and 2020.

The fourth and final question is the nature of center–periphery relations. In the twenty years since the collapse of the USSR, power first swung to the regions and then shifted back to the center. Will the relationship continue to swing in this manner like a pendulum, or will it find a more stable equilibrium? In the current situation, it seems that the center took more power than it can handle and that it is now necessary for it to find some way to change the situation to avoid falling into a period of prolonged stagnation. Clearly, institutional change is necessary to give the regions more representation in federal policymaking. Giving the regional elites a larger voice would require undoing many of the changes that Putin made since he came to power in 2000.

Russia 2020

This concluding section examines two possible scenarios for the future development of center–periphery relations through 2020. The first plots out current trends ten years into the future. The second focuses on an optimistic outcome for Russia.

The Inertia Scenario

The inertia scenario starts with the assumption that the economic situation for Russia remains difficult: While rising energy prices bring in more income, growth remains relatively sluggish. As in the past, the Kremlin continues to emphasize maintaining central control and political stability rather than economic development as the main goal. The federal leadership continues to rely on appointed governors from outside the regions where they work. Accordingly, the governors do not represent regional interests, but rather those of Moscow. The results are more street protests at the regional level and increased activities by political groups against the background of a stagnating political system. In the past, these protests typically targeted higher taxes, more expensive utility bills, general corruption, unemployment, and a general drop in living standards. These largely economic-based protests will also eventually lead to political demands. Protesters are likely to come out more often to express discontent with incompetent governors sent to them by Moscow. Overall, the federal government's inability to deal with this growing discontent will lead to a much greater use of repressive force. Nevertheless, despite this rising tide of political activity, most individuals will be focused on improving their private economic situation rather than seeking to enact broader social progress and political reform.

In the 2011 parliamentary and 2012 presidential elections, the political machines that once were so efficient in turning out the vote for United Russia and the Kremlin-designated candidate for president will be less effective. Rather, there will be a stronger protest vote that will not necessarily benefit any of the opposition candidates in particular but will take away support from the official United Russia candidate. However, while popular support drops off, United Russia and the officially approved presidential candidate will still win the elections and continue the political stagnation.

The country's institutions will continue to languish. Russia's extensive corruption will remain an important factor in the context of center–periphery relations. In practical terms, the pervasive informal economy will undermine federal control over what happens in the regions. A bureaucracy that lives mainly to serve its own interests has little use for central directives. A key factor in this corruption will be the implementation of big projects across Russia. In such projects, the corruption is on a massive scale. For example, blogger Alexei Navalny published an Accounting Chamber report exposing extensive corruption in the construction of the Eastern Siberia–Pacific Ocean pipeline, with the amount of money stolen in the billions of dollars.[25] Similar problems can be expected with the 2012 Asia-Pacific Economic Cooperation forum summit in Vladivostok, which cost $6 billion, and the Olympic games to be held in Sochi in 2014 at a cost of $12 billion in public funds. These extensive networks of corruption have undermined efforts for regional development.

Similarly, infrastructure disasters can exacerbate relations between the center and the regions. For example, the August 17, 2009, flood at the Sayano-Shushenskaya hydropower plant killed 75 people and caused billions of dollars in damage. Explosions on May 8 and 9, 2010, at the Raspadskaya's flagship coal mine near Mezhdurechensk city in Kemerovo Oblast, Russia's largest underground mine, killed more than 90 miners and rescuers and did significant damage to Russia's steel industry as it sought to take advantage of rising international prices.[26] The center will need to respond quickly to address these kinds of problems if it hopes to avoid the spread of discontent. During the final days of the Soviet Union, the coal miners played a major role in laying out the population's grievances against the regime. If they are serious enough, such infrastructure failures could serve as a trigger for a broader political crisis.

Although the center makes an effort to appoint members of the titular ethnic group as leaders in the ethnically defined republics, its choices have not always proven successful. Governors who do not understand the ethnic nuances of the regions where they work are likely to provoke an ethnic mobilization among the population. Because the people will have no formal mechanisms through which to voice their displeasure, they will resort to street demonstrations, which will prove politically destabilizing. As a consequence of these rallies, Russian nationalist groups are likely to become more prominent in Russia's big cities. These groups will play on fears of Islam and immigrants to drive even more nationalistic policies in the center, potentially creating a negative feedback loop with the regions.

Overall, the failure to reform the political system, combined with the continued leadership of Putin and Medvedev and the ongoing reliance on appointed governors will create growing public pressure for change on the federal government and its governors. This pressure will likely destabilize the system, causing the federal government to make a variety of concessions to the regions in an unorganized manner, and thus further undermining efforts to enact coherent economic reforms.

The Optimistic Scenario

Even if the economic situation remained difficult as in the inertia scenario, a more optimistic possibility for Russia's development would result from a split within the federal elite, with those prioritizing economic modernization gaining the advantage over advocates of maintaining extensive political control. However, despite the emphasis on economic growth, there would continue to be a lack of agreement among federal elites about how best to diversify the Russian economy. Although those in favor of maintaining political control seek to keep the main focus on the energy industry, seeing it as a reliable source of income that will make it possible to shore up their political power,[27] advocates of greater diversification argue that the development of new industries and economic sectors will help pluralize the political system and support such innovations as a way to increase their political weight within the system.[28]

In these conditions, the federal leaders would still insist on appointing governors, but would do so in a way that takes regional interests much more into account than current appointees. The governors would typically have strong connections to the regions they lead and would serve as advocates for their regions at the federal level, bringing resources from that level home to their regions. They would take care to meet the interests of regional businesses but also work to increase the level of competition so that regional markets could expand over time.

Although regional elections would still be highly controlled, there would be greater opportunities for regional elites to capture their local branches of United Russia and use this organization to gain additional political representation. With a greater voice in the Duma and Federation Council, regional interests could use their time in Moscow to more effectively lobby the presidential administration and government to adopt policies that better reflect regional interests.

Under this more sensitive approach, the federal leadership would rely more heavily on republican governors who are well versed in the ethnic politics of their regions and are careful to avoid provoking tensions. Finally, this greater representation for regional interests would stabilize the existing institutions so that there would be less pressure for radical reform. Although a return to gubernatorial elections would be optimal, it is not politically feasible in the next ten years, so a more sensitive use of presidential appointments would be the most workable solution within the framework of Russia's Putinist system.

Notes

1. Irina Busygina and Mikhail Filippov, "Problema vynuzhdennoi federalizma" [The problem of forced federalism], *Pro et Contra*, no. 46 (May–August 2009): 125–38.

2. Andrei Zakharov, "Rossiiskii federalism kak 'spyashii' institute" [Russian federalism as a 'sleeping' institution], *Novoe literaturnoe obozrenie*, n.d., www.nlobooks.ru/rus/nz-online/619/1829/1838.

3. See chapter 10 in this volume, by Vladimir Milov.

4. Joel C. Moses, "Russian Local Politics in the Putin-Medvedev Era," *Europe-Asia Studies* 62, no. 9 (2010): 1437.

5. Peter Reddaway, "Historical and Political Context," in *The Dynamics of Russian Politics: Putin's Reforms of Federal-Regional Relations*, Volume 1, edited by Peter Reddaway and Robert W. Orttung (Lanham, Md.: Rowman & Littlefield, 2004), 10.

6. Alla E. Chirikova, "Regional'nye elity v sovremennoi Rossii: Kontseptual'nye diskussii i politicheskaia praktika" [Regional elites in contemporary Russia: conceptual discussions and political practice], *Rossiia i sovremennyi mir*, no. 1 (2009): 154–72. This article has been republished in English: Alla E. Chirikova, "Regional Elites in Contemporary Russia," *Russian Politics and Law* 48, no. 1 (January–February 2010): 21–39; the citation here is on 37.

7. Darrell Slider, "Medvedev and the Governors," *Russian Analytical Digest*, no. 86, November 16, 2010.

8. International Institute of Political Expertise (MIPE) and the Minchenko GR consulting agency, "5 let sisteme naznacheniya glav regionov v RF" [5 years of the system of appointing regional heads in the Russian Federation], March 17, 2010, www.stratagema.org/issledovaniya.php?nws=anz117770801488.

9. See chapter 7 in this volume, by Kirill Rogov.

10. Rostislav F. Turovskii, "Praktiki naznacheniia gubernatorov," *Politiia*, no. 2 (2009): 72–89; republished in English translation as Rostislav F. Turovskii, "How Russian Governors Are Appointed," *Russian Politics and Law* 48, no. 1 (January–February 2010): 58–79, http://minchenko.ru/news/news_36.html.

11. Olga Kryshtanovskaya, "Dmitrii Medvedev postavil na omolozhenie deistvuyushie elity" [Dmitry Medvedev banked on a younger elite], Kreml.org, October 4, 2010.

12. See Vladimir Milov's blog: http://v-milov.livejournal.com/293396.html.

13. Eugene Huskey, "Nomenklatura Lite? The Cadres Reserve" (Kadrovyi reserv), Russian Public Administration, National Council for Eurasian and East European Research, October 24, 2003, www.ucis.pitt.edu/nceeer/2003-817-04-2-Huskey.pdf.

14. Moses, "Russian Local Politics," 1445.

15. No author, "Khu iz mister Khamitov?" *Moskovskii komsomolets*, July 17, 2010, www.mk.ru/politics/article/2010/07/16/517080-hu-iz-mister-hamitov.html.

16. Moses, "Russian Local Politics," 1438.

17. Vitaly Ivanov, "Medvedev i gubernatory " [Medvedev and the governors], *Izvestia*, March 9, 2010, http://izvestia.ru/comment/article3139413.

18. Levada Center, "Rossiyane ob izmenenii vybornogo zakonodatel'stva" [Russians on the changes in the electoral legislation], June 26, 2009, www.levada.ru/press/2009062604.html.

19. Ora John Reuter, "The Politics of Dominant Party Formation: United Russia and Russia's Governors," *Europe-Asia Studies* 62, no. 2 (March 2010): 295.

20. Andrey Polunin, "Carnegie Center: Medvedev's Reforms Are Minor Cosmetic Changes" (interview with Nikolay Petrov), *Svobodnaya Pressa*, November 24, 2010.

21. Maksim Glikin and Natalia Kostenko, "Sekret naznacheniya," *Vedomosti*, March 18, 2010 and http://minchenko.ru/news/news_36.html.

22. Glikin and Kostenko, "Sekret naznacheniya."

23. Moses, "Russian Local Politics," 1441.

24. Andrey Polunin, "Black Lists of Untouchables Are Growing—In 15 Years Russia's Media Will Be Like North Korea's" (interview with Boris Timoshenko, head of the Glasnost Defense Foundation's regional network), *Svobodnaya Pressa*, April 23, 2010, available at www.svpressa.ru.

25. Alexey Navalny, "Kak pilat v Transneft" [How they steal in Transneft], November 16, 2010, http://navalny.livejournal.com/526563.html.

26. Ilya Khrenikov, "Raspadskaya Pledges Coal Supply to Russia After Blast," *Bloomberg Businessweek*, May 21, 2010, www.businessweek.com/news/2010-05-21/raspadskaya-pledges-coal-supply-to-russia-after-blast-update2-.html.

27. Thad Dunning, "Resource Dependence, Economic Performance, and Political Stability," *Journal of Conflict Resolution* 49, no. 4 (August 2005): 451–82.

28. This argument differs substantially from the line of reasoning proposed by Clifford Gaddy and Barry Ickes. They claim that the debate over diversification is simply an attempt by various people to gain control of the energy rents. But they overlook the political consequences of an economy heavily dependent on resource income. Such an economy favors an authoritarian system and helps to perpetuate it. See Clifford G. Gaddy and Barry W. Ickes, "Russia After the Global Financial Crisis," *Eurasian Geography and Economics* 51, no. 3 (2010): 281–311.

the CONTINUING REVOLUTION *in* RUSSIAN MILITARY AFFAIRS: TOWARD 2020

Pavel K. Baev

A particular feature of the intellectual exercise of drawing possible trajectories for the transformation of the Russian Armed Forces toward 2020 is the very short basis for extrapolation. Normally, making a reasonably sound ten-year forecast requires data for a similar period, and preferably twice that. In principle, the two post-Soviet decades of Russia's history provide exactly this basis for prognostication. However, the problem is that since the fall of 2008, the Russian military organization has entered into a phase of reforms so radical in their aims that they can only be compared with Yegor Gaidar's "shock therapy" that reshaped Russia's economy in the years 1992–1993.[1]

In hindsight, the wisdom of launching such far-reaching and extra-painful reforms exactly at the start of a devastating economic crisis looks questionable at best. It has been driven forward with remarkable determination but has, nevertheless, run into serious problems—and its prospects are not good. What makes it impossible to construct the usual "muddle-through" scenario, which would extrapolate the current trends with the necessary downsizing of goals and extension of deadlines, is the increasingly obvious paradox that the logic of revolutionary changes in the military structures is compatible with neither the economic foundation nor the political superstructure.

Indeed, the sharp contraction of Russia's economy in 2009 proved not only the vulnerability of its energy and metal sectors to fluctuations in world prices but also the impossibility of reproducing the "golden era" of petro-prosperity of the early 2000s. It can thus be taken for a fact that the amount of resources available for modernizing the armed forces in this decade would be strictly limited, whether the grand plan for Russia's "modernization" progresses or not. As for the political part of the problem, it stands to reason that a deeply corrupt "overmanaged democracy" (as three experts have recently defined it) is not only incapable but also uninterested in building a modern combat-capable military structure.[2] Such a self-confident and emboldened army would inevitably become a powerful political actor pursuing its own agenda, while the Kremlin could find it increasingly difficult to keep the top brass under control.

This nonsustainability of the ongoing reforms creates a methodological problem for analysis, because the unavoidable changes in building up the armed forces becomes a dependent variable determined by the very uncertain transformation of the political regime and the even more fluid prospects for economic recovery or stagnation. In chapter 18, Aleksander Golts tackles this problem by constructing scenarios that combine military and political developments; this chapter attempts a different method of simplifying the overdetermined development. It makes two basic assumptions: (1) that the current political regime will survive until 2020, while the awkward construct of the "tandem" is abandoned and Vladimir Putin returns to the position of commander in chief; and (2) that the economy settles on a pattern of slow growth, without any major new spasms. Neither of these assumptions is rock-solid, and this author has argued on many occasions that the breakdown of the "petro-prosperity" model has generated a profound crisis of the political system of "Putinism," which has exhausted its rationale.[3] It may be useful, nevertheless, to contemplate what shifts in the military buildup are possible within the existing and fairly rigid political-economic framework.

The aim of this chapter is thus to examine the narrow range of options for transformation of the Russian Armed Forces toward 2020 that is limited by the condition of domestic stability and perpetuation of the nondemocratic regime built by and presided over by Vladimir Putin. What would determine choices for prioritizing this or that direction in transforming the armed forces in this period of state stagnation are changes in the security situation, particularly external challenges. Russia has enjoyed an opportune environment of low security threats (except for domestic crises of high intensity), but this favorable condition would hardly last into the third decade of its post-Soviet existence. Events—like the August 2008 war with Georgia, the violent destabilization of the North Caucasus in 2009, or the bloodbath in the Osh region of Kyrgyzstan in June 2010—would defy Moscow's basic preference for the status quo and demand military responses. The character of these responses will depend on the available instruments—and also influence their construction and calibration. The chapter starts with a brief evaluation of the initial results of the ongoing reforms, and then separately examines the nuclear and conventional capabilities, finally arriving at a brief net assessment of the risks that the Russian army would need to mobilize against.

Reform Goes Beyond the Point of No Return but Runs Into Trouble

The launch of breathtakingly radical reforms in the armed forces in October 2008 was quite unexpected, particularly because the top brass had every reason to expect rewards for the spectacular victory over Georgia two months earlier. In hindsight, however, it appears obvious that the preparatory work started soon after Putin's famous "Munich Speech" in February 2007, when Sergei Ivanov was replaced as defense minister by Anatoly Serdyukov—an improbable choice given Serdyukov's lack of knowledge about military matters and the fact that he did not belong to any of the siloviki clans that formed Putin's inner circle. The initial phase of the reform, and in particular the painful cut of the officer corps by no less than half, has been scrutinized in many analyses, so there is hardly any need for another description of this beginning.[4]

What is relevant, however, is an attempt at net assessment of the achievements and setbacks of the military perestroika, particularly because official reporting is uniformly upbeat, while the Defense Ministry refuses to engage in any debates on the results and further directions of its efforts. This extreme closeness of decisionmaking perhaps betrays the insecurity of the reformers, which stems not only from their isolation in the military organization but also from their very uncertain political support. Indeed, President Dmitri Medvedev performs the role of commander in chief far from convincingly and avoids addressing the major issues for military reform (the term "reform" is actually never used), demonstrating attention mostly to social problems, like providing housing for officers. He also seeks to elaborate the ideas of an "innovative army" as an element of his "modernization" discourse, for instance, setting the goal for increasing the share of modern weapons systems to 70 percent. It is characteristic, however, that only two sentences in his manifesto-article "Go Russia!" concern military matters: "Of course Russia will be well armed. Well enough so that it does not occur to anyone to threaten us or our allies."[5] As for Prime Minister Putin, he frequently deals with specific questions of armaments research and development but generally steers clear of strategic matters, indicating that troubles with building up the armed forces are outside his area of responsibility.

The privilege of "ownership" of the revolutionary reform is thus declined by the ruling duumvirate and remains with Defense Minister Serdyukov, who has shown remarkable determination in pushing forward unpopular changes and overcoming the resistance in the military bureaucracy. He has never pretended to understand esoteric strategic paradigms, and he thus keeps the focus on practical questions like cutting out a rational proportion between the number of officers and soldiers. He has established proper control over military expenditures and closed many loopholes in the cash flow, but he still cannot secure the necessary level of financing for the costly reorganizations. Quite probably, at the planning stage money did not look like a problem, but launching his project in fall 2008, Serdyukov was hardly blind to the unfolding economic disaster and had to promise that the changes would be accomplished without extra increases in the already-approved defense budget.[6]

This "economically correct" promise, combined with the "politically correct" priority for funding the housing program for the made-redundant officers, produced many distortions in the design of the army's "new look," particularly regarding the curtailing of the program for "professionalization" of the "permanent readiness" units. These distortions could have been corrected in the second or third year of reforms, but state finances are set to remain tight, and even the exemption from sequestration granted for the military budget by the commander in chief, who does not want to appear negligent of security needs, cannot provide sufficient investment in military modernization. This may be particularly obvious with the delays and reductions in the ambitious procurement plans, but in fact the sharp decline of combat-worthiness is the most worrisome development.[7]

These increasingly apparent negative consequences of reshaping the Russian armed forces are easily predictable and could have been explained away as consequences of the initial disorganization inevitable in any deep reform process, and particularly one hampered by insufficient funding. But what makes the problem far worse in this case is the lack of any coherent vision of what the "new look" army would actually look like. Serdyukov is an effective enforcer but certainly not a visionary; hardly anybody in the narrow circle of trusted aides shared by the two duumvirs has a sound understanding of military organization; and the General Staff, traditionally the main depositary of strategic wisdom, has been badly damaged by multiple cadre reshufflings. This astounding deficit of military expertise in the small and isolated team of reformers leaves much space for doubt about whether they are capable of comprehending the strategic consequences of their results-oriented efforts. For that matter, it is rather obvious that the disbandment of hundreds of the "reduced strength" units (which had long since degenerated into empty shells containing depots of unusable armaments) implies that Russia no longer has even a theoretical capacity for conducting a large-scale mobilization, which essentially means that it is not preparing for a large-scale conventional war either with NATO or with China; it is unclear, nevertheless, whether the High Command has internalized this plain strategic fact.[8]

What should have established a solid foundation for the suddenly rushed reconfiguration was the Military Doctrine, and the postponement of its approval until February 2010 was interpreted by informed commentators as extra-careful theorizing of shifts in the security environment.[9] There was overwhelming disappointment with the text of this fundamental document, as it provides no useful guidelines for building up the armed forces and, in keeping with the tradition set by previous editions, postulates that they should be ready to engage and prevail in any and every possible hostility. The list of "threats" is compiled from entirely abstract notions, and the list of "dangers" (which is a new term with a rather unclear theoretical rationale) consists of equally imprecise entries with a single exception— NATO is identified as a source of dual danger; its "global ambitions" are seen as detrimental to Russia's interests, as is its "infrastructure."[10]

This single specific point in the strikingly low-content document has little relevance to the real restructuring of the military's capabilities (as is shown later and in greater detail in chapter 18) and appears to be a pro forma concession to the traditional doctrinal framework.[11] As such, it indicates a profound confusion in military-strategic mindsets, which is generated by the swift execution of reforms without any coherent connection between assessed threats and planned capabilities. This confusion inevitably translates into mistrust among the top brass in the changes that they are forced to implement that goes far deeper than the usual grumbling of a conservative uniformed hierarchy. Facing this discontent and even sabotage, Serdyukov has executed several rounds of purges among the High Command (certainly with Medvedev's and Putin's consent), replacing all the top generals and promoting the more agreeable commanders, which often involves compromising the quality of leadership.[12]

By the end of Medvedev's presidency, the process of reforms is approaching a fork in the road of radical but narrowly focused changes, where the "more-of-the-same" path is no longer available. Serious problems with manning the army, the combat-worthiness of the newly built brigades, and the modernization of the key weapons systems and equipment have accumulated to such a burden that a hard political decision is necessary to shoulder it. One way forward involves the choice to downsize the total strength of 750,000 personnel, reducing the draft to a reserve-building practice and shifting the emphasis to professionalization, and increasing the investment in new technologies. It appears, however, that the readiness to enforce changes is nearly exhausted in the ruling duumvirate, which needs to secure political calm for the next self-reformatting in 2012. That leaves as a more probable choice the partial reverse of the reforms, including the extension of the draft service period to eighteen months, an increase in the number of units and reconstitution of divisions, and the recall to service of a few dozens of fired generals, while Serdyukov would get the sack. This would still require an increase in financing the 1-million-strong armed forces, but it could ease the immediate tensions and exorcise the specter of "military opposition" that has emerged due to widespread discontent in the ranks and in the numerous cohorts of retirees. The unmodernized army could regain some combat-readiness but the deep-rooted manning and degradation problems would come back in the second half of the 2010s.

Nuclear Disarmament Is Set to Continue Unless an Acute Challenge Strikes

The pivotal importance of nuclear weapons for guaranteeing Russia's security is one of the fundamental postulates of its macrostrategic dogma that is ritually confirmed in all key documents and speeches. Putin emphasized it forcefully in the autumnal phase of his presidency, declaring in the 2006 address to the Parliament: "Over the next five years we will have to significantly increase the number of modern long-range aircraft, submarines, and launch systems in our strategic nuclear forces."[13] Medvedev is staying with this message, despite its obvious incompatibility with the idea of a "nuclear-free world" that is being revived by U.S. president Barack Obama.[14] This reliance on the "absolute weapon" is nevertheless far more controversial than the mental habit of connecting great power status with the possession of a vast nuclear arsenal would admit.

The basic dilemma is that maintaining nuclear capabilities and the supporting infrastructure on a level that is seen as sufficient requires greater resource allocation than the political leadership or the majority of generals are prepared to provide. This creates a permanent tug-of-war between strategic and conventional forces for priority funding, which goes beyond a healthy competition and shapes what could be called a "mother of vicious circles" in reforming the armed forces. Indeed, the weakness of conventional capabilities necessitates greater reliance on nuclear instruments, which is translated into their greater share of the defense budget, which in turn further aggravates the problems with conventional forces.[15] In principle, investments in nuclear weapons are supposed to generate greater returns (which are known as "bigger-bang-for-the-buck" output), but in fact the net result of the channeling of massive resources into strategic modernization is far from impressive.

It should be pointed out that while the scope of financing has been steadily growing throughout the 2000s, the priority for strategic forces has been quite unstable. At the start of Putin's "era," the Kosovo war delivered hard evidence of the irrelevance of nuclear instruments for projecting Russia's power, and the war in Chechnya necessitated a prioritization of funding for ground forces, so Defense Minister Igor Sergeev, a staunch supporter of Strategic Rocket Forces, was fired after a bitter quarrel with Chief of the General Staff Anatoly Kvashnin.[16] Sergeev's main legacy is the remarkably successful missile Topol-M (SS-27), which was developed in the 1980s and will most probably constitute the only operational intercontinental ballistic missile (ICBM) by 2020. The deployment of silo-based missiles started in 1997, and the road-mobile version was deployed in late 2006, while since mid-2010, a multiple-warhead (MIRVed) modification known as Yars (RS-24) has been entering service.[17] Although the missile is reliable and relatively cheap, its production at the Votkinsk plant has been maintained at the level of six to seven units a year, which is below the economically optimal output of 30 missiles. As a result, the total number of ICBMs has declined, from about 750 at the start of the 2000s to 370 in 2010, and is set to come down to below 200 by 2020, as the extended service lives of heavy SS-18s and SS-19s come to an end and all solid-fuel SS-25s expire.

This trend means that Russia does not need to execute any additional measures to meet the targets for reductions set in the Prague Treaty and is in fact objectively interested in negotiating a new parity-based deal with the United States.[18] What could weaken the U.S. interest in accepting new binding commitments is the uncertain future of the two other legs of Russia's strategic triad. It is the navy that has since the mid-2000s become the main recipient of extra funding as the Bulava missile became Putin's pet project—and ripened into the most spectacular failure of the strategic modernization. Two tests in October 2010 and one in June 2011 were successful, but the record of malfunctioning is so long that the possibility of a dead end for this hugely expensive program must be taken into serious consideration.[19] Politically unacceptable as it may be, the technical flaws in the Bulava design could cause not only a decade-long delay with the deployment of a new-generation Borey-class strategic submarines but also a crucial weakening of the naval component of strategic deterrence.[20]

Indeed, all five Delta III-class submarines must be retired by 2015, and of the remaining six Delta IV-class submarines, none can last longer than 2020; it will take only one serious accident (and the record of those is long, with *Komsomolets* and *Kursk*—both newly built submarines—making the largest entries) to get this feeble fleet grounded—perhaps forever. Political demand to get the unfortunate *Yuri Dolgoruky* (the keel was laid in 1996) on combat patrolling with unreliable missiles could overrule all risk assessments and bring to a sudden closure the strategic role of the Russian navy.

The situation with the air force is different but no less uncertain. The Long-Range Aviation has traditionally been the weakest leg of the strategic triad, and only in mid-2007 did Putin discover its value defined by the high visibility of flights close to U.S. or UK airspace, or indeed visits to Venezuela. With all this attention, there are no plans for upgrading these capabilities, which are set to decline sharply by 2020. Indeed, hardly any of the 63 turbo-prop Tu-95MS (Bear-H) planes would last that long (reliable as they are), and the 13 Tu-160 (Blackjack) most probably would be reequipped for conventional missions, particularly because all 84 substrategic Tu-22Ms (Backfires) would also be retired. Plans for organizing the serial production of Tu-160s at the Kazan plant have been quietly abandoned, and the more recent promises about deploying a new stealth-technology-based strategic bomber are very vague.[21] It has to be mentioned that Russian long-range aviation has been very lucky in not having a single bad accident while performing strategic patrolling (on average, one or two plane flights a month since August 2007), particularly taking into consideration the dismal air force safety record. Even if this luck would not run out, the viability of strategic air capabilities is doubtful.

Perhaps the most controversial part of the strategic deterrence system is the anti–missile defense, and the essence of Russian worries, which might seem not entirely rational, was perfectly captured by Putin:[22]

As everyone knows, our American partners are building a global missile-defense system, and we aren't. But missile-defense and strategic offensive weapons are closely interrelated issues. A balance of forces was what kept aggression at bay and preserved peace during the Cold War. The missile and air defense systems and offensive weapons systems contribute equally to this balance. If we do not develop a missile defense system, the risk arises that our partners will feel entirely secure and protected against our offensive weapons systems. If the balance I mentioned is disrupted, they will feel able to act with impunity, increasing the level of aggression in politics and, incidentally, in the economy.

Putin is not entirely correct in asserting that Russia is not working on its own strategic defense because there is great amount of conceptualizing of the integrated air space defense system and significant investment in deploying the S-400 antimissile complex and developing a more capable S-500 weapons system.[23] There has also been remarkably successful work on constructing a new network of strategic radars and a less successful but more ambitious program to create the satellite navigation system GLONASS, which should enable the Russian armed forces to make a quantum leap in high-precision targeting.[24] There is no space here to elaborate on the various and multiple shortcomings in the programs under implementation, but the bottom line is that Russia's air defense system has deteriorated to such a degree that an upgrade to an air space system is simply a figment of the imagination, which brings nice profits to many interested parties.[25] A symmetric answer to the probable U.S. decision to start full-scale deployment of a strategic "shield" is, therefore, not available.

The most inexplicable paradox in the Russian nuclear posture involves nonstrategic or tactical nuclear weapons (TNW), the exact number of which is not known but has been estimated to be no less than 2,000 and no more than 4,000 warheads.[26] The point of paradox is that official documents and statements never mention any role for these weapons, and the training of the Russian armed forces does not include any exercises for their possible use—but Moscow resolutely refuses to discuss any framework for their possible negotiated reduction.[27] The only part of this arsenal that has a specific function are naval torpedoes and antiship cruise missiles, which grant the much-diminished Russian navy a chance to make a hit on several U.S. aircraft carrier battle groups. It is possible to speculate about the statement of Nikolai Patrushev, the secretary of the Security Council, who revealed that in the classified part of the Military Doctrine, "conditions for the use of nuclear weapons for repelling aggression with the use of conventional weapons are corrected not only for a large-scale but also for a regional or even a local war," and further indicated that "in situations critical for national security, the possibility of a preemptive (preventive) nuclear strike on the aggressor is not ruled out."[28] It is also possible to suggest that the irreducible weakness of the conventional forces creates the psychological need for a greater reliance on nuclear deterrence that should be flexible to cover the maximum variety of possible contingencies. It appears probable, nevertheless, that given sufficient reassurance from NATO to avoid the impression of unilateral concessions, talks on TNW reductions could produce a series of deals as soon as the mid-2010s.

The scope and composition of the Russian nuclear arsenal by 2020 might appear reasonably predictable, given that the key programs have significant inertia and the life cycles of all weapons systems are well known. The main uncertainty is created by the Bulava project, which determines the very existence of the naval component of strategic forces. Providing that this unfortunate missile is perfected, Russia would have four operational Borey-class submarines and six Delta-IV submarines (scheduled for retirement by 2025) divided between the Northern and Pacific fleets. If, however, the project fails, some desperate measures—like retrofitting the *Yuri Dolgoruky* and her sister submarines for the liquid-fuel Sineva missile (SS-N-23, which Delta-IV subs carry)—could be undertaken, but the reliability of naval platforms would be severely compromised. The only way to compensate for this weakness is to increase the production of Topol-M and Yars IBCMs to 15 to 20 units a year, which would secure an expansion of the Strategic Rocket Forces. The much-reduced air component of the current triad would most probably be completely reoriented toward conventional missions. As for the TNW, their usefulness, without resuming nuclear tests, would become so problematic that most of the warheads would need to be decommissioned with or without international negotiations.

This "technical" trajectory could be altered by various events, two of which could be identified as fairly probable and definitely capable of having a high impact. The first one is the above-mentioned U.S. decision on the deployment of a full-scale antimissile system based on revolutionary new technologies for interception. This development would not create any direct threat to Russia, but the self-made trap of security thinking in terms of mutual deterrence is set to snap without fail. The Russian leadership, unable to follow suit, would feel forced to respond with extra effort to strengthen offensive capabilities, which would require channeling massive additional resources into every component of strategic forces, and primarily the land-based missiles, where adequate returns are guaranteed. The Prague Treaty will be canceled, and the viability of the Intermediate Nuclear Forces (INF) Treaty (1987) also becomes problematic, even if Moscow cannot be interested in a return of U.S. intermediate-range land-based missiles to Europe.

Another drastic change in the nuclear posture would result from a serious deterioration of Russian-Chinese relations. The return to confrontation could be caused by a Chinese intervention in a violent conflict in Central Asia, or by a series of anti-Chinese pogroms in the chronically depressed Far East, or by a chain of border incidents—or indeed by any combination of these triggers, but it will inevitably sharply accentuate the already-present (but never officially acknowledged) perception of the high vulnerability of the Eastern theater. Only nuclear instruments could help in neutralizing this threat, and the main emphasis could be placed on nonstrategic capabilities, so that a withdrawal from the INF Treaty could become necessary. Facing the imperative of redeploying maximum possible forces to the East, Russia would have to rely on partnership with NATO, and even the deployment of an antimissile system by the United States would become an irrelevant security challenge.

Conventional Forces: Still in Multidimensional Limbo

Serdyukov's bold and brutal reform has barely touched the nuclear capabilities but has had a massive impact on the conventional forces, and first of all Ground Forces. It was probably inevitable that cuts, restructuring, and officer cadre decimation would cause serious disorganization, but in reality the scope of decline in combat capabilities has turned out to be far greater than was expected (or, indeed, has been admitted)—and the recovery in the new organizational structures is by no means certain. Expert assessments of the operability of new brigades and the integrity of the chain of command have turned increasingly negative, but the High Command resolutely refuses to engage in any discussions on the implementation of the reform plan, while commander-in-chief Medvedev pays only superficial attention to military issues.[29] What makes it possible to deny the crisis in military modernization is the generally benign security situation, which presents no immediate tasks for the armed forces; however, when in the spring of 2010 the violent disorder in Kyrgyzstan, formally one of Russia's closest allies, involved the question of peace enforcement, it quickly transpired that there is no capacity for such deployment.[30] Further development of this military crisis is determined by the interplay between three variables: recruitment, equipment, and financing.

Russia's demographic decline, which is deepening despite the political campaign for boosting fertility, is the fundamental cause of difficulties with manning the army, while the growth of the middle class (continuing despite the recession) objectively weakens support for and the acceptability of the draft system.[31] The unforeseen but, in hindsight, inevitable consequence of the emphasis on cutting down the officer corps by more than half on the first stage of reform was a sharp drop in the number of soldiers serving on contract (*kontraktniki*), first of all due to shrinking funding for this program.[32] The sound proposition for building a cohort of professional sergeants was also reduced to one experimental school, while the demotion of newly graduated lieutenants to sergeant positions has brought much disgruntlement.[33] Stopgap measures could camouflage the problem for a couple of years, but after 2012 the choice must be made between an extension of the conscript service to eighteen or twenty-four months or a determined effort to professionalize the majority of combat units. Only the latter option answers to the requirements of an "innovative army," but it also implies downsizing to the target figure of 750,000 for total strength.

For twenty years, since the collapse of the USSR, the Russian army was able to live on the weapons systems and material reserves produced by the enormous Soviet military machine. This "low-or-no" investment period has come to an end. The problem is not that only 15 to 20 percent of armaments can be defined as "modern" (this definition is always conveniently imprecise) but also that poor maintenance has rendered much of the equipment and infrastructure unreliable or unusable. Medvedev has set the task of increasing the share of "modern" weapons systems to 30 percent, focusing particularly on communication technologies; this task can be accomplished by scrapping redundant dilapidated "assets," but as for introducing high-technology command, control, communications, and information systems, the army in its present shape clearly cannot cope with those.[34] The military industry is able to cover most of the immediate needs of the armed forces, but it has good reasons to prioritize export orders, while powerful lobbies connected with Deputy Prime Minister Sergei Ivanov push for higher prices on their products, mostly based on Soviet designs, and fight against the plans to increase the importing of armaments.[35] Putin has always been generous with promises of military hardware, but the short period of reform has seen an unprecedented avalanche of "defense orders"—hundreds of helicopters and T-90/T-95 tanks, Ruslan transport planes and "fifth-generation" fighters, several aircraft carriers, and the French helicopter-carrier *Mistral*; a minimally realistic assessment shows that deliveries on this spectacular wish list remain problematic.

Financing is supposed to be the most manageable but in fact is the most uncertain variable in this combination, not to mention the fierce squabbles inside the military bureaucracy for the distribution of the allocated funds—and the lack of reliable information on the execution of the defense budget. Quite possibly, low returns on the steadily increasing investments in the military might have influenced Putin's decision to replace Ivanov with ruble-wise Serdyukov as defense minister. The latter probably budgeted for more generous funding of his reform endeavor, but it is truly remarkable that the sharp contraction of state income in 2009 did not cause any cuts in the money flow to the Ministry of Defense coffers. Further priorities in resource allocation are, nevertheless, impossible to foresee, and the reevaluation of the State Armaments Program for 2011–2020 provide a perfect example: In May 2010, Putin confirmed the figure of 13 trillion rubles (about $400 billion) as the final estimate, but in June one of Sedyukov's deputies asserted that Medvedev's order to increase the share of "modern" weapons to 70 percent would cost 36 trillion rubles, and in July a compromise target of 20 trillion was suggested.[36] Just a year later, leading defense industry enterprises went public with claims that the implementation of the approved acquisition plans was sabotaged—aiming these accusations directly at Serdyukov.[37] Russia's economic future does not look particularly bright, and it is clear that the median trajectory of slow and uneven growth will involve many hard choices between "must-have" weapons systems, optimal levels of contract service and drafted troops, and affordable demonstrations of military "muscle."

It is the ground forces that are currently the most affected by Serdyukov's reforms and could face further setbacks due to sudden cuts in funding, swings between politically prioritized armaments programs, and "economizing" on costly professionalization. It is significant, however, that one component of this traditionally central part of the armed forces has been exempted from experiments with the "new look"—the airborne troops (Vozdushno-Desantnye Voiska, VDV). General Vladimir Shamanov, a veteran of the Chechen wars and a key advocate of reforms, was appointed commander of the VDV in May 2009 and immediately asserted that airborne divisions would not be downsized to brigades and no officer positions would be cut.[38] The VDV remain the most, and perhaps the only, combat-capable part of the ground forces. But their numbers remain small, so they can only spearhead combat deployment even in a local conflict. The "Vostok-2010" exercises demonstrated that newly formed brigades need not only time but also much investment of effort in building the noncommissioned officer/sergeant core to become combat-worthy units, while in the Eastern theater, a shift back to the regiment/division structure makes much sense.[39] The weapons inventory of the ground forces is old but fairly durable, so their most urgent technical need is for modern communications equipment. The central problem, however, is personnel, and every attempt to solve it "on the cheap"—that is, by expanding conscription—would generate tensions in society and increase the costs that would eventually have to be paid for building a usable force that invariably bears the brunt of every war along with peacekeeping.

The air force faces a very different set of problems that are only tangentially related to Serdyukov's reforms, though the disbandment of its regiments and divisions and creating instead the rather administrative air bases is a questionable improvement that quite probably will be reversed. Two main issues in this component of conventional forces that are recognized as crucial for operations in modern warfare are combat training and the replacement of weapons systems. Greater emphasis on the former since the mid-2000s has resulted in a significant increase in accidents caused by the very slow progress with the latter; the crash of two Su-27 fighter jets from the Vityazi (Russian Knights) pilot group in August 2009 highlighted these problems.[40] An unexpected gift for the Russian air force in 2009 were 34 MiG-29s, which were delivered to the domestic market when Algeria refused to honor the contract for purchasing them, but it is difficult to count on more surprises of this sort. The feasibility of current plans to acquire so many planes of various kinds (including the "fifth-generation" fighter) so that the whole fleet will be renewed by 2020 looks very doubtful; the only reference point is the fact that the delivery of two Su-34s in 2008 was the first real acquisition in more than fifteen years.[41] Setting priorities is going to be the key issue; for that matter, the transfer of Army Aviation to the Air Force in the mid-2000s caused a sustained deprioritization of helicopter units, but now the task of increasing the mobility of the army brigades can only be accomplished by investing in helicopters— very much against the parochial interests of the Air Force Command.[42] The worst option is a constant change of priorities, which would undermine the stability of the key programs.

The navy is mostly out of reach of Serdyukov's reforms, but it faces an acute problem of manpower quality because it is impossible to make an able sailor from a conscript serving twelve months. This problem attracts less attention than the dramatic shrinking of the list of seaworthy ships due to aging—a situation so severe that nearly all vintage landing ships and minesweepers will have to be retired before 2020.[43] Maintenance and repairs are another major problem, even in the strategically pivotal Northern Fleet, and it is further complicated by the wide variety of vessel types (for instance, there are seven frigates of six different classes). Shipbuilding was severely dislocated due to a total lack of orders in the 1990s, and it continues to be affected by the very high concentration of funding on the Bulava/Borey program. It can be safely assumed that the plans for building several (or even one) aircraft carriers fall into the category of wishful thinking, but the politically motivated plan for buying French Mistral helicopter carriers and building two or three ships of this type might come true and radically change the composition of the Russian navy.[44] The proposition for strengthening the Caspian Flotilla has apparently been abandoned, the Baltic Fleet is set to be downsized to a symbolic squadron, and the key point now is how to rebuild the barely seaworthy Black Sea Fleet, which is set to stay in Sevastopol to save the expenses of constructing a new naval base in Novorossiysk.[45] Admirals now have little political clout, and they are hardly going to gain any, so the future of the navy depends upon erratic "patriotic" ambitions to "show the flag" dampened by rare sober calculations of costs.

Overall, the prospects for conventional forces are extremely mosaic given that the programs for the different branches are uncoordinated, poorly compatible, and often compete for funding that is less than generous. As the war with Georgia demonstrated, a capacity for joint operations is practically nonexistent; for that matter, at least half of the surprisingly high losses of aircraft could be attributed to "friendly fire."[46] Seeking to enhance this capacity, Serdyukov has opted to enact in the new phase of his reform the old plan for forming four strategic commands—East, West, South, and Center—instead of the traditional Soviet organization of military districts.[47] This plan makes good sense, though several past attempts to implement it failed over bureaucratic resistance, but the reformers probably have scant understanding of how, for instance, the subordination of the Northern Fleet to the Center Command would work in practice. The political will to make hard choices remains a preciously rare commodity in the further reshaping of the ground forces, the air force, and the navy, though it will be necessary for rebuilding their diminishing combat-worthiness.

Conclusion: Events on Top of Reforms

One piece of political wisdom attributed to U.S. president Harry S. Truman is "A president either is constantly on top of events or, if he hesitates, events will soon be on top of him." The Russian leadership in the coming decade has only a slim chance to be on top of events as it seeks to preserve the status quo regime that has exhausted its potential for modernization and resists the pressure to change. This means that reforms of the military organization will be driven not by a rational strategy corrected by interservice/intraservice feuds but by emergency tasks generated by suddenly erupting crises.

It is impossible to predict the scope and timing of such events that are by definition unpredictable, but it might make sense to isolate several possible violent cataclysms in Russia's neighborhood in order to suggest a brief net assessment of their impact on the armed forces' transformation. To take one of the most current examples, Moscow opted against any intervention in the state failure in Kyrgyzstan in the spring and summer of 2010, but its response to a similar implosion in Turkmenistan would probably be more proactive. President Gurbanguly Berdymukhammedov has canceled some odious features of the country's despotic regime, but his grasp on power remains infirm, and a clash of clans vying for a greater share of rent might trigger an explosion of public discontent. Russia's interests in this state are defined by its rich reserves of natural gas—but several neighbors are similarly interested. Russia would hardly be able to dissuade Uzbekistan from taking control over the eastern part of troubled Turkmenistan, but it would try its best to prevent a move from Iran. Several battalions could be deployed by sea and air rather quickly, and then reinforced by a brigade or two, but the main challenge for this operation would be logistics. This would require an allocation of extra resources to the much-neglected rear services, and also a modest strengthening of the Caspian Flotilla.

One key precondition for such order-restoring intervention is that the ground forces are not engaged in any other mission, as they were in Chechnya from the mid-1990s to the mid-2000s. The current escalation of instability and terrorist attacks in the North Caucasus indicates that this region would remain the source of multiple security challenges as new tensions interplay with "frozen conflicts" while Moscow remains very sensitive to any risks pertaining to the preparations to the 2014 Winter Olympic games in Sochi. The August 2008 Russian-Georgian war could hardly be taken as a "lessons-learned" model, and Russia must be prepared for a wide range of conflicts, including, for instance, a confrontation between Azerbaijan and Iran. This requires building a strong, multitasking grouping of forces with an emphasis on mobility, command, control, communications, and information capabilities as well as combat readiness, which can only be achieved by professionalizing several motor-rifle, marine, and airborne brigades. The building up of the Russian military presence in South Ossetia, Abkhazia, and, possibly, Armenia would effectively preclude any progress in reviving the Conventional Armed Forces in Europe Treaty.

One major crisis that the Russian leadership considers as probable is the disintegration of Ukraine (portrayed as an "artificial state") as a result of another political spasm similar to the Orange Revolution of November and December 2004. It is possible to argue that Ukraine has accumulated experience in managing its political and economic turmoil, but it is clear that Russia is not preparing for any military response to Ukraine's imagined breakdown/breakup. The main parameter of a hypothetic "brotherly" intervention is the large number of troops that would be needed to stabilize a country of such size, so a significant increase in the draft would be imperative. The only feasible scenario for this train of thought is the secession of Crimea, which might be supported by a timely arrival of a few Russian battalions; the political price of this low-cost "military solution" would be certain to be heavy. Another crisis that the Russian leadership does not want to contemplate is a "color revolution" in Belarus, where the life cycle of the populist regime of Alexander Lukashenko might come to a sudden end. The opposition to this "last dictatorship" in Europe might count on moral and material support from the West, and Moscow, despite its pronounced dislike of Lukashenko, could feel obliged to come to the rescue with military means. The key task would be to secure the western and northern borders of Belarus in order to isolate the "Union state" from Western interference, and a "nuclear umbrella" made of a few dozen TNW might be seen as essential for preventing any real confrontation with NATO.

Russia cannot take the current "more-of-the-same" low-risk security environment for granted, and it can ill afford the luxury of manipulating conflicts and simulating mobilization against convenient challenges. The rationality of decisionmaking in weak authoritarian regimes is never solid, so shallow ambitions often overrule elementary "cost-efficiency" calculations and expediency gives way to pragmatism. This reality is likely to affect the sustainability of military reforms negatively. There is also a danger that technical accidents could reach a catastrophic scale, due largely to the willingness to relax the criteria for "unacceptable risk"—for instance, in staging large-scale air parades over Moscow. Russia has entered a decade of uncertainty with a seriously disorganized and profoundly disgruntled army—a state that does not bode well for its domestic stability.

Notes

1. One sound assessment of the ongoing military reform is given by Vitaly Shlykov, "The Secrets of Serdyukov's Blitzkrieg," *Russia in Global Affairs*, January–March 2010, 29–48. Also see my most recent analysis: Pavel K. Baev, "Military Reform Against Heavy Odds," in *Russia after the Global Economic Crisis*, edited by Anders Åslund, Sergei Guryev, and Andrew Kuchins (Washington: Peterson Institute, 2010).

2. See Nikolai Petrov, Masha Lipman, and Henry E. Hale, "Overmanaged Democracy in Russia: Governance Implications of Hybrid Regimes," Carnegie Paper 106 (Washington, D.C.: Carnegie Endowment for International Peace, 2010).

3. See the archive of my weekly columns in the *Eurasia Daily Monitor*, www.jamestown. org/programs/edm.

4. One good discussion is presented in "Current Issues and Logic of the Military Reform" (in Russian), *Nezavisimoe voennoe obozrenie*, April 24–May 14, 2009. Hereafter, unless noted, all articles and the like cited from Russian publications are in Russian; the article titles are simply translated here for the reader's convenience.

5. The extensive debates on this article published in the liberal *Gazeta.ru* hardly touched on military issues; see www.gazeta.ru/subjects/3260384.shtml.

6. On the initial cost estimates, see Vadim Solovyev and Vladimir Ivanov, "Reform Turns in an Unpredictable Direction," *Nezavisimoe voennoe obozrenie*, May 29, 2009.

7. This problem is emphasized by Anatoly Tsyganok, "Main Problems of the Russian Army," Polit.ru, June 10, 2010, http://polit.ru/author/2010/06/10/army_print.html.

8. On this, see Aleksandr Hramchihin, "All in All: 85 Permanent Readiness Brigades," *Nezavisimoe voennoe obozrenie*, October 16, 2009; and Stanislav Kuvaldin, "Army for a Modest Power," *Expert*, October 12, 2009.

9. See "Doctrinal Uncertainty," *Nezavisimoe voennoe obozrenie*, October 16, 2009.

10. One attentive analysis of this casuistic is given by Keir Gilles, "The Military Doctrine of the Russian Federation," *Research Review*, NATO Defense College, February 2010, www.ndc.nato.int/research/series.php?icode=9.

11. This is consistent with the anti-NATO guidelines of the National Security Strategy (approved in May 2009), but it is hardly compatible with the new aims of Russia's foreign policy as outlined by Medvedev in the summer of 2010; see Vladimir Solovyev, "Not According to this MID," *Kommersant*, July 13, 2010.

12. On the group firing in the summer of 2010, see Pavel Felgengauer, "Rearmament Declared the Main Issue in Russian Military Reform," *Eurasia Daily Monitor*, June 24, 2010.

13. For the official English translation of this address, see http://archive.kremlin.ru/eng/ speeches/2006/05/10/1823_type70029type82912_105566.shtml.

14. One argument on harmfulness of the antinuclear movement is Sergei Karaganov, "Global Zero and Common Sense," *Russia in Global Affairs*, April/June 2010, http://eng. globalaffairs.ru/number/Global_Zero_and_Common_Sense-14889.

15. On this, see Leonid Orlenko, "National Security and Modernization of the Army," *Nezavisimoe voennoe obozrenie*, July 11, 2006.

16. For a sympathetic view on Sergeev's lost cause, see Aleksandr Golts, "The Last Chance of a Technocrat," *Itogi*, July 28, 2000.

17. Updated data of great value can be found on Pavel Podvig's blog, "Russian Strategic Nuclear Forces," http://russianforces.org.

18. One concise and competent assessment of the yet-to-be-ratified document is given by Alexei Arbatov and Vladimir Dvorkin, "New START: A Step in the Right Direction," Moscow Carnegie Center Briefing Paper, June 2010.

19. Deputy Prime Minister Sergei Ivanov revealed that 40 percent of the total defense budget was allocated to the Navy, primarily for its strategic submarines. See "Ivanov: Lion's Share of the MoD Budget Goes to the Navy," *RIA-Novosti*, June 3, 2009, http://rian.ru/defense_safety/20090603/173122482.html.

20. See Albert Dubrovin and Sergei Makeev, "Bulava Might Still Fly but Will Not Fly High," *Nezavisimoe voennoe obozrenie*, December 11, 2010.

21. See Mikhail Rastopshin, "Imitation of the Process of Building New-Look Weapons," *Nezavisimoe voennoe obozrenie*, October 23, 2009; and Ilya Kramnik, "Long-Range Aviation: Prospects for Strategic Planes," *RIA-Novosti*, December 23, 2009, http://rian.ru/analytics/20091223/201029231.html.

22. For the official translation of the conversation with journalists on December 29, 2009, see http://premier.gov.ru/eng/visits/ru/8759/events/8815.

23. On the problems with research and development of the S-400 *Triumph* surface-to-air missile complexes, see "'Triumph' Without a Triumph," information memo, December 16, 2009, http://pro-spe-ro.livejournal.com/260.html.

24. See Viktor Myasnikov, "GLONASS for All of Us," *Nezavisimoe voennoe obozrenie*, June 4, 2010; much information is available on the website www.glonassgsm.ru.

25. On the dismal state of the Russian air defense system, which currently can intercept at best 20 percent of aircraft or missiles targeting Moscow, see Oleg Vladykin, "Holes in Space Defense," *Nezavisimoe voennoe obozrenie*, May 21, 2010.

26. One reliable update analysis of this issue is given by Johan Bergenäs, Miles A. Pomper, William C. Potter, and Nikolai N. Sokov, "Reducing and Regulating Tactical (Nonstrategic) Nuclear Weapons in Europe: Moving Forward?" *CNS Report*, Monterey Institute of International Studies, April 2010, http://cns.miis.edu/opapers/pdfs/reducing_tnw_april_2010.pdf.

27. An insightful take on this issue is given by Alexei Arbatov, "Tactical Nuclear Weapons: Problems and Solution," *Voenno-promyshlenny kuryer*, May 5–11, 2010.

28. See Vladimir Mamontov, "Russia Is Changing, and Its Military Doctrine Is Changing Also," interview with Nikolai Patrushev, *Izvestia*, October 14, 2009.

29. See, for instance, Albert Aleksandrov, "Not the Last Reform in the History of the Russian Army," *Nezavisimoe voennoe obozrenie*, May 28, 2010; and Vladimir Evseev, "Stages in Military Reform: What Next?" *Nezavisimoe voennoe obozrenie*, July 16, 2010.

30. On the proposition of establishing a Russian military base in the conflict-torn Osh region, see Grigory Mikhailov and Viktoria Panfilova, "Kyrgyzstan Uses Russia as a Shield," *Nezavisimaya gazeta*, July 9, 2010.

31. According to data gathered by the Levada Center, the low point in public support for conscription (27 percent) was registered in 2002; the reduction of the draft period to twelve months secured an increase to 47 percent in 2009, but already in 2010, the figure came down to 39 percent, while 54 percent preferred the contract system. See Levada Center, "The Army, Conscription, and the LDPR Initiative," July 14, 2010, www.levada.ru/press/2010071401.html.

32. See Vladimir Ivanov, "Kontraktniki Are Reduced to the Minimum," *Nezavisimoe voennoe obozrenie*, July 2, 2010; and Ilya Kramnik, "The Army Gets Conscripts Instead of Kontraktniki," *RIA-Novosti*, May 13, 2010.

33. See Nikolai Poroskov, "From Officers to Sergeants," *Vremya novostei*, July 1, 2010.

34. See Oleg Vladykin, "Equipment Beyond Backwardness," *Nezavisimoe voennoe obozrenie*, May 28, 2010.

35. See Alexandr Konovalov, "Hard Defense Posture," *Ogonyok*, November 9, 2009.

36. See "Astronomers in Uniform," *Vedomosti*, July 22, 2010; for my take, see Pavel Baev, "*Lynx* Braces for a Jump," *New Times*, July 5, 2010.

37. Viktor Myasnikov, "The failure of defense order: price war, corruption and arms-twisting," *Nezavisimoe voennoe obozrenie*, July 22, 2011.

38. See Oleg Vladykin, "Flank Maneuver of the Paratroopers," *Nezavisimaya gazeta*, June 4, 2010.

39. One critical evaluation of these exercises is given by Aleksandr Khramchihin, "Inadequate Vostok," *Nezavisimoe voennoe obozrenie*, July 23, 2010.

40. See Igor Naumov, "*Sukhoi* Counts Losses," *Nezavisimaya Gazeta*, August 19, 2009.

41. On the current promises, see Viktor Litovkin, "20 Trillion for 10 Years," *Nezavisimoe voennoe obozrenie*, July 23, 2010.

42. The need in expanding the fleet of helicopters was acknowledged after the *Vostok*-2010 exercises; see Vladimir Sherbakov, "Mi-26 Makes a Claim for Leadership," *Nezavisimoe voennoe obozrenie*, July 23, 2010.

43. One competent assessment of the naval posture is given by Mikhail Barabanov and Mikhail Lukin, "Where the Russian Navy Is Going," *Kommersant-Vlast*, February 25, 2008.

44. Many professionals are skeptical about this plan; see Yuri Kirillov, "Does Mistral Fit into the Russian Navy?" *Nezavisimoe voennoe obozrenie*, May 25, 2010.

45. See Pavel Borisov, "Celebrating a New Fleet," *Lenta.ru*, June 25, 2010, http://lenta.ru/articles/2010/06/25/fleet.

46. See Anton Lavrov, "Russian Air Force Losses in the Five-Day War with Georgia," in *Tanki Avgusta* [The Tanks of August], edited by Mikhail Barabanov (Moscow: Center for Analysis of Strategies and Technologies, 2009), 109–18.

47. See Ilya Kramnik, "New Command System Is in the Making," *RIA-Novosti*, July 15, 2010, http://rian.ru/analytics/20100715/255118238.html.

the ARMED FORCES in 2020: MODERN or SOVIET?

Alexander Golts

In the next decade, Russian military and political leaders will face a difficult dilemma: to decide whether or not it is necessary to divert substantial economic resources to the modernization of the armed forces at a time when there is virtually no military threat. In 2010–2011, the Russian armed forces will approach a point of bifurcation where the country's military and political leadership will need to choose, with a greater or lesser degree of certainty, one of two or three scenarios for future development. Meanwhile, it is not out of the question that these scenarios will directly contradict one another. As such, the state of the Russian army in ten years will directly depend on which scenario is chosen.

The authorities' choice will be determined by a number of objective and subjective factors. Among the objective factors, one must first consider the demographic situation: The young men who could begin their service in 2020 have already been born, and their numbers cannot change. In 2011, the country will have 648,000 eighteen-year-olds; in 2012, 662,000; in 2013, 641,000; in 2014, 613,000; in 2015, 592,000; and so on, descending.[1] The number of eighteen-year-olds will begin to increase slightly only in 2022–2023. This means that any plan for the structure of the armed forces should (though it is far from certain that it will) consider the growing shortage of the male population in the most productive age range, between eighteen and thirty years old. In this chapter, I try to predict the impact the demographic factor could have on each of the scenarios for the development of the armed forces.

Yet another objective factor is the current revolution in military affairs. The essence of this revolution (also referred to as the era of wars of the sixth generation) is that apart from land, sea, air, and outer space, there is a new arena for warfare: information. Information technology gives its possessors comprehensive, highly detailed information about their enemy's actions; it allows them to strike their enemy from hundreds or thousands of miles away using "smart" weapons. Robotic instruments of armed conflict are undergoing intensive development. Under these circumstances, the armed forces, in accordance with scientific and technological achievements, require a high level of education and training for all military personnel. The army, in meeting these requirements, cannot be as large as the Russian leadership is currently planning. Neither now, nor in the coming years, will Russia have a million people with the requisite skills.

Finally, there is the objective factor that the nuclear-missile facilities inherited from the Soviet Union (even in the event that they are significantly reduced in the next ten years as a result of unavoidable deterioration) will for the foreseeable future remain a reliable guarantee that no state will risk committing an act of aggression against the country. It is enough for Russia to declare (as has already been done in the military doctrine[2]) that in the event of aggression that it cannot stop with conventional armed forces, it is prepared to use nuclear weapons first. This can provide a credible deterrent to any potential aggressor.

At the same time, all this does not mean that threats to Russian security are entirely absent. It would seem that the primary threats come from Central Asia. The very likely defeat of U.S. and NATO forces in Afghanistan will inevitably lead to instability, and even to the fall of the weak authoritarian regimes of the Central Asian republics. As a result of such a course of events, the area around the Russian-Kazakh border will become flooded with tens of thousands, if not hundreds of thousands, of refugees within a matter of months. Events on the border between Kyrgyzstan and Uzbekistan will look like child's play compared with what would happen in Russia's Orenburg region in the event of civil wars in Central Asia. The possibility of armed conflict on the Korean Peninsula—in which the use of nuclear weapons cannot be excluded—represents another serious threat to security.

The problem, however, is that these challenges are quite difficult to answer by military means. The crisis in Kyrgyzstan, where Russia essentially refused to provide military assistance to the country's provisional government, demonstrated that Moscow is not prepared to participate in conflict resolution at an early stage using military force. Therefore, in the event of serious crises, the army will be condemned to support essentially nonmilitary functions: receiving refugees, disarming gangs of deserters, and protecting against weapons of mass destruction.

As a result, in the next decade, Russian military and political leaders will face a difficult dilemma: whether or not it is necessary to divert substantial economic resources to the modernization of the armed forces at a time when there is virtually no military threat.[3] Moreover, the choice is complicated by the fact that new technology seriously devaluing the significance of nuclear weapons could arrive in the middle of the next century. Thus, the way Russia uses the "security window" formed in 2010–2020 is fundamentally important for the future of the country's national security.

First among the subjective factors is the country's domestic political development. In the event that Russia moves toward an increasingly rigid authoritarian model, this will involve a revival and strengthening of militaristic tendencies in both foreign policy and military doctrine. The strengthening of authoritarianism will inevitably be accompanied by a deterioration in relations with the West. And aggravation with criticism from the outside is just as inevitably voiced in military terms by Russian leaders; they are beginning to picture Russia as a besieged camp where every citizen is first and foremost a soldier.

It is clear that the Russian authorities are aware that they face no threat of the sort that can be repelled by "traditional" military means. That is precisely why the armed forces periodically become the subject of all manner of public relations campaigns associated with Russia's foreign policy actions. It is enough to recall the threats of President Medvedev to deploy the Iskander tactical missiles in the Kaliningrad region, or the flights of strategic bombers in Venezuela. None of this made any sense militarily. The hope was that, on the one hand, they would demonstrate Russia's military might, while, on the other hand, they could remain confident that the United States and NATO would not take these threats seriously.

Russian leaders must make a choice: either prepare the armed forces to respond to real threats, or preserve them as a sort of imperial symbol of the bygone power of the USSR. The nature of this choice is not at all ambiguous. In one case, they must delegate financial resources to developing means to deploy troops and to creating rapid response forces and associated support structures. In the other case, all resources must be directed toward maintaining a semblance of nuclear parity with the United States.

The obvious difference between the Russian armed forces and the country's other government institutions lies in the fact that their effectiveness cannot be verified in times of peace. Thus, the population may harbor the illusion that victims—in the form of those dead and injured as a result of the hazing of conscripts—along with the billions of dollars wasted, are not in vain. And this circumstance reduces social pressure on the government.

Finally and most important, the future of the Russian army will to a large degree depend on the direction in which the military reforms currently under way proceed.

Serdyukov's Reforms

Of all the military reforms undertaken during the past twenty years, those that began in 2008 represent the most radical attempt to modernize the armed forces. Proceeding under the slogan of "optimization"—that is, the elimination of disparities ostensibly resulting from the collapse of the Soviet army and the mass layoffs of the 1990s—it represents the first attempt at a final rejection of the framework of a mass-mobilization army (a framework that was realized in building the Russian armed forces during the past fifty years).

Under this reform, which should be completed in 2012, 205,000 of 355,000 officer positions were to be eliminated. In the army, all skeleton units will be eliminated. As a result, their numbers will be reduced by a factor of 11. Of the army's 1,187 units, 189 remain today. All in all, in accordance with the reforms, only 6,000 of the 26,000 separate units of the armed forces remain.[4] Moreover, the reductions will continue into the future. According to the press, it is planned that the armed forces will retain only 2,500 units.[5] The scale of the reductions are such (as it stands now, two-thirds of the officers of the armed forces have been dismissed) that it has become clear that, contrary to official statements, this has nothing to do with ordinary "optimization." The elimination of reduced-personnel units and the dismissal of surplus numbers of officers means that the Russian political leadership has decided to abandon the idea of mass mobilization for good. If not long ago defending the country in the event of aggression meant mobilizing 4 to 8 million reservists, then today the army, according to its former commander in chief, Vladimir Boldyrev, plans to deploy only 60 brigades (about 300,000 people).[6] According to the chief of the General Staff, Nikolai Makarov, in the event of war, a total of 700,000 reservists are to be mobilized.[7]

Under these circumstances, it would be logical to expect a phasing out of the draft and a gradual transition to the formation of voluntary armed forces. Indeed, the main reason for the existence of a conscription-based army is the preparation of a trained reserve, available on demand in order to increase the size of the armed forces several times over. In situations where the number of reservists makes up about two-thirds of the size of the army in peacetime (which is characteristic of voluntary, but not conscription-based, armed forces), the draft simply does not make sense. If, in the event of military action, only 700,000 reservists are to be called to duty, then why spend a huge amount of resources to train 750,000 conscripts each year if no one is planning to call on them, even in a time of war?

In addition, it is clear that if the one-year term of service by draft is retained, the combat capability of the Russian army will be highly doubtful. Every six months, half the troops will be replaced, so that at any given moment a significant part of the military will consist of untrained recruits. By preserving the draft, the "constant readiness" of every unit that has been put forth as the most important goal of the reforms—Chief of the General Staff Makarov even argued that, now, any unit is prepared to execute an order within an hour of receiving it—will be limited by the fact that, numerically, they will all be fully staffed in accordance with the wartime troop list.

However, contrary to the clear logic of military development, Defense Ministry leaders insisted that in the coming years, not only will the draft not be scaled back but on the contrary, it would be expanded. To ensure recruitment in the armed forces amid a sharp reduction in conscripts, the head of the Main Organization and Mobilization Directorate of the General Staff, Vasily Smirnov, proposed at a Federation Council hearing to increase the draft age limit from the current twenty-seven years to thirty years. The spring conscription period would be extended until August 1, which would make the draft effectively year-round. Seventy percent of colleges and universities would forfeit the right to offer draft deferments, which would allow the military to draft first- and second-year students at the majority of the country's colleges and universities. Finally, a proposal has been made to reject a practice that has been inconvenient for the Ministry of Defense, whereby each potential recruit is delivered a summons that he must personally sign. A proposal has been made to send them an Internet mobile text message notification, and in the event that a recruit does not report to the military recruitment office, he will be subject to criminal prosecution.[8]

It is unlikely these measures will fill the ranks of the army, but maintaining the current draft system will inevitably result in a collapse of recruitment into the armed forces. This will allow the generals, in rejecting the reforms, to justify a return to the Soviet approach to military development.

Furthermore, it is possible that by the end of 2011, the government will not have fulfilled the social obligations it took on with respect to both dismissed and active officers. First and foremost, this concerns the allocation of housing.[9] It emerged that about half of those who were given vouchers for an apartment in 2009 did not receive housing.[10] Bearing in mind that we are talking about 200,000 people, their dissatisfaction may represent a political risk for Putin and Medvedev (who so far have supported the military reformers).

In addition, social pressure will inevitably grow among the active officers in the armed forces themselves. Because of an excess of officers in 2009, 4,700 military school graduates were granted only sergeant positions. Given that approximately 40,000 officers have been forcibly retired, these lieutenants will not have any opportunity for promotion. Moreover, because of the overabundance of officers, as of this writing, trainees for officer positions will no longer be accepted (instead, military schools will be engaged in training professional sergeants).[11] As a result, as has already happened several times, the political leadership may decide to curtail the reforms.

In addition, of fundamental importance is the question of whether or not the Kremlin and the military leadership will attempt to implement an ambitious rearmament program. This concerns their intention to replace 80 percent (though, by other data, 70 percent) of the military's weapons stock by 2020. At a time when the organization of military production is completely ineffective and when the Ministry of Defense insists on the necessity of producing the full range of weapons, an attempt to begin mass production will inevitably turn into a giant waste of resources,[12] which may also lead to a deceleration or complete cessation of reforms. Evidence of the depth of the crisis in the military-industrial sector can be seen in the unprecedented conflict between the leadership of military-industrial corporations and the leadership of the Ministry of Defense. Vladimir Popovkin, while serving as Deputy Defense Minister, said publicly that his goal was to secure for the army the weapons it required, and not to keep ineffective military-industrial companies afloat. Under this logic, the Ministry of Defense decided to buy the French helicopter carrier *Mistral*. "We do not have the docks necessary to build an aircraft carrier," said Popovkin. "But when negotiations with the French began, there was an uproar. The people were saying, 'You can't do that.' We will supposedly destroy the domestic shipbuilding industry. But what should we do if the industry can't do what we need?"[13]

The weak point of the reform is that it is extremely controversial. As mentioned above, until recently, the Defense Ministry leadership insisted that the armed forces would be formed mainly by conscription; thereby making it clear that the federal program envisaging a partial transfer of the armed forces to a service contract had failed. This assertion was followed by a 180 degree turn: First, on March 18, 2011, Defense Minister Anatoly Serdyukov declared that the Russian armed forces should have 425,000 contract soldiers, while only a few months earlier it had been suggested that 100,000 was enough.[14] A little later, the same Chief of the General Staff Makarov stated that the Russian army is conceived as a volunteer force, and as such, conscripts should not exceed 10–15 percent of the total number in the armed forces.[15] With this approach, the draft is needed only to select candidates for the future contract soldier positions.

There is also inconsistency regarding the size of the officer corps. In the first two years of the reform, the Ministry of Defense fired around 205,000 "redundant officers." Then, under the pretext of creating air and space defense forces (a dubious excuse at best), it was announced that the size of the officer corps would be increased by another 70,000.[16]

These twists and turns can be explained by Russia's being an authoritarian state. The authorities do not feel the need to explain to the public why military reform is needed. After all, only the support of the top political leadership is needed to make it happen. The lack of public involvement, however, also means that the ruling tandem can stop the reform at any point they see fit or when they decide that it is fraught with too much political risk. It is not accidental that the decision to increase the size of the officer corps was made after paratrooper veterans staged protest rallies under anti-government slogans. For this reason it's still impossible to say whether Russian military reform has passed the point of no return.

The factors discussed above and the way in which they interact will determine the shape of the Russian armed forces in 2020. In this context, three alternative options for scenarios can be envisioned.

The First Option: Positive, Practically Impossible

The first option can be realized only given a liberalized government. According to this scenario, the "Serdyukov" reforms, as planned, are successfully implemented by the end of 2012. Over the course of the ensuing three to five years, the country's leadership recognizes the futility of preserving the draft. It is abundantly clear that maintaining an armed forces of 1 million soldiers and officers unavoidably condemns service members to living in poverty. Calculations show that even by allocating 3 to 4 percent of GDP to military expenditures, Russia can maintain armed forces of no more than 500,000 to 600,000 troops. As a result, the foundation for the revival of a mass-mobilization army is eliminated. The draft gradually dies out.

Simultaneously, conditions are created for a transition to an armed forces based on voluntary recruitment. Several educational institutions are created similar to the already-functioning Center for the Training of Sergeants at the Ryazan Airborne Academy, where special attention is given not so much to technical subjects as to the basics of management, psychology, and pedagogy. In these centers, future sergeants receive an identical basic vocational education. As a result, every year the armed forces grows by several thousand professional junior commanders. It is the sergeants who bring professional morale to the barracks—not that of mercenaries, but of professional soldiers whose job it is to defend their homeland. Regulations are developed that clearly establish a system for progressing through the service as a sergeant, laying down a hierarchy of ranks and positions that creates a reliable basis for professional and career development.

The system of military education and the officers' progression through the service is radically changed. In military training centers, officers of the armed forces receive a foundational education in the humanities and sciences. The former allows commanders to understand their place in a rapidly changing world and to take responsibility for their subordinates, while an education in the sciences enables them to understand the workings of modern weapons systems. The system of career advancement and the procedure for appointment to senior positions become competitive and transparent. A system of continuous education is developed for officers, as advancing through the ranks is no longer based solely on seniority but also on qualifications. A soldier competing for a higher position knows that preference is given to the individual who has attained a higher qualification and achieved success in the preparation of his units and subunits.

The use of increasingly sophisticated weapons and equipment requires longer periods of training, which is virtually impossible if the armed forces are made up of conscripts serving for one year. In accordance with the growing professionalization of the armed forces, they are transformed into a social ladder that allows ambitious young men from small towns to receive an education. Service in the army ceases to be a "tax" and is no longer viewed as a system of negative socialization.

Within the framework of military reform, the functions of the Ministry of Defense, the General Staff, and the armed forces as a whole are successfully separated.[17] The Ministry of Defense becomes a department shaped mainly by competent civil servants. Its mission is to translate the tasks of the armed forces, formed by the country's political leadership, into the language of military orders. These civil servants formulate the technical policies of the Ministry of Defense, in addition to procuring arms and military equipment.

The leadership of the armed forces is carried out in the form of orders that follow from the Ministry of Defense through the General Staff directly to the four joint strategic commands (JSC) of the armed forces. Given such organization, the General Staff does not have direct operational control of the JSCs. Its objectives are limited to managing the country's strategic nuclear forces and space forces, coordinating actions among the JSCs, organizing the use of the reserve force of the supreme commander, and providing strategic planning and advice to the minister of defense and the country's political leadership. The General Staff is involved in the assessment of military threats, and most important, in the development of proposals for countering them as well as for preventing war. The assessment of the military and political situation as well as of the plans and capabilities of a potential opponent is formed on the basis of information received from the Main Intelligence Directorate, which is directly subordinate to the Ministry of Defense, in consultation with the Security Council.

The rejection of a mass-mobilization army leads to fundamental changes in the structure of the armed forces. Military districts, whose primary function had been to conduct mass mobilization, are eliminated. Troops are consolidated into joint strategic commands ("East," "West," "South," and "Center"), which include the army, the air force, and the navy. Control over large swaths of territory is ensured not by the size of the armed forces but by surveillance from outer space, the ability of troops to deploy and relocate quickly, the technical resources for the operational deployment of forces, and of course by modern long-range, high-precision ("smart") weapons. To ensure such deployment and the possibility of troop movements, combat-ready forces are created and heavy-weapons depots are deployed in advance in the areas under threat (first and foremost, the Caucasus region and the regions adjacent to the Russian-Kazakh and Russian-Chinese borders, and also along the border with North Korea).

That said, the country's leadership is aware that the regular armed forces can secure a victory only in a local, or at best a regional, conflict. A full guarantee of security during the period of radical reform of the armed forces is provided only by nuclear weapons, the backbone that will support the forthcoming decade. However, the country's nuclear policies must also undergo radical changes. As a result of rapprochement with the West, Russia rejects costly attempts to maintain nuclear parity with the United

States. Its nuclear capability is reduced to 100 to 200 carriers and 400 to 600 warheads. Moscow, to the extent possible, participates in the creation of a global missile defense system built by NATO at the initiative of the United States, and installs into it Russia's own S-400 air defense systems and missile warning systems. Cooperation with the West also extends to the prevention of armed conflicts in Central Asia (where the situation will probably be exacerbated following the likely withdrawal of U.S. and NATO troops from Afghanistan) and the Caucasus.

The government begins a radical reform of the military-industrial complex. Under these reforms, Putin's concept of a state-owned corporation is rejected (today, the state-owned corporations represent a sort of "collective" in which one relatively successful company contains more than a dozen factories that are close to bankruptcy). An industrial cooperative is formed on the basis of a small number of priority projects that are desperately needed to maintain the combat readiness of the armed forces. In doing this, the government finances not corporations but, rather, specific projects. Under these projects, a revolution in military affairs is achieved. First and foremost, these are projects concerning tactical control, communications, and intelligence systems. Specific enterprises and their subcontractors are reequipped technically as part of these projects' realization. The political will for reform can be achieved only through strict civil control, which in turn is based on parliamentary control (which, of course, is impossible under the current system of government in which representative bodies have been transformed into an appendage of the executive branch). This would require the adoption of a law "on civil control" to provide "positive" oversight over the spheres of defense and security. Parliament—with the help of independent experts engaged for the purposes of providing professional analysis of specific problems in military structuring and determining the direction of military and technical development—critically evaluates the proposals of the Ministry of Defense, the law enforcement agencies, and the special services, and allows only those programs that correspond to the country's interests and opportunities to receive financing. Thus, public policy in the field of defense and security is formed openly and publicly.

At the same time, military expenditures must be as detailed and open as possible, which requires that legislators radically revise a number of laws—in particular, the Budget Code and the law "On State Secrets," as well as a number of regulations. The military budget must not only comply with the UN standard on states' military expenditures but must also be substantially broader and more detailed so that lawmakers and their outside experts are able to understand and evaluate the main trends in the development of the armed forces, their supply of weapons, and the provision of a range of allowances to service members.[18] (The current classification of military expenditures in the Russian Federation does not comply even with the UN standard, and contains only the most general and vague wording.) And the report itself, detailing the military expenditures of the Russian Federation, is sent to the UN, bypassing the State Duma. In this case, international officials have (albeit with some lag) more information than the legislators do when they vote for the budget.

Parliament should be given the function of "negative" control—that is, a legally enforceable right of control over how the previously appropriated funds are spent. Civil control is not limited to the parliamentary level. It would seem necessary to establish an ombudsman for the armed forces, whose responsibilities would include monitoring compliance with the social and political rights of service members.

In addition, it is essential to create institutes of independent expertise in the area of defense and security. These think tanks should provide objective analysis of the processes taking shape in the field and develop recommendations not dictated by the ministries concerned. At the same time, such research centers should also establish educational institutions that would prepare not only future researchers but also civilian specialists who are competent in the field of defense and security. It is precisely these specialists who should make up the staff of civil servants in the Ministry of Defense.

It is clear that the radical military reform described above (in order to be successful, it must be accompanied by the demilitarization of all the remaining so-called power structures[19]) will represent a decisive break not only from the Soviet tradition of the armed forces but also from three centuries of an entrenched Russian military culture based on the idea of compulsory service, and also from the political system in which the main priority is neither effectiveness nor the expansion of opportunities for citizens but, rather, the consolidation of a political monopoly. These reforms, which fundamentally change the relationship between citizens and the state, cannot but give rise to determined resistance not only from the commanding officers of all the "power structures" but also from most of the officer corps.

This option can be realized only given a radical change in the political regime. If one considers the specific, deeply militaristic nature of the current system of power, the transformations described above must become a primary element of internal political change.

The Second Option: Negative, Unlikely

If the authoritarian regime grows stronger, the "Serdyukov" reforms will be abandoned. The reason for this abandonment will be the collapse that will reach the system of conscription in the next two to three years. According to estimates from specialists at the laboratory for military studies at the Institute for the Economy in Transition under the leadership of Vitaly Tsymbal, the size of the draft was virtually equal to the number of young men who had turned eighteen. For some time, the draft can be maintained, as it is now, by "selecting" slightly older young people—recent college graduates, "draft dodgers," and so on. However, at the turn of 2013–2014, the entire draft pool will be completely exhausted, even from a purely quantitative perspective (figure 18.1).

This does not take into account that about one-third of young people are relieved of duty for medical reasons, while another third are granted a deferment in order to attend university. It is unlikely that the authorities will risk abolishing the "educational" deferment before the 2012 presidential election. Consequently, the collapse of the conscription system will occur at the turn of 2012 and 2013.

As a result of an artificially created emergency, the generals will be able to justify the need for a return to two- and even three-year terms of service—and then, in the event of a growing confrontation with the West, a return to the mobilization model for organizing the armed forces. Having proved unable to fulfill their social obligations to the forcibly dismissed officers, the government returns them to military service. And to guarantee them positions, reduced-force cadre units will be restored. There is no

FIGURE 18.1   *Intensity of the military draft in the Russian Armed Forces*

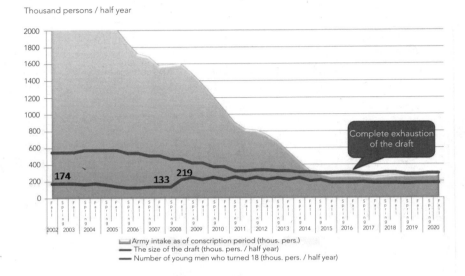

Thousand persons / half year

Army intake as of conscription period (thous. pers.)
The size of the draft (thous. pers. / half year)
Number of young men who turned 18 (thous. pers. / half year)

longer any discussion of reforming the military-industrial complex. The functioning of the military industry is by no means built on market principles. To provide the defense industry with hardware components and materials, all the country's factories, regardless of their form of ownership, receive so-called mobilization assignments as in Soviet times. In essence, this is a new, extremely heavy tax, the size of which varies according to the size of bribes given to the officials deciding the mobilization assignment.

However, all these measures cannot guarantee military power in its modern sense. The armed forces will be a sort of sham Soviet mobilization army—first and foremost because the mobilization reserve will be entirely exhausted. The demographic situation will not allow for a million-strong army. Military and political leaders plow ever farther down the path suggested by the current head of the Main Organization and Mobilization Directorate. They attempt to further tighten the rules of the draft. For example, they forbid accepting young people into jobs or university who have not yet passed through the army's "school of life" (with the exception of a few; officially, they are those who are extremely important for the government, while in reality, the exception is simply a means to exempt the children of senior officials from military service). In the same spirit of a militarized police state, the proposal of the General Staff is sustained, so far delivered only unofficially; the proposal seeks to prohibit the issuance of passports to anyone without a military identification card (this would require either changes in visa policies with a number of countries that belong to the Commonwealth of Independent States, or the conclusion of an agreement on extradition—not of criminals, but of conscripts). Law enforcement agencies (which have so far resisted this with all their power[20]) will be obligated to try to catch draft dodgers and deserters.

It is clear that such measures cannot bring any positive results (even in terms of manning the army). Only the number of bribes given to escape military service will grow, and many times over. Then the government, like it or not, will need to abandon the few remaining trappings of democracy— citizens' freedom of movement, for example.

Recreating the mobilization model returns the Russian army to the situation described by Vladimir Putin when, in an address to the Federal Assembly, he recalled the circumstances surrounding the beginning of the second Chechen war: "In order to effectively respond to the terrorists, we needed to assemble a force of at least 65,000 people. And in the whole army, in the combat-ready subunits, there were 55,000, and those were scattered across the country. The army has 1.4 million people, and no one to fight. And here they sent unseasoned boys out under fire."[21]

All the while, the armed forces continue to receive, in the best case, isolated deliveries of "modern" military technology: in reality, it is called modern only because it was never manufactured. But it was developed no later than the end of the 1980s.

The realization of the "Soviet" scenario means that the Russian army will lose almost all its combat capability. It will remain only as a sort of militaristic symbol and also as a tool that demonstrates the subordination of the citizen to the state. However, such a course of events is impossible without a deterioration of relations between Russia and the United States, and with other countries of the West. In the event of growing confrontation, the main task will be to maintain nuclear parity with the United States at all costs, which, as in the late 1970s, would consume a substantial portion of the country's oil revenues.

Such a scenario is unlikely. Its realization assumes a drastic curtailment not only of the political rights, but also the personal rights of Russian citizens, which would entail a radical breach of contract between the people and the government (which is based, among other things, on the non-interference of the government in private life). Furthermore, the realization of the mobilization scenario condemns the Russian ruling class—especially the bureaucracy—to give up the level of consumption to which they have become accustomed. Finally, the mobilization scenario draws Russia into a sort of new arms race, which, even if only undertaken superficially, is capable of completely destroying the domestic economy. Undoubtedly, the mobilization scenario will radically change the system of relations between government and business. Today, business reluctantly funds various state projects, from Skolkovo to the construction of homes for fire victims. However, in the event of the realization of the mobilization scenario, such relatively moderate requisitions by the state will inevitably be replaced by substantially harsher burdens on business. And when a real threat to business arises, the owners will begin to act much more forcefully.

The Third Option: Intermediate, Most Likely

The "Serdyukov" reforms follow the path typical of the majority of Russian reforms. They focus on meeting certain formal measures and characteristics (in the case of military reform, this includes the size of the armed forces, the number of units, the new structure, and so on), and at the same time avoid making decisions that would require radical changes in the country's political and social life.

It is very likely that so-called restructuring, as well as the elimination of reduced-strength units and the dismissal of thousands of "redundant" officers, will all take place under the reforms. Joint strategic commands will be created, to which a diverse range of forces will report: the army, the air force, and the navy. Three dozen of the military's institutions of higher education will also be eliminated, and ten military training centers will be built on their basis.

However, the internal logic of the reforms contradicts the main priority, mentioned above: The authorities seek to avoid major changes in the political and social spheres. This is precisely why the Ministry of Defense is not abandoning the draft. The authorities do not dare resort to such draconian measures, forming the army at the expense of conscripts. The rules of the draft are virtually unchanged. As a result, the reduction of the armed forces continues nonetheless. But it has a "secretive" nature. Given Russia's effective exit from the Treaty on Conventional Armed Forces in Europe, which envisioned information sharing about the size of the armed forces and the number of units in the European part of Russia, the sole source of data about the armed forces is the Ministry of Defense itself, which provides a substantial opportunity for manipulating the figures. Officially, the Defense Ministry claims that the size of the armed forces remains at the level of 1 million soldiers. In reality, the number has been reduced to 500,000 to 600,000. The draft will reduce the number of conscripts to 200,000 to 300,000, from which practically all forces will be formed. That these forces are not actually combat ready does not worry the Russian authorities; large-scale war is impossible.

The process of professionalization, not imposed from the top, is beginning to gradually break through from the bottom. The actual security of the country is ensured by the strategic missile forces, where the officer corps dominates. Using the rules specified in the new Strategic Arms Reduction Treaty (New START), which govern the allowances for strategic weapons and the exchange of data, Russia is seeking to create the illusion of quantitative parity with the United States and to maintain the image that Moscow is able to provide nuclear deterrence of Washington. To achieve both its domestic and foreign policy goals, Russian leaders periodically resort to military rhetoric—but, as is the case now, such rhetoric is not followed by any actions that could seriously perturb the West, which has sufficient data to form an adequate picture of Russia's military potential.

The ability to counteract risks emerging on the local and regional levels is provided by ten paratrooper battalions made up of contract soldiers (at present, according to Airborne Forces commander Colonel-General Vladimir Shamanov, there are five such battalions).[22] In addition, the best officers and professional sergeants are sent to a limited number of "elite" units and commands. There they get relatively new weapons and military equipment. Thus, a "core" is formed in the general-purpose forces: one to two airborne divisions; three to four army brigades; several squadrons of multifunctional fighters (for the purposes of propaganda, it can be claimed that these are fifth-generation fighters); and navy forces, the flagship of which is the *Mistral* helicopter-carrier. These commands are designated for prevailing in local conflicts, such as those in Georgia and Chechnya. Also, the target of development is the Military Space Forces, whose satellite formation must ensure the effectiveness both of the strategic missile forces and the main attack units of the general-purpose forces. This part of the Russian army can be considered modernized and will more or less develop normally.

The rest—a large part of the armed forces—will exist in a state of partial stagnation. If Serdyukov's ideas about the humanization of conscription in the army (two days off every week, exemption from duties servicing military units, and even from guard duty) and enhanced physical training are realized, then conditions in the military units will begin to resemble those of a sports camp rather than a prison.

But this achievement, which is certainly valuable in its own right, will only slightly affect the level of combat readiness of the units composed of these conscripts. It is clear that in one year of service, conscripts will be able to learn only the most basic aspects of their military specialty. Claims by military leaders that training in military disciplines begins in school with the system of the Voluntary Association for Assistance to the Army, Air Force, and Navy, are not convincing. There is no mechanism for compulsory military training in school. As a result, at any given time, half the personnel (those who have served more than six months) will hardly be combat ready, while the other half (those who have served less than six months) will not be prepared for combat at all.

Preserving the draft also distorts the meaning of officers' service, if they indeed wish to establish the principle of continuous education at the heart of such service. After all, officers will be condemned to repeat the basics of combat training with the new recruits each year (if not every six months). For the younger officers, it will be neither possible nor necessary to prove their professional worth. And it is unlikely that a troop commander will be motivated to improve if he is condemned to circulate through the most primitive elements of combat training. At the same time, imbalances in the ratio between the numbers of officers and of ordinary soldiers are once again arising in the armed forces—one officer will account for two to three privates.

If one considers the very low level of education of new recruits (even according to official data, the number of recruits with a high school education is at most 70 percent),[23] then this means that any revolution in military affairs will be impossible in the overwhelming majority of units of the Russian army. But then no modern technology can be put into mass production, and thus the production of weapons, even in theory, cannot be profitable.

Preserving a conscription-based army also contradicts the modern approach to organizing the armed forces. The main question is whether military districts will be eliminated with the creation of the four strategic commands. At present, it appears that this question has not been resolved. However, it is fundamentally important. During the past 150 years, the most important function of the military districts has been to conduct mass mobilization within their respective territories in the event of a military threat, and to undertake the subsequent management of those troops. If military planning is, as before, based on mass mobilization, and this function is transferred to the strategic commands, then the new structure will be just as ungainly as the current military districts. By preserving the mobilization structure of the armed forces, the plan for troop engagement will necessarily be tied to the completion of the process of forming reserve units. After all, until that moment, the troops of the strategic command will not be fit for military action, even though the number of reservists constitutes only two-thirds of the number of units during peacetime. If the military districts are preserved as structures responsible for forming units of reservists in the event of war, then conflicts will inevitably arise during the organization of military operations given their reassignment to the strategic commands.

Such a scenario creates an extremely volatile situation. In the absence of a real military threat, the armed forces could evolve, extremely slowly, in a positive direction. However, any military clash will demonstrate the weakness of the Russian army, which could result in a return to the negative scenario.

Notes

1. V. Yevseev, "Otsrochki ot voennoi sluzhby: Segodnya i zavtra" (Deferment from Military Service: Today and Tomorrow), *Otechestvennye zapiski,* no. 5, 2005, www.strana-oz.ru/?numid=26&article=1155.

2. See "Military Doctrine of the Russian Federation," www.scrf.gov.ru/documents/33.html.

3. The theory concerning a military threat, in particular from NATO, has been used very successfully by the Russian leadership in voicing its aggravation in any given conflict situation.

4. V. Litovkin, "Parad ne zatormozil reform" (The parade has not slowed reform), *Nezavisimaya gazeta,* May 14, 2010, http://nvo.ng.ru/realty/2010-05-14/1_parad.html.

5. Ibid.

6. L. Khairemdinov, "Vremya mobilnosti" (A time of mobility), *Krasnaya zvezda,* October 1, 2009, www.redstar.ru/2009/10/01_10/1_05.html.

7. D. Telmanov, "V sleduyuschem godu zarplata leitenanta sostavit 50 tisyach rublei" (Next year, the salary of lieutenants will amount to 50 thousand rubles), Gazeta.ru, November 14, 2008, www.gzt.ru/topnews/politics/-v-sleduyuschem-godu-zarplata-leitenantov-sostavit-/208438.html.

8. "Rossiya otkazalas' ot professionalnoyi armii—vooruzhennie sili vozvrashchayutsya k sovetskomu obraztsu" (Russia said no to a professional army—the armed forces are returning to the Soviet model), Newsru.com, May 14, 2010, www.newsru.com/russia/14may2010/army.html.

9. It is provided for all who have served twenty years and have a right to a pension, as well as for those who served more than ten years and were dismissed in connection with so-called restructuring (that is, through no fault of their own, but as a result of the changing attitudes of the authorities regarding the composition of the military).

10. V. Mukhin, "Voenno-protestnaya oborona" (Military protest defense), *Nezavisimaya gazeta,* May 17, 2010, www.ng.ru/politics/2010-05-17/2_oborona.html.

11. See "Rossiiskie voennye vuzy dva goda ne budut gotovit' ofitserov" (Russian military colleges will not train officers for two years), REGNUM News Agency, August 30, 2010, www.regnum.ru/news/polit/1320193.html.

12. At State Duma hearings dedicated to a new armament program (four previous ones had failed), acting chief of armaments of the Russian army Lieutenant-General Oleg Frolov said that the program would require 36 trillion rubles, and not 13 as originally planned.

13. Yu. Gavrilov, "Istrebitel 'ekonomklassa'" (An "economy-class" fighter), *Rossiyskaya gazeta,* September 8, 2009, www.rg.ru/2009/09/08/popovkin.html.

14. "Serdyukov obyavil ob uvelichenii chisla kontraktnikov v armii do 425 tisyach chelovek" (Serdyukov announced an increase in the number of those on contract military service to reach 425 thousand people), Gazeta.ru, March 18, 2011, www.gazeta.ru/news/lenta/2011/03/18/n_1752697.shtml.

15. V. Vyzhutovich, "Armiya s chelovecheskim litsom" (An army with a human face), *Rossiyskaya gazeta*, April 15, 2011, www.rg.ru/2011/04/15/armia.htmlhttp://www.rg.ru/2011/04/15/armia.html.

16. "Serdukov reshil nabrat' 70.000 tisyach ofitserov" (Serdyukov decided to recruit 70,000 officers), *Svobodnaya pressa*, September 8, 2011, www.svpressa.ru/society/article/38374.

17. The functions of the Ministry of Defense and the General Staff currently intersect in many places. The main thing is that both the ministry and the General Staff maintain the right of operational leadership of the troops.

18. Currently, the budget of the Russian Ministry of Defense fits on 20 pages, while, for example, in Germany it fills a separate volume of 190 pages. In the United States, it takes up more than ten volumes.

19. Successful military reform is possible only in the event that the armed forces and its command hierarchy, along with its requirement for the unconditional execution of orders and so on, is recognized as a unique institution and part of a democratic society. In the present circumstances, where military service is required in more than ten ministries of the Russian Federation and where more than half the people in uniform serve in these ministries, the idea of the "special" status of service members is blurred; society offers them special benefits in appreciation for the fact that, for the sake of national security, they condemn themselves to a number of limitations.

20. See, for example, the interview with Moscow chief of police Vladimir Kolokoltsev: M. Falaleyev, "Sluzhebnoye sootvetstvie" (Official compliance), *Rossiyskaya gazeta*, April 28, 2010, www.rg.ru/2010/04/28/kolokolcev.html.

21. Vladimir Putin, Address to the Federal Assembly of the Russian Federation, May 10, 2006, www.kremlin.ru/appears/2006/05/10/1357_type63372type63374type82634_105546.shtml.

22. V. Khudoleev, "Aeromobilnost, vozvedennaya v absolyut" (Air mobility, raised to an absolute), *Krasnaya zvezda*, May 27, 2010.

23. "Kazhdiy tretiy prizyvnik ne goden k sluzhbe po sostoyaniyu zdoroviya" (Every third conscript physically unfit for service), Botkinskyi hospital website, July 13, 2009, www.botkinmoscow.ru/rus/news/1638.html.

REGIONS

PART V

CHAPTER NINETEEN

RUSSIA'S REGIONS and CITIES: SCENARIOS for 2020

Natalia Zubarevich

A ten-year forecast of regional socioeconomic development is much easier and safer for an expert's reputation than political predictions. Space is inertial, and Russian space in particular—due to weak infrastructure, great differences in the level of development, low mobility of the population, and other reasons.

Scholars specializing in regional studies are lucky with their object of research: Even a Soviet textbook on economic geography can still serve as a source of information. But, true to the law of compensation, regional policy is the sphere where the Russian authorities unleash their imaginations, and thus try to implement way-out projects at all costs—though it is clear from the start that this kind of exercise will not bear fruit. The number of inadequate development strategies and programs (for sectors, regions, and cities) is so great that it is difficult to discern weighted assessments in this debris-littered landscape. A strict dichotomy prevails—either the country will disintegrate; or "everything will be all right," and the party's plans will become the people's plans (and, adding modern realities to this Soviet-era slogan, business's plans).

In this chapter, I outline politically neutral scenarios for urban and regional development, taking into account both the real "corridor of opportunities," as determined by intrinsic factors and trends, and the impact of the government's regional policies. Each scenario has its own spatial development picture and carries its own risks.

Basic Factors in Spatial Development: You Cannot Jump Higher Than Your Head

The prospects for Russia's regions are determined, in the first instance, by those basic factors that create advantages for or barriers to spatial development. Paul Krugman, the founder of the "new economic geography," delineated two groups of these factors:[1]

- "First nature" factors: endowment with natural resources that are demanded by a market (minerals, land), and advantageous geographic location (within agglomerations, close to seas, land borders, and international trade routes) permitting lower transportation costs.
- "Second nature" factors: agglomeration effects and high population density, resulting in economies of scale; a developed infrastructure that shrinks economic distance; human capital (the population's education, health, work motivation, mobility, and ability to adapt); institutions influencing the entrepreneurial climate, population mobility, the spread of innovation, and so on.

All these factors affect the development of Russia's regions and cities, though in varying combinations and to varying degrees. A particularity of regional development in this country is the elevated role of "first nature" factors, first and foremost its endowment with the oil and gas resources that are highest in demand in the global marketplace. "Second nature" factors, like the geographical location factor, work in most instances as barriers to development. Russia is distinguished by a small number of cities, especially large ones with a population of more than 250,000 (74 of 1,090 Russian cities), and so the agglomeration effect is only manifested weakly, with the exception of the biggest agglomerations (Moscow and Saint Petersburg). A huge barrier is linked with undeveloped infrastructure and the great distance of the major part of the country's territory from transportation routes. The scale of the economic periphery is huge, even in the country's more densely settled European part (which makes up more than 40 percent of its territory).[2] Another barrier is constituted by depopulation in three-fourths of the country's regions and the ubiquitous deterioration of its human capital. The influence of basic factors of and barriers to spatial development should be taken into primary consideration when forecasts are being developed. Quick changes, including a noticeable weakening of the barrier effect of "second nature" factors and, even more, a reduction in the scale of the periphery, will not occur by 2020.

In this context, institutions look like a more flexible factor, but path dependency plays a negative role here. Moreover, Russian institutions influence spatial development more strongly than it seems at first glance. The new economic geography established that the concentration of population and economic assets in a country's biggest city is determined not just by the agglomeration factor, which entails growing economies of scale, and the city's central location within the national transportation network, which lowers transportation costs.[3] This socioeconomic concentration also depends on the concentration of political power; more pluralistic systems are characterized by a lower concentration in the central city than are dictatorships. A more uniform distribution of cities' size is also a distinctive characteristic of states with a federal system. But Russia is still an authoritarian state and a federation only in name, and therefore the overconcentration of population and economic activity in the Moscow agglomeration only increases. Only a change of the political system could reverse this trend.

It also must be noted that in more open economies, the biggest cities' populations are smaller than in closed ones. Closed markets and a high level of trade protectionism facilitate the emergence of big central cities.[4] Russia's economy even today—to say nothing of the past—can be regarded as open only nominally, just because the country exports oil, gas, and metals. And when there is a low level of openness, it is better for firms to locate their new manufacturing facilities close to the central agglomeration to tap the advantages of the centralized market—especially when the transportation network is inadequate and transportation costs are high. True to this theory, nearly all the new production facilities built by foreign car manufacturers in Russia are concentrated near Moscow (in Kaluga) and Saint Petersburg. Only growing openness could initiate the deconcentration of production. And even then it would not happen overnight, because the mobility of production factors and development of nonresource exports are also necessary.

The emergence of new "leader regions" is connected with technological breakthroughs that can change the economic map and facilitate regional development. But an economic breakthrough on the wave of new technologies requires something more than factors favorable for business development like lower wages in the region. A system of effective institutions, strong motivation, and entrepreneurship is needed as well. Russia has big problems with all these, so one should not expect technology-driven shifts in spatial development in this decade.

The development of territorial clusters is premised on increasing global economic integration and a reduction of transaction costs, facilitating the concentration of firms in a given sector and deepening specialization.[5] In the absence of these institutional factors, cluster policy has no perspectives.

Institutions influence innovation as well. Richard Florida shows that the development of modern cities is promoted by their heterogeneity, diverse social environments, and concentration of the creative class, which possesses the various skills needed for thriving urban areas.[6] The inmigration of professionals with various specializations stimulates new knowledge accumulation and economic growth. These migrants are especially attracted by a diverse and tolerant urban environment. Russia is not a very tolerant country, but phobias toward migrants are not regarded by the authorities and public as a barrier to innovation-driven development, though they can become such a barrier even in Moscow, where the atmosphere for creative people is most favorable.

According to theory, sustainable regional development is possible only with the improvement of institutions and opening of the economy. Even bad infrastructure is not such a strong barrier—it can be redeveloped on the basis of economic growth. Theory also postulates that growth is never uniform territorially:[7] Investors prefer regions with a competitive advantage, where the return on capital is bigger. Global experience also shows that investments in strong territories boost the development of the whole country.

Trends in the Development of Russia's Regions, 2000–2010: Basic Factors Are Working

Existing inequalities and trends represent a secondary basis for forecasting, insofar as spatial development is very inertial. The leading role played by basic factors of spatial development was apparent both in the period of economic growth during the 2000s and during the economic crisis of 2008 and 2009. During the years of economic growth, three or four groups of territories developed more solidly.

These groups of territories included, in the first place, the *agglomerations of the two federal cities*, Moscow and Saint Petersburg. The prominence of these two agglomerations is a consequence not only of the agglomeration effect but also of their special institutional advantages. Under Russia's overcentralized administrative system, Moscow's status as the capital has promoted the concentration of head offices of Russian businesses in the city, a huge influx of tax revenues to the city budget, a large number of highly paid jobs, and significantly higher-than-average incomes for the population. In the 2000s, development accelerated in the Moscow region thanks to agglomeration advantages and the overflow of capital from the central city. In Saint Petersburg, the effect of scale has been less strongly manifested. Federal authorities have attempted to stimulate the city's development by special institutional means, transferring there the head offices of a portion of the major companies to increase the city's budgetary revenues and to create new, highly paid jobs; but the result (apart from the growth in the city's budgetary revenues) has not been very noticeable. The Leningrad region developed more dynamically, making use of the dual advantage of its coastal location on the routes of trade with Europe, and the agglomeration effect, though these factors were sufficient only for the accelerated development of the western, coastal portion of the region, within the bounds of the Saint Petersburg agglomeration. A consequence of the dynamic development of the country's two largest agglomerations is that they accounted for 75 to 80 percent of all migration within Russia in the period 2007–2009, including 55 to 60 percent in the Moscow agglomeration.

Second, ten to twelve regions with economies that had an export-oriented structure, and a high number of industries extracting natural resources, developed more solidly. Among them one may single out the autonomous *okrugs* of the Tyumen region (the region itself receives large tax revenues as a rentier, though its economy is weak). The leaders of the second tier are the Tatarstan and Bashkortostan republics, the Krasnoyarsk and Perm *krays*, the Samara region, and several leading metallurgical regions, where revenues have increased thanks to the rapid rise in world prices for raw materials. In the early 2000s, the favorable state of the world market partially compensated these regions for the loss of revenue caused by the Kremlin's policy of overconcentration of tax receipts in the federal budget. In the dynamic of their gross regional product, however, these regions did not distinguish themselves from the average rate of economic growth for the country as a whole. The only regions that grew more quickly were Tatarstan, thanks to its institutional advantages (including a regional oil-extracting company and special financial support from the federal budget), and the Sverdlovsk region (which had a combination of the low base effect following the strong fall in the economy in the 1990s and the favorable state of prices for metals in the 2000s).

A special case is the regions where new drilling for oil and gas has been undertaken—the Sakhalin region and the Nenets autonomous *okrug*—where rates of economic growth have been very high. The Sakhalin region developed on the basis of an institutional factor: Large-scale foreign investments (up to 20 percent of all foreign investment in Russia in the early and middle 2000s) flowed in after the conclusion of production-sharing agreements. This made it possible to almost double the volume of the region's industrial production in ten years, and the volume of the gross regional product by a factor of 1.8 at comparable prices.

The positive impact of the seaside position on global trade routes started to manifest itself only in the early 2000s, and is localized in several western and southern regions of Russia. By itself, this factor so far cannot stimulate regional development due to enormous barriers, especially in the eastern part of the country. Additional girders are needed—either institutional, like the status of a special economic zone (the Kaliningrad region), or proximity to a big agglomeration (the Leningrad region). For the southern Russian regions (Krasnodar *krai*), the growth factors also included better land resources and a positive climate for the development of the agricultural sector, a denser population, and a relatively developed infrastructure, as well as human capital (the population's capacity for enterprise).

Among the numerically dominant group of regions that are "average" in their level of development (which are about two-thirds of the Russian Federation's subject regions), it is difficult to distinguish the basic factors that are stimulating development. Although the dynamic of economic growth in these regions has varied, overall they have either repeated the countrywide average trend or fallen behind with respect to it. In the poorly developed regions, faster economic growth has been enabled by large-scale financial aid from the federal budget; such growth cannot be sustained.

Of the cities other than the federal centers, regional centers have developed more quickly, especially the largest ones (with populations of 700,000 to 1 million), as well as those company towns most important for business that have economies exclusively based on branches of export industries, with higher incomes among the population and in their budgets. Among the regional capitals, Krasnodar and Yekaterinburg have been growth "champions," as measured by socioeconomic indicators (per capita volume of trade, paid services, and housing construction). The status of a regional center has represented an advantage, but this institutional factor has not been bolstered by a rapid growth of investments, also for institutional reasons. Regional centers are classified as municipalities and are very limited in their budgetary revenues. Their development has been hampered by the monopolization and corruption of the land market and the housing construction industry, and by barriers to the development of small businesses and migration. The concentration of service functions in the regional centers has occurred against a backdrop of the decay of small and peripheral towns located outside the boundaries of agglomerations.

The regions' economic disparity, defined according to the per capita gross regional product, grew in the early 2000s, but in the second half of the decade, with the beginning of the boom in oil revenues and the strengthening of federal redistribution policy, it has been somewhat reduced.[8] Interregional differences in the population's income showed an even more pronounced trend of the same kind: They fell substantially, especially in the last years before the economic crisis, thanks to the strengthening of the redistribution policy and growth in the volume of transfers from the federal budget.

The economic crisis of 2008–2009 has been felt in Russia's regions to varying degrees.[9] The crisis has had the least effect on the poorly developed regions and those that are well endowed, where the legal economy is dominated by the budgetary service sector, which is stably funded by transfers from the federal budget. The dynamic of industrial production in the Far East was more stable, insofar as the purging of uncompetitive producers had already occurred, during the economic crisis of the 1990s. In the moderately developed regions, the depth of the fall caused by the economic crisis has been defined by the structure of the economy, and the regions specializing in machine building and textiles—they are all located in the European part of the country—have suffered most. Their uncompetitive industries are coming out of the crisis very slowly. In developed regions with diversified economies, the recession was more moderate, and they had rebounded from it almost completely by the middle of 2010. Regions attractive for investors (the Kaluga, Leningrad, Belgorod regions) recovered even faster. In the leading oil-producing regions, those with the most favorable industrial dynamic, the fall was minimal, while growth continued in those regions with new projects for oil and gas extraction.

The Volga regions, the Urals, and the central regions have been geographically the most affected by the economic crisis (as reflected in the rate of industrial decline and the situation of the labor market). The authorities strove to prevent the growth of social tension, and tried to maintain employment in industrial enterprises with financial aid and administrative prohibitions. As a result, the level of hidden unemployment (including partial employment and employment in public works) in these regions has overtaken officially registered unemployment. If all forms of unemployment are taken together, then in the most severely affected regions, along the Volga and in the Urals, the level of unemployment reached that of indicators during the 1998 economic crisis; in other words, the cycle of crisis repeated itself, but without a purge of ineffective jobs.

The economic crisis of 2008–2009 differed from the preceding crises of the 1990s in that it had a weak effect on the population's incomes. After a small dip, incomes had rebounded to the precrisis level by the end of 2009. This is a consequence of state policy: The state had accumulated large financial reserves during the period of economic growth, and it used a part of these reserves to mitigate the social effects of the crisis. During 2009, the budgetary expenditures of Russian regions on social policy increased by a third, thanks to the growth of federal transfers for this purpose. Incomes and consumption were growing fastest in the poorly developed national republics, while the regions suffering from deep industrial recession caused by the crisis experienced a fall of incomes due to the growth of both open and hidden unemployment. The same thing happened in the leading oil- and gas-producing regions, where the elements of variable pay (wage supplements, bonuses, and awards) were significantly curtailed, and in the major agglomerations, where employment is dominated by the service sector. And so the labor market reacted with the greatest flexibility to the economic crisis, with layoffs and a fall in wage levels.

Overall, the new economic crisis exhibited fairly obvious trends. Regions with a production monoprofile experienced the greatest decline in the real sector of their economies in connection with the crisis (and will experience this as new crises occur), dependent as they are on fluctuations in the business cycle and global prices for raw and semiprocessed materials, as did regions with unreformed or uncompetitive manufacturing industries, located mainly in European Russia. The large financial cushion accumulated by the federal budget helped to support employment and partly revenues in those regions. But if such a cushion would not be available, new crises would follow the typical scenario of the 1990s: a steep decline in the population's real wages and incomes (after the crisis of 1998, these were reduced in real terms by a third). As in the 1990s, labor markets reacted to the latest crisis with a reduction of employment, but it was often in the form of hidden unemployment, especially in regions with labor-intensive industries. It would appear that such a reaction to crises will also occur in the future, which slows employment reform and the growth of economic mobility among the populations of regions with uncompetitive economic branches. Regional trends in response to economic crises, conditioned by basic developmental factors, including institutional ones, would hardly change by 2020.

The Government's Regional Policy and Spatial Development: Public Relations and the "Saw-Cut"

The impact of the authorities' regional policy is easy to assess and predict. Its priorities are not yet elaborated in Russia, and relevant instruments work poorly; therefore, regional development is influenced primarily by general economic and social policies. As a development factor, state regional policy by itself has played a very limited role.

In the 1990s and early 2000s, the main task of regional policy in Russia was to flatten interregional differences, but the federal budget's resources were limited, and the equalizing effect turned out to be minimal. In the mid-2000s, amid fast economic growth, the government announced a transition to a stimulative regional policy. New priorities changed rapidly— the support of "growth-driving" regions, which were to be selected by the federal authorities, was followed by proposals to create agglomerations (mostly by administrative methods), cluster policy, and so on. All these undertakings were copied from foreign experience, often inadequately, and as a result remained on paper.

The document "Strategy for Russia's Development Until 2020," which was issued in mid-2000, included—for the first time since the Soviet era—a section on regional development. It was prepared by the Ministry of Regional Development, and with its abundance of "big projects"—with a special stress on developing the eastern regions—resembled the documents of the Soviet State Planning Committee. It was as if the federal and regional authorities had not noticed that private businesses had become the main investors in the country, and tried to paint a picture of a "rosy future," ignoring the potential economic efficiency and profitability of their proposed projects. The implementation of the Comprehensive Development Program for the Sakha Republic (Yakutia), for instance, required resources comparable to all foreign investments in Russia in 2008.

State action on spatial development by means of the standard instruments of regional policy has not generated any results: Programs remained on paper, and the special economic zones have not been very successful; and attempts to create artificial agglomerations have failed, as has cluster policy resembling Soviet plans for territorial production complexes—and in both cases failure could be expected from the start.

Stimulative regional policy in the 2000s has been limited to the implementation of political priorities. One of them concerns political public relations projects: The financing of preparations for the Olympics in Sochi and the Asia-Pacific Economic Cooperation (APEC) Summit in Vladivostok was growing rapidly, even during the crisis. Total spending for the APEC Summit is equivalent to 10 percent of all Russian regions' budget expenditures in 2009. The soccer World Cup will cost even more. Support for the politically unstable North Caucasus republics, especially Chechnya, is also a political priority. The republic's per capita budget expenditures are 25 percent higher than the national average and 2.5 times higher than the average for the Southern Federal District—and 90 percent of Chechnya's budget is financed by federal transfers. The development of the Far East, declared as a priority task, amounted to increased budget financing for Vladivostok and the Kuril Islands.

The strongest influence on regional development is exerted by inter-budgetary distribution and the federal authorities' social policy. These could hardly be defined as equalization policies, as the aforementioned task does not seem to be a priority in this context. Response to the crisis was mostly limited to an increase of federal transfers to regional budgets (by a third in 2009) and "manual control"—that is, an unformalized one with opaque criteria—over the distribution of these resources. During the acute phase of the crisis, budget incomes in 60 percent of the regions were growing; therefore, inefficient spending also increased. Expenditures on social benefits, for instance, grew by 67 percent from 2008 to 2010.

Financial assistance to crisis-plagued company towns, however, was small and was provided in an extremely bureaucratic manner: The selection of recipient cities took a whole year; and all company towns were ordered to elaborate comprehensive investment plans that had minimum chances of being implemented. The lion's share of budgetary resources allocated for assistance to company towns was received by the city of Togliatti—to solve the problems of the Avtovaz car factory there. Employment support, as far as resource distribution among the regions in concerned, was more adequate, because political risks in this sphere were too high. The financing of a large-scale public works program, however, contributed to the conservation of ineffective employment patterns in the regions. As a result, the institutional design of support for the regions during the crisis was characterized by high costs and the low efficiency of federal transfers. And there are no stimuli available to change this design—except through a depletion of financial resources.

Forecasting Scenarios:
A Contraction of Economic Space Is Inevitable

One's forecast can be based on a standard range of scenarios—optimistic, inertial, and pessimistic—in order to subsequently superimpose Russian spatial specifics upon each trend, with different combinations of development factors and barriers. But whatever the combination, one point needs to be understood clearly: *The basic development trend will be a contraction of habitable and economic space.*

In all probability, an *inertial scenario* of development will be realized in Russia, which will continue the trends in spatial development that have already been formed. Its macroeconomic backdrop is the fading recovery growth following the decline due to the economic crisis of 2008–2009 and the country's relatively low rates of growth in the new decade, caused by the stabilization of oil prices and the slower increase of global demand for natural resources. Against such a backdrop, spatial development will most probably follow entirely predictable trends, independent of the regional policy implemented by the authorities.

Moscow's hypertrophied role, and the concentration of financial and human resources in the city, will be preserved. The Moscow agglomeration will develop rapidly and spread, engulfing the surrounding *raions* of neighboring regions. Artificial innovation projects like Skolkovo will not change the economic profile of the territories surrounding the capital; service, logistics, and recreation and industrial sectors will develop still further, oriented toward the huge market in the capital. Saint Petersburg's development will depend more heavily on federal financial resources and institutional support, and on the transfer of head offices of major companies—which are big taxpayers—to the northern capital. These measures, however, are not enough for sustainable growth; the city is hindered by the institutional barriers common across the country, which block the development of the services sector and the inflow of investments. Efforts to turn the northern capital into an industrial center for the production of cars will inevitably come up against the problem of the lack of a qualified and relatively inexpensive workforce, and the necessity of its transfer from other regions of Russia, or the other countries that belong to the Commonwealth of Independent States, and provision of special training. It is unlikely that assembly-line car production will significantly raise the city's budgetary revenues, and its contribution to the city's development will not be great.

The leading regions of Russia's Fuel and Energy Complex (FEC) will maintain their position in the group of leaders by dint of maintaining extraction volumes (this will not become an acute problem before 2020). But their populations will age, natural population growth will fall, and the flow of youth migrating out of the regions will increase, because few highly skilled jobs are being created in the regions of the FEC (an economy based on the extraction of natural resources is not labor-intensive). Those migrating out are already mixing with a migratory current of unskilled workers from the republics of the Northern Caucasus and Central Asia, which will inevitably increase social tensions and the problems of drug addiction, and will place a burden on the population's social welfare system.

A sizable number of the regions in the group of second-tier leaders could fall back into the middle group. For the leading metallurgical regions, this would be a consequence of a fall in global competitiveness, due to aging Soviet industrial assets, and cost increases caused by rises in the prices of oil and raw materials. Various multifunctional industrial regions have already begun to move downward, first and foremost the Samara region (with a drop in competitiveness of the automobile industry) and the Perm region (with the exhaustion of mineral resources and the absence of major new investments).

Under conditions of relative political stability in the Caucasus, the major southern regions with predominantly Russian populations will continue to have faster growth, thanks to their stable advantages: a more developed infrastructure, the presence of seaports, and natural resource advantages consisting of better soil and climate conditions for agriculture. The Sochi Olympic Games will probably, in fact, hinder the South's stable growth, through the disproportionate concentration of investment in one spot, and the inevitable problems of unprofitability that will affect the sporting and other facilities after the completion of this project of Putin's.

The numerous group of developmentally "average" regions will remain as it is, with a slight rotation up (a few regions with an advantageous coastal location, and the southern industrial and agricultural regions) or down (partially depressed regions specializing in machine construction or textiles).

The depopulation of non-black-earth regions and other peripheral territories of European Russia will increase, on account of high natural losses; the concentration of the population in regional centers and other major cities will continue, above all in the agglomerations of federal cities. It will not be possible to solve the problem of peripheral decay, due to the population's low mobility, and barriers in urban housing markets.

Despite ambitious federal programs, the contraction of habitable space will continue, as will the decay of all settlement systems in the Far East and the Baikal region. The economy of the eastern regions will be even more polarized; alongside the centers of growth (Vladivostok, Khabarovsk, and, to a lesser extent, other regional capitals, leading ports, and areas where raw materials are extracted for export), the rest of the territory will see its infrastructure decay and its population drop. In the event that federal budget revenues increase, it will be possible to renew costly infrastructure projects in the East and the North, but a dismal economic fate awaits them. Newly built facilities will probably generate losses rather than profits.

The republics of the North Caucasus will remain a "black hole" of budgetary finance, but they will experience an increase in outward migration of young people seeking work in other regions of Russia, which will somewhat alleviate the problem of unemployment, given the recent establishment of a declining birthrate (excluding the period when it was stimulated from 2007 to 2009). This valve, however, will not start to open for the poorly developed republics of Siberia (Tyva and Altai), due to their distant location, and stronger cultural barriers. As before, Chechnya will remain a favorite for financing from the federal budget, but Ingushetia and Dagestan could join it, depending on the political situation.

The *worst-case scenario* will not only strengthen the above-mentioned tendencies toward peripheral decay but will also sharply reduce the number of growth zones with good prospects, due to worsening institutional conditions and declining investment. If the political regime decays, which is quite possible, this scenario could become a reality. Here I briefly outline the most dangerous trends of spatial development for the future.

The capital agglomeration of Moscow will see a rapid worsening of the quality of life due to problems of infrastructure and ecology, if the current rate of population growth is maintained. The decay of the social environment could encourage the emigration of the population's most competitive segments—youth, and those with high levels of education and higher incomes.

In the coming decades, an accelerated contraction of habitable space in peripheral territories should not be expected; the prospect of their depopulation is longer term, by 2030–2050. A different adaptive strategy is more likely for the populations of peripheral territories of different types (the aging population of the non-black-earth regions and eastern and northern regions), which has already been formed, and will be strengthened. This is the reduction of legal employment, providing job security and benefits, and the growth of self-employment among the population, making use of traditional sources of income: land resources (supplementary individual cultivation), forest produce (the collection of mushrooms and berries), forest resources (illegal timber cutting in the taiga), and fish (illegal fishing in the Far East, in Siberian rivers, and in the Astrakhan region). The archaic shift in employment structure not only facilitates the decay of human capital but also contributes to the growth of ineffectual budgetary expenditures to support the social infrastructure in the economically moribund territories and social welfare for their populations (unemployment benefits, social security payments, and so on).

The growth of tension, ethnic conflicts, and clan phenomena in the republics of the North Caucasus will stimulate the current of outward migration of educated and more modernized urban dwellers to other regions. This loss of "modernizing agents" will reproduce and strengthen traditionalism and conflicts. At the same time, the flow of unskilled workers, forced out of their own regions and into the biggest urban agglomerations by conflicts and a lack of work, will grow stronger.

Economic growth in the major cities that are regional centers will slow down sharply due to a dearth of investment and the worsening of institutional conditions. This will lead to an even greater concentration of human capital in the federal cities. Even more important, this will limit the opportunities for transfer to the regions of impulses toward all forms and types of modernization—of consumption, of behavior, of values. In Russia, big central cities are the most important "translators" of innovations, facilitating their movement down through the hierarchy of towns in their immediate regions, and thence into the surrounding areas.

This collection of problems is a sufficient basis on which to forecast a substantial drop in human capital in Russia; and without this capital, the country will not be able to develop normally.

The *optimistic scenario* of stable investment-driven growth is possible only given a significant amelioration of institutions (defense of private property rights, decreased corruption, and so on) and the growth of openness in the country's economy. Even poor infrastructure is a less rigid barrier, because it can be developed as economic growth occurs; the Sakhalin region has offered an example of this.

Under the optimistic scenario, the polarization of spatial development is also present. Economic growth is not equal across territories; investors are more attracted to regions with competitive advantages that permit faster and greater returns on their investments. The spatial configuration of these competitive advantages (development factors) will scarcely change in the course of a single decade; in Russia, they are especially inertial. As a consequence, essentially the same territories indicated in the inertial scenario (see above) will be points of growth. Given a decrease in institutional barriers, however, the speed and quality of their development will increase. Moreover, the number of dynamically developing territories will grow as a function of positive change in the balance of factors for and barriers to development.

Interregional inequalities, especially in the initial phase of investment-driven growth, will grow stronger because the regions with few competitive advantages will lag behind. But the scale of growth inequalities will not be as great as it was in the 1990s and early 2000s. The problems of the regions that lag can be solved not only with the aid of stimulative regional policy (which is often far from successful, even in developed countries) but also, in the first instance, with the aid of redistributive social policy (social welfare) and policy targeting the growth of human capital. There is a central principle for such policy: You need to help people, not regions.

So as not be repetitive, I distinguish seven characteristics of the optimistic forecast for spatial development that differ from those of the inertial forecast. *First is the expansion of the geography of realizable natural resource advantages.* Because Russia's natural resource endowment remains its most significant advantage, the realization of the optimistic scenario will hasten the development of gas- and oil-producing and transit regions in the European North (the Murmansk region, the Nenets autonomous *okrug*, and the Komi republic), Siberia (the Yamal-Nenets autonomous *okrug* and the Krasnoyarsk *krai*), and the Far East (Yakutia and the Sakhalin region), thanks to joint projects with foreign companies for the extraction of fuel using Western technology. Fertile land resources will also be exploited more efficiently. This will constitute a basis for the rapid growth of the agricultural sector and food processing in the regions of the European South, and then in the regions around the Volga and in the southern area of West Siberia, which are further from export routes. State support will help to strengthen the position of Russian producers in the global food market.

Second is the rapid expansion of the Moscow agglomeration's economic zone. This process is actively proceeding, but has so far encompassed only the border areas of neighboring regions along major highways and the urban centers of some regions with better investment climates. With a reduction of barriers, all the regions around Moscow will receive an additional flow of investment aimed at creating goods and services for the enormous market in the capital agglomeration. A second component of this process is road building to reduce economic distance; it will be implemented by the government in partnership with business.

Third is the acceleration of the development of regional urban centers. Growing consumer demand will stimulate the growth of Russian and foreign investment in the service and food production sectors and other import-replacing industries of major regional urban centers and in their suburban zones. First to attract investment resources will be those cities with a million inhabitants or more, and those with populations close in size, which will compete for investors and human capital. This will, first, reduce the Moscow agglomeration's hypertrophied role; second, the competitive development of the regional urban centers will accelerate the process of modernization of municipal institutions.

Fourth is the emergence of innovation-driven development centers beyond the Moscow agglomeration. This role can be played by several big Russian cities (Tomsk, Novosibirsk, Yekaterinburg, and so on) that have preserved a significant potential in various branches of science. Developing demand for innovation within the country is a longer-term task; but with the improvement of the investment climate, venture financing from domestic and foreign sources will be available. In the aforementioned cities, high-quality universities with research facilities and an effective system of stimulus for academic activities will develop. These innovation centers, however, will not be numerous, given that the concentration of higher-quality human capital is low in most big Russian cities.

Fifth is the realization of the advantages of proximity to developed countries. In the northwestern regions that border European Union countries, lowering the barrier function of the border and improving the investment climate will facilitate the flow of investments to timber-processing industries and to more labor-intensive manufacturing industries producing for export, as well as for the markets of the Saint Petersburg agglomeration and other Russian regions. This is a typical development trend for the border regions in the countries of Central and Eastern Europe, which heretofore has not been realized in Russia because of institutional barriers.

Sixth is the expansion of advantages of coastal and transit situations. In contrast to the western and southern coastal regions, the coastal zones in the more populous regions of the Far East (the Primorsk and Khabarovsk regions and Sakhalin) have so far not made use of their advantages because of strong institutional barriers and a less developed infrastructure. A reduction of the institutional barriers of "gangster capitalism" will permit the attraction of necessary investments in infrastructure, which, coordinated with rational state infrastructure projects, will create the necessary conditions for the development of business. The influx of Chinese investments and the adequately controlled attraction of labor will also assist the economic growth of the Far East, including both its major cities and the agricultural sector.

And seventh is the increased efficiency of regional policy in peripheral territories. Under all kinds of scenarios, Russia will retain extensive peripheral spaces, but the state can stimulate the population's mobility, making migration easier (for youth, in the first instance). Moreover, more effective forms—both mobile and fixed—of social services will develop to aid vulnerable groups among the populations of peripheral territories.

It is rather hard to believe in this rosy picture. But in other countries, such as Poland and the Czech Republic, similar trends are already present and analogous development-stimulating measures have been successful.

Modernization Risks: The Spatial Dimension

The modernization of institutions—with property rights guarantees, independence for the judiciary and media, a reduction of corruption, and the like—is a basic condition for implementing the optimistic scenario. Another necessary condition is a rejection of the overcentralized governance system and, in the long term, a transition to real federalism. Institutional modernization always involves risks that should be foreseen in advance. Irina Busygina and Mikhail Filippov think that a long period of economic losses will be inevitable on the road to federalism, and emphasize the problem of "early winners," which, having received an advantage, lose the stimulus for the continuation of reforms.[10]

A transition to real federalism is a very complex problem that needs a separate analysis. As far as risks of decentralization are concerned, the experience of "the turbulent 1990s" is often mentioned—growing differences in the regions' socioeconomic development, a possibility of the transformation of territories where control is nearly lost into the equivalents of failed states, and, in the extreme case, the disintegration of the country itself. But a cocktail of real problems and horror stories, with which the electorate is treated, cannot be the basis for a serious analysis of risks and ways to minimize them.

Interregional economic inequality would indeed increase due to the differences in their competitive advantages; but, apart from the several years of the oil boom, it was growing under overcentralized governance as well. A massive redistribution of oil incomes deepened dependency of the lagging regions rather than stimulated their economic development. A decentralization of the tax system combined with the modernization of the institutional environment gives more competitive regions a chance to increase the pace of development, attracting investments from businesses, improving infrastructure, and accelerating economic growth in the country as a whole.

The transition to real federalism, however, involves a serious risk, which is also predetermined by the laws of spatial development. Russia has clear competitive advantages as far as its natural resources endowment is concerned; therefore, the opening of its economy will lead to a flow of foreign investments primarily into resource-extracting industries and regions. Consequently, the resource orientation of the national economy can increase, and the leading oil- and gas-producing regions will differ from the others even more by the level of economic development, and "fatten" on the resource rent. The current mechanism of rent concentration (that is, the mineral extraction tax) at the federal level, with its consequent redistribution, more or less solves this problem (in contrast to the special position of Moscow, fattening on the rent of its status as a capital), but flexibility will be needed to maintain an effective balance in the relations between the center and the regions in the changing economic conditions.

Growing social inequality among the regions (in employment, incomes, and access to social services) constitutes another, similarly serious risk of decentralization. In the 2000s, interregional inequality in incomes was reduced, and the Russians appreciated this. There are no easy solutions for this politically sensitive problem, but the situation is not hopeless. Unlike the 1990s, mechanisms providing social security and the growth of human capital in the less developed regions are already in place today. The first of them is a transition to targeted social support; now, its share of overall social benefits is only 25 percent. Second, Russia will need to master the mechanism of income control, like the one existing in developed countries. Third, optimization of the social welfare institutions network is needed, and it should be done thoroughly rather than as a campaign under orders from above, as happens now. Fourth, population mobility should be increased by stimulating educational and labor migration, by developing mortgage mechanisms, and by reducing the corruption surcharge in the urban land and construction markets, which will lower housing prices. Fifth, opportunities for self-employment and support for small businesses should be enhanced. All these measures are quite familiar, but in Russia's conditions they have been implemented slowly and badly.

Decentralization will force regions and cities to compete more actively for investments and human capital, and this is a very strong stimulus to modernize social institutions, improving conditions for the development of medium-sized and small businesses. Of course, there will be winners and losers in this competition. The latter will obviously face risks of social instability, but there are mechanisms to mitigate them. The competitive election system is able, though only with a considerable time lag, to ensure the rotation of authorities and thus enhance the quality of regional or city government. Moreover, Russian law allows the imposition of federal authority on regions with acute budget problems due to bad governance, which lowers the risk of their deterioration into failed states.

If all the aforementioned mechanisms work badly (which is quite possible at the initial stage of decentralization), how many Russian regions will emerge as losers and experience with high probability the negative consequences of growing social inequality? International experience makes it possible to calculate the approximate scale of risks. A World Bank report sums up the long-term trends of regional inequality in the developed countries, and demonstrates that the growth of income inequality stops when per capita GDP exceeds $10,000.[11] At this level of development, a country acquires the necessary resources for redistributive social policies. In Russia, per capita GDP in 2008 reached $16,000 at purchasing power parity (PPP), and even during the crisis, in 2009, remained near the $15,000 level. But this is an average figure; in half the regions, per capita gross regional product (GRP) at PPP in 2008 was lower than $10,000. Barriers inherent in the Russian space—the vast territory, low population density, and poorly developed urban network—should not be forgotten either. To overcome them, state social expenditures should be considerably higher than in developed European countries. All this means that at least half of Russia's regions may lose from decentralization. At this moment, it is impossible to predict whether the mechanisms ensuring social security and the development of human capital in these regions could start to work efficiently before the whole system slips out of control. But if nothing is done, the whole declining country will get out of control—or end up in the "dustbin of history."

Notes

1. Paul R. Krugman, "First Nature, Second Nature, and Metropolitan Location," *Journal of Regional Science* 33 (1993): 129–44.

2. T. G. Nefedova, *Selskaya Rossiya na pereputie: Geographicheskie ocherky* (Rural Russia at the crossroads: Geographical essays) (Moscow: Novoye Izdatelstvo, 2003).

3. Paul R. Krugman, "Urban Concentration: The Role of Increasing Returns and Transport Costs," *International Regional Science Review* 19, nos. 1–2 (1996): 5–30.

4. Paul R. Krugman and R. E. Livas, "Trade Policy and the Third World Metropolis," *Journal of Development Economics* 49 (1996): 137–50.

5. Territorial clusters are defined as territorially localized groups of enterprises belonging to the same industry or interconnected industries. They develop more rapidly by exchanging information, qualified personnel, technologies, and best practices, they use common infrastructure—this is a certain symbiosis of competition and collaboration.

6. Richard Florida, *The Rise of the Creative Class: And How It's Transforming Work, Leisure, and Everyday Life* (New York: Basic Books, 2002).

7. M. Fujita, P. Krugman, and A. J. Venables, *The Spatial Economy: Cities, Regions, and International Trade* (Cambridge, Mass.: MIT Press, 2000).

8. N. V. Zubarevich, *Regiony Rossii: Neravenstvo, Crisis, Modernizatsiya* (Russia's regions: inequality, crisis, modernization) (Moscow: Nezavisimy Institut Sotsialnoi Politiki, 2010).

9. N. Zubarevich, "Stabilizatsia Bez Modernizatsii" (Stabilization without modernization), *Pro et Contra*, no. 3 (2010): 49.

10. I. Busygina and M. Filippov, "Problemy Vynuzhdenoi Federalizatsii" (The problems of federalization out of necessity), *Pro et Contra*, nos. 3–4 (2009): 46.

11. World Bank, *World Development Report 2009: Reshaping Economic Geography* (New York: Oxford University Press for the World Bank, 2009).

CHAPTER TWENTY

POLITICAL SYSTEMS *in* *the* RUSSIAN REGIONS *in* 2020

Alexandr Kynev

One of the biggest factors that shaped political development in the Russian regions during the 1990s and 2000s were the events of October 1993, when lower-level soviets, including the Moscow City Soviet, had their powers revoked by presidential decree, and many regional soviets dissolved themselves or were dissolved by the governors. The presidential decrees did not affect the republics, but many of them were run by authoritarian regimes that had been in place since the communist days and were headed by former local party bosses who had simply changed their job titles. The new Russian Constitution instituted a hyperpresidential republic with a very weak Parliament, and a similar system was replicated in the regions. In many regions, governors were a key force in making the regional power system more authoritarian through the part they played in drafting election laws and organizing election campaigns, and later in adopting regional charters (constitutions).

Regional leaders' influence and their political ambitions grew rapidly as Boris Yeltsin neared the end of his time in office. This was reflected in the 1999 parliamentary elections with the creation of Fatherland–All Russia (OVR)—the "regional leaders' party." The federal authorities responded by forming the Medved (Bear) Bloc in 1999, headed by newly appointed prime minister Vladimir Putin. As we know, the alliance of regional elites headed by Yuri Luzhkov, Yevgeny Primakov, and Mintimer Shaimiyev lost this battle.

Having succeeded Yeltsin as president, Putin lost no time in acting to weaken the political clout of the regional elites, who lost the battle for federal power in 1999. The reform of federal relations began, shifting the balance of power between the federal and regional authorities sharply in the federal authorities' favor. The next decade saw the regions' political and institutional independence substantially undermined.

Aside from the federal authorities, who sought to establish a firm hold over a country with overly strong regional elites and restore a common legal space, the heads of the big federal business organizations (including the so-called oligarchs) also had an interest in this, as they wanted to pursue economic expansion in the regions. The federal leaders of political parties also had an interest in weakening the regional authoritarian regimes, hoping to thereby expand their influence on regional political life.

The first step in reforming federal relations was to create the federal districts and place the law enforcement and security services outside the governors' control. The next step was to introduce the possibility of "federal intervention," which gave the federal authorities the right to dissolve a regional parliament by passing the required federal law, and gave the president the right to dismiss regional heads. But these provisions came with many restrictions designed to guarantee against arbitrary action, and it is not by chance that these measures were never used once during the next four years.

Reforming the Federation Council was another step. Instead of being formed by regional heads, the upper chamber of Parliament was to be made up of representatives delegated by the regions instead. Half the Federation Council's members were elected by the regional parliaments, and the other half were appointed by the executive heads in the regions. As a result, the Federation Council ended up filled with people who were there more to lobby for particular sectors' interests rather than represent the regions, and, what is more, the new members were to a large extent under the control of the presidential administration. This lowered the Federation Council's prestige and also the quality of its lawmaking work.

The federal authorities tried to unify the country's system of administrative and territorial divisions by getting rid of the regions made up of more than one entity. They succeeded in abolishing six autonomous districts, which were absorbed into the Perm, Irkutsk, Kamchatka, and Chita regions, and Krasnoyarsk Territory. But Nenets Autonomous District re-fused to be absorbed into Arkhangelsk Region, and the same was true of Khanty Mansiisk and Yamalo-Nenets autonomous districts and Tyumen Region. These autonomous districts, which have developed oil and gas production industries, simply agreed to pay more revenue to the two re-gions of which they are formally part, but the merger process went no further than this. As for the former autonomous districts, they became ad-ministrative units with "special status" that varied from one case to an-other depending on the results of political bargaining. Rather than ending asymmetry, the merger process has in fact only made it greater.

Essentially, instead of the old semifeudal system, in which the regional authorities had full power over their regions in return for political loyalty to the sovereign (the president), a system of parallel verticals was estab-lished that was agency based and corporate, and was built around various federal organizations. These verticals soon also spread into social and po-litical life.

Electoral reform became an integral part of the federal authorities' new regional policy. New federal laws were drafted and passed in 2001–2003: On Political Parties, On Basic Guarantees of Russian Citizens' Electoral Rights and the Right to Take Part in Referendums, On Elections of Depu-ties to the Russian Federation State Duma, and On Russian Federation Presidential Elections.

Work on creating a single "party of power" began in parallel to the legal reforms. By forcing the regional bureaucracies into submission and oblig-ing them to support United Russia, the federal authorities first weakened and then eliminated the competition between administrative resources that had to some extent compensated for an as-yet-underdeveloped com-petition between political parties. Unlike in regimes that are truly domi-nated by a particular political party, the party regime formed in the 2000s is more of a regime of total domination by the executive branch. The party, imitating the role of dominant force, in fact plays an auxiliary part in this system and is in a dependent and subordinate position with regard to the executive authorities.

The creation of a "vertical" of electoral commissions was another step in electoral reform. Local government bodies no longer had a part in forming the electoral commissions that organized federal and regional elections. Electoral commissions were formed mostly on a hierarchical basis instead, with the higher-level commissions forming the lower ones.

The package of reform measures that Putin introduced in 2004, after the Beslan tragedy, abolished the direct elections of regional governors, who were instead to be nominated by the president and approved by regional parliaments. These reforms also introduced the proportional system for elections to the State Duma.

By abolishing direct gubernatorial elections, the federal authorities "killed two birds with one stone," dealing a crushing blow to the regions' political independence and at the same time replacing "uncontrolled" renewal of regional authorities with a "controlled" process. Not only did this limit people's right to take part in governing the country, but it also led (especially in tandem with the regional governors joining United Russia en masse) to greater mobilization of administrative resources in the next round of federal elections.

The demands political parties had to meet were toughened at the same time. Under the December 2004 law, parties had a year to bring their membership up to least 50,000 (at least 500 members in more than half the regions, and at least 250 members in the others). The new law's authors made no secret of the fact that their aim was to prevent the creation of new parties and liquidate most of the existing ones.

In 1999, 139 national political parties and groups were entitled to take part in the elections to the State Duma. The adoption of the new law on political parties saw this number drop to 44 political parties and 20 national public movements (as part of election blocs) in the 2003 State Duma election. By the start of 2006, however, after checks of party membership, only 19 parties remained. A new round of streamlining began after the State Duma election in 2007, because parties that received less than 2 percent of votes in the election had to pay vast sums of money for air time and newspaper space, which in the past they had been allocated for free. By the start of 2009, only 7 parties remained, including 6 of the old parties—United Russia, the Communist Party (KPRF), LDPR, A Just Russia, Patriots of Russia, and Yabloko—and one new party, Right Cause, formed by the merger of 3 earlier existing parties. Right Cause, which was created with overt help from the Kremlin, is the only new party since 2006 to have managed to meet the draconian registration requirements set by the Law

On Political Parties, though people have and are still making numerous attempts to establish new parties.

Starting in 2004, the authorities increasingly pressured the elites into party membership, while at the same time rolling back a genuine multi-party system. This left the regional elites with even less room for maneuver in their search for political partners with whom to take part in federal and regional elections.

The regional elites and the federal authorities fought an ongoing position battle during the 2000s. The regional elites attempted to sidestep the restrictions imposed by the federal authorities, and they adapted their tactics to the new rules of the game. But the federal authorities responded by closing emerging loopholes and tightening their control over events. With the introduction of the mixed-member electoral system for regional elections, the regional elites began establishing control over federal parties' formal branches, but the real battle in the regions between the various interest groups (clans, clients, business groups) continued under the new system.

The tougher rules made it no surprise that in most regions, only parties represented in the State Duma—United Russia, KPRF, LDPR, and A Just Russia—took part in the 2010 regional elections. Only these parties could afford not to worry about the legal obstacles because the law puts them in a privileged position by exempting them from having to collect signatures or pay collateral when registering their regional lists.

By 2008–2010, changes in the quality of regional government, brought about by the abolition of direct gubernatorial elections, were visible. During Putin's time in office, for 29 new gubernatorial appointments, there were 11 "voluntary" resignations, 12 cases of governors reaching the end of their terms, 3 dismissals, 1 promotion (Sergei Sobyanin), and 2 deaths (Mikhail Yevdokimov and Viktor Shershunov). In a total of 83 regions, there were 27 governors appointed between February 2005 and May 2008[1] (32.5 percent of regional leaders overall). Governors' roles underwent a change in quality that saw them transform from politicians into executive administrators. Even in cases when directly elected governors remained in office, their loss of political independence and the need to approve key appointments with the regional administration became ever more apparent. This change in the governors' quality and the weakening of their ties with regional elites is reflected most clearly in the appointment of governors from outside the region—people with no ties to the region they are sent to head. Of the 29 new appointees between February 2005 and May 2008, 16 can be considered to be in this category.

It was in the North Caucasus republics that the authorities treaded most carefully with regard to the old regional elites' interests, fearful of stepping on the wrong toes, losing control of the situation, and potentially destabilizing the region with an ill-thought-through appointment.

What emerges clearly is that the regions that gave least cause for complaint during the 1990s and had the least violations of federal law suffered most from the new gubernatorial appointments policy, while the leadership of regions that violated federal law had their interests taken into account most of all under the new policy.

Governors lost a lot of their independence in forming the regional administrations. First, many of them were forced to sacrifice key members of their administrations to keep their own positions safe; and second, new deputies were appointed in a number of regional administrations, often people brought in from outside to act as "inspectors" keeping watch on the governor. New governors appointed from outside the region were almost always followed by colleagues and friends from their home region, who would take up official posts, and by active expansion into the region of business with links to the new governors. Rather than trying to consolidate the regional elites, new governors appoint to key posts people they trust personally, or representatives of the groups within the federal elites or state corporations to which they owe their appointments.

The change in governors' institutional status did not affect their importance for the federal authorities in guaranteeing the outcome of federal elections. In some cases, the electoral factor stopped the federal authorities from going ahead and replacing particular governors. Total control over the regional elites and electoral process in a number of the republics (Tatarstan, Bashkortostan, Dagestan, and so on) and in regions such as Tyumen and Rostov made the heads of these regions essentially irreplaceable for the federal authorities. The federal authorities' desire to keep control of the electoral process competed with their desire to overhaul the regional elites.

By the time Dmitri Medvedev became president in 2008, the governors had three main responsibilities:

- Formally ensuring enforcement of federal laws in the regions and carrying out federal reforms with minimum deviation from the course set by the federal authorities.
- Ensuring that the main state corporations' interests are taken into account and helping them to carry out their plans and strategies (private-sector big business interests are taken into account as long as they do not clash with state corporations' interests). This takes place on a reciprocal basis, with the corporations taking the governor's personal interests and those of his entourage into account.
- Ensuring maximum votes for the federal party of power in elections in the region at any price.

Also important to note is the system of "parallel verticals." Competition between the different verticals has partially begun to replace other competition mechanisms, creating some room for local communities to defend their interests, but these gaps between the verticals are temporary and tied to particular situations, and are in no way connected to any real orientation by the verticals toward local community interests.

At the same time, the stronger verticals gradually began crushing the weaker ones. The strongest verticals are those formed by the Prosecutor General's Office, the Investigative Committee, the Interior Ministry, and the Federal Security Service (FSB).

Local government heads have ended up in an ambiguous situation in the Russian regional power system. On the one hand, inclusion of the governors in the "executive vertical" system has made mayors (especially the mayors of regional centers) the obvious next target for inclusion in the "vertical." Passage of the new federal law On General Principles of Local Government Organization in the Russian Federation in 2003 intensified this process, regulating the various municipal government organization models and introducing provisions such as the possibility of bringing in hired "city managers" to head municipal administrations. But on the other hand, the municipal reform, the declared goal of which was to bring the municipal bodies closer to local people, substantially decentralized the regional government system and expanded the number of people involved in local government.

Abolition of direct gubernatorial elections and single-seat electorates in elections to the State Duma, along with the increase (enforced from above) of the role played by tightly regulated political parties in elections to regional parliaments, contributed to a gradual shift in the center of real political competition from the regional parliaments to the local government bodies, which control real economic activity at the grassroots level. These local bodies gradually become the main centers of political dissent, and the fact that a number of large cities were headed by successful entrepreneurs and charismatic public politicians only added to the scandals and conflicts.

There had been conflicts between regional governors and mayors since the early 1990s, but they took on a clear symbolic character in the second half of the 2000s. Conflicts with the mayors of regional capitals are practically unavoidable, given that in most regions the regional capital ends up having to subsidize the other towns in the region, inevitably raising the mayors' ire. Land allocation is another source of conflict. It is practically impossible today to run a large city without violating any of the various regulations, and an inspection of any local administration will reveal violations, if one wishes to find them. Conflicts arise not only with the mayors of regional capitals but also with the heads of any more or less significant towns.

Thus the second component of municipal reform, which changed the local government bodies' public role, increasingly clashed with the first component with its centralizing and unifying aims. It therefore came as no surprise that after the federal and regional electoral regulations were tightened, the local government election system was the next in line. This system was gradually brought into the party vertical. Starting in 2005, the main trend in elections to municipal representative bodies was the gradual introduction of a mixed or fully proportional representation system.

Changing Trends Under Medvedev

By the time Medvedev became president, the quantitative changes brought about by eliminating regional authorities' political independence were increasingly transforming into qualitative changes. Local elites and citizens were increasingly discontented with the unification carried out and the ill-conceived personnel decisions (above all, appointing governors from outside the region), which ignored the regions' specific circumstances, and the social and economic crisis further added to a rise in the protest mood.

Local anger over appointments led to Medvedev's taking a more cautious line in choosing candidates for governor. The federal authorities attempted to find a "golden mean," looking for candidates who were part of the federal elite while at the same time had ties to the region in question or to neighboring regions. But this more cautious approach did not stem the discontent over the appointment of people from outside the regions.

Renewal of the body of governors as a whole accelerated. In the spring of 2009, when it looked as though the country had got through the worst of the crisis, the federal authorities decided to cast aside the caution that had been holding them back from replacing governors at a faster pace.

Large-scale replacement of governors (as a rule, governors in the most important regions are replaced, while those in less important regions are allowed to stay on for a new term) practically always means local personnel revolutions. The new governors get rid of their predecessors' teams and dismantle their administration models. Thus, against a backdrop of ongoing crisis and gradual rise in public discontent, the federal authorities, having finally seized the opportunity to mold the regional elites to their taste, are undermining the foundations of the very stability and administrative control that justified building the various power verticals in the first place. With limited human resources options, and no public legitimacy and skill in public political competition, the new governors make all manner of management and public relations mistakes. They often end up unable to mobilize public support for their policies, or win over local business, and willingly or unwillingly provoke ever new conflicts and scandals.

In dismantling on such a large scale the old regional elites and depriving the regions of what remained of their political independence, the federal authorities are unwittingly dismantling the regional autocracies, which will inevitably destabilize and eventually even topple the federal autocracy. The regional elites that many federal officials loathe so deeply are in reality their Siamese twins. Drunk on a sense of total power, the federal authorities may dislike them, but they cannot survive without them. For the federal authorities, the battle with the regions will turn into a battle against their own selves, and this will inevitably have an impact on election results further down the line.

The unpredictable gubernatorial appointments policy, which resembles a game of Russian roulette, does not mean that the candidates themselves are worse than those appointed during the period 2005–2009. More likely the contrary in fact is true because, objectively, the quality of candidates has improved compared with the previous period. In many cases the regional elites were in need of a substantial shakeup, and people such as the former Communist Party officials still running the Yamalo-Nenets Autonomous District needed to be replaced. But this does not change the fact that the vertical structure, in dividing the elite and demoralizing regional government, weakens its own foundations.

The enforced and often publicly ill-explained shakeup of the regional elites turns the federal authorities into the target for public anger. In the public's eyes, the federal authorities bear full responsibility not only for successes but also for the obvious failures that occur, for forming regional administrations based on client principles, and for the appointment to regional administrations of officials for no explainable reason other than personal and corporate connections to the new governor and those who lobbied for his appointment.

Changes have taken place in the election system, including elections to regional parliaments. On Medvedev's initiative, the need to pay collateral to take part in elections was abolished for elections at all levels. This leaves only two means of registering: the preferential terms for candidates from parties represented in the State Duma; and the collection of signatures, with all the associated draconian requirements involved, which makes registration completely dependent on the whim of regional or local authorities.

The way the Federation Council is formed changed starting January 1, 2011, with only deputies from regional and local councils now able to be delegated there. And the regions now have the right to recall their representatives from the Federation Council.

A law came into force in February 2009 depriving public organizations of the right to have candidates run for them in local elections under the proportional representation system. They were given instead the possibility of concluding agreements with political parties on having their candidates make up to 15 percent of the party list, but these agreements carry no firm guarantees.

Despite a few symbolic defeats for United Russia starting from the autumn of 2008 in regional and local elections and an overall drop in votes for the party following the social and economic crisis, earlier trends, in particular expansion of the proportional representation system, remained in place. Medvedev outlined several proposals for political reform in the regions in his 2009 annual presidential address:

1. Standardized size of regional parliaments. Under the new law, after September 1, 2011, regional parliaments will be formed on the basis of 15 to 50 deputies for regions with a total voter population of less than 500,000; 25 to 70 deputies for regions with 500,000 to 1 million voters; 35 to 90 deputies for regions with 1 to 2 million voters; and 45 to 110 deputies for regions with more than 2 million voters. Eight regions (the republics of Adygeya, Bashkortostan, North Ossetia-Alania, Tyva, Khakasia, Karachaevo-Cherkessia, Kabardino-Balkaria, and Udmurtia) will have to reduce the size of their parliaments (ranging from cutting 2 seats in Kabardino-Balkaria to 25 seats in Khakasia). Eleven regions (Khabarovsk Territory, Kemerovo, Penza, Saratov, Tver, Tyumen, and Ulyanovsk regions; Moscow City; and Nenets, Khanty-Mansiisk, and Chukotka autonomous districts) will need to increase the size of their parliaments (from 1 seat in Tyumen Region and up to 10 seats in Penza Region and Moscow).

2. Guarantees for all parties represented in regional parliaments, the possibility of forming fractions, and the possibility of filling posts for deputies working on a permanent basis and in leadership positions.

3. Guaranteed representation in parliament for parties that received more than 5 percent of the vote in regional elections. Each party in such a case gets one seat in parliament. Given that most regional parliaments have around 40 to 50 seats, this essentially amounts to lowering the threshold for entry into parliament.

4. Parties not represented in the State Duma but with fractions in regional parliaments are exempted from having to collect signatures in order to register to take part in regional elections. In reality,

this exemption concerns only Patriots of Russia in a few regional parliaments.

5. Introduction of a new practice that would see legislative authorities at all levels meet at least once a year to listen to and discuss the proposals of parties not represented in the parliaments. Parties not represented in the parliaments will have the guaranteed possibility of taking part on an ongoing basis in the work of the central and regional electoral commissions.

6. Tougher rules on early voting in local elections, along the lines of rules for federal elections, and tighter regulation of the use of certificates entitling voters to vote in another location.

7. Guarantees for equal media coverage of the activities of parties represented in the regional parliaments.

8. Nationwide introduction of a practice requiring governors to make an annual report to the regional parliament (though the governors cannot be held responsible for the results of the reports, and the regional parliaments cannot dismiss them).

One of the noticeable recent trends is a sharp increase in abolition of direct mayoral elections. The biggest conflicts were over attempts to abolish mayoral elections in towns in Sverdlovsk Region and Khanty-Mansiisk Autonomous District. Decisions to abolish mayoral elections caused big protests in Perm and Chelyabinsk. Dzerzhinsk and Surgut succeeded in stopping the abolition of direct mayoral elections, and so did Yekaterinburg for a time. Since late 2009, Nizhny Novgorod, Perm, Chelyabinsk, Smolensk, Blagoveshchensk, Elista, Vladimir, and Kurgan have joined the list of towns where mayors are no longer elected by popular vote. By July 2011, direct mayoral elections had been abolished in the administrative centers of 46 out of 79 regions of the Russian Federation (four regions: Moscow, Saint Petersburg, Moskovskaya oblast, and Leningradskaya oblast do not have administrative centers or municipalities). During Dmitri Medvedev's presidency, the enlargement of regions was stopped, but administrative borders were modified, with certain regions taking over parts of other regions' territories. The most noteworthy example was a takeover of a sizable chunk of Moskovskaya oblast by Moscow in summer of 2011; as a result the territory of Moscow became 2.4 times larger. A new Federal district (North Caucasus Federal District, NCFD) was created and some of the presidential envoys have been replaced by civilians (the original appointees were retired generals), three of them former governors.

The system of "parallel verticals" remained practically unchanged: the verticals that are more closely tied to the federal center (the interior, the procuracy, and some others) effectively resisted the attempts of less important verticals (Rostekhnadzor [technological inspection], Rosprirodnadzor [environment inspection], and so on) to increase their own influence in the regions.

Certain "specialized" officials of regional administrations, such as the heads of regional finance departments or deputy governors in charge of domestic politics, and those responsible for election campaigns are appointed following close consultation with the respective federal agency. This practice has become even more common lately; as a result, the regional officials in question are not only members of local administrations, but are also incorporated in the respective "specialized" subordination vertical.

Future Prospects:
Between Unitary Federalism and Real Federalism

The first of the big decision points that will shape the future of the regional political system during the next decade is the choice between continuing the policies of the 2000s, based on dismantling real federalism and building a de facto unitary state with an ever-increasing number of binding legal norms and increasing uniformity and standardization of regional policy in a constantly growing number of areas, or the return of elements of real federalism with stronger institutional political independence in the regions.

Based on the current trends, the second option looks far less realistic. Even if it were the chosen option, there would still be many different possible development scenarios. Going by the experience of the last two decades and the big part played by informal practices, if regions did get the chance to substantially increase their political independence, one could expect to see a broad range of regional political systems emerge, from heavy-handed authoritarian regimes based on inherited personal power to essentially parliamentary republics. The big issue for this option, then, would be the question of formal limitations to prevent developments from taking unwanted turns. These limitations could include limited numbers of terms for regional heads, or restrictions on electing close relatives as successors, such as are in place in some Latin American countries.

Regional political practices will continue to be diverse, even with the far more likely development scenario of continuing the current "unitary federalism" policy (from authoritarian Chechnya to relatively liberal Perm Territory and Kirov Region), given the existing diversity of regional social and economic composition, political cultures, ethnic and religious make-up, and so on. Ten years is obviously not long enough to have stamped out or significantly weakened this diversity of informal practices. Historically, all attempts, acting out of whatever aims and interests, to impose standard-ized institutional solutions on the whole vast Russian territory have always led to the formal institutional system and the real political practice becom-ing two rather different things.

If the current policy of maximum uniformity of regional political sys-tems continues, the big issue that would arise (in turn creating "second-tier" development scenarios) is, what is this policy actually for? Is the aim to build "executive verticals" in all regions right down to the last village council, or is it to give all regions a common set for formal democratic institutions, by, for example, giving regional parliaments a bigger say in forming regional governments, introducing direct elections for members of the Federation Council and so on?

In the end, the two options produce four possible scenarios, which are shown in table 20.1. Why does the inertia-based scenario of continuing the "unitary federalism" policy seem most realistic, because the forces seeking real rather than cosmetic political change make up only a frac-tion of the current ruling elite? It would take time, too, to dismantle what has been methodically and systematically put in place during these last ten years. There are no visible initiators of potential revolutionary change in regional politics, nor supporters of any weight among the federal elite. This means that the system's internal problems and contradictions will continue to build up, and the system itself will gradually decay and lose its effectiveness. With politics now so much less public, rather than ad-dressing real problems, regional officials will increasingly keep them in

TABLE 20.1 *The Four Possible Scenarios Produced by the Two Options*

OPTION	SCENARIO
Real federalism	Restrictions introduced to prevent deviant scenarios
	Minimum restrictions
Unitary federalism	Further strengthening of the executive vertical
	Unification in the aim of guaranteeing a common set of formal democratic institutions in all regions

the shadows, out of sight of the federal authorities, who will thus receive an increasingly less objective picture of the real state of affairs in many regions. Personnel problems will also worsen, because there will be no source of new people to bring into the system, and this will sooner or later cause the system's failure. But this gradual process of decay could unfold over a very long time frame.

Of course there is always hope for change, but experience shows that the most pragmatic approach when building plans and strategies is to start from the worst-case scenario: It is better to overestimate negative trends than to underestimate them. One should, therefore, take the "unitary federalism" inertia-based scenario as the foundation and look at other scenarios as alternatives with much less chance of actually taking place.

Some among the democratically minded public hoped that the change of president would open the road to progress and restore if not all then at least part of the country's democratic institutions. Medvedev's image-building campaign drew in part on these unconscious hopes. But life has shown that Medvedev is, first, very limited in his room for maneuver, and that the federal leadership remains a creature of "many heads and entrances"; and second, that whatever positive changes have been made under Medvedev have been insignificant and mostly decorative in nature, and have gone hand in hand with further worsening in the state of Russia's democratic institutions. This worsening situation is reflected in the increase of the presidential and State Duma mandates, reduction in the Constitutional Court's independence, fewer possibilities for using jury trials, public organizations' loss of their right to put forward independent lists of candidates to run in municipal elections, mass-scale abolition of direct mayoral elections, and expansion of the FSB's and Interior Ministry's powers. Given that in 2012, either Medvedev will be reelected for a second term, of six years this time, or Putin will return as president, the inertia scenario looks set to continue at least until 2018.

As the authorities see it, "modernization" is above all about pursuing technological innovation while continuing to tighten the screws of "managed democracy." Medvedev is essentially continuing the policy of the ongoing enforced standardization of regional political institutions and dismantling even formal attributes of federalism, such as the regions' right to decide themselves on the size of their parliaments, independently appoint senior officials, and so on. The federal authorities are still trying to cut all the regions to fit the same abstract model for an ever bigger number of parameters.

As for the question of what future shape this unitary federalism will take, this is a lot less clear. The situation looks as follows regarding the main parameters:

- *Election or appointment of regional governors:* Given the widespread discontent with various appointment decisions (practice shows that governors usually have two or three years before policies that ignore the local elites' interests start to spark big protests), there is reason to expect an increase in the number of regions where protests against specific governors break out. This could encourage changes to the procedures for gubernatorial appointments, by expanding parliaments' powers to select candidates, for example, or pass a vote of no confidence in particular governors or executive administration officials.

- *Expansion of parliaments' powers:* This is most likely, through granting them greater involvement in choosing governors, but at the same there is a continued trend for deprofessionalization of the regional parliaments through the fewer numbers of deputies working on a permanent basis, and changes to the regional government formation process have not increased parliaments' influence as yet. The introduction of selection of city managers has also not increased representative bodies' power, because the regional executive authorities hold a third of the seats on the tender committees.

- *Limits on use of particular types of electoral system in the regions:* There are no signs yet that the standardization process is coming to a halt; on the contrary, the number of restrictions looks set to increase.
- *Changes to electoral procedures for electing deputies to the Federal Assembly (State Duma and Federation Council):* It is possible that if United Russia's ratings fall, the federal authorities might agree to return to a mixed system or even introduce a full single-seat electorate system (perhaps with only parties still having the right to put forward candidates). A return in whatever form to direct elections of Federation Council members would increase their public profile and independence from governors, which in turn would make governors more dependent on public opinion in the regions.
- *Changes to legislation on political parties:* The policy of a "managed multiparty system" will probably continue.
- *Limits on local government organization models:* Proposals have already sounded on getting rid of separate administrative organizations in municipal districts' administrative centers (in other words, the district administration head would run the district center directly), and there are a growing number of cases of district councils being formed through indirect elections (deputies at the village level delegate representatives to the district council). These examples reflect a clear trend toward reducing local government bodies' influence and bringing them under the regional authorities' tighter control. But there can be no doubt that parties other than United Russia will continue to lobby for the expansion of the proportional representation system.
- *Changes to procedures for appointing the heads of federal executive bodies' regional offices:* This looks unlikely, as the federal authorities are hardly likely to be willing to let go of their hard-won control over these appointments.
- *Federal policy on mergers of regions:* The merger process will probably not continue.

Overall therefore, on most counts (especially as concerns local government), steps will probably continue to strengthen the executive vertical, but in some areas (choosing regional governors) circumstances could pressure the authorities to introduce some elements of democratization while continuing to implement their standardization policies.

Note

1. Twenty-nine, if one takes into account that there were two appointments in a row in the Irkutsk region, and the governor of Koryakia, which later merged with Kamchatka.

CHAPTER TWENTY-ONE

2020: THE LAST CHANCE *for the* NORTH CAUCASUS?

Alexey Malashenko

This attempt to predict the state of affairs in the Russian North Caucasus in ten years' time is based on two probable scenarios—an optimistic one, and an inertia-based, or negative, one. Neither scenario is likely to unfold in full measure due to the contradictory and even mutually exclusive trends in the region's internal situation, and also the effect of the subjective factor that is individual politicians' acts and decisions. In the semi-traditional Caucasus society, this personal factor has always played a big and sometimes decisive role.

The North Caucasus is part of Russia and it is not easy to predict what Russia as a whole will look like in 2020. Any prediction carries risks and can always be easily challenged today. Only when the time actually comes can we see if we were right or not. Looking back at the forecasts made about the North Caucasus in the early 1990s, we see that the bleakest of them did indeed prove correct; but at the same time, we can be thankful at least that the worst-case scenario did not happen and the North Caucasus did not withdraw from the Russian Federation or sink into total civil war. But it is true that two wars in Chechnya and a series of bloody local conflicts "made up" for this.

The general futurological mood of twenty years ago was largely negative and focused mostly on what kind of crisis would emerge and how it would develop in the region. By 2010, this now familiar barrel of pessimism got a spoonful of optimism added to it in the form of new government proposals for tackling the region's problems. The dual-scenario approach is thus fully justified in this case. But rather than examining each scenario separately, I have chosen to examine each of the region's key issues in the context of the two scenarios.

Moscow's "Reset" Caucasus Policy

At the end of 2009, Moscow announced a "reset" in its Caucasus policy. The establishment of the new North Caucasus Federal District (NCFD) and the appointment of Alexander Khloponin as the presidential envoy there raised new hopes for improvement in the region. At the same time, however, this step was a sign that the federal authorities recognized that their previous policy had failed and that they had to abandon it, or at least radically adjust it.

The motivation behind the new policy was that grouping regions with similar problems together in a single federal district would help to find comprehensive strategies for their resolution. All the regions face big social and economic difficulties and also political tension and the presence of armed opposition and radical Islam. It is not by chance that some call the new district the "Islamic district." Forming the NCFD was supposed to facilitate the search for a common solution to the region's problems.

The appointment of the governor of Krasnoyarsk Territory, Alexander Khloponin, as the presidential envoy in the new district was also symbolic. The main arguments in his favor were his successful record in Krasnoyarsk and the fact that he was not involved in any way in North Caucasus politics, not part of any of the intrigues going on there, and independent from the local elites, which would give him the chance to make independent decisions and remain outside the entrenched system of clan and bureaucratic interests and corruption schemes. Khloponin was raised to the level of deputy prime minister, which also boosted his influence and authority. It was announced that he would focus above all on his work on resolving the region's social and economic problems.

But the new policy and appointment had inherent drawbacks right from the start. Not all the region's politicians agreed with the idea of forming the NCFD, and the fact that Khloponin does not know the Caucasus works not just to his advantage but also against him. Publicly, of course, everyone expressed unanimous support for Moscow's new course. Said Amirov, the mayor of Makhachkala, called it "one of the president's most effective and well-thought-out strategic moves."[1] The president of Karachaevo-Cherkessia, Boris Ebzeyev, described it as "an absolutely justified and necessary" decision.[2] And Arsen Kanokov, the head of Kabardino-Balkaria, called Khloponin's appointment "original and very successful."[3] Be it on the conscience of these speakers to say just how sincere their words really were. In any case, the local elites were obliged to back Moscow's personnel decisions, if only because their own fates depended on it. In reality, the idea of an "envoy from Moscow" with broad powers, come to put their activities under closer scrutiny, including financial scrutiny, had the local politicians worried. A case in particular here was the president of Chechnya, Ramzan Kadyrov, who had established a trusting informal relationship with Prime Minister Vladimir Putin, and for whom Khloponin signified the arrival of an additional "intermediary" link in the chain of communication with the country's top leadership. This was something for which he had no need at all, all the more so because Khloponin was a *presidential* envoy, and thus not the prime minister's man.

Khloponin's appointment was a sign of the authorities' increasing desperation. But at the same time, it raised hopes that this new figure from outside the region would somehow find the magic solution to its problems. The official optimistic "Khloponin scenario" looks fragile and artificial. Some have even suggested that the Putin-Medvedev tandem chose this course as a means of shrugging off responsibility for the Caucasus, shifting the burden instead to a successful manager brought in from outside. At the 2009–2010 crossroads, Khloponin looked like either a "political kamikaze" or a Soviet-era agriculture minister, doomed from the outset to permanent crisis.[4]

But the NCFD's establishment and Khloponin's appointment nevertheless mark the starting point for a potentially optimistic scenario and an assessment of just how realistic its implementation could be. The alternative is an inertia-based development of events—in other words, the probability that life in the North Caucasus will continue much as it is today.

The impression at the start of 2010 was that the new policy consisted of a parallel dual approach—with, on the one hand, a social and economic dimension and innovation drive, for which Khloponin is responsible, and, on the other hand, the efforts to maintain stability and fight terrorism, which remain as active as ever. These efforts are the responsibility of the security forces and law enforcement agencies, which prefer to keep using their familiar methods.

A New Approach to Maintaining Stability

A new approach to maintaining stability is not clearly outlined in any way in the "Khloponin scenario." But devising and implementing a new approach in this area is essential for an *optimistic scenario* to have a chance of success. These measures are needed to stabilize the situation and facilitate the implementation of new social and economic policies.

What is needed, specifically? First of all, limits need to be set on the force component of the federal authorities' policy. Security operations using force and counterterrorist operations have been going on in the region since early 2000, and though it was possible to justify this approach at the start of the decade, it has largely worn itself out now and meets with the hostility and fear of the local population, thus fueling an increase in latent and open support for the armed insurgents. Local civilians often suffer in these operations, as a number of examples in 2010 made clear (one of the starkest of which were the deaths of wild garlic pickers killed during a counterterrorist operation in Ingushetia). It is impossible, sadly, to completely eliminate the risk of civilian casualties, but it is vitally important to try to minimize the possibility of civilian casualties during counterterrorist operations.

Second, law enforcement officers must show full respect for the law, and must not be allowed to detain people unlawfully or use torture. The practice of collective punishment inflicted on the families of opposition members must also be ended (from June 2008 to June 2009, there were 26 cases of "arson as punishment" reported in Chechnya).[5]

Third, a nonstandard and more flexible approach needs to be taken to recognize the radicals as an opposition force and establish a differentiated approach to the various members of the protest movement, rather than simply lumping them all together under the label of "bandits."

Fourth, a normal environment must be created for contacts and maintaining dialogue with opposition-minded Muslims and supporters of nontraditional Islam, including those who follow fundamentalist or other ideologies.

Practice in implementing these kinds of measures has already built up on an informal basis. Conciliatory initiatives undertaken by local politicians—such as the president of Ingushetia, Yunus-bek Yevkurov—have been helpful in lowering the tension. Yevkurov has already appealed to Khloponin to grant amnesty or pardon members of the underground movements who have not committed serious crimes and want to return to normal life. Arsen Kanokov and Ramzan Kadyrov have also stated their willingness to pardon (grant amnesty to) those of their opponents who seek to mend their ways.

Fifth, members of the armed underground accused of committing crimes must be tried in open court trials. This would give the authorities greater opportunities for justifying the wisdom of their actions, including actions involving force, and at the same time would deprive the extremists of their aura of heroes fighting for a just cause.

Sixth, and finally, the authorities must recognize their own mistakes and punish those responsible for them. This would boost their authority in the public's eyes from the low level it is at today.

Of course, it is no easy thing to start making concessions and put the focus on reconciliation after so many years of confrontation and brutal action on both sides. It is especially difficult to do so in a situation of continuing terrorism. On the basis of data currently available to the public in Russia, the American researcher Gordon Khan drew up a table showing the dynamic of terrorist attacks and their consequences in the North Caucasus in 2008–2009. During this period, the number of terrorist attacks went up by 24 percent in Chechnya, 27 percent in Ingushetia, and 132 percent in Dagestan. The situation was somewhat brighter in Kabardino-Balkaria, where they fell by 18 percent, in Karachaevo-Cherkessia, where the figure was down by 60 percent, and in North Ossetia, which saw a decrease of 89 percent. But overall, the number of terrorist attacks in the North Caucasus as a whole increased by 37 percent.[6] In 2010, terrorists not only stepped up their activity but took it beyond the region, too, killing 40 people in a double attack in the Moscow metro in March of that year.

Terrorist attacks are a sadly regular occurrence in the region itself. In 2009 and 2010, attempts were made on the lives of three presidents of Caucasus republics, railway lines were the targets of blasts, and in July 2010, terrorists attacked the Baksan hydroelectric power station in Kabardino-Balkaria. All this shows that the extremists still have a lot of strength, whether in military-technical terms or in terms of human resources. In a way, their renewed activeness can be seen as a response to Moscow's attempt to implement its new policies. The radicals have long since learned to deal with crackdowns and increased use of force, and it is not this they fear, but rather the prospect that the authorities will relax their use of force and thereby marginalize the extremists and make it harder for them to recruit new supporters.

Trying to achieve complete unification under the aegis of the local Islamic authorities is a futile undertaking. Islam was always heterogeneous in terms of theology and ideological principles. The optimistic scenario here calls not for reaching a consensus between the various currents but for setting the discussion primarily on a theological track. It would be impossible (and unnecessary) to completely depoliticize Islam, all the more given the Islamic leanings of some of the region's secular authorities, above all Ramzan Kadyrov.

The measures listed above that would be needed for the optimistic scenario to go ahead might seem naive and unattainable in the near future. There are clear risks involved, the biggest of which (as my critics will surely point out) is that if the authorities do actually take this course, their adversaries could interpret it as a sign of weakness.

At the same time, it is not going to be possible to achieve a complete victory over the radical religious opposition in the next decade. The biggest realistic goal that the optimistic scenario can hope to achieve is to weaken the protest movement and deprive it of its systematic supply of new resources and support from among the region's young people. As for terrorist attacks, if the authorities follow a reasonable course of action, terrorist attacks will become less systematic, and the armed insurgents' new tactic of attacking infrastructure sites, which emerged in 2009, will also end up a failure.

The *inertia scenario* as applied to security and stability is the complete antithesis of the optimistic scenario, in that the authorities would not implement the measures listed above and would continue a strategy dominated by the use of force. Even with slight adjustments, a continuation of this policy would provoke a counterreaction from the opposition. Events would continue to unfold in a tit-for-tat spiral, fueling the local population's discontent even further and corroding its confidence in the federal and local authorities' ability to stabilize the situation.

In May 2010, Khloponin said that he is ready to take part in the appointment of any federal officials. At the same time, his entourage has become full of new deputies and advisers from among the ranks of law enforcement and security officials. Khloponin has appointed Arkady Yedelev as one of his advisers, head of the Interior Ministry in the NCFD Yevgeny Lazebin has kept his job, and the list could go on.[7] The authorities in Moscow give the impression of letting Khloponin take care of the purely economic side of things, while leaving security in the hands of proponents of the old line. The Law on Amendments to the Federal Law on the Federal Security Service only adds to this situation, because it gives the FSB "the right to issue official warnings to physical individuals about the inadmissibility of actions that create the conditions for committing crimes." The law has drawn a mixed reaction in Russia in general, but people in the North Caucasus see it as being directed above all against themselves and thus have taken it as yet another sign of the authorities' lack of trust toward them.

Some statements by federal politicians have also drawn negative reactions in the North Caucasus. One example was President Dmitri Medvedev's comment that even those "who cook soup and wash clothes" should be counted as terrorists' accomplices. Another example came from Khloponin, who said that "bandits, hiding behind the mask of terrorism and religious extremism . . . are organizing criminal groups involved in carving up assets." How are people in the North Caucasus to interpret such words? They get the sense that the authorities really do see their region as no more than a bandits' lair. This kind of approach is guaranteed to keep the inertia scenario going.

Not even eliminating the radical opposition's leaders could really turn the tide in this situation. This was illustrated by the recent wave of terrorism that followed the killing in early 2010 of prominent underground leaders such as Said Buryatsky and Anzor Astemirov. Of course, the security forces will continue these kinds of operations and will even clinch new successes, but it is clear that for every radical leader killed, a new one takes his place: Buryatsky and Astemirov were themselves part of this young generation.

One direct question that often comes up in the debate over putting the emphasis on force, or following the more cautious "soft" line, is whether or not it is possible to spread Ramzan Kadyrov's hard-line policy to the entire North Caucasus region. Most politicians and experts think that extending Chechnya's "peacemaking" experience to the whole region would be dangerous and carry big risks of counterresponses and social upheavals. What is more, the situation in Chechnya itself is not all peaceful, and Kadyrov from time to time talks about the "devils" still battling away in his republic. He estimates their number at about 50 to 70 people, but military sources put the number of armed insurgents in the hundreds. According to Gordon Khan's calculations, 34 rebels were killed in Chechnya in 2008, and 98 in 2009, while 37 rebels were captured in 2008, and 43 in 2009.[8] In August 2010, Chechnya's interior minister, Ruslan Alkhanov, said that 48 rebels had been killed and 128 captured since the beginning of the year. No one knows exactly how many people are fighting against Kadyrov, but it is clear that they have the support of part of the population, including some in Kadyrov's own entourage.

But in Moscow and in the North Caucasus itself, some sections of opinion are spellbound by what Kadyrov has achieved in using hard-line methods to attain a higher level of stability than in Dagestan or Ingushetia. Some in these republics say that Kadyrov's methods might not be to many people's liking, but they have brought order to Chechnya, and with time, perhaps even tougher measures might be needed to help normalize the situation in the other republics.

It is entirely possible that extending Kadyrov's methods to other republics in the region could at first achieve some results, but in the long run this policy would only ultimately worsen the situation, including through exacerbating interethnic tension, which in Dagestan, for example, would result in real tragedy. In such a case, the inertia scenario would become catastrophic. Instability would take on a firmly chronic nature (as one Caucasus politician said, a real "civil war" would spread through the region) and become politically "routine," with flare-ups of terrorism in the region itself and around the country. Social upheavals would spread to the currently relatively prosperous western part of the region, where the conditions for serious problems are already emerging.

Chechnya's case is thus something of an exception, because it is above all the result of two wars, overcoming the consequences of which called for extraordinary measures.

The Top Priority for the Federal Authorities

The top priority for the federal authorities now is to resolve the region's social and economic problems. This cannot be achieved overnight. At best it will take a decade, and there is no guarantee that improvement in the economic situation will automatically lead to religious extremism's fading away and clear up the differences between the authorities and society. Politics, religion, the macroeconomy and microeconomy, and unemployment are all interrelated, but the relations between them are far from linear. As analyst Sergei Makedonov put it, "It is not people digging around in rubbish heaps that go and become terrorists, and it is high time we realize this. . . . Terrorists are not people who have trouble getting a job. People join the radicals because they have no means of political expression and self-realization."[9] The idea that the economy alone can serve as the engine that will pull the Caucasus back on the right road is fundamentally mistaken. "Khloponin's miracle"—if it ever happens—will take place only in conjunction with sorting out the region's political problems. The efforts to modernize the North Caucasus are about to begin in a situation when the region is still caught up in a demodernization process.

The *optimistic scenario* entails real change above all at the political level. One of these changes is to bridge the gap between society and the authorities, whether local or federal. This can be done by making local governments transparent, having local leaders take part in public roundtables, and giving people the chance to ask them questions via the Internet. Officials must be accountable before the public, and there must be public supervision of their decisions and their implementation. Legislative institutions work more effectively, and parties are more active, when they are less closely tied to the local clans. Nongovernmental organizations need to have normal conditions for their work, and the law must guarantee these organizations' independence and possibility to work unhindered.

Distribution of financial resources—from the federal budget above all, but also from local budgets—must be kept under strict control. For instance, at the United Russia regional conference in Pyatigorsk in 2010, Olga Timofeyeva, a deputy from the Stavropol City Duma, appealed to the prime minister, saying directly that half of the money sent to develop the North Caucasus "would be stolen yet again."[10] Vladimir Putin made no response, obviously aware of this problem's eternal nature (before him, Boris Yeltsin publicly lamented that he did not know where the money sent to the Caucasus actually ended up). Compliance with federal laws would create barriers preventing this kind of misappropriation of financial resources.

Relations between the authorities and society must be regulated by the law alone, and it is strict compliance with the law that will determine the region's social and economic development. But the big difficulty is to make the laws work in an environment that makes this kind of compliance hard to enforce. The federal authorities play the main part here.

(In fact, there are problems with enforcing the laws and ensuring compliance with them throughout the entire country, which makes it doubly difficult to enforce them in the region. But we are talking here about a future ideal model for the North Caucasus and, indeed, for the whole of Russia.)

If the laws are fully enforced, this will help to rein in corruption. As the head of the Volgograd Region's Interior Ministry put it, the decision to give Khloponin "unprecedented powers" was also made in order "to liquidate the corruption problem."[11] The level of corruption will inevitably remain higher in the North Caucasus than in the rest of Russia, and this can be explained by the traditional nature of society there, the habit of looking at official posts as a source of material well-being, and nepotism. Corruption is intrinsically bound up with the shadow economy, which in the former Southern Federal District, the NCFD's predecessor, accounted for 40 to 60 percent of the economy (two times more than in Russia as a whole). In 2004, shadow economy revenues in the Southern Federal District were comparable to the amounts of state subsidies sent to the district's regions.[12] Over the last five years, the shadow economy has not decreased, but, on the contrary, has grown even bigger. It is this gray sector, unaccounted for by official statistics, that has prevented the North Caucasus from going into complete economic collapse and is in many ways the local population's means of survival. Each region's economic weight must be taken into consideration when efforts are made to build relations with the NCFD, all the more so because the local authorities, in their bids to get more financial aid out of the federal authorities, deliberately keep quiet about the shadow economy's role and try to make their republics look poorer in Moscow's eyes than they are in reality.

By 2020, neither the shadow economy nor the corruption problem will have been eliminated. They cannot ever be completely eliminated. This is probably the key to understanding Putin's bit of black humor at the above-mentioned United Russia party conference, where he was asked, "What should we do with people guilty of corruption?" and he replied, "Hang them, I suppose" (though he then added that "this is not our method").

The course to take in this context would be to legalize a substantial (perhaps even the greater) part of the shadow economy, and make corruption more "predictable," that is, at least work on the principle of "officials getting their due according to their rank." This kind of practice is already being tried in Chechnya.

Rather than trying to eliminate these problems, the goal should therefore be to put limits on them and bring them under some kind of control. Unlike empty slogans of the "we shall vanquish corruption!" type, this is a realistic goal.

There is not really any point in describing the development of events if the *inertia scenario* prevails. To list just a few of the more obvious circumstances, the gap between the public and the authorities would continue to grow, the laws would not work, and systemic corruption would remain in place, becoming, along with the clan network system, the main mechanism for distributing financial resources and administrative posts. The shadow economy would expand further throughout the economy in general, and the economy itself would turn into a genuine "black hole," into which federal budget money would simply vanish.

The federal authorities would have only nominal control of the region, which would be exercised primarily through personal ties between members of the Moscow and local elites, with the latter seeing their position grow much stronger. The local elites' increasing independence would not lead to actual separatist ideas emerging, but would create a situation of "internal separatism," with the existence of regions only semigoverned or not governed at all in any real way through the federal power system.

Sooner or later, the federal authorities would realize this problem and attempt yet again to "restore order to the Caucasus," but this attempt to restore constitutional order would turn out to be a very painful process and come at a big risk of serious and perhaps even irresolvable conflicts.

The Question of Borders

The question of borders between the different republics and within some of the regions is still not completely settled. First and foremost is the problem of the border between Ingushetia and North Ossetia. With the help of federal officials, the two republics' presidents have made efforts during the last two years to settle the territorial disputes over the Prigorodny District. In the *optimistic scenario*, this problem would be completely settled, and this is possible in principle. The current consensus among the Ossetian and Ingush elites would be of help in resolving this dispute, as would the fact that people on both sides are tired of the constant tension and, unlike in the 1990s, no longer feel so mutually aggrieved.

The situation is also volatile, albeit to a lesser extent, along the borders between Ingushetia and Chechnya, and between Chechnya and Dagestan. If the local politicians reach agreements, the border issue will not play any noticeable role.

Within the republics, the best course would be to work toward a consensus to settle the question of whether to establish ethnic enclaves, and maintain ongoing contacts with organizations representing ethnic minorities' interests. Interethnic differences in some of the republics would in this way end up taking a peripheral place in political life, flaring up only sporadically, when provoked by radically minded individuals.

Under the *inertia scenario*, border disputes would lead to serious interethnic clashes and destabilize the situation throughout the region. An Ossetian/Ingush conflict would provoke confrontation along broader lines that would eventually also entangle Chechnya, which has always taken a paternalist view of Ingushetia and where there is support for the idea of restoring the Soviet-era Checheno-Ingush Autonomous Republic's borders (with Chechnya playing the dominant role). Conflict could also take on a religious dimension given that the majority of Ossetians are Christians (there have already been attempts to play on the religious side of things). The Chechen leadership would make restoring Checheno-Ingushetia one of its main slogans. Its ambitions would grow, and so too would demands that the border between Chechnya and Dagestan also be revised.

If conflict resumes between the Ossetians and the Ingush, the Kudars, people from South Ossetia who played a significant part in the 1992 tragedy, would once again be drawn in, and the idea of Greater Ossetia—the creation of a unified Republic of Ossetia within the Russian Federation—would also undergo a revival.

Some among the Cherkess people (aside from the Cherkess themselves, they include also the Kabardinian, Adyg, Shapsug, Ubykh, and Abkhaz people) could renew calls for the creation of a Republic of Cherkessia as a separate region within the Russian Federation, and, even more radically, could call for the establishment of "Greater Cherkessia."

There would be increasing tension in interethnic relations between the Cherkess peoples and their neighbors in Karachaevo-Cherkessia and Kabardino-Balkaria. The situation is aggravated by the fact that the Karachai and Balkar groups opposing the Cherkess and Kabardinians are more Islamized and have links to senior figures in the Caucasus Emirate.

Not only would the situation in the North Caucasus itself deteriorate, but so would Russian-Georgian relations, and this would all have a negative impact on Russia's international standing, because it would face accusations not only of recognizing separatists but also of ambitions to annex part of Georgia's territory.

The Caucasus Muslims would have growing grievances against Russia, charging it with taking enormous risks for the sake of supporting the Ossetians and Abkhaz when it cannot even manage to settle its own internal problems. Various forces would take easy advantage of the border issues to destabilize the situation in and around the region.

The 2014 Sochi Olympics

The 2014 Sochi Olympics should also be examined in the context of both the optimistic and inertia scenarios. Preparations for the games have already provoked a flare-up of the Cherkess issue, which had seemed to have become no more than a smoldering remnant of old grievances.

Under the *optimistic scenario*, there would be efforts to defuse the tension brought about by increasingly active Cherkess organizations opposed to the Olympics, which they say are to take place "on Cherkess graves"— because tens of thousands of migrants from the Caucasus, fleeing Russia in the nineteenth century, died and were buried in these places.

It is still entirely possible to prevent tensions from escalating today and to stop the conflict from entering an active phase. This will require efforts by both the local and federal authorities. The authorities should show some sensitivity toward the Cherkess people's historical grievances. At the same time, they must make efforts to prevent interethnic tension from escalating in Karachaevo-Cherkessia and Kabardino-Balkaria, especially over the issue of dividing up administrative posts. Seemingly secondary issues such as using Cherkess and Caucasus symbols during the Olympics and their preparation are also important because they would help to give Russia's Cherkess community a more positive view of the Olympics and would perhaps even encourage members of the Cherkess diaspora to come to Sochi. This would improve Russia's image in general, and not just in the Muslim world.

Under the *inertia scenario*, the Sochi Olympics would remain an added destabilizing factor in the region. If the federal authorities ignore the Cherkess people's opinions, this will create an increasingly negative attitude toward the games and could provoke opponents of the event into taking more decisive action. We would most likely see various meetings and demonstrations, which will become more frequent as the Olympics draw closer. But more desperate responses are also possible, including terrorist attacks, in the preparation for the games, and during the event itself.

The Caucasus Emirate and radically minded Cherkess groups could very likely start coordinating their actions. So far, there has been no sign of such cooperation, because the calls to establish "Greater Cherkessia" are at odds with the Caucasus Emirate leaders' main goal of uniting the

Caucasus on the basis of Islam. But it is entirely possible that they could come to some agreement in the interests of fighting a common enemy—the Russian authorities. If this kind of cooperation emerges, even if only temporarily, it could hinder the Olympics from taking place or lead to tragic events during the games.

Terrorist attacks directed against the Olympics would be very hard to prevent, in the experts' view, and would also have the effect of discrediting Moscow's policy in the North Caucasus and its ability in general to achieve any fundamental improvement in the situation there. Russia would end up looking like the weak link in the international antiterrorist effort. The repercussions of a negative scenario as far as the Olympics are concerned would be hard to overestimate. In this book, we are looking at events within the time frame until 2020, but the repercussions could go well beyond that time.

Predicting What the North Caucasus Will Look Like in 2020

One cannot predict what the North Caucasus will look like in 2020 without taking into account the influence of local tradition on the situation in the region, and this influence is growing very fast. Ethnocultural tradition and religion (Islam) are inseparable from politics in the North Caucasus. This is something one should recognize as a given and not build illusions about establishing genuine secularism in the region in the foreseeable future, all the more so by 2020. This is already recognized de facto by all involved in the Caucasus and its issues.

How will tradition influence the social and political situation in the region in the *optimistic scenario*? This influence will remain and grow quite strong, even if economic modernization is successful, law and order are restored, and the education system and so on are overhauled and revived. But in a positive environment in which the federal laws are respected, the authorities attempt to guarantee social justice, and the local population sees that the authorities really are acting in the people's interests, tradition's influence will remain largely confined to family life and behavioral ethics. Islam will be less politicized, and there will be less demand for its protest potential.

The creation and stable and effective operation of a modern tourism sector would offer work to tens of thousands of people (building the five planned ski resorts alone would create 160,000 jobs[13]), but would also give local people the chance to use advanced technology and meet new people.

The federal authorities see the possibilities for putting local tradition to effective use. It was not by chance that Dmitri Medvedev instructed Khloponin in 2010 to examine the possibility of establishing a council of elders in the NCFD.

A rational and measured approach to tradition would also help to get the ethnic Russian population more involved in Caucasus affairs. The idea here would not be to get those Russians who left the Caucasus to return, but to encourage specialists from other Russian regions to come to the Caucasus (which would be comparable in a way to the programs for developing the virgin soil regions in the 1950s, with the difference that the Russians would come to the region, attracted by high wages, and would not settle permanently).

Tradition's increasing hold on society would come to a halt, and an optimum balance would emerge between tradition and modernization. This stable symbiosis would play a positive part in ensuring social stability and helping to overcome the region's identity crisis. People in the region would start to see general Russian civic values in a more positive and reasonable light, and the region would lose its dubious fame as a kind of "internal abroad," becoming a full-fledged but unique part of Russia.

The *inertia scenario* would see the region irreversibly continue its descent into traditionalism. Tradition would become the main factor regulating social relations. The demodernization of society would pass the point of no return, and the region would turn completely into an "internal abroad."

The influence of Sharia law would increase, given that it represents a comprehensive system that reaches all spheres of legal life. Federal laws would be applied only formally, if at all. Even now, the use of *adat* and other traditional laws already poses a frequent challenge to the Russian Constitution.[14]

The Sufi brotherhoods—Nakshabandia, Kadiria, and Shazilia—would become definitively politicized. They would gain legitimate influence in the region's politics, all the more so because many politicians in Dagestan are *murids* (followers) of Sufi sheikhs. Secular government would give way to or simply merge with traditional institutions such as Sharia courts and councils of elders.

At the same time, the authorities themselves will use tradition as a convenient instrument for maintaining control over society. The state will intervene actively in religious affairs. Most consistent in this respect is Ramzan Kadyrov, who already started pursuing this policy in the 2000s. Yunus-bek Yevkurov in Ingushetia has also made no secret of his interest in traditional institutions, as could be seen from his unexpected statement in 2010 that the local clans (*teips*) could play a part in developing tourism by overseeing the reconstruction of Ingushetia's famous towers.

Competition between nontraditional (Salafist and fundamentalist) Islam and traditional Sufi Islam would continue, but there would be increasing cooperation between the rival groups in order to reach the common goal of spreading Islam and Sharia to the whole of society. This kind of cooperation is already going on in covert fashion today, but it would become systematic and public.

All of this creates a fertile environment for the Islamic opposition. Society would end up polarized, because not everyone welcomes the idea of Islamization, let alone the use of Sharia law. Supporters of a secular state would end up in the minority.

The growing influence of tradition is not confined to the North Caucasus alone. A similar process is under way in Central Asia—in Tajikistan, Uzbekistan, and Kyrgyzstan, where Islam is having an increasingly visible influence on society and politics. Specialists think that the return to tradition in Tajikistan has now become irreversible.

Tradition, especially religious tradition, is self-sufficient, and its followers no longer seek to be a part of the Russian Federation's legal and cultural framework. Tradition will turn into an instrument used in confrontation with the federal authorities. Hypertrophied tradition would make it impossible to maintain control of the state of affairs in the region. It would be equally hard to control the actions of politicians such as Kadyrov, some of whose statements are already provocative. The ruling elites would remain loyal to Moscow, but deep within Caucasus society the idea of possible political sovereignty would gradually take root—a return to the 1990s.

Other Factors for Development Scenarios

Social and economic development scenarios—whether optimistic or inertia—can be examined only in connection with success or failure in political life, relations between the authorities and the public, efforts to build
stability, and the degree to which Islam—or, rather, its more radical currents—is involved in social and political life. If these things are not taken
as a whole, the new economic and social strategy will end up being no
more than utopian wishful thinking.

On January 23, 2010, at a meeting on the NCFD's economic development, Khloponin outlined five policy priorities: (1) Develop a comprehensive strategy for the whole region and use it as the foundation for drafting
clear development plans for each republic individually; (2) adopt special
measures to improve the region's investment climate (establish regional
and industrial parks); (3) have the federal agencies and natural monopolies draw up special infrastructure development investment programs; (4)
improve people's quality of life, including local development; and (5) put
the local government and civil service in order.[15]

One can add to this list a number of issues that have been repeatedly
raised by the federal authorities and by Khloponin: dramatically reducing
unemployment, modernizing the agriculture sector, targeted mobilization
of local resources, establishing a common Caucasus market, setting up
special economic zones, and improving the education system. The plan
that has been most coherently and clearly set out so far is that for developing tourism, which is receiving 480 billion rubles in funding.

What stands out among Khloponin's priorities is that putting government in order is the last point on the list. By the time he had been in the
job a few months, however, he realized that the political issue was the main
task to address. But his initial plans and vision are very symbolic in the
way they reveal his lack of understanding of and failure to take into account the specific situation in the Caucasus.

The heads of the republics proposed a vast 126 projects all at once at
the United Russia interregional conference (20 were designated "priority projects," and 6 were given "urgent priority" status). The strangely
long list of projects that had to be examined strikes a cautionary note and

creates an impression that the whole idea of rebuilding the Caucasus is only a rather amorphous notion.

The *optimistic scenario* naturally does not mean that all the priorities listed above will be fulfilled. It would be enough to resolve the following tasks:

- Establish a reliable investment climate, above all through ensuring stable state guarantees for private investors.
- Create the 400,000 jobs that Putin promised.
- Put a big and well-developed tourism cluster into operation.
- Fundamentally improve the situation in agriculture.
- Create the conditions for small business development.

Resolving the other tasks depends on first resolving these main priorities. If these efforts are successful, the region's economies will start to grow, internal investment will emerge, and various production businesses, including in the food processing sector, will develop. Economic activity at the local level will help to bring down unemployment.

People's living standards will increase, and opportunities will emerge for developing social infrastructure and improving the situation in culture and sports. The possibility will also emerge to finally start taking steps to deal with the region's disastrous environmental situation. Also, the number of young people leaving the Caucasus for Russia's central regions will drop. Above all, if the optimistic scenario goes ahead, it will have the much-hoped-for general effect of checking negative trends and giving people hope and belief in the future.

In the *inertia scenario*, the objectives listed above would remain unfulfilled.

I want to make separate note of one circumstance that could end up playing a cruel joke on those putting their bets on tourism development in the region. It is possible to develop a large-scale and unique tourism cluster in the North Caucasus. The scale of the plans is evident from the project to build a road network linking Mineralniye Vody, Karachaevo-Cherkessia, and Kabardino-Balkaria. Khloponin has spoken of the need to build three-star hotels there and has emphasized his desire to develop mass tourism. But the question is, even if the necessary infrastructure is built, how attractive will it be for Russian tourists, and how competitive will it be in terms of price and service? The Caucasus traditions of hospitality and professional customer service are not one and the same thing, and it costs less to have a good-quality vacation in Turkey or Europe than in Russia, and so the tourism cluster's development might end up falling far short of the hoped-for results.

An Interim Scenario of Chronic Stagnation and Protracted Demodernization

Of course, aside from the two scenarios at either extreme, there is also an interim scenario of chronic stagnation and protracted demodernization, which would be slightly mitigated by infusions from the federal budget. A situation of permanent instability would settle in. But this would be no case of "classic stagnation." Negative trends would continue to develop and, though at a slower pace, the region would continue its movement toward collapse. This interim scenario is thus closer to the inertia scenario and is essentially its final phase.

The Context for the Scenarios

Development scenarios for events in the North Caucasus need to be looked at in the broadest possible context. The North Caucasus as a part of the Soviet Union was in a completely different situation from the North Caucasus as a part of the Russian Federation. The Soviet system leveled out the various specific nuances of interethnic and religious relations, arbitrarily set internal borders, and brought entire peoples to the brink of extinction. The modernization carried out during the Soviet period did help the region to develop, but, as throughout the whole country, this development was limited and ultimately led to a dead end. Social transformation slowly but surely turned into social stagnation, with many problems remaining unresolved, pushed out of sight, and waiting for the moment when they would burst back into the open. This moment came when the Soviet Union collapsed.

"There is nothing unusual about what is taking place today in the North Caucasus," writes the political analyst Igor Yakovenko. "It would be strange if these events did not happen. The calls to 'live in peace with each other' and the vows of destinies bonded together forever . . . are pointless."[16] The Russian federal authorities have yet to propose a way out of the dead end in which the North Caucasus has found itself. This is not just the fault of the central government, which has made many mistakes, including criminal mistakes, in the region. But the central government is partly to blame, for in spite of the above-mentioned vows and mantras, a real understanding of the truth cannot be achieved in just a decade or two (the prerevolutionary Russian Empire spent a whole century coming to this understanding).

Resolving the Caucasus's problems will also take a long time, more than a generation's lifetime. Even the optimists think that terrorism will continue to be a problem over the next fifteen to twenty years. When packaged in religious form, terrorism is not a chance mutation that can be surgically removed but is a natural product of the historical process and the result of numerous mistakes made by politicians on all sides—Muslim, European, American, and Russian.

The region's problems are a complex mix of many dimensions—economic, domestic politics, stability, interethnic relations, identity crises, collisions within Islam, and relations with the federal authorities. Only by starting to untangle in a competent fashion this complex mix can we eventually reach an understanding of what the North Caucasus should become and what basic place it will take, in the broad sense, within the new Russia.

The optimistic scenario for 2020 could be the region's last chance.

Notes

1. See "Mer Makhachkaly nazval sozdanie SKFO odnim iz samykh effektivnykh strate-gicheskikh hodov Medvedeva" (The mayor of Makhachkala called forming the NCFD one of Medvedev's most effective strategic moves), regnum.ru, January 21, 2010, www. regnum.ru/news/1245062.html.

2. See "Glava Karachaevo-Cherkessii: reshenie o sozdanii SKFO – opravdannoe i neob-khodimoe" (The President of Karachayevo-Cherkessia: the decision to form the NCFD is justified and necessary), regnum.ru, January 21, 2010, www.regnum.ru/news/1244908. html.

3. See "Arsen Kanokov: 'Naznachenie Khloponina—reshenie neordinarnoe i ves'ma udachnoe'" (Arsen Kanokov: Khloponin's appointment is original and very successful decision), regnum.ru, January 19, 2010, www.regnum.ru/news/1244287.html.

4. Alexei Malashenko, "Priletit vdrug Volshebnik . . ." (Suddenly, a magician appears . . .), *Nezavisimaya gazeta*, December 1, 2009.

5. See Human Rights Watch, www.htw.org/ru.

6. Gordon Khan, "Comparing the Level of Caucasus Emirate Terrorist Activity in 2008 and 2009," *Islam, Islamism and Politics in Eurasia*, no. 8, February 5, 2010.

7. Ivan Sukhov, "Vsya vlast polpredu" (All power to the presidential envoy), *Vremya novostei*, May 17, 2010.

8. Khan, "Comparing the Level of Caucasus Emirate Terrorist Activity."

9. See www.regnum.ru/news/1246097.html.

10. Lyudmila Kovalevskaya, "Putin at the Conference in Kislovodsk: The NCFD Will Get a Large-Scale Ski Resort Network," *Stavropol Pravda*, July 9, 2010, www.stapravda. ru/20100708/putin_na_konferentsii_v_kislovodske_v_skfo_poyavitsya_masshtabny_ 46523.html.

11. See "Usileniye silovogo bloka na Severnom Kavkaze neizbejno: mnenie" (Strengthen-ing of the power bloc in the Southern Caucasus is unavoidable: an opinion), regnum.ru, January 25, 2010, www.regnum.ru/news/1246107.html.

12. V. V. Glushkov, "The Shadow Economy as a Risk Factor in the Russian Economy's Mod-ernization" and "Multidimensional and Asymmetric Development in the Economies of Russia's Southern Regions: Modernization Risks and Transformation Mechanisms," papers presented at the Second All-Russian Scientific Conference, April 6–10, 2006; Dombai (Karachay-Cherkess Republic), 314.

13. Andrei Kolesnikov, "Bisnes dolzhen uiti v gory" (Business must take to the mountains), *Kommersant*, July 7, 2010.

14. Renee Gendron, "Alternative Dispute Resolution in the North Caucasus," *Caucasian Review of International Affairs* 3, no. 4 (Autumn 2009): 335.

15. See "Ideya sozdaniya osobykh ekonomicheskikh zon na Kavkaze mozhet provalit'sya – ekspert" (The idea of setting up special economic zones in the Caucasus may fail), Regnum.ru, January 25, 2010, www.regnum.ru/news/1246047.html.

16. I. G. Yakovenko, *Rossiiskoye gosudarstvo: Natsionalniye interesy, granitsy, perspektivy* (The Russian state: Interests, borders, future prospects) (Moscow: Khronograf, 2008), 248.

SOCIETY *and* CIVIL SOCIETY

PART VI

CHAPTER TWENTY-TWO

SOCIETY, POLITICS, and the SEARCH for COMMUNITY in RUSSIA

Samuel A. Greene

The degree to which contemporary discussions of Russia avoid dealing with Russian society is striking.[1] This was not always (and is still not entirely) the case. Cultural historians in particular have long studied the evolution, revolutionary dismantling, and partial persistence of the institutions underpinning social relations, and the end of the Soviet Union brought a revival of interest in the long story of Russian society. The difficulties of Russia's post-Soviet transition, however, and its "failure" to democratize, have led many to take society out of the picture: Because the social factors that may have led to Russia's retrenched authoritarianism seemed so deterministic and path-dependent, social scientists have often preferred to ignore them, looking instead either to agency or to the impact of formal political institutions, present and past. Even the long-running argument about Russians' supposedly weak social capital and overall lack of trust is generally explained as a result not of societal factors but of political choices made by elites, mostly over the course of the twentieth century.

I will not deal here with the question of whether those disciplinary and methodological preferences were as intellectually robust as they were politically correct; much of the social science done in and on Russia in recent years has been excellent and enlightening. Nor would I suggest that no (or even not enough) attention is being paid to Russian society; indeed, fascinating work continues to be produced by sociologists and anthropologists of various ilk. But the vogue for politics and political economy has meant that this social research, when put in the broader context of Russian area studies, is almost inevitably reduced to a dependent variable. Certainly, politics and the political economy do produce social results. My task here, however, is to demonstrate that social factors may also produce political results.

On the surface, this seems obvious enough. The transformation of economic grievance into political mobilization in Pikalevo, Zabaikalsk, and other so-called *monogoroda*—towns heavily dependent on a single industry for employment and revenue—and also in larger cities, including Vladivostok and Kaliningrad, forced the Russian government to react, through a combination of co-optation and repression, where it would probably have preferred to remain aloof. The regional elections in the fall of 2009 provided a second illustration of the hypothesis that complete political complacency cannot be expected of the population if the government does not hold up its economic side of the bargain. Perhaps more importantly, however, the elections may have demonstrated the remarkable degree to which a large section of the population, if not the majority, is willing to buy into the system even when it falters. And finally, the reemergence of the motorists' movement—with new tactics and new leadership but the same demands—reflects the ability of Russian society to generate and sustain grassroots engagement and, indeed, to set at least a portion of the political agenda in a sustained manner, despite what we think we know about social capital and trust.

But these examples are almost too obvious. The question I want to address here is as follows: Are there fundamental social processes under way that have the potential to drive the evolution of the Russian state and, if so, how might that occur during the next ten years? In this chapter, I outline what I believe to be "four and a half" key phenomena and then lay out two basic scenarios for how they might evolve—one that is inertial (but not static), in which current trends continue; and another in which certain key changes occur that allow society and state–society relations in Russia to develop along a normatively more "optimistic" pathway to 2020.

Four and a Half Key Social Phenomena

Before I launch into a discussion of the "four and a half" key social phenomena that I argue will shape Russia's future, I should explain two basic assumptions that underpin my understanding of Russian society. The first has to do with deinstitutionalization: Russia is not entirely devoid of social institutions, but it is close. In treating institutions here, I take the sociological definition of an institution as a set of ingrained rules and norms governing behavior for individuals or groups of individuals that allows one to predict with reasonable accuracy what the reaction will be to any given action. Thus, in saying that Russia is almost devoid of institutions, I do not refer to the myriad establishments laid out on paper, enshrined in bricks and mortar, and endowed with budgets of varying generosity; rather, I refer to the fact that none of these "paper" institutions—whether the law in general, the apparatus of the state, or higher education or the Russian Orthodox Church—allows Russian citizens to predict with reasonable accuracy how any given social or state–societal interaction will proceed. Moreover, with the partial exception of the Caucasus and other long-standing ethnic communities in the Urals, Siberia, and the far north, the Soviet Union and the turmoil of transition together succeeded in eviscerating whatever horizontal social institutions may have existed in the past, whether religious, ethnic, tribal, land-based, familial, or other.

The second assumption flows from the first: In a deinstitutionalized environment, certainty is at a premium, and the balance between certainty and uncertainty is the key commodity in any social interaction. This increases the relative trust placed in people who may be termed *nashi*—ours—and reduces trust in people who may be considered *chuzhie*—other (although it may have no discernible impact on the overall stock of trust). This endows those able through their status or station to manufacture and manipulate uncertainty with a tremendous degree of power. And this catastrophically lowers the appetite for risk.

That last point about risk leads directly to the first of the four and a half key phenomena. There is a common myth in the discussion of Russian politics—and particularly Russian civil society and civic engagement—that Russians are passive. This is not true: Russians are aggressively immobile. The difference is more than semantic. Passive people may not be easily led, but they are relatively easily pushed. Aggressively immobile people are difficult to move in any circumstances, precisely because their immobility is strategic and rational. An environment bereft of social institutions is one in which there are few if any shared and replicable pathways to success. As a result, the relative comfort and prosperity that any Russian citizen may enjoy is the result of a singular, unique set of circumstances, owing exclusively to that citizen's ability to cope with her or his uncertain environment (the order of the pronouns here is not arbitrary; women are generally significantly better at coping in Russia than men). Change, then, threatens to undermine these achievements, potentially forcing the citizen to start again in the face of uncertainty—a wholly unattractive prospect. This is true on both the micro and macro levels. Russians living in failing cities such as Pikalevo are thus unwilling to leave not because they feel good about their prospects at home but because they have no certainty that they will be able to navigate a new set of bureaucratic and other formal and informal relationships in a new setting. Similarly, Russians oppose liberalizing and democratizing reforms not because they are happy with the status quo of political and economic monopolization but because any large-scale change risks sweeping away achievements built on extremely shallow foundations.

The second phenomenon is the particular way in which the so-called resource curse has manifested itself in Russia: Rather than fuel outright repression (à la Myanmar) or heavy-handed populism (à la Venezuela), the abundance of natural resources and the associated rent flows have cushioned a mutually agreeable divorce between the government and its people, following seven decades of overly intimate relations. It is often said that the implicit Putin-era social contract in Russia has been one in which the population agree to ignore politics in return for economic growth. I would modify that somewhat: The implicit social contract, if there is one, affords maximum autonomy to both sides of the bargain, provided neither significantly impinges on the interests and comfort of the other. It is an inherently fraught arrangement, however, similar to Soviet-era divorces in which irreconcilable spouses were forced to continue living in the same apartment; there is bound to be some friction. Oil, gas, and the economic growth they generate provide some lubrication, but there remain limits to the degree of alienation that is possible. The fact of shared space becomes most evident on Russia's roads, where the elite and ordinary citizens live on two sides of an almost institutionalized lawlessness, in which the elite are forbidden nothing and the non-elite have no recourse.

The third phenomenon is thus increasing friction. The more the elite and the non-elite crystallize and defend their own individual achievements—whether in the form of armored motorcades or high fences around even modest private landholdings—the more conflict becomes inevitable. The debasing of the public space in order to maintain the private—what Michael Burawoy referred to as "involution"—helped people cope with the tumult of transition, but as Russia's "new normal" has been established and appetites begin to grow again, there is a creeping privatization of the commons.[2] It is not only the roads that have seemingly become the private domain of the elite, together with the lives of those who happen to be on them. Moscow's sidewalks and courtyards are continually and repeatedly privatized by anyone who wants to park a car. Public nature reserves become the private hunting grounds of anyone with sufficient access to a helicopter, and the country's forests are littered with the remains of countless picnics, as though the forest itself were disposable. This relentless extension of the rules of elite and mass private behavior into Russia's shared social spaces is an irritant for all involved, as each individual encounters behavior consonant with his or her own behavior but dissonant with his or her personal interests. The natural reaction is an attempt to extend, provided the means are available, the power of one's professed (but not performed) social norms onto others—an attempt that, given Russia's lack of functioning social and sociopolitical institutions, is doomed to fail and produce only more irritation.

The fourth phenomenon is a relatively new means of coping with the second and third phenomena, what I will call "individual modernization." The advent of globalization—by which I mean not so much trade and economic interdependence as global communication and global culture—opens up avenues that were not available to Soviet-era dissidents. Certainly, gaining access through illicit radio reception or samizdat to the world beyond the USSR was an important part of both challenging the Soviet regime and building an autonomous moral space outside its ideological boundaries but inside its geographical borders. But the end of censorship, the opening of borders, and the growing availability of the

Internet and other communication technologies has fed an explosion of individual strategies of identity formation within modern Russia. Especially in Moscow, but not only there, adherents can be found for all the fashion trends, schools of thought, political and social undercurrents, and economic projects present in the world at large. Young, educated, dynamic, and mobile Russians—as well as a good many of their older compatriots—are seemingly as likely to identify themselves with a global meaning as with a local one. This is true in much of the world, but in the Russian context of deinstitutionalization, state/society alienation, and the constant friction of the public space, it takes on particular importance: While remaining physically present in Russia (or at least resident), Russians may take themselves socially, politically, and intellectually out of the Russian space. The consequences of this are contradictory. On the one hand, this is potentially tremendously liberating for a large number of the country's best and brightest. On the other hand, however, it greatly lowers the degree to which those same best and brightest may be willing to invest in the modernization of Russia's own social space.

The "half" phenomenon, finally, lies somewhere between the third and the fourth phenomena just described and is this: Despite its faults, Russia's current system of social and political relations has its adherents. These are not just those in the elite and below it who are consistently able to maximize their benefit from the manufacture and manipulation of uncertainty. Even those who are not on the winning end of that bargain invest in the system's survival. Witness, for example, an appeal made in June 2010 by a group of schoolteachers in the town of Voskresensk, not far from Moscow, to President Dmitri Medvedev. The teachers, who were drafted into serving on the local board of elections during the municipal elections in October 2009, now find themselves at the center of an investigation into electoral fraud in which they themselves admit they were complicit. What they want from Medvedev, though, is not to right the wrong but an intercession simply to prevent them from being prosecuted. Referring to the hundreds of thousands of ordinary Russians who, like the Voskresensk teachers, helped falsify elections in 2009, human rights activist Sergei Kovalev told Ekho Moskvy radio that "lying has ceased to be a means of hiding the truth and has become instead a ritual of loyalty and patriotism." That may be overstating the case; the Voskresensk teachers are unlikely to have acted out of any great patriotism, and they were probably threatened with dismissal or at least docked pay if they did not cooperate. But the reality is, when faced with a situation in which they could protect their positions by cooperating with the investigation in service of the truth, they chose instead to seek shelter in the lie. This is a deeper degree of co-optation than we see among the young men and women who join Nashi and other government-run youth groups in exchange for a trip to a lake and money on a cellphone account; the latter is simply opportunistic, while the former is calculated.

Understanding the Politics of Society

Much of the discussion of states and societies—and thus of politics—is guided by the standard Weberian definition of a state, with its emphasis on the effective monopolization of legitimate violence. In this conceptualization, the state is almost always seen as the active party, seeking to generate and maximize its power, whereas society is at best confined to the role of resistance to or acceptance of that power and, thus, the legitimization of the state's monopoly on forceful coercion. The "systems" approach launched by Talcott Parsons went some distance toward elucidating the complex interrelations between political and societal actors and institutions that underpin this arrangement, but it has been roundly criticized for a teleological assumption that some systems are developed and others are developing, with all trajectories leading to a similar (read Western) endpoint.

This chapter is guided by a somewhat different conception, proposed by Joel Migdal under the headline "State in Society"—in other words, the conceit that states, broadly speaking, are rooted in and derivative of the societies they purport to govern. Migdal places the emphasis on "process—on the ongoing struggles among shifting coalitions over the rules for daily behavior":

> These processes determine how societies and states create and maintain distinct ways of structuring day-to-day life—the nature of the rules that govern people's behavior, whom they benefit and whom they disadvantage, which sorts of elements unite people

and which divide them, what shared meaning people hold about their relations with others and about their place in the world. And these processes also ordain the ways that rules and patterns of domination and subordination are challenged and change.[3]

Migdal, in turn, draws importantly on Edward Shils's use of the concept of community. Thus, Shils writes that

> . . . a community is not just a group of concrete and particular persons; it is, more fundamentally, a group of persons acquiring their significance by their embodiment of values which transcend them and by their conformity with standards and rules from which they derive their dignity.[4]

To Migdal, it is this process of creation of community that ultimately guides the formation of states. The crucial aspects of this relationship are brought into particularly sharp focus in social, political, and economic environments undergoing rapid change, such as Russia. In these sorts of settings, it is perhaps to be expected that citizens—individually *and* collectively—have a difficult time arriving at the shared rules of behavior, and thus shared values, that lead to community. Migdal writes:

> In such bewildering and fragmented settings, individuals must respond not only to the constraints and opportunities posed by one organization but by many. Some of these organizations exist side by side peacefully, but others are struggling actively with one another over what the rules of the game should be. Individuals thus confront a fundamental lack of coherence in their social worlds, with various organizations proposing contradictory values and modes of behavior. Models that assume a fundamental unity underlying one's actions, feelings, and thoughts are inadequate for explaining the diverse strategies people use in acting within these heterogeneous organizational settings.[5]

The "four and a half" social phenomena outlined above illustrate how this dilemma plays out in Russia. With the fracturing of the public space, the flattening of the hierarchies that governed Soviet interactions, and the dismantling of the institutions of certainty in social life, citizens in all social strata retreated from the public space, fortified their private spaces, and then engaged in a privatization of the commons. This spectacular devaluation of community is self-reinforcing, proving to all participants that their strategies are justified and correct, precisely because everyone else's strategies are simultaneously identical (in their individualism) and threatening (in their rejection of the communal).

But this is not to say that Russians are valueless. With the evaporation of broad social institutions, citizens and elites alike have fallen back on residual institutions. Thus, the particularistic networks and arrangements of family, friendship, clan, ethnicity, and *chin* hold more value than other arrangements—such as law-bound institutions—that might inculcate more universalistic values. An excellent illustration of how this works is provided by an anthropological study of a remote community in Siberia, where David Anderson found "numerous examples of institutions which truly mediate civil, political and economic interests," in large part because he did not look for them in the formalistic, "differentiated" categories proposed by the mainstream civil society literature, but rather by observing everyday life in the town.[6] These institutions, however, are highly particular, pertaining either to ethnic or uniquely local economic and social circumstances. The challenge for Russia is thus to aggregate the trust generated in such institutions into forms that can be linked and propagated at a national level.

It could (and, indeed, has been) argued that the fault in this failure to aggregate trust lies in a problem of values—or, more precisely, of culture—that has roots considerably deeper than those of the present political arrangement. Because the object of this chapter is to look, however tentatively, into the future, I must deal with the suggestion that it is determined by the past. The most systematic argument for path-dependency in Russia has been put forward by Oleg Kharkhordin, Mikhail Afanasev, and Richard Pipes, who write (separately) that Orthodox, absolutist, and patrimonial models of social interaction are, to quote Pipes, "rooted in the failure of Russian statehood to evolve from a private into a public institution" and thus encourage not the consolidation of community but, in the words of Kharkhordin, the "diffusion of civic life."[7]

There is some debate as to the source of such "archaic" tendencies, with Kharkhordin and others suggesting that the dominance of the old is a result of the failure of the new, whereas Afanasev argues that the new fails precisely because of the dominance of the old. And it is exactly because of this fundamental and irreconcilable disagreement that the historicist argument holds little or no explanatory value for contemporary phenomena in Russia. When Russians today face challenges in social interactions, they are confronted simultaneously and inseparably with the dominance of the old and the failure of the new. Thus, in guiding decisions regarding social interactions, neither of these phenomena is causally prior to the other. In other words, Russian citizens inevitably make decisions based on factors that are present *now*, and it is this immediacy that both gives meaning to the past and creates the future.

Immediacy, of course, is the fundamental concept of game theory, an approach that models human behavior in social settings based on the rapid resolution of present dilemmas based on the unambiguous evaluation of past experiences and future consequences. The political game theorist Margaret Levi uses game-theoretical approaches to argue that citizens exercise "contingent consent" vis-à-vis the demands of their states—which, in our conceptualization, are the reflections of the rules set or accepted by communities—and that the propensity to consent increases in proportion to the degree to which "citizens perceive the government to be trustworthy," "the proportion of other citizens complying," and the ability of "citizens [to] receive information confirming" the prior two indicators.[8]

Following Levi, Charles Tilly asks the question "How have members of trust networks defended themselves and their resources against predation?"—which is particularly relevant to Russia, where predation has become the dominant strategy of certain groups of elites. The answer, Tilly finds through a broad comparative study, is a combination of three strategies: "The *concealment* strategy . . . fortifies the boundary between insiders and outsiders by means of secrecy and dissimulation. The *clientage* strategy . . . depends on some power holder's patronage, usually at a handsome price, for defense against other potential predators. *Dissimulation* . . . involves conceding just enough compliance with rulers' demands and regulations to hold off close surveillance and expropriation."[9]

In essence, all these strategies are an escape from politics, because in the system to which they pertain, politics is a game of predation. In other words, what one observes in Russia can be explained as a natural reaction both to the anticommunal rules of behavior that encourage authoritarianism and the ways in which that authoritarian rule is exercised. Democratization, then, is a story of the reintegration of citizens into politics through the regeneration of a meaningful political community:

> To the extent that people integrate their trust networks into public politics, they come to rely on governmental performance for maintenance of those networks. They also gain power, individual and collective, through the connections to government those networks mediate. They acquire an unbreakable interest in governmental performance. The political stakes matter. Paying taxes, buying governmental securities, yielding private information to officials, depending on government for benefits, and releasing network members for military service cement that interest and promote active bargaining over the terms of its fulfillment.[10]

It is thus a mistake to assume, as many normative and historicist theorists do, that rules derive from values. Indeed, it is the other way around: Rules are written to make human interactions more effective and predictable (at least for those writing the rules), and when they prove themselves to be sufficiently beneficial to a sufficiently large (or powerful) group of people in a community, over time they evolve into values. The question for the remainder of this chapter is "What are the factors that could drive a shift in Russia from the dominance of the individual to the value of the communal?"

Russia 2020: Scenarios for the Future

From where we stand today, there appear to be two potential scenarios for the future: one inertial, in which existing trends continue until they descend into outright crisis; and a second, in which a few key factors shift and a more "optimistic" storyline emerges. I start with the first, as a baseline. To call this scenario inertial, however, is not to say that it is static; social processes cannot simply stand still, and it is unfathomable that nothing at all—or even nothing significant—would change over the next ten years.

In the inertial scenario, all the phenomena described above remain in place: aggressive immobility, state/society alienation, increasing social friction, blossoming individual modernization, and an active conservative constituency. Over time, as the state's retrograde apparatus becomes increasingly ineffective and continuing political and economic monopolies reduce marginal economic growth to nearly zero, social friction increases and comfortable alienation becomes harder and harder to maintain.

To an extent, we can already see this scenario unfolding. The nationalist riots that gripped Moscow in December 2010 bear witness to virtually all the phenomena described above. Rioters in the hundreds and thousands, many of whom perceive themselves to be victims of marginalization and relative deprivation, and who are unable to partake of the economic glamour that has become so conspicuous in the capital, moved concertedly and violently into the public space, claiming the commons for their own. The authorities did their best to ignore them; President Dmitri Medvedev "tweeted" first about an Elton John concert, and only then about the riots, promising blandly that those guilty would be punished; Prime Minister Vladimir Putin remained all but silent on the issue for several days. In the end, however, this separation could not be maintained: Riot police engaged, political interventions were held, pressure was applied.

The broader lesson that was learned, however, was that the commons, like nature, abhor a vacuum. Individuals, whether ordinary citizens or the elite, may temporarily enjoy the delusion that the space between their private refuges—the streets on which they drive, the metro in which they commute, the squares on which they walk—are empty, airless, and soundless; but they are not. The fact of rioters in the streets and in the metro, the omnipresent but largely invisible threat of violence and personal harm, compounded by the absence of trusted sources of information, for a time turned the commons into the jungle, a state of nature in which life could indeed be "nasty, brutish, and short." And until the rioters themselves went home, nobody—not the public, not the state—had the power to restore order.

Returning to the scenario, this increasing friction eventually pushes the state into a more forward relationship with society, first to set rules in defense of elite privilege, and then to regulate social relations themselves to maintain stability. But because nothing changes within the state itself—the active conservative constituency is sufficient to overcome any pressure from the creative and entrepreneurial classes, whose political ties with Russia are increasingly weak—this amounts to a reprivatization of the commons, rather than a deprivatization. Thus, non-elite individuals are pushed out of the common space, in the name of harmony and stability, but are then increasingly deprived of access to it altogether, as the captured state redistributes the benefits of the public space to the elite.

Is it not possible that Russian citizens, seeing the commons increasingly occupied by the elite, would react and demand change, much as did Egyptians and Tunisians in January and February 2011? In theory, yes. Often, the failure of Russians—and, indeed, of people in underdeveloped countries around the world—to place "sufficient" value on the commons is explained with reference to poverty, which theoretically prejudices particular and material interests over those that are universal and ephemeral. Unfortunately, there is insufficient rigorous research on poverty, or deprivation more broadly, in Russia and its impact on political engagement that would allow us to draw robust conclusions. However, research in India shows that poverty is correlated neither with a lack of support for democracy nor with levels of "political efficacy and . . . participation"; however, significantly correlated are levels of education, information, social capital, and access. Similar results have been reported in Africa and other parts of South Asia.[11] And developments in North Africa have underscored the validity of these findings.

It is not, however, that simple. An uprising from below will trigger a response from above. Indeed, Adam Przeworski argues that the problem of poverty and democracy resides not with the poor but with the rich:

> Increased participation of the poor is a threat to democracy only in situations where elites, fearing drastic redistribution, are prone to overthrow democracy. For the poor themselves, democracy might be the only viable means to get what they want. Yet, if they act precipitously, they may lose even that chance.[12]

The situation Przeworski describes fits Russia almost perfectly. A slow crisis may be expected to encourage splits within the elite, with those less certain of their future either exiting the system or lobbying for gradual change, much as the so-called 1960s generation did in the USSR, emboldened by the Khrushchevian "thaw" and frustrated by Brezhnevite stagnation. But such politically lethargic change will look to the masses like inertia (which, in effect, it is), and any uprising in response will make no distinction between the relatively more and less conservative members of the old guard. (Russian society tried to make that distinction once and is quite convinced that it did so in vain.) The result will be a reconsolidation of the elite (minus, perhaps, whatever marginal portion jumps ship) in defense of its status and privilege and a standoff with the mobilized sections of the public, the outcome of which is deeply uncertain.

This, then, is a scenario of alienation pushed to its limits, generating conflict and dragging the state into a futile and counterproductive authoritarian engagement with society. The result by 2020 will be a Russia with a severely fractured political and social space, a stagnant economy, and extremely low levels of political identification between citizens and the state to which they nominally belong. But because of the aggressive immobility of both the masses and the elite, the only way out of this situation will be through a profound and protracted crisis, sufficiently decimating individuals' prosperity and comfort that change will begin to look relatively more attractive. Given, however, that change will come in a climate of political alienation, the absence of a true public sphere, and the lack of legitimate, ingrained horizontal social institutions, it is highly unlikely that change will be democratic.

The second, more "optimistic" scenario likewise assumes that all four and a half key social phenomena remain in place but supposes one crucial difference. At some point early in the second decade of the twenty-first century, say in 2011 or 2012, the Russian government, faced with increasing social (and, indeed, intra-elite) tensions and a continually faltering economy, pushes toward maximum economic integration with the West, particularly with the European Union, and the latter reciprocates. Thus, Russia would join the World Trade Organization, conclude a free investment and trade deal with the European Union, drop visa requirements for EU citizens, and obtain visa-free travel for its own citizens to Europe. Over time, a growing number of Russian citizens would begin to form institutional relationships and strategies based on their newfound unfettered access to the European space, for education, entrepreneurship, investment, and other purposes, compensating for the lack of institutions at home.

Russian entrepreneurs in various spheres—whether in business, education, research, or even government—do not suffer from a lack of good ideas. What they do lack, however, is an institutional environment that makes it attractive to invest in those ideas while not leaving Russia. In this regard, supporting Skolkovo and other official "modernization" projects is not enough. There is no reason to believe that the new institutions created in Russia under the banner of modernization will differ in their essence from those institutions that already exist, distorting and manipulating the law to empower officials and disenfranchise citizens.

The approach to "democratizing" Russia to date has focused on identifying the potential stakeholders in new institutions and attempting to mobilize them to reform existing ones. The problem with this approach is that it ignores the fact that existing institutions have their own stakeholders and that they, unlike the potential stakeholders of as-yet-nonexistent institutions, are already empowered. But a lowering of the barriers to the individual-level integration of Russians living in Russia into the European institutional space would have the consequence of allowing Russians to become stakeholders in European institutions. Already, certain Russians settle their commercial disputes in London and their human rights cases in Strasbourg. Russian business makes ample use of the European financial system. And elites and well-off members of the masses also avail themselves of European education, health care, and recreation.

How this would look would depend to a great degree on the creativity of policymakers in Europe. But allowing more and more Russians—and particularly those in business and academia who have the potential to drive change at home—to rely on the stability and usability of European legal and institutional frameworks to support investment in their own ideas and strategies will have two important implications domestically. First, it will enrich and empower the internationally integrated members of Russia's middle class (the internationally integrated members of Russia's elite being already rich and powerful) relative to the broader conservative constituency, dislodging them from the aggressive immobility described above.

Of particular importance, integrated citizens will gain an institutional foundation for their prosperity and comfort that nonintegrated citizens do not enjoy, increasing the attractiveness of integration for others and demonstrating a realistic, obtainable, and, crucially, institutionalized pathway for achieving success.

Second, it will draw into sharper focus the losses in opportunity cost that these same internationally integrated citizens will suffer as a result of Russia's own deinstitutionalization. Even with lowered barriers to integration with Europe, the transaction costs of relying on European institutions would still be higher than they would be if similar institutions functioned in Russia. The resulting pressure for institutional reform and harmonization may not be overtly political, but it would have the potential to revitalize public interest in the commons, and thus in community, by demonstrating a shared interest in a public good.

Taken together, this is sufficient to produce a consolidated domestic constituency for change, which will gradually drag a retrograde and reluctant (but not belligerent) state into modernity. It will be a difficult road, and it will not be completed by 2020. But if Russia and its partners are open to integration—and if we reverse the standard logic that demands democracy as a prerequisite for integration—there may yet be a way out of inertia.

Notes

1. Witness, for example, the most recent major volume on political "transition," *Democracy and Authoritarianism in the Postcommunist World*, edited by Valerie Bunce, Michael McFaul, and Kathryn Stoner-Weiss (Cambridge: Cambridge University Press, 2010). Of the twelve chapters, only one truly deals with society, and that, by Tsveta Petrova, is about Bulgaria.

2. M. Burawoy, P. Krotov, et al., "Involution and Destitution in Capitalist Russia," *Ethnography* 1, no. 1 (2000): 43–69.

3. Joel Migdal, *State in Society* (Cambridge: Cambridge University Press, 2001), 11.

4. E. Shils, *Center and Periphery: Essays in Macrosociology* (Chicago: University of Chicago Press, 1975), 138, cited by Migdal, *State in Society*, 6.

5. Migdal, *State in Society*, 190.

6. D. G. Anderson, "Bringing Civil Society to an Uncivilised Place," in *Civil Society: Challenging Western Models*, edited by C. Hann and E. Dunn (London: Routledge, 1996), 115.

7. M. N. Afanasev, *Opasnaia Rossiia. Traditsii samovlast'ia segodnia* (Moscow: RGGU, 2001); O. Kharkhordin, "First Europe-Asia Lecture: Civil Society and Orthodox Christianity," *Europe-Asia Studies* 50, no. 6 (1998): 949–68; R. Pipes, *Russian Conservatism and Its Critics. A Study in Political Culture* (New Haven, Conn.: Yale University Press, 2005).

8. M. Levi, *Consent, Dissent, and Patriotism* (Cambridge: Cambridge University Press, 1997), 21, cited by C. Tilly, *Trust and Rule* (Cambridge: Cambridge University Press, 1997), 19.

9. Tilly, *Trust and Rule*, 83–84.

10. Ibid., 135.

11. A. Krishna, "Do Poor People Care Less for Democracy?" in *Poverty, Participation, and Democracy*, edited by A. Krishna (Cambridge: Cambridge University Press, 2008), 92.

12. A. Przeworski, "The Poor and the Viability of Democracy" in *Poverty*, ed. Krishna, 126.

the INERTIA *of* PASSIVE ADAPTATION

Lev Gudkov

The demand for forecasts that we see so clearly today in many quarters of Russian society has its roots in the growing awareness of Russia's stagnation in recent years under the rule of Vladimir Putin and his team. The sense of perspective has been lost. No one knows where change will come from, and there is no sense of the forces that could transform the current situation. This makes those in and around the elite (no matter what their party or ideological views) particularly sensitive to any forms of social protest, and always on the lookout for tensions that could lead to social upheaval, or for signs of conflict at the top, within the Medvedev-Putin tandem itself, that could signal potential change ahead. In this context, attempts to monitor and predict what could change and to what degree are a way of explaining the present and, to a lesser extent, of revising the means of conducting political analysis.

The Amorphous Nature of Russia's Social Structure

There are no grounds for expecting change in Russian society's social morphology during the next ten years. The institutional reforms that could have transformed society's composition either have been halted or declared but not actually carried out. Starting in the 2000s, social change ceased to be a targeted policy of the kind it had been in the first half of the 1990s. The population's passive adaptation to the changes resulting from the Russian authorities' contradictory policies became the dominant feature in social behavior.

During the past fifteen years, the biggest changes that have affected the population's life have been the Soviet defense industry's degradation and the associated deindustrialization. Qualified industrial workers' share of the adult population fell from 32 percent at the start of the 1990s to 19 percent in the first half of the 2000s. During the Soviet era, those termed "qualified workers" formed the model "middle class," and their mind-set, values, and way of life became the ideologically approved norm through propaganda and education efforts. These values and this mind-set were imposed on other groups, which accepted them to some extent as a set of reference points for mass demand and views. The post-Soviet deindustrialization process opened the road for growth in the trade and service sectors, which filled the shortages and failings of the planned economy. But at the same time, it accelerated the erosion and decay of the Soviet system of references and examples, and the distribution of income and status—and thus of the entire social order. This process dealt a particularly severe blow to the lower echelons of the Soviet bureaucracy and to those engaged in science, education, health, and culture.

The rapid development of trade and services led to the emergence of new zones of intensive social exchange, expanding market relations, and the formation of a new social infrastructure. It also signaled the emergence of new priorities, and changes in mass demand and behavior models— but only "where the money is." The reorganization of power that involved a redistribution and privatization of state assets, on the contrary, did not change the closed nature of Russian politics and government, which continued to be beyond the public's sight and control. The material interests of the most active and best organized groups—those in the civil service and business—are linked above all today to possibilities for access to power (and obtaining privileges and preferences), and not to conditions that would ensure effective government and a working economy. These groups are motivated by the desire to hold onto and consolidate their social status, which discredits the very concept of earned and recognized social promotion and wealth. Any movement up the social hierarchy can be achieved and preserved only with the authorities' approval. This creates a lack of cultural (moral, legal, and ideological) means for enjoying and justifying the social capital that has already been accumulated, such as a recognition of inalienable property rights, reputation, and recognition of having earned a particular status in the social hierarchy. In other words, the amorphous nature of Russian society's social stratification reflects the weak legitimacy of the central institutions (government, administration, property, law), and it is balanced only by the development and use of means to neutralize or suppress mass discontent. This explains why, in the general public's mind, the social order continues to be perceived as "unfair" and morally and legally dubious. In other words, as they see it, "ordinary people" have absolutely no influence on society at all, and therefore they have no incentive to become more productive and seek new developments.

If the institutional framework determining the rules and subordination within a society are habitually closed, and the mechanisms for social and career promotion are opaque, the result is to erase and blur the sociocultural differences between various groups and statuses. In Russia, this happens despite the huge gap in incomes, which is much wider than in . European countries or the United States (even official statistics put it at 17-fold, whereas independent estimates put it at 27-fold or more). Russian sociologists and economists make an "objective" classification of the social structure, and distinguish among different social classes, strata, and groups on the basis of education, the nature of the labor they perform, and their property status, but these distinctions only have conventional value and are not underpinned by clear cultural distinguishing signs within each stratum or barriers between them. The current regime has proclaimed the "middle class" the guarantor of social and political stability and the driving force of "innovation" and "modernization," but these declarations are no more than ideological assertions not backed up by any real evidence. This class does not exist as a collective force in the mass public consciousness or in social practice. Meanwhile, local and regional differences in conditions of life seem "natural" and self-evident, and are not considered as "social" in nature or as something that can be changed. Most people consider these differences of more importance than individual and family class and social differences—that is to say, more important than a particular person or small group's position on the labor market and in property relations.

The Institutional System's Rigidity

The institutional system that emerged in Russia under Putin suppresses the social conditions for development and creates an unfavorable environment for long-term and stable economic growth. This applies above all to the institutions that are supposed to protect property rights—the courts and law enforcement agencies—but fail to accomplish these tasks and thus cannot protect the relations at the foundation of any economic activity.

Today's business environment and conditions give rise to monopolistic practices and limit competition, inciting businesspeople to concentrate on making the biggest short-term profits they can, knowing that the balance of forces at the top is an unstable construction and could change at any minute. In such a situation, today's business favorites could easily become tomorrow's outcasts. Favoritism on the part of the state authorities and their intervention in the economy, price controls, obstacles in the way of foreign investors, along with the inevitable corruption that ensues, all create a fertile breeding ground for strong anticompetition incentives. In this environment, the stock market cannot fulfill its basic function of acting as a mechanism for redistributing capital in the economy and channeling people's savings into investment.

The number of small businesses is an even more important indicator of an economy's development potential. During the "fat" years under Putin, the number of small businesses increased by 62 percent, reaching slightly more than 1.3 million in 2009. The small business sector employs 9 million people today—12 percent of the workforce. Back in 1999, when Mikhail Kasyanov was prime minister, the Higher School of Economics estimated, based on recovery growth trends, that "by 2005–2006, the number of registered small businesses in Russia could reach around 4 million and employ up to 32–35 million people. Their share of GDP could increase from the current 12 percent to at least 35 percent.[1] But this did not happen[2]—which attests not only to the liberal economists' unjustified hopes but also to the continuing unfavorable business environment.

As long as the economy is dominated by the state authorities, whose top priority is to keep power in the hands of a narrow circle of people, those controlling private capital will not want to or be able to take risks, preferring instead to invest in sectors under the authorities' "protection." Thus, growth is concentrated mostly in sectors not connected to the general public's prosperity. This trend, though not weakening the state power system as such, does ultimately make the state less effective.

A total of 70 percent of the population do not have savings (and another 12 to 15 percent have only small savings, only enough to cover basic needs for three to six months). Most people (at least three-quarters of the population) live from payday to payday, or from one pension payment to the next. This does not encourage attempts to save in order to improve one's own situation and lifestyle, and investment in the future (for instance, in health care and in children's education). This indicates that the gratification mechanisms characteristic of market relations are not working for most of the Russian population. In other words, the country does not have a common national market for labor and capital.

This situation makes it hard for complex forms of social organization, such as public solidarity (for example, civil society, legal awareness, and cooperation between the generations through pension funds and insurance societies) to develop. It also hampers the development of long-term planning in life, fighting for collective life goals or improvements, autonomous justice, and optimized education. The low level of mobility indicates serious obstacles—an underdeveloped labor market and problems with housing and infrastructure, including the road network—in the way of developing a market economy and a rule-of-law state. A huge share of the population does not have the resources for changing their long-established way of life and cannot move to where there are better opportunities for finding work and improving, or at least having the hope of improving, their conditions and quality of life.

The greater part of the population (62 percent) lives in villages and small towns.[3] Life in these places is very different from life in the big cities (which are home to 20 percent of the population). The differences between the main urban centers and the social periphery arise not so much from the difference in income as from prevailing consumer behaviors and lifestyles, and the information environment's limits, which all help to shape social interaction, political preferences, and the like. The poor periphery forms a zone characterized by chronic social depression and stagnation-induced tension, social anomie, and pathology. People in the provinces are far more dependent on the authorities and thus on the domination of paternalist-state ideas and preferences, with all the accompanying illusions and expectations. These groups form the main pool of voters. Their numbers far outweigh those who support liberal parties, and they form the support base for conservative politics.

People in medium-sized and big cities have been much more deeply affected by social change, as can be seen by how the urban labor market and consumer behavior have undergone noticeable transformations. Only very slowly are "classes" of entrepreneurs and "free farmers" starting to emerge. Specialists at the Levada Center put the proportion of entrepreneurs at only 4 to 5 percent of the adult population. The reasons for this situation are obvious: The market economy cannot function without public trust in financial institutions, which in turn cannot function without legal institutions and courts independent of the executive and legislative branches of power.

Two opposing tendencies thus characterize Russia's post-Soviet modernization. Some parts of society are quick to take on the simplest and most widespread forms of Western mass culture and consumption (to a lesser degree technology and communications, and even less—financial relations). But at the same time, there is a process of involution or degeneration of the Soviet-era or earlier complex forms of social life (for example, fundamental science and culture). The consumer boom reached about 25 to 27 percent of the population during the years 2003 to 2007, but in the same period the numbers of people considered among the upper layers of the Soviet intelligentsia shrank. A lack of financing and the brain drain led to a drop in the number of people engaged in science, innovative industry, and research and development.[4]

Most people share the idea that the social upheavals of the last twenty years have taken something important from them without giving them anything in return (see table 23.1). The most well-off groups' (the upper 20 percent of the population) increasing prosperity is little related to any real increase in the economy's effectiveness, and their ever-growing prosperity thus only deepens the social differentiation in people's incomes. The main source of their prosperity is redistribution of the "administrative rent"—in other words, their ability to turn the resources of state power into their own assets, in which closeness to the authorities plays a crucial part. The situation of economically influential groups and others close to the authorities

TABLE 23.1   *Have You Personally and Your Family Gained or Lost from the Changes in Russia Since 1992?*

YEAR AND MONTH OF SURVEY	1999 DEC.	2002 NOV.	2006 DEC.	2007 DEC.	2008 APRIL	2009 DEC.
Gained	10	20	22	29	36	23
Lost	74	70	57	41	37	50
Don't know	16	10	21	30	27	27

As a percentage of the number of people surveyed, $N = 1,600$.

depends less on their business skills, labor productivity, or ability to optimize management than on their connections with officials at various levels.

The provinces are "frozen" in a state of degradation, but the center (this is, the biggest cities) is developing fast.[5] This helps to perpetuate and entrench Soviet-era values and mentality, also reproducing them among younger people, and generates persistent social envy (that is, envy of the "rich" people in the big cities), inferiority complexes, wariness about anything new and unusual, and a rise in isolationist and nationalist views.

Putin's Policy of Conservatism

Modification of the Institutions of Power

Opponents to the current regime, and outside observers, usually criticize the government system's ineffectiveness and rigidity, the corrupt bureaucracy, the lack of qualified civil servants, the opaqueness of the budget and distribution of financial flows, the gap between declared political goals and the actual results achieved, and the shift in emphasis from aims to methods in the exercise of government. But these critics overlook the most important social aspects and functions of state institutions, namely, the socialization of new generations, who will inherit the political culture that has taken shape.

The 1990s saw the former Soviet-era nomenklatura's different factions engage in fierce battles for power. The result was to destroy only the peripheral state administration structures. The Soviet system's central institutions, on which the organization of power and the social order's legitimacy were dependent, proved far more resistant. The brief transition period of democracy under Boris Yeltsin (1992–1996) gave way to Putin's "managed democracy." At the start of the 2000s, the former Soviet Communist Party and economic nomenklatura were pushed out by new groups—the "chekists," "siloviki," and new government-appointed "oligarchs." These groups had no need either for an ideology of building a "new society" or for integration with Western democracies. They proclaimed a policy based on political conservatism (that is, social stability and a strong state), traditionalism (defense of national traditions and values, strong families, Orthodoxy, anti-Western thinking, and restoration of Russia's status as a great power), and "unity of the people and government"—in other words, suppression of the opposition, managed elections, and using the media for propaganda purposes.

The way the state administration system was organized underwent some modifications, but the system's nature, expressed through its self-sufficiency (vertical distribution of powers) and lack of political accountability—that is to say, its lack of any mechanisms enabling public control of its activities, including the possibility of a change of government—remained unchanged. Also unchanged was the power system's lack of differentiation among the different branches of power, which left the legislative and judicial branches dependent on the executive authorities.[6]

New Techniques for Manipulating Society

New techniques for manipulating society are widely used for maintaining social order. These techniques are based on depoliticizing, de-ideologizing, neutralizing, and sterilizing public opinion and suppressing the autonomy of any influential groups. The Kremlin administration's main task is to prevent the public from gaining an independent potential capability to call the authorities to account or get them replaced. Various obstacles preventing people from establishing the horizontal ties without which civil society cannot develop have had the effect of fragmenting society and reducing the amount of solidarity and trust among people and groups. Total control of the broadcast media has turned television into a powerful propaganda instrument with a beefed-up entertainment component used to help "keep the masses quiet." This artificially lowers TV viewers' intellectual level. Political parties not on the Kremlin's approved list have been squeezed from the public stage, and society has sunk into a state of apathy. People were receptive to this kind of manipulation from the outset, given that the experience of adapting to life in a repressive state over the decades of Soviet power had become deeply rooted in the mass public's identity, and also in society and culture. All this has created a situation in which people do not see any connection between the quality of their own lives and their participation in political life.

Mass Perception of the Current Authorities

Public opinion surveys show that there was growing public demand at the end of the 1990s and start of the 2000s for things such as "order," a "strong hand," and respect for the laws, all of which a strong personalized power system would hopefully be able to guarantee.[7] Respondents thought that this kind of power system could—and had a duty to—prevent administrative arbitrariness on the part of the government, regional governors, local authorities, police, and even criminal groups. The frustrations and uncertainty that the general instability and absence of control in the country were having on everyday life inevitably provoked public discontent with those who had initiated the changes that had led them to this situation. The anomie that began in the first half of the 1990s increased as the decade went by and was echoed by public demoralization and widespread cynicism. These moods were the result not only of losing perestroika-era illusions by the mid-1990s but also a reaction to the abruptness and rough edges of market relations, for which democratic politicians or democratically minded sections of the public had been ready. Feelings of social and intellectual helplessness, vulnerability, and disorientation were transformed in the public consciousness into hopes for a strong leader with real authority (see table 23.2), who would be able to convince people that a better future was in sight and all they had to do was accept and follow his lead. These hopes found comfort in Putin's rhetoric of state paternalism,

TABLE 23.2   *What Do You Think the President and Government Should Do in the Current Crisis Situation, and With Which of the Views Below Do You Agree Most of All?*

'Tighten the screws' and keep tight control of political and economic life	53
Give people the freedom to pursue their own affairs and make sure only that they do not break the laws	33
Don't know	14

January 2001, $N = 1,600$, as a % of total number of respondents.

restoration of the Soviet past, and national projects, without which the efforts to centralize state administration and limit the autonomy of various groups and institutions would have been difficult.

Overall, the mass mentality that has taken shape today could be described as conditional acceptance of unchecked state power based primarily on neotraditionalist and nonmodern institutions. The most important of these institutions are the "national leader"; the Orthodox Church, which sanctions the symbolic status of those in power; the security forces with their emergency powers, that is, powers not limited by the law; a "technical" government that does not have political status and importance of its own but just carries out the "national leaders'" will; and the armed forces, as one of the state's main embodiments of historical memory and techniques of mass compulsion. The regime's stability comes not so much from broad public support and approval as from a simple lack of overt resistance. The prevailing public attitude toward Putin is one of no clearly expressed antipathy, or of refusal to make any kind of assessment of his activity. As Hannah Arendt noted, passive submission to totalitarian or repressive regimes is equivalent to supporting and approving them.[8]

The public takes a negative view of the other state and public institutions. In the public's eyes, the courts, police, trade unions, and political parties are not there to serve their needs and interests but to protect the interests of those in power, keep control over society, or pursue their own selfish interests. Only no-alternative institutions representing the national whole or the force of legal compulsion (such as Putin and the Orthodox Church) benefit from the public's confidence (social support capital).

TABLE 23.3 *Which Groups of the Population Does Vladimir Putin Rely On for Support, in Your View?*

| YEAR OF SURVEY | 2000 | 2001 | 2003 | 2005 | 2010 |
MONTH	OCT.	JULY	JULY	JULY	OCT.
'Siloviki': intelligence services, army, police	54	43	51	51	35
Yeltsin's former inner circle, 'the family'	25	22	25	19	11
'Oligarchs', bankers, big business	24	15	27	25	31
'Directors' corps': heads of big companies	16	16	20	23	23
Civil service, bureaucracy	12	15	21	26	25
'Ordinary people': employees, workers, farm workers	12	15	15	18	16
'Middle class': people with a good income	10	16	19	23	21
Intelligentsia	5	10	8	12	9
Cultural and scientific elite	4	8	9	11	8
Everyone without exception	5	7	7	5	8
Don't know	13	18	11	12	12

As a percentage of total number of respondents, $N=1,600$, Oct. 2000; July 2001, 2003, 2005; ranked based on 2000.

Putin does not simply rely on these forces for support, but, in the public's view, "expresses" their interests (see table 23.3). The growing inclination toward authoritarianism in the late 1990s and early 2000s was not just a reaction to a serious crisis but also a partial restoration of the earlier paternalistic culture (the ratio of authoritarian and paternalistic ideas and their contrary notions is approximately 2:1 or even 3:1; see table 23.4). Nothing points at the moment to any future emergence of new groups with different social, economic, political, and ideological demands, and thus no change to the authoritarian-paternalist mentality is in sight for now. The current authorities have enough mass support to keep themselves in power at least until the middle of the next cycle (after the 2012 election), even if people's living standards go into a protracted decline.[9]

TABLE 23.4 *Does the Fact That Vladimir Putin Has Concentrated Almost All Power in His Hands Benefit Russia, or Will it Not Bring Russia Any Benefits?*

YEAR AND MONTH OF SURVEY	2004 MARCH	2005 DEC.	2006 SEPT.	2007 OCT.	2009 JULY	2010 JULY
Benefits Russia	68	57	61	66	63	52
Will not benefit Russia	20	29	24	20	16	22

$N = 1,600.$

By suppressing social and political discussion and not allowing freedom of information, the authoritarian regime sterilizes and marginalizes the whole idea of a political future. The growing neotraditionalism brings in its wake persistent mass indifference to the regime's declared political aims and to politics itself.[10] Possibilities for planning one's life are highly limited because systematic planning is possible only if there are effectively functioning official (legal) institutions. The extent of paternalist thinking is proportionate in the reverse to the country's ability to function as an effective modern state. Because the public's alienation from politics has built up not just over the last fifteen years but is also deeply rooted in the Soviet-era experience over three generations, it cannot be overcome in just a matter of months in the event of an upsurge in social friction or even a severe crisis. Experience shows that even if the conditions are right and there is no obvious repression, public groups turn active and protest moods grow only very slowly, over a period of many years. Repoliticizing society would take more than just the liberal-minded politicians, businesspeople, technocrats, and intellectuals in Moscow and the other main centers realizing that the system needs radical transformation. For change to happen, influential groups with an interest in changing the regime, for whatever reason, would need to emerge within the power structure itself.

Only 9 percent of survey respondents expressed "great interest" in political events and processes. The majority (52 percent) said they have no interest in politics, and the remaining 39 percent said they had only a very "moderate" interest. At the same time, 54 percent said they "do not understand politics." People in Russia believe that they have no means for expressing their interests and demands—the currently active political parties, trade unions, and politicians fail to perform this task. Eighty percent of respondents said that the current politicians are interested only in getting themselves elected, and not in carrying out the policies that the voters really want (8 percent disagree with this, and 7 percent said they "don't know"; April 2010, $N = 1,600$). Sixty-eight percent said they do not believe that ordinary people like them can achieve their aims and defend their interests by taking part in meetings and demonstrations today. Nongovernmental organizations (NGOs) have been discredited by official propaganda that depicts them as agents of Western influence or as disguised commercial organizations pursuing selfish aims under the guise of charity work.

The Kremlin and regional administrations firmly and consistently nip in the bud any possibility of protest groups gathering influence, taking action as soon as such groups begin to emerge. Without social organization, protests remain sporadic and brief, isolated hotbeds of collective discontent that inevitably take the tactic of appealing to the paternalist authorities and addressing complaints about the bosses to those very same bosses. The authorities are quick to pick up on these complaints and put on a performance of "personal intervention" and "dealing with isolated shortcomings and abuses." The Putin regime uses its chosen new techniques for maintaining power and mass-scale manipulation of the public to atomize society and show that social solidarity is possible only within the government-approved framework—within United Russia and veterans' associations, say, or within politically sterilized organizations such as the Russian Union of Industrialists and Entrepreneurs, the Public Council, soccer fans' clubs, and the like.

The reverse side of these relations between the authorities and the public is that they produce a persistent widespread lack of confidence in the individuals who make up the state organizations, and also a lack of respect or even antipathy toward the authorities (see table 23.5). This explains why 75 percent of respondents do not want to take part in political and public action, even when it pursues the goal of addressing problems in the towns or districts where they live. The lack of free and fair elections and referendums, pressure on NGOs, censorship in the main media, and so on all set the limits within which sitting patiently and taking the view that political life does not concern them becomes the fullest expression of popular

TABLE 23.5 *Which of the Following Best Describes the People Currently in Power in Your View?*

	1994	1997	2000	2001	2004	2005	2006	2007	2008	2009	2010
A	47	59	38	52	53	64	51	60	31	31	43
B	16	15	11	11	14	11	12	9	11	13	11
C	18	11	11	12	9	10	10	11	13	13	10
D	4	4	17	10	13	6	12	10	26	23	18
Don't know	15	11	23	15	11	9	15	10	19	20	19

$N = 1,600$

(A) People concerned only with their own material and career ambitions.

(B) Honest but weak people who do not know how to use power properly and ensure order in the country.

(C) Honest but not very competent people who do not know how to get the country out of economic crisis.

(D) A good team of politicians taking the country along the right road.

wisdom and a tactic of passive adaptation to the system. The majority of respondents (54 percent) do not therefore consider themselves responsible for what is happening in the country.

Adaptation's Reductive Nature: A Deceitful Scheme

Both sides build their relations on mutual deceit, although the members of the general public feel that they bear a lot less responsibility for this than do the authorities. The public holds a widespread view that the population, albeit under duress, fulfills to a greater extent the main provisions of the "social contract" than does the state. The ratio of those who comply with the "contract" and those who do not is 2:1 with regard to the general public, but people take a more negative view of how the state respects its obligation, producing a ratio of 1:2. This negative view of the state's respect for its commitments in turn serves as a justification for breaking the law and going against the social order, which only furthers the decaying influence on Russians' legal awareness.

This idea of mutual deceit has become familiar on all sides, and this kind of behavior is therefore not the object of any particular public outrage or disapproval, but is instead seen as something "normal." One could say that this sort of social convention is what holds up the general political consensus in Soviet and post-Soviet Russia, extending its reach to all areas of public life, from elections to the economy. Society has no control over the authorities (this is the view of 80 percent of the people, with 9 percent saying there is public control, and 11 percent who did not know).

The authorities can maintain their domination and effective hold on power only by systematically suppressing any public consciousness of their own worth—that is, by sterilizing the motivations and aspirations for success, higher forms of social recognition, and gratification from activity and social behavior. The authorities try to inculcate in people the value of "being just an ordinary person," of "being the same as everyone else." The result is that society has practically no mechanisms for encouraging and recognizing innovative behavior. The now-established practice whereby it is not society, nor even specialized professional groups, but the corrupt state itself that decides what constitutes "property," "morals," "culture," "law," "merit," and "achievement" is, in the public's mind, a sign of the elite's degradation and sterilization. The state authorities appoint their servile supporters to play the part of the "elite," thus discrediting the very value of creative achievement, knowledge, law, productiveness, and innovative development. In the end, this distorts the entire system of values and gratification, turning it on its head.

Protest Moods as a Factor for Change

A large section of society (the most depressed and poorest sections for the most part—people in the countryside and small towns affected by social degradation) feel no need for social, political, and economic change. Even special studies show that these groups today, as during the Soviet era, have no real incentive to intensify their labor.

Society manages to balance between a familiar combination of "semi-satisfaction" and chronic irritation that has never reached a critical threshold during the past decade. Even during the toughest times in the mid-1990s, protest activity remained low and was not in itself a factor that could change the system of power. Today, after the global financial and economic crisis of 2008–2009, society shows no signs of growing tension; thus, 36 percent of respondents said they are happy in general with their lives, 40 percent said they are happy with some things in their lives but not with others, and 24 percent said they are not happy with their lives. When it came to assessing their material situation, 59 percent described themselves as "average" (taking the general level they see around them as the reference point; that is, being "no different from everyone else" is the main evaluation criterion), only 13 percent described their situation as good, and 24 percent assessed their situation as bad. Forty-nine percent of respondents said that nothing had changed in their family's life over these last years, 18 percent said their life has improved, and 32 percent said their life is worse than it was before. The overall mood can be summed up by the formula "life is hard, but still bearable," to which 56 percent subscribed, whereas 27 percent said that "things are not so bad" and only 15 percent said that "we've had enough and just can't keep living this way any longer" (21 percent could not decide and did not answer the question). In other words, stability is ensured, keeping the public locked within the narrow framework of a routine and little-changing life. This life creates few demands but makes it comparatively easier to satisfy what demands there are. This section of society does not know other living standards and does not take them as a reference point.

The level of chronic irritation is relatively high but does not convert into actual action. Meanwhile, the authorities learn how to react to openly expressed dissatisfaction and thus reduce the tension somewhat, though without dealing with its root causes. Diffuse irritation does not threaten the system's functioning. On the contrary, it is built into the system of relations between the authorities and their subjects. Despite the superficial opinions some might hold, vague and nonspecifically targeted discontent plays a part in keeping the regime going and intact. This kind of discontent does not seek to overthrow the system as such but only to replace "bad" bosses and managers with "good and honest" ones. Kitchen talk and smokers' room conversations play an even more important latent role in maintaining order and stability. They reflect not simply society's passiveness in an authoritarian environment, or act as a vent for discontent, but also form the kind of surrogate political and social activeness typical of closed societies, and are a sign of civil society's emasculation.

The education system plays an ambiguous role. Unquestionably, it transmits social knowledge and, in part, is a source of modernizing examples. But at the same time, the opportunism of a social elite that sees all change as linked solely to the authorities and their transformation undermines its moral authority and prestige in society. As a result, there are no influential figures able to help the public work out what is going on and map out future directions. In the 1990s, there was still a dose of idealism or romanticism with regard to "democracy," but by the second half of the 2000s, educated people were far more likely than other social groups in Russia to express nationalistic, clericalist, or conservative views, playing up to the ruling elite's preferred line. Possibilities for articulating and representing group interests in the public sphere had all but vanished (the existence of a handful of independent newspapers with limited circulations does little to change the picture, and the Internet does not significantly change anything either). The decrease in political activeness and civic solidarity that Russia has witnessed in recent years is the result not just of pressure from the authorities on political parties not part of the Kremlin circle but also of pressure on NGOs and public organizations. The fact that parties, autonomous NGOs, and public organizations have no access to channels for interacting with the public (above all, national television channels and universities) has also played a big part in this decline. The number of civil society organizations has gone down considerably in recent years (going by official statistics), while the number of people working in NGOs and the number of volunteers have stayed remained relatively stable but not high—1.5 to 2 percent of the population. The disappearance of politics as a practice, civil society, and the possibility of expressing group views and interests has paralyzed Russian society and left it in what has become a familiar state of apathy and stupor.

People are far more likely to support economic demands and action than political ones. Thus the potential for political protest is low (and is clearly exaggerated by the opposition, which hopes for political change through protest, and by opposition-minded journalists). Between 12 and 18 percent of people declare their readiness to take part in protests, but fewer than 1 percent (over the course of 2010) actually took part in meetings and demonstrations. Unskilled people and low-income earners, along with people in the small towns and rural areas, are the groups with the highest frustration levels, but their self-organization potential is extremely low due to lack of knowledge and experience in consolidating opinion and taking active measures to stand up for their rights. They therefore do not constitute a threat to the regime. But the authorities nevertheless fear mass protests and respond to them in a nervy and sometimes irrational fashion.

The likelihood of mass political action organized by the opposition, or protests based on economic demands, is not high. But the same cannot be said about the danger of sudden upsurges in ethnic tension, in which social protest combines with mass xenophobia. Sudden bursts of hostility, conflicts, and pogroms signal a return to forms of social behavior more primitive even than those prevalent during the Soviet years. These social phenomena are not a sustainable situation and cannot continue for long, but they are a sign of how systematic efforts to keep the political dimension out of public life create an environment that, to use Niklas Luman's words, takes a "reduction of complexity" and leads to a barbarization of society.[11]

Conclusion

By trying to impose its control on Russia's political competition mechanisms, the media, public organizations, the courts, and other institutions, the current regime suppresses social and structural differentiation and thus cuts off the possibilities for transforming the system through modernization. This situation increases conservative outlooks and compensatory nationalism, and it also strengthens paternalist state, antiliberal, and anti-Western moods in society. Political apathy is on the rise in society, following the pattern already seen in other countries with transition authority regimes. Ideological domination has given way to political technology for keeping the public passive and limiting its demands. The public has no confidence in parties or civil society organizations and does not believe in the possibility of change. Society adapts to changes not by diversifying and becoming more complex in its makeup, structure, and cultural and values range but by lowering human and intellectual potential and simplifying the institutions that ensure the basic rules for interaction within society.

Groups seeking modernization emerge constantly in Russian society (seeking institutional reform in important areas such as the legal, court, and law enforcement systems, and the armed forces). They are also aware that the economy will continue to degrade irreversibly without consistent efforts to reduce the state's presence. But their calls and efforts run up against the self-preservation instincts of the ruling circles, the elite's opportunism, and the apathy of a public whose moral and cultural horizons are limited by the tasks of simple day-to-day survival. The problem for the future of post-totalitarian societies of this kind is that government in such societies is not just a technical apparatus for public administration but is also a symbolic institution that embodies and perpetuates fundamental concepts of human nature and the values of collective behavior. Justifying this order (agreeing with the use of force by the state) is akin to accepting the practice of systematic values disqualification of the subject people, depriving them of their own self-worth and right to freedom, and going along with the authorities' refusal to recognize them as independent actors with rights of their own, including the right to life, education, the right to defend their own interests, and so on.

The possibility of change emerges only when new generations have built up enough social and cultural capital and reached a point at which the fear of destitution and the threat of a return to the ascetic times of the Soviet-era planned economy with its chronic shortages cease to act as a values regulator. Discontent with protracted stagnation and the patriotic rhetoric of Russia's return to great power status will provide the impetus for change. But this prospect will emerge only with the arrival of the next generation of young people, who will push aside today's young generation, dubbed the "Putin youth," and this will not happen until sometime in the mid-2020s.

In the medium perspective, as defined by the electoral cycles, if one takes the period 2015–2020—the period from the middle of the next electoral cycle until the end of the following election campaign—one can outline several likely development scenarios for Russia:

- The prospect of lengthy recession following the 2008 crisis forces the country's leaders to make *systemic changes in political life and check the development of an increasingly authoritarian regime*. This would signal a return to plans for radical reform of the political system, courts, and law enforcement agencies; restoration of media freedom; holding fair and competitive elections; and the development of self-government and civil society. This is the best scenario for Russia's national interests, but it is also the least likely, given the intellectual and moral state of the Russian elite, the people in the upper levels of power, and the political culture of the larger part of Russian society.

- A prolonged crisis accompanied by a substantial drop in living standards during the next five to seven years will *destabilize* the economy (by putting too great a burden on the budget) and also the *regime itself*, which will be unable to cope with the growing social problems. This will increase conflict among the different groups with influence—above all, between the regional elites and the federal authorities.

- *An increase in state repression and authoritarianism* is a more likely scenario, but its time frame can only be limited; too repressive a regime would not be able to cope with the increasing social tension and the ensuing breakdowns in government. The current regime has learned to be more flexible in its approach than was the Soviet regime.

- The most likely scenario of all is that the country will enter a period of chronic stagnation or ongoing crisis, and fluctuate between bouts of increasing social tension and improvements in the situation. The country's leaders will be forced to make partial changes to the political system and laws, and they will thus variously tighten and relax the state's control over society and the economy. But these steps will not affect the system's actual foundations—the vertical power hierarchy on which it is built, and the concentration of government powers in the hands of the current small and nontransparent circle.

Notes

1. A. Yu. Chepurenko, "Small Business in Russia," *Mir Rossii* 10, no. 4 (2001): 130–60.

2. The number of small businesses has been falling since 2007. See "Social-economic situation in Russia," Federal'naya Sluzhba Gosudarstvennoy Statistiki (Federal State Statistics Service), www.gks.ru/bgd/regl/b09_01/Isswww.exe/stg/d08/pred-3.htm.

3. Small towns are defined as towns with fewer than 250,000 people.

4. The number of people engaged in scientific research and development has declined from 1.5 million in 1990 to 760,000 in 2008.

5. Moscow and Saint Petersburg account today for 75 to 80 percent (about two-thirds in Moscow) of all books published in Russia. The collapse of the old book distribution system and low purchasing power in the regions means that new books do not reach towns with fewer than 250,000 people, not to mention the rural areas. There is a greater diversity of publications today (the number of first editions has been at around 110,000 to 120,000 titles during the last few years, which is 2.5 times more than during the Soviet period), but print runs have fallen two-fold to three-fold. This information flow is available only to a relatively small section of the population in the big cities. As a result, the number of regular readers in the country has dropped from 29 to 22 percent compared with the Soviet period, and the number of people who do not read books or magazines at all increased from 44 percent to 54 percent from 1990 to 2009. The number of people who regularly buy books has gone down from 12 to 4 percent during the past ten years, and the number of people who do not buy books has increased from 30 to 60 percent. Only 10 percent of the adult population use libraries today. See B. Dubin and N. Zorkaya, "Reading 2008," based on sociological research carried out by the Levada Center, 2008.

6. O. V. Kryshtanovskaya, "Sovietization of Russia: 2000–2008," *Eurasian Review* 2 (November 2009): 95–134.

7. Levada Center, "Obshchstvennoe mneniye" (Public opinion), 2010, 31, table 3.4.11 and 41, table 3.7.16.

8. Hannah Arendt, *Eichmann in Jerusalem: A Report on the Banality of Evil* (New York: Viking Press, 1963), 120.

9. During the last two years, the country's top leaders have had a "complete confidence" and approval rating of 65 to 70 percent.

10. This was the attitude, for example, that people took toward the national projects, or to Medvedev's declarations on modernization. The number of skeptics was 1.5 to 2 times higher than the number of those who believed that implementing the national projects would improve the situation in the areas concerned. Replying to the question "How will the money allocated for these projects be spent?" 13 percent to 14 percent said "effectively and productively"; 68 percent to 70 percent said "ineffectively" or "it will be stolen." Levada Center, "Obshchestvennoye mneniye" (Public opinion), 2008, 52–53.

11. Niklas Luman, *Soziale Systeme. Grundriss einer allgemeinen Theorie* (Frankfurt: Surkamp, 1984), 50.

the NOMENKLATURA
and the ELITE

Nikolay Petrov

The private and/or personal dimension of the processes unfolding in Russia is one of the keys to understanding the country's future development. This chapter seeks to show, first, that there have been big changes vis-à-vis the nomenklatura and the elite; and, second, that these changes have often been in different directions at the federal and regional levels. In the first case, the main trend has been the transformation of the administrative staff into the ruling elite; in the second case, the situation has been the other way around.

To simplify the present situation, it could be described as a wishy-washy state somewhere between two human models—the nomenklatura and the elite.[1] The current Russian system was in large part inherited from the Soviet nomenklatura apparatus, and thus preserves a certain similarity. However, today there are no resources dedicated to Soviet-style repression, and without this "stick"—that is, without an external mechanism of control and selection—today's "nomenklatura" is inevitably transformed into an elite.

The principal difference between the new system and the Soviet-Stalinist one is the Chekist component, which absorbs all other elements. This leads to a dramatic weakening of internal controls, and a legal relativism with increasing tendencies of the criminal state.

The inertial scenario with the buildup of problems and conflicts, which leads to a deepening of fissures between the characteristics of the "nomenklatura" and "elite," can result in a collapse of the system.

Changing Concepts of the Elite

The very concept of the "elite" in the context of today's Russia is not something on which everyone agrees. There is a point of view that due to the elimination of the elite—which took place twice in the last century—Russian society has been left without an elite altogether. Applying this to the present-day scenario, many experts prefer to term them "the so-called elites."

Without going into the discussion of how rooted and good the Russian elites are, the extent to which they are the "cream of society," what role they claim to play in society, how society accepts them in this role, and so on, instead I start with a functional definition of "elite." According to this understanding, belonging to the elite faction is a function of an individual's power and influence, without any tight conditions of intellect or moral and ethical qualities. In most cases, with such an approach the members are the "elite" as defined by their position in the administrative system. The current members of the Russian elite can, therefore, be referred to as "bosses."[2]

The total supersession of elites—"from rags to riches" and vice versa—has happened more than once during the last century, and has proven to be obviously too much for the country. And the matter has not been restricted to persons alone—there has also been a loss of mechanisms of replacement and responsibility. Thus begins "the effect of recutting," when in place of good timber grow flattened undergrowth, weeds, and bushes. Nothing has remained from the old, prerevolutionary elite, neither in the country (for obvious reasons) nor in exile, where the third and fourth generations have completely delinked themselves from their Russian roots (unlike, say, in the Baltic countries, where the second generation turned its attention homeward on a significant scale).

Many of today's "bosses" are the "children of the 1980s," the younger generation of the last Soviet elite. They came to power as a result of the collapse of the USSR, which pushed out of power their senior colleagues, the actual communist leadership. Appearing on the edge of the system, they were simultaneously its gravediggers and heirs. Their internal organization bears a horizontal, corporate-clan character, and is devoid of roots, tailing up the depth of the cultural layer.

At some point during the period of perestroika, there emerged in the public and media space some descendants of the Russian nobility. But their appearance was short-lived and failed to add diversity to the Russian elites or restore its pre-Bolshevik roots—perhaps because seventy years of the communist rule had virtually destroyed the remains of imperial Russia and there was, in fact, nothing to bring back. Or perhaps because, unlike some of the former communist countries, Russia did not enact lustration laws (investigating and removing former Party officials and other members of the elite from their positions), and the continuity from the Soviet elites to the post-Soviet ones was too strong. In addition, unlike the Baltic countries, Georgia, or Armenia, the Russian diaspora in the West would not return to the motherland to join the ranks of the postcommunist Russian elites.

Instead of restoring the roots, we have a postmodern image of a rather unnatural alliance between the old and the "new." The "heir" of the House of Romanov, Georgy Romanov became the adviser to the former KGB lieutenant colonel Vladimir Strzhalkovsky, who had earlier received a confirmation of his hereditary nobility by Georgy's mother, Grand Duchess Maria Vladimirovna.[3] This may have seemed curious, if not for the security officers' reasoning that they are the modern nobility, and the desire of the majority of the representatives of the ruling elite to, by hook or crook, get academic degrees and titles, membership in large and numerous "intermediate" academies, and so on.

The distinction between the rank-based elite and the hereditary one is important: the latter implies autonomous weight (aside from the official title), and a measure of responsibility. The quality of elites is defined by the proportion of the rank-based elite versus the hereditary. It is bad when there are no "social climbers," and even worse when everyone is a social climber.

What Russia has now is some kind of nomenklatura system, but with weak internal controls and regeneration, and without the well-established external mechanisms that were overseen by secret services in the nomenklatura system. In the 1990s, first the old system was suppressed and partially removed, and then it was partially recovered—neonomenklaturization.[4] The problem is that not all the elements of the old system were restored; above all, the methods of selection and training, as well as regeneration, were not. At the same time, the system was adapted toward the institution of private property, with the alignment of the mechanisms of enrichment—the conversion of power into property, along with expropriation of property from those who had been trusted to hold it but who would not observe the informal rules of the nomenklatura world.

Without external shocks and the cleansing of the nomenklatura system, which has no built-in mechanism of regeneration and renewal, along with the absence of protection from inbreeding, the system is prone to rapid degeneration. This is precisely what we are witnessing.

The Nomenklatura System as It Is

The phenomenon of the nomenklatura system is poorly understood, despite the presence of a number of brilliant papers on this topic.[5] This system is a specially arranged organization for the recruitment, replacement, and operation of personnel. And it constitutes a vicious cycle: Once a person gets in, he or she never leaves it. In a sense, the nomenklatura system has achieved gigantic proportions and logical perfection and thus acts as the group that exerts semi-criminal control over society.

The nomenklatura system has several necessary and sufficient conditions:

- vertical subordination (entailing centralism and hierarchy), with different levels and the presence of "overseers" at every level;[6]
- closed entry and exit;
- a hierarchical caste system with strict codes of internal conduct and exemption from following strict external rules;
- internal rules of career development, following which growth—or at least maintaining status regardless of "external" performance indicators—is guaranteed.

Here it is useful to consider an analogy. If the construction of an Egyptian pyramid had used a modern method of erecting a tall building, then the result would be very reminiscent of the "nomenklatura pyramid," which grows from the bottom up and has strong horizontal and vertical structural links. The design is very stable and it's virtually impossible to destroy the pyramid by removing blocks from top, side, or bottom. The pyramid will be damaged when it stops its normal regeneration—recruitment of new nomenklatura personnel. Then the base of the pyramid will begin to narrow. But the pyramid will collapse only if there is a radical change in the principles whereby its management personnel are developed.

On the stories of the nomenklatura pyramid, all movements take place along horizontal walkways. There are escalators, but the down escalators are missing. From each story, you can move outside—to the business world, for example. Not to just any business; however, but one that is closely associated with government agencies, this association between private business and government tends to be informal. Those who leave in an orderly way proscribed by the "rules" remain in "active reserve" and retain the ability to log on to the same or even higher floor. For an outsider or a newcomer, penetrating into the nomenklatura from the sides rather than from below is much more difficult because of the corporate character of the system. Like the cell membrane, the outer envelope of the nomenklatura pyramid is much more open to output than input, and easily allows insiders to move inside, while for strangers entry is barred.

The post-Soviet nomenklatura differs from the Soviet one, first, because of the presence of a business wing adapted specifically to its post-Soviet pyramidal structure, and, second, due to the fact that the pyramid is part of the external world—with respect to both the bureaucracy and the country itself (with a transition to freely convertible currency as a universal equivalent to received benefits). This business wing provides room for maneuver, which previously did not exist. This wing allows nomenklatura members to take occasional breaks in their nomenklatura careers and switch to the business sector in order to have a legitimate source of enrichment. When they come back to civil service they can leave their businesses to their near and dear.

This pyramid is inhabited by bureaucrats from different areas as well as businesspeople appointed by them—often from their own ranks—who by virtue of their origin are virtually tied to the state apparatus and its controlled resources.

A normally functioning nomenklatura system needs a constant rotation of personnel. This is what strengthens it both horizontally and vertically, allowing it to maintain rigidity and unity. The particularity of the current system lies in the fact that it is not able to do this for itself—and without external renewal mechanisms, it will rapidly degrade.

The nomenklatura is a "state within a state," with its own laws (ranging from traffic rules to the penal code) and rules of conduct, its own network of shops and ateliers, and its own motor depots and resorts. With the transition from the nomenklatura system to the capitalist variant, there is less need for a special infrastructure and no need at all for the top-tier elites. Instead of the homegrown infrastructure, the elite gets the means to access the world of global luxury, wealth, and prestige.

Within this system, a strict adherence to the rules—which requires, above all, loyalty to both the system and the boss—guarantees the preservation of one's status and one's job security. The guarantee of employment to maintain or improve one's status is not charity, as it may seem, but instead is an effective strategy vis-à-vis the system. This is because, for the system, the length of service, and the conformity and dependability of individual elements, are more important than their self-contained, individual effectiveness. Strengthening ties between the individual elements and their transformation into the national network, which always moves horizontally, is also an important part of the overall strategy that assures the unity of the nomenklatura system across the country.

Therefore, for an official in the nomenklatura, "being at fault" in a significant way means that the official can be pushed to the edge, or even completely dropped off the operating platform and put into the reserves, or dismissed from appointed office. But he or she usually does not leave the "club," in the end being protected by the system in some way. Here one can see the workings of a kind of collective responsibility, which has been demonstrated more than once by the State Duma deputies, who did not wish "to surrender their people" at the request of the prosecutor general, who is more powerful and better positioned. This does not mean that the "stick" does not exist—the system penalizes and punishes severely, but it usually does not give up, does not reject its people, and does not let them out. It is no coincidence that the authorities even have a penal colony of their own.

The life of the nomenklatura system is continuous, not discrete. Nevertheless, from time to time there is a reconfiguration in the system, coupled with a sharp increase in domestic competition. This could be observed before the 2007–2008 election cycle, when the deputy finance minister, Sergei Storchak, the right-hand man of the head of the Federal Drug Control Service, General Alexander Bulbov, and later the head himself, General Viktor Cherkesov, became victims of the fight between verticals. In anticipation of the 2011–2012 election cycle, the nomenklatura battle intensified and began to spill into the public arena.

In the capitalist version, the perks of the nomenklatura are replaced by the idea of a "right to corruption," whereby extracting benefits from the provision of services becomes the norm and is not associated with the risk of incurring penalties. However, if the earlier payments and benefits were used as a "leash," with a transition to a market economy and corrupt rent seeking, supervisors in the nomenklatura system have largely lost direct leverage over their subordinates. Nevertheless, weaning from corrupt rents, the system continues to "keep them on the hook" under the threats exercised in the past. In combination with more publicity and elements of the market, this creates the illusion of novelty.

The Nomenklatura Under Putin

The nomenklatura system, like any other human resources system, can operate only in conditions of stability. Thus, during the first "revolutionary" years of the new Russia, it was, on the one hand, broken, and on the other hand, paralyzed and not as noticeable. By the mid-1990s, it largely recovered, but with the political stabilization after Vladimir Putin came to power, it was strengthened and now manifests itself in full.

What is fundamentally new for today's system is that the nomenklatura involves not only a mass replacement of the old staff by people from "the security organs," something that had happened before, but also the total elimination of internal controls at all levels, which in Soviet times was carried out within the framework of two major opposing subsystems—the

Communist Party and the KGB.[7] The subordination of all other secret police systems, alongside a sharp weakening of internal controls, was a consequence of the dangerous combination of entrusting both the establishment of rules and their enforcement in one pair of hands. As is characteristic of special services, the legal relativism with the primacy of expediency and the lawfulness of "intracorporate" concepts under the law lead to the practical blurring of the distinction between the nomenklatura system and criminals. As a result, instead of the closed orders to which Stalin referred, the system has turned into a gigantic semi-criminal group.[8]

Under Putin, the overall stabilization, reconstruction, and restoration of damaged structures became the reasons for strengthening the nomenklatura. For example, envoys in the federal districts partly compensated for damage caused by the introduction of a direct nomenklatura system for the election of governors. Elected governors themselves broke down the nomenklatura system, and this affected its other elements. Therefore, the election of regional governors had to be canceled just like the direct election of mayors—who are also considered "breakable" vis-à-vis the system—and is now being dismantled. With the restoration of the power vertical, the political system has passed the point of bifurcation, and development is now going according to the nomenklatura scenario.

The nomenklatura system, first of all, signifies control over all positions of power, directly or indirectly, from a single center—whether it is called the Central Committee of the Communist Party of the Soviet Union or the Presidential Administration. The imposition of major personnel decisions beyond the limits of the apparatus, whether it is real competition for posts or the formation of a government by the parliamentary majority, or the true independence of the courts at any level range—all these developments weaken and eventually destroy the nomenklatura system. A real rather than a decorative democracy is fundamentally opposed to the nomenklatura system.

In comparison with the Soviet period, the current nomenklatura system shows more dynamism, as well as an interspersion of well-formed phases of career development—more sectoral and spatial, with less stability and staging. Many of its members mushroom out of nowhere, or out of someone's personal network—and leave, though not so much to just any place as to the business world.

The nomenklatura is a kind of army, in which each individual is not a person but a function. The most important things in the nomenklatura system are clarity, obedience, and adherence to the charter of internal service. In recent years, these features have become more than obvious in the system of appointments. It can be observed in full measure in the configuration of the Duma majority, and even more so in the appointment of managers in the United Russia Party.

The nomenklatura system is not afraid of powerful institutions, but only to the extent that they remain dependent on it. In this sense, predictably, institutions and related players have been consistently weakened under Putin, and the list includes all relatively independent political players except the president himself—whether it is the State Duma, the federation council, the oligarchs, or the regional governors. Similarly, there has been a natural emergence and strengthening of players whose role is not determined by the Constitution but personally, by their guarantor; among these are the security council in the early stages, authorized representatives of the president in federal districts, the state council, the accounting chamber, and so on. Their presence in the political arena testifies to the intensification of the position of the nomenklatura system.

The nomenklatura system is not afraid of business owners either; but if they depend on power, it assigns and reassigns them. Under the new conditions, the court of law becomes an increasingly important tool in the nomenklatura system, and begins to act as a means of redistribution of property and power. Therefore, in principle, any judicial reform carried out by the current regime cannot be geared toward strengthening the independence of the court.

Mikhail Gorbachev started the process of the destruction of the nomenklatura; Boris Yeltsin pulled out its ideological core, and restored it to the upper stories, partially losing control over the lower ones. As a result, the pyramid lost its integrity and solidity, and small "pyramid-ettes" formed at the regional level. Under Putin, the pyramid was restored as a whole structure, but with limited functionality; it has no system-dualism, based on the presence of two fiercely competitive systems of power and control—the administrative party and the secret police. Furthermore, the current system does not have a functioning system of replacement.

The Problem of Personnel

The approach to the problem of personnel shows clear evidence of how the government seeks and finds the simplest and most primitive solutions, and they often prove to be inadequate in addressing the complexity of the situation. Faced with a shortage of human resources, the administration has not started restoring the mechanisms that ensure their regeneration and has instead elected the nomenklatura approach, the so-called personnel reserve.

Presidential training programs had already been introduced under Yeltsin. The activation of work in keeping with the preparation of the personnel reserve—first of the United Russia Party, and then of the president—has coincided with a sharp reduction in the space of public policy and a further strengthening of the role of government in all spheres. An example of how this looks in practice can be drawn from the early 2009 announcement of hundreds of members of the presidential personnel reserve, which made a favorable impression on the experts and the public.[9] The "personnel reserves"—both presidential and those of United Russia—made an attempt to solve the problem, but they carried out their measures in unsuitable ways, with the notorious manual control.

In comparison with the formation of the presidential reserve, the recruitment of personnel in the establishment of newly appointed Moscow mayor Sergey Sobyanin looked almost like a violation of the accepted norms of the system. "Selection of the Moscow team does not depend on personal acquaintance," said Sobyanin. "Even people whom I did not know before coming to Moscow came. And, incidentally, it was the same situation in Tyumen, and the same situation in the Russian government. I invited people, not because they are my fellow villagers or fellow students or friends, but because of a completely different principle. I pick them by profession."[10]

So, instead of a public mechanism, this was an announcement of the results of a nonpublic procedure. Any "personnel reserve" is nothing more than a declaration of intent. The inefficient system is not able to effectively select personnel. Such a problem reminds one of Baron Munchausen, who tried pulling himself out of the swamp by his hair. The problem is not that the mechanism of selection is absent; it is there but it is ineffective, and even counterproductive. This is most clearly manifested in the appointment of governors, because their failures are more apparent and obvious than of those personnel who sit in the depths of the bureaucratic apparatus. The more unsuccessful appointments took place in the Irkutsk and the Far East regions, where the governors had to be changed, without waiting until the end of their mandate.[11]

The people who are currently sitting in different positions may not be competent, but that is not the point; the point is that the actual system design is such that these people cannot form an effective working mechanism.

One reason for the personnel shortage is the lack of public policy as an effective mechanism for their selection and training—in the form of elections, political competition, and so on. Another equally important reason is negative selection, whereby the system discards the best and relatively independent players and picks the worst—but absolutely loyal—ones. People like Boris Nemtsov, Vladimir Milov, Vladimir Ryzhkov, and Mikhail Kasyanov are left out, simply because the system rejects people with personal weight and a certain autonomy, that is, those who make up the elite, not the nomenklatura. All gubernatorial "heavyweights," who were objectively strong leaders, can be added to the list of these opposition politicians who have been rejected by the system because they were deemed too independent.

In recent times, the element of nepotism has drastically risen in the personnel ranks. Apart from the fact that this phenomenon indicates the breaking of ties and times, and of corporations, along with the system's archaism, it is also a factor in the destruction of the nomenklatura system, transforming it into the elite. The Dubik brothers,[12] Turchak father and son,[13] Vorobyov father and sons,[14] father-in-law and son-in-law Zubkov-Serdyukov, the wife of Viktor Khristenko—Tatyana Golikova, and the Rotenberg brothers all can serve as examples.[15]

The abundance of relatives in the system reflects not only the staffing proposal but also supply and demand—a shortage of people who can be relied upon even in the absence of selection and training, along the same lines of the Komsomol. At the same time, it reflects a crisis in the nomenklatura system.

The Nomenklatura Versus the Elite

As opposed to the self-developing and self-sustaining system of the administrative elite, supporting the nomenklatura system requires constant input from external forces. Therefore, so that the nomenklatura does not become the elite, it must be treated just as one would treat a park to maintain it, always cutting the trees, replacing the old ones with new ones and so on.

The essence of the elite lies in its internally sustained reproduction—in the transfer of resources and status, and a sense of responsibility. A prerequisite for this is the relative stability of socioeconomic conditions and social stratification.

The revolutionary change in the political model in the late 1980s and early 1990s gave rise to a sharp weakening of the elite's succession. Even if specific persons have retained control of the levers of power, the institutions have been broken, and, therefore, succession has been disrupted. If at first, there was a hacking of the elite caste space and the "injection of new blood" in terms of the emergence of new persons with higher education, scientific and technical intellectuals, soldiers, and journalists, then later the situation stabilized; the system either incorporated them by forcing them to adopt its rules of the game or weeded them out. Today in the upper echelons of the political elite, almost no one who was incorporated into postcommunist Russia from the late Soviet version is left.[16]

"New power," like "new money," does not automatically entitle the bearer to a sense of responsibility—whether it is narrowly corporate or more systemwide.[17] The psychology of a part-time worker is characteristic of "new power" representatives; interest in the regeneration of the system in the long term is simply absent. The social fabric of this elite is fresh and shallow—it has little or no stable intergenerational ties, and it could not stand the test of time. In today's elite officers, among figures who still exercise influence without having a "portfolio," are, perhaps, only Alexander Voloshin, Yevgeny Yasin, Yevgeny Primakov, and the like.

The behavior of elites is determined by a dual system of coordinates. There are external rules and limits from the side of society, and there are internal rules from the side of corporations. There is a law that is both external (for all) and internal (concepts). Staying in the nomenklatura system, they are immune from punishment for violations of external regulations, but only if the violations do not affect the nomenklatura's more senior members.[18] Violators of corporate rules become outcasts and are subject to common law.[19] The current internal law is tailored more for the functional convenience of the existing elites than for their regeneration and survival.

By cultivating its representatives and itself outside the boundaries of the law, the nomenklatura system becomes similar to the criminal underworld. Among the signs of similarity are the weakness or even absence of formal institutions, which are replaced by the weight of authority exercised by informal rules; a powerful power unit, which plays an active role in business disputes; industry sectors/territories for fostering; and the need for personal loyalty toward the leader, distinct elements of nepotism, and the robustness of violators of the corporate "code of honor."

The splicing of power and property makes gray schemes and shady relationships inevitable and necessary, and promotes the direct and indirect adoption of nomenklatura principles of organization and norms of an informal community, including a conspiracy of silence, the "inner court of honor," pooled cash funds, and so on. First and foremost, this is characteristic of the power bloc of the nomenklatura, for both business shelters and organized criminal groups. In some cases, there is even direct bonding of "authoritative businessmen" with political power, particularly at the municipal level, but also reaching much higher levels.[20]

For normal selection mechanisms, it is essential that the completion of recruitment into the nomenklatura system be based on more meritocratic principles, and that external mechanisms of renewal be more open and dynamic. However, Putin's nomenklatura system has neither the first nor the second. Instead, there is artificial selection, and culling and pushing become significant to the process, and thus potentially dangerous to the system of people. Like the body, which because of a lack of certain enzymes loses its ability to digest, the nomenklatura system rejects the human material, which under other circumstances could have contributed to the country's prosperity.

The emerging elite is a natural antagonist of the nomenklatura; and from here emerges the ultimate desire to at all costs shut out independent candidates from gaining access to power relative to the nomenklatura system's players. Thus, among the many facets in the "Khodorkovsky case," conflict with the nomenklatura system is more important than the redistribution of property; this was fully confirmed by the second trial of Mikhail Khodorkovsky and Platon Lebedev. Chichvarkin's harassment is an example of a different kind, but it also fits into the same pattern of systemic conflict between the nomenklatura and the emerging independent elite. In many cases, the general business lesson is that in each case the business goes not to a bright individual but to a more systematic player.

The Nomenklatura Children as a Threat to the System

Entry and exit are two key elements of any open system. If there is a serious problem with entry when it comes to recruiting and training young people, then at the exit the system more or less works, providing places in public administration or the private corporate sphere for those who leave active work life. The same role—to one extent or another—is served by the Federation Council, the diplomatic services, and various quasi-state funds for generals in uniform, or without, guaranteeing an upgrading of the personnel based on a "soft" model, that is, without executions and purges.

Recently, the system has actively incorporated automatic upgrade mechanisms—the sixty-five-year milestone for civil servants, and fifty-five to sixty years for generals; and an age limit for the personnel reserve (forty years), limiting the tenure to two to three terms (and in some places already at five years) for federal officials in the regions, now including governors. Rotational arrangements are to play a similar role, where at the time of appointment, governors, prosecutors, judges, and others are gradually introduced to the practice of serving two terms and then moving to another region.

A generational change is already under way; the "young" of the perestroika era are leaving, and there has been an inflow of fresh blood. However, no matter to what extent this is guaranteed by the nomenklatura's propagandist segment, this fresh blood to a large extent is an active and ambitious but poorly educated group, which is often associated with the Storm Troopers or the Red Guards.[21]

Systemic mechanisms to climb up the public administration ladder do not exist. The Kremlin youth movement that pretends to replicate this role does not fulfill this task. Making a career in the public service worked only for a few members of Nashi and the "Young Guards": Vasily Yakemenko, who took over as minister of youth; and Ruslan Gattarov, who took over the post of the senator for the Chelyabinsk region. Careers in the Nashi United Russia segments are often promoted by "old" power and resources, as was the case of a prominent United Russia member Andrei Vorobyov, the son of a deputy minister of emergencies, or another prominent party member Andrei Turchak, who is currently the governor of the Pskov region and the son of Putin's judo partner.

The administrative elites rely exclusively on cash as vehicles of capital accumulation and its transfer to their children. It would seem that the direct conversion of power into property—which one could call conversion-1—would be essential to ensure the stability and a relatively independent position of the elites. However, this does not happen because property rights are not defined, the enrichment occurs rapidly, and, as a rule, in circumvention of the law, and relations are generally built on the nomenklatura "concepts," again in an extrajudicial manner. Without any real rule of law and secure protection of private property, billions of dollars make their way to the various members of the system, but this money can easily be taken away. Hence, there is a need for a conversion-2, which comes with blistering business careers being pursued by the current bosses' children, who en masse join banks and state companies.

Children are a reliable indicator of a sociopolitical system. If the children of the former Soviet elite sought to pursue careers that would take them to the West (hence the choice of education at the Moscow State Institute of International Relations, schools of journalism, and departments of foreign languages), then the children of the current nomenklatura "take the banks" and large businesses; moreover, this is not only a relative guarantee for the future but also part of building family chains, which is an essential element of the capitalization of their parents' administrative resources and the legalization of family income.[22]

It is precisely the children of the nomenklatura fathers who are entering businesses and acting as the gravediggers of the system. Businesses, and even the state, allow a person to cease to be solely a function of his office—thus breaking the framework of the nomenklatura system. After all, capital that cannot be taken away with the post is independent of position and power, and, therefore, is less dependent on the system.

Regarding "fathers and sons," there emerges the problem of not only the destruction of the system but also generational breakdown. The second generation is the most problematic. The parents' meritocracy, even when it has downsides, is transformed into a "golden youth" version with painful complexes for the children.

Network Structures

In the presence of weak institutions, and of openly political mechanisms in competition for the mechanisms of recruitment, the elite largely begins to take on a network character, which is reflected in its structure. In such a case, networks can be horizontal (for example, the "Saint Petersburg" type) or vertical (for example, the corporate variety), and they may overlap, which leads to the formation of "Saint Petersburg Chekists," "Saint Petersburg operators," and "Saint Petersburg liberals."[23]

First and foremost, corporate expansion and intrusion on the part of the security forces is the essential element of the network. The expansion of security forces may be industrial—Olga Kryshtanovskaya and Stephen White call this "militocratic" and "spatial."[24] A striking example of the latter are the "Boevoe Bratstvo/Combat Brotherhood" veterans of local wars and conflicts in the Moscow region.

Elements of the network structures existed in Stalin's time, but back then the working mechanisms of regeneration ensured a constant flow of fresh blood into the power elite. Under "developed Putinism," networking has became the main mechanism of recruitment.

Because of Russia's vast territory, major networks covering the whole country must necessarily be hierarchical. In this case, the network structure transforms into a pyramid, where for each high-level figure, there is an entire array of more junior personnel.

The public reception rooms of presidential envoys, which were established in 2001–2002, have become the pioneer of hierarchical network structures of a new type. Later, the reception rooms of the local chapters of the United Russia Party and of the party chairman followed.

New network management structures of a semiformal nature began appearing in 2005; this was the impetus for mass protests against the monetization of benefits and the "Orange Revolution." It was then that networks of civil society—from the top of the Russian Public Chamber (July 2005), public district councils (and some public advice agencies), and public houses at regional and municipal levels—began forming. This is when the authorities created many youth organizations, such as Walking Together, Nashi, and the Young Guards of United Russia.

An example of a project management structure is the Council for National Projects (launched in October 2005; the Presidium, with Dmitri Medvedev as the head, was created in July 2006), with regional structures headed by governors, and to a lesser extent, the local government councils, the Cossacks, and the commission on modernization.

On the eve of the elections and transfer of power, two special network structures were built, and governors were appointed at the regional level: the National Antiterrorism Committee (NAC, February 2006), and the National Anti-Drug Committee (NADC, October 2007). These committees still work, but the peak of their activity has passed. In 2010, anti-corruption was added to the vertical with the relevant committees being formed.

In addition to the aforementioned network structures—such as the Public Chamber, the NAC, and the NADC—which grow from the top down, there is another type of a network, where federal-level structures try to subjugate relatively autonomous structures in the regions. This, for example, is the case of the Russian Accounts Chamber that has reinforced the coordination and organizational functions relative to the regional chambers, leading to the gradual establishment of the vertical.

If networks, particularly spatial ones, do not break the nomenklatura system, then they grow through it, severely complicating it. The nomenklatura system is extremely centralized and unified; it is not supposed to have roots in the territory, and even less to sprout into it.

The hypertrophic development of networks leads to a fall in the system's efficiency, causing its decay, which provokes an unnatural competition—between networks and clientele, for example, the one that unfolded between the attorney general's office and the Investigative Committee that seceded from it—and leads to negative selection.

Quasi-Political Bureau: Nomenklatura and Elite Vertical

The nomenklatura system is rigidly structured along vertical lines. At the same time, the corporate-network structure is just as characteristic of the elite. In modern Russia, as in the criminal world, with its hard-hierarchical "families," there exist coordination mechanisms at the level of their leaders.

With the state's total control, decisionmaking is relatively simple. In the case of multistructuralism, as right now, there is a need for diversity in conciliatory procedures and mechanisms. Herein lies the weakest point of the current neonomenklatura system. In the era of the Communist Party, formal mechanisms existed, such as the bureau and plenary sessions of the party committees. Today, they have been replaced by mechanisms of informal communication like survey voting, which was actively exercised in the late Brezhnev era.

In recent years, discussions about the need for the existence of a main center that harmonizes the interests of different factions has intensified. Earlier, Olga Kryshtanovskaya compared the security council with the Politburo as if they were Areopagus leaders. This comparison is not entirely correct; because the Soviet Politburo was the apex of the all-powerful Central Committee apparatus and not simply a group of politicians, as is the current status of the security council. However, if we add the bureau of the government to the latter, the decisionmakers in the presidential administration and a few oligarchs—both public and private—then, perhaps, we can say that the nomenklatura elite jointly takes the most important decisions.

According to Evgeny Minchenko, the current "Politburo," like an informal body of collective leadership, includes about three dozen representatives of the administrative, power, and business elites, from which about one-tenth are members of the right and the remaining are candidates (see figure 24.1). In addition, there is the Central Committee, which includes several dozen people who are usually orbiting members and alternate members of the Politburo.[25] This structure lacks functionality. It features not as many managers as it has owners and shareholders, of large corporations, who may or may not manage the affairs on a regular basis but intervene only when it is needed. The managers here are representatives of major shareholders in the government and the presidential administration and operational management.

FIGURE 24.1 *Models of Putin's Elites*

"Solar system"

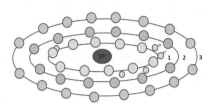

"Politbureau"

1. Inner circle (partners): *Kovalchuk, Rotenberg, Timchenko,* <u>Kudrin</u>, <u>Fursenko</u>, <u>Strzhalkovsky</u>, *Berlusconi, Abramovich,* + <u>Sechin</u> <u>Sobyanin</u>, *Varnig, Litvinenko.*
2. Intermediate circle (junior partners): <u>*Miller*</u>, *Yevtushenkov, Aven, Deripaska,* <u>*Gref*</u>, <u>*Zubkov*</u>, <u>*Yakunin*</u>, <u>*Chemezov*</u>, <u>*Tokarev*</u>, <u>*Chubais*</u>, *Yakovlev.*
3. Outer circle (loyal servants): Gryzlov, Matviyenko, <u>Surkov</u>, <u>Volodin</u>, <u>Kozak</u>, <u>Golikova</u>, <u>V. Ivanov</u>, <u>Serdyukov</u>, <u>Bastrykin</u>, <u>S. Ivanov</u>, <u>Bortnikov</u>, <u>Nurgaliyev</u>.

1. Full members: <u>Putin</u>, <u>Medvedev</u>, <u>Sechin</u>, <u>Kudrin</u>, <u>Naryshkin</u>, <u>Surkov</u>, <u>Sobyanin</u>, *Kovalchuk, Timchenko, Abramovich, Usmanov.*
2. Candidates: vice-premiers and presidential envoys to federal districts, siloviki, heads of state corporations, speakers of the parliament, presidential staff, patriarch.
3. Central Committee members: ministers and governors.

"The Kremlin towers"

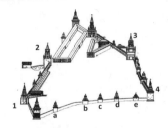

Business-political clans:
Towers: Saint Petersburg's Chekists-1 (Sechin); Saint Petersburg's Chekists-2 (Ivanov-Patrushev); Saint Petersburg's economists (Kudrin); Saint Petersburg's lawyers (Medvedev).
Turrets: Orthodox Chekists (Yakunin), Saint Petersburg's physicists (Kovalchuk), Reiman's group, Voloshin's group, Zolotov-Cherkesov's group.

In italics—private business figures; in underscored italics—state corporations figures; in underscored regular type—state officials

Vladimir Pribylovsky makes an interesting observation that "in contrast to the Politburo of the CPSU, the Politburo of the party of 'Putin's oligarchy' never gets ready together. The members and alternate members of this Politburo engage in decisionmaking through individual meetings with general secretary–first oligarch (vertical), and they issue their recommendations on the basis of clan gatherings (horizontal). This, on a larger scale, resembles the royal council of a feudal monarch rather than the Politburo of a totalitarian general secretary."[26]

In addition to the framework of "Putin's political bureau," which showcases the system's principal shareholders and managers, who participate in the formulation of major decisions, there are other frameworks operating. These frameworks, similarly, reflect the device at the core of Putin's elite, but by using other methodological principles. In one, there is a model of sustainable business and political clans (Kremlin towers), and the other follows a "planetary" model, wherein the elites derive power not through strong ties with each other but by virtue of their position relative to Vladimir Putin, who plays the role of the center of the system.

The Kremlin Towers Model

One of the ways in which the elite space can be structured is by selecting groups based on sustainable business, kinship, career, and other relationships. The model with four or five towers (or entrances) is the most generalized. This is a first-order structure, which can be extended to a more detailed form.

In the framework, the business political clans can be seen and identified with the names of the most influential and powerful emerging figures, as well as dominant corporations. The structure of the clans is composed of figures at various levels of government and business. Almost all the clans have a "Saint Petersburg" affiliation, which reflects contemporary political realities.

Putting the different figures under one roof does not mean that they enjoy close relationships. Dedicated clans have a compound, hierarchical structure, and do not exclude internal competition or alliances with "external" players. In their time, these associations were classified by Vladimir Pribylovsky in connection with the coalitions around different candidates for the post of a successor in 2008.

The Planetary Model

If one can call the "tower" model genetic because it relies on family and business ties, then the planetary model is more likely a position-functional one. At any given time, some planets revolving around Putin—the center of the system—may form ad hoc groups; but after a while, they can disperse in different directions, and the picture changes.

The first circle of policymakers is made up of those whom Putin trusts, and with whom he regularly meets and discusses problems and plans, and those who develop and implement these business plans. This is "collective Putin."

The second circle is made up of those individuals whose advice Putin takes (or whose opinions he listens to), those whom he can always contact directly to arrange a meeting to ask for help, and get it.

The third circle is made of the "trusted servants," which may drop out of their cages at any given moment, and who, unlike the members of the first two circles, do not enjoy job security.

The planetary system is not static but dynamic in its idiosyncrasy and can be described more in terms of "entry" and "exit" than the transition from one orbit to another. Such transitions almost never occur. There are also two exit options: the honored—the "retirees," with safeguards to protect them (for example, in the case of the former head of presidential administration Alexander Voloshin and the former prime minister Mikhail Fradkov), or the infamous—the "traitors," who are left without any guarantees, as was the case of former prime minister Mikhail Kasyanov and former head of the Federal Drug Control Service Viktor Cherkesov.

It should be noted that these frameworks are not so much alternatives but complements to each other. They complement each other, focusing on the different features and characteristics of the organization of the elite and the various aspects of its operation.

The State Council, its Presidium, and similarly a following commission of the prime minister, provide the framework for interaction between federal and regional elites. United Russia, in the capacities of regional and supraregional structures, is more of a negotiating platform for business-political clans, at both high and low levels, than a vertical structure that permeates all levels. Furthermore, the party is not represented at either the highest or lowest levels. However, these differences do not seem to be fundamental. Even in Soviet times, the verticals were not of equal standing; in addition to the party and secret police, there was a secondary organization. Now the administrative excellence of the Chekist vertical is the foundation, and the party is secondary.

During Soviet times, the nomenklatura system was a hierarchical variant of spatial control over corporate governance. It is roughly the same situation today. In this sense, the state corporation is, on the one hand, replicating successful experiences from the point of view of Gazprom, and, on the other hand, it is reviving the Soviet ministries as the owners of business corporations.

The Heterogeneity of the Elites

Different segments and strata of the elite develop unevenly. For a part of the business elite, dynamism, openness, and a focus on Western standards are fundamental characteristics; by contrast, the security officials are characterized by maximum secrecy; and administrative elites are somewhere in between them. As for the political elite, in recent years they have lost their independence, transforming into essentially business-administrative elites. There is also the phenomenon of natural selection—the quality of business elites is higher; open competition among them is more common, and the criteria for efficiency are better defined.

The notion that the effect of minimizing public policy started a weeding out of the political elites and replacing them with security forces is not entirely precise. The weeding-out, at first, really happened, but then those security officers who took over the positions of administrative—if not political—elites also took over to a large extent the functions of their predecessors who were not from the security forces, including, to some degree, in opposition to their former colleagues, who were law enforcers. The point here is the effect of regeneration, like the earthworm, when the severed body part is restored together with all its functions. Another thing is that in the absence of public policy and because of a paramilitary mentality, with the crossover to a "citizen," the security forces created for themselves a new sphere of behavior from the old. This, in fact, is the essence of a "militocracy."

Within the elite, there are generational differences—not so much of age as of genetics. In recent years, there has been a squeezing out of the current elite (this has particularly affected the governors) who had experience in public political activities. This means, among other things, that the existing elites are less ready for direct dialogue with citizens, and that the restoration of public policy shock and the attrition rate among them is the same as in the late 1980s.

Alongside social elevators, operating within the strata, there are "tracks": business, public administration, and politics (so far wedged out). What is new is not so much individuals' transitions from one track to another but rather the significant increase in the frequency and recurrence of such transitions. There are spillovers between segments and strata, and migration and cross-pollination.

The heterogeneity of the elites in recent years has increased, but this is not the main problem. The problem is multistructuralism and the presence of contradictions between the individual elements and blocks. The three coexisting, fundamentally different systems—the elite, the nomenklatura, and the feudal system of "grant for sustenance" *kormlenie* (whereby senior controlling positions in corporations and the regions are routinely used as a source of self-enrichment)—are pulling in different directions.

The Regional Component

In the 1990s, the Russian regions were essentially closed political systems, and regional officials almost always remained in their regions; if they moved from one position to another, these movements were confined within the borders of their own administrative unit. In the 2000s, the regions "opened up," and this defined the way regional elites were transformed. The mobility of the elites increased, both between the regions and between the regions and Moscow. Relatively autonomous and rooted regional figures have been consistently replaced by Moscow-appointed officials.

Regional elites are no longer autarchic; instead, they have increasingly become a mix of locals and outsiders. This is largely due to the appointment to gubernatorial positions of "carpetbaggers," who commonly bring outsiders to fill in administrative positions. A recent trend has been to infuse "Moscow blood"; large groups of Muscovites arrive in regional administrations, where they work in "shifts" by traveling between the region where they work and Moscow, where their families remain behind.

This is especially true of the political sections of local administrations. Regional elites usually come to dominate when the "alien graft" is incom-

TABLE 24.1   *Key Federal Positions in the Regions of Russia: Ties with the Local Elites and Term of Service in the Region (as of January 1, 2011)*

TIES AND TERM	CONNECTION TO REGION	TERM IN OFFICE
Regional head	3.9	5.1
CFI	3.2	3.6
UVD chief	1.5	3.6
Prosecutor	1.7	3.8
SKR	3.6	2.7
FSB	1.3	2.7
Judge	3.8	8.2
United Russia secretary	4.7	2.5
All positions	2.9	4.1

Note: The degree of connection to the region was measured on a scale from 1 to 5 and averaged across the regions: 1 is a "carpetbagger," an official who had no ties to the region whatsoever; 2 is essentially an outsider having ethnic ties with the region or born there; 3 is an outsider who had worked in the region for some time and has grown some ties; 4 is a "native," a member of the local establishment who had, however, worked in another region before his or her appointment; and 5 is a "native" who made a professional career in the region.

petent, so "locals" join forces to stand up against the "carpetbaggers." If the alien team is good, locals can merge with it. A serious flaw of this system is that outside managers inevitably develop the mentality of temporary workers; because they are not permanently based in the region and have no ties there, their time horizon is shorter than that of the locals.

Table 24.1 illustrates the extent to which federal officials are ingrained in the regional political and executive elites. The table shows that the most embedded among the federal appointees are the secretaries of the board of the United Russia Party; but at the same time, they have the shortest tenure in office, and, perhaps, minimum weight. The regional head, who has the longest tenure in office after the judges, no longer comes from the local elite, and the security forces and law enforcement forces have little to do with the head in general.

There is an expansion of corporate elite organization at the regional level on a spatial basis (here the elite becomes the personnel!), along with the successive "decapitation" of the regional elite, depriving them of their natural leaders—the authoritative figures, representing the interests of all regional elites at the center. Initially, regional heads served in such a capacity. But then, when the heads were appointed, all these positions were increasingly taken over by new figures in the region, and the informal role of the seniors changed to speakers in regional parliaments and mayors of cities. In 2010, with the adoption of the practice of replacing the positions of speakers with the regional secretaries of United Russia's political council, the autonomy, authority, and duration of tenure were significantly reduced. The transition from the system of directly elected mayors of regional capitals to the model of city managers incentivizes the mayors to leave.

As something new appears, something old disappears. Thus, the regional mechanism of "peerage"—which existed during Soviet times, and for some time after that—practically disappeared when the regional head, leaving the post, moved to a higher position in the central apparatus, providing a stronger link between the federal and regional elites. Regarding dismissed regional chiefs, Moscow shows no concern except in the case of a few exceptions—unless someone is sent to the Federation Council, but this is usually nothing more than a part of an "exit package" from the office. Here, in part, operates the mechanism of "grants for sustenance," suggesting that each governor must take care of himself or herself, building a personal fortune during the years of service.

What Next?

In this ten-year time horizon, the systemic contradictions between the elements of the "elite" and the elements of the "nomenklatura" have been amplified, and their peaceful coexistence seems increasingly difficult. The proportions will inevitably vary in either direction. Given the recent shifts, the elements of the nomenklatura will, perhaps, prevail. This is a dissolution of choices—first gubernatorial, and now mayoral; a revival of mechanisms of horizontal rotation of most federal agencies' heads in the regions; and in full measure a revival of the nomenklatura's system of personnel reserves.

Transformation into an elite is promoted, perhaps, only by nepotism and a mechanism of inheritance through a capitalization of the position of authority with subsequent handover of the capital to one's relatives and removal of the capital from under the system's control. However, even one of these may be sufficient to destroy the system from within. The resulting dynamics are determined by several key factors and processes:

1. increasing the possibility of resolving the contradictions and conflicts, primarily those of a generational nature, and similarly those that exist between the three main factions of security officials, and public-administrative and business elites;
2. the ability of the system's mechanisms, including the regeneration of the elite bloc to improve itself in order to survive;
3. the ongoing de-Sovietization—psychological in their heads, as well as across institutions.

Let us consider three important factors in greater detail. The first factor is generational conflict between those who came in earnest and the chief fathers and their grown-up children, who have been around for a long time, which can develop in three ways: (1) the "lost generation" phenomenon, whereby under the circumstances of a free migrational deflux, a lost generation can become much more serious and have a lasting effect; (2) a complete (revolutionary) replacement of fathers by children; and (3) a partial replacement of fathers by children.

The situation is worse with conflict between factions; the dominance of the faction security officials (and within them, that of the Chekists) within the nomenklatura system cannot be abolished in an evolutionary way, and this eventually will lead to its demise. However, if the nomenklatura will be transformed into the elite, the system can outgrow this defect, even if the process is not painless.

The second factor is that the system will need to build a regeneration mechanism, including the recruitment, training, and dismissing of staff members. Right now, this is the weakest aspect, because there are no normal elections as an external and public mechanism of competition. Those mechanisms that are implemented are experimental: The personnel reserve and, working with it, the quasi-primaries of United Russia and Nashi are far from efficient, even in a simple and direct way. Meanwhile, the gradual degradation of the Soviet educational infrastructure will at some point lead to its complete collapse, finally depriving the system of human resources.

The current elite will undergo further degeneration. Its replacement, and a significant upgrade, seems inevitable. A voluntary upgrade would be preferable, for it will provide an element of continuity and training.

And the third factor is that, in ten years, there will be a natural renewal of the elite. In 2020, 30 years after the collapse of the Soviet Union, almost no one will be left of those who formed or got into the elite in the Soviet era. However, because the Soviet mechanism has not been removed and remains in effect, there is, on the one hand, the regeneration of the elements of the nomenklatura's consciousness, and, on the other hand, a loss of self-defense instincts, which have survived in those who grew up in the USSR.

What will the situation look like in the inertial scenario? It should be noted that inertia does not mean the preservation of the current system's parameters but their rapid deterioration. This process involves a decline in quality because of a lack of competitive mechanisms, and this can lead to adverse selection and degradation, along with a progressive erosion of the most active and independent parts of the citizenry abroad. Consequently, the inertial development represents the expansion of the corporate-network mechanisms of recruiting (for example, the expansion of "people from Saint Petersburg" and the "Chekists") at the expense of all others; and thus archaism, along with tribalism, nepotism, and loyalty, will be given priority over efficiency.

Among the positive trends, one can speak of interspersion—both corporate, between the civil-administrative and business elites; and spatial, between the different regions of the country.

In general, this leads to a significant decrease in the quality of the elites and in their effectiveness.

The counter-elite will also weaken because if there is no regular alternation of the elites in power, they are marginalized. Moreover, in the absence of an outside flow into the elite, its ability to regenerate itself shrinks.

The weakness of competition between the elite and the marginalized counter-elite is the main problem for the system. The current elites are threatened not by their opponents but by degradation—in their own generation and that of their children, with the possibility of losing power because of its inefficient use. Due to the lack of public competition and inbreeding, degradation "naturally" increases adverse selection. There is also a mirror image problem; if the existing elite does not meet its aims noncompetitively, then it prevents the promotion of more deserving candidates. The negative effect is twofold: Society's potential as a whole is still not fully realized, and the most active and enterprising elites get frustrated and leave the country.

The coming together of all these problems and internal contradictions in the inertial scenario may lead to a collapse.

How to Influence the System's Development?

The personnel bloc of the political system cannot survive in its present form, and is certainly not capable of living for another ten years. A hybrid of the nomenklatura and elites, and its underlying foundations, is not viable even in the medium term; one way or the other, it will end up in a heap of scrap.

There are two main options:

1. Remove the surviving parts of the nomenklatura system.
2. Bring it up to a level where it has the ability to regenerate itself, and subordinate the interests of the whole system.

It always boils down to the control unit, either externally, and governmentally, to strengthen the nomenklatura system; or as an intra-elitist function, to strengthen the elite system.

The workings of the nomenklatura system are ineffective but still quite apparently functional. If one tries to keep this system, one must equip it with the mechanisms of external cleansing, without which it is doomed to rapid degradation. But neither elites nor leaders are willing to do this— there is no political will or resources. Palliative measures taken by, say, the introduction of elements of an artificial competition, whether qualification requirements for the transition to a certain level or optional primaries, cannot fully solve the problem. Similarly, the problem cannot be solved by substituting elections by sociological surveys—the latter can only delay the degradation. Without destroying the nomenklatura system, transition to a system of public competition is impossible. For a shake-up and to maintain a constant shape, it is necessary to hold elections and separate powers.

To improve the quality of the elite and its level of professionalism, it is not enough to stop the practice of adding power elites to administrative elites; it is also essential to make the business elite the most dynamic and advanced. There should be an increase in the flow of civilians toward joining power structures, as is the case with the Ministry of Defense.

It is necessary to strengthen the elements of corporatism and regionalism combined with public openness, such as officers' assemblies, boards of judges, a lawyers' association, and an association of civil servants. Corporate responsibility with its supporting institutions should be developed, including courts of honor, reputation, corporate titles, and marks of distinction. A person's position in the system should not be fully contingent on his or her formal position; to this end, other frameworks—both corporate and territorial—should be created. A number of social networks—of fellow students, members of professional corporations, and the like—may be developed beyond the virtual realms. These measures can help regenerate the social fabric, which is extremely thin right now.

It is necessary to strengthen the autonomy of the elite's individual members, to eliminate their dependence on a superior system with the help of qualifying examinations as a basis for promotion. Standard terms of office tenure and rotation should be clearly worked out. It is essential to restore and expand the elements of eligibility, including direct elections for various positions on the basis of the citizens' will, as well as free indirect elections.

Particular attention should be paid to education and training. The creation and maintenance of traditions, including family and official ties, will need to follow.[27] Figuratively speaking, it is necessary to introduce a high inheritance tax regime, making everything official and pulling the system out of the shadows. There is a need to develop and implement a fundamentally different system of motivation and incentives, both positive and negative.

Finally, a member of the elite is a product of the system, and an important factor determining its work. You can seat any person you like behind the wheel of a primitive Soviet Lada—even Schumacher—but it is hardly reasonable to expect that he or she will win the race. Changes in the elite system must occur simultaneously with changes in the system of political mechanics. At the same time, one must ensure that both systems become capable of self-development.

Notes

1. Here and later we will focus mainly on the administrative elite.

2. In his time, P. Kropotkin suggested the use of this referring to power elites in general. Here I focus on the fact that a person's sense of belonging to the elite is defined by factors that are external—positions that are given and those that can be eliminated.

3. In September 2005, the head of the House of Romanov, Grand Duchess Maria Vladimirovna, accepted a request for confirmation of Vladimir Strzhalkovsky's hereditary nobility, and the hereditary nobility of his sister and her son Eugene (at the same time nobility was granted to a few more people from the KGB/FSB—in particular, the director of the FSB, Nikolai Patrushev; the former director of the Federal Security Service, Sergei Stepashin; and the nobility of the widow and daughters of Anatoly Sobchak was also confirmed. Ironically, it was Patrushev, congratulating the staff, saying it was the day of the FSB Chekists, who addressed them as the "new nobility." Andrei Soldatov and Irina Borogan drew on this term to name their new book on the FSB; see Andrei Soldatov and Irina Borogan, *The New Nobility: Essays in the History of the FSB*, authorized English translation (Moscow: OOO United Press, 2011), 298; and Andrei Soldatov and Irina Borogan, *The New Nobility: The Restoration of Russia's Security State and the Enduring Legacy of the KGB* (New York: PublicAffairs, 2010).

4. It should be noted that different parts of the old nomenklatura system have been changed to varying degrees in these years. At least, these changes have affected more private police, and especially the FSB, which in part served in the role of "sanctuaries" that have retained the nomenklatura mechanisms and rules even in the times of change and have subsequently contributed to their restoration in other areas.

5. See, for example, M. S. Voslensky, *Nomenklatura: The Ruling Class of the Soviet Union* (Moscow: Sovetskaya Rossiya in cooperation with October, 1991).

6. There have always been a few verticals; the main one in the Soviet system was the party, now it is the FSB tower.

7. For example, in connection with the 1969 appointment of the chairman of the KGB in Azerbaijan, Heydar Aliyev, to the post of first secretary, in just three years 2000 (!) KGB officers were appointed to senior positions in the country. From the display name of the individual elements of the system to the system itself, it has not changed and even corruption, which was being fought against, very soon exceeded the previous level. Ilya Zemtsov, *The Party or Mafia? (An Embezzled Republic)* (Paris: Les Editeurs Reunis, 1976).

8. In 1921, a draft of the plan booklet "On the Political Strategy and Tactics of the Russian Communists" (first printed in 1952), Stalin gave his definition of the party: "The Communist Party is a kind of 'Order of the Sword' in the Soviet State, and it directs the organs of the latter and inspires their activities."

9. According to the explanations of the head of the Russian presidential administration, Sergey Naryshkin, the administration along with Vladislav Surkov identified about two hundred experts—respectable people, whose names, however, were not made public. Everything was absolutely nonpublic. Each of these experts has compiled a list of those

whom he or she deems most worthy. And then the president's administration compiled these lists together with the stated purpose of forming the "presidential thousand." At the beginning, a hundred of the most positive and attractive people were selected, and it was announced that it was the "personnel reserve" of the president. All 1,000 people did not manage this, but at the end of 2009 a new list with an additional 5,000 names emerged. Some from this "reserve" were entrusted with tasks (training courses, holding various meetings with senior government officials, discussions). Later, however, it came down to a formal report regarding the appointment and career advancement of people from these numbers.

10. Sergey Sobyanin's interview in *Echo Moskvi*, March 16, 2011, www.echo.msk.ru/programs/beseda/750466-echo.

11. This refers to the former governor of Irkutsk Alexander Tishanin (2005–2008), the brother-in-law of Vladimir Yakunin (now in the administration of Russian Railways), and Alexei Kuzmitsky (2007–2011), the former governor of Kamchatka (2007–2011), who according to several publications is a relative of Viktor Ivanov, and Nikolai Kolesov of Amur (2007–2008), who landed in the business "Rostexnologii."

12. Sergei Dubik is the head of the Russian presidential administration on civil service and personnel, and his brother Nikolai Dubik, a university classmate of Igor Shuvalov, is the head of the Legal Department of Gazprom and the CEO of RosUkrE.

13. Anatoly Turchak has engaged in judo with Vladimir Putin, and is the president of the holding company "!Leninist" and the head of the CSE in Saint Petersburg; Andrei Turchak is a former leader of the "Young Guard" of the United Russia Party and the governor of the Pskov Region.

14. Yuri Vorobyov is the former deputy crisis situations minister, and the vice speaker of the northern fleet; his son Andrei Vorobyov is the chairman of the United Russia Party's central executive committee.

15. Arkady Rotenberg has engaged in judo with Vladimir Putin and is the former CEO of the sports club "Yanvar-Neva," in which capacity he was appointed by Vladimir Putin and Gennady Timchenko; he is also the owner of Stroygazmontazh, which works on a contract from Gazprom; his brother Roman Rotenberg is a businessman, co-owner of the bank "Severnoi morskoi put'" and vice president of the Russian Judo Federation; finally, Arkady Rotenberg's son Igor is the director of the Department of Assets of Russian Railways, and Roman Rotenberg's son Boris is a senior manager of Gazpromexport.

16. At the federal level, it is, perhaps, only V. Zorkin and S. Stepashin.

17. With respect to "new power" being like "new money," could one also say "nouveau riche—nouveau pauvre"?

18. This is the telling story of businessman Matthew Urin, whose guards in November 2010 in Rublevka beat up a driver cutting off his car, apparently in connection with Gazprom, and rumor has it, that this was in connection with Prime Minister Vladimir Putin's family. His and his guards' arrest was followed by a review of licenses not only for the agency's security guards but also in five of Urin's banks, where they found serious violations.

19. This includes Minister of Justice Vladimir Kovalev (dismissed in 1997), Prosecutor General Yuri Skuratov (1999), Prime Minister Mikhail Kasyanov (2004), and Moscow mayor Yuri Luzhkov (2010)—each of whom is in violation of corporate rules and is being prosecuted.

20. Last year produced many examples of this kind, including the cases of the Kushchevskaya village, Gus Crystal, Engels, and Astrakhan.

21. One can count Vyacheslav Volodin, the brothers Boris and Basil Yakimenko, Alexei Chesnakov, Valery Fedorov, Alexei Chadayev, and Vitaly Ivanov. And this list could easily be expanded.

22. The younger son of Deputy Prime Minister Sergei Ivanov is deputy chairman of the board of Gazprombank, the elder son—Alexander—is a director at Vnesheconombank; Peter Fradkov—son of a former prime minister—also works at Vnesheconombank; the son of FSB director Bortnikov is the chairman of the board of directors at "VTB North-West"; the son of Valentina Matvienko, Sergey Matvienko, was vice president of Vneshtorgbank and vice president and part owner of the Saint Petersburg Bank (until July 2010); the son of N. Patrushev, Dmitry Patrushev, was at Rosselxozbank; the son of Yuri Kovalchuk, Boris Kovalchuk, is chairman of the board of directors at "INTER RAO UES"; Murov's son, Andrey Murov, is the CEO of Pulkovo airport; and the son of Yakunin, Andrei Yakunin, is the head of the investment company Venture Investments & Yield Management. Direct inheritance from the transfer of post from father to son, and the distribution of leadership positions to families/clans, still occurs only in the Caucasus.

23. An excellent example of a project, all the members of which have become significant public figures and businessmen, is the case of the corporate "Ozero"; the list of its founders includes Vladimir Putin, Sergei A. Fursenko, Vladimir Yakunin, and Y. Kovalchuk.

24. See, for example, Olga Kryshtanovskaya and Stephen White, "Putin's Militocracy," *Post-Soviet Affairs* 19, no. 4 (October–December 2003): 289–306.

25. See "Politolog: V rossiiskom rukovodstve est 'politbyuro' i 'TSK'" (Political Scientist: There is a "Politbureau" and "Central Committee" in the Current Russian leadership), event summary, December 12, 2010, www.rosbalt.ru/moscow/2010/12/09/799055.html.

26. See Yevgeny Minchenko, "Pribylovskiy pro Politbyuro" (Pribylovskiy about the Politbureau), personal blog, December 10, 2011, http://minchenko.ru/blog/ruspolitics/2010/12/10/ruspolitics_474.html.

27. Interestingly, in most of the ministries, departments, and regional administrations, there has recently appeared a trend of putting together a portrait gallery of the different managers, dating back in history to Catherine the Great's time. Although this is nothing more than following fashion, the managers' projected association with historical figures promotes a sense of dignity and responsibility.

the EVOLUTION *of* CIVIC ACTIVENESS

Jens Siegert

*We admire the finished and complete, and undervalue what is still
in the process of formation.*

—Friedrich Nietzsche[1]

Only an increasingly closed political system that goes as far as actual political repression would be able to stop the continued development of civil
society in Russia. Such a scenario cannot be completely ruled out at the
moment, but it is not very probable.

The constitutional right to freedom of association is one of the big differences between the current Russian regime and the Soviet regime, even
if, in practice, this right is severely constrained by the authorities. This
concerns political parties above all, but also applies to civil society organizations, of which there are now several hundred thousand. These autonomous organizations, which are independent from the state, are examined
in this chapter as constituting the main component of civil society.

As most scholars, politicians, and experts use it, the term "civil society" refers to a social partnership between individuals and families on
the one hand, and the state on the other. The term refers to people who
have voluntarily formed an association to carry out together socially useful activity or philanthropic work. This definition of civil society excludes
organizations carrying out economic activity with the purpose of drawing

profits. This definition also places no importance on the institutional forms these organizations take. They do not have to have an official legal status and can operate without having the state's approval. The underlying principle of civil society is that it be voluntary, autonomous from the state authorities, and without a fixed organizational structure; its composition is always in the process of change, and this is what gives it such diversity.

Civil society actors and nonstate organizations are an essential part of the political system because they notice and identify problems in society earlier than do the state authorities (if the latter even become aware at all). Simplifying somewhat, one can divide civil society actors into three main groups:

- Nongovernmental organizations (NGOs) operating in the space between the state and society, that is, playing an intermediary role.
- Groups involved in building up social capital; this includes self-help groups, veterans' associations, cultural groups, sports clubs, and so on, as well as Christian bodies and other religious groups (which represent a specific case by virtue of the particular relations they have with the state authorities).
- Nongovernmental charitable organizations, such as cooperatives and church organizations providing social assistance. This category also includes the Red Cross, in particular.

In theory, all these organizations are parts of civil society, but such a broad definition is impractical for the purposes of making a more detailed analysis of relations between the state and civil society. In this chapter, therefore, I concentrate on the first group—that is, the organizations that perform an intermediary function between the state authorities and society, which are usually referred to as NGOs.

The areas in which NGOs work can be called the focus of civil society activeness. The public's involvement in NGOs' activities—their desire and need to act in the public good—makes it possible to say that NGOs are the bearers of a new political culture. In cases where the public recognizes that NGOs' activities are genuinely useful for society, this can give rise to legitimate new forms of social and political interaction.

Civil society organizations help to establish trust between public actors. Trust is an ephemeral factor that reduces the transaction costs and facilitates the diversity of public structures and relations in society. In today's increasingly complex societies, trust is becoming increasingly important. Today, neither the state authorities nor public groups, and even more so individuals, can foresee all the consequences and ensuing risks that their actions could have. Therefore, to be able to act in the public sphere, they all need to trust their own and others' professional judgment. Trust is therefore the "lubricant" for public progress, above all economic progress. Without this lubricant the wheels turn more slowly, action is less effective, and there is a constant threat of breakdown.

This is why in modern societies, whether in the private or public sphere, coercion (or the framework providing for it) is being increasingly replaced by trust as the prime resource for managing and resolving conflicts. However, going against this trend, Russian society is dominated by an atmosphere of complete distrust on all sides. This distrust is directed primarily against the state authorities and economic actors, but it also extends to public organizations. Paradoxically, this mistrustful attitude is often linked to the altruistic principles that underlie social and political efforts.

NGOs in Russia

The development of Russian civil society can be divided into an initial phase, three subsequent development phases in the 1990s and 2000s, and an interim period. Here, I first briefly describe each phase's main features, and then on their basis I propose possible development scenarios for the future.

The First Phase: Perestroika and the End of the USSR

In theory, real and effective democracy needs a full-fledged civil society. This is a normative hypothesis and an empirical observation—vice versa would be a decreasing sense of common spirit, embodied in public initiatives, that poses a threat to democracy. Western democracies have been expressing fears for quite some time now that people's desire and need to act in the common good could decrease, which would eventually weaken democracy. This has given rise to discussions on how to support public activeness in modern societies that are becoming ever more individualistic and focused on individual consumption.

In modern Russia, as in other postauthoritarian societies, the problem is even more complicated: There is either no tradition of civic activeness at all, or it has been kept suppressed for a long time. The question is thus not one of preventing a decrease in civic activity or trying to stimulate its development, but above all of making this kind of activity legitimate and attractive in the eyes of the public. At the same time, one should not forget that, paradoxically, it was in Eastern Europe that the concept of "civil society" reemerged.[2] This concept was closely linked to the gradual erosion of that region's communist regimes starting in the 1970s and to the emergence of internal "civil" and nonviolent resistance in its countries.

Formally speaking, public organizations also existed in the Soviet Union, but of course they were not independent from the state. Though outwardly similar to public organizations in other countries, they did not and could not perform the functions described above. The Soviet authorities kept strict control of civil, or rather, social activeness. Independent activity was prohibited, but what is prohibited exists nevertheless—otherwise, why prohibit it in the first place? The post-Stalin USSR, for example, saw the emergence of autonomous spaces, small at first, but gradually growing bigger. The most prominent dissidents were the predecessors of today's civic activists. But these spaces were concentrated in the cultural sphere, in the well-known kitchen discussions, for example. One can also include here the informal groups involved in environmental protection.

Soviet society started opening under Mikhail Gorbachev, slowly at first, but then picking up the pace until it became a great rush. A huge number of organizations not controlled by the state emerged. By the fall of 1990, according to estimates given by *Pravda*, the Soviet Union had more than 11,000 organizations that were independent from the state authorities.

Rise and Fall Under Yeltsin

Many civic activists were already carrying out intermediary functions between the state authorities and society before the Soviet Union's collapse.

In 1989, many activists were elected to the Congress of People's Deputies and became members of the Supreme Soviet or were given government posts. Many of these first NGOs gave their backing to Boris Yeltsin, thus placing their hopes on the more democratically minded part of the Soviet nomenklatura. This was a coalition similar to those that took shape in many postcommunist countries at the early stage of transformation. Later, these coalitions often became problematic, not so much for the old elite as for the new democrats.

This new union turned out to not be very durable in the young Russian Federation as well. Its collapse was brought on by three events: the constitutional showdown in the autumn of 1993, the first Chechen war, and the 1996 presidential election.

In 1993, after the Supreme Soviet was dissolved with the help of tanks, a new Constitution was adopted following a referendum, and it served as the foundation for electing post-Soviet Russia's first State Duma. These events, which are still the subject of much debate, had far-reaching consequences because many people in Russia did not see the new Constitution as legitimate. As a result of Yeltsin's "undemocratic" actions, members of the liberal camp, often also referred to as the "democratic" camp, along with NGOs, do not have much support in Russian society and are often accused of having double standards.

The first Chechen war, launched in December 1994 on Yeltsin's decision, further worsened relations between the Kremlin and the NGOs. Right from the start, human rights groups were harsh in their criticism of the bloody war, with its accompanying mass human rights violations and aims that remained unclear to the Russian public. The 1996 presidential elections saw the divided allies—the NGOs and the Kremlin—close ranks once again against the estimated threat of a communist return to power.

Many NGOs supported Yeltsin in the election only to keep votes from going to the Communist Party candidate, Gennady Zyuganov, who, according to the polls in the spring of 1996, stood a real chance of victory. This alliance also included a small group of big businesspeople and bankers, who financed Yeltsin's campaign in return for new opportunities for enrichment—in particular, by buying from the state's large reserves of oil, gas, and other raw materials at rigged auctions with bargain prices. These were the members of the group who became known as the oligarchs, and in the public mind they became closely associated with—and at the same time compromised—the ideas of democracy and freedom that most of the NGOs promoted.

The 1996 presidential election sparked debate within some of the NGOs about their attitude toward the political parties and Yeltsin's presidential administration, which called itself democratic. Particularly fierce debate took place within Memorial, one of the country's biggest human rights organizations, which strongly criticized the first Chechen war. Stormy debate went on over whether the danger of a communist return to power was sufficient justification for calls to support Yeltsin, despite the bloody and unjust war in Chechnya. Most of the organization's staff and activists opposed supporting Yeltsin, but said they should call the public's attention to the danger that a communist victory represented. Some of Memorial's members, who did not wish to support a president who was waging war in Chechnya, left the organization. The debate was the first time that Russia's NGOs found themselves facing the challenge of how to maintain the independence they needed while at the same time reconciling their moral principles with political expediency.

The 1996 presidential election, especially the alliance between the political authorities and big business that it produced, had a great influence on how Russians viewed democracy in general and NGOs in particular. The memory of these events plays a big part in shaping public opinion to this day, above all because fundamental democratic principles were violated in the name of protecting democracy and preventing a communist victory.

Two years later, in August 1998, this Russian government, which claimed to be democratic, ended up insolvent and declared a partial default. This reinforced in many people's minds the idea, which persists to this day, that the supposedly democratic regime that governed them was really just a dressed up form of authoritarian, economically incompetent, and socially unjust government. The narrow "specialization" of the country's NGOs added to this perception. In the 1990s, practically no influential NGOs focused on economic and social issues. The exceptions were organizations such as the Russian Confederation of Consumers' Societies, which attempted to reach an agreement with the government to compensate people for their savings that had lost their value as a result of the 1998 default, but they were little noticed by the general public. Perhaps this was partly a result of the legacy left by Soviet propaganda, which presented social justice and political freedom in either/or terms.

The result was that by the end of the decade, relations had soured between the state authorities and the NGOs. NGOs have less need to reconcile moral principles and realpolitik compromises than do actual politicians. After all, their influence is determined not by high office and the state's backing but by an overall good reputation in society and having the public's trust, and these are things that are hard to win and easy to lose. During the last period of Yeltsin's presidency, the state authorities and the NGOs mutually ignored each other.

Russia saw the emergence in the 1990s of quite a few NGOs that won recognition at national and international levels (primarily environmental and human rights organizations), but the number of people taking part in their work remained much smaller than in Western countries. There are three reasons for this. First, public involvement depends on the level of economic prosperity, and Russia in the 1990s had undergone a disastrous economic decline. Second, the Soviet practice of imitating civic activeness by "mobilizing" the public to take part in activity organized from above still made its legacy felt and was one of the reasons explaining the public apathy of much of the population. The third reason had its roots in the tradition of informal self-help networks of friends and family that operated in areas for the most part outside the state's reach. There was no need to establish NGOs to keep this tradition going, and indeed it was these informal networks that helped people survive in the 1990s.

Putin's First Term: Reining In the NGOs

By the time Vladimir Putin became president, Russia's NGOs had largely shaken off the state's pressure, but this situation did not last long. After his arrival in power, Putin began systematic efforts to bring under the Kremlin's control sections of the Russian public political sphere that had previously functioned perhaps not entirely autonomously but had at least been controlled by various power centers rather than a single center. Civil society actors also became a focus of this new campaign.

At the end of 1999, in Putin's political program article titled "Russia at the Threshold of the New Millennium," one of the demands he listed was "the creation of conditions facilitating development in Russia of a full-fledged civil society to balance and keep watch on the authorities."[3] He declared this an essential condition for building a "strong state," noting that "one of the main priorities is to build a partnership between the executive authorities and civil society." He also made other statements praising democracy and civil society. But after coming to power, it was this same Putin who made the first attempts to bring the NGOs to heel or impose corporate dependency on them. The more prominent among the NGOs responded by establishing regional and supraregional coalitions, the most well known of which was the People's Assembly, made up of mostly Moscow-based NGOs such as Memorial, the Moscow Helsinki Group, the Foundation for the Defense of Glasnost, and the Social and Environmental Union. During the first part of Putin's first term, the Kremlin recognized some of the leaders of these NGOs as negotiation partners.

The first serious attempt to bring the independent NGOs under state control, as part of the so-called managed democracy policy, came with the convocation of the Civic Assembly, which had been initiated by the Kremlin in 2001. NGOs that were deemed "unconstructive" from the Kremlin's point of view were excluded from this project from the start. But the attempt to establish a "civil society representative office" under state control did not succeed. In the summer of 2001, the People's Assembly was brought in to take part in organizing the Civic Forum, apparently not so much because of the influence of the NGOs themselves as of a decision from within the presidential administration and motivated by internal struggles inside the Kremlin.

The Civic Forum was organized at the end of November 2001. The forum was the state authorities' idea, but the participants included about 3,000 representatives of NGOs and 1,500 journalists and guests from throughout the whole country. They discussed more than 20 different subjects at the Kremlin, from armed forces reform and refugees to environmental protection policy. State and NGO representatives agreed to establish "platforms for communication" on each issue, but most of these plans never actually saw the light of day.

At the start of the decade, the government and the NGOs held talks and discussions on new tax legislation, because earlier laws had removed the differences between "commercial" and "noncommercial" organizations and treated commercial organizations and NGOs the same way. The talks brought no result, however, and the Tax Code entered into force at the start of 2002. The peace that the Kremlin and the NGOs concluded at the Civic Forum lasted until the end of the fall of 2003. Two events put cracks in it: the arrest of businessman Mikhail Khodorkovsky, and the change of power in Ukraine following mass public protests.

Khodorkovsky used the Open Russia Foundation that he had established to provide large-scale financing to NGO projects without seeking the Kremlin's approval on who or what to finance. His arrest marked a particularly clear political turning point, as one can see today, and dashed NGOs' hopes for long-term and stable financing from internal Russian sources, because it was perceived as a clear signal to all other potential domestic grantmakers not to donate to independent NGOs. On May 26, 2004, Putin said in his Annual Address to the Federal Assembly that "thousands of civil groups and associations exist and work constructively in Russia, but far from all of them are focused on protecting people's real interests. For some of them, the main priority is to get grants from prominent foreign funds, while the objective of others is to serve dubious group and commercial interests, and meanwhile, the country and its people's biggest problems go unnoticed."[4]

On November 21, 2007, making his main speech before the State Duma election, Putin expressed his views in even harsher terms:

> Some oppose us and do not want us to carry out our plans because they have completely different goals and a different vision of Russia's future. They need a weak and ailing state, a disorganized, disoriented and divided society, in order to do their deals behind its back and reap dividends at our expense. Sadly, there are some in our country who feed like jackals off foreign embassies and diplomatic missions, hoping for the support of foreign funds and governments rather than that of their own people."[5]

Most members of the Russian ruling elite saw the toppling of Ukraine's government as a defeat for the West and a failure of Russia's policy. As the Kremlin saw it, NGOs supported by Western donors had played a big part in the Ukrainian events.

Despite the rising tension, relations between the state and the NGOs retained a degree of ambiguity for a while longer, and in some cases civil society organizations developed working relationships with the authorities, above all with regional administrations, but sometimes also with central government agencies. The presidential administration's actions were tactically motivated, however. The Kremlin saw in NGOs a potential political threat, but at the same time had to find a way of working together with them, given that the Putin government's main priority was to pull Russia out of its crisis and restore it to a status worthy of a great power. The economic modernization that was much touted at the start and middle of Putin's time in office, at the rhetorical level in any event, would be possible only with civil society's active participation.

The Russian elite's difficulty was how to strike a balance between providing the economic freedom needed for effective development while at the same time preventing this freedom from spreading to political and public life. Efforts concentrated at first mostly on restricting political freedom, preventing political competition, and ensuring that the ruling group kept its monopoly hold on power. But it is harder to restrict civil society's activeness. The question is where one draws the line between civil society activity and politics—that is, which kind of activity to allow, and which to prohibit. There is no "natural" border between the two. Any kind of public and civic activeness also has a political dimension. Civil society's diversity, lack of clear organizational structure, constantly changing nature, and wide range of forms and activities all further complicate the situation.

In the end, the state actors chose the "hands-on management" method as their means of establishing control over civil society. This choice comes with the risk that the authorities will be tempted to turn the screws ever tighter. But at the same time, paradoxically, it weakens possibilities for control—or deviates more and more often from its original aims. The result is that there is either "too much" control, with independent civil society groups coming under too much pressure from above and thus unable to modernize, or "too little" control, with civil society actors slipping free of state oversight and becoming a threat to the political regime.

Putin's Second Term: Controlled Civil Society

Despite not yet having put down deep roots and not having broad-based public support, Russian civil society nonetheless showed itself capable of putting up substantial resistance during Putin's first term. There are four reasons for this.

First, increasing control over political life and control of the mass media left the Kremlin facing a lack of information about the situation in the country. The coalition of NGOs provided an effective information channel without being a political alternative to the government, which thus did not perceive it as a threat.

Second, the NGOs focused on areas that had been left largely forgotten after the old Soviet system collapsed. The new Russian government had not yet brought these areas back under its own wing. This concerned work with the elderly, former political prisoners and their families, drug addicts, and so on—in other words, areas where there was a need for people to work using nonrepressive methods in the new nonauthoritarian environment. The NGOs had the advantage of being able to help spread modern social work methods, and from this point of view, the state authorities saw possibilities for successful and relatively safe cooperation with the NGOs.

Third, during Putin's first term (right up until 2004), the NGOs managed to take advantage of conflicts within the ruling elite to resolve public problems. Various groups within the ruling elite also used the NGOs as an instrument and—most probably involuntary—ally in their internal power struggles.

And fourth, backed by statements from the West, which criticized restrictions on democratic freedoms and human rights, those NGOs that were independent of the authorities took an open political stance within the country.

Relations between the Kremlin and NGOs soured quickly after the change of power in Ukraine in the winter of 2004–2005. This led directly to the establishment of the state-controlled Public Council at the start of 2006, and also the adoption of the new law on NGOs, which came into force in April that same year. Both initiatives had a considerable negative impact on the environment in which NGOs operated. They also sent society a clear signal that NGOs were under suspicion as a potential source of "danger" for the state. The authorities at every level had what amounted to instructions to increase their criticism of the NGOs, step up control of their activities, and make it harder for them to work. The main purpose of the new law on NGOs was to tighten control, while the Public Council was about delegitimizing the NGOs not represented in it, above all those among them whose activities had political overtones.

The law on NGOs brought under a single set of provisions and reinforced the various instruments through which the state could control NGOs' activities. This led to self-censorship within the NGOs themselves (as yet, there have been no reliable studies on the nature and scale of this self-censorship) and considerably raised the barriers to establishing NGOs. For the time being, the authorities used the new law's provisions less to ban or close down organizations and more as a permanent threat, carrying out numerous checks into their activities and issuing "warnings." After the second warning, the state authorities have the right to close the NGO. The paradoxical response to systematic state pressure has been an increase in the number of informal organizations not officially registered by the state, although there are no exact figures on this count.

The establishment of the Public Council, in which state-approved "civil society representatives" represent civil society in general, produced contradictory results. The attempt to use the Public Council as a means to delegitimize independent NGOs not represented on the council has not produced the hoped-for results with the Russian public, and has not gone down well with foreign observers.

The loyal NGOs represented on the Public Council receive quite generous funding from the state; but to justify their "civil society" status and not just become another branch of state power, they must try at least to do some "real" work and use the state's funds to address people's problems or at least act on behalf of the public to bring these problems to the authorities' attention. This makes the Public Council more difficult to manage, and at the same time helps to strengthen NGOs' legitimacy, including that of those NGOs that are critical of the authorities. The Public Council has thus to some extent produced the opposite result to that desired in that its work has legitimized civil society activity, albeit if under state control.

The increased control over political life, especially over the political party system, and the almost complete lack of political space free of the

Kremlin's control have turned Russian NGOs into a sort of surrogate for opposition political parties. In a number of cases (this situation continues today), they have found themselves playing the part of the opposition, of a channel for communication between the political elite and society, and of the voice of particular interests.

This situation has created a type of NGO in Russia that is practically unknown in developed democracies—organizations acting as mediators between the state authorities and the public. Some of these communication channels have been given institutional form—for example, the Presidential Human Rights Commission, which was set up in 2002 with Ella Pamfilova as chairwoman. In 2004, the commission was reorganized as the Presidential Council for Developing Institutions of the Civil Society and of Human Rights. Up until the end of Putin's presidency, the council's members included a number of people from influential opposition NGOs.

The Interim Period: Medvedev's Modernization Rhetoric

In February 2009, almost a year after he became president, Dmitri Medvedev approved a renewed list of members for Pamfilova's Presidential Council, almost half of whom were now people known for their uncompromising criticism of the Kremlin. These appointments were seen at that moment as a "liberal signal" from Medvedev. With the council's help, some of the provisions in the 2006 law on NGOs that had been particularly hampering the work of small NGOs were amended, and some efforts were made to reduce the red tape making it hard to establish new NGOs. Pamfilova stepped down as the council's chairwoman in the summer of 2010. The circumstances surrounding the appointment of her successor, Mikhail Fedotov, showed that the Kremlin still wanted to maintain contacts with opposition-minded NGOs.

Surveys show that civil society activity is not particularly prestigious in Russia today. But at the same time, an as yet diffuse sense of discontent is growing in society as people become sick of slow-moving reform, corruption, bureaucratic arbitrariness, and the Kremlin's monopoly on power. The economic crisis has made problems linked to the political system more visible, and President Medvedev has responded by proposing a renewed version of modernization rhetoric reminiscent of that heard during Putin's first term.

Democratic and legal traditions vary from one country to another, but the growing influence of civil society is a general trend. In England, the landowning gentry's struggle against the crown for its rights, above all property rights, led to the development of the rule of law. In Germany, the movement to unite small principalities into a larger whole saw the emergence of the burghers as a group in society, and this development also ultimately led to the emergence of the rule of law with a unified state administration at its head. In both cases, however, the desire of new economically active groups in society to establish common rules limiting, in particular, the state's powers, also played a crucial role.

Russia's development in this respect is closer to the German model, but with the difference that the most active participants in the Russian rent-based economy play a subordinate role. New forms of civic activeness have emerged in many areas, but most people, if they are willing at all to get involved, only do so with respect to issues that concern them personally. In other words, their actions are a response to interference in their private lives: Car owners protest against the traffic police's arbitrariness; and local residents protest against speculative real estate deals, ever denser construction in cities, or, as in Khimki, the destruction of a forest that had been a recreation area for the residents. The number of public movements of this kind has increased in the last couple of years—2009 saw protests against higher duties on imported secondhand cars in the Far East; 2010 saw more than 10,000 people in Kaliningrad protest against the state's social policy, and in Moscow there were meetings against the arbitrary construction and the thoughtless demolition of architectural monuments. And not just small limited-scale public groups got involved in these protest movements; they also mobilized the small circle of people principally opposed to an authoritarian state.

At the same time, most Russians do not support the people demonstrating in defense of Article 31 of the Russian Constitution and do not approve of Russian liberals' and Western observers' heightened attention to violations of these activists' rights. Nevertheless, the atmosphere among NGOs had become unsettled by the middle of Medvedev's presidential term, and there was a growing sense in their midst that change was ahead—only what kind of change, and who would be its agent?

The answer comes to some extent in the development of protest movements during recent years. Some of these initiatives have been at least partially successful. In some cases, protests have drawn attention beyond the specific region where they take place, and in a number of instances when the organizers have managed to expand the social base, they have forced the state authorities into a compromise. Protests by small groups of environmentalists—for example, against plans to lay the East Siberian–Pacific Ocean oil pipeline to the north of Lake Baikal—got the general public's attention, in this case because of Baikal's symbolic significance for the whole region. This broad public support forced the Russian leadership into changing the pipeline's route.

There was a similar situation with respect to the construction of the Moscow–Saint Petersburg highway through the Khimki Forest. The public protests in this case took on a political dimension because of the proximity to Moscow, and because the interests of the local people, who would suffer from the forest's destruction, coincided with the interests of environmentalists and the political opposition. The authorities were forced to respond to the activists and make a number of compromises, even if the decision to build the road through the forest remained in force.

These examples reflect a general strategy: When public tension grows, the authorities take steps to make contact with the public activists and even agree to some concessions. But these concessions are either of a technical nature or simply a means of buying time. Once the tension dies down again, the initial plan goes ahead. At the same time, the authorities generally lose no time in cracking down on political challenges, or anything they perceive as political challenges.

What is interesting is that in both the above-noted cases, the state authorities and the general public perceived the environmental protests as "nonpolitical" and thus legitimate, in spite of the authorities' effective ban on political activity. As long as environmentalists do not cross the line of what the authorities consider potentially dangerous "politics" in their actions, the organizers of environmental protests have some freedom to maneuver, and this makes it difficult for the state to simply brush them aside.

The fact that this is true not just of the two above-noted cases gives us reason to conclude that when it comes to environmental issues, the authorities do not give "politics" such a broad definition as they do in other areas.

Similar developments took place in Germany in the 1970s. The movement opposed to building nuclear power plants united environmentalists, radical leftist students, farmers whose interests were affected by the construction, and respectable members of the middle class—above all people representing socially important professions such as doctors, pastors, and teachers. The German authorities of the time could have easily discredited protests by only environmentalists as "absurd," and only by students as the work of "leftist radicals" or "communist-inspired" extremists (in Russia, the label "extremist manifestation" would be used instead), but the fact that there was involvement from a much broader range of social groups made this impossible.

Two Development Scenarios

There are many public organizations, nongovernmental and not under state control, working in Russia today. In this respect, Russia is a lot closer to civil society than was the Soviet Union in its final period, or even the new Russian Federation of the early 1990s. Furthermore, the new trend is the emergence of grassroots initiatives reminiscent of the "new social movements" that formed in the 1950s and 1960s in the developed industrial countries of the West. But there has so far been little interaction between the bigger Russian NGOs and the new "grassroots initiatives."

In a situation where the political opposition is weak and political activity is severely restricted in general, the NGOs display three types of behavior with regard to the authorities. The first is open cooperation with the authorities (such NGOs often end up partially merging with GONGOs—that is, "government-organized NGOs," the abbreviation designating pseudopublic organizations set up or initiated by the state authorities). The second group is made up of NGOs that think it necessary to maintain limited cooperation with the authorities and keep communications channels with them open in order to resolve practical issues and in some cases discuss issues of principle. The third group is close to the so-called opposition outside the system and makes contact with the authorities only to resolve purely practical matters. Of course, there is no clear line between these three groups, and individual NGOs can build their relations with the authorities using two, or sometimes even all three, of these models.

Each of these three groups has its own institutionalized communications channels with the authorities: The first group maintains contact with the authorities primarily through the Public Chamber, the second goes through the Presidential Council for Developing Civil Society and Human Rights, and the third prefers to work through Russian Federation human rights ombudsman Vladimir Lukin and his expert council.

Whichever development scenario Russia follows, the evolution of its civil society will be closely linked to its political development. A brief analysis of the two development scenarios—the inertia scenario and the optimistic scenario—is presented here.

Under the optimistic scenario, civil society will help to gradually democratize and open up Russia. If, however, events take a pessimistic turn, the NGOs will fall victim to further attempts at authoritarian consolidation of the political system.

In this context, the inertia scenario should be seen as the direction developments will take if the current political course remains unchanged. Steps to give the political system greater openness would create the conditions for more optimistic development, but are not so likely.

Paradoxically, both scenarios can help civil society organizations to develop further. The only way to stop this development would be to close off the political system to the extent of resorting to actual political repression. Such a development cannot be completely ruled out in the current situation, but it is not likely.

The Inertia Scenario

If the inertia scenario goes ahead, social, economic, infrastructure, and other problems could worsen, and this would most likely lead to increasing protests in society. The authorities and the NGOs would come into periodic confrontation depending on the political situation, economic and foreign policy situation, and the way election campaigns go. As has been the case so far, various different interests would compete in state policy. If this scenario were to be realized, the authorities will try to get the NGOs on their side as useful mechanisms for diagnosing and helping to smooth out conflicts, but at the same time, they will try to keep control over the NGOs as part of the political opposition. That the NGOs have in part been transformed into elements of the political opposition is a result of the policies pursued by these same state authorities, which make greater efforts to discredit civil society while at the same time establishing more and more new GONGOs.

The demands on NGOs' professional activities will continue to increase, and this will raise their overall level of self-organization. The main danger in this scenario is that a worsening economic, political, and social situation could push the NGO community toward an increasingly radical stance. The state would probably react in such a case by tightening the political screws, which would reduce NGOs' potential to help settle political problems in society, and force the authorities to go even further in their repressions. Civil society could end up going into regression, with many civil society actors withdrawing into the political opposition, while the NGOs that heretofore focused on cooperation and problem solving would have an ever harder time keeping a stable footing in the changing situation.

The Optimistic Scenario

A cautious and gradual opening up of the political system could create a greater need for strong NGOs than the other development scenarios. This has all the more relevance today as, over the last years, the members of the ruling elite, in their attempt to keep their hold on power, have systematically removed from the political stage many actors who could have served as intermediaries between the state and society and between the government and the opposition. Actors from the NGOs could step in to fill this gap—and most likely will indeed do so. For civil society, this would be a long and complex process, but one that would ultimately probably prove beneficial. For the foreseeable future at least, NGOs will need to take on a role not naturally theirs—that of surrogate political opposition, and at the same time take part in drawing up and securing new rules and procedures for settling disputes with the authorities.

In this situation, NGOs' level of self-organization would be likely to grow. At the same time, as the political system opens up, a "brain drain" would start as activists leave NGOs for the political party and parliamentary stages.

Increased opportunities for freely financing NGOs inside Russia will help to develop general public support for their activities. Greater professionalism in the NGOs and a stronger emphasis on analytical work as a result of the reduced "political burden" could also help to bolster public support for their activities.

Civil society organizations generally cover a large political spectrum, from radical opposition groups to organizations loyal to the authorities. Russia's NGOs today tend more toward the extremes of the political spectrum. This division into "loyal" (constructive) and "nonloyal" (unconstructive) organizations is partly a distinction created by the authorities for their own advantage, and partly society's response to political prohibitions. It is a largely artificial division and will probably become less visible and acute.

This scenario could also see more regular involvement of NGOs in discussing current issues of state administration, and this is something that is already happening in a few areas.[6]

Notes

1. Quoted from Friedrich Nietzsche, "Chelovecheskoyeslishkomcheloveskoye," in *Collected Works in Two Volumes* (Russian), (Moscow: Mysl, 1990), vol. 1.

2. The term "civil society" dates back a long time and was actively used in the nineteenth century. In the twentieth century, the term was not much used for a while in sociological and political discourse until the emergence of dissident movements in Eastern Europe.

3. Vladimir Putin, "Rossianarubezhetysyacheletii," *Nezavisimaya Gazeta*, December 30, 1999, www.ng.ru/politics/1999-12-30/4_millenium.html#.

4. Vladimir Putin, "Address to the Russian Federation Federal Assembly," Moscow, May 26, 2004, http://archive.kremlin.ru/appears/2004/05/26/0003_type63372type63374type 82634_71501.shtml.

5. Vladimir Putin, "Speech at a Forum of the Russian President's Supporters," Moscow, November 21, 2007, http://archive.kremlin.ru/appears/2007/11/21/1558_type63374 type63376type82634_153636.shtml.

6. This happens in organizing the civil alternative to military service, for example. There is also partial involvement in carrying out military reform, fighting drug addiction, and, to a much lesser extent, in reforming the prison system.

IDEOLOGY
and CULTURE

PART VII

CHAPTER TWENTY-SIX

RUSSIA *and the* NEW "RUSSIAN WORLD"

Igor Zevelev

As the first decade of the new century came to a close, ethnic Russian nationalism had not become a serious political force inside Russia itself, and did not have any real influence on policy toward Russia's neighbors. Could this situation change by 2020?

The Soviet Union's collapse left millions of people who considered themselves Russians divided by political borders. For the first time in many centuries, these people found themselves scattered across a number of countries neighboring Russia. Starting in 1992, Russia pursued what could be described as a cautious and restrained policy toward this new challenge. Russia did not give its support to irredentist demands in Crimea, northern Kazakhstan, or other regions with a compact Russian population. Russia's first attempt to protect its citizens and "compatriots" abroad with the help of military force came in August 2008 in South Ossetia and Abkhazia, where Russians make up only about 2 percent of the population. But does this mean that the ethnic factor does not play any significant part in Russia's policies in the post-Soviet region?

How Russia views the fact that about a quarter of the people who call themselves Russians live outside the Russian Federation, more than half of them in neighboring countries, theoretically could become one of the biggest factors in developing the Russian state's identity and in the system of international relations that takes shape in Eurasia during the decade up

The views expressed in this article are those of the author and do not necessarily reflect the views of the MacArthur Foundation.

through 2020. But this factor has remained just a possibility—or, rather, just one possible scenario for the future.

Two main approaches to this situation—which has become known as the "Russian question"—have taken shape in Russia today. First, there are moderate notions of "diasporas" and the "Russian world";[1] and second, there is a radical nationalist discourse of the "divided people," though this concept has not so far had any substantial impact on actual policy. If one examines these two approaches in the broader context of how Russian identity has developed during the past two hundred years, with some simplification one can say that they reflect two basic approaches that have long been traditional in Russia: that of the nation-state, and that of the nation-ethnos.[2] These two concepts will most probably be continuing their coexistence and interaction in 2020. But the question is how they will develop, what respective shares they will have in the overall equation, and what consequences the resulting national identity configuration will have for international security.[3] As things stood in 2010, Russian ethnic nationalism had not become a serious political force inside Russia itself and did not have any real influence on its policy toward its neighbors. Various non-ethnic aspects of Russian identity—imperial, Soviet, civilizational, universalist—all continue to play substantial roles. Could this situation change by 2020? What impact would possible democratization have on ethnic Russian nationalism's development, and what part will the new "Russian world" play in this whole process?

Two Scenarios for Compatriots and the "Russian World" in Russia's Policy Through 2020

Two different but overlapping discourses have given rise to the concepts of "compatriots" and the "Russian world." The concept of "compatriots" began emerging in 1994 as a specific policy expressed primarily in laws, state programs, and foreign policy action.[4] The concept of the "Russian world," though its roots go back further, only became a part of active public discourse in 2007.[5] It is a much broader concept, which carries strong philosophical and world outlook connotations, and has a greater connection to public, not just state, activity. The concept of compatriots is based on laws and legal regulations, whereas the concept of the "Russian world" is based primarily on self-identity.[6] The two concepts overlap in the free choices made by those who feel a connection with Russia in one way or another. Putting together the Russians in the "near abroad"—the former Soviet republics—with Russian émigrés and former Soviet citizens in general makes the concepts of "compatriots" and the "Russian world" very hazy and at the same time reflects the authorities' attempts to soften the issue's sharper edges.[7] In this chapter, I look at what is called the "Russian world," that is, those Russians (in the sense of those whose cultural identity is Russian) whom the collapse of the Soviet Union left outside the Russian Federation's borders.

The issue of Russians abroad has undergone considerable change during the brief historical span since the Soviet Union's collapse. In 1992, the issue of compatriots abroad was only a sideline in Russian policy and public opinion. But gradually, in 1993 and 1994, it became an important part of the discourse on the Russian nation and increasingly prominent in domestic and foreign policy rhetoric. The five years from 1995 to 2000 were ones of trial and error in putting together a real policy in this area. During the period 2000–2010, the concept of "compatriots" took on what could well prove to be its definitive place and role in Russian official discourse and policy for many years to come. Plans to carry out a decisive policy toward the Russian diaspora communities (such as introducing dual citizenship officially recognized by the neighboring countries) did not go ahead, and other initiatives such as strengthening ties with Russians abroad remained modest in scope and content. This situation might change over the second decade of the twenty-first century, if there is a change in Russia's national identity and a transformation in the political system.

The coming decade could see two main development scenarios for Russia and the new "Russian world": continuation of a moderate "state-centered" approach, the inertia scenario; and adoption of the notion of a "divided people" as the foundation for state policy, the disaster scenario. A liberal alternative could be possible in the form of a gradual and relatively slow transformation of the inertia scenario as its transnational components begin to emerge and gather strength.

The inertia scenario, in essence, would continue the situation in which the main impulses come from the Russian Federation, which sees the

"Russian world" above all from the point of view of its own state interests. President Dmitri Medvedev spoke of this at the Third World Congress of Compatriots: "The main thing is common concern for Russia, for the Russian Federation's future, and essentially our common future."[8]

In the inertia scenario, the discourse in this area, though tense on the intellectual level, remains marginalized, and policy toward compatriots remains halfhearted and not very effective. The central issue as far as specific policy goes is how liberal (or stringent) the immigration and citizenship laws will be. These issues are about battles among the different state agencies rather than political battles.

What is the likelihood that the moderate, state-centered approach will continue during the coming years and that the compatriots issue will remain in its current background state? This will depend on three groups of factors: the situation and activities of the Russian communities in Russia's neighboring countries, the nature of interstate relations in the post-Soviet area, and the direction of changes in Russian domestic and foreign policy. When examined together as they stood in 2010, these combined factors suggest that the current moderate trend will continue during the medium term.

The decisive factors in the situation of Russians and, more broadly, the Russian-speaking communities in the post-Soviet area is the absence of direct violence against them from the local "indigenous" population, their low level of mobilization, and their fragmented nature. There are almost no visible horizontal ties between the different Russian communities. The differences between these communities give no hope that these ties will appear in the future. The communities differ greatly in size, way of life, and level of integration into the local society. They do not have a common adversary or a common vision of the future, and each is poorly organized. The vague lines between ethnic Russians and Russian-speaking groups is another factor of considerable importance holding back their political mobilization along ethnic lines. This all strengthens the likelihood that the inertia scenario will continue.

Efforts to seek political unity, solidarity, and cooperation as an ethnic minority are something completely new for a people who used to constitute the dominant ethnic group in their own country. To some extent, the situation is different in Latvia and Estonia, where an intellectual discourse on the Russian-speaking minorities has developed, and small political parties representing their interests have emerged. But their activities concentrate entirely on resolving issues within the context of Latvian and Estonian statehood, and to an increasing extent with the European Union, and are little connected to Russia and its concept of "compatriots." Without Russia's involvement, the problems faced by the Russian communities in the post-Soviet area will mostly likely remain only of local significance.

The nature of interstate relations in the post-Soviet area has so far helped to ensure that the issue of the Russians left outside Russia itself, for all the differences in approach, has never become the focus of any acute confrontation within the Commonwealth of Independent States (CIS). In the period 2003–2010, for example, Russia, for the sake of maintaining relations with Turkmenistan and pursuing its own gas interests, closed its eyes to Ashgabat's flagrant violations of the rights of people with dual Turkmen-Russian citizenship. Agreements between the CIS countries, visa-free travel between most of them, and the psychological impression of sharing a common historical legacy have kept the issue from growing inflamed.

Theoretically, the governments of the former Soviet republics could provoke a sharp response from Russia if they were to encourage or initiate serious incidents that could threaten the Russian population's physical security. But in the absence of such unlikely developments, the chance remains negligible that the Russian government will make more active use of its position as the strong player in relations with the "near abroad" in order to protect the Russian communities' interests or use the Russian issue to put direct pressure on neighboring countries' governments.

In the inertia scenario, the compatriots issue will not often become the center of the Russian president's and prime minister's attention, unless crisis situations arise. This means that policy in most cases will be shaped at the lower levels in the Russian power hierarchy.

Different state institutions take different views of the issue. Real policy on compatriots during the coming years will be shaped by the interactions among four interest groups, each of which is represented in the government bodies: humanitarian, "soft power," law enforcement, and economic interests. The different state agencies and public groups advocating these four positions differ in their motivations, and each will try to make its vision of the issue the main driving force in shaping official policy.[9]

Civil society groups and institutions, such as the Presidential Council for Civil Society Development and Human Rights and the human rights ombudsman, will make humanitarian concerns their chief motive. This will translate into efforts to protect the rights of the Russian-speaking populations of the neighboring countries and immigrants in Russia, and also efforts to liberalize Russia's citizenship laws. But at the same time, it needs to be noted that the human rights community in general has shown itself relatively indifferent to the issues facing compatriots abroad.

The soft power component could be expressed through reinforced instruments to support compatriots abroad with the aim of increasing Russia's influence in the post-Soviet area. But the Russian Foreign Ministry does not have the relevant experience and will most likely also seek to keep the compatriots issue running primarily along humanitarian lines and work through multilateral international institutions. The Russian authorities have not yet learned in full measure how to use soft power in interstate relations, and the potential of Russians abroad as an instrument of influence will most probably not be put to effective use during the coming decade. Evidence of this can be seen, in particular, in the Russian Federation Foreign Policy Concept of 2008, which places the compatriots issue in the same section as humanitarian cooperation and human rights.[10] As the main ministry responsible for working with compatriots abroad, the Foreign Ministry takes a contradictory position.[11] Russian diplomats have not entirely succeeded in combining the development of interstate relations with support for their compatriots abroad, which is often and not without justification perceived in neighboring countries as an attempt to meddle in their affairs. The situation in this respect partially resembles U.S. diplomacy's attempts to defend human rights. The aim in establishing a new federal agency, Rossotrudnichestvo (Russian Cooperation Agency), and the Russian World Foundation was to lessen this contradiction.

The amendments to the Law on Compatriots, passed in 2010 in the form that the Foreign Ministry wanted, have bolstered the likelihood that the inertia scenario will continue. In accordance with the law's new wording, those who want Russia to consider them compatriots must carry out particular public or professional activities to maintain the Russian language and other languages of the Russian Federation's peoples, develop Russian culture abroad, and strengthen friendly relations between their countries of residence and Russia.[12] The law's critics say that to maintain ties with their historic motherland, Russians abroad need to become "professional compatriots" who prove their identity not through faith, language, and conscience but by serving Russian diplomacy's interests of the moment.[13]

The Russian Interior Ministry will follow its law enforcement motives by making efforts to curb migration from the southern republics and to prevent people from using the status of compatriot to make it easier to get Russian citizenship. The law enforcement and security agencies' analytical divisions appear to be preoccupied by the rise in crime and interethnic tension, but these kinds of restrictive practices inevitably run up against the resistance of economic actors interested in a cheap labor force with good knowledge of the Russian language. So long as Russia continues to show relatively high growth in labor-intensive sectors, the government's economic officials will be forced to take a more liberal line that facilitates temporary economic migration and helps some compatriots get permanent residence in Russia.

No matter how the four different main lines in Russian policy sketched above come together, the state machine overall will continue the moderate line. The situation could change only at the political level. The issue of the diasporas and Russia's responsibility for their fate is present in theoretical discussions on state building and nation building. Is there a way for more radical approaches to infiltrate the spheres where real policy is developed? What conditions would be needed to break off the inertia scenario and transform it into a nationalist scenario?

As was noted above, the diaspora issue is not one of Russia's main policy priorities, but specific conditions could bring it to the fore. The experience of nationalist movements in other regions shows that the authorities can use slogans about reuniting the nation as a tool for mobilizing the public and winning themselves support at the moment they most need it. Thus a number of different political forces hoping for voter support could use the reunification issue as a rhetorical tool, proclaiming it as a key issue for Russia's national interests and security. But two factors prevent them from doing so.

First, the economic boom of the early 2000s made abstract ideas about the Russian people far less attractive than the idea of increasing Russia's own prosperity. The situation was reminiscent of Austria following the collapse of its empire after World War I, when most ordinary people and members of the elite thought not about restoring a lost empire but about simply surviving, or getting richer. Although Vladimir Putin revived some imperial symbols, few people were ready to sacrifice their own material well-being for the sake of a geopolitical comeback.

Second, the power system Putin built leaves very little room for political activity independent of the Kremlin. The ruling elite sees ethnonationalism as a threat to the Russian state's internal integrity, does not think in narrow ethnic terms, and is not interested in strengthening parties and movements advocating ethnonationalist slogans.

However, there are groups and currents in Russian society that could potentially cast shadows over the future of the current policy of restraint. Much will depend on the direction taken by the search for a national identity in Russia. Russians' sense of ethnic self-awareness became more visible after the Soviet Union's collapse stripped the country of its imperial trappings. Russian ethnonationalism is not an organized political force, but it could quickly become powerful, especially if the need to construct a *nation*-state becomes a leading theme in political discussions. In both Soviet and post-Soviet academic circles and in the public awareness, the political term "nation" never had a civic so much as a strong ethnic connotation. As has happened so often in Europe's history, when shared culture or blood comes to be seen as the foundation for an imagined political community, such a direction could ultimately lead to calls to unite all Russians under the rule of a single country.

Attempts to redefine Russia in more specifically ethnic terms, as has happened in the other former Soviet republics, could become the most dangerous step yet in Russia's entire post-Soviet history. Carrying out such a political project could undermine its internal integrity and lead to a revision of its borders.

The experience of other countries shows that it is usually ethnonationalists who set about nation building on the ruins of empires. For instance, Ataturk's Turkey began its experiment in building a nation-state with the deportations of Armenian, Greek, and Kurdish minorities.[14] Many Austrians welcomed Hitler's Anschluss after having lived for twenty years in a small postimperial country. After Yugoslavia collapsed, Serbia and Croatia took a course of aggressive nationalism and began redrawing the lines of the post-Yugoslav political map. All the former Soviet republics nurtured ethnopolitical myths whereby the country was proclaimed as the motherland of its "indigenous" population. In all these cases, it was the tradition of historical romanticism, according to which humanity can be neatly divided into nations based on culture or ethnicity, each with its sacred rights, that served as the theoretical basis for these policies.

The period following the Soviet Union's collapse seemed to offer favorable conditions for reinforcing Russians' ethnic awareness and their dominant role in forming Russia's new national identity. Ethnic Russians accounted for about 80 percent of the population at the start of the twenty-first century (compared with 43 percent in the Russian Empire in the late nineteenth century, and 50 percent in the Soviet Union), and were therefore unquestionably the dominant ethnic group in their country for the first time in two hundred years. The share of ethnic Russians in the population will decline somewhat by 2020, however, due to a faster natural growth rate among other ethnic groups and to migration. And during this period, the Russian language will also see its position weaken in some of the republics within the Russian Federation. These trends could fuel ethnic Russian nationalism.

Russian ethnic nationalism received a powerful intellectual boost from the works of Alexander Solzhenitsyn, who became the first prominent thinker to challenge the country's supranational traditions in their imperial form. The severe economic crisis of the 1990s and the difficulties that ethnic Russians faced at that time in the former Soviet republics undergoing their own ethnonationalist transformation created receptive conditions for political mobilization centering on this issue.

Among the factors expanding the broad base for ethnic Russian nationalism in recent years has been the increasingly prominent influx of migrants to the big Russian cities. From a formal legal point of view, migration from Central Asia and the South Caucasus is a completely different thing from internal migration from the North Caucasus. But in the mass public awareness, they blend into a single phenomenon—the "flood" of non-Russians who come to occupy socially visible niches in small-scale trade and services and in semilegal or illegal business and related criminal activities.[15] This perception of migration fuels xenophobia and extremist groups' activities. Public opinion surveys by the Levada Center show that the number of Russians who think restrictions should be placed on migration rose from 45 percent in 2002 to 61 percent in 2009.[16]

The issue of the "divided" Russian people that had such a big place in the nationalist discourse in the 1990s gradually began to fade into the background, taking second place to internal problems and threats in Russia. But the 2010s will likely see issues such as migration, Islam, and the situation of Russians in the national republics gain new importance, while the situation with the Russian diasporas in the neighboring countries has already stabilized to a substantial extent. Some of the ethnic Russians and Russian speakers, above all from Central Asia and the South Caucasus, have moved to the Russian Federation. Some have adapted to their new situation. They have not become the target of direct violence in any of the post-Soviet republics, and there have thus not been any grounds for nationalist mobilization in Russia. The Russian language's status, opportunities for cultural development, preserving one's identity, and not facing discrimination in neighboring countries are all important issues, of course, but they do not have sufficient potential to mobilize the public when set against the serious social and ethnic challenges inside Russia itself. Furthermore, no matter how great the temptation, there is no way the situation in Ukraine and Belarus can be reduced to purely ethnic terms. The historical, cultural, and linguistic closeness of the eastern Slavic peoples makes it that much harder to push political demagogy, which usually has more success in simpler situations that are easy to present in black-and-white terms.

Ethnic Russian nationalism as it stands at the start of the twenty-first century manifests itself primarily as xenophobia. Marginal skinhead groups direct their energy at intimidating and perpetrating violence against migrants from the Caucasus and Central Asia. The Moscow and Saint Petersburg regions have seen a particularly high number of crimes committed for racist and neo-Nazi motives.[17] The extremists find a relatively favorable public atmosphere for their activities. According to opinion polls carried out by the Levada Center, the share of people who to whatever extent agree with the idea of "Russia for the Russians" rose from 43 percent in 1998 to 54 percent in 2009.[18]

The Russian authorities have attempted to seize the initiative from the extremist groups by launching discussions on the native population's interests and the notion of Russians as the ethnic group forming the state's main foundation. Putin formerly used the term "native people" to refer to the small indigenous peoples of Siberia, but in 2006 he started using it to refer to all Russian citizens as opposed to the migrants: "We need to think about the interests of our native people of course. If we fail to do this, . . . it would give an excuse and open the way for various radical organizations to try to take the stage."[19] In 2006, after the ethnic riots in Kondopoga and as the anti-Georgian campaign got under way, Russian officials kindled xenophobic sentiments in their statements on a number of occasions, but these kinds of public declarations soon stopped.

In 2007, the political party United Russia launched its own "Russian project" using different concepts such as "state-forming people" and "ethnic nucleus."[20] But these issues faded into the background again with the transfer of presidential power to Dmitri Medvedev and Putin's move to the prime minister's job. The smooth and peaceful handover of power (unlike the competitive situation in free and fair elections) gave the authorities no need to look for an issue with which to mobilize voters.

However, it is a very dangerous thing that the ethnically charged issue of the Russian people and their role has emerged at all in official Russian discourse. That Russians' sense of identity as an ethnic group was only partially formed was one of the main reasons explaining why the Soviet Union's collapse was an overall peaceful process, especially compared with the bloodshed that accompanied the disintegration of another socialist federation, Yugoslavia, in which the Serbs had a clearer vision of their own identity. Perhaps leaving the Russian people without clearly defined borders in official discourse and the public consciousness is the only possible peaceful solution to the "Russian question" since the Soviet Union's collapse. Paradoxically, Moscow's inconsistent and tangled relations with the republics within the Russian Federation, and its moderate and at times totally ineffective policy toward the Russians living in the "near abroad," do more to help maintain peace and security in the post-Soviet area than would attempts to develop a clearer approach to building a nation-state. Radicals could always take over the slogan of building a civic nation and soon cast the "civic" part of it aside.

The nationalist opposition's most radical demands on the moderate line so far have been based on the concept of the divided Russian people and their right to reunification. Most prominent in developing this idea have been Natalia Narochnitskaya, Ksenia Myalo, Viktor Asyuchits, and Alexander Sevastyanov, and politicians such as Vladimir Zhirinovsky, Gennady Zyuganov, Yuri Luzhkov, and Sergei Baburin. Several attempts were made to give this concept legislative form during the period 1998–2001. State Duma committees discussed several bills—On the Russian People's National and Cultural Development; On the Russian People's Right to Self-Determination, Sovereignty Throughout Russia's Territory, and Reunification in a Single State; and On the Russian People. But none of these bills became law. The reality of state building gave the country completely different tasks to tackle, and pragmatism always won the day over narrow groups of politicians with their specific ideological demands. The establishment of rigid presidential control over the legislative branch in 2003 marginalized the discourse on the Russian people and their right to reunification.

The possibility that pluralism could emerge in Russian politics during the 2010s could return the issue of the divided Russian people to the political stage. The emergence of political parties based on this platform cannot be ruled out. The experiences of Israel, Austria, Hungary, and a number of other countries have shown that sometimes even small nationalist parties can acquire a disproportionately strong influence, as more moderate political parties form alliances with them in order to secure a parliamentary majority.

All forms of supranational projects—whether empire, the Soviet Union, Slavic-Orthodox civilization, or Dostoyevsky's "universal man"—are always a product of the elite. The concept of the nation, both as an ethnic and a civil notion, is more democratic. If Russian society starts to become more democratic after 2010, the balance in the two components of Russian identity—that of the supranational state, and that of ethnonationalism—could shift toward the latter. This would be in keeping with the general trend in the world. In this situation, the idea of a "divided nation" could take a central place in foreign policy, with disastrous results for the region's stability.

An Instrument of International Influence

Russian leaders have proclaimed on numerous occasions their aim to turn the Russians living abroad into an instrument of Russia's soft power and to build up the transnational "Russian world," which encompasses the whole of "Russia's multiethnic people" and compatriots abroad.[21] Russia's political elite takes the view that formulating this issue in terms of the political nation and using soft power could bring the country big advantages in the next decade.

Many diasporas, especially in the United States, do indeed work in the interests of their historic homeland. This has been the case for the Jewish, Armenian, Greek, Chinese, Baltic, and Central European diasporas, for example. This is what makes the individual citizens of foreign countries members of these diasporas, when seen as a political category. Russia now has the chance to help form a Russian diaspora made up of Russians and members of other ethnic groups with links to the Russian Federation. There have already been some steps in this direction in the form of political discourse and laws during the twenty years since the Soviet Union's collapse, but they have yet to be reinforced by a consistent policy, and have yielded only modest results so far.

To form an active diaspora during the next decade, Russia would need to show its interest in pursuing this objective and its willingness to act in the interests of its members. Laws making it possible to convert the status of compatriot into that of Russian Federation citizen and their real application in practice would be a big breakthrough in this direction. Before 2010, the laws and programs for compatriots had no connection at all to citizenship laws and migration policy, but the new draft of the law on compatriots that came into force in 2010 makes it possible for some categories of people to obtain Russian citizenship through simplified procedures exempting them from having to meet the requirements on the number of years resident in Russia. Actually implementing these provisions, however, would involve making the required amendments to the law on citizenship. The effort to make it easier for compatriots to obtain Russian citizenship will also encounter resistance from people who are opposed to the idea of increasing numbers of non-ethnic Russians from neighboring countries, especially the South Caucasus and Central Asia, who are moving to Russia.

The status of compatriot needs to offer the opportunity of eventually resettling in Russia—otherwise it would make no sense for many people in the post-Soviet area.[22] Further changes to the laws would make it possible to achieve the objectives initially pursued by the failed dual citizenship strategy. First, it would be a support to those who choose to remain in the neighboring countries, giving them a sense of having a special link to Russia and the "emergency option" of being able to move there if the situation in their current country of residence were to worsen. Second, for those compatriots wanting to move, it would help smooth the way and help bring into Russia qualified Russian-speaking workers who could somewhat compensate for the drop in Russia's population in the coming decade.

Russia's law enforcement agencies have so far successfully blocked any attempts to liberalize procedures for obtaining Russian citizenship, although corruption has made it possible to get around the stringent rules. The internal, primarily interagency, battles over this issue will continue during the coming decade.

The intellectual challenge that Solzhenitsyn raised against the supranational tradition in its imperial and Soviet forms was still without an answer at the start of the twenty-first century. But starting in 2008, for the first time since the Soviet Union's collapse, the Russian authorities began speaking in terms of a big supranational project. Russian foreign policy's basic world vision was more and more formulated in terms of Russia's identity as a civilization. Continuing the traditions of the nineteenth and early twentieth centuries, Russia came to this view not through reflection on the "divided" nature of the Russian people and their interaction with the neighboring peoples but as a result of increasing tension in relations with the West. Unsuccessful attempts to become an independent part of a Greater West and the realization that these failures might be due to more than just the current circumstances on the international stage forced the Russian elite to reconsider the country's place in the world. Moreover, claims to great power status obliged the Russian authorities to attempt to formulate their foreign policy goals in terms that go beyond the framework of national interests.[23]

The Russian authorities found that the ideological concept of civilizations fitted closely with their own thinking. In the nineteenth century, it was generally conservatives who talked of Russia as a distinct civilization, especially Nikolai Danilevsky and Konstantin Leontiev. In modern times, the late American conservative, Samuel Huntington, formulated an outlook in terms of civilizations.

The Russian authorities today have come up with two possible approaches to Russia's identity as a civilization. The first was expressed for the first time by President Medvedev in his speech in Berlin in June 2008, when he said that "the end of the Cold War has opened the way for developing genuinely equal cooperation between Russia, the European Union and North America as the three branches of European civilization."[24] Foreign Minister Sergei Lavrov, while repeating this idea of three branches of European civilization, declared at the same time that adopting Western values is just one possible choice. In Lavrov's words, Russia will follow a road "based on the premise that competition is becoming truly global and taking on a civilizational dimension, that is to say, value references and development models are also within the sphere of competition today."[25] In the summer of 2009, in an interview with a Latvian Russian-language newspaper, Lavrov used the term "greater Russian civilization."[26]

The authorities give the impression of really not seeing any big contradiction between these two approaches. In the Russian establishment's eyes, they are not mutually exclusive but, rather, complement each other. One approach is for the West's consumption, whereas the other is for Russia's neighbors, compatriots, and the Russian world. The premise that Russia is a separate big civilization makes it easy to fend off criticism of modern Russia's system of government and democratic shortcomings. At the same time, it offers a modern twenty-first-century interpretation of the "Russian question": Russian civilization is Russia, along with the Russian world, which includes everyone who feels a pull toward Russian culture. In this context, the premise of the Russians as a divided people sounds archaic. The choice between the two approaches to Russia's civilizational identity during the coming decade will ultimately depend on pragmatic concerns, chief among which will more likely be relations with the West rather than with Russia's immediate neighbors.

Success in "influencing the surrounding world with the help of its civilizational, humanitarian, cultural, foreign policy, and other kinds of attraction," as Lavrov calls for, would require Russia to make use of and draw on the universalist humanitarian traditions of the country's intellectual heritage. If Russia does not offer the world universal human values, it has no hope of learning how to use soft power in international relations in the new century.

However, historical experience shows that even if Russia does manage to provide a universal basis for the way in which it projects its image on the international stage, it could still end up not meeting the hoped-for response. During the last three centuries, Russian culture has formed within an imperial framework, and its key distinguishing feature has been what Dostoyevsky called "universalism." This helped to bring it worldwide recognition. Having left provincialism and narrowness far behind, Russian culture easily absorbed the achievements of other cultures, above all those of Europe, and gave humanity many great works. But at the same time, attempts at cultural and other types of inclusion of everything and everyone in a limitless "universal" Russia always came into conflict with the aspirations of neighboring peoples, who for the most part did not wish to be used as the material for a universalist project, in which they saw what amounted to their Russification and a threat to their very survival. Such messianic traditions shaped by historical and cultural circumstances are clearly not suited to the new geopolitical, economic, and demographic situation of today's Russia.

The modernization strategy that has become the basis of Dmitri Medvedev's political identity has a chance of becoming the main pillar supporting an emerging discourse on Russia's future in the coming decade. If this does happen, rhetoric about Russian identity and civilization will fade into the background as practical tasks take center stage. The issue of Russia and the new Russian World will remain politically marginal.

Notes

1. The correct way to write the term "Russian world" has not been settled yet. Documents signed by the Russian president give it in quotation marks and with a lowercase "world," while the Foreign Ministry documents write it Russian World—without quotation marks and with a capitalized "World."

2. Without going into the debates on the substance of the terms "nation" and "nation-state," I note only that I share the position of Alexei Miller and other authors, who, based on the discursive nature of these concepts, think that a nation-state has not yet fully taken shape in Russia. See, for example, *Naslediye imperii i buduchschee Rossii* (The imperial legacy and Russia's future), edited by A. I. Miller (Moscow: Novoye literaturnoye obozreniye, 2008).

3. See Igor Zevelev, "Budushchee Rossii: Natsia ili tsivilizatsia?" (Russia's future: Nation or civilization?), *Rossia v globalnoy politike*, no. 5 (September–October 2009).

4. The term "compatriots abroad" was brought into official use by Boris Yeltsin and Andrei Kozyrev a little earlier, in 1992. In Russian discourse, "compatriots" usually refers to those who live outside the Russian Federation but are conscious of historical, cultural, and linguistic ties with Russia and want to keep these ties regardless of what citizenship they may hold.

5. The term "Russian World" appeared in Russian publications at the end of the 1990s. It started appearing in Foreign Ministry documents and presidential speeches from the mid-2000s. The concept of "Russian World" usually refers to the networks of people and communities outside the Russian Federation that are in one way or another involved in the Russian cultural and language environment. See the numerous documents and publications by the Russian World Foundation (www.russkiymir.ru), and also see S. Panteleyev, "'Russky mir' kak setevaya struktura: Teoria i praktika" (Russian World as a network structure: Theory and practice), www.ia-centr.ru/archive/public_details 0edc.html?id=1062.

6. See V. Tishkov, "Russky Mir: Smysl i strategia Rossii" (Russian World: Sense and strategy for Russia), in *Povestka dnya dlya Rossii*, edited by V. Nikononv (Moscow: Forum, 2009), 185–228.

7. The strongly supranational interpretation of the Russian World concept that dominates in official circles and in the foundation of the same name is fiercely rejected by ethno-nationalists. See, for example, Y. Yefimova, "'Russky mir' bez russkykh?" (The "Russian World" without Russians?), *Zolotoi lev*, nos. 175–76, www.zlev.ru/index.php?p=a rticle&nomer=6&article=198.

8. Third World Congress of Compatriots, December 1, 2009, www.kremlin.ru/news/6187.

9. See I. Zevelev, "Sootechestvenniki v rossiiskoi politike na postsovetskom prostranstve" (Compatriots in Russia's policy in the post-Soviet area), *Rossia v globalnom politike*, no. 1 (January–February 2008).

10. "Russian Federation Foreign Policy Concept," www.ln.mid.ru/ns-osndoc.nsf/0e9272bef a34209743256c630042d1aa/d48737161a0bc944c32574870048d8f7?OpenDocument.

11. This issue and that of ties with compatriots have been repeatedly raised by Konstantin Zatulin, the chairman of the State Duma Committee on CIS Affairs.

12. Federal Law FZ 179 of July 23, 2010, "On Amendments to the Federal Law on Russian Federation State Policy Toward Compatriots Abroad," www.ln.mid.ru/ns-dgpch.nsf/215 bdcc93123ae8343256da400379e66/efc22f59432c7795c3257776003a376c?OpenDocu ment.

13. M. Kolerov, "Pochemu Rossia otkazivayetsya ot sootechestvennikov i ot sebya" (Why Russia is renouncing its compatriots and itself), www.regnum.ru/news/1308005.html.

14. The danger of the "Turkish model" being applied to Russia and turning the former imperial center into a nation-state has been emphasized in particular by Anatol Lieven, "Restraining NATO: Ukraine, Russia, and the West," *Washington Quarterly*, Autumn 1997, 73–74.

15. According to the heads of the Federal Migration Service's senior officials, of the 5 million migrants working in Russian 2010, 4 million were working in violation of the laws; see www.interfax.ru/society/news.asp?id=153666.

16. Levada Center, *Public Opinion—2009* (Moscow: Levada Center, 2009), 148.

17. Sova Center, *Xenophobia, Freedom of Conscience and Anti-Extremism in Russia in 2008* (Moscow: Sova Center, 2009), 7.

18. Levada Center, *Public Opinion*, 147.

19. Transcript of third meeting with members of the Valdai International Discussion Club, September 9, 2006, www.kremlin.ru/text/appears/2006/09/111114.shtml.

20. I. Demidov, "Mnogonatsional'naya gosudarstvennost' nevozmozhna bez nalichiya nekoego etnicheskogo 'yadra'" (Multiethnic statehood not possible without an "ethnic nucleus"), United Russia website (no longer available).

21. See Putin's, Medvedev's, and Lavrov's statements on the Russian World in, respectively, "Opening Remarks at the World Congress of Compatriots Abroad," October 24, 2006, www.kremlin.ru/text/appears/2006/10/112923; "Third World Congress of Compatriots"; and "Transcript of Speech and News Conference by Russian Foreign Minister Sergei Lavrov After a Conference on the Results of Russia's Diplomacy in 2006," Moscow, December 20, 2006, www.mid.ru/brp_4.nsf/2fee282eb6df40e643256999005e6e8c/6a 48399f78e81296c325724d003d22fe?OpenDocument.

22. Many countries—including Armenia, Bulgaria, Germany, Hungary, Israel, Ireland, Serbia, Turkey, Finland, and Croatia—make it quite easy for people belonging to the main ethnic group's diaspora to obtain citizenship. See J. Muller, "My i oni" (Us and them), *Rossia v globalnoy politike*, no. 3, May–June 2008.

23. See Zevelev, "Budushchee Rossii."

24. Speech at meeting with German political, parliamentary, and public representatives, June 5, 2008, www.kremlin.ru/transcripts/320.

25. Theses set out in a speech by Russian foreign minister Sergei Lavrov at the International Symposium Russia in the Twenty-First Century, Moscow, June 20, 2008, www.ln.mid.ru/Brp_4.nsf/arh/8825DB13898CD2E4C325746E0057BB9E?OpenDocument.

This thesis was repeated almost word for word in the Russian Federation Foreign Policy Concept approved on July 12, 2008.

26. See "MID Rossii pozdravil gazetu 'Vesti segodnya' i vspomnil o 'bol'shoy rossiyskoy tsivilizatsii'" (MFA of Russia congratulated newspaper "Vesti segodnya" on jubilee and remembered "big Russian civilization"), ves.lv, July 26, 2009, www.ves.lv/article/88022.

CHAPTER TWENTY-SEVEN

SOCIETY *and the* STATE *on the* INTERNET: *a* CALL *for* CHANGE

Alexey Sidorenko

In the coming decade, the Internet will become the most important factor influencing the social and political situation in Russia. For now, both society and the state are still getting used to the new technology, trying both new and old mechanisms to communicate and to fight with each other. The state is attempting to impose elements of control over the virtual social sphere, though not always successfully. By itself, the virtual social environment is simultaneously both poisonous and constructive. Civil society and proto–civil society formations of a new sort are being created within it: regional forums, groups on the social networking media website Vkontakte, and communities formed by thematic projects. At the same time, the information space—with its susceptibility to manipulation and its very lowbrow culture of online interaction—is forcing many analysts to wonder whether it is able to introduce changes not only into the state's political structure but also into society itself—or whether it, along with other areas, will be brought under the state's control.

In attempting to predict exactly how the Internet will influence Russians' lives, two variables must be kept in mind: the state, and society. Under the influence of the Internet, serious changes are taking place both in society and in the state. Because of the differing internal political logics of these two domains, the "reaction to the Internet" can occasionally be explosive. If the Internet's decentralized structure makes it possible to build a more democratic society even in a not entirely democratic country, then for the state's hierarchical (and in the Russian case, superhierarchical) structure, a conditioned reflex springs into action, replacing the seemingly chaotic order of network interactions with a centralized, hierarchical model. It is in this contradiction that one finds the space of possibilities determining the development of the two domains.

The State

The Internet in Russia is no longer statistically insignificant. At the end of 2011, approximately 46 percent of Russians are using the Internet; moreover, broadband Internet access has been growing rapidly since 2006, and mobile Internet access since 2008.[1] According to a study by the Public Opinion Foundation, by 2014, 71 percent of the country's adult population could have access to the Internet, though there is every reason to believe that the growth in the number of users will pause after reaching 65 to 68 percent.[2]

The level of penetration for mobile Internet devices is currently 20 percent,[3] and is constantly growing.[4] Despite this high growth rate, Internet use in Russia currently lags behind that in the majority of European countries.[5] In recent years, blogs and social networks covering approximately 80 percent of Russian Internet users have become widespread.

Russia's largest Internet portals have already caught up with several federal television channels: Yandex has a daily audience of 24 to 26 million people,[6] and Vkontakte attracts 20 million.[7] The Russian blogosphere includes more than 7.4 million bloggers (in 2008, there were only about half as many, at 3.8 million, while in the early 2000s, the total number of bloggers numbered only in the thousands).[8] Approximately 93 percent of Russian-speaking bloggers live in Russia, and 7 percent reside abroad.

The four major blog platforms—LiveJournal, LiveInternet, Blogs.Mail.ru, and Ya.ru—contain 76 percent of all Russian-language blogs.[9] The largest of these, LiveJournal, continues to dominate, primarily due to the fact that it houses the vast majority of bloggers writing on social and political topics. However, after two Distributed Denial of Service attacks on LiveJournal (in April and July 2011), a significant number of users "multiplied," creating duplicate profiles on the Western social networks Google+ and Facebook.[10]

The impact of the Internet on the Russian economy is still relatively small. According to estimates by the Boston Consulting Group, the Internet's contribution to Russian GDP in 2009 stood at 1.6 percent, or 2.1 percent excluding oil and gas ($19.3 billion).[11] Compared with the global average value (3.4 percent of gross domestic product), Russia's commercial Internet remains in the cohort of those lagging behind. Working against Russia are the country's vast geographical expanse, poor infrastructure, and unstable postal service (a key issue for the development of online shopping). As is the case throughout the world, the Internet primarily helps small and medium-sized business, because it allows these businesses to avoid the costs associated with the positioning and marketing of goods. The Boston Consulting Group's researchers predict that the Internet's contribution to GDP will expand to 3.7 percent (5.1 percent excluding the oil and gas sector) by 2015.[12]

Despite the relatively small impact of the Internet on the Russian economy, one can confidently assert that the period when the Russian Internet audience could be considered statistically insignificant ended at the turn of 2009–2010.

The Arab Spring, Social Networking Policies, and Growing Paranoia

As the role of the Internet grows, the authorities increasingly speak of expanding their control over it. The events of the "Arab Spring," along with the unrest in Manezh Square in Moscow and in relatively prosperous England, once again fueled the anxiety of politicians throughout the world (and in Russia) regarding regime stability amid the growing influence of the World Wide Web. In 2011, a number of Russian public figures (including the minister of internal affairs, Rashid Nurgaliyev; the prosecutor general, Yuri Chaika; and the head of the Russian youth organization Rosmolodezh, Vasily Yakimenko) called for control over the Internet.

The Internet may be giving in to manipulation, but not as readily as television and print journalism. Bloggers and commentators themselves are analyzing the news and creating alternative narratives, which at times are very critical of the authorities. This was especially evident during the campaigns in the traditional media deployed against the popular bloggers Alexey Navalny and Yevgeny Roizman. The defamation of these online politicians was quite successful on television and in the newspapers, but on the Internet, such mudslinging was met with the almost immediate exposure of those behind the attacks. This "viral power" makes online politicians more effective than traditional opposition figures.

Despite these temporary victories, however, the collar around online social networking freedom is being tightened with a series of slow movements, which are at times imperceptible but are strategically effective.

The Shrinking Space of Online Social Networking Freedom

One can tentatively divide the ways in which online social networking freedom is being curtailed into the following categories:

- Control over comments in media portals registered as mass media, by Roskomnadzor, the Federal Agency for the Supervision of Communications, IT (Information Technology), and Media.
- Suppression of "extremist" activities, by the Prosecutor's Office / Police / FSB.
- Tracking users, by the police / FSB.
- The strategic control of key media assets, by pro-Kremlin oligarchs.
- Promotion of the idea of "national sovereignty" on the Internet, by the Ministry of Communications / Ministry of Foreign Affairs.

Missing from this list are a number of areas that are difficult to connect directly with the state's activities—including the activities of the pro-Kremlin youth movement Nashi, whose members engage not only in discrediting Internet politicians but also in acquiring paid promotions for their own posts, trolling, and so on.[13] Although Distributed Denial of Service attacks on publicly important websites are difficult to directly connect to state action, owing to such attacks' decentralized nature, the state benefits from such "hidden" acts in the majority of cases—given that the attacks are able to neutralize negative information, whose dissemination the state seeks to limit.

It is worth noting that not only are the methods of curtailment of Internet freedom growing, but so also is the number of those doing the curtailing (that is, the state ministries whose available methods and authority include the possibility of removing network resources). For example, since March 2011, the police have had such authority (under the law "On the Police").

Cracking Down on Bloggers' "Extremist" Comments

Unlike traditional media, online publications have a relatively higher degree of freedom, though since 2010 the state has also heightened its pressure on freedom of expression online. In 2009–2010, the number of convictions of bloggers based on extremist articles grew, and Roskomnadzor was granted the right to issue warnings to online media for anonymous comments, which resulted in websites' transition to a system whereby comments would be moderated and discussion platforms would be transferred to separate discussion forums and the like.[14]

Moreover, in 2011, first Roskomnadzor and then the Ministry of Defense announced a contract for the development of software to scan and detect "extremist" comments automatically, which would further extend the ability of government entities not only to control actual "extremism" (no matter how dubious the definition thereof) but also to monitor online activists. Thus were born the state's so-called contract campaigns against bloggers and the like.

The Prosecution of Bloggers

From January 2009 through October 2011, 23 criminal cases were initiated against bloggers,[15] and 12 arrests were made.[16] Despite the fact that most bloggers are put on probation, the danger of a real prison sentence often hangs over them. For example, in June 2011 the blogger Alaudin Dudko, who had been arrested in 2010, was charged with possessing explosives and narcotics and was sentenced to six years in prison. Before Dudko, the most serious sentence a blogger had received for his or her online activity was two years in a penal colony, which was the sentence imposed on Irek Murtazin, a politician and blogger from Tatarstan (Murtazin was subsequently released on parole).

Most personal prosecution of bloggers takes place at the regional level, especially when bloggers criticize regional authorities. The two most hostile regions for online activity are the Republic of Komi and Kemerovo.

Monitoring Users: More Dangerous Than Censorship

With respect to the personal prosecution of bloggers, the particular concern is not so much even the filtering of individual voices or the pressure on individuals through their hosting platforms but rather the tendency to monitor users. The cases in which groups on the social networking website Vkontakte have been shut down demonstrate the close attention the security forces pay to the site. In addition, reckless statements made on the Internet are often used by the Ministry of Internal Affairs (MVD) to establish a criminal case for combating extremism with a capital "E." The Internet provides a phenomenal opportunity to monitor, manipulate, and prevent online activism. Before our very eyes, state agencies are becoming familiar with the "dark side" of the Internet, albeit not particularly skillfully.

The case of Yandex-money, which began to unfold in April 2011, is an example of the growing interest in the opposition activities of bloggers. The FSB requested data connected with people who had donated to Alexey Navalny's Rospil project. Additionally, judging by media reports, the FSB gave these personal data to activists in the Nashi youth movement, who began calling Navalny's supporters to learn their motives. The FSB has never explained either the basis on which these data were requested from Yandex or why the agency gave this information to Nashi.

The Strategic Risks of Russian Internet Platforms

All social networks on the Web and major online publications are somehow or another connected with the large Russian business structures. In May 2010, Alisher Usmanov owned 50 percent of the company SUP (the operator of LiveJournal, which, as noted above, is the largest Russian blog platform) as well as 35 percent of Digital Sky Technologies (which has been renamed Mail.ru Group), which owns the social networking websites Odnoklassniki and Vkontakte in addition to a number of shares of similar sites throughout the world. Mikhail Prokhorov owned the largest news website, RosBiznesKonsalting (RBK); Vladimir Potanin owned 19 percent of Rambler; and Gazprom-media owned RuTube, the Russian equivalent of YouTube.

Ownership of not-always-profitable online services does not have a direct impact on freedom of expression on the Internet, though it creates potential risks for users' self-expression. As the experience of the past several years has shown, being included among the assets of large holding companies provides no special protection for platforms. Even the influence of Usmanov's media empire could neither protect LiveJournal from attacks nor ensure that the crime would be investigated—or even that a criminal case would be filed in Russia.

One must give credit to the Internet users who, despite a preference for Russian Internet platforms (or for those platforms controlled by Russian businesses), in the event of danger or the inoperability of one or another platform, simply move to another one, often one based in the West. In the most striking example, which took place in connection with the attacks on LiveJournal, the most popular bloggers took just over one and a half months to regain their audience on Google+.

The Impact on the Global Internet Architecture

The attempts of the modern Russian state to limit freedom on the Internet are not limited solely to domestic measures. If the introduction of Cyrillic domain names in December 2010 can be seen not only within the context of "isolationist discourse" but also as a measure to make the Internet more accessible to less-educated segments of society, then other Russian initiatives for reforming international Internet governance are much more alarming. The issue primarily concerns the struggle for recognition of the concept of "national sovereignty" on the Internet and a "National Segment" of the Internet, which, according to several experts, is not only contrary to the Internet's decentralized architecture but could also become a long-term risk to the Internet's existence as a universal network in general.[17]

In May 2011, the Interparliamentary Assembly of the Commonwealth of Independent States published Framework Law No. 36-9, "On the Basis for Regulating the Internet."[18] Although this law has no legal force, it is the recommended template for similar laws "on the Internet" in the Commonwealth. Included in the law is the right of states to annul the registration of domain names that "violate national law or the public order in other states, or are used by the domain's administrator to carry out activities prohibited by national law"—in other words, the possibility of closing domains in other countries at the demand of the state.

In September 2011, Russia—along with China, Uzbekistan, and Tajikistan—proposed the International Code of Conduct for Information Security to the UN secretary-general (it is worth noting that two countries from among the signatories, Uzbekistan and China, are recognized by the human rights organization Reporters Without Borders as "enemies of the Internet").[19] In point (c) of this proposed code, the signatories commit to cooperate "in curbing the dissemination of information that incites terrorism, secessionism or extremism or that undermines other countries' political, economic and social stability, as well as their spiritual and cultural environment"—that is, the widest possible range of actions.

There is every reason to believe that the path toward the sovereignization of the Internet is one of the long-term factors in the political situation surrounding the Internet not only in Russia but also abroad.

Key Trends for the State's Internet Policy

Given the discussion above, it is possible to identify several key trends that will define the course of the state's policy on the Internet in the near and medium terms:

- *Parallel processes of concern and involvement* in the virtual environment. Both a growth in the actual use of large online services and also fear and suspicion of the medium will have a place within the ranks of the government elite. The simultaneity of the processes is important, because it will limit any attempts to accelerate the process of control over the Internet.
- *The ever-growing de facto and legislative regulation* of the Internet, both in the domestic Russian legal space and in the world arena.
- *E-government* and electronic public services will grow, but they will be slowed (compared with other countries) by the institutional

structure of the Russian bureaucracy and domestic opposition in the stagnant environment of Russian officials.

Society

The impact of the Internet is especially great in those cultures where traditions of freedom and individualism have not been strong.[20] The various effects manifested in the form of network activism, the strengthening of trust among participants in a network community, and the uncontrolled development and transformation of national and local identities as well as of predominantly youth-based creativity, are all echoes of the global trends toward societal change.

Network Activism and Crowd Sourcing

According to the research of the American scholar Mary Joyce, the number of cases of online activism (that is, blog campaigns or, as the Russian online activist Marina Litvinovich calls them, "blog waves") are growing exponentially in Russia (figure 27.1). At the same time, the institutionalization of online communities is occurring across the board, while traditional social movements are "going online," which ultimately enables them to find more supporters.

FIGURE 27.1   *Number of Activism Cases in Russia, 2006–2010*

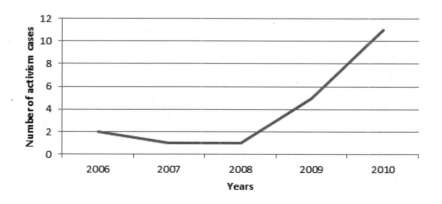

TABLE 27.1 *Russian Civil Crowd-Sourcing Portals, 2009–2011*

2009	2010	THIRD QUARTER, 2011
88003333350.ru (now kartanarushenyi.rf)	dalslovo.ru	vzyatochnik.info
taktaktak.ru	rospil.info	roskomvzyatka.ru
	democrator.ru	gdecasino.org
	streetjournal.org	rynda.org
	lizaalert.org	rosyama.ru
	russian-fires.ru	Ushahidi.rf

Note: This list may be incomplete and may not include smaller portals.

Source: Compiled by the author.

In 2010 and 2011, crowd-sourcing portals underwent a stage of development—if in 2009 it was possible to find only two crowd-sourcing portals, in 2011 six new ones had been created (resulting in a total of 14) (see table 27.1).

"Blog waves" and communities undergoing institutionalization (crowd-sourcing projects are just one example, along with LiveJournal communities and regional forums) are extremely important, both as mechanisms for and elements of the formation of Russian online society. What Sam Greene calls "individual modernization" (see chapter 22)—that is, the choice of autonomous individual strategies—is taking place precisely in close contact with these phenomena. At the same time, not only is individual modernization taking place within communities, but also the modernization (or, more precisely, the reconstruction) of new collective groups is under way. However, in contrast to the penetration of the Internet, this trend still remains at the level of statistical insignificance—the model could begin to work, or it could become just an element of online culture at the turn of the decade.

The Creation of New Spaces

It is widely believed that "withdrawal into the Internet" is a sort of domestic immigration, a form of escapism that ultimately negatively affects political and social changes offline—that is, in the so-called real world. But as we have seen from the examples of Germany and other countries where the process of the "networkization" of politics has gone further than in the rest of the world, the politics of the future is inseparable from the online agitation, online debates, and the commonality of issues that can be grouped under the label "the paradigm of online politics."[21]

Russians, without knowing it, are not emigrating—and even those who do emigrate "with their feet" in real life most often remain in the Russian-language virtual space. They create new virtual spaces. And it is in these spaces that the very interesting processes of the exchange of values, experiences, and examples between "those who have remained" and the "immigrants" take place.

Incidentally, the participation of immigrants from Arab countries who were in Europe had an impact on the online agitation during the "Arab Spring" and on the coverage of these events in the West. Immigrant bloggers created a sort of bridge that brought Western values and standards to their compatriots, who had no other opportunity to learn about democracy and human rights. A good example is Sami Ben Gharbia, the editor of the Tunisian portal Nawaat.org, who before the revolution in Tunisia was forced to live for almost fourteen years in exile and was able to return home only after the events of the winter and spring of 2011. His website was extremely important for changing the situation in the country (later, his services were recognized with an award from Reporters Without Borders) because of its coverage of the self-immolation of the Tunisian fruit vendor Mohamed Bouazizi and the subsequent protests.

As immigration from Russia continues (first of all, as would be expected, as "soft immigration"—that is, without officially changing one's citizenship), the number of people who are ready to talk about life abroad expands.[22] Of course, not all immigrants, by a long shot, believe in democracy or human rights, and many are guided more by the material conveniences afforded by their new place of residence—though they still experience a different reality.

The concentration of an ever-increasing number of Russians in the same virtual space creates a situation whereby supporters of a liberal model of development have not only the opportunity to express their ideas but also to dominate.

Yet another effect is the use of online platforms for choosing an electoral strategy not used in the previous electoral cycle. Thus, during the course of the summer of 2011, many famous bloggers and "traditional" politicians actively participated in defining strategy—either to boycott elections (the "Nakh-nakh" movement, and others) or to vote for any party except for United Russia (the so-called Navalny option). It is entirely possible that in the future, similar joint—and most important, free—discussions could significantly influence the behavior of "online society."

A New Generation of Protopoliticians

Under conditions in which the media are controlled by a select few, the Internet plays the role of a "vent" (to use Gregory Asmolov's image), which serves as an outlet for the energy of Russian activists who do not have an opportunity to realize themselves in the "real" world (it is not possible to express this word "real" without quotation marks, because for many people, online life has become real). Such activists trace out a remarkable trajectory—they become popular online, are noticed at the federal level, and then are co-opted into the regional or federal elite. If the co-option is not successful, these new leaders of public opinion begin being persecuted.

An extreme case is evident in Belarus, where after the suppression of all possible opposition, the special forces went after the moderators of revolutionary groups on the Vkontakte website that had attracted very impressive memberships—between 100,000 and 200,000.

Many of today's moderators of decidedly nonpolitical communities and forums are in essence "protopoliticians"; that is, quite often, these are independent people who are critical of power and who often have carefully distanced themselves from politics—as does, for example, the "blue bucket" movement. The issue is that the cost of participation in political life is too high—it involves slanderous campaigns in the traditional media, which online activists can still somehow manage, along with very real criminal cases (as in the case of Alexey Navalny, who is still under investigation in the Kirov region).

In a situation where the ratings both of the United Russia Party and of Vladimir Putin are falling, the entire "traditional opposition" has been discredited, and the majority of opposition politicians have negative ratings, a "black hole" has been formed in the representation of the middle class (according to Mikhail Dmitriev).[23] It is precisely this black hole that can be filled by those who for the time being remain online protopoliticians, who are often popular bloggers or moderators of online communities and thus possess transparency and the trust of their readers.

Navalny, a federal celebrity who is hardly prominent in the polls of the Levada Center, is one of the most striking examples of a protopolitician (and, broadly speaking, is already a real politician). Not having made his career in "traditional" politics (indeed, he was expelled from the most liberal party, while the People (Narod) movement was generally not popular), he became extremely popular online. Despite the fact that only about 6 percent of Russians know Navalny himself, the slogan he coined—the "party of crooks and thieves"—is recognized by at least 31 percent of the population.[24]

The Desacralization of the Notion of Power

One of the effects of the Internet and of online services is the nascent recognition of the axiom that "code is law" ("code" being the primary regulator of cyberspace) and the consequent understanding of many things, including government functions, as simply services. This is an extremely important psychological transition that is essential for desacralizing power. Moreover, this understanding means that these things are seen not just as services but as online services, which repositions users (that is, citizens) not so far from administrators (officials). It is precisely along these lines that a number of online projects have been created, such as rosyama.ru, streetjournal.org, and terron.ru/roads.

The most serious such recognition is presented in the book *Cloudy Democracy* by the Urals politician Leonid Volkov. Online activists are applying Internet technology to create alternative forms of self-government. Such forms are significantly more effective and transparent than "traditional" mechanisms of public administration. This contrast, which is becoming apparent to an ever-expanding circle of individuals, on the one hand undermines support for the bureaucratic class and on the other hand leads to efforts to push for the recognition of the necessity of change in government.

An important attempt to reimagine democracy can be found in "crowd funding," or online fund-raising. One feature of 2011 was the success of crowd-funding campaigns—including fund-raising for the Rospil project and for the publication of Boris Nemtsov's report criticizing the Putin regime and exposing its alleged wrongdoings—which raised a total of 8 million rubles, a record for Russian online activism. This is not quite a trend, because other similar projects have not met with similar success (for example, fund-raising for EJ.ru and oldmos.ru). After Navalny's success, the Duma proceeded to reform the legislation concerning electronic money, clearly with the goal of reducing the potential opportunities for online crowd funding. Although these phenomena instilled confidence in Internet politicians, most important, they showed that in virtual Russia, an "ideal democracy" based on citizens' voluntary contributions is possible.

The Main Scenarios

If, at the end of 2010, the decision in Russia concerning the role of online society and the country's situation with respect to the Internet was resting with the government (at the time, I proposed the dichotomy of China and Estonia as representing two polarized strategies vis-à-vis the Internet[25]), then today the ball is in society's court.

In 2011, the government decided not to make any sudden moves, and despite slowly rolling in the direction of the Chinese pole (that is, toward the limitation of online freedom), it remained within the scope of the "inertial variant" of development (a partial restriction of freedoms, and the independent development of online society).

Four Bifurcations

In general, the multiplicity of scenarios associated with the Internet, politics, and society can be summarized as a succession of four bifurcations (figure 27.2). Of course, it is clear that this is an approximation and that actual life will be more complicated. The first point of bifurcation comes after the 2011 elections. It will become clear whether the solidarity of online society will manifest itself in the form of unusually high levels of

FIGURE 27.2   *The Four Bifurcations*

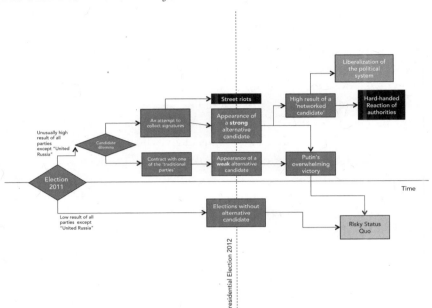

votes for parties other than United Russia—in other words, whether the "Navalny option" can affect the election results. If it cannot, then there is a direct route toward an uncontested presidential election.

If, at this first point of bifurcation, the "Navalny option" does not succeed and the Russian presidential elections indeed turn out to be uncontested, then there is every reason to expect the resumption of a state that can tentatively be called the "risky status quo," wherein the degree of "riskiness" will rise as Vladimir Putin grows older. Internet risks in this case are tied to nationalist and/or neo-Nazi mobilization and its outbreaks, to episodes of ethnic violence, and also to outbreaks of civil (not nationalist) activity as a result of various natural and human-made emergencies or of failed economic policies. The danger of the risky status quo lies in the fact that spontaneous protests that are not channeled into any state or social outlets can appear for any reason—moreover, not only in authoritarian countries but also in relatively democratic countries such as the United States, with its Occupy Wall Street movement.

Second, if one assumes that the "Navalny option" succeeds at the first point of bifurcation and that United Russia receives unexpectedly few votes (it is not about United Russia being defeated, but simply of a result less than 45 to 50 percent, which in a symbolic sense would mean a significant weakening of the position of the ruling party), then the situation could develop in the following way. Inspired by their own success and joined in solidarity, the members of online society would have trouble in the presidential elections ("the candidate's dilemma")—they would have to either attempt to use all available means to collect the required number of signatures (as the experience of the PARNAS party demonstrated, the possibility of the Central Election Committee, TsIK, rejecting signatures is very strong) or to negotiate with one of the traditional parties where the risk of losing control (as in the case of the party A Just Cause, or Pravoe Delo) will always be strong.

Third, an agreement with one of the parties would likely mean a weak candidate, and as a result, an unconditional victory for Putin at the election, which in turn would mark a return to the state described above as a "risky status quo."

However, one can assume another option: The "online opposition" refuses to compromise with one of the parties, and by means of online mobilization is able to collect signatures (the blogosphere consists of approximately 7 million plus approximately 112,000 active bloggers, and modern technology enables this) and put forward its own candidate. If the signatures are accepted by the Central Election Committee, then the candidate goes to the election; if not, then street demonstrations are entirely possible—perhaps not immediately, but closer to summer.

Fourth, if the candidate from the "online opposition" loses badly to Putin, then this will deliver a strong blow to the very idea of online mobilization (however, bloggers' confidence will be restored quickly enough). If an alternative candidate wins enough votes to be symbolically significant (that is, approximately 20–25 percent), then the country will move forward to the next junction: Either the authorities will scour the whole online space immediately after the election, or, in a less likely move, will make concessions and liberalize the political system.

The Situation after 2012

If there are three "entry points" in 2012, then it is clear that the number of variations and combinations of variations will grow (figure 27.3). In two cases (the "toughening of the system" and the "risky status quo"), it is likely that there will be a transition toward a repetitive, cyclical scenario. In the case of the "toughening of the system," this is a cycle of "stagnation—thaw—stagnation" that can potentially continue within the bounds of a single Kondratieff cycle (that is, through 2030).[26] After the conclusion of a given Kondratieff cycle, changes seem inevitable, but their analysis is beyond our time frame.

Within the scope of the planning horizon used in this book, the only possible violation is the situation in 2015–2016, when the presidential elections in Belarus could provoke a "Belarusian Spring" and the victory of an alternative candidate. Together with demographic changes and the possible deterioration of the economic situation, this could trigger the "demonstration effect" (for a prime recent example, the Arab Spring has

FIGURE 27.3   *The Three Entry Points*

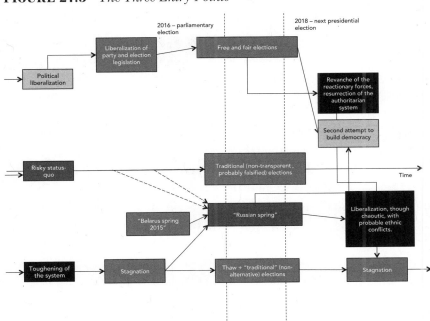

spread among the Arab states precisely because of this demonstration effect) and lead to a "Russian Spring."

I say "Russian" Spring because there is reason to believe that in connection with the toughening of the system after 2012, only the nationalist political culture will survive, while the liberal political culture will be definitively suppressed and/or forced out of the country. Its participation in the "Russian Spring" could lead either to chaotic liberalization and democratization, which would be replaced either by ethnic conflicts (the Serbian scenario) or (which, however, is very unlikely) the building of a democratic society on the model of the Eastern European nation-states (the Czechoslovak scenario). In either event, one can say that the toughening of the system in 2012 could lead to territorial changes in 2018.

The state of "risky status quo" could also quite possibly become cyclical and repeat itself through 2020 and beyond. The riskiness lies in the constant danger of falling back to the scenario of a "Russian Spring." But this is less likely than the case with the strengthening of the political situation after 2012. The lack of reforms (the essence of the status quo) in this period will continue to intensify the risks. The electoral period in this case will be passed through with the use of "traditional electoral technologies."

In the case of the "liberalization of the system" in 2012, one must expect changes in party and electoral legislation, along with alternative elections in 2016–2018. It is possible, however, that revanchist forces could come to power through the elections, and these could be capable of returning the country to a state of stagnation in the self-repeating cycle of "stagnation and thaw"—with the only difference being that such a regime would only function while the existing technical and economic realities were maintained (that is, through 2030–2040).

If this stagnation does not occur, however, then for the first time in many years Russia can attempt to build a democracy from the ground up. To find this path even with the series of extremely simplified points of bifurcation sketched above would not be simple; it seems (and in this case the author does not hide his prodemocratic sentiments), however, that this will be the only possible scenario for the successful and bloodless integration of the country into the subplanetary system of global democratic governance, which by that time will encompass the most developed macro regions on Earth.

Notes

1. "Internet-auditoriya rastyot bystree, chem ozhidalos'" (Internet audience grows faster than expected), press release, Public Opinion Foundation, June 15, 2011, http://bd.fom.ru/report/cat/smi/smi_int/pressr_150611.

2. This conclusion was reached by the author based on an analysis of the structure of population dispersal and the country's demographic structure.

3. "Proniknovenie 3G telefonov v RF prevysilo vse prognozy" (The extent of 3G phones in the RF has exceeded all estimates), October 27, 2010, http://rumetrika.rambler.ru/review/0/4544.

4. Mobile Internet access is particularly important for villages, where for many reasons, it is too expensive to install broadband Internet access.

5. "Rossiya ustupaet pochti vsem evropeyskim stranam po proniknoveniyu Interneta" (The extent of Internet use in Russia lags behind that of the majority of European countries), November 10, 2010, http://rumetrika.rambler.ru/review/0/4560.

6. "Reklama na Yandekse" (Advertising on Yandex), http://advertising.yandex.ru/advertiser/research/tns.xml.

7. "Znakomstva i obschenie" (Acquaintances and intercourse), www.liveinternet.ru/rating/ru/meeting/day.html.

8. *Blogosfera Runeta*, Vesna 2009 (Runet's Blogosphere, Spring 2009), information newsletter, http://download.yandex.ru/company/yandex_on_blogosphere_spring_2009.pdf.

9. See ibid.

10. Distributed Denial of Service is an attack on a computing system with the goal of pushing it to the point of failure. It attempts to create conditions whereupon ordinary users of the system cannot access the system's resources (the servers), or where access is made difficult.

11. Bartolomeo Banche, Vladislav Boutenco, and Olga Kotsur, *Russia Online: How the Internet Is Transforming the Russian Economy* (Moscow: Boston Consulting Group, 2011), www.bcg.ru/documents/file79164.pdf.

12. Ibid.

13. Trolling is the practice of posting provocative messages with the aim of starting a conflict between discussion participants by means of inflicting mutual insults, leading a discussion away from the realm of civilized discourse, and ultimately discrediting the author's original message.

14. It is worth noting that even the promise Dmitri Medvedev gave to bloggers in April 2011 to look into the matter did not improve the situation.

15. These are the author's calculations.

16. Including the arrest of activists from the group Voina (War); the Internet served as the main channel for the distribution of information about its installations.

17. The National Segment of the Internet is understood as "domains that are recognized, as prescribed by national legislation, as national domains of the state; Internet resources located in other domains or not belonging to any domain, whose hosting is provided within the territory of the state; and national network operators and service providers"; CIS Interparliamentary Assembly model law "On the Basis for Regulating the Internet," Article 2.

18. Model'niy zakon "Ob osnovakh regulirovaniya Interneta" (Framework Law "On the Basis for Regulating the Internet"), Interparliamentary Assembly of the CIS, May 16, 2011, www.iacis.ru/html/?id=22&pag=792&nid=1.

19. Letter dated September 12, 2011, from the permanent representatives of China, the Russian Federation, Tajikistan, and Uzbekistan to the United Nations, addressed to the secretary-general, http://blog.internetgovernance.org/pdf/UN-infosec-code.pdf.

20. This concerns a sort of "base effect." The Internet has had the most shocking effect on those cultures in which free communication and a lack of hierarchy are not characteristic, as evidenced by the events of the "Arab Spring."

21. In September 2011, the Pirate Party of Germany, having carried out agitation only on the Internet and concerning itself primarily with questions of importance for the online paradigm, received 8.5 percent of the votes in the election for the Berlin City Council, coming out ahead of a member of Angela Merkel's Free Democrat coalition.

22. Anastasiya Kornya, "Neuyutnaya Rossiya" (Uncomfortable Russia), *Vedomosti*, June 10, 2011, www.vedomosti.ru/newspaper/article/256238/neuyutnaya_rossiya.

23. "Rossiyane o predstavitelyakh oppozitsii" (Russia's citizens of the opposition), press release, Levada Center, March 25, 2011, www.levada.ru/press/2011032507.html.

24. "O partii 'Edinaya Rossiya'" (On the party "United Russia"), press release, Levada Center, May 5, 2011, www.levada.ru/press/2011050501.html.

25. Alexey Sidorenko, "Nastoyaschee i buduschee rossiyskogo Interneta: Suschestvuyuschee polozhenie, regional'naya proektsiya, perspektivy" (The present and future of the Russian Internet: The current state, regional projections, and prospects), *Vestnik obshchestvennogo mneniya* (Russian Public Opinion Herald), no. 3, July–September 2010, http://ecsocman.edu.ru/data/2011/03/17/1268219842/Pages%20from%20vom3-5.pdf.

26. A Kondratieff cycle is a sinusoidal-like cycle in the modern capitalist world economy that lasts for forty to fifty years. On the basis of previous policy changes associated with the end or beginning of economic cycles, it seems logical to assume that any authoritarian-imposed political cyclicity will be finished within the scope of a single Kondratieff cycle.

CONCLUSIONS

Maria Lipman and Nikolay Petrov

The Putin era is over. Vladimir Putin may still remain Russia's uncontested national leader eleven years after he first became the president. Moreover, in 2011 he appears to have secured another twelve years of the presidency for himself. Yet, the political and economic system created under Putin's leadership in the first decade of the twenty-first century has largely exhausted itself. It is not capable of dealing with rapidly changing conditions, and Putin and his team will need to make many modifications if they hope to stay in power in the years ahead.

To hold on to power, Putin masterminded a system of governance in a highly favorable financial situation. The prices of raw materials increased, providing ever-growing revenues that led to rapid economic growth. The authorities could buy whatever they needed at any moment—from citizens' trust to solutions to any problems that appeared. As a result, the political system and system of governance became, on the one hand, extremely primitive, while on the other hand, they became extremely unwieldy, because given the poorly functioning system, an individual approach to management needed to be applied in each case. The government will have to change the current political management to match the increasing complexity of Russia's socioeconomic and technological environment.

In the coming decade, the system will likely have to respond to a variety of crises, which might facilitate a strengthening of the system and increase its complexity, or it could lead to a loss of control over the country and the replacement of the current system with a new one. But it is a thankless task to warn the authorities of the danger and call on them to be responsible before their people. It's an equally thankless task to try to guess today when and how the crisis will occur. It seemed to us more productive to opt for a more academic approach and investigate the factors that are determining the development of Russia today, the crossroads that lie ahead, and the risks that appear on the various paths. This is the approach that has been taken by the participants of Russia-2020, although our interpretations of ongoing events and actions are not always well-integrated and thus sometimes openly contradict one another.

The balance between descriptivism and prescriptivism in the scenarios was decided largely in favor of the former. This will allow the reader to formulate his or her own opinion about the future of the country, which might differ from the opinion of the authors.

Scenarios for 2020

As we considered possible developmental trajectories for Russia until 2020, in addition to our own scenarios, we also analyzed the overall framework and four key elements: drivers, triggers, crossroads, and risks.

The External Framework

The main external framework is the world political and economic order and the place Russia holds in this order. The Russian economy, and consequently the Russian political system, is highly dependent on the world economy, especially on the price of mineral resources, primarily oil, gas, and other hydrocarbons. The influence of the latter is nonlinear; in fact, it is multidirectional. Higher prices might lead to a worsening of the "Russian sickness" connected with the primitivization of the economy, but they also might affect the entire political system. Another result of high prices for energy resources might be a decline in world economic development and lower demand for raw materials, which, in turn, might undermine the economic model based on them.

Developments in the post-Soviet arena, including in Russia's imme-diate neighbors, are of crucial importance. Sometimes these are supple-mental sources of power (joint labor, capital, and consumer markets), and sometimes they are a source of weakness (competition for labor and the attention of the West).

In contrast to the Soviet Union, Russia is an open system. Today the country must compete fiercely for financial and human capital from abroad as well as hold onto its own capital.

Drivers

The functioning of the system is contingent on the economy and the mode of governance. To keep the system afloat, the economy must provide a constantly growing influx of financial resources. Likewise, the stability of the system depends on the quality of governance: To maintain stabil-ity, the quality has to be improved. These two factors are interrelated: in recent years, governance has steadily deteriorated, but growing financial resources compensated for its ineffectiveness. If resources dwindle and can no longer compensate for the deficiency, tension in the system will increase, which will necessitate urgent reform. In this situation, even a small malfunction in either the economy or the form of governance might lead to a serious systemic crisis and a new trajectory.

Neither the Russian elites nor the citizens are a vehicle of national de-velopment. In the absence of internal sources of energy, the system follows a reactive mode of development. If such internal drivers of development do not emerge, there will be no mechanism to guide it toward becoming a constructive force.

Triggers

Mechanisms of change are most likely to be triggered by malfunctions in governance and domestic political crises, along with steam let off by an overheated, tense system—for example, increased interethnic tension in the Caucasus that slips out of control. Triggers might be attempts to tighten the screws, or to the contrary might be attempts to loosen them, or threads so worn that the screws no longer turn at all. A systemic malfunction leading to a noninertial scenario of development might be caused by asymmetry in the changes and actions of various parts of the system. This might occur when social policies become stricter in 2012–2013 in conjunction with undeveloped political parties and no channels for society to let off steam. A strong trigger might be set off by relatively free elections, such as the elections of 1989. It is not necessary for there to be one strong tremor. Several smaller factors pushing the system to change might be sufficient.

Risks

External risks include economic and political destabilization in the world that entail an economic crisis or a drop in demand for resources, which, as the events of 2008 and 2009 demonstrated, hit the Russian economy hard. Another external risk is serious destabilization along the Russian borders, which is a particularly severe threat in Central Asia.

Such a crisis might also set off numerous internal risks. The most significant internal risk lies in the tangled knot of problems in the North Caucasus—including a further escalation of tension and terrorist activity in the North Caucasus republics, worsening interethnic conflicts, and large-scale terrorist attacks in Moscow and other major cities. In many ways, the North Caucausus challenges are simply Russian problems pushed to the extreme—weak institutions, corruption, and so on. Other crises might be human-made accidents and disasters caused by the exhausted infrastructure, especially in health care and education, where the situation, which has steadily worsened during the last twenty years, might drastically decline in the next decade. We note here that financial and governance instruments cannot prevent or significantly mitigate the negative consequences of these challenges, but they might, in an unfavorable confluence of circumstances, seriously exacerbate them.

When we look at the risks Russia faces from a historical perspective, we see how remarkably unchanged they are. Almost two hundred years ago, writer Nikolai Gogol said that Russia's main problems were fools and bad roads. The same can be said today—although now the fools are called "bureaucracy" and the bad roads are called "infrastructure." There are also, however, new risks, which are largely functions of the globalized

FIGURE 1   *Tree of Probable Scenarios*

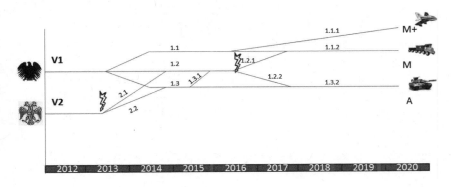

world: the steady emigration of the most entrepreneurial segments of the population, and the country's dependence on foreign markets.

Y-tracks

As shown in the tree of probable scenarios presented in figure 1, the closest chronological "planned" crossroads for Russia is the 2012 presidential election.

At the outset of our project in fall 2010, we acted on the premise that Vladimir Putin would remain Russia's leader after the 2012 elections.

Originally we considered two variants:

V1. The positions of the formal leader and real leader will be combined;
V2. The formal and real leaders remain different people (tandem rule).[1]

We agreed, however, that V2 is not sustainable and, therefore, V1 is much more likely.

Our line of reasoning proved correct one year later, in September 2011, when president Medvedev announced that he would step down after his first term and Putin would run for president in 2012.

The choice of V1 over V2 can be explained by the fact that the "tandem rule" of 2008–2011 complicated or even blocked opportunities for political maneuvering. Therefore a switch back to a single primary source of decisionmaking authority can be seen as an attempt to deal with the growing inefficiency of governance.

The next crossroads will be reached in 2013–2014 (or earlier) (see figure 1), when the authorities will be forced to make changes to the country's social policies—cutting back on expenditures as the state's economic capabilities contract. A consequence of this will be the restructuring of the relationship between the leadership and society. At this stage, we see three possible variants lying ahead:

V1.1 Reactive modernization
V1.2 Stagnation with elements of political modernization
V1.3 Strengthening of authoritarian tendencies
(authoritarianization)

In all three variants it is practically impossible to avoid increased political competition; this will require a (currently absent) mechanism for reconciling the interests of the main interest groups (including regional ones). In the case of authoritarianization (V1.3), political competition is a destructive factor that undermines the foundations of the personified and unitary regime. There is also an option of rapid maneuvering with shock therapy and a return to the paternalistic model, but it is less likely.

The third crossroads that we envisioned falls on the electoral cycle of 2016–2018. At this point each of the three variants mentioned above branches out into a variety of paths. Reactive modernization (V1.1) might continue, remaining under the control of the ruling elite (V1.1.2), or it might become V1.1.1: Modernization + "Gorbachev-style," in which the process started at the top spins out of control. When Stagnation (V1.2) goes through economic and political crises, it changes to either Moderate Modernization (V1.1.2) or to V1.2.2: Authoritarianization.

It is useful to describe the variants of development in more detail.

Reactive modernization—for example, World Trade Organization accession and joining the OECD, as well as the development of the Customs Union—will enhance the significance of the external framework and impose binding obligations on Russia. This would reduce the opportunity to change the rules "in process," ease the pressure caused by the arbitrary treatment of business, and stimulate competition. Law enforcement practices will improve as a result of the presence of foreign players, but also because government and business will no longer be closely interlinked. The role of the judiciary and the representative branches will rise; public politics will reemerge. Political parties represented in the Duma will be ensured a fair share of Cabinet positions. Elections will begin to make a difference; the number of elective offices will grow. Elements of federalism will be reinstituted—tax revenues will be redistributed so regions can rely on their own tax base. Regional leaders will be directly elected; the upper house, the Federation Council, will be reorganized to better represent regional interests. Governing functions will be redistributed from the top downward between different levels of authority. Local government will be consolidated. With people's real incomes growing, the tax rates will increase and taxation will become more differentiated.

Stagnation with elements of political modernization is an inertial scenario. The framework defined by tight government control over business and society remains in place, but some elements of public politics begin to emerge. This includes the enactment of primary elections, a return of direct mayoral elections, and a shift away from a purely proportional electoral system at the lower (municipal), medium (regional), and even higher (federal) levels. Control can be eased over some other elements of the electoral system, such as the registration of political party slates and candidates, parties' electoral hurdles, and so on. While the budgetary system and the appointments of regional leaders remain overcentralized, mechanisms of financial assistance to the regions will be improved, and the interests of regional political elites will be better taken into account.

Under *authoritarianization*, the government deals with emerging problems, including social unrest, by resorting to police-state methods. The party and electoral system are locked in their current state; elections are turned into purely ritualistic ceremonies aimed at legitimizing the political status quo. A crackdown on the education system provides for enhanced unification and brainwashing. "Nashi" (a Kremlin-masterminded youth group), the youth section of United Russia, and other youth organizations are transformed into Komsomol-like structures and are actively used by the government as an instrument of state control over younger constituencies and, in the mode of the Chinese cultural revolution, as a tool of pressure and intimidation of the elites. Other elements include the enlargement of the administrative regions through the rearrangement of regional borders. Freedom of travel is constrained and foreign policy becomes more confrontational.

Uneven development in each vector of change and intensifying contradictions between the vectors may produce crises.

A real two-party system cannot be created as long as the political parties are controlled from above. The framework of managed modernization could be broken if the system weakens, if there is a schism among the elites, or if citizens are encouraged to get politically involved. In *Modernization+* (V.1.2.1–V.1.1.1), there would be also a true separation of powers and strengthening of institutions, along with the emergence of other, increasingly autonomous centers of influence. This scenario implies a transformation of the existing system. The Parliament would have real control over the actions of the government, including the security and defense structures. The judiciary branch would become more independent, and federalism more robust. However, when the state is forced to confront unavoidable crises, Modernization+ might easily morph into Authoritarianization, as happened in 1993.

Under *Authoritarianization* (V.1.3–V.1.3.1), elections would be totally emasculated and become a kind of ritual demonstration of loyalty. The transition to a one-and-a-half-party system with imitation political parties would be complete. The models for this kind of development are Belarus, Kazakhstan, and several other post-Soviet regimes. Regions might be enlarged for ease of governance, or federal districts be turned into full-fledged levels of power. The actions of various power verticals (top-to-bottom power structures) would be coordinated more strictly, and the structures would be enlarged. A politburo-like entity would be created to reconcile the interests of the various clans. In this scenario, the role of the security structures would be strengthened and include vetting and maintaining control over the elites.

Thus, in the 2010s Russia faces three main crossroads: the election of the president and configuration of power in 2012; the choice of social-economic course and political models in 2012–2014; and the choice of the configuration of power in 2016–2018. By the end of this decade these three crossroads might produce three main development trajectories: Moderate Modernization (V1.1.2–V1.2.1); Modernization+ (V1.1.1), and Authoritarianization (V1.2.2.)

The main point of bifurcation is the choice of political-economic model for the next decade. The leadership was still making this choice in late 2011, but the final picture will not be clear until after the 2012 presidential elections. The configuration of power in 2011–2012—first and foremost, the end of the tandem rule and Putin's return to the topmost position— seems to be *informed by* that choice rather than being the starting point for making it. In other words, the pattern of governance dictated the structure of the leadership for the next decade, not the other way around. The Russian leaders appear to have made that choice as early as in 2010. At that point they had an opportunity to compare the potentials of the two key models— the so-called "traditionalist" model (redistribution of rents from extraction and refinement of natural resources, carried out under strict government control) and the "modernization" model. With the growth of world prices on energy resources, the technological and geopolitical potential of the "raw materials" model seemed to be far from exhausted. This persuaded the business and political elites that there was no urgency in transitioning to an alternative strategy.

Turbulence associated with the decreased resources can be put off, but such tactics will be costly. The choice between reforming now or putting it off until later can be described as Gorbachev's dilemma.

A question arises how the timing of the launch of unpopular reforms will shape the trajectory. If procrastination is the choice, the existing problems will be aggravated, and some options for future development may be closed. For instance, if the further postponement of reforms push- es a critical mass of Russia's potential agents of modernization to leave the country, this can hinder or even block the opportunity to modernize. In addition, such a policy would progressively deplete available financial resources even before Russia entered a period of turbulence; meanwhile a shortage of resources in an unstable situation is especially dangerous since it reduces the capacity for maneuver. The government, however, is still likely to stave off reform, the mentioned risks notwithstanding. Rus- sia's decisionmakers are "short-distance runners," and generally refrain from setting strategic goals, opting instead for tactical decisions taken as situations arise. In 2008–2011 Russia "bought" a deferment from the crisis: The government did not opt for economic restructuring and instead increased social spending. If the crisis had been short-lived and the world economy had quickly recovered, this would have created favorable conditions in Russia for the delayed management of the consequences of the crisis. But things turned out quite differently.

The extension of the presidential term from four to six years enacted in 2008 seems to indicate that the Kremlin is preparing to launch unpopular measures at the outset of the 2012–2018 tenure; the government may expect that by the end of the six-year period, any negative sentiments would be forgotten. However, the 2014 Olympic Games in Sochi appear to conflict with such a timeline. Conceived as a global demonstration of the achievements of Putin-led Russia, in particular in the North Caucasus, the period of the Olympic Games and the years preceding them are hardly an appropriate time for policy moves fraught with the potential for destabilization.

With regard to periods of turbulence, it is important to keep in mind the asynchronous development of the Russian regions. Turbulence will hurt them at different stages of development, and the effects will vary quite significantly region to region. Putin's government has always refrained from taking steps that might lead to a simultaneous deterioration of living standards throughout Russia to avoid the risk of simultaneous protests. This concern is likely to remain, resulting in the government's choosing the "traditionalist" option over the "modernization" one. Thus, for the next decade, modernization will remain, in the best case, a way to prop up the effectiveness of the "rents" model. This bodes ill, because the intra-systemic contradictions in this situation are only going to grow.

The Resulting Likely Scenarios

To sum up, three likely, realistic pictures of Russia in 2020 can be visualized:

1. A moderately modernized Russia—"Early Putin," or "Putin the Reformer"

2. Russia in radical modernization mode—"Perestroika-2", or "Neo-Gorbachev"

3. Russia on the way to a resurgent dictatorship—"Stalin-lite"

A moderately modernized Russia (Early Putin, Putin the Reformer) is a 2020 option that can be seen as the inertial one, an evolution of the current course. It implies that most key elements of the currently existing political system remain in place, with a somewhat enhanced role and independence for the political parties, including a transformation of United Russia into something of a dominant party. This would mean a more robust separation of powers and an intensification of political competition. Higher competition increases the likelihood of repoliticization and more active political participation. Thereby the new spiral turn signals a return—with some reservations—to the situation of 2002–2003. Some elements of federalism are restored, including direct elections of regional leaders and a transformation of the upper chamber of the Federal Assembly into an organ of genuine regional representation. The economy will have a more solid market character as the government reduces its involvement in economic life. Meanwhile, the social sphere will continue to decline as a result of a protracted deterioration of the quality of health care and education, and the continued outflow of the entrepreneurial groups from Russia. In foreign policy, Russia will refrain from binding partnerships and integrationism and will go on with a balancing act between the main global centers of power. There is no nationally shared ideology; instead there is an ideological mix consisting of elements borrowed from different époques and concepts.

The "moderate" nature of this scenario does not rule out crises. The latter can be generated if changes are irregular and one sphere is modified faster than others. Such changes can increasingly come into conflict with each other, first and foremost, as a result of a separation of powers horizontally and vertically. This can lead to a correction of certain elements within the framework of the moderate modernization; or the trajectory can shift to Modernization Plus/Perestroika-2 or Authoritarization.

In Perestroika-2 (Neo-Gorbachev), political parties are still controlled "from above"; a fully fledged two- or three-party system will take a radical modernization that will also imply a genuine separation of powers and a consolidation of political institutions. In particular, this would mean a gradual transformation of the parliament into a relevant representative body that is able to ensure accountability of the executive branch, including the accountability of the "power" ministries. The parliamentary pattern of governance appears to meet these functions better. Federalism is reinstated, with powerful and influential municipal and regional levels; these levels of governance are assured of sufficient tax revenues that enable them to perform a broad range of functions. Business is separated from political power. The state's functions are significantly reduced. The societal forces gain an additional boost; social and territorial mobility is growing. Although migration within the country is growing, fewer people show an interest in leaving Russia altogether. Foreign policy shifts toward European integrationism. This kind of scenario, like Gorbachev's perestroika, can be self-sustaining, with the initial effort aimed at improving the existing system and causing an avalanche effect.

Radical modernization will face more hurdles related to irregular development than any other scenario. This means that if such a course were to be adopted, crises would be highly likely. Some of them could strengthen the system, but others can push the trajectory toward authoritarianization.

"Stalin-lite," or Russia slipping toward dictatorship, implies the rise of personalistic elements in the political system, and thus a complete evisceration of elections, which should be fully transformed into a ritual of pledging allegiance. A one-and-a-half party system will finally take shape, with political parties being reduced to mere imitations. This would mean a drift toward some of the post-Soviet regimes, such as Belarus or Kazakhstan. The authoritarian framework may be expected to launch an enlargement of the administrative regions—for the sake of more practicable governance. Another possible move, if the authoritarian model were to be adopted, would be to turn Russia's eight federal districts into a fully fledged "level" of government authority. In any case, centralizing and unitary trends will be enhanced. This mode of governance will call for a more rigid coordination of various government "verticals" and their enlargement, along with the establishment of a "politburo" whose mission will be to reconcile the interests of major "clans." The role of the power agency will inevitably grow; and to make up for the missing political competition, a mechanism of "purges" will be introduced.

For the national economy, this would mean a greater role for state corporations and "crony businesses" highly dependent on the political elites. The rent-seeking model will be further consolidated; with rent distribution tightly regulated by the centralized government. State–society relations will be further informed by the paternalistic pattern; and the "besieged fortress" mind-set will be broadly disseminated. The "dissenting" constituencies will be pushed to leave the country. This will be accompanied by a rise of nationalist/xenophobic sentiments and a threat of interethnic clashes leading to disintegration and a de-facto separation of some of the ethnic regions. Relations with the outside world will also bear elements of confrontation.

In the "Stalin-lite" scenario, conflicts and crises can be provoked by the internal competition of the elite "clans" and corporations, and by irregular development along with the essential limits of centralized management of a country as vast as Russia. Another factor of crises is the inevitable further decline of the efficiency of governance and a failure to respond to external challenges.

Scenario Malfunctions and Transitions, or Wild-Card Scenarios

While the political calendar will designate possible turning points—and therefore, also points of bifurcation—there might be a broad range of concrete scenarios that would represent variations within the three main pathways. These scenarios would be set in motion by a change in the external framework, the effect of risk factors, or malfunctions in the system caused by either governance decisions or unforeseen circumstances.

Several of these scenarios, such as Russia's admittance to the World Trade Organization, may be forecasted with significant certainty in the near future. But it's impossible to rationally predict the likelihood or time that other "elements of turbulence" might appear. This, however, does not mean that they should not be taken into consideration.

Given these factors, it is useful to look at several of the possible "wild-card" scenarios that might occur separately or in various combinations.

Wild Card Scenario:
Second Wave of the World Crisis and a Drop in Raw Materials Prices

A significant and long-term drop in prices for raw materials would cause a radical cut in government spending and a revision of social obligations—which even now the government cannot meet in full measure. This would imply the need to tighten the budgetary belt, both for the elite (which would set off a sharp intensification of intra-elite conflicts) and for citizens (which would spur more active public politics). Because the structure of the economy and the entire construction of the system is based on a high income from commodities, such developments would require a systemic overhaul.

The intra-elite conflict will spill out to the public realm. The federal television channels—which since the early 2000s have remained the chief and indivisible political resource of the leadership and the key instrument for imposing the sense of the leadership's being unchallenged and uncontested—will become a venue of political competition and genuine debate. The conflicting elites will reach out to the people, seeking to muster constituencies and forcing people to make political choices. The scenario in question can evolve as a major political crisis, with Putin's government resorting to repression in seeking to restore "order." Putin's leadership can be pushed out by radical nationalist forces condemning Putin's government for "selling out to the West" or by a liberal wing declaring him responsible for wasting natural resources and failing to prevent a national decline. But even in the best-case scenario, a reinstatement of the traditional pattern—centralized government and a monopoly of power—should never be ruled out. Russian politics has been too radically de-institutionalized in the 2000s and the people have been pushed too far away from political participation to expect a smooth transition to a moderate, reasonably democratic polity. In the Russian environment, gradual repoliticization is preferable to crisis developments, yet crises are far from ruled out.

Wild Card Scenario: Russia Without Putin

To test the sustainability of the regime, we conducted the mental experiment of removing or replacing the main players. Russia currently does not pass this sustainability test, and if Putin left the political arena or were significantly weakened by a sharp decline in his popularity rating, drastic destabilization would be likely to follow. If Putin somehow disappears from the scene, he will leave behind a highly powerful and deeply entrenched inner circle. We are talking about a powerful group of business/banking tycoons with a state security background who have accumulated enormous wealth (that is, they are dollar billionaires) and clout during Putin's tenure. Keeping them in place would be deadly for any new ruler, but challenging them would mean destabilizing the country; it could be highly risky for the top leader and would likely cause a fierce, and possibly bloody, political struggle. Anyone trying to take Putin's place as supreme arbiter will thus face a highly competitive battle. Another option would be a change of the entire configuration with empowerment of some of the previously weak institutions, such as the upper house of the parliament or the military, but this would also be bound to cause a major destabilization. This intra-elite battle for power with weak institutionalization could be compared—with obvious reservations—to the one that took place after Stalin's death. Eventually this might come down to either a "new Putin" or a split in the ruling elite.

Wild Card Scenario: Destabilization of Neighbors

The personalized regimes in the majority of the countries neighboring Russia—in Belarus, in the Caucasus, and in Central Asia—mean that the departure of a leader almost inevitably leads to destabilization. The transfer of power could be particularly difficult in the Central Asian countries, where a high risk of civil war and humanitarian disaster entail direct political and economic risks for Russia. After the Arab Spring, similar scenarios are also being considered for Central Asia—given that some of the region's leaders have been in power for about two decades and have run authoritarian and even despotic regimes, while the socioeconomic situation in most of those countries remains dire and radical Islam is on the rise. Apparently in preparation for such developments Russia has consolidated the Organization of the Treaty of Collective Security, which can be used to quash street protests and upheaval. In addition to a direct threat of imported instability, the government can be anticipated to opt for preventive crackdowns inside Russia—similar to the measures taken in response to "color revolutions" in some of the former Soviet states. Such a scenario, especially if it is not successful, could increase the risk of confrontation with both the West and China. This might push Russia to make foreign policy choices that it has heretofore been unwilling to make. This would also call for a choice between liberalization and authoritarianization at home. The prospect of a Russia-led use of force against mass protests in the streets of Tashkent or Ashgabat raises serious concerns about migrant workers' communities in Russia and their relations with local populations in Moscow and other urban centers.

Wild Card Scenario: Soft Dissolution

In a scenario of soft dissolution, decentralization/regionalization would either spin out of control or be barely controlled. This would be possible if the political system were to continue its degradation and the center were to become weak in the long term, as it did in the 1990s. This scenario, which is not at all ruled out, is, in essence, the roll-out of the Chechen model to other regions, either through the expansion of Chechnya and/or the creation of analogous models beyond its borders. Despite widespread opinion to the contrary, this scenario would not be set in motion by separatism, but rather by hyper-centralization—inflexibility combined with the center's attempts to carry out functions that it is incapable of achieving.

This might result in some regions seceding de facto or de jure from the unified sovereign state. The most obvious candidates are borderline territories in Russia's Far East and the North Caucasus. The government is aware of this risk, and thus it has launched major investment-rich projects in the Russian Far East. However, this has hardly stopped the depopulation trend, with the most energetic and entrepreneurial groups moving westward to European Russia. With the depletion of resources, Russia may find itself unable to pour still more cash into these regions, which would leave them weak and easily attracted by geographically much closer and economically interested neighbors such as China. Because this kind of soft secessionism does not necessarily need physical separation, some internal regions, such as certain ethnic republics, can evolve as an "internal abroad," the way this has already happened with Tatarstan, Bashkortostan, and others in the early 1990s. If such processes begin to unfold, they may

608

be used as a powerful political issue in the intra-elite struggle. This line of development could then make a transition into one of three further scenarios: real dissolution, federalization, or (with a change in the external framework) recentralization. Each of these scenarios is fraught with foreign policy complications, as some of the more independent regions would be likely to pursue foreign policies that are be at variance with that of the federal government.

Wild Card Scenario: Schism in the Elite

Competition among elite groups has intensified and will become even more intense in the future. A schism is fairly likely, especially if the arbiter is weakened. Rivalry is likely to rise among business-political clans as the state pie gets smaller. Even today, there is a battle among power verticals (that is, command structures), and it might very well spin out of control. If, in the scenario we call soft dissolution, territories were to be broken up, corporate and governmental groups would break up.

The scenario of Russia without Putin or the scenario of a weak Putin as a result of a depletion of resources (see first scenario above) and further deterioration of the economic governance and crumbling infrastructure would lead to a schism in the ruling elites. This schism could lead either to a victory of one of the elite groups over others (with the other groups subordinated to it), or a strengthening of the corporate model of state governance. In the latter case, the state power and assets will be divided between major elite clans in a negotiated deal, with each of them having its own piece of the state pie.

Wild Card Scenario: Destabilization in Moscow

Due to the harsh and ill-considered policies of the federal authorities, Moscow is one of the regions that may destabilize. Indeed, destabilization is possible in every region; but in Moscow, as the capital city, the effect would be far more intense because of the hyper-centralization, the hypertrophied role of Moscow, and the enormous ramifications of events in the capital. The concentration of critically minded, vocal, wealthy, and entrepreneurial Russians has already led to several prominent civic initiatives, such as Blue Buckets (a drivers' movement against driving privileges for "big shots" in Moscow's heavy traffic); charity groups, and environmental groups such as Khimki Forest protesters (a group protesting a road building project slated to cut through a natural landmark forest). Though strictly political initiatives are scarce, the drive for and skills of organization and information sharing are certainly growing, and antigovernment sentiments are high and unconstrained. It may be envisaged that a powerful socioeconomic or even political trigger would push broader protests around issues such as lawlessness, the abuse of police or government authority, a government malfunction, or a crackdown/attack on a popular figure. Back in 2009, rigged elections to the Moscow city Duma left people largely unimpressed—and with frustration growing, the next time, election organizers may not get away with it as easily. The December 2010 large-scale nationalistic demonstrations in downtown Moscow can be seen as a harbinger of even more dangerous developments. A crackdown by Moscow mayor Sergey Sobyanin might provoke major outrage. When former Mayor Yuri Luzhkov's Moscow team was routed, a schism appeared in the elite groups and external governance had to be forcibly introduced. This, combined with growing discontent among Muscovites, might produce a crisis in Moscow that could spill over into a nationwide crisis.

Wild Card Scenario: A Third War in the Caucasus

The current "simmering" civil war in the North Caucasus will not subside. The North Caucasus policy has reached an impasse; violence is a daily routine, with subversive acts, terrorist attacks, abductions, and assassinations combined with Islamic radicalization. Terrorist attacks are a constant threat outside the North Caucasus, with two that took place in Moscow less than a year apart in 2010–2011. Armed clashes in the North Caucasus republics are reported on a regular basis, and a larger-scale unraveling is not improbable. The highly personalized, leader-centered system at the federal level and at the regional level in the North Caucasus make the system hostage to leaders' personalities and their relations. This is especially true of Vladimir Putin and the leader of Chechnya, Ramzan Kadyrov. Putin relies on Kadyrov for relative safety outside his territory and lets him get away with an abominable human rights record on his territory and inexplicable assassinations of his rivals and adversaries—for example, in Moscow, Vienna, or in the Arab world. An aggravation in the North Caucasus may pose a hard dilemma: A crackdown is sure to backfire, and the weak federal authorities risk further emboldening Kadyrov. Rising xenophobic nationalism in Moscow and other big cities further aggravates the problem of the North Caucasus.

The only reasonable, though not necessarily successful, policy in the North Caucasus would take a long-term investment in socioeconomic and humanitarian/cultural development at least aimed at saving the next generation from radicalization. But Russia's government management in general is not strategic; rather it tends to entail short-term mending of problems as they emerge. This is especially true of the North Caucasus, in view of the Winter Olympic Games scheduled for Sochi in 2014. The Games set an artificial deadline: Security in the North Caucasus before and during the Games is a top-priority goal that must be achieved at any cost. This detracts attention from any long-term plans; in addition, huge budget allocations in the North Caucasus in the run-up to the Olympics further aggravates the corruption, egregious in this region even by Russian standards, and undermines any positive initiative that might be launched.

The Kremlin's reliance on local elites inevitably leads to the archaicization of the political elite (Chechenization, Dagestanization, and so on); in the meantime, the security services are increasingly staffed by outside, non-Caucasus personnel, which generates risks of mass-scale social rebellion. If Russia is spared such a terrible outcome before the 2014 Olympic Games, an important factor of destabilization will be the inevitable post-Olympics drop in federal subsidies, which have ballooned during preparations for the Games.

Wild Card Scenario: Nationalist Coup

Throughout the 2000s, the Russian leadership prudently refrained from playing the nationalist card. The few exceptions where the government opted for nationalist rhetoric and/or policies were short-lived. The appearance of Kremlin-sanctioned nationalist rhetoric ahead of the parliamentary campaign of 2011 was also promptly halted. Xenophobic nationalism is easily the only universal sentiment shared by a broad majority of the Russian public, the only idea that can bring together the otherwise predominantly cynical Russian community. The desire to preempt xenophobic/nationalist activism before it bursts out from below is understandable, as is the attempt of the government to channel these xenophobic attitudes and coopt the nationalist constituencies. However, if the government abandons the prudence of the 2010s and opts for nationalist policies and rhetoric, it risks unleashing ethnic violence, which already is not uncommon in Russian cities, and ethnic minorities are highly likely to respond in kind. Nationalism could also be encouraged if Russians were squeezed out of the Caucasus and if the scenario of war in the Caucasus (see above) occurred. Another important factor is Russia's potential transformation into a nation-state and analogous processes in a number of republics in Russia with primarily one ethnic group. This could lead to a battle of nationalisms, as we saw during events in one of Moscow's central squares in late 2010 and in the North Caucasus. Political factors that would precipitate a nationalist coup include the departure of Vladimir Zhirinovsky ("nationalism lite") from the political arena along with a strong showing of nationalist forces in relatively free elections.

Wild Card Scenario: European Choice

The European choice scenario would include accession to the World Trade Organization and the Organization for Economic Cooperation and Development, as well as closer cooperation with Western nations and international organizations. Such a choice, however, would take an essential shift in Russia's stand, which is currently informed by distrust and suspicion of the West as an agent seeking to weaken Russia and take advantage of it. This world outlook is traditional for Russia; it implies that relations with outside players must not include any binding obligations or agreements. A shift toward policies based on trust, alliances, and partnerships looks barely likely today. Moreover, in contrast to the nationalist scenario, this one could only be carried out from above. It could be triggered by a deeply unfavorable economic trend, but even so not as a direct policy choice but rather as a result of an economic crisis caused by dire straits, with westernizing forces playing the upper hand in the ensuing domestic political crisis.

Such a European choice would be bound to be highly beneficial for Russian development, with those modernized constituencies that are currently isolated from decisionmaking attracted by the opportunity to make a difference. It would also be beneficial for shaping a more rational foreign policy in which Russia, based on alliances with the West, could figure out its role in Asia and elsewhere and switch from ad hoc, reactive policies to more proactive ones in various regions of the world. A more definitive rapprochement with the West might facilitate more gradual—or, to the contrary, a more drastic and mass-scale—political reform in diverse spheres, ranging from federalization to a rise in political competition. However, it might also strengthen the nationalist mood, antagonize entrenched anti-Western interests, and even lead to a nationalist coup scenario.

Wild Card Scenario: A Bloggers' Revolution

This scenario of a bloggers' revolution implies not bloggers per se, but, more generally, the advanced and younger constituencies' uncontrolled, snowballing reaction to the clumsy actions of the authorities—for example, falsification of election results on a mass scale, limitations placed on the Internet's social networks, or harsh actions against bloggers and other civil society activists. It is important to bear in mind that while there's little interest in politics among such groups, especially among the younger constituencies, they tend to take for granted the individual freedoms permitted in postcommunist Russia—and an encroachment on these freedoms might inflame strong outrage. In this particular case, today's instantaneous communication technologies could come in handy for organized action. The events of the recent "Arab Spring," combined with a number of successful Internet campaigns (Aleksey Navalny's anticorruption Website "Rospil"; an anti-United Russia campaign branding the chief pro-Kremlin force "a party of swindlers and thieves") put the government on the alert, increasing the risk of an escalating confrontation between it and the bloggers. This is probably the kind of trigger that can set off a socio-political avalanche, similar to the scenario of destabilization in Moscow.

If we apply the inertial model (defining inertia not as the extrapolation of linear trends but as the cyclical fluctuations of the last two decades), then in 2013–2015 there will be a change in the model of relations between state and society, and the center and the regions, resulting from a growing discrepancy between a modernizing postcommunist society and the essentially paternalistic, backward pattern of governance.

Last Thoughts

The intellectual exercise undertaken by our team—despite a broad diversity of views on the further development of Russia in very different dimensions—has demonstrated a kind of common vision of the nation's prospects for the next decade. It has shown that there are still various options on the table. Meanwhile, the opening decade of the 2010s appears critical: if Russia misses the still-existing opportunities for full-fledged modernization, some of them may be closed for an indefinite period of time.

This book presents the conclusions from the first stage of an enormous research project. It is not a monolith, but a series of authorial sketches done from a range of positions and in a range of styles. Thus, it is an unfolding conversation—lively and varied, with internal contradictions and arguments—that we invite our readers to join.

Note

1. It was clear by the end of 2010 that the Putin-Medvedev tandem as it was launched in 2008 outlived its role for all intents and purposes. This role was positive for the economy: when Vladimir Putin assumed the post of prime minster, the duo-centricity of the presidential and prime minister's governments came to an end. However, in domestic politics the tandem blocked any possible change to the system. In terms of the regime's image, the chance to improve it through rhetorical efforts and declarations of intent have also been exhausted.

INDEX

B

INDEX

INDEX

elimination of direct, 263
provided basis for building
   democracy across Russia's vast
   territory, 340
Putin canceling future, 334
Gulag, 27, 167
Gusinsky, Vladimir, 258, 260

H

habitable space, contraction of, 408
hands-on management method, state
   actors choosing, 540
Hanson, Stephen, 28
hard power, 11
health and education systems, reform
   of, 16
health care, deterioration of quality of,
   603
heavy manufacturing sector, 170
heavyweights
   gubernatorial rejected by system, 509
   interests of, 70
helicopter units, deprioritization of, 364
hierarchical caste system, 502
hierarchical levels, sites of conjugation
   between, 315
higher education, 152–153
high-technology-driven growth, 158
historic reconciliation, with countries of
   Central and Eastern Europe, 60
Hitler, 8
horizontal connections, shrinkage of, 320
horizontal rotations, 317
horizontal social institutions,
   eviscerated, 461
horizontal ties, 484–485, 556
housing, allocation to officers, 376
housing and infrastructure, as obstacles,
   481
housing construction industry, 401
housing program, for made-redundant
   officers, 352
housing stock, percent privately owned,
   152

human capital, 396
   decay of, 409
   deterioration of, 397
   substantial drop in, 410
   targeting growth of, 410
human resources, shortage of, 508
human rights, importance compared to
   order, 136–138
human rights community, 558
human rights groups, criticism of first
   Chechen war, 535
humanitarian concerns, of civil society
   groups and institutions, 558
Hungary, 34
Huntington, Samuel, 567
hybrid and authoritarian regimes, 257
hyper-centralization, scenario set in
   motion by, 608
hypermilitarized economy, 166

I

ICBMs (intercontinental ballistic
   missiles), 356
ideal democracy, possible in virtual
   Russia, 586
ideational stands, United Russia
   associated with certain, 265
identity formation, explosion of
   individual strategies of, 464
ideological domination, giving way to
   political technology, 494
immediacy, fundamental concept of
   game theory, 468
immigrant bloggers, creating a sort of
   bridge, 583
imperial division, method of allocating
   deputies' seats, 299
implicit social contract, affording
   maximum autonomy, 462
imports, 132, 153
imposed consensus, 140
   framework of, 220
   notion of, 148
   rules of, 145

O

CONTRIBUTORS

Pavel Baev is a research professor at the Peace Research Institute (PRIO) in Oslo, Norway.

Thomas de Waal is a senior associate in the Russia and Eurasia Program at the Carnegie Endowment for International Peace, Washington, DC.

Georgi Derluguian is a professor of sociology at New York University.

Clifford Gaddy is a senior fellow at the Brookings Institution in Washington, D.C.

Vladimir Gelman is a professor at the European University at St. Petersburg, Russia.

Alexander Golts is deputy editor of the Russian online publication *Yezhednevny Zhurnal* ("Daily Magazine").

Thomas Graham is an analyst who served on the U.S. National Security Council staff from 2002 to 2007.

Samuel Greene is director of the Center for the Study of New Media & Society at the New Economic School in Moscow.

Lev Gudkov is the director of the Levada Center, an independent, non-governmental polling and sociological research organization in Moscow.

Henry Hale is director of the Institute for European, Russian, and Eurasian Studies at the George Washington University in Washington, D.C.

Barry Ickes is a professor of economics at Pennsylvania State University.

Alexandr Kynev is the director of regional programs at the Foundation for Information Policy Development, Moscow.

Maria Lipman is editor-in-chief of Carnegie Moscow Center's *Pro et Contra* journal.

Fyodor Lukyanov is editor-in-chief of the *Rossiya v global'noy politike* (Russia in Global Affairs) journal.

Boris Makarenko is chairman of the board of the Center for Political Technologies in Moscow.

Alexey Malashenko is a scholar-in-residence at the Carnegie Moscow Center.

Vladimir Milov is president of the Institute of Energy Policy in Moscow.

Arkady Moshes is program director of the EU's Eastern Neighborhood and Russia research program at the Finnish Institute of International Affairs.

Robert Orttung is assistant director of the Institute for European, Russian, and Eurasian Studies at the George Washington University, Washington, D.C.

Nikolay Petrov is a scholar-in-residence at the Carnegie Moscow Center.

Kirill Rogov is a leading research fellow at the Yegor T. Gaidar Institute for Economic Policy in Moscow.

CONTRIBUTORS

Richard Sakwa is a professor of Russian and European politics at the University of Kent, United Kingdom.

Alexey Sidorenko is the editor of the RuNet Echo project, GlobalVoicesOnline.org.

Jens Siegert is the director of the Russia office of the Heinrich Böll Foundation.

Daniel Treisman is a professor of political science at the University of California, Los Angeles.

Dmitri Trenin is the director of the Carnegie Moscow Center.

Immanuel Wallerstein is a distinguished research professor at Yale University.

Igor Zevelev is the director of the Moscow office of the John D. and Catherine T. MacArthur Foundation.

Natalia Zubarevich is a professor at Moscow State University and director of the regional program at the Independent Institute for Social Policy.